D1561265

ELEMENTARY PRINCIPLES OF BEHAVIOR

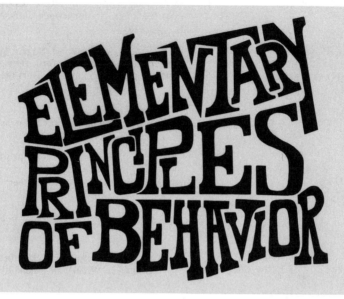

Donald L. Whaley
North Texas State University

Richard W. Malott
Western Michigan University

Prentice-Hall, Inc., Englewood Cliffs, New Jersey

©1971
by PRENTICE-HALL, Inc.,
Englewood Cliffs, New Jersey

All rights reserved. No part of this book
may be reproduced in any form or by any means,
without permission in writing from the publisher.

Printed in the United States of America

ISBN: 0-13-259499-4

Library of Congress Catalog Card Number: 78-149209

10 9 8 7 6 5 4 3 2 1

Copyright © 1968, 1969, 1970 by
Donald L. Whaley and Richard W. Malott

Photographs by James E. Smith

PRENTICE-HALL INTERNATIONAL, INC., *London*
PRENTICE-HALL OF AUSTRALIA, PTY. LTD., *Sydney*
PRENTICE-HALL OF CANADA, LTD., *Toronto*
PRENTICE-HALL OF INDIA PRIVATE LIMITED, *New Delhi*
PRENTICE-HALL OF JAPAN, INC., *Tokyo*

CONTENTS

FOREWORD   vii

ACKNOWLEDGMENTS   xi

1
Hors d'oeuvre   3

2
Conditioning   19

3
Extinction   37

4
Response Differentiation and Superstitious Behavior   61

5
Shaping, the Method of Successive Approximation   79

6
Schedules of Reinforcement   101

7
Time-Dependent Schedules of Reinforcement   127

8
Stimulus Discrimination   147

9
Stimulus Generalization and Concept Formation   171

10
Fading   195

11
Techniques Involving Gradual Change—
(Shaping, Fading, and Attenuation of Reinforcer)   207

12
Imitation   223

13
Stimulus Control and Verbal Behavior   247

14
Generalization of Reinforcement Therapy   263

15
Conditioned Reinforcement and the Token Economy   277

16
Stimulus-Response Chains   293

17
Factors Influencing the Effectiveness of Reinforcers   305

18
Punishment Produced by Contingent Stimulation   329

19
Punishment Produced by Contingent Withdrawal
of a Positive Reinforcer   351

20
Escape and Avoidance   373

21
Respondent Conditioning   399

22
An Application of the Principles of Behavior
to Education   417

23
Conclusions   439

INDEX   449

FOREWORD

In all ages, science has awaited the education of individuals who will become scientists. How much longer, anxiously and patiently, has education awaited science? Reinforcement theory has demonstrated with unquestionable authority that learning need not be painful, boring, or restricted to a select group of individuals whose specific personal histories have shaped them to be "heroic scholars." Learning can be easy progress, with fluidity and direction, and it can even be "fun." A learned person need not first be a hero.

This volume seeks to teach principles of psychology to ordinary, undedicated, unenlightened, noninspired, nonheroic, beginning college students. We have found these individuals a wonderful group and we are dedicated to teaching them psychology. In doing so, we do not intend to forego a mastery on their part of what we feel are the critical and often difficult principles of science. Rigor cannot be sacrificed for the sake of fun. We propose to demonstrate that the two are not mutually exclusive; we suggest even that the dedicated student will find he is learning more, but doing so with considerable ease and interest.

In an attempt to implement the aims outlined above, it will be found that the format of this volume differs from the typical general psychology text. The style is intentionally informal and more closely resembles that of popular magazines than introductory textbooks. It has been our experience that beginning college students prefer this informal style to the more academic idiom. We are attempting to avoid the language barrier which so frequently creates communication difficulty between faculty and students.

Perhaps more important than the popular stylistics is the emphasis on a "living" content. Most of the studies reported are concerned with the application of the analysis of behavior to human affairs. Only those animal studies which have obvious immediate relevance to human behavior are cited and highlighted.

As with most books which attempt to program the learning process, materials are presented in a graded manner, beginning with simple concepts and terms and growing in complexity as the student grows in his ability to accommodate added complexity.

Physically, the book is divided into reading assignments. Each reading assignment consists of text material, a set of questions pertaining to the text, and notes. The text material comprises the core of the material presented to the student. If a student can answer the questions without referring back to the text, he has, at least for the moment, mastered the material. The notes, we feel, will be an important feature of the book; herein, details deleted from the main text are elaborated along with speculations and a few pet ideas of the authors. It is hoped that the notes will serve the purpose of maintaining the interest of the more inquisitive student as in many ways they have maintained the behavior of the authors.

The book is self-contained and may be used as a core textbook or as a supplement to another text. It is arranged in such a manner as to facilitate correspondence with other sources.

As presented here, this volume has gone through an extensive testing procedure similar to that often employed with programmed texts. Students were repeatedly examined in terms of their ability to answer questions based on the text. If they did poorly, this was taken as an indication that the material was not clear, was improperly paced, or had sequential flaws in presentation. It was consequently rewritten until questions were answered in an acceptable manner. Dozens of evaluations were elicited from the students in terms of how they liked various portions of the text, the interest evoked, and suggested changes. The outcome of these evaluations are reflected in this volume.

To the Student

Upon being complimented for his speaking of Italian, an American in a Hemingway story remarked how easy a language it was to speak. "Ah, yes," the Italian major who had paid him the compliment said. "Why, then, do you not take up the grammar?"

Most of you have been talking to, discussing, observing, and generally interacting with people all your lives. Many of you, I am sure, find that people are easy to understand. Perhaps, like Hemingway's hero, it is time for you to learn the grammar. For there are rules and principles to understanding human behavior which are formally subsumed under the term "psychology."

Like the principles of grammar, the principles of psychology are not intrinsically simple. New terms must be learned, new concepts mastered, and more importantly, old notions you bring with you discarded, the latter sometimes not without a grimace.

In teaching you the grammar of behavioral psychology, we will try as hard as we can to keep away from abstract, unrelated materials. We intend to make psychology as near and dear to you as possible by making it relevant to you and to real problems, aspirations, and ambitions. We hope that in the end you will do more than parrot facts of psychology, facts of unknown origin and value. Rather, we desire that you will know the principles of the science of psychology and be capable of evaluating not only the facts that are given to you in this book, but also new ones that are presented to you in popular media, the pronouncements of experts, and by the kid in the student union.

D. L. W.
R. W. M.

ACKNOWLEDGMENTS

We gratefully acknowledge the editorial assistance of Lyla Jansen, Judy Morton, Penny Zlutnick, Karen Smith, Kathy Janczarek, Linda Hilton, Nancy Head, and Ernie Ponicki. We also wish to thank Janet Klinkers and James Palm for their help.

Our special appreciation goes to David Thorne for the cartoons; to Patience Vaughan and Shirley Bale, who conceived the graphics; and to Ernie Ponicki for the poems.

ELEMENTARY PRINCIPLES OF BEHAVIOR

HORS D'OEUVRE

Psychological Causes of Starvation

Mary was 37 years old, five feet four inches tall, and weighed only 47 pounds.[1] She was admitted to the hospital because she was dying of starvation.

At the age of 11 Mary weighed 120 pounds and was considered chubby. Her weight remained at about 120 pounds until she was married at the age of 18, at which time her family physician warned her that she was sexually under-developed and that her marriage might "make this worse, or might make it better." The couple lived in California where her husband was in the military service. Since this was during World War II when living conditions were not very pleasant, they lived in a small crowded apartment with no facilities for cooking and had to eat their meals in cheap restaurants. Mary was also having trouble adjusting to the sexual aspects of married life and was very homesick. Consequently, she made the long trip from California to Virginia several times to visit her family. After the first few months of her marriage, she started eating less and began losing weight at an alarming rate. A physician suggested that if she lost any more weight she should return home and live with her family, which she did.

Society would normally criticize a woman for leaving her husband to return to her parents, except if this were done for reasons of health. Mary was having problems adjusting to her husband and was living in fairly uncomfortable conditions. In addition, she was homesick. The doctor had provided her with a legitimate reason for doing what she really wanted to do. She could escape from her unhappy marriage and at the same time be rewarded by returning to the comfortable environment of her family. Furthermore, she could do this without being punished by society's scorn.

At this point we can only speculate, but it seems very plausible that she ate

1. This section based on Bachrach, A. J., Erwin, W. J., and Mohr, J. P. The control of eating behavior in an anorexic by operant conditioning techniques. In L. P. Ullman and L. Krasner (Eds.), *Case Studies in Behavior Modification.* New York: Holt, Rinehart and Winston, 1965, 153–163.

poorly because she was rewarded by being able to escape from her marriage and return to her family home without suffering criticism. You should not think that Mary was consciously trying to lose weight. Probably she would have been shocked had it been suggested that she was losing weight in order to have an excuse to return home. Nonetheless, those factors may have been the primary causes of her failure to eat.

In this example, we have seen that Mary's poor eating was caused by what happened to her when she did not eat. This is one of the most important notions that you will learn in this course. Rewards and punishments play a major role in our everyday lives.

When Mary returned home she continued to lose weight. Probably because of her eating problem, she received more attention than she had prior to her marriage. If a person eats normally, no one pays much attention to him. However, if he refuses to eat, he will receive quite a bit of attention. Friends and relatives will talk to the person who eats poorly and try to coax him to eat more. It is very rewarding to have someone pay attention to us. It is quite plausible that Mary continued to eat poorly because people paid more attention to her under those circumstances than when she ate normally. Once again, we see that rewards might have been a major factor affecting the way that Mary behaved. In this case, not eating resulted in being rewarded by attention from the family. Therefore, poor eating was more likely to occur in the future.

Between the ages of 18 and 37, Mary went from 120 pounds to 47 pounds, which is an amazing demonstration of how powerful the social reward of attention can be in controlling the behavior of a human being.

At this point, it was felt that if Mary did not gain weight, she would literally starve to death. Since no medical reasons could be found for her weight loss, a new type of therapy was tried whereby she would receive social rewards only when she ate and not when she refused to eat.

Mary was placed in a room containing only the bare essentials, and social contact was kept at a minimum. Mary was in such poor physical condition that she could not move from her bed without help. She was served three meals a day. During each meal she had a companion; however, the companion would only talk to her after she had made a response that was to be rewarded. Conversation with the dinner companion served as a reward. Initially, whenever Mary lifted her fork in preparation for taking a bite of food, the companion would chat briefly with her. At any other time, the companion would refuse to say anything. After Mary was frequently reaching for bites of food, she was required to raise the food to her mouth before being rewarded by a few seconds of conversation. When this response was occurring fairly often, the companion would converse only after she had chewed some food, and eventually the companion would talk to her only after she had taken a piece of food, raised it to her mouth, chewed, and swallowed it. In addition to conversation, she was rewarded by being allowed to listen to the radio or phonograph, or to watch television when her meal was completed. Whenever Mary refused to eat any of her meal, she was not allowed to partake of this entertainment. At first, she was required only to eat a bite or two of food, but eventually she was required to eat everything on her plate before being rewarded with the entertainment.

At later dates, if she ate all of the food on her plate, she could choose what food she wanted at her next meal, could invite one of the other patients in to eat with her during her next meal, and could eat in the dining room with the other patients during the next meal. Other social rewards were gradually introduced. These consisted of walking around the hospital grounds with a companion and receiving visits from her family and others. Receiving mail and having her hair shampooed and set were also used as rewards. After three months of treatment, Mary had gained 14 pounds.

When Mary returned home, her family was instructed to continue giving her social rewards such as praise and attention when she ate and to ignore her when she did not eat at mealtime. At the end of a year of treatment in her parent's home, she weighed 88 pounds and was able to participate in a relatively normal and useful social and professional life.

Thumbsucking

How can we eliminate thumbsucking in young children? This is a common question. A common solution is to cover the child's hands with gloves or put them in cardboard tubes. However, that method is like cutting off his thumbs to prevent him from sucking them.

The principle of rewarding an individual for not doing something—as Mary was rewarded initially for not eating—was applied in the case of Roger, a five-year-old nursery school boy who persistently sucked his thumb.[2]

Over several days, Roger was observed as he watched animated cartoons. His thumb was in his mouth all of the time. Since Roger seemed to enjoy looking at the cartoons, it was decided that showing the cartoons would be used as a reward for his not sucking his thumb.

Roger sat in a chair in front of the motion picture screen for about three-quarters of an hour. For the first few minutes, the cartoons were shown continuously regardless of whether or not he sucked his thumb. He did in fact suck his thumb continuously. The cartoons were then turned off and were turned on again only when Roger took his thumb out of his mouth. After this procedure was repeated several times, Roger sucked his thumb only about one-half of the time. This experiment demonstrates that thumbsucking can probably be reduced by rewarding the child when he does not suck his thumb.

Reclaiming a Small Girl from an Institution for the Retarded

In the past, very little has been done to train or educate the retarded. A few years ago, however, it was shown that these individuals could learn and be trained through special techniques and methods.

2. This section based on Baer, D. M. Laboratory control of thumbsucking by withdrawal and representation of reinforcement. *Journal of the Experimental Analysis of Behavior*, 1962, 5, 525–528.

Following this precedent, a group of psychologists began an intensive training program with Sue, a young retarded girl who could not speak a sentence or name objects but who was able to mimic words spoken by someone else.[3] She had extreme difficulty in walking and was unable to perform even simple movements with her hands. Attempts were made to give her intelligence tests, but she was so lacking in skills that her IQ was zero. She was untestable. The experimenters then began a lengthy procedure aimed at increasing Sue's language skills and her ability to discriminate and name objects. At the same time, they trained her to perform tasks such as playing games and working puzzles.

Language training included the frequent use of candies as rewards. The experimenter uttered a word and if Sue repeated it she was rewarded with a small piece of candy and perhaps a pat on the head and the word "good." After months of this procedure, she was able to name objects and finally to express herself in short sentences.

The training of physical skills was also extremely important. Because Sue had poorly developed leg muscles and very poor coordination, she did not enjoy attempting to ride a bicycle or other physical activities. The experimenters decided to make it worth her while to participate by using candies as rewards. They mounted a bicycle in a stationary position on a frame so that the wheels would turn if the foot-pedals were pushed down. In the initial stages they rewarded Sue for just sitting on the bike. In the next stage, an automatic candy dispenser delivered a small piece of candy each time she turned the wheels of the bicycle around for five revolutions. After she had perfected this, the requirement gradually increased until the wheels had to be turned around many times before a piece of candy was dispensed. At the same time, and by small degrees, the amount of pressure on the back wheel was adjusted so that it took much more effort to turn the pedals. After some months of this training, Sue's muscles had developed considerably and she spent many hours turning the wheels of the bicycle and consuming the candy with great satisfaction. When she had gained the required coordination and strength in her legs, the bicycle was taken down from its stationary position and through the use of rewards, she was taught how to ride it out on the driveway of the institution. Once Sue learned how to ride rewards were no longer necessary, and she rode for hours in much the same way that normal children do, for the pleasure and enjoyment of riding.

At the termination of hundreds of hours of training with rewards, Sue progressed to the point where she could be tested with a standard intelligence test. Her intelligence quotient had risen enough to allow her discharge from the institution and her placement in a special class in the public school system. There is good reason to believe Sue would still be in that institution if the intensive reward training had not been undertaken.

In the cases described above we have seen how rewards play an important part in bringing about desired changes in the behavior of people.

But not all things or events in the world are rewarding. In fact, some experiences are so painful that we do all we can to avoid them. Psychologists also use these aversive situations to bring about behavior changes and while they are

3. This section based on Risley, T. Personal communication.

somewhat uncomfortable to the person on whom they are employed, they can be judiciously used to contribute to his overall behavioral and physical health. The following cases demonstrate the use of mildly unpleasant events to modify behavior.

Punishment of Self-mutilation Behavior

Self-mutilation is difficult to understand because it persists even though the consequences are often extremely painful and harmful to the individual.[4] Observations of psychotic children give us a plausible reason for this: they hurt themselves simply to get attention. The psychotic child usually comes from a family that is preoccupied with other things and has little time to spend with him. However, if the child should accidentally fall down, the parents may rush over and pick him up, thereby giving him more attention than he would otherwise receive. Since he has been rewarded for falling down, he may fall down again. After this has happened a few times, the family may start ignoring the child until an occasion when he falls down and bangs his head. Once again the parents may rush to shower him with love and attention and then gradually ignore him as before. Eventually the child may bang his head with such force that he injures himself and again receives the attention of his parents. The child may continue injuring himself indefinitely, as long as he is rewarded for self-injury by the attention of his parents.

Processes similar to this probably occur with most children but have little lasting effect and do not develop to the point of truly self-injurious behavior. On the occasions when self-injurious behavior does develop, the child is usually placed under physical restraint in a hospital.

Dickie was a small, good-looking nine-year-old boy whose appearance was marred by many bruises and abrasions on his face and head. When the psychologist first saw Dickie, he was in the hospital ward of an institution for the mentally retarded where he had been placed because of a serious concussion resulting from beating his head against a concrete floor. This self-injurious behavior had started early in Dickie's life and had developed into a threat to his welfare. He had to be constantly supervised and often there had been no other recourse but to restrain him or restrict his activities to a crib, thus preventing him from developing many normal skills.

One might expect that the pain resulting from the head banging would serve to punish Dickie and make it less likely that he would continue this self-injurious behavior. However, he probably gradually developed the dangerous head-banging response over a period of several days. Therefore, Dickie probably got used to the pain that resulted from head banging, so that it was not a very effective punisher. Since the punishment was of a specific nature, the psychologist speculated that if a new type of punishment could be arranged when Dickie began to bang his head, this might serve to suppress or lessen his rate of head banging.

4. This section based on Cowart, J., and Whaley, D. Punishment of self-mutilation behavior. Unpublished manuscript.

Dickie was brought to a special room fitted with a floor mat in order to protect him from hurting himself severely, and was allowed to bang his head as often as he wished for an hour, during which time he banged his head 1,440 times. After this recording period, small shock leads were placed on his leg and a mild shock was delivered each time he banged his head. The first time he banged his head and was given a shock, Dickie stopped abruptly and looked about the room in a puzzled manner. He did not bang his head for a full three minutes, and then made three contacts with the floor in quick succession, receiving a mild shock after each one. He again stopped his head-banging activity for three minutes. At the end of that time he made one more contact, received a shock, and did not bang his head for the remainder of the one-hour session. On subsequent sessions, after a shock was given the first time Dickie banged his head, he abandoned this behavior. Soon the head banging had stopped completely and the mat was removed from the room. Later, a successful attempt was made to prevent Dickie from banging his head in other areas of the ward.

Currently Dickie no longer needs to be restrained or confined and has not been observed to bang his head since the treatment was terminated; therefore, in his case, punishment was a very effective technique for eliminating undesirable behavior. The psychologist working with Dickie stressed that the shock used was mild and, compared to the harm and possible danger involved in Dickie's head banging, was certainly justified.

An Animal Experiment on the Effects of Rewards and Punishments

In the preceding study we saw how the processes of reward and punishment may work in opposite directions. It was guessed that Dickie's head banging occurred because it was followed by the relatively small reward of attention. It was also guessed that the severe pain normally resulting from head banging was not a very effective punishment because the severity of the pain had been only gradually increased. This may seem like wild speculation; consequently it is important that these notions be tested with an experiment in the laboratory. The question is: will an individual continue to respond when the response is occasionally followed by a small reward and always followed by a large punishment? If we are able to demonstrate this in the laboratory, then we will have more confidence in our analysis of Dickie's problem.

We would not want to use humans in such an experiment because of the pain involved; therefore, animals were used as subjects. Past research has shown that nearly all of the results of animal experimentation are just as true of humans as they are of animals. In this experiment pigeons were used as subjects. The research was conducted by Dr. Nathan Azrin at Anna State Hospital, Anna, Illinois.[5]

If we had walked into Dr. Azrin's laboratory a few years ago, we might have

5. This section based on Azrin, N. H. Punishment and recovery during fixed-ratio performance. *Journal of the Experimental Analysis of Behavior*, 1959, 2, 301–305.

seen a pigeon inside a box pecking at a small disc. On some of the occasions when the pigeon pecked the disc, it fluttered its wings, lurched violently, and almost fell down. Upon closer examination, we would have noticed a pair of wires connected to the pigeon. Through these wires he received a brief but intense shock each time he pecked the disc. The shock was powerful enough that it almost knocked the animal down. Yet the bird kept pecking the disc and getting shocks. Why was the animal pecking the disc if he was being punished for it, and for that matter, why would the animal peck the disc even if he were not being punished? Eventually we would have noticed that occasionally when the pigeon pecked the disc an electrically operated feeder delivered some food. In other words, the bird was occasionally given a very small reward for pecking the disc, and in spite of the fact that he was receiving a severe shock, he continued pecking the disc.

The answer to our experimental question is that it is possible to get an organism to take a tremendous amount of punishment each time it responds even though it only occasionally receives a very small reward. This is in agreement with our guess that Dickie was banging his head because of the small social reward. Furthermore, the only way that a pigeon can be gotten to respond in spite of such high intensity shocks is by gradually increasing their intensity. If the pigeon had first been trained to make the response with only the reward present, and had we then abruptly introduced the high intensity shock, the animal would have stopped responding altogether. This supports our notion that Dickie was able to stand such violent head banging because the force of the head banging was only gradually increased.

Relief from Prolonged Sneezing

Sneezing is an extremely violent activity involving one's whole body and, if prolonged, can be tiring, uncomfortable, and conceivably of great danger to the individual.

A 17-year-old girl was admitted to the hospital for a minor checkup.[6] While she was in the hospital, workmen were painting an area adjacent to her room. Fumes from the paint entered her nostrils, causing her to sneeze violently several times. On the day after she was discharged and returned home she began to sneeze quite frequently. At first neither her parents nor her physician were concerned about it, because it is not uncommon for a person to sneeze for many hours as a result of minor irritation.

The sneezing continued for several days at intervals ranging from once every several minutes to once every few seconds. Her parents became alarmed and took her to the hospital. Allergists and other specialists were called in on the case but to no avail. The sneezing continued.

6. This section based on Kushner, M. Faradic aversive controls in clinical practice. In C. Neuringer and J. L. Michael (Eds.), *Behavior Modification in Clinical Psychology*. New York: Appleton-Century-Crofts, 1968.

At the end of six months, the girl was still sneezing at a high frequency although some one hundred specialists had been consulted. They had tried hypnosis, drug therapy, minor operations involving packings in her nostrils and mouth cavities, psychiatry, and prolonged uses of sprays and antihistamine preparations. One physician administered a sleep-inducing drug which made her sleep for several days. During the big sleep she did not sneeze but as soon as she awakened her sneezing began anew.

At this point a group of psychologists from a nearby VA hospital were brought on the case. They based their procedures on the assumption that although the sneezing had caused the young lady many hours of discomfort, some aspect of the sneezing was rewarding. Besides providing some momentary relief from the irritation, the sneezing provided the girl with more attention than she had ever received in her life. Possibly the attention was enough reward to cause the sneezing to continue. The psychologists hung a special microphone from the young girl's neck. Although she was free to talk or laugh normally, when she sneezed the microphone was activated and a mild shock was delivered to her forearm. The shock began as soon as the sneeze was emitted and lasted for half a second after its cessation. Within a few hours the sneezing became less frequent, and six hours later it had stopped completely. For the first time in six months other than during the big sleep, the girl spent a full night and day without a single sneeze. Two days later she was discharged from the hospital and, with occasional subsequent applications of the shock apparatus, her sneezing remained under control.

One might have expected the procedure to have failed because the sneezing itself must have been very uncomfortable without the addition of shock. However, the discomfort ordinarily associated with the sneezing was not directly linked to the sneeze as such, but occurred some time after the sneeze or at treatment times when the sneeze was not actively occurring. Therefore, by pairing the shock directly with the sneeze, the punishment was most effective.

The months of extreme discomfort, the thousands of medications, and the many hours of painful and inconvenient treatment the girl had received were terminated by the judicious application of a few brief and mild electric shocks. The total time that the teenager actually received shocks during the entire treatment was less than three minutes.

Control of Crying and Whining Behavior by Withdrawing Attention

All children cry at one time or another. Often the crying is associated with a bump, cut, or other physical contact with the environment. Some children seem to cry, whine, and carry on for no good reason, and in doing so create much discomfort and anguish for those around them. These children manage to get more than their measure of attention from teachers, parents, and others.

The staff at a nursery school became concerned about the persistent crying and whining of four-year-old Bill, who attended nursery school sessions in the mornings.[7] Bill was observed several mornings and the frequency of crying episodes recorded. On the average, eight episodes occurred each morning. During the observation period, they also discovered that Bill's whining and crying resulted in almost immediate attention from teachers, who hurried to comfort and cajole him until he stopped crying.

The nursery school teachers consulted with Dr. Montrose Wolf and designed a program for Bill. It was decided that Bill persisted in his crying because, in effect, his minor tantrums were being rewarded with the immediate attention of the nursery school teacher who lavished kindness and affection on him. The program the group adopted consisted simply of ignoring Bill whenever he began to cry without cause. Bill still received his share of attention and affection from the nursery school teacher, but never when he was crying.

This procedure was carried out for ten days during which time the number of crying episodes dwindled to almost zero. During the last five days of the ten-day period, only one incident occurred. Due to the effectiveness of the simple technique of removing the reward which seemed to be maintaining the behavior sequence, Bill ceased to be a problem.

Summary

In this chapter we have seen how several apparently diverse behavior problems—starvation, thumbsucking, mental retardation, self-mutilation, sneezing, and crying—were alleviated by relatively simple but effective behavioral techniques. The following consistencies in the cases reported warrant emphasis.

1. In all of the instances, emphasis was placed on what the individual was actually doing. The psychologist seeking to bring about changes in his behavior did not spend long hours in interviews, theorizing, or speculating as to what the patient must be thinking or feeling, but rather observed him and recorded what he did and what occurred as a result of his actions.

2. Rewards played a significant role in the measures taken to bring about changes in the individuals. Mary began to eat when eating was rewarded by conversation and the opportunity to view television. Bill's crying and whining ceased when they failed to produce attention as they had previously done. Roger's thumbsucking diminished greatly when it resulted in the termination of the opportunity to watch cartoons.

3. An unpleasant event, a mild electric shock, brought about termination of sneezing and self-mutilation. In both cases, the shock was produced swiftly and reliably by these behaviors.

4. In all of the cases presented, the giving of reward, the removal of reward, or the presentation of an unpleasant shock took place immediately after the patient's action or behavior. In effect therefore, his actions produced the punishment or rewards. Since the psychologists involved in these cases were successful in

7. This section based on Hart, B., Allen, K., Buell, J., Harris, F., and Wolf, M. Effects of social reinforcement on operant crying. *Journal of Experimental Child Psychology*, 1964, *1*, 145–153.

dealing with these behaviors in this manner, a generalization can be drawn from these examples: actions are frequently either stopped or increased as a result of the effects they produce on the individual. Stated in a less wordy manner, behavior is controlled by its consequences.

The four points presented above are of the utmost importance in the study of how and why organisms act as they do. They will appear again and again in many contexts throughout the remainder of this text.

The next section contains a list of questions designed to help you review this chapter. It will take you only a few minutes to go through these questions. We strongly recommend that at this point you do so. You will find that you are able to answer almost every question. If there is a question whose answer you are not sure of, it will be an easy matter to check back in the chapter and find the answer. You need not bother to write down the answers. You may also find this useful as a way of reviewing the chapter just before a quiz or exam, since it is probable that most of the points covered in the quizzes or exams will be covered in this list of questions.

QUESTIONS

1. Between the ages of 11 and 18 years, Mary weighed approximately: (a) 40 pounds; (b) 80 pounds; (c) 120 pounds; (d) 160 pounds.
2. Briefly describe the conditions in which Mary lived in the first few months of her marriage.
3. What did the physician tell Mary that she should do if she lost any more weight?
4. What was the reward for Mary's eating poorly?
5. Was Mary consciously trying to lose weight?
6. Rewards and punishments are of almost no importance in the everyday lives of normal people: (a) True; (b) False.
7. When Mary returned home to her parents, did she immediately stop losing weight?
8. What is the relationship between eating and receiving attention?
9. What was suggested as the reason for Mary's continuing to eat poorly when she returned home?
10. From the time Mary was 18 until she was 37 years old, her weight dropped from 120 pounds to: (a) 117 pounds; (b) 47 pounds; (c) 87 pounds; (d) 107 pounds.
11. In treating Mary in the hospital, conversation with the dinner companion served as a: (a) punishment; (b) reward; (c) pep talk before the meal was served; (d) distracting influence which interfered with eating.
12. Describe the various stages used to get Mary to swallow the food starting with simply lifting her fork in preparation for taking a bite of food.
13. Describe the changes in requirements of Mary's behavior before she would be rewarded with the opportunity to listen to the radio or phonograph or to watch TV.
14. When Mary returned home, what were the instructions the family was given?
15. The authors advocate putting cardboard tubes on a child's hands to prevent thumbsucking. (a) True; (b) False.
16. Before the psychologist started working with Roger, roughly how much of the time did he spend with his thumb in his mouth while watching animated cartoons?

17. What was the reward which Roger received when he was not sucking his thumb?

18. Initially, Sue's IQ was: (a) 0; (b) 10; (c) 20; (d) 40; (e) 80.

19. Describe Sue's initial verbal skills.

20. Briefly describe the language training procedure.

21. What were the rewards?

22. What language skills did she have after the training?

23. In general, Sue's training was based on: (a) rewards; (b) punishments; (c) a combination of rewards and punishments; (d) none of the above.

24. What specific activity was used in teaching Sue physical skills?

25. Briefly describe the sequence of stages used to teach Sue to ride a bicycle.

26. Were they able to discontinue the special candy reward for riding the bicycle?

27. At the end of the treatment, what happened to Sue?

28. What was Dickie's behavioral problem?

29. Specifically, what was the self-mutilation response?

30. One of the characteristics of the psychotic child is that his family is usually pre-occupied with other things and has little time to spend with him. (a) True; (b) False.

31. Briefly describe how violent self-abusive behavior can be developed in a child.

32. Indicate the probable reward for such behavior.

33. Why was not the pain for head banging a very effective punisher?

34. It was speculated that if a new type of punishment could be arranged when Dickie began to bang his head, it might serve to suppress or lessen his rate of head banging. (a) True; (b) False.

35. Before the treatment, how many times would Dickie bang his head in one hour? (a) 14; (b) 144; (c) 1440; (d) 14,400.

36. What specific punishment did the psychologist use when Dickie banged his head?

37. On the first day that shock punishment was used, approximately how many times did he bang his head? (a) 5; (b) 50; (c) 500; (d) 5000.

38. The psychologists were able to eliminate Dickie's head banging in the special room but not when he was placed back in the ward. (a) True; (b) False.

39. What species of animal is used in the animal experiment?

40. What was the general question which the experiment was trying to answer?

41. How does this question relate to Dickie's problem?

42. Why was an animal used instead of humans in this experiment?

43. Are the results of most animal psychological experiments applicable to humans?

44. In the pigeon experiment discussed, what was the response which was rewarded?

45. What was the reward?

46. What was the punishment?

47. How can you get an animal to take a large amount of punishment if they only occasionally receives a small reward?

48. What would happen if the pigeon had first been trained to make the response with only the reward present and then we had abruptly introduced the high intensity shock?

49. Approximately how many specialists were consulted about the girl's sneezing?

50. What were the two *possible* rewards for sneezing?

51. Briefly describe the procedure used for eliminating the sneezing.

52. Approximately how many days of treatment were required to eliminate the sneezing?

53. Roughly how much total time did the patient receive shock during conditioning? (a) 3 seconds; (b) 3 minutes; (c) 3 hours; (d) 30 hours.
54. Before the treatment started, what did the teachers normally do when Bill had a temper tantrum?
55. Would you say his temper tantrums were being rewarded or punished?
56. After the treatment was started, what did the teachers do when Bill had a temper tantrum?
57. How long did the procedure last? (a) one day; (b) ten days; (c) one hundred days; (d) one year.
58. Was the procedure effective in dealing with the crying behavior?
59. In all of the studies reported, the psychologists spent long hours theorizing and speculating about what the patient must be thinking or feeling before they attempted any therapy. (a) True; (b) False.
60. What were the three basic procedures used to modify behavior in the preceding studies?
61. What specific behaviors were modified by the use of giving rewards?
62. What behaviors were modified by the removal of reward?
63. What behaviors were modified by the presentation of unpleasant shock?
64. What is the single most important psychological generalization which can be drawn from these studies?
65. Give an example from your everyday life in which behavior has been controlled by the giving of rewards.
66. Give an example of how behavior could be modified by the withdrawal of rewards.
67. Give an example in which behavior can be modified by the use of punishment.

In most classes this will conclude the formally assigned part of the chapter. However, some of you may find it useful to read the next section, which is headed Notes. Such a section will be present at the end of each chapter. Details not included in the main text are elaborated upon here. The Notes section sometimes contains topics which are a little too advanced to include in the regular part of the chapter; they may sometimes also be a little too speculative. In any case these sections include items which we personally find interesting. Many students may not choose to read these extra few pages; however for those of you who have nothing better to do with your time, we hope that you enjoy them.

NOTES

Psychological Causes of Starvation

We have avoided using technical terms in this first chapter. However, there are usually no everyday terms exactly equivalent to the technical terms; if they were equivalent, there would be no need to develop a technical vocabulary. The term *reward* was used in place of the technical term *reinforcement*. A reward is something which gives *pleasure* or *satisfaction*. Unfortunately, the terms *pleasure* and *satisfaction* cannot be clearly defined. To find out if something was rewarding one could ask the individual involved whether it was pleasant and satisfying. In the past, an attempt was made to build a science of psychology by asking such questions of individuals. Unfortunately the results collected in this manner were unreliable and difficult to interpret. If one person says something is satisfying and another says it is not, we do not know whether the individuals are being affected differently, whether they mean slightly different things by the word satisfying, or even whether one of them is lying. Another difficulty with relying on the individual's verbal report is that we cannot use that technique in experiments with animals. We expect the laws of biology to apply to animals as well as to man. Similarly, it is scientifically desirable that the laws of behavior should apply to animals as well as man. For these reasons, psychologists have developed other techniques for collecting data.

We have seen that the notions of pleasure and satisfaction, in the meaning of the term *reward*, are unacceptable to the science of psychology; however, reward may also be defined as something that is given for a job well done. It is this meaning of reward that the psychologist retains in the term *reinforcement*. A reinforcer is given after the completion of a response or a sequence of responses. However, in order for something to qualify as a reinforcer, it must have a reinforcing or strengthening effect. A reinforcer follows a response and makes it more likely that the response will occur again in the future. This definition of a reinforcer says nothing about *why* a stimulus event acts as a reinforcer; it says nothing about satisfaction or pleasure; it merely says *what* a reinforcer is.

My name is Xenogeopholus
I'm crazy today.
 Have you ever thought
Maybe I like it that way?
It's neat to be nuts
 Fun to be flipped
 Great to be gone
 Tough to be tripped
Happiness is a warm puppy
 A wet guppy
 A rubber boot
 A hunk of coal
 A Pie in the face
  Is my only goal.

Guess I'll talk
 Go for a walk
 Take some chalk
 Mark the walls
 Scream down halls
 Slide down stairs
 Scramble chairs
 Pull out hairs
 And raise a fuss.
That should get attention
 For Xenogeopholus.

It has sometimes been suggested that the notion of reinforcement is not useful because its application always involves circular reasoning. For example, to the question "Why is that child always crying?" the answer might be "He cries because he is reinforced by his parents' attention for crying." To the question "How do you know that the parents' attention is reinforcing the crying?", an erroneous circular answer would be, "I know that the attention is acting as a reinforcer because the child is always crying." This reasoning is circular because the notion of reinforcement is being used to explain the child's crying and the child's crying is being used as proof that a reinforcement is involved. A more appropriate answer to the last question would be: "Attention is acting as a reinforcer because when parents pay attention to their children for crying, the children spend much more time crying than when parents give no attention for such behavior." The way to determine whether a stimulus is acting as a reinforcer is simply to try it and see. If the response occurs more frequently when it is followed by the stimulus than when it is not, then, by definition, the stimulus is a reinforcer.

Mary's therapy was based on the notion that by successively reinforcing responses which more closely resemble the desired response, an individual may be guided to the desired response. This method is known as *successive approximations,* and will be discussed in detail in later chapters.

Thumbsucking

In the study of thumbsucking, a relationship had to be established between the termination of the cartoons and the thumbsucking response. When the cartoons went off, the boy removed his thumb from his mouth. The experimenters presumed this response was due to the punishing effect of the cartoon termination; however, the child might also simply have been upset and annoyed when the cartoons happened to end, and therefore pulled his thumb from his mouth. In order to establish a relationship between these two events, the child was subjected to alternate periods during which the cartoons were turned on and then off. The on-off cycle was independent of whether or not the child was thumbsucking. This control procedure did not affect the thumbsucking rate. Later, when cartoon termination was made contingent on thumbsucking, a reduction was observed which brings to light an important aspect of learning. If an individual's behavior is to be affected by reward or punishment, reward and punishment must be closely related in temporal sequence to the response.

The thumbsucking study is an example of the relation between positive reinforcement and punishment. The subject was rewarded for not sucking his thumb by the presentation of the cartoons; or conversely, he was punished for sucking his thumb by the removal of cartoons. In other experiments this reciprocal relationship may be less clear, but in almost all cases the procedures can be viewed either as positive reinforcement or as punishment. This study differs from most laboratory experiments with animals. For example, when a pigeon is pecking a key for food, each peck is a discreet and temporally circumscribed response of short duration. Thumbsucking, however, is an ongoing response; the child may keep his thumb in his mouth for hours. Similarly, reinforcement in the form of food for the pigeon is present for only a few brief seconds and is then removed. The reinforcement of the cartoons in the thumbsucking experiment continued for a long duration. The discreet nature of the usual response and reinforcement may account for the difficulty of seeing the reciprocal relation between punishment and reinforcement in most animal experiments.

Punishment of Self-mutilation Behavior

It was stressed that a behavior pattern similar in many respects to Dickie's could be arranged experimentally in the laboratory with a pigeon. Dickie persisted in banging his head and had sustained pain and physical damage for the reward of attention and social contact. The pigeon pecked a key that delivered an immediate shock to him, but eventually yielded a reward in the form of food. He maintained the pecking and suffered the attendant pain for a small amount of reinforcement. If the pigeon were to be placed on this schedule for years, a new pigeon doctor, not familiar with his history and how he became so deviant, might treat the pigeon in much the same way Dickie was treated. A different type of punishment in addition could be delivered on each key peck. The new punishment could be a physical blow, perhaps delivered by a small hammer. Under these conditions it would be expected that the key pecking would decrease just as Dickie's head banging decreased.

Relief from Prolonged Sneezing

It is interesting that sneezing, which is considered to be reflexive in nature and not under the voluntary control of the individual, can be modified or suppressed by contingent punishment. Aversive conditioning is being applied to similar problems with great success.

Control of Crying and Whining Behavior
by Withdrawing Attention

Crying is classified as operant or respondent. Respondent crying is that which is obviously the direct consequence of physical injury, occurs immediately after the injury, and does not depend on the presence of other people or particular circumstances. Operant crying on the other hand is not primarily associated with injury and does not occur unless others are present. Often the child will look around to ascertain the presence of others before he begins to cry. The occurrence of both kinds of crying can be modified by the proper contingencies; however, the operant type of crying is more immediately amenable to control.

In treating Bill, the experimenters did not terminate the study at the point indicated in the text. Although only one crying episode occurred in the last five-day period, some doubts still existed as to whether the removal of attention was the cause. It was conceivable that events occurring at home, a change in the child's physical condition, or other unidentified variables coincided with the removal of attention and might be the real cause of the diminution of crying behavior. In order to demonstrate that withholding of attention was the pertinent variable, the procedure was reversed, and the original conditions observed prior to the experiment were reinstated. That is, each crying or whining episode was reinforced with immediate attention. As a result, the frequency of crying rose dramatically and assumed the original high rate, demonstrating that the removal of attention was the critical factor. When attention was once more withheld crying again diminished to near zero frequency and remained at that level.

CONDITIONING

consumable reinforcers (such as food) . . .

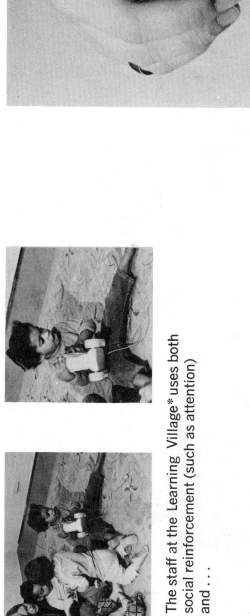

The staff at the Learning Village* uses both social reinforcement (such as attention) and . . .

* These photographs were taken at the Learning Village—an educational day-care center directed by Dr. Ulrich of Western Michigan University.

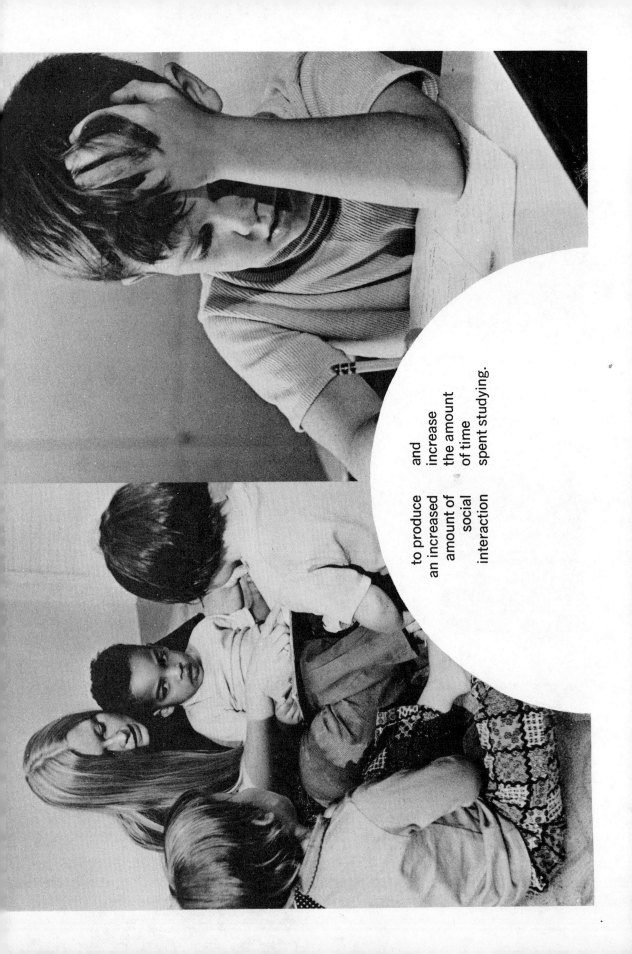

to produce
an increased
amount of
social
interaction

and
increase
the amount
of time
spent studying.

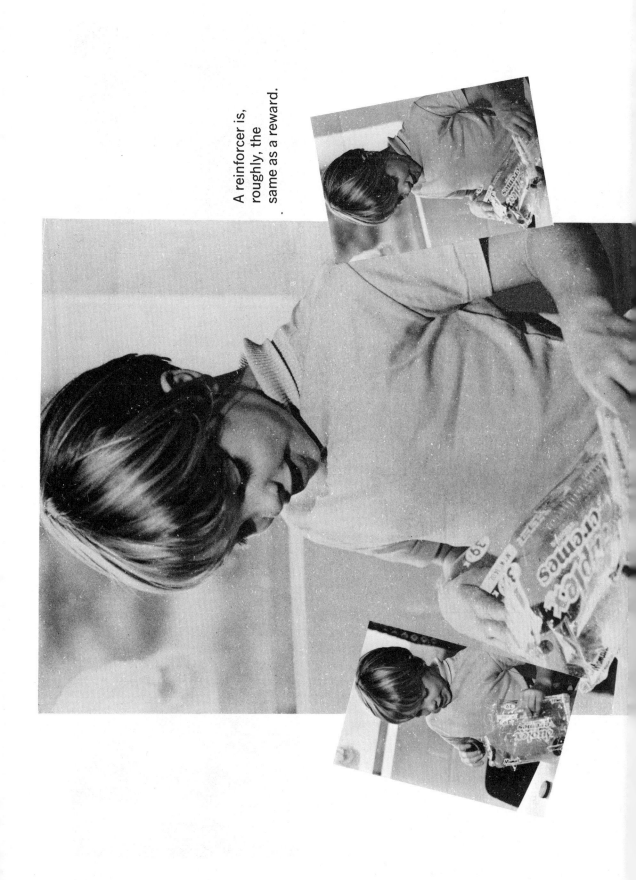

A reinforcer is, roughly, the same as a reward.

A substance is not
always a reinforcer
to different people . . .

or to the same
person at
different times.

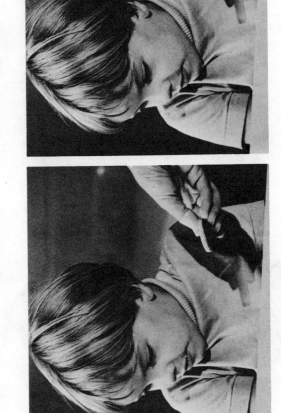

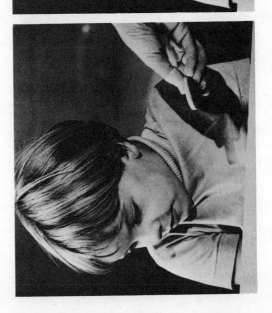

A reinforcer increases the frequency of a response.

A reinforcer must immediately follow a response.

and the rate increases . . . .

immediately after a response . . .

When a reinforcer is introduced . . .

CONDITIONING
is said to occur

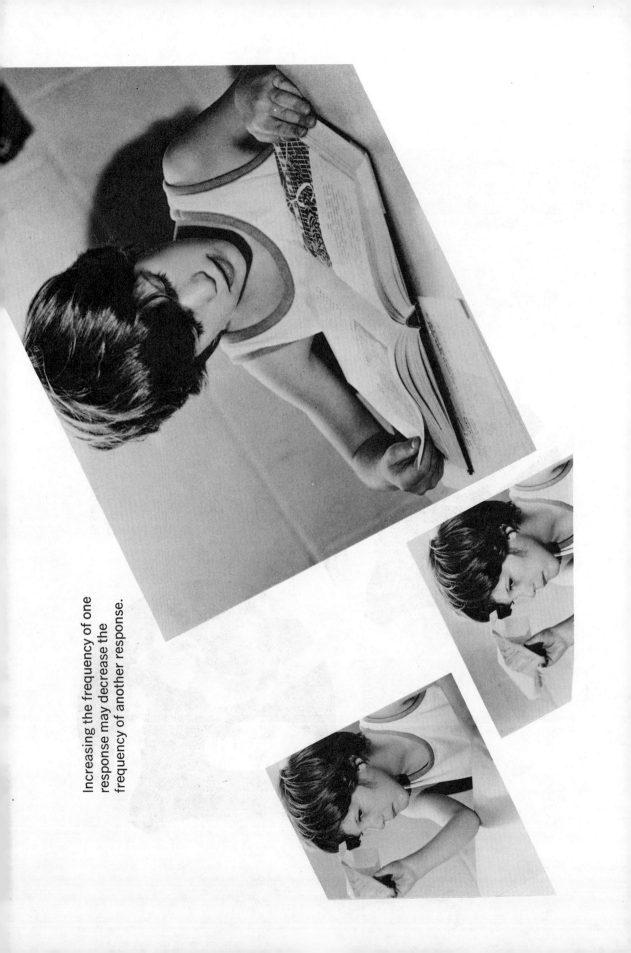

Increasing the frequency of one response may decrease the frequency of another response.

A single response or a class of responses (for instance, a class made up of all types of social interaction) may be reinforced.

CONDITIONING CONDITIONING CONDITIONING
NING CONDITIONING CONDITIONING CONDITIG
CONDITIONING CONDITIONING CONDITIONING
NING CONDITIONING CONDITIONING CONDITIO
CONDITIONING CONDITIONING CONDITIONING
NING CONDITIONING CONDITIONING CONDITI
NING CONDITIONING CONDITIONING CONDITI
CONDITIONING CONDITIONING CONDITIONING
NING CONDITIONING   CONDITI
CONDITIONING CONDITIONING CONDITIONING
        ING   CONDITIONING
            CONDITIONING
CONDITIONING   CONDITIONING
COND   CONDITIONING   IONING
NING CONDITIONING CONDITIONING CONDITI
CONDITIONING CONDITIONING
NING CONDITIONING CONDITIONING CONDITI
CONDITIONING   CONDITIONING
NING   CONDITIONING
                CONDITIONING
NING
CONDITIONING CONDITIONING
                CONDITIONING
    CONDITIONING
            CONDITIONING CONDITIONING
CONDITIONING
    CONDITIONING   CONDITI

CONDITIONING

CONDITIONING

In one of J. D. Salinger's stories, a child genius named Teddy is asked if he loves his parents.

> Teddy thought it over. "You know what the word 'affinity' means?" he asked, turning to Nicholson.
> "I have a rough idea," Nicholson said dryly.
> "I have a strong affinity for them. They're my parents, I mean, and we're all part of each other's harmony and everything," Teddy said.[1]

Like Teddy, most of us are not able to dichotomize our relationships with the world neatly into a like-dislike system. The fact that we do persist in many kinds of activities is probably more important than how we feel about them. The primary question is why and how our behavior is maintained day in and day out, and under what conditions we begin new activities and forsake old ones.

In the study of psychology, years of observation and experimentation have led us to believe the determining factor in the behavior of an individual is what follows the behavior. If the behavior yields a reward for an individual, the behavior will be retained and increase in frequency.

When we analyze behavior, however, we no longer use the term "reward" since an object, privilege, or dispensation offered by the giver as a "reward" may not be viewed in the same manner by the recipient. For example, an explorer who was visiting a primitive tribe became a local hero when he saved the chief's son from sure death by drowning. Needless to say, the chief was grateful and sought to reward him for his behavior by giving the finest gift he could think of—an extremely plump and giddy native woman who was the chief's most prized wife. When the explorer saw his "reward" his heart almost stopped; he immediately took a private but solemn oath never to play the part of the hero again.

In order to avoid a difference of opinion between a giver and receiver as to

1. From Salinger, J. D. *Nine Stories.* Boston: Little Brown and Company, 1953, 285.

what constitutes a reward, psychologists use the term *positive reinforcement*. The thing which is given is called a *reinforcer* and may take the form, for example, of a candy bar, a $50 gold piece, or a ticket to a play. For a given individual, however, none of these things may be a reinforcer. The thing which is given is a positive reinforcer only if it increases the frequency of a response or behavioral act it follows. In the example above, the chief's reward was not a positive reinforcer because it did not tend to strengthen or increase in frequency the hero-like behavior of the explorer. In actuality, the explorer's "hero responses" were less likely to occur than before the "reward" was given.

Positive Reinforcement with a Vegetative Idiot

Today, positive reinforcement is the single most effective technique in the treatment and training of retardates.[2] It is a comment on the newness of psychology as a science that the first important study of the efficacy of positive reinforcement in the modification of retardate behavior was done as late as 1949. The study, which was conducted by Dr. Paul Fuller, involved an 18-year-old boy who was described in the institution records as a "vegetative idiot." The boy lay constantly on his back and was unable to roll over. He could open his mouth, blink his eyes, move his arms, and, in an extremely limited manner, manipulate his head and shoulders. His trunk and legs were entirely immobile. He had never been heard to make a sound, and could not chew food placed in his mouth, although he did have a few underdeveloped teeth. For 18 years his diet had consisted of liquids and semisolids. It is easy to see why the term "vegetable" had often been applied to him.

At the time Dr. Fuller began his experiment, most of the institution's staff, and indeed, most of the professionals in the field of mental retardation, felt it was doomed to fail.

"A human vegetable such as this simply cannot learn," they typically said. "No method, old or new, will succeed!"

Dr. Fuller asserted that success or failure was something which could be determined after positive reinforcement had been tried. It remained to be seen. After observing their subject closely for some time in an effort to find a movement or response which the boy did with consistency, he and his assistants ultimately noticed that the retardate raised his right arm from a horizontal to a vertical position from time to time and with some regularity of movement. The frequency with which he raised his arm was observed and recorded for 20 minutes. It took place on an average of once per minute.

During the next ten minutes, something entirely new was done with the boy. A syringe filled with a warm sugar-milk solution was brought near his mouth. On previous occasions a similar solution had been fed to him in a cup and he had appeared to enjoy it. Perhaps it would serve as a positive reinforcer. Each time

2. This section based on Fuller, P. R. Operant conditioning of a vegetative human organism. *American Journal of Psychology*, 1949, 62, 587–90.

the boy raised his arm, a small amount of the sugar-milk solution was squirted into his mouth. Thus, each time he raised his arm, the solution followed reliably and consistently. If delivery of the sweetened and warmed milk was a positive reinforcer, the frequency of arm raising should have increased. Dr. Fuller and his assistants found exactly that. After 45 presentations of the solution, the average frequency of arm raising had increased from 1.0 to 1.12 times per minute. The next morning, after the completion of another session, the average frequency of arm raising had increased to 3.0 per minute, exactly three times greater than the frequency initially observed. It was apparent that the boy was less a "vegetable" and more a human being whose behavior could be modified by the proper technique; in this case, positive reinforcement.

In the experiment described above, sugar-milk solution was consistently presented following each occurrence of arm raising in close temporal association. Since the frequency with which the boy raised his arm increased, the sugar-and milk solution can be called a reinforcer. Each presentation of the solution therefore constituted a reinforcement. For other individuals, sweetened and warmed milk might prove to be far from a reinforcer; perhaps you would prefer a Coca-Cola or even a draft beer.

The procedure of introducing a positive reinforcer immediately following a response with a resultant increase in the frequency of that response is called *conditioning*. A response whose frequency has been increased in this manner is said to have been *conditioned.* In the study presented above, the raising of the arm was followed with warm sugar-milk and subsequently the frequency of arm raising increased; thus *conditioning* occurred. The boy's arm raising was *conditioned*. It might reasonably be said that the boy in Dr. Fuller's experiment merely *learned* to raise his arm more frequently, but psychologists prefer to use the term conditioning to describe what happens under these conditions, and to reject the older and less explicit term *learning*.

The term "learning" is roughly defined as "a change in behavior brought about by experience." It can be seen that "learning" is a much broader term than "conditioning," covering the plethora of activities and skills animals and men acquire through contact with their environment. Included within this category are the complex processes of verbal and symbolic skills in logic, and spoken and written language.

The meaning of "conditioning" is much more specific and exact than learning. Conditioning is also easier to understand; it is the increase in the frequency of a response which has been recently associated with a positive reinforcer under explicit conditions. In the future, when we know all there is to know about experience and its effect on behavior, we may find that all learning consists of compounds and combinations of simple responses that have arisen through conditioning.

Today, psychologists still use the term "learning" when behavioral changes due to unknown or undefined experience occur. It is a useful term at times, but when scientific explicitness and rigor are sought, they employ the more restrictive term "conditioning." In the following pages of this book, "conditioning" will be the mode, with a reference to "learning" here and again.

Conditioning with positive reinforcement involves more than finding an object or commodity which a person will work for. For conditioning to occur, the potential reinforcer must be presented closely after the occurrence of the behavior that is to be increased. Failure to present the potential reinforcer closely after the response will result in little or no increase in the frequency of the response, that is, in little or no conditioning. Unless applied properly, a potential reinforcer will fail to make the grade—it will not be a positive reinforcer, regardless of its potential, and conditioning will not occur.

The Importance of Immediacy of Positive Reinforcement in Conditioning

Everyone is impressed by the speed with which young children seem to acquire new skills. Most people erroneously believe, however, that infants cannot be taught directly, although they develop on their own. It is obvious that if the proper techniques are used with infants, any number of skills or behaviors can be conditioned.

One researcher demonstrated that consistently presenting bottles of milk to four-month-old infants each time they turned their heads dramatically increased the frequency of their head-turning behavior.[3] With a similar group of infants, he also showed that the same number of milk presentations was completely ineffective in conditioning head-turning behavior if the presentations of milk did not deliberately and consistently follow each head-turning response.

Three groups of ten infants each were employed in the study. Each baby in the first group was given a bottle immediately after he turned his head to the right. Upon receiving the bottle, the infant was allowed to nurse it for three seconds. The second group was treated in exactly the same manner as the first except that turning the head to the left produced the milk bottle. The babies in the third group were given bottles on a random schedule with complete disregard for their head-turning behavior.

The results were striking and conclusive. The milk served as a positive reinforcer of great effectiveness for the first two groups. Right head turning and left head turning increased tremendously in the respective groups. Milk presentations failed to condition head-turning behavior in the third group where milk was randomly presented. In the third group, the milk did not serve as a positive reinforcer.

We can conclude from this study that something that is offered or presented can be called a reinforcer only if it conditions the behavior with which it has been associated, and that it will become a reinforcer only if it is associated properly with the response. As will be shown, the optimum association of a positive reinforcer and a response occurs when the positive reinforcer follows the response immediately.

3. This section based on Siqueland, E. R. Operant conditioning of head turning in four month old infants. *Psychological Science*, 1964, *1*, 223–224.

The Use of Television Viewing as a Positive Reinforcer for "Coming When Called"

Until now, we have spoken only of positive reinforcers which can be consumed or swallowed. Edible things comprise only a small part of our environment. Many other items which cannot be eaten will serve as well and sometimes better than consumables as positive reinforcers.

While I was enrolled as a graduate student at Florida State University, I was able to see for myself how an everyday thing such as the opportunity to view television could be employed as a very effective positive reinforcer.[4] The case involved a nine-year-old boy who was brought to the Human Development Clinic where I was serving a practicum. It was the practice at the clinic for each fledgling psychologist to be assigned a case along with a supervisor who served as consultant, teacher, confidant, and in general, bailed him out if the going got tough. I was quite pleased to be assigned Dr. Todd Risley as a supervisor for even at this time he had a fine reputation in the field of behavior modification.

The boy, whose name was John, was brought to the clinic by his mother, who confessed that she was at her wit's end in trying to cope with her son. The aspect of John's behavior which caused her the most discomfort was his consistent failure to heed her when she attempted to call him in from play. She usually called him at least a half a dozen times and then finally was forced to roam about the neighborhood in search of him. By that time she was upset and found herself speaking more harshly to the boy than she intended. Later she often felt guilty and apologetic for having been overly harsh. There was a practical side to the problem, however. Meals often cooled before John appeared. Important appointments and telephone calls were missed because of the time consumed in rounding up John from his neighborhood haunts. For the same reason that the mother found her harsh words offensive, she was unwilling to spank him or even threaten physical contact as a measure of control. She came to the clinic seeking a means of controlling her child other than by spankings or harsh words.

The first thing we did was to ask the mother to keep accurate records of her son's behavior in regard to his response to her calling. We furnished her with forms drawn up specifically for this purpose and contacted her daily the first week to assure ourselves that recording was done correctly and reliably. The procedure consisted of the following: a standard type of call was to be given consistently by the mother from the same location on the back porch with the call given only once on each occasion. Also, John's mother limited the number of calls she would make during this phase of the treatment to four calls daily, a total of 28 calls each week. If John appeared at the back porch within ten minutes after the call, a plus mark was recorded on the mother's data sheet. If he failed to appear within ten minutes, a minus mark was recorded. The mother recorded this information

4. This section based on Whaley, D. L., and Risley, T. The use of television viewing opportunity in the control of problem behavior. Unpublished manuscript.

daily for four consecutive weeks during which time she was not receiving any active help with her problem. If her son did not appear after she had waited the ten minutes, she was faced with the old task of finding and bringing him home.

The next task was to find an object or privilege that would be a positive reinforcer for John. After several hours of discussion with John's parents, we learned that John greatly enjoyed watching television. John's parents had kept his television viewing to a minimum and had to some extent controlled the type of program he was permitted to watch. They were, however, willing to allow him more viewing time up to a certain point, and to give him almost unfettered choice as to the particular programs he watched, if in doing so his behavior could be controlled.

For the next four weeks, the opportunity to view television was offered to John under the following conditions. If John appeared within ten minutes after the standard call, he received a plus mark which signified a five-minute privilege of television viewing. If he did not arrive within ten minutes, no credit was given. Since John's mother felt that coming to meals on time was particularly important, an additional incentive was offered: for complying with a call to dinner within the limit, John received 15 minutes in which to view television. John could accumulate his viewing time and use it in a block during the prime evening programs or, if he wished, he could use it at various times during the day, provided it did not interfere with the household schedule. Figure 2-1 represents the initial four weeks of observation and the following four weeks in which television-viewing opportunity followed an answer to call. The vertical axis, or *ordinate*, is broken down into segments that correspond to the frequency with which John answered a call within the imposed time limit. The horizontal axis, or *abscissa*, is broken into eight segments that correspond to the eight weeks under discussion. The vertical broken line separates the first four weeks during which initial observations

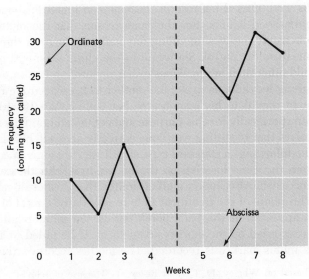

Figure 2-1   Noncumulative record

were made from the second four weeks during which television was introduced as a consequence.

The rapid increase in answering the call of his mother in the second four weeks illustrates that the television-viewing opportunity employed in this manner was a powerful positive reinforcer for John's behavior.

Another method of presenting behavioral information is by means of a cumulative graph, or *cumulative record* (see Fig. 2-2).

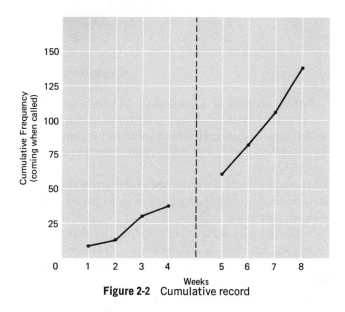

Figure 2-2   Cumulative record

Again the vertical axis is called the ordinate and the horizontal axis, the abscissa. The ordinate is labeled "cumulative frequency" and differs from the first figure whose ordinate was labeled "frequency." The labeling and segmentations of the abscissas for both figures are identical. The cumulative graph differs from Figure 2-1 in that the frequency observed for each week is added to the frequency observed for the preceding weeks. The sum of these is then added to the frequency for the next week, etc. The frequencies are very low during the first four weeks when no viewing time was offered as a consequence of coming when called. As a result, the tilt, or slope, of the data line is slight and does not differ a great deal from the horizontal plane, or abscissa. At the beginning of the fifth week, when television viewing was instituted, the frequencies cumulate rapidly and consequently the slope of the line is more diagonal. The change in the slope of the data line for the first four weeks compared to the slope of the line for the last four weeks tells the researcher that considerable conditioning has taken place. Cumulative graphs are used extensively in describing behavior and behavioral change.

The use of television viewing as a positive reinforcer turned out to be so successful that John's mother proceeded to use the same type of positive reinforcement for a number of John's other behavior problems. Perhaps equally as dramatic as the change in John's behavior was the change in his mother's attitude. Having learned how to exert a gentle but firm influence on her son, she found that she enjoyed him much more.

Positive reinforcement is an extremely powerful factor in our lives. Thus far in this chapter, we have seen how effective it is in conditioning simple arm raising and head turning and the more complex response of coming when called. In the following two cases in which positive reinforcement was used to condition a whole class of responses we will see that the resulting changes were so comprehensive that one might almost say the basic personalities of the two individuals were changed.

Conditioning Play Behavior

During Mark's first six months at a preschool, he rarely participated in play involving physical activity.[5] He was clumsy, and his occasional attempts at playing with other children were failures. He spent most of his time at school wandering about listlessly, sampling first one activity and then another, seemingly unimpressed and unentertained.

It might be thought that Mark was either fundamentally shy, retiring, clumsy and nonphysical, or that he simply had not had a proper opportunity for play behavior to be conditioned.

When Mark tried to play with other children, he disrupted their games because of his poor physical and social behavior. Whenever this happened, the teachers attempted to persuade him to do something more constructive. Since attention is usually a powerful positive reinforcer, the teachers may have inadvertently increased Mark's undesirable behavior of aimless wandering and disruption of the other children's play. It is likely that the undesirable behavior was continuing because of the teachers' social reinforcement.

Physical activity is important in our culture since so much social interaction centers around active sports and games. A child who cannot participate in these recreations is deprived of an opportunity for the conditioning of important social skills, which will be of use both to the child and to the adult in later life.

The teachers at the preschool resolved to try positive reinforcement to condition the desirable behavior. When feasible, this solution is very effective. In the present case, the preschool teachers decided first to condition a specific type of activity that consisted of playing on a large climbing frame, monkey bars, located on the playground.

The teachers used their attention as the positive reinforcer. When giving reinforcement, the teacher on duty stood within ten feet of Mark, watched him, spoke to him, smiled at him, touched him, or brought him other pieces of play equipment. When reinforcement was not being given, the teacher turned away and involved herself in other activities.

5. This section based on Johnston, Margaret K., Kelly, C., Harris, Florence R., and Wolf, M. N. An application of reinforcement principles to the development of motor skills of a young child. Unpublished manuscript.

For nine days the teacher on duty carefully watched Mark during the outdoor play periods before reinforcing climbing behavior. During those nine days Mark never climbed on the monkey bars and he touched them only once. He spent less than 1 percent of his time in contact with the monkey bars, 25 percent of his time simply standing still or walking around, and 75 percent of his time in such quiet activities as playing in the sandbox.

In order to get Mark to the monkey bars, the teacher decided to reinforce responses which brought him closer to the bars. Whenever the youngster approached or walked by the monkey bars, reinforcing attention was presented. Gradually he came closer to and stayed longer near the monkey bars. As this happened, the teacher became more selective and required that Mark be closer to the monkey bars and stay there longer before giving a reinforcer. Eventually he touched the frame and then began climbing it. From then on reinforcers were given only for the climbing response.

The response approximation procedure took place on the first day of conditioning. During that day, Mark was in actual contact with the monkey bars about 2 percent of the time. By the ninth day of the treatment, he was climbing the monkey bars 67 percent of the time that he was outdoors. This procedure was therefore very effective in increasing the amount of Mark's climbing behavior. In addition, Mark's skill at climbing also showed considerable improvement.

The treatment described thus far was incomplete, however, since it was not enough that Mark participated only in climbing monkey bars and in none of the other forms of physical activity. Furthermore, the teacher could not be standing around giving a reinforcer *every* time Mark was physically active. Therefore, a final phase of the treatment was instituted.

In the initial phase, the teacher provided reinforcement by paying attention to Mark as long as he was climbing on the monkey bars. During the final phase, she reinforced the climbing response only every other time that it occurred; and gradually she increased the number of times that Mark had to play on the monkey bars before she paid attention to him. At the same time, the teacher slowly reduced the amount of time she spent paying attention to Mark. At first she paid attention to him as long as he was playing on the monkey bars. Eventually she was staying with Mark and paying attention to him only briefly on any particular occasion of reinforcement. By the end of this phase of the treatment, Mark was receiving no more attention for playing on the monkey bars than were the other children in the preschool. During this phase, the teacher also gave social reinforcement to Mark for all other forms of vigorous play using other equipment. His acts of climbing ladders, suspended and inclined boards, packing boxes, trees, and other frames were also conditioned. During the four days of the final phase, Mark spent about a third of his time outdoors playing vigorously with the equipment. Prior to the treatment he had spent less than a tenth of his time in that way.

When Mark returned to the preschool in the fall of the next year, he continued vigorous and active play with the equipment over half of his outdoor time. Conditioning appeared to have had a lasting effect on Mark's play behavior. It is probable that once he developed a high rate of climbing behavior, such activity was maintained by the social and physical reinforcers that are normally available for climbing. When participating effectively in physical play, Mark was in a more favorable position for his social behavior to be conditioned.

Conditioning Study Behavior

In the preceding section we saw that it was undesirable for a child to be inactive. Excessive activity, or "hyperactivity," however, may be just as undesirable. There is a happy medium between too little and too much activity.

Earl was a hyperactive child whose parents and grandparents had been extremely brutal and cruel toward him.[6] His skull had been fractured before he was one year old; as a result, he suffered brain damage. When he was three years old, Earl was adopted by parents who were much kinder; however, he still had adjustment problems. When he was nine, he had not progressed beyond the second grade and was almost always misbehaving in the classroom. He was easily distracted and worked only short periods of time. Earl's hyperactivity took the form of talking, pushing, hitting, pinching, looking about the room and out the window, leaving his desk, tapping, squirming, and fiddling with objects. In addition, he was aggressive, pinched other children, and threw himself into groups of children, disrupting their work or play. One extreme form of disruptive behavior which he occasionally engaged in was shoving of his desk around the classroom, pushing aside all the children and desks in his way. Because Earl was an aggressive nine-year-old in a classroom of seven-year-olds, the other children consciously avoided him.

He was referred to Dr. Gerald Patterson at the University of Oregon Psychology Clinic. The traditional way of dealing with a child's behavior problems is to bring the child into the clinic and work with him there; however, Dr. Patterson went to the second grade classroom and worked with Earl in the setting where the boy's problems occurred.

If we want a person to behave normally, we should use positive reinforcement to condition normal behavior. Undoubtedly Earl was receiving a lot of reinforcing attention for his misbehavior. Therefore, strong positive reinforcers had to be used to condition more normal behavior. Dr. Patterson used M&M candies and pennies as reinforcers. You will find that, for the psychologist, M&M candies are very popular reinforcers—they reportedly melt in the child's mouth and not in the psychologist's hand. The normal behavior to be conditioned was attending properly to the school work. A small box containing a light bulb and a counter was placed on Earl's desk. Earl was told that at the end of each ten-second interval, if he had paid attention to his work for the entire time, the light would flash and the counter would add a count. Each time this happened he had earned one M&M or one penny and these would be given to him at the end of each lesson. The daily lessons lasted from five to thirty minutes.

6. This section based on Patterson, G. R. An application of conditioning techniques to the control of a hyperactive child. In P. Ullman and L. Krasner (Eds.), *Case Studies in Behavior Modification*. New York: Holt, Rinehart and Winston, 1965, 370–375.

Dr. Patterson solved the problem of what to do with the other children in the classroom by actively enlisting their help. The students were told that some of the pennies and candy which Earl earned for working hard and paying attention to his lessons were to be shared with all of them and that they could help Earl earn more if they did not distract him when he was working.

The decision of enlisting the help of the other students provided the additional bonus of social reinforcement. At the end of each conditioning session when the score was announced, the students applauded Earl. They also frequently walked by his desk to check the counter and to see how many reinforcers he had earned and spoke approvingly to him, thereby giving him the added reinforcement for which anyone would work even harder.

Before conditioning started, Earl spent 25 percent of his time making disruptive or inattentive responses. By the end of the ten days of conditioning, he misbehaved less than 5 percent of the time, which is about average for the normal child. In fact, near the end of the experiment, Earl was observed for a two-hour period; he was the best behaved child in the classroom. He was also less hyperactive and destructive on the playground and actually played with the other children rather than just hurling himself at them. Four months later, he was still much quieter in the classroom, and for the first time, other children were coming to his home to play. In addition, he was making progress in a remedial reading program.

Summary

In this chapter, we introduced the use of *positive reinforcement* in conditioning. We described studies in which positive reinforcers of a consumable nature were used to condition the behavior of a severely regressed retardate and of normal infants. Nonedible positive reinforcers were shown to be effective in conditioning a young boy's responsiveness to his mother's call, in conditioning active and productive play in a child, and in conditioning study behavior in a hyperactive child. From these cases the following points warrant emphasis.

1. The most important key to understanding, controlling, and predicting the behavior of individuals is the identifying or arranging of events that follow the behavior in question.

2. The term *positive reinforcer* is roughly synonymous with the more common term *reward*: however, a reward may or may not be a positive reinforcer. Only those events or objects that follow a behavior and subsequently increase the frequency of that behavior are defined as positive reinforcers.

3. An object, privilege, or dispensation that has been observed to be a positive reinforcer under some conditions and for some individuals may not act as a positive reinforcer for other individuals and under other conditions.

4. If an object or privilege with potential positive reinforcement qualities is to become a positive reinforcer, it must immediately follow the response to be conditioned.

5. Positive reinforcement may be used not only to condition specific re-

sponses but also to condition whole classes of responses. A *response class* is a set of responses that have something in common, for example, active play. A change in a response class may be so pervasive as to modify the character of the individual.

6. Conditioning one response class may have the indirect effect of decreasing the frequency of another response class.

7. In order to describe and study behavioral patterns and response frequencies, the data may be represented graphically. Two types of graphs have been introduced. In one type of graph, frequencies of response for each subsequent period of time are plotted independently and correspond directly with a specific time interval. In a second type of graph, called a *cumulative graph* or *record*, the frequency for each time period is added to the frequencies for the previous time periods. This method of representation has the advantage of demonstrating behavioral changes in a quick and dramatic way.

QUESTIONS

1. What is the problem with simply asking people what they like?
2. What is probably more important than having people say what they do and do not like?
3. After years of experimentation and observation, what do psychologists feel is the most important factor in the behavior of organisms?
4. Why was the term "reward" discarded by scientific psychology?
5. What term is roughly equivalent to "reward" and in what important properties does its definition differ from that of reward?
6. In the anecdote, why was the chief's reward not also a positive reinforcer? (Hint: Use the definition of a positive reinforcer in answering the question.)
7. In the section entitled "Positive Reinforcement with a Vegetative Idiot," describe the work of Dr. Fuller, the researcher who was among the first to demonstrate the effects of positive reinforcement on a profoundly retarded individual. Approximately how long ago did he do this study?
8. Describe the behavior which caused the subject in Dr. Fuller's experiment to be labeled a vegetative idiot.
9. What was Dr. Fuller's reply to suggestions that positive reinforcement would not work with a profoundly regressed retardate?
10. What response did Dr. Fuller and his assistants condition, and what was the positive reinforcer used?
11. What is the importance of positive reinforcement in the training and treatment of retardates today?
12. In the section entitled "The Importance of Immediacy in Positive Reinforcement in Conditioning," what was the prevalent feeling of most people about conditioning infants?
13. What response was conditioned in the study with the infants, and what reinforcer was employed?
14. How did the procedure in the experiment differ for each of the three groups of infants?
15. In which of the three groups did the response fail to increase, and why did the failure occur?

16. In order for a potential positive reinforcer to be effective, where should it be placed in time in its association with the response?

17. In the section entitled "The Use of Television Viewing as a Positive Reinforcer for 'Coming When Called'," why was John brought to the Human Development Clinic?

18. Why was John's mother reluctant to use spankings as a means of control?

19. What was the first thing the experimenter had the mother do?

20. In the study above, what constituted a "standard call?"

21. What did John's mother observe and record during the first four weeks?

22. What condition in John's home contributed most to making a television-viewing opportunity a positive reinforcer for him?

23. On a graph similar to that in Figure 2-1 and 2-2, what is the vertical line called? What is the horizontal line called?

24. What type of graph is presented in Figure 2-2?

25. How does a cumulative graph differ from the graph in Figure 2-1?

26. How do the labels of the ordinate of the two types of graphs differ, and what do the labels signify?

27. What aspect of the data line in the cumulative graph gives the experimenter immediate knowledge of change in frequency of response?

28. In the study on conditioning play behavior, describe Mark's initial behavior.

29. Before conditioning started, what were the preschool teachers doing that probably helped maintain Mark's undesirable behavior?

30. Why was it important to change Mark's behavior?

31. What specific response did the teachers condition?

32. What positive reinforcer did the teachers use?

33. What were the two limitations of the first part of the treatment, and how were they overcome?

34. In general terms, what were the results of the treatment at the end of the school year, and what were the results when Mark returned after summer vacation?

35. In the section on conditioning study behavior, describe Earl's behavior before conditioning started.

36. Did Dr. Patterson's treatment of Earl consist of having interviews with him at the psychology clinic?

37. What specific types of responses was Dr. Patterson trying to condition?

38. What did the box on Earl's desk do? Describe the relationship between what the box did and Earl's behavior.

39. What reinforcers did Dr. Patterson use with Earl?

40. The difficulty that is usually anticipated by teachers when Dr. Patterson's approach is suggested is the problem of what to do with the other children in the classroom. (a) True; (b) False.

41. In what way did Dr. Patterson get around this difficulty?

42. What did the other students in the class do to help Earl's conditioning process?

43. Briefly describe the results of the treatment.

44. Define positive reinforcement.

45. Define conditioning.

46. Give ten examples of stimuli which you think would act as positive reinforcers for yourself.

47. Give two everyday examples of conditioning which were not mentioned in this book.

48. Why is it that grades at the end of the semester are often not very effective reinforcers in maintaining studying behavior?

49. How could grades be more effectively used to maintain adequate studying behavior?

50. Think of some other reinforcers which might be used instead of grades for controlling the studying behavior of college students.

51. Think of a conditioning experiment that you could perform on your roommate.

52. What are some things which you think would be reinforcing to your psychology teachers?

53. What are some potential reinforcers for your psychology teacher which you have control of?

54. What is a response which you would like to see conditioned in your psychology teacher?

55. How would you arrange those potential reinforcers to condition that response?

56. Do you really think you should?

57. Do you think smiling and looking attentive to what he is saying is a reinforcer for your psychology professor?

58. Do you think that you could condition some *harmless* response in your professor by smiling and looking attentive immediately after each occurrence of the response during the lecture?

59. How could you reinforce dismissing class early?

NOTES

Positive Reinforcement with a Vegetative Idiot

It is surprising for many people to find that psychology is such a young, albeit energetic science. Sometimes a single study or experimental finding, which in the scope of the history of human behavior took place only yesterday, has such a sweeping impact that its manifestations proliferate geometrically almost overnight. Such an experiment was the one conducted by Dr. Paul Fuller. The demonstration that a profoundly retarded and handicapped individual could be taught by means of positive reinforcement was a hallmark in the field of mental retardation. Today the application of reinforcement techniques similar to those used by Fuller is the single most effective tool for the training and behavioral treatment of retardates. In numerous institutions throughout the country, retarded individuals are being taught complex skills and behaviors which, prior to Fuller's study, were considered impossible. The limitation in the efficacy of reinforcement techniques has yet to be established as each day new uses are discovered and explored. In later chapters, some of the more recent findings pertaining to the retarded will be presented.

Operant and Respondent Conditioning

We have been talking about one general type of conditioning procedure called *operant conditioning*. *Operant conditioning* is the process in which a reinforcer immediately follows a response with a reinforcer being defined as an event or object that increases the rate of a response which it follows. Another general type of conditioning procedure is called *respondent conditioning*. In respondent conditioning, a reinforcing stimulus is one which reliably elicits *brings out* a particular response, but need not increase the rate of a response which it follows. For example, a tap on the knee by a doctor's hammer elicits a slight knee-jerk response; yet the knee tap probably would not act as a reinforcer in an operant conditioning procedure. In respondent conditioning, a reinforcing stimulus is paired with a neutral stimulus; after repeated pairings of the two stimuli, the neutral stimulus acquires the characteristics of the reinforcing stimulus, with the neutral stimulus now eliciting the response. For example, if a bell is rung each time just before the doctor taps the knee, eventually the bell should elicit the knee jerk response.

The term *conditioning* was initially associated with respondent conditioning and later extended to cover the concept of operant conditioning. It is unfortunate that the words *conditioning* and *reinforcement* are used in both situations since fundamentally different processes may be involved.

Conditioning was initially introduced as a technical psychological term through a mistranslation of the work of the Russian physiologist, Ivan Pavlov. He spoke of an unconditional stimulus and a conditional stimulus. The unconditional stimulus, such as the tap of the doctor's hammer, was one which normally elicited a particular response. The conditional stimulus was only a stimulus for the knee jerk response if it had been paired with the unconditional stimulus or knee tap. Regrettably conditional and unconditional were mistranslated as conditioned and unconditioned, and by now the wrong terms have become so well entrenched in American psychological literature that it is doubtful they will be removed.

The Importance of Immediacy of Positive Reinforcement in Conditioning

The restrictive but technically sound use of the term *positive reinforcer* to describe an event or object that conditions the response it follows has created difficulty among students and professors alike. Most of the problem arises because an event can only be called a reinforcer if it functions to reinforce. If it does not condition the response it follows then, by definition, it is not a positive reinforcer.

The difficulty is compounded because some stimuli function as reinforcers for numerous responses, for numerous individuals, and under varied conditions. These stimuli could be called positive reinforcers in an abstract or hypothetical sense. If commodity X has been observed to act as a positive reinforcer a number of times in the past, it is probable that it will also serve as a positive reinforcer in the future. Candy has been called a universal positive reinforcer because it functions as a positive reinforcer for many individuals and for a wide range of behaviors and conditions. For some individuals, however, candy will not be a reinforcer. Therefore, an object or substance can only be called a reinforcer if it has been demonstrated to function as a reinforcer in the specific case at hand. When one speaks of commodities such as candy in the abstract or hypothetical sense, they are referred to as *potential positive reinforcers*.

Semantic confusion arises from words that may be made from the infinitive *to reinforce*. An object or event which acts as a *reinforcer*, that is, increases the frequency of the response it follows, is said to be a *reinforcing* object or event. The act of delivering a quantity of the reinforcer is called *reinforcement*. Reinforcement, however, is sometimes used to refer to a bit or chunk of a reinforcer which is delivered. In short, *reinforcement* becomes not the act of delivering but rather a small piece of the reinforcer itself.

The Use of Television Viewing as a Positive Reinforcer
For "Coming When Called"

The manufacturer of a gelatin dessert claims that his product is desirable even after a large meal. Regardless of the veracity of the manufacturer's claims, the notion he brings up is important where positive reinforcers are considered. In order for most consumable positive reinforcers to be effective, the subject should have been deprived of food for a certain period of time prior to the experiment. The experimental procedure of withholding a specific object so that later it will serve as a positive reinforcer is called *deprivation*.

In the study on the vegetative human organism reported in this chapter, the subject had been without nourishment for 15 hours. Under these conditions, the warm sugar-milk solution was a highly effective positive reinforcer. If Dr. Fuller had attempted his experiment immediately after his subject had received the regular institution meal, it is unlikely that the solution would have been effective. In all instances where edible substances are to be presented, it is incumbent on the experimenter to insure an adequate period of deprivation prior to the experimental procedure. Even if M&Ms, other small candies, or the gelatin dessert are used, deprivation remains an important factor. Regardless of whether or not the subject has just completed a large meal, if candies are the potential reinforcer, he must be deprived of the candies themselves if they are to be effective. If the large meal had consisted of nothing but gelatinous dessert or candies, it is unlikely that these substances would serve as positive reinforcers immediately after the meal.

With events, objects, or privileges that are not consumable, the role of deprivation becomes confusing. In the study above in which John received positive reinforcement in the form of the television-viewing opportunity, deprivation played an important part. In John's home television viewing was always a privilege. If, as in many homes, television-viewing opportunity had always been available, its presentation would not likely have been a reinforcing event. A period of deprivation would have to be established in such a situation and then television viewing would take on a different value for the individual.

In a similar way, the attention of or interaction with other persons of significance is not always found to be a positive reinforcer. For a child, the attention of a nursery school teacher would lack effectiveness as a positive reinforcer if the teacher had just completed a three-hour individual session with that child. In most school settings, attention is an effective positive reinforcer because the existence of other children who both require and seek out the teacher's attention ensures that each child will be relatively deprived of attention. It is this nearly constant deprivation which makes the teacher's interactions with the child so effective as a positive reinforcer.

The cumulative graph presented in Figure 2-2 was plotted with the help of a watch and hand counter. Times and frequencies were recorded on a data sheet and then plotted in graph form with much the same appearance as they have in the text. In the behavioral laboratory, this inconvenient method of representing data in a cumulative graph is replaced by a device which automatically accumulates responses as a function of time. This electronic recorder is often referred to as an "XY" recorder, because the marking pen moves both in a vertical and horizontal plane. Typically the behavioral scientist does not refer to this type of recorder as an "XY" recorder, but rather as a "cumulative recorder." Its primary benefit to the researcher is that it gives him an immediate and permanent record which he may monitor in an ongoing fashion, or may save for detailed study later.

Conditioning Play Behavior

In working with Mark, attention was used as a learned or *conditioned positive reinforcer*. Receiving attention is probably a positive reinforcer because it has previously been associated with other positive reinforcers like food and comfort. Reinforcers such as food are unlearned or *unconditioned positive reinforcers*. As we shall see later, many of the experiments with humans make use of conditioned reinforcers.

The failure of Mark's play behavior to be properly conditioned prior to the experiment raises an interesting question about the nature of play. Mark Twain noted the thin line between work and play. He observed that wealthy sportsmen paid a considerable amount of money to drive mule trains along a treacherous route because the task was said to be a sport. When the task was called work, people insisted on being paid for driving the mule trains.

The difference between work and play is not based on the activity itself, but rather on the positive reinforcement the activity produces. When the reinforcement is money, the task is work. At first glance, we might say that play contains its own reinforcement; play, by definition, is simply fun to perform. Additional positive reinforcement should not be, but frequently is, needed to get an individual to play. Most often play is a social activity. For example, sports are usually competitive, and, contrary to the old adage that "It's not whether you win or lose but how you play the game that counts," the major reinforcement for playing is derived from winning the game. A consistent loser may be induced to continue playing the game for a while on the basis of other conditioned social reinforcers such as frequent though untruthful comments about how well he is playing.

The need for extra reinforcement may be readily observed in faculty sports at a university. It is a ritual for a few men to spend many of their noon hours at the gym fighting the middle-age spread. However, the reduction of the middle-age spread, which is supposed to be the reinforcer, rarely occurs, and social reinforcers are necessary to maintain the act of going to the gym. A faculty member rarely goes to the gym to play on the handball court by himself. Although he could reduce his weight and perform the actual physical activities of the sport alone, there is no opportunity to win and no opportunity to receive praise. Occasionally a professor does go to the gym and work out by himself, but when he returns to his office, he usually lets his colleagues know what gallant efforts he made, thereby attempting to pick up a few delayed, but nonetheless desirable, positive reinforcers.

The need for extra reinforcement to maintain play behavior may be observed not only in college professors but also in retarded children who have not had the background of social reinforcement necessary to condition play behavior. It becomes apparent when they are presented with the opportunity to play that the activity itself is not reinforcing. They must be taught how to "have fun."

If you have not looked at sports and play in these terms you may find it interesting over the next few years to remember this analysis and see to what extent it applies.

A psychologist developed a variation on the distinction between work and play with his four-year-old son, Bill. Every night, the father came home from work with his briefcase full of papers and mail. After supper, Bill would persistently request that he be allowed to help his father work. Finally, the father would give in and allow Bill to take the papers and mail out of the briefcase and help sort them to the accompaniment of much social reinforcement from his father. This activity had all the earmarks of a game except that both the father and son called it work. It would be interesting to see if Bill's eagerness to work generalizes to other situations as he matures.

3

Now that we have covered the principle of conditioning, you may wish to observe the behavior of your fellow man with this principle in mind. Such an exercise will be amusing, interesting, and sometimes disquieting. There is one unfortunate illustration of the principle of conditioning that you are likely to encounter. It occurs in almost every family with young children. This is the conditioning of crying behavior. When a child is in pain, he cries, and the parent attends to him. Since the attention is reinforcing, the crying response eventually becomes conditioned. Then crying occurs even when pain is absent. Most mothers say that they can discriminate between crying due to obvious pain and crying conditioned by attention. Still they continue reinforcing the conditioned crying.

Sooner or later, you will run across this sort of thing. As a beginning psychologist, your most immediate reaction will be to try to dissuade the parents from any further conditioning of their child's crying behavior. Let me pass on a word of advice, hard won through bitter experience: in such situations, "Silence is golden." Parents do not reinforce that sort of assistance from psychology students; much to our dismay, they do not even reinforce this valuable help from psychology professors!

Suppose you do find a parent who wishes to eliminate the conditioned crying behavior. Is this possible or will the child be a "crybaby" the rest of his life? Can you erase a child's unfortunate history of reinforcement for crying? The rate of the crying response increased when reinforcement was given; perhaps the rate will decrease when reinforcement is withheld. Incidentally, you should not be confused by our use of "rate." When we are counting the number of responses in a given period of time, we most often speak of "the rate of response" instead of "the frequency of the response."

37

The Elimination of an Infant's Temper Tantrums

The boy was seriously ill for the first 18 months of his life; during that time, he received an unusually large amount of attention from his concerned parents. These circumstances were ideal for crying behavior to become conditioned, and it did.[1] In fact, the crying behavior became so well conditioned that the term "temper tantrum" would not be inappropriate. Conditions became so bad that the infant became the tyrant of the household; he had his parents under perfect control.

When they put their son to bed, the parents had to keep him company until he went to sleep. This usually took from one and a half to two hours. Now the parents were very loving, but no matter how loving the parents, they are bound to find it a little dull spending so much time watching their child go to sleep. Occasionally these bedside vigils would get to be too much; the patient parent would lose his patience and foolishly try to slip from the bedroom. The parent would barely have time to get the bedroom door closed before regretting the rash attempt at freedom. Boredom was better than the pandemonium which broke loose. At other times, the parents would try for a compromise. They would stay in the room, but attempt to sneak in a more reinforcing activity such as reading to themselves. Oh, foolish parents! Did they really think they could escape the watchful eye of the young tyrant? He was satisfied with nothing less than the complete attention of his subjects. The racket which the infant raised made reading impossible.

By the time the child was 21 months old, the parents were completely discouraged. If things kept going the way they were, they were liable to cease being loving parents; it is difficult to love a child who is making life miserable for you, even if it is your own child. They wanted to do something about this problem.

Their sitting in the bedroom and paying attention to the child probably served as a positive reinforcer for his crying behavior. Under Dr. C. D. Williams' guidance, they stopped the presumed reinforcement to see if the crying behavior would cease. The procedure consisted of leaving the child awake in the bedroom by himself. On the first day, he screamed and raged for 45 minutes before going to sleep! The parents certainly displayed an unusual amount of perseverance. Most parents who try a procedure like this can tolerate the crying for only a few minutes before they return to comfort the child, and inadvertently reinforce the crying behavior. But the parents had considerable confidence in the procedure and perhaps a good pair of earmuffs; they held to their resolve. Over a period of days, the crying behavior gradually decreased. By the tenth time the child was put to bed, there was not even a whimper. The child simply smiled pleasantly as his parents left the room. They could hear him making happy sounds while he was falling asleep.

About a week later, an aunt put the child to bed and left the room as usual. The boy immediately began screaming and fussing. The aunt gave in; she re-

1. This section based on Williams, C. D. The elimination of tantrum behavior by extinction procedures. *Journal of Abnormal and Social Psychology*, 1959, 59, 269.

turned to the room and remained there while the child went to sleep. That was all the reinforcement needed. After only one instance of backsliding, it was necessary to go through the whole extinction process again. In fact, the next time the child was put to bed, he cried for 50 minutes before going to sleep. But everything was in good order by the ninth time, when this crying was finally eliminated once and for all. In less than two weeks, they had eliminated a problem which had been making their lives miserable for more than three months.

At the time this case was reported, the child was three years and nine months. He had had no further bedtime tantrums and had grown into a friendly, expressive, outgoing youngster.

The course of the treatment is summarized in the cumulative record in Figure 3-1. The gradual decrease in the amount of time spent crying is shown by

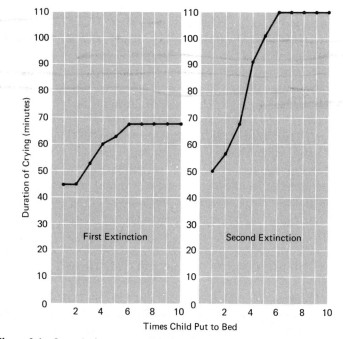

Figure 3-1 Cumulative record. Elimination of an infant's temper tantrums

the decrease in the slope of the curve. The abrupt increase in crying following the unfortunate episode with the aunt can be seen in the sharp increase in the slope of the cumulative record. When the crying behavior again decreased, the slope also decreased to a zero slope. Since this is a cumulative record, the curve never returns to the zero value on the ordinate; i.e., it never falls back to the abscissa. It is important that you learn to read these cumulative records, as they are very useful in presenting psychological data. If you are still having some difficulty in reading these graphs, you may wish to refer to the noncumulative graph of the same data shown in Figure 3-2.

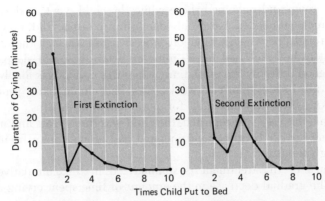

Figure 3-2 Noncumulative record. Elimination of an infant's temper tantrums

Dr. Williams used a well-established method to decrease the rate of occurrence of the response. It is called "extinction." The *extinction procedure* consists of withholding the reinforcement for a conditioned response. The typical *extinction behavior* is a gradual reduction in the rate of response, as a result of the extinction procedure, until the response is finally occurring no more often than it had prior to conditioning. The response is extinguished like the flame of a candle.

Students sometimes misuse the words "to extinguish." When they should say, "His response was extinguished," they mistakenly say "He was extinguished." These two sentences have greatly different meanings. If Dr. Williams had recommended extinction of the young boy instead of extinction of the crying behavior, he might now be in jail instead of the university.

The Elimination of Temper Tantrums in the Classroom

Elaine Zimmerman used the extinction procedure to eliminate conditioned crying behavior in an emotionally disturbed 11-year-old boy.[2] He was a student in her special English class for emotionally disturbed children. His frequent temper tantrums involved crying, kicking, and screaming. This behavior always disrupted the class. It was a common occurrence to see the attendants dragging the boy down the hall to his classes with him kicking and screaming all the way. He could invariably attract a large audience of staff members by throwing himself on the floor in front of the classroom and continuing his tantrum. The audience would watch him and comment as he lay on the floor kicking and screaming. A favorite hypothesis of the less imaginative onlookers was that these tantrums occurred when the boy was teased or frustrated. Since Mrs. Zimmerman was the

2. This section based on Zimmerman, Elaine H., and Zimmerman, J. The alteration of behavior in a special classroom situation. *Journal of the Experimental Analysis of Behavior*, 1962, 5, 59–60.

wife of an experimental psychologist, she had a different hypothesis. She noticed that the temper tantrums were not particularly associated with the child's being teased or frustrated. However, she did see that he received a tremendous amount of attention as a consequence of them. As you have undoubtedly anticipated, Mrs. Zimmerman felt that this attention might be acting as a reinforcer for the temper tantrum behavior. She decided to use an extinction procedure.

The next time a tantrum occurred outside her classroom, Mrs. Zimmerman asked the attendants to bring the boy into the room. The attendants placed the boy at his desk and left the room. Mrs. Zimmerman closed the door and waited. She told the boy that when he had finished crying, they could start working. The boy cried for seven or eight minutes and then said that he was ready to work. Mrs. Zimmerman went to his desk to help him with his English exercises, and the boy was very cooperative for the remainder of the class period. After several weeks of extinction, the tantrums in the English class disappeared completely.

You may recall from Chapter 1 that a nursery school student's conditioned crying behavior was also eliminated by the withholding of attention; that is another example of the process of extinction.

By now we have seen that the crying response seems to occur initially without conditioning; however it can become inadvertently conditioned and cause a great deal of difficulty. We also learned that such behavior can be eliminated by withholding reinforcement.

Now we will look at another response not normally thought of as conditionable. This is the vomiting response. We shall see that vomiting can be conditioned and extinguished like any other response. It will also be shown that it is helpful to recondition and re-extinguish the behavior when trying to find the relevant reinforcers.

Extinction of Vomiting Behavior in a Retarded Child

Laura was a nine-year-old girl who could not speak and was diagnosed as "suffering from mental retardation, cerebral palsy, aphasia, hyper-irritability, and brain damage."[3] She was admitted to the Rainier School, an institution for the retarded in the state of Washington. When the child first arrived at the institution, she had a strange tendency to vomit with an unusually high frequency, but within a few weeks the rate of vomiting decreased to once or twice per month. Soon the vomiting was forgotten. After she had been at the school for six months, Laura was enrolled in a beginning class which met every day. A month later, she began vomiting occasionally in class, and within three months, she vomited nearly every day. Laura became quite a marksman with her vomiting and had particular favorite targets. These included the teacher's desk, the table at which other members of the class were seated, and her own clothes when she had removed them.

3. This section based on Wolf, M., Burnbrauer, J., Lawler, Miriam, and Williams, T. The operant extinction, reinstatement, and re-extinction of vomiting behavior in the retarded child. Unpublished manuscript, 1967.

During each vomiting episode, Laura also screamed, tore her clothes, and destroyed nearly everything she could. Laura frequently vomited on her dress; whenever this happened the teacher took her back to the residence hall. Drug therapy was tried, but it was of no help. At the end of three months, Laura was permanently excused from class because of her vomiting.

Two months later, a brave teacher volunteered to take Laura into her own class with the idea that Dr. Montrose Wolf and his colleagues would help her. A physician indicated that Laura's vomiting was not due to medical factors. It is usually felt that vomiting is a response which cannot be controlled by reinforcement procedures; however, Dr. Wolf decided to see if that was the case. He guessed that Laura's vomiting had been conditioned by its reinforcing consequences. As you can well imagine, her vomiting was a response which attracted attention even in an institution for the retarded where bizarre behavior is the rule. They decided to withhold the special attention which was being paid her and to stop taking her from the classroom, since this might be reinforcing the vomiting response. The only attention she received due to her vomiting was when the mess was removed. This was done as soon as possible for obvious reasons.

At the beginning of the extinction procedure, Laura vomited many times in each daily one and one-half hour class period. The frequency of vomiting was so great that in one single class period she vomited a total of 21 times. The teacher who put up with this in order to help Laura is certainly to be admired. Her faith in the effectiveness of extinction was eventually reinforced; by the end of 30 days, the rate of vomiting had gradually decreased to zero. Surely the teacher breathed a sigh of relief when the behavior was finally extinguished and no vomiting occurred for more than 50 class periods.

Dr. Wolf and his colleagues wanted to be absolutely certain that the vomiting was a conditioned response, reinforced by the teacher's attention and Laura's removal from the classroom. This was important because they had to advise the residence hall personnel and future teachers on how to manage Laura's behavior in case she ever started vomiting again. Since this treatment was so new and radical, they needed to have very convincing evidence that it was effective. You can imagine how difficult it would be to convince a teacher, not enlightened about the principles of reinforcement, that the way to stop Laura from vomiting is to simply let her continue to vomit as much as she "wants" to.

It is possible that the extinction procedure had nothing to do with the decrease in the frequency of the vomiting response. It may be that the elimination of Laura's vomiting was due to entirely different factors, having nothing to do with her removal from the classroom. The fact that there was a decrease in the frequency of vomiting when the extinction procedure was started and the teacher stopped taking Laura from the classroom might have been a mere coincidence. Suppose an attempt were made to condition the response again and then to extinguish it for a second time. The rate should go up when the response was reconditioned and down when it was re-extinguished. If this happened, we would have a good deal more confidence that removal from the classroom was acting as reinforcement for the vomiting response; we could be fairly certain that we were not dealing with a coincidence.

Dr. Wolf had guessed that Laura's removal from the classroom reinforced her vomiting. If this were true, the teacher should have been able to recondition the response by taking Laura back to the residence hall each time that she vomited.

In order to condition the vomiting behavior again, it was necessary to wait until a vomiting response occurred. The extinction procedure was so effective that they had to wait for over 50 class periods before Laura vomited. At that point, they started reconditioning the vomiting response. The teacher continued reinforcing the vomiting response for 58 class periods. As soon as Laura vomited once, she was taken out of the class for the rest of the day. This meant that she could vomit no more than once per day during the conditioning period. At the end of the previous extinction phase, over 50 consecutive class periods had elapsed without Laura's vomiting once. Subsequently, the conditioning phase lasted 58 days and the vomiting occurred on 23 of these days. Toward the end of the conditioning, Laura was vomiting nearly every day.

Needless to say, Dr. Wolf, his colleagues, and certainly the classroom teacher were unwilling to let things stand at that. They insisted on extinguishing the response again. If they were successful with this final extinction phase, two goals would have been reached. They would have clearly demonstrated that Laura's removal from the classroom was reinforcing the vomiting response and they would, once again, have eliminated the serious problem from which Laura suffered. If Laura's vomiting could be eliminated, it would be unnecessary to curtail her education by permanently excusing her from school.

During this final extinction phase, Laura was kept in the class for the entire one and one-half hour period. She was no longer limited to a mere one vomit per class session, and she certainly took advantage of this opportunity. Vomiting occurred at an extremely high rate; as many as 29 vomiting responses occurred in a single class period during the first part of this extinction phase. It may seem strange that the response rate should be higher during the first part of extinction than it was during the previous conditioning phase, but remember that Laura was limited to only one vomiting response per class period during the conditioning phase. The effectivenesss of this conditioning could not really be demonstrated until she was allowed to vomit as often as she wanted. Eventually, however, the extinction procedure took effect and the rate of vomiting decreased to zero; by the end of the 34 class periods in extinction, the vomiting behavior was completely eliminated. The presumed reinforcer was removal from the classroom. We have seen that as the presumed reinforcement was withheld, presented, and finally withheld again, the frequency of vomiting decreased, increased, and finally decreased. This evidence should be sufficient to convince the most skeptical that removal from the classroom reinforced the vomiting response.

The treatment is summarized in the cumulative record in Figure 3-3. The high rate of vomiting during the initial extinction phase is seen in the very steep slope of the cumulative record. The process of extinction is reflected in the gradual decrease in the slope of the record until it finally has a slope of zero. At that point, the line is horizontal. During the conditioning phase, large sections of the cumulative record have a slope approximating the maximum of one response per class period. When the limitation of the number of responses per class period is re-

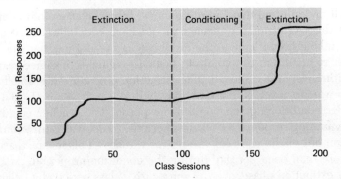

Figure 3-3 Cumulative record. Extinction of vomiting behavior in a retarded child

moved, during the final extinction phase, the initial slope of the cumulative record is extremely high. It gradually drops again to a slope of zero as the extinction continues.

If you are still having difficulty reading the cumulative response record, it may be helpful to compare it with the same data plotted noncumulatively in Figure 3-4.

Although it was very important to cure Laura of her particular vomiting problem, the study has even greater significance. Its major value lies in the fact that vomiting of this sort is a common problem among young children. The present study not only demonstrates that such vomiting may be a conditioned response, but also suggests a method of eliminating vomiting which has wide general application. In the enactment of the simple procedure of extinction, an important treatment has been given to clinical psychology. When using a new treatment for the first time, the therapist almost has a moral obligation to collect data and perform the treatment so that it can be published as a scientific experiment which demonstrates the effectiveness of the therapy. In so doing, he not only helps the individual under study, but may also indirectly help hundreds or even thousands of other individuals. Such long-range concerns characterize the clinical psychologist who is also a scientist. When he treats the therapy as an experiment,

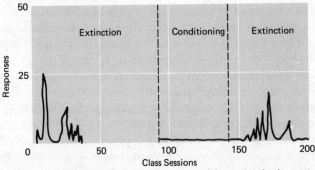

Figure 3-4 Noncumulative record. Extinction of vomiting behavior in a retarded child

he is not only showing concern for the welfare of an individual person but also for that of humanity in general.

We have been dealing primarily with the behavior of children. The next study will be concerned with two adult female mental patients. We have not been too surprised to learn that behaviors like head turning and arm raising are under the control of reinforcement processes. However we might not have anticipated that crying and vomiting could be conditioned and extinguished just as readily. Similarly, in this next study, we probably would expect that the behavior of visiting the nurses' office too frequently might be a conditioned response; however, it takes considerable imagination to anticipate that bizarre psychotic talk was also a conditioned response just like any other.

The Use of Extinction Procedures in a Mental Hospital

Most of the work in this book is quite recent and has been done in the last ten years. During this time new techniques have been developed, some of which may determine the course of psychology for the next one hundred years. It is reinforcing to be involved in a science when it is beginning to break through barriers to knowledge. For example, we are just now coming to grips with the problems of mental illness.

One of the first studies demonstrating a new approach in this area was published by Drs. Teodoro Ayllon and Jack Michael in 1959.[4] I was a graduate student in experimental psychology at the time. I remember that my fellow graduate students and I were elated by the article. We saw this as the forerunner of the application of scientifically established principles to the treatment of mental patients. These scientific principles were developed in the laboratory as a result of experiments with animals. This was the very kind of work which we ourselves were doing, and it was pleasing to see the results being applied to significant human problems. People who are involved in basic scientific research, such as we were, are frequently criticized by those who are unable to see any relevance to human affairs in such research. The work of Ayllon and Michael readily demonstrated the relevance. However, we felt that the article had greater significance than helping convince the skeptics that our efforts were not in vain.

The article demonstrated that a strong bond might be developed between clinical psychology and experimental or scientific psychology. Clinical medicine is based on the sciences of biology and chemistry, and engineering is based on the science of physics. We were afraid that clinical psychology did not have its scientific base, and for that reason might never attain the effectiveness of those other applied areas.

There are very good reasons why an applied field such as clinical psychology should be closely tied to a basic research field like experimental psychology. The scientific procedures available to the experimental psychologist make it possible

4. This section based on Ayllon, T., and Michael, J. The psychiatric nurse as a behavioral engineer. *Journal of the Experimental Analysis of Behavior*, 1959, 2, 323–334.

to discover valid laws of behavior. Clinical psychologists can then confidently apply these well established laws to the problems that confront them. In the past, much of the practice of clinical psychologists was based on intuition and vague, unsubstantiated hunches. In some cases intuition might be correct, and in others it might not. Unless clinical practice is based on scientifically established principles of behavior, consistently effective treatments will rarely be developed. The recent increase in the amount of scientifically sound clinical work seems to have justified our early excitement. The article by Ayllon and Michael is now one of the most widely reprinted and referred to articles in the field, although it initially attracted the attention of only a few.

When Teodoro Ayllon was a graduate student in clinical psychology, he had an opportunity to do his internship at the Saskatchewan Hospital in Canada. While there, he did the research for his Ph.D. thesis. Dr. Michael was his thesis advisor.

Like many pioneers in psychology, Dr. Ayllon had to work against many obstacles; prejudices, engendered by tradition, had to be overcome. The other personnel on the project had all been trained in an ineffectual standard approach to the treatment of mental patients. They felt that the patients' problems were symptoms of deep-rooted "psychic" disorders and not the result of unfortunate conditioning histories. They were all very skeptical about the project and did not think that appropriate behavior could be conditioned.

The mental patients were women, most of whom had been in the hospital for several years. At that time, it was felt that a patient who had been in the hospital so long could not be "reached." Such patients were placed on the back wards and given minimal treatment. In this initial work, Ayllon and Michael did not attempt a comprehensive cure of the patients' behavior problems but rather concentrated on the specific behaviors which were creating the most difficulty in the hospital. We will discuss only two of the cases. The first case involves Lucille, a woman who had a strange way of making a nuisance of herself.

For the two preceding years, Lucille had been making frequent uninvited visits to the nurses' office. These visits greatly interfered with the nurses' work. They felt very strongly that she should stop pestering them, but nothing they tried had any effect. Usually when she entered the office she was taken by the hand and led out or else actually pushed back into the ward where she belonged. Since Lucille had been classified as a mental defective and seemed hopeless, the nurses had become resigned to their fate. As one nurse put it, "It's difficult to tell her anything, because she can't understand—she's too dumb."

The psychologists decided that entering the nurses' office was a response, controlled by its consequences like any other response. Therefore some reinforcement must maintain it. When confronted with a problem of this sort, the first thing you should do is look at the events which consistently follow the undesirable behavior. These events probably constitute the reinforcer. In the present case, the undesirable behavior was entering the nurses' office and the event which normally followed was Lucille's being forced back out of the office. In this rather abrupt manner, the nurses were paying attention to Lucille. It might seem to you that this sort of attention could not be very reinforcing; however, it is since the back wards of most mental hospitals are devoid of much social reinforcement in the form of attention from the nurses. Generally the best way to get attention is to behave in a crazy fashion. This unfortunate aspect of life in a mental hospital probably contributes to the maintenance and even the conditioning of undesirable behavior in many mental patients. If leading and pushing Lucille out of the office served as the reinforcer, then the best procedure would be to extinguish the response by no longer paying attention to her when she entered the office. It may seem strange that the best way to stop Lucille from coming into the office was to stop trying to get rid of her.

During the week before extinction started, Lucille entered the nurses' office an average of 16 times a day. You can well imagine that the nurses were a little reluctant to try the extinction procedure, but they finally agreed to. During extinction, each time that Lucille came into the office the nurses continued their activity as if she were not there. After a few minutes, Lucille would leave and the nurses would breathe a sigh of relief. Over the eight weeks of extinction, the frequency of entering the nurses' office gradually decreased from 16 times a day to only twice a day. The extinction procedure was very effective.

This shows dramatically how behavioral experts were unable to solve a problem for two years; yet when the simple procedures of reinforcement, conditioning, and extinction were used, the behavior problem readily disappeared.

Helen's case involved an even more unusual behavior problem. She had a high rate of psychotic or bizarre talk which had persisted for the last three years. Her conversation was primarily about an imagined illegitimate child and the men who she claimed were constantly pursuing her. The nurses felt that she had "nothing else to talk about." Such a diagnosis had been of very little use in helping Helen with her behavior problem. Her psychotic talk became so annoying that in the four months prior to treatment, the other patients had frequently beaten her in an effort to keep her quiet. She was described by one of the psychiatrists as a "delusional patient who feels she must push her troubles onto someone else, and by doing so she feels that she is free."

We are used to thinking of psychotic talk as reflecting some internal turmoil or distorted perception. Consequently, it is difficult for us to consider it as a complex conditioned response like any other conditioned response. Most of the studies that you have read thus far had not been published when this treatment was performed. It took intellectually independent people with considerable imagination to think of psychotic talk as being a conditioned response. It also took courage to actually test a treatment for psychotic talk based on this conception since a treatment had never been tried before.

The nurses frequently paid attention to Helen when she talked in a psychotic manner. They would listen to her in an attempt to get at the "roots of her problem." When they did not actually listen, they would at least nod and remark, "Yes, I understand," etc. Such attention, which is normally reinforcing, is particularly so in the bleak environment of the back ward of a mental hospital.

During the treatment, the nurses ignored Helen whenever she talked in a psychotic manner and paid attention to her only when she talked normally. This treatment involved both the extinction of psychotic talk and the conditioning of normal talk.

During the week prior to the treatment, 91 percent of Helen's talk was psychotic. By the end of the first nine weeks of treatment, the psychotic talk dropped to less than 25 percent. This is a dramatic change, particularly considering the complex nature of the response and the fact that it had been occurring at a high rate for at least three years.

Some unforeseen events which had an undesirable effect took place during the last three weeks of the treatment. In the tenth week, Helen talked to a social worker who reinforced the psychotic talk. As Helen told one of the nurses, "Well, you're not listening to me. I'll have to go see Miss _____ again because she told me that if she could listen to my past, she could help me." Evidently the reinforcement for psychotic talk generalized to the ward, because the amount of psychotic talk doubled to become about 50 percent of the total talk. Other sources of unauthorized reinforcement occurred when a volunteer ladies' organization came to entertain the patients and when a hospital employee came to visit the ward. In both cases, the visitors reinforced the psychotic talk by paying attention to Helen when it occurred. Incidentally, a term which some psychologists use for unauthorized or "illegal" reinforcement is "bootleg reinforcement." Many social sciences attempt to usurp the prestige of the physical sciences by borrowing their technical terms. We are not sure about the status of a science that borrows its terms from the gangster argot of the prohibition era.

Since this was a pioneering study, it was not followed through to the extent that it might have been. Since this early work, Dr. Ayllon and Dr. E. Haughton have shown that psychotic talk can be essentially eliminated if more control is obtained over the patient's sources of reinforcement and the control is maintained for a prolonged period of time.[5]

Before concluding this chapter, it seems desirable to discuss a common source of confusion, the differences between the procedures for obtaining extinction behavior and forgetting.

Extinction and Forgetting

One of Dr. Donald Proctor's most famous cases is that of Jack B. When Dr. Proctor's receptionist arrived at the office one morning, she found Mr. B. impatiently waiting at the door. He was obviously very distraught and upset. The receptionist invited him into the waiting room and offered him a seat. As a matter of routine, she asked what his problem was. He was reluctant to discuss it but finally replied, "My problem is that I can't remember anything. I'm always forgetting." The nurse nodded sympathetically and informed him that Dr. Proctor would be available in a few minutes.

As soon as the doctor was free, Mr. B. was ushered into his office. "Now then, Mr. B.," asked Dr. Proctor, "what seems to be your problem?"

Mr. B. twitched nervously and confessed, "I forgot."

In order to understand the concept of forgetting, it is helpful to distinguish

5. Ayllon, T., and Haughton, E. Modification of symptomatic verbal behavior of mental patients. *Behaviour Research and Therapy*, 1964, 2, 87–97.

between the procedure to produce forgetting and the act of forgetting itself. We say that we have forgotten or cannot remember something if we are unable to make the appropriate response when it is called for. There is more to it than that. Forgetting is supposed to be a decrease in the likelihood that a response will occur as a result of that response's not having been made for a long period of time. We can say that the *forgetting procedure* consists of preventing a response from occurring for a period of time after it has been conditioned. In the fictitious, but, we hope, humorous case of Mr. Jack B., a period of time elapsed between his stating the problem to the receptionist and his failure to make the same response to the psychologist. Presumably the mere passage of time was sufficient to eliminate the response of saying, "My problem is that I can't remember anything." When this forgetting procedure eliminates a response, we say *forgetting* has occurred.

You recall that the "extinction procedure" consists of allowing the response to occur without reinforcement after it has been conditioned. If the extinction procedure eliminates a response, then extinction behavior has occurred.

The difference between the two procedures is as follows: in the forgetting procedure, the response is prevented from occurring for a period of time. In the extinction procedure the response is allowed to occur but reinforcement is withheld. Forgetting and extinction behavior are similar in that they both consist of a decrement in the rate of the response. They are different in that forgetting is due to the lack of an opportunity to respond and extinction is due to responding without reinforcement.

The psychological term "forgetting" is a very common everyday term, whereas the psychological term "extinction" is not such a common term. You might think that "forgetting" is much more important; it should receive more emphasis than "extinction." Perhaps an experiment by Dr. B. F. Skinner of Harvard University will indicate why this is not the case.[6]

Dr. Skinner conditioned several pigeons to peck a particular spot on a target. The response was reinforced by the occasional presentation of some birdseed. After accurate pecking had been well conditioned, the birds retired to their pigeon coop for six years. When the birds were presented with the target again and given an opportunity to respond, they did so immediately and with the utmost accuracy. Dr. Skinner was unable to get his pigeons to forget the target-pecking response even though they had not had an opportunity to practice it for six years.

Now, you may feel that you forget things nearly every day. Does this mean that you would be better off if you had a bird brain like Skinner's pigeons? Probably not. Once you have learned to drive a car, ride a bicycle, roller skate, or dance, you will not forget it even though it might have been years since you had occasion to demonstrate such skills. On the other hand, if you learn to drive a car on the right-hand side of the road in the United States and then spend some time driving on the left-hand side in England, you had better be careful when you return to this country. It may look like you have forgotten that you should drive on the right-hand side of the road, but in fact what has happened is that driving on the left-hand side of the road was conditioned and driving on the right-hand side

6. Skinner, B. F. Pigeons in a pelican. *American Psychologist*, 1960, *15*, 28–37.

of the road was extinguished or punished. If the response of driving on the right-hand side of the road is not rapidly extinguished in England, then you will be.

When it appears that you have forgotten the phone number of your former boy friend or girl friend, in fact what has happened is that that particular series of number responses has been extinguished and other responses have been conditioned in its place. Such processes of extinction and reconditioning can be extremely complex when they involve verbal material, but extinction and conditioning seem to account for all cases of apparent forgetting. Many laboratory experiments have been conducted on verbal learning which support this notion.

With this in mind, note that Dr. Skinner's experiment shows that when you prevent extinction from occurring and you prevent any other response from being learned, a response decrement is not obtained. It would appear that there is really no such thing as pure forgetting. It is to be understood in terms of the extinction of one response and the learning of other incompatible responses.

Summary

In this chapter we have studied the extinction of a wide variety of responses with both children and adults. We have seen that the crying responses of a young child and even an infant can be conditioned and extinguished. The main points covered in this chapter are:

1. First the process of extinction was considered. The *extinction procedure* consists of withholding reinforcement for a conditioned response. The typical *extinction behavior* is a gradual decrement in the rate of the response until it occurs no more often than it did prior to conditioning.

2. Then forgetting was considered. The forgetting procedure consists of preventing the occurrence of a response for a period of time. *Forgetting behavior* is a decrease in the rate of response following a period when the response did not occur.

3. Finally, forgetting was compared with extinction. Forgetting behavior and extinction behavior are similar in that they are both decreases in response rate. However the forgetting procedure and the extinction procedure differ. The forgetting procedure involves the prevention of the occurrence of the response, whereas the extinction procedure allows the response to occur without the reinforcement.

4. The forgetting procedure does not in fact seem to lead to forgetting behavior. What commonly appears to be forgetting is due to extinction and the conditioning of incompatible responses.

5. Many psychological therapists also act as scientists and collect reliable data on the effectiveness of their treatments. In the long run, they help many more people than those they deal with at first hand.

6. Applied fields such as clinical psychology should be closely tied to basic research fields such as experimental psychology. This allows for the development of much more effective treatments.

QUESTIONS

1. What is the unfortunate illustration of the principle of conditioning which can be observed in almost every family with young children?
2. Can most mothers discriminate between crying due to pain and conditioned crying?
3. Dr. Williams was specifically concerned with temper tantrums which the child threw on particular times during the daily routine. What were these occasions?
4. What was the reinforcement for the temper tantrums?
5. What happened when the parents attempted to read while waiting for their son to go to sleep?
6. What did the parents attempt to do to eliminate their child's problem?
7. What was the result of the treatment?
8. What was the first thing that the child did when his aunt put him to bed and left the room?
9. What was the aunt's response to this behavior of the child?
10. What was the consequence of the aunt's response the next time that the child was put to bed?
11. What were the long-term effects of the treatment?
12. What is the technical term for the procedure which Dr. Williams recommended?
13. Give a rough definition of the extinction procedure.
14. Give a rough definition of extinction behavior.
15. What mistake do students commonly make when using this term?
16. What problem did we discuss that Mrs. Zimmerman dealt with in her English class for emotionally disturbed children?
17. What were some of the things that happened as a consequence of the little boy's undesirable behavior?
18. These consequences might be summed up by saying that the child received a large amount of at_____ when he misbehaved.
19. What did Mrs. Zimmerman think was the effect of these usual consequences?
20. How did Mrs. Zimmerman deal with the problem?
21. What is the technical term describing the procedure which she used?
22. What were the results of this procedure in her classroom?
23. What problem did Laura, the retarded girl, have which was dealt with in this chapter?
24. This vomiting behavior eventually began occurring primarily in one place. Where was this?
25. What things usually happened to Laura as a consequence of her vomiting in the classroom?
26. Dr. Wolf guessed that attention and removal from the classroom were acting as a re_____ for Laura's undesirable behavior.
27. What is the technical term for the initial procedure which Dr. Wolf used to treat Laura's problem?
28. Specifically, how was this initial procedure carried out?
29. What were the results of this initial procedure? In other words, describe the frequency of the response during the first part of this phase and during the final part.

30. There were actually three major phases to this treatment. What is the technical term describing the second phase?
31. Specifically what was done during this second phase?
32. What happened to the frequency of occurrence of behavior during this phase?
33. Why was the conditioning phase added?
34. What is the technical name to describe the third and final phase of the treatment?
35. Specifically what was done in this final phase?
36. Why were the results of the conditioning phase more apparent during the initial part of the re-extinction phase of the treatment?
37. What was the behavior like during the final few days of this terminal extinction treatment?
38. Why was this terminal extinction treatment added?
39. Can you draw a cumulative graph summarizing the results of this study and label the ordinate and abscissa? Similarly, can you draw a noncumulative graph? If you do not think that you can, you should take a look at the graphs again.
40. What should the scientist-clinician do who is not only concerned about a particular individual but with all of mankind?
41. Most of the research reported in this book was done in the preceding century. (a) True; (b) False.
42. In what way did the work in the mental hospital by Dr. Ayllon and Dr. Michael help the basic researchers justify their efforts?
43. Has there been a long and close relationship between clinical and experimental psychology?
44. What did this work in the mental hospital indicate about the possible relationship between clinical psychology and experimental psychology?
45. In the past, much of the practice of clinical psychologists was based on intuition and other vague, unsubstantiated hunches. (a) True; (b) False.
46. In what way can experimental psychology help clinical psychology?
47. The work done by Dr. Ayllon and Dr. Michael was made particularly easy because all of the personnel on the project were in complete agreement with the scientists and had a good deal of confidence in the success of the outcome. (a) True; (b) False.
48. How long had most of the patients been in the mental hospital? (a) Several days; (b) Several weeks; (c) Several months; (d) Several years.
49. What was the general attitude toward the likelihood of a cure for such patients?
50. What was usually done with them?
51. Did Drs. Ayllon and Michael attempt a comprehensive cure of the patients' behavior problems so that they would be completely normal again and could leave the mental hospital?
52. Describe the problem Lucille created at the nurses' office.
53. Prior to the treatment, in what specific ways did the nurses usually respond to Lucille when she entered the office?
54. What was the reinforcement for Lucille's frequent entrances into the nurses' office?
55. In general, how should one behave if he wishes to get attention in a mental hospital?
56. How does getting attention for behaving abnormally affect the development of normal behavior?
57. What is the technical term for the procedure used to treat Lucille?
58. Specifically, what did the nurses do during this treatment?

59. What were the results?

60. Describe Helen's verbal behavior; what sorts of things did she talk about?

61. What was the reinforcement for her bizarre verbal behavior?

62. Describe the treatment used and give the technical name.

63. What were the initial results of the treatment?

64. How did the social worker cause difficulties during the end of Helen's treatment?

65. What is "bootleg reinforcement?"

66. Give at least a rough definition of the forgetting procedure.

67. Give a rough definition of forgetting behavior.

68. In what way is forgetting behavior like extinction behavior?

69. In what way is the forgetting procedure different from the extinction procedure?

70. Can you think of a better joke about forgetting? If you can, will you send it to the authors; they would appreciate it.

71. What response did Dr. Skinner condition with the pigeons?

72. Once the responses were conditioned, what did Dr. Skinner do with the pigeons?

73. What is the technical name for the process which Dr. Skinner was trying to demonstrate?

74. What was the final test that Dr. Skinner performed with the pigeons?

75. What were the results of this final stage of the experiment?

76. What are the implications of Dr. Skinner's experiment for forgetting?

77. Two things are usually occurring when we think that something has been forgotten. What are those two things?

78. Can you think of an irritating response which someone you know frequently makes? If you cannot, think a little harder. If you can, what is that response?

79. What do you think frequently occurs as a consequence of the response? Incidentally, the consequence need not occur every time in order to be important.

80. Do you think this consequence can act as a reinforcer for the response?

81. Can this potential reinforcer be withheld so that the response might be extinguished?

82. Give two more examples like the above, but be sure to cite examples in which you could personally make certain that the reinforcement is withheld.

83. Now think of behavior on your part which you would like to see eliminated.

84. What is the reinforcement for that behavior?

85. Do you have control over the reinforcement, or does someone else? If someone else has control over the reinforcement, could you arrange it so that they would withhold the reinforcement for this behavior?

86. Now work through another example of behavior of yours which you would like to see eliminated. Be sure to select some behavior for which you or someone else can withhold the reinforcement.

NOTES

The Elimination of an Infant's Temper Tantrums

Most psychologists are just as bad as other people about reinforcing their children's crying behavior. This seems to be true even when they realize that they are conditioning the crying. In other words, psychologists are just like everyone else, or almost like everyone else. In any case, they find their children's crying just as aversive and upsetting as most parents do. Like other children, the psychologist's child is also able to control his parents quite well by throwing temper tantrums. A psychologist-parent will do whatever is necessary to terminate the aversive stimulation. One of the easiest and most acceptable ways of terminating crying behavior is to comfort the child. Comforting and paying attention to the child has the short-term consequence of allowing the parent to escape from the aversive crying. The short-term consequence maintains that behavior on the part of knowledgeable parents, even when the parents are psychologists and presumably know better. The behavior continues in spite of the fact that it has the long-term consequence of causing crying to occur more frequently in the future. Because of their eagerness to escape the immediate crying, the parents act in a manner which exposes them to a greater total amount of crying in the long run. Unfortunately, this seems to be a very general problem. Our behavior is usually under the control of short-term consequences when we would be better off if the long-term consequences were in control.

Extinction of Vomiting Behavior in a Retarded Child

Usually when a scientist performs an experiment, he wishes to conclude that the results of the experiment are due to something he did. He is always worried about the danger of a wrong interpretation of his results. Perhaps the results were due to chance.

In the study of vomiting behavior, the decrease in Laura's vomiting might not have been due to the removal of the presumed reinforcer. The fact that the decrease in response rate occurred at the same time that the reinforcement was withheld could have been a coincidence. We can present and withhold reinforcement several times; if each time that we do this, the response increases or decreases accordingly, then it is very likely that the reinforcement is controlling the response. It is very unlikely that the results are due to chance. We saw how Dr. Wolf and his colleagues used this procedure. They extinguished, conditioned, and finally re-extinguished the vomiting response in order to eliminate even the shadow of a doubt that the vomiting was being controlled by removal from the classroom. A similar approach was used by Dr. Fuller. After he had conditioned the arm-raising response in the vegetative idiot, he successfully extinguished the response. He did this to strengthen his case that the warm milk acted as the reinforcer in the initial conditioning.

In another experiment, in Chapter 2, the head-turning response was conditioned in four-month-old infants. After this was done, the response was extinguished and then once again conditioned. This procedure also supports the notion that the *presumed* reinforcer was in fact an *effective reinforcer*.

We also saw in Chapter 2 that play behavior could be conditioned through the use of social reinforcement. After that part of the study was completed, the monkey bar-climbing response was extinguished and then reconditioned to make certain that the social reinforcement was really controlling the response and that conditioning was occurring.

It is scientifically useful to be able to show that when we present and withhold reinforcement, the response rate increases and decreases. This helps us demonstrate that the reinforcement is really controlling the behavior. The use of extinction as a check to ensure that the true reinforcer is being manipulated has become a widely applied technique.

Occasionally, it is undesirable to use an extinction procedure to help pinpoint the

The cumulative recorder is a winner
A novel invention of B.F. Skinner
It records responses for you, Brother,
And piles them on top of one another.
Displayed in orderly togetherness
It wipes out mess
    Ends duress
    Adds Finesse
      To your best guess
        Of what's happening.
Check the curve
It's really strange
    No uppers and downers
The only change
    Is the slope gets high.
Each R adds on
    and that is why
With one quick scope
You can state
    That the steeper the slope
    The faster the rate.
      (And if there's no responding
      The slope is straight.)
Just one more thing
    And you'll be set.
We haven't mentioned
    The hatch mark yet.
That southeast mark is plain indeed
One more record for your need.
It counts the times the subject thrived
On something for which he's been deprived.

relevant reinforcers. For example, sometimes extinction of the conditioned response might directly or indirectly cause physical harm to the individual being worked with. In other cases, an extinction procedure is simply not possible. Once a response has been conditioned, it may be maintained by reinforcers which the experimenter cannot control. For example, if an enterprising young man were to condition amorous behavior on the part of his pretty girlfriend, she would probably have no trouble finding other boys to reinforce such behavior if he decided to extinguish it.

In addition to the extinction procedure, there is another sort of check on whether or not conditioning has occurred. It should be performed but usually is not. Just because the response increases in the presence of the presumed reinforcer and decreases in its absence, it does not follow that conditioning is taking place. In order for conditioning to occur, it is normally necessary for the reinforcer to follow the response immediately.

Consider the experiment on arm raising with the vegetative idiot. It is possible that simply squirting the warm sweetened milk in his mouth made the idiot more active and therefore increased the rate of arm raising. Perhaps when the milk was withheld he became less active and the frequency of his arm raising decreased. In other words, the presentation of milk was probably the event which increased the arm raising. However, this result may not have been due to the reinforcing property of the milk nor to the fact that the milk immediately followed the response. The increased frequency of arm raising might not have been due to conditioning and the decrease might not have been due to extinction. What could we do to check the possibility that it was not necessary for the milk to follow the response immediately in order for the response to increase in frequency? In other words, how can we find out whether or not conditioning really occurred? We could present the presumed reinforcer randomly so that it would rarely follow the response. We would squirt some milk in the mouth of the vegetative idiot every now and then regardless of whether or not he had just raised his arm. If this produced an increase in the frequency of arm raising, we would conclude that conditioning had not really taken place. On the other hand, if arm raising did not increase, we would have very powerful evidence that conditioning had taken place.

The experiment on conditioned head turning in infants illustrates this. The group that had the reinforcement delivered randomly was actually a test group to determine whether it was necessary for the reinforcement to follow the response immediately. As it turned out, this group did not learn the head-turning response; therefore it can be concluded that conditioning, in fact, occurred for the other groups.

In some respects the researcher was like a man wearing suspenders and a belt; in order to be doubly safe, he also used another technique for demonstrating that conditioning was really occurring. For one group, he attempted to condition head turning to the right but he recorded the frequency of head turns to the left as well as to the right. For that group he found that right head turns increased in frequency more than left head turns during conditioning. Comparable results were obtained for the left-turning group. It would be difficult to interpret this data as anything other than strong evidence for conditioning.

An expression which is frequently used in this context is *control group* or *control procedure*. In the past most psychological research involved large groups of subjects. For example, one group of subjects might receive reinforcement immediately following the response. This is called the "experimental group," the group for which conditioning is to be obtained. The other group of subjects would have reinforcement randomly presented. That would be the "control group," the group where conditioning could not occur. If the response rate increased more in the experimental group than in the control group, then conditioning had been obtained. The control group was treated exactly like the experimental group except for the one crucial factor of immediate reinforcement. In other words the control group controls for all extraneous factors which might have produced an increase in response rate.

In the last few years psychology has made many advances and now it is usually not necessary to use large groups of subjects in experiments. In fact, most of the research we have reported here has made use of a single subject and could not have been done if large groups were used. Can you imagine finding one hundred children who had conditioned vomiting responses and who were available for experimentation? Half of them would be the experimental group that would receive extinction for vomiting. The other half would be the control group that would be treated as they always had been. Even if one hundred young vomiters had been available for the experiment, I doubt that anyone would have been willing to put up with them. Fortunately, we are now able to do research with single subjects. Instead of speaking of "control groups," we speak of "control procedures." Dr. Wolf first extinguished the vomiting response. Then as a control procedure to demonstrate the effectiveness of the reinforcement, removal from the classroom, he reconditioned the response. As another control procedure, he finally re-extinguished the response. When we use a control procedure with a single subject, we speak of the subject as "serving as his own control."

The general procedure of controlling for the effects of unknown factors is one of the most important in science. It is one of the major techniques which has made the scientific method the most useful way of finding out about the world.

Behavior such as vomiting, which involves the smooth muscles and not the striated skeletal muscles, is usually classed as respondent behavior. It is felt that respondent conditioning, discussed in the notes of Chapter 2 and in Chapter 21, is a most effective way of modifying respondent behavior. Prior to this study, the only attempts at conditioning the vomiting response have used respondent conditioning procedures. This is why the success of the operant conditioning procedure is so surprising.

The Use of Extinction Procedures in a Mental Hospital

Scientists engaged in basic research are pleased to see the results of their work applied to the betterment of mankind; it certainly helps them account for their efforts to the laymen. However in most cases, they do not feel that such applications are necessary in order to justify their work to themselves. They feel that basic research is of value if it adds to the knowledge and systematic development of science without regard to its ultimate applicability to human affairs. This sort of motivation is difficult for many beginning students to understand. However, if you ever have the opportunity to become involved in a basic research project, you will soon see that these scientific problems are every bit as interesting and challenging as are the problems outside the laboratory.

For years the psychologists doing basic research insisted on working with rats and pigeons in the laboratory. Paradoxically, their work has laid the foundations for the development of a psychology which can be effectively applied to human affairs. Those psychologists who concerned themselves exclusively with the problems of mankind did so with very little success. Ironically, the scientists who erroneously gave the impression of caring little about man's ultimate welfare are now contributing the most to it.

Before the psychologists in basic research realized that they had anything to contribute outside the laboratory, they were most vociferous about the virtues of pure science and disdainful of anyone concerned with the everyday world. Now that the experimental psychologists see that they have something to contribute to the outside world, they are as eager to do so as anyone else. At this point, if there is any danger, it may be that the laboratory scientist will find the social reinforcement involved in applied psychology too much to resist. If too many leave their "ivory towers," we may soon run out of new scientific developments which can be applied to human affairs.

Helen's talk about her illegitimate children and the men who were pursuing her is typical of the sexual emphasis to be found in the bizarre talk of mental patients. This has traditionally been taken as indicative of the patients' underlying sexual disturbances. However, an analysis of psychotic talk in terms of conditioning yields a different picture. The mental patient, like anyone else, will exhibit any behavior in his repertoire if it is reinforced. When a patient's audience pays particular attention to talk with sexual implications, that sort of talk will be reinforced and will occur most frequently. If "deep-seated" sexual disturbances are involved, they may not be in the mental patient.

Extinction Behavior #1

Extinction Behavior #2

Extinction Behavior #3

Extinction Behavior #4

Extinction Behavior #5

Extinction Behavior #6

4

An apocryphal baseball story concerns the New York Yankee star Mickey Mantle and an unidentified rookie in the same club. The rookie had been carefully watching Mantle's powerful swing and secretly practicing it for months. Just as he was sure he had it perfected, an opportunity to try it out occurred in an early season home game. When the rookie's turn came to bat, the opposing pitcher delivered three straight pitches and the young rookie swung an equal number of times, striking out in style.

"I can't understand it," he said to Mantle later. "I spent months trying to learn how to swing like you. I guess I don't have it yet."

Mantle smiled slightly when he heard this. "You know 'how' all right kid," he said. "Now you should learn 'when.'"

In understanding behavior, as in understanding baseball, the "when" is an extremely important consideration, particularly if the "when" involves the delivery of a substance which has the power of being a positive reinforcer.

In a previous chapter, it was emphasized that a positive reinforcer must immediately follow the response if conditioning is to occur. Infants who were given a bottle without delay after turning their heads exhibited an increase in head-turning responses. Infants who were given the bottle at times completely unrelated to head turning did not increase their frequency of head turning. Thus the "when" of the delivery of a potential reinforcer determines whether or not conditioning will occur.

A further, and perhaps more sweeping, point should be made. If the experimenter in the study above had been interested in raising the frequency of responses other than head turning, milk would have served equally as well as a positive reinforcer. In a deprived infant, the delivery of milk will doubtlessly condition any response it consistently follows. It can be stated as a general rule that *any substance or event which has been demonstrated to be a positive reinforcer for one response will, in all likelihood, condition any response it regularly and immediately follows.*

61

In order to illustrate the rule stated above, it is expedient to entertain the following imaginary state of affairs. Suppose you are a young and smashingly handsome man-about-town and one of the foremost connoisseurs of feminine loveliness. After years of searching through all of the exotic capitals of the world, you find in Beruit, Ohio, a girl whose beauty and grace are absolutely unsurpassable. Above all else, you must win her favor or you will become a monk. Others have tried before you. Diamonds, furs, sports cars, Paris gowns, have been offered by scores of enamored suitors, but to no avail. Both they and their gifts were coolly rejected while she stood sublimely detached, watching as enrollments in monasteries became overabundant. Being devilishly clever, you do not come prepared with anything so common as diamonds and mink. You bring instead the ultimate weapon, the one thing no mortal woman can possibly resist, a full book of trading stamps. Unlike the run-of-the-mill rogue, you do not immediately throw both yourself and your precious trading stamps at her feet. You know the principle of positive reinforcement and realize what an enormous power you have at your disposal. You observe her behavior carefully throughout the evening, biding your time, watching cunningly, craftily, as at various times she lights a cigarette, flashes her magnificent eyes, blows her nose, opens her purse, crosses her legs, winds her watch, and furrows her brow. You wait. Finally it happens! She approaches you, runs her fingernails through your tousled hair, and snuggles lightly next to you. With a lightning-fast response, you pull forth the book of trading stamps, and place it firmly in her lap. When she sees the stamps her blasé look changes to one of ecstasy, and she makes small yelps of joy. Suddenly she stops, stares at you puzzled, quizzically, as if seeing you for the first time. You chuckle to yourself.

You have reinforced her snuggling and tousling behavior. It will happen again and again. Not without a certain smugness, you pat the pocket where the other books of trading stamps remain for instant use. Her fingers approach your hair. . . .

You have learned from playing the part of the hero in the story that the instant a positive reinforcer is delivered determines the behavior which will become conditioned. A slight miscue in timing and our *bon vivant* might have spent the evening with a young lady who seemed to do nothing but wind her watch, open her purse, or blow her nose.

Psychologists are keenly aware of the "fickle" nature of reinforcement. They know it will increase the frequency of virtually any response it follows, and as a result they are ultra-careful in ensuring that the positive reinforcer they employ follows the response, and only the response, they want to condition.

Other individuals who are not familiar with positive reinforcement are not at all careful about when they give presents, rewards, or other potential reinforcers. In fact, potential reinforcers are most commonly given us with total disregard for the response we have just completed. This situation gives rise to the possibility of "accidental" conditioning, which results when a positive reinforcer and response become inadvertently associated.

"Superstition" in the Pigeon

Dr. B. F. Skinner was one of the first psychologists to mention the possibility of "accidental" conditioning. He was the very first to demonstrate it scientifically. But Dr. Skinner's reputation is due to more than that. His name, above all others, can most intimately be associated with positive reinforcement. At a time when many psychologists were floundering in a morass of mentalistic explanations of behavior, Dr. Skinner was among those pioneering a movement to make psychology a science.

In order to demonstrate the power of positive reinforcement to condition any response with which it was associated, regardless of why or how the association came about, Dr. Skinner set up the following experiment.[1] A pigeon was placed in an experimental chamber with dimensions just large enough for him to make a half-dozen paces in any direction. At one end of the chamber, a small hinged trough—called the hopper—could be swung up to an opening in the bottom of the chamber. The pigeon could poke his beak through the floor opening and into the hopper. Ordinarily, however, the hopper was extended downward beyond the pigeon's reach. The hopper was filled with grain which had on numerous occasions been shown to be a powerful positive reinforcer for grain-deprived pigeons. Soon after the bird was placed in the box, a timer set for a 15-second interval was energized. At the end of each 15-second interval, the hopper came up for a few seconds and remained within the pigeon's reach, allowing him time to eat the grain. Typically, pigeons in this apparatus hear the hopper on its way up and immediately stop what they are doing and make a beeline for the feeding area. It is crucial to note that the grain hopper came up at the end of each 15-second interval, regardless of what the bird was doing. In fact, the operation of the hopper was completely independent of the bird's behavior and would have occurred even if the box were empty.

The first bird was placed in the box and at once began to strut about exploring first this corner, then that, scratching on the floor, pecking here and then there, and in general reconnoitering the box.

After 15 seconds had elapsed, the hopper came up for the first time. Just prior to this, the pigeon made an abrupt counterclockwise turn. The counterclockwise turn was accidentally associated in time with the action of the hopper and was reinforced. In a few seconds, the hopper was retracted and the pigeon once again strutted about the box. Soon, however, he began to make counterclockwise turns; the turning was the behavior followed a short time before by the appearance of the grain hopper. He had completed two, perhaps three, counterclockwise turns when the 15-second interval again expired and the hopper swung up within his reach.

From that time on, the bird exhibited a fixed or stereotyped pattern of behavior which involved rapid and persistent counterclockwise turning motions. If

1. This section based on Skinner, B. F. Superstition in the pigeon. *Journal of Experimental Psychology*, 1948, *38*, 168–172.

an observer who was not familiar with what had taken place was allowed to view this "whirling dervish," he would doubtless suggest the bird was disoriented, silly, or intoxicated. The turning pattern was broken only when the hopper was presented, at which time the bird went without hesitation for the grain.

In a similar fashion, accidental reinforcement in another bird conditioned a head-tossing response which looked much like that of a bull tossing an imaginary matador on his horns. After a few instances in which this behavior received accidental positive reinforcement, it occurred with great precision and regularity whenever the pigeon was placed in the box. Other pigeons developed a pendulum motion with their heads, swinging them to and fro as if keeping time to an unknown and unheard melody.

Dr. Skinner thought long before labeling the behavior which came about through accidental associations of reinforcement and response. He finally applied the expression "superstitious behavior." He gave it this name because it greatly reminded him of superstitious notions occurring in most cultures. Just as a man associates walking under a ladder or having a black cat cross his path with bad luck, the pigeon associated the bizarre behavior he engaged in with the presentation of the grain hopper. There is much to be said for Dr. Skinner's analogy between what the pigeon does under these circumstances and superstitions in humans.

In various battlegrounds of World War I, cigarette-smoking behavior came under the control of similar accidental associations. Where active engagements were in progress, it was not considered safe to strike a match at night except for a brief period, because the light could be seen by the enemy and give him a target on which to train his rifle. If a match burned just long enough to light one cigarette, there was little time for the enemy to draw his bead. The lighting of two cigarettes from the same match still did not afford the sniper time to pinpoint a target. If the match remained burning for a longer period of time, long enough to light a third cigarette, there was time to aim and fire. Trained on the locus of the light, the bullet sought the soldier whose cigarette had last been lighted. In this peculiar way the superstition of "bad luck to light three on a match" reportedly was born. Today, the superstition is far removed from the conditions where it arose. There is no longer any real reason to believe a bullet is waiting for the third to light from the same match. Yet the idea persists as superstition, being transmitted through the social context of our culture.

Accidental association of response and positive reinforcers probably contributes to human behavior in ways other than superstition. We have spoken exclusively of positive reinforcers which are programmed by an experimenter. However, only a small portion of the positive reinforcers human beings receive are delivered as carefully and as explicitly as those in the laboratory. More often, positive reinforcers in the form of rewards or favors are presented at times far in advance or arrears of the act of behavior for which they are ostensibly delivered.

Generally, gifts or presents are given when the giver feels charitable, benevolent, or guilty, and are not concerned with a specific response on the part of the recipient. In other instances, gifts are associated with birthdays, Christmas, and other fixed calendar occasions which are likewise independent of the recipient's behavior.

Often when I am away from home, in the laboratory, or teaching class, I am reminded of my young daughter and how much she pleases me with her beguiling manner and provocative little-girl ways. At these times, I am moved to buy her a small gift or present by way of demonstrating a father's appreciation. Usually I give her this reward as soon as I arrive home in the evenings with little or no regard for the activities in which she was busily engaged before my arrival. The present could become accidentally paired with any number of behaviors. If my present-bringing were frequent enough, it is conceivable that my daughter could become quite superstitious about the relationship between what she does and the delivery of the reinforcing objects I bring to her. This situation can arise because my bringing home of gifts, which are potential reinforcers, is independent of what she is doing at the time I arrived home. By and large, whether she receives a gift, and when she receives it, is completely out of her control.

So far, I am relieved to say, I have not often observed her play the part of "the whirling dervish" like Dr. Skinner's pigeon. On the other hand, from time to time I see quite peculiar behavior whose origin mystifies me. There is a tendency to attribute these "out of the blue" responses to interactions at school or the influences of her little friends. When they are particularly "weird," I blame them on her mother's relatives.

Psychologists have yet to seriously tackle the problem of accidental conditioning and how it relates to the development of human behavior. Presently most of our notions regarding the phenomenon in humans are purely speculative.

Response Differentiation with Positive Reinforcement in a Middle-aged College Professor

It will undoubtedly have occurred to the reader by now that positive reinforcement can be an extremely powerful tool in controlling the behavior of others. A psychology professor with whom the authors are intimately acquainted came to be controlled by a class of students who used the same reinforcement techniques on him he had taught them only a few weeks before. The method they used entails the special use of positive reinforcement called *differential reinforcement*.

The impetus for the class to modify their professor's behavior arose because he traditionally stood like a stump on one side of the classroom while he lectured, refusing to move even a foot toward the opposite wall. Students on the nonpreferred side felt neglected and often had to strain their ears to hear. Students on the preferred side soon grew a little weary of having him breathe down their necks for the full 50 minutes of the lecture. One student in the class decided to get quantitative data on his lecturing behavior. During the 50-minute period, the professor spent an average of 46 minutes lecturing to the preferred right side of the classroom. Furthermore, almost all the time remaining was spent at the podium in the middle of the room. On the rare occasions when he did venture to the opposite side of the room, it was to write on that section of the blackboard.

The students got together one evening before class and agreed on the following scheme. They would reinforce the professor when and only when he stood at the far left side of the room—the side he typically avoided as though it were diseased. He would not receive reinforcement while lecturing from any other place. The students had little difficulty deciding which potential positive reinforcer to use on their unwitting mentor. Like most professors, theirs thought there was no more beautiful sight in the world than the smiling face of a student intently hanging on each word of wisdom put forth, devouring it like a succulent morsel.

Accordingly, the pact was made. Whenever the professor lectured from the far left side of the room, 35 faces beamed up at him, smiling in rapt attention. If he ventured from that spot to his favored haunt in the far right side of the room, each of the students suddenly became engrossed in note-taking, rarely if ever looking up from their books.

When class convened, the professor went directly to his favorite corner and began to lecture. All eyes looked down and remained there for ten minutes or so. At the end of this time, several terms were written on the blackboard. In order to complete the list, he was forced to move to the far left side of the room. When he turned from the blackboard to the class, it was like the sunshine suddenly breaking through on a cloudy day. He seemed to hold the attention of each student in the palm of his hand as each word followed the other like pearls on a string. He remained on that very spot for almost five minutes. As he moved to the other side, his attentive audience immediately fell away. The next several minutes were spent in pacing behavior in which he strode from one side of the room to the other. When 20 minutes remained in the period, he stopped at the appropriate spot and lectured from there until the end of the class. After class the students checked their records. He had spent a total of 28 minutes on the "smiley" side of the room. This was compared to an average of less than a minute at times in previous class periods when attention was not specifically arranged to follow lecture position. It was the teacher who had been taught.

In the next class period the students confessed their conspiracy to their subject. After threatening to flunk the whole class, he calmed down and admitted that it had been a good demonstration, even if it had been at his expense. He had been completely unaware of what was going on. He had noticed the initial lethargy but attributed it to a class time which was scheduled right after the evening meal. He had likewise noticed the great increase in attention during the end of the hour, but felt that this was strictly the result of the glowing facts he was presenting at the time.

The method used by the class on the professor is called *differential reinforcement. It consists of reinforcing only one member or response from a response class and neglecting all other members.*

But before we can discuss the salient aspects of differential reinforcement and relate them to the change in the professor's behavior we should first know and understand another term. This term is *response class.*

Let us assume that it is the first day on the job for you as part of the psychology staff in the mental hospital. Your supervisor, who, like most psychologists, is handsome, witty, congenial, intelligent, brave, clean, and reverent, assigns you the following task: you are to observe a new patient through the closed-circuit television camera for a period of four hours and report his responses. After 15 minutes or less of observation and four or five severe seizures of writer's cramp, you decide a detailed written description of each single response is out of the question. Quickly you devise a scheme, for grouping similar responses together and merely make a tally on your sheet when one of those responses occurs. Yankee ingenuity wins out. You have discovered the meaning, use, and utility of *response class*.

In the simplest terms, a response class is a grouping of all responses which have at least one characteristic in common.

Responses have many characteristics, however. Furthermore, they may be grouped into response classes along any of these characteristics. One of the most obvious characteristics of responses is the movements they involve. Anyone could see that one eye blink was pretty much, muscle-wise, like another eye blink. Even early psychologists could see this. Consequently, early psychology was primarily concerned with eye blinks, finger lifts, leg flexions, and knee jerks.

It is still common to find responses categorized into response classes in terms of movements. Today response classes grouped along this dimension generally involve "gross" body movements as opposed to the isolated movements of specific parts of the anatomy studied by early psychologists. It is more prevalent today to hear of a "turning response," "climbing response," or "rocking response" than it is to hear of a leg flexion or knee jerk.

Another important characteristic of responses which is popularly employed to categorize them into response classes is the *effect they have on the environment*. All of the things people do can conceivably be classified along this dimension. Just as people come to be "known by the deeds they do," so do responses come to be known and classified by the "deeds" or effects they perform on the environment.

One effect which may be brought about by a response is the ringing of a doorbell. All responses which result in ringing the doorbell can be classified, for want of a more imaginative term, into the response class called "doorbell-ringing responses." Now most of us are content to ring the door bell with our index finger. We could make the bell ring, however, by depressing the button with our little finger, thumb, giant toe, elbow, forehead, knee, nose, chin, or buttocks; the latter, not without some difficulty. Each of these responses may encompass entirely different movements or contortions, as the case may be. They all have the similarity of yielding a common result, the ringing of the doorbell. Each of these responses, having the same *effect on the environment*, can be said to belong to the same response class, namely that class termed "doorbell-ringing response."

It is convenient and meaningful to analyze the lecturing behavior of the professor we have recently discussed into this type of response class designation.

Each location taken by him as he delivered his lecture can be called a "location" response. Since there are numerous locations he could have taken and yet delivered his lecture to the students, each specific location can be thought of as a single "location" response from a large response class comprised of the many location responses possible.

Differential reinforcement consists of reinforcing one response from a response class and neglecting to reinforce all other members of that class. The students selected one location response and systematically presented reinforcement when this response was made. When lecturing from any other location, the professor found the noses of his students buried deep in their notebooks. He received no reinforcement for making other location responses.

The results of the response differentiation procedure can be clearly shown in the professor's behavior. Initially he had favored one lecture location response, although making other location responses occasionally. The class selectively reinforced one location response and not others. By the end of the hour, the professor spent all of his time making the location response the class had reinforced. Of all the possible location responses the professor could make, one became *differentiated* due to selective positive reinforcement by the students. It should now be clear why the procedure is called *differential reinforcement.* Another term whose meaning should fairly jump out at the student now is *response differentiation.* Of course this refers to a typical result when one member of a response class is differentially reinforced and reinforcement withheld from others. Thus, through *differential reinforcement, response differentiation* comes about.

While the student will undoubtedly bask in the knowledge that differential reinforcement can enable him to control his teacher or professor, the technique is far from limited to this use. The wide complex of positive reinforcers which our culture and society have to offer us are frequently dispensed in such a manner that they engender response differentiation. In the arts, positive reinforcement in the form of public accolades, recognition, and good pay are stingily guarded, and offered only for responses of excellence. If most of us were to exhibit our singing responses at the Metropolitan Opera, we would likely find the patrons in the audience prepared to do practically anything but reinforce our behavior.

Attaining skill in an athletic event or sport involves a long process of response differentiation. The inexperienced golfer begins his golfing career by addressing the ball with a wide variety of swinging responses from the general class of golf club swings. Occasionally one of these responses is differentially reinforced by a golf ball that soars straight and true toward the green. After years of differential reinforcement, a standard swing becomes differentiated which more often than not results in positive reinforcement, and a low golf score.

Nature herself is a tight-fisted old girl who is extremely selective in the responses she will reinforce. An engineer studies the laws of nature before he makes the response of building a bridge. If his years of study have correctly differentiated his responses, Nature herself will reinforce him and his bridge will endure. If the wrong response is made, reinforcement will be withheld. The bridge will fall into the water with the first moderate breeze. A hunter approaches his deadly prey armed with nothing but a spear. If his response is not precise, he may lose much more than an opportunity for reinforcement.

A conversation between two people is a situation in which each of the participants differentially reinforces the verbal responses of the other. It is no accident that we converse on one topic with Jack or Bill and converse on a different topic with our Aunt Hattie. A good conversationalist is one who makes verbal responses which others positively reinforce with interest, amusement, or fascination. A poor conversationalist is one whose verbal responses have never become differentiated. He can never seem to say things which bring forth reinforcement from the listener. Perhaps he has not had enough practice at conversation. This is another way of saying that not enough differential reinforcement has been given his verbal responses. In a moment we will see how verbal behavior can be modified in a therapy situation by differential reinforcement. But first, one last time, let us make sure the student has these concepts down.

Responses which share a common characteristic can be said to belong to the same *response class*. A procedure which involves reinforcing one response class member and failing to reinforce others is called *differential reinforcement*. Differential reinforcement results in an increase in the rate of the reinforced response relative to the rate of other members in the response class. This result is called *response differentiation*.

The Unwitting Use of Differential Reinforcement by a Psychotherapist

Psychotherapy is a very special conversational situation, arranged to help a patient with his problems.

There is a great deal of disagreement, even among people who spend the major portion of their life in administering psychotherapy, as to exactly what goes on in the therapy session. They will generally agree, however, that the course of a successful treatment assumes the following progression. During initial sessions, the patient appears to be confused and somewhat agitated. He makes many statements expressing his dissatisfaction with himself and his environment; many of his verbalizations concern his difficulties in coping with and understanding his world. Gradually, these confused and distressed statements drop out of his verbal behavior and are replaced with other statements which are generally more optimistic and reflect on his own behavior in a more reasonable manner. Ultimately, the patient becomes even more aware of his behavior and is able to express some notions as to the cause of his difficulties. The patient leaves therapy with a new optimism. Often he makes changes in his environment which greatly decrease the conflicts he encounters.

One group of therapists, generally referred to by the term "nondirective therapists," feel that the therapist does not exert an active role in the changes which come about in the process of therapy. The goal of the therapist is merely to provide a sympathetic and permissive ear to the patient. The patient responds to this subtle and kindly influence by solving his own problems and gaining insight into his conflicts. In effect, the patient "heals" himself.

Other psychologists and psychiatrists see the therapist in a much more active role in the psychotherapy session. They assert that the patient does not magically and spontaneously begin to make more healthy and constructive verbal responses. Rather, his verbal responses are selectively chosen by differential reinforcement provided by the therapist. Verbal responses of the patient which show understanding of his problems and clarify exactly what his feelings are regarding himself and others are reinforced with verbal responses of the therapist which radiate warmth, agreement, and understanding. Verbal responses of the patient which revolve around themes of confusion, pessimism, and inability to comprehend his own behavior do not receive positive reinforcement from the therapist. The therapist responds to these verbalizations with silence and cool indifference. Assume, for instance, that the patient makes the following verbal responses:

Patient: I just don't know how I feel about my parents. . . . Surely they love me. . . . Yes! I know they love me! Why just yesterday they bought me a new swing, sliding board, and monkey bars.

Therapist: (Sits up abruptly, leans toward the patient with interest, smiles at him slightly.) Uh-huh, I guess you're saying, "My parents must love me or else they would not worry about providing me with recreation."

Patient: Yes. . . . that's it. One thing puzzles me. . . . Doctor, why should my parents give the workmen orders to have the recreation equipment placed in the middle of the freeway?

Therapist: (Coughs, looks out the window, subtly changes the subject.) You didn't happen to see the Ed Sullivan Show last night, did you? There was this dog act that was really great. . . .

Dr. Carl Rogers is the leading proponent for the "nondirective" view of successful psychotherapy. It is Dr. Rogers' opinion that the therapy session is really a set of *uniform conditions* which are "facilitative of personal growth and integration." He contends that his patients begin to verbalize in a "healthier" way because of the general therapeutic climate and not because of differential positive reinforcement of acceptable verbal behavior.

One researcher, Dr. Charles Truax, elected to see if what Dr. Rogers said was true, or if, in fact, he did differentially reinforce the verbal behavior of his clients without being aware of it.[2]

Several recordings of Dr. Rogers' therapy sessions with a long term patient were analyzed by Dr. Truax and his assistants. First these recordings were analyzed in terms of the statements made by the patient. Each of these statements were categorized in terms of content. Nine different categories were found. One category including statements by the patient which reflected on his progress in learning to discriminate about himself and his feelings. Another category was made up of statements arranged along a continuum of clarity to ambiguity.

Next Dr. Rogers' response to each of these statements was analyzed. It was found that in five of the nine categories he did respond differently, providing positive reinforcement in the form of understanding, warmth, and affirmation to "healthy" statements, and neglecting to do so if statements were not "healthy." In the category of clarity-ambiguity, for instance, he offered positive reinforce-

2. This section based on Truax, C. B. Reinforcement and non-reinforcement in Rogerian psychotherapy. *Journal of Abnormal and Social Psychology,* 1966, *71,* 1–9.

ment for statements which reflected clarity, but withheld reinforcement from ambiguous statements. As a result of providing warmth, understanding, and affirmation to some statements and neglecting to do so to others, it was found generally by Dr. Truax that the former increased in frequency while the latter did not. Dr. Truax concluded that regardless of what Dr. Rogers said, the data indicated that he differentially reinforced his patients' responses when they were consistent with his notion of "healthy."

The therapy process apparently involves differential reinforcement. The patient is reinforced for saying the right things. He receives reinforcement as long as he stays "on the right verbal track," but not when he makes statements which are confused, self-deprecating, pessimistic, or generally unhealthy. As therapy continues, the patient's healthy verbal behavior begins to generalize to areas outside the session. He is more optimistic, relaxed, and clearer than before. Friends and acquaintances see this change and respond to it favorably, thus reinforcing his new personality. Soon it can be maintained by persons other than the therapist, and therapy may be terminated.

The fact that Dr. Rogers has been shown to use differential reinforcement in the treatment of his clients in no way detracts from his skill or competency as a psychotherapist. His reputation as one of the foremost influences in the field of clinical psychology is well deserved. The discovery that differential reinforcement does play an important role in a complex interaction like psychotherapy underlines its importance in human behavior.

> Before reaching the top
>
> If it goes down
>
> Is out of order
>
> A cum recorder

Summary

In this chapter, we have emphasized and clarified the importance of positive reinforcement in the control and analysis of behavior. Within this context, the following points deserve mentioning.

1. A quantity or event identified as a positive reinforcer for one response, if programmed to follow another response, may condition the new response as easily as the first.

2. Psychologists and other individuals who know the principle of positive reinforcement may intentionally deliver positive reinforcement after a specific

response they wish conditioned. On other occasions positive reinforcers may be delivered by agencies or individuals without explicit intention of associating them with a particular response. In some cases, pairings of positive reinforcers and behaviors come about quite by accident. Behavior which becomes conditioned in this manner has been called *superstitious behavior* by Dr. B. F. Skinner.

3. The term *response class* was introduced. It was defined as: *a grouping of all responses which have at least one characteristic in common.* Since responses have many characteristics, there are many different ways they can be formed into response classes. Two characteristics of responses which are prevalently employed by psychologists to classify responses are: A) Movements: responses with similar movements are classified into the same response class. Classes grouped this way are knee jerks, eye blinks, turning responses, climbing responses, etc. B) The effects responses have on the environment: responses may be placed in the same response class if they have the same effect on the environment. One example discussed was "doorbell-ringing responses."

4. *Response differentiation* comes about when one member of a response class is positively reinforced while other members are not reinforced. In this manner, the reinforced response becomes differentiated and occurs with greater frequency than other nonreinforced responses of the response class. A college professor's lecture location became differentiated through selective reinforcement.

5. The process of reinforcing only one response and neglecting to reinforce other responses of that class is called *differential reinforcement*. Through the process of *differential reinforcement* of one response in a response class, *response differentiation* takes place.

6. The importance of *response differentiation* and its pervasiveness in human behavior was discussed. Fine arts, sports, and vocations which involve interaction with natural elements were pointed out as instances where *differential reinforcement* soon begets responses of specific quality and excellence.

7. The role of *differential reinforcement* was elaborated further. Psychotherapy is a special situation in which conversation is established to bring about therapeutic changes in verbalizations. Regardless of the statements and assertations of Dr. Carl Rogers and followers of "nondirective therapy," it was found that the therapeutic situation involved precise and *differential reinforcement*. Changes taking place in the patient's verbal behavior can thus be classified as another example of *response differentiation*.

QUESTIONS

1. If a substance or event which has been shown to be a positive reinforcer for one response is arranged to follow another response, what, in all likelihood, will occur to the second response?
2. In the imaginary story, what did the young man use as a positive reinforcer?
3. What responses did he condition with this positive reinforcer?
4. What would have happened if he had "miscued" and paired the reinforcer with another of the responses the girl made during the evening?

5. What is meant by the notion that a positive reinforcer is "fickle"?

6. People who are not familiar with the principles of positive reinforcement are usually careful in selecting a certain time to award gifts or presents which are potential reinforcers. (a) True; (b) False.

7. By and large, the fact that potential positive reinforcers are given with little regard for what the individual is doing at the time gives rise to the possibility of _____ _____ conditioning.

8. Who was the first psychologist to demonstrate accidental conditioning scientifically?

9. In order to demonstrate accidental conditioning, what experimental animals did Dr. Skinner use?

10. What type of enclosure were they placed in during the experiment?

11. What type of substance was used as a positive reinforcer?

12. What device delivered this substance to the birds?

13. How often was reinforcement made available to the pigeons?

14. Which of the following statements is true about the delivery of reinforcement? (a) The pigeon had to peck a lighted key before reinforcement was presented; (b) The hopper containing reinforcement was presented by a timer completely independent of the pigeon's behavior; (c) This information was not given in the text; (d) The pigeon had to look at the experimenter before he was reinforced.

15. How often was the grain presented to the pigeon?

16. In the first pigeon discussed, what was the behavior with which reinforcement became accidentally associated?

17. As a result of this association, what stereotyped behavior pattern did the pigeon develop?

18. Name two bizarre behavior patterns which became conditioned in other pigeons due to accidental associations.

19. What did Dr. Skinner label behavior which came about through this type of accidental conditioning?

20. What human behavior did it remind him of which encouraged him to give it his label?

21. Briefly describe the situation which reportedly gave rise to the superstition that three on a match was unlucky.

22. Gifts are always given for specific behaviors. (a) True; (b) False.

23. Being psychologists, the authors of this text are always careful about when they offer gifts or presents. (a) True; (b) False.

24. The author's little girl had turned into a "whirling dervish" as a result of accidental conditioning. (a) True; (b) False.

25. Where does the author place the blame for the "weird" behavior he occasionally observes in his daughter?

26. Accidental conditioning is one of the oldest areas of research in psychology. (a) True; (b) False.

27. In the article in which a middle-aged college professor was conditioned, who took it upon themselves to do the conditioning?

28. What aspect of the professor's behavior did the students find irritating and therefore decide to change?

29. On the average, in a 50-minute lecture session, how many minutes did the professor stand on the preferred side of the room? (a) 10 minutes; (b) 26 minutes; (c) 46 minutes; (d) 2½ hours.

30. On what extremely rare occasion did the professor go to the nonpreferred side of the room prior to conditioning?

31. What did the class decide to use as a positive reinforcer?

32. What behavior on the part of the professor was consistently reinforced?

33. Were any other behaviors reinforced also? (a) Yes; (b) No.

34. At the conclusion of the study, how much time had the professor spent on the "smiley" side of the room? (a) 5 minutes; (b) 28 minutes; (c) 1 minute; (d) 50 minutes.

35. The professor, being well-versed in conditioning procedures, knew precisely what the class was doing. (a) True; (b) False.

36. The name of the method employing positive reinforcement used by the class is called _____ _____.

37. Briefly describe what the method entails.

38. Which of the following does not belong to the same response class? (a) Ringing the doorbell with the index finger; (b) Ringing the doorbell with the left giant toe; (c) Ringing the doorbell with buttocks; (d) Knocking on the door with knuckles.

39. In the professor's case, what response class did the students deal with?

40. What response of this class did they selectively reinforce?

41. The procedure of selectively reinforcing one response and neglecting to reinforce others is called _____ reinforcement.

42. Differential reinforcement of one response in a response class brings about the result of _____ _____.

43. Thus, it can be said that through differential reinforcement, response differentiation comes about. (a) True; (b) False.

44. Briefly explain how response differentiation plays an important role in singing, golfing, and bridge building.

45. The fact that we talk on one topic with Jack or Bill and converse on a different topic with Aunt Hattie shows that conversation is another case of: (a) bridge building; (b) response differentiation; (c) extinction; (d) response class.

46. A poor conversationalist is one whose verbal responses have never become: (a) reinforced; (b) extinguished; (c) differentiated; (d) vocal.

47. A very special conversation situation which is arranged ostensibly to help the patient with his problems is called _____.

48. Which statement would most accurately summarize the position of a nondirective therapist? (a) The therapist plays no active role in therapy; (b) The therapist modifies the behavior of his client through differential reinforcement.

49. Which of the following statements would a psychotherapist probably reinforce? (a) I hate myself and others as well; (b) I understand now why I have such a difficult time at work; (c) I change into a vampire bat by night and a werewolf by day; (d) No one really loves me; (e) I feel much more kindly toward my enemies than I used to.

50. Who is the leading figure in nondirective therapy whose tapes Dr. Truax analyzed?

51. How many categories of statements did Dr. Truax find in Dr. Rogers' tapes?

52. In how many of these categories did Dr. Rogers differentially reinforce his client's verbalizations?

53. What happened to the frequency of statements in four of these five categories?

54. Did Dr. Truax's findings tend to support a nondirective approach theory of psychotherapy or did it tend to support a reinforcement theory?

NOTES
"Superstition" in the Pigeon

In an early part of this chapter, it was stated that "any substance or event which has been demonstrated to be a positive reinforcer for one response will, *in all likeli-hood*, condition any response it regularly and immediately follows." The qualifying phrase, "in all likelihood" refers to the finding that a substance which will act as a positive reinforcer and condition one response may in some rare circumstances not act as a positive reinforcer for another response. A common-sense example of two such responses follows: one involves supreme effort on the part of the respondent and the other involves little or minimal effort on the part of the respondent. A small food pellet delivered to a rat for pressing a lever will condition this response even within situations where very wide ranges of force are needed to depress the lever. If the force required to depress the lever is increased to the point where the rodent must all but strain him-self, the probability is very low that a reinforcement of the size and quantity previously used will reinforce this super-response. In order to condition this new response, perhaps a bigger reinforcer or even a new reinforcing substance may have to be employed. With few exceptions, however, the statement in the text is true. We can generally ex-pect a positive reinforcer to be instrumental in conditioning any number of responses.

Dr. Skinner's label of "superstitious" behavior, which is applied to behaviors con-ditioned by accidental pairing of responses with positive reinforcement, has stuck in the literature. His demonstration of the phenomenon with pigeons was highly dramatic and engendered a myriad of speculations regarding its relevance to human behavior and particularly human behavior disorders. The aspect of the pigeons' behavior which produced the greatest interest was the unique and bizarre quality of their response patterns. If an outsider, unfamiliar with the experimental production of these behaviors, were to view the "superstitious" pigeons, he would probably speculate that the birds were abnormal or even psychotic. The fact that persons in mental hospitals often mani-fest qualitatively similar bizarre behavior patterns offers the possibility that these behaviors were shaped in much the same way as those of Dr. Skinner's pigeons.

That many mental patients have histories of inconsistent parental influence adds further provocativeness to this notion. A popular way to characterize an inconsistent parent is to say that he is an individual whose behavior toward his child is, by and large, independent of the child's behavior. Rewards are given at times when the parent is feeling euphoric, or perhaps guilty, in his neglect or imagined neglect of his child. Such times may not coincide with desirable behaviors on the part of the child. In a similar fashion, punishment or other abuse is administered when the parent suffers from a "hard day" or has the "blues." In short, rewards or punishments are given indepen-dently of the child's behavior and therefore, at least on a theoretical level, the possibili-ties for superstitious patterns are greatly enhanced. While this hypothesis seems at least credible, it has yet to find scientific or experimental substantiation. It remains for future researchers to determine exactly what relationship noncontingent reinforce-ment and punishment ultimately have to human behavior problems.

Superstitious behavior, as observed in the pigeon, probably has less relevance to human superstitions than it does to the general notion that human beings are character-istically ignorant of the causes of the events which impinge on them. Therefore, there is a great opportunity to ascribe causal powers to other events which are related only through happenstance. Superstitions which are not idiosyncratic and can be found in the public domain were not gained firsthand; they reflect acculturation and social influence. Someone who stresses the unsavory aspects of black cats crossing paths probably has no personal reason to mistrust or denounce black cats. His ideas can be traced back to the early influence of parents or other significant individuals. It is probably a safe bet, however, that at one time or another popular superstitions did actually obtain for some individuals. The case of "three on a match" exemplifies how such a superstition may be engendered from a set of circumstances where bad luck did seem to afflict the third on a match. Perhaps some religious laws began in the same way. The reluctance of some religious groups to eat pork initially may have been a rule with great survival value in days before a government inspected meat. Today, the law persists as a form of religious and cultural heritage. The reader who is further interested in the topic of superstition in both pigeons and men may wish to consult Dr. R. J. Herrnstein's chapter in Honig's book *Operant Behavior: Areas of Research and Application.*

It is true that a positive reinforcer *most directly* reinforces that behavior which it immediately follows. Other responses occurring sometime *before* reinforcement may be strengthened as well. Strengthening of responses which occur after reinforcement has theoretically been labeled "backward conditioning." In point of fact, this has never been demonstrated. It is safe to say that responses which follow the reinforcing event will simply not be affected or modified by its introduction. Responses occurring sometime before reinforcement may be strengthened, however, and the degree of strengthening appears to be a function of how coincident the responses are with the reinforcing event. In order to illustrate this point, let us assume that a child makes three responses which we may label A, B, and C. Response A, a nose twitch, occurs first. It is followed by response B, which is a puckering of the lips, and which is followed finally by response C, a furrowing of the brow. Let us assume that the positive reinforcer is an M&M candy and it is presented immediately after response C, the furrowing of the brow. If reinforcement is delivered regularly in this fashion, we would of course expect response C to increase in frequency. In a less dramatic way, however, response B, which is the mouth-puckering response, will also increase in frequency. To an even lesser degree than response C or B, response A will increase in frequency. The fact that the positive reinforcer is less effective for responses as they become further removed from it in time is called the *gradient of reinforcement.* The reinforcing property of the event can be described as a decreasing gradient from response C to response A.

To be most effective, a reinforcer should immediately follow the response it is to condition. The interval of time between the response and the delivery of positive reinforcement is called the *delay of reinforcement.* Inasmuch as the delay of reinforcement is short, the positive reinforcer will be highly effective, and inasmuch as the delay of reinforcement is long, the positive reinforcer will be less effective.

The Unwitting Use of Differentiation Reinforcement by a Psychotherapist

The research of Dr. Traux contributed a long-awaited bit of information to the body of psychological knowledge. The controversy between those therapists adhering to Dr. Rogers' nondirective position and other groups of therapists who are sensitive to positive reinforcement and its principles went on for many years without resolution.

Dr. Truax's findings favor the reinforcement idea of verbal interactions whether they be at home, in school, at social gatherings, or in the therapy setting. It was difficult for those adhering to a reinforcement explanation to subscribe to the notion that the therapist in his office, under the conditions of therapy, defined a situation which was in some mystical way different from other behavioral situations. Dr. Truax's confirmation that the basic principles of behavioral psychology apply in the therapy session as well as outside brings to bear the possibility of further scientific analysis into the care and treatment of emotionally disturbed persons. By couching psychotherapy in a scientific framework, it can be made more effective and its principles specified so that they may be more easily taught to students and apprentice therapists.

5

SHAPING, THE METHOD OF SUCCESSIVE APPROXIMATION

In the last chapter, we witnessed a perfect group of scoundrels as they controlled the lecturing behavior of their professor. They differentially offered smiles and attention when he delivered his lecture from one location, but withheld their smiling countenances at all other locations. As a result of this use of differential reinforcement, the professor's lecture location responses underwent the process of response differentiation. Although nonetheless boring, his lectures were delivered from the location the class had ordained.

If the students had waited two or three weeks longer before hatching their evil plot, they would have learned, as you are about to learn, that positive reinforcement can be used to achieve even more dramatic behavioral changes than simple differentiation. Through the proper use of positive reinforcement, *entirely new* responses and behavioral sequences, which the subject has never been seen to exhibit before, can be brought into his active repertoire. In one study, positive reinforcement was employed in this capacity to bring speech to a psychotic in a mental institution.

Application of Positive Reinforcement to Reinstate Verbal Behavior in a Psychotic

A psychotic is an individual who is almost always retained in a mental hospital. He is distinguished by severe disruptions in his behavior which deviate considerably from behavior patterns you or I exhibit. Often psychotics have a history of hurting themselves or others or appear to be so lethargic that they must be cared for and watched over almost constantly. Some psychotics become so "regressed" after being placed in an institution that they even lose speech and become mute.

One such man, whom we shall call Andrew, was diagnosed as a catatonic schizophrenic.[1] He was admitted to the hospital when he was 21 years old and from the day of his admission did not utter a word.

He had been silent for 19 years. It was only by accident that the psychologist got the clue which enabled him to recondition Andrew's verbal behavior. Andrew, along with some patients who were able to talk, was assigned to a group therapy session in which patients are encouraged to verbalize their feelings about being in the institution and discuss their problems with other patients. Some of the staff in the institution thought it was sadly inappropriate for Andrew to be present, for he did not speak, and therefore could not lessen his burden of problems in this manner. In one group session the attending psychologist removed a package of cigarettes from his pocket and in doing so inadvertently dropped a stick of chewing gum on the floor. Andrew's eyes, which had normally been impassive and unresponsive, showed a glint of interest in the chewing gum. Later the psychologist thought about Andrew's behavior. If chewing gum had been effective in bringing Andrew out of his private world, perhaps it would also serve as a positive reinforcer.

During the next two weeks, this hypothesis was discovered to be well founded. Periodically in the group sessions, a stick of gum was held before Andrew's face. The psychologist waited until Andrew's eyes moved toward it. When this occurred, he immediately relinquished the stick of gum to Andrew, who opened his mouth and chewed it with alacrity. The gum served as a positive reinforcer, for Andrew began to look at the psychologist more and more often. At the end of two weeks, Andrew cast his eyes toward the psychologist each time he produced a stick of gum.

Having demonstrated that chewing gum was a positive reinforcer, the psychologist elected to use this simple but obviously powerful tool to reinstate verbal behavior in Andrew's life.

Even with the extraordinary and somewhat unexpected positive reinforcing effect of chewing gum, the task of reinstating Andrew's verbal behavior was not a simple one. Before a behavior can be reinforced, it must first occur, and Andrew had not initiated speech for more than 19 years. A less knowledgeable psychologist than the one working with Andrew might have approached him in the following manner:

"Andrew, I have some gum here. If only you'll begin to talk, I'll see that you get a piece of it."

Such an approach would have been doomed to failure before it started, and the psychologists consulting on Andrew's case knew this beforehand. The technique they adopted is far more subtle. It is known in the nomenclature of psychology as the *method of successive approximation*. The first step in the technique involves a decision on the part of the psychologist and his assistants as to a final behavior pattern they would like to see their patient acquire and maintain. The choice of the final behavior pattern may be purely arbitrary. In clinical psychology, where the welfare of human beings is at stake, the final behavior is always

1. This section based on Isaacs, W., Thomas, J., and Goldiamond, I. Application of operant conditioning to reinstate verbal behavior in psychotics. *Journal of Speech and Hearing Disorders,* 1960, 25, 8–12.

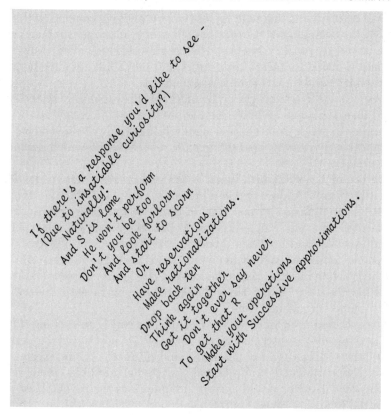

If there's a response you'd like to see -
(Due to insatiable curiosity?)
Naturally!
And S is lame
He won't perform
Don't you be too
And look forlorn
Or
Have reservations.
Make rationalizations.
Drop back ten
Think again
Get it together
Don't ever say never
To get that R
Make your operations
Start with Successive approximations.

one that will hasten the patient's rehabilitation. This final behavior is called the *terminal behavior* or the *terminal response*. It is a sort of target the psychologist aims for in his treatment program. The terminal behavior selected for Andrew was fluent and appropriate speech.

After the terminal behavior is agreed upon, the individual on whom the technique is to be employed is observed closely in order to identify an *initial response* which is related to the terminal response along some meaningful dimension. Unlike the terminal response, which the patient does not currently emit, the initial response must be made by the subject in the here and now. Further, it must take place with at least a minimal frequency.

After an initial response is identified, it is conditioned and soon occurs with regularity. At that time, it is abandoned and another response which more closely approximates the terminal behavior is selected and likewise conditioned. This procedure continues until the terminal behavior is observed to occur, whereupon it is reinforced directly.

In accordance with the method of successive approximation, an initial response was selected for Andrew. Early in the third week, the experimenter saw Andrew make a slight movement of his lips. Immediately the psychologist pulled forth a stick of gum and reinforced this lip movement. By the end of that week,

Andrew was regularly making both lip movements and eye contacts with the psychologist. At the beginning of the fourth week, a new and more strenuous requirement was placed on Andrew before chewing gum was delivered. Now Andrew not only had to make contact with his eyes and move his lips, but he also was required to emit a vocal sound of one sort or another.

The experimenter waited patiently until the first sound spontaneously occurred and then was quick in delivering the positive reinforcer to Andrew. By the end of the fourth week, Andrew was regularly making eye movements toward the experimenter, moving his lips, and making a vocal sound which resembled, of all things, a croak.

At the beginning of the fifth week, a new requirement was made. The psychologist waited until Andrew made a croaking sound and then he urged, "Say gum, gum." Andrew began to make his croaking sound after the psychologist's prompt, as if taking a cue from a director. At first, the croak was not much different from those which had been heard before. The experimenter hesitated until the croaking sound faintly resembled the word "gum" and then he gave Andrew his reinforcement. On the next occasion, he insisted that Andrew's vocalization sound even more like the word "gum." He withheld reinforcement until Andrew had all but approximated verbalizing "gum."

During a session near the sixth week of the treatment, an exciting thing happened. The psychologist had just given Andrew the now usual request to say "gum." Andrew suddenly said quite clearly and distinctly, "Gum, please." Before the session had terminated, Andrew was answering questions about his name and his age and thereafter would answer any questions the psychologist directed to him. In the following days, Andrew continued to chat with the psychologist, both during the session and at other times and places within the institution.

But the psychologist's job was not yet over. For one thing, Andrew had not shown the slightest inclination to speak to anyone else. Verbal behavior is of limited value if it is restricted to interactions with only one person. Accordingly, the psychologist sought to get Andrew to have verbal interactions with other persons. A nurse came to Andrew's room one day and it was noticed that Andrew smiled at her. The psychologist asked her to visit Andrew daily. After a month he began to answer her questions and thus made a first step in generalizing his verbal behavior to other people.

At this time, a problem came up in Andrew's treatment. The difficulty should be mentioned here because it is typical of a far more general problem than pertains strictly to Andrew. A volunteer worker who regularly spent several hours a week at the institution was working on Andrew's ward. One sunny day, Andrew brought her his coat and hat and indicated through gestures that he desired to go outside. Wishing to be of maximum service to her patients, the volunteer quickly interpreted his gestures and took him outside. This interaction gave the psychologist some insight into his reluctance to verbalize and also suggested a method of getting Andrew to speak in a reasonable manner to others who approached him. One of the reasons Andrew did not speak to the volunteer worker was simply that he did not have to speak. Through gestures, and primarily through the volunteer worker's swift and astute interpretation of his desires, Andrew received what he wanted without having to talk. By and large, this situation prevailed in other areas of the institution. Since Andrew did not talk, attendants and institution personnel assumed he was not capable and were more than eager to interpret his gestures and signals. This situation is not one that was unique to Andrew nor was it unique to the institution where Andrew was maintained. It is a disquieting but nonetheless true fact that unless people have a good reason to do something, they are not likely to do it. Andrew had begun to talk to the psychologist only when the psychologist had made it "worth his while" with a chewing gum reinforcement.

An anecdote can perhaps exemplify the general problem in a more humorous way.

Two fine people were married, and in a short while their union was blessed with a son. The son was handsome and appeared healthy in all respects. His proud parents were overjoyed. As time went on, however, the child exhibited no inclination to speak or communicate verbally. Although trips to specialists had revealed there was no physical cause for silence, the boy, whose name was Johnny, simply did not speak. His parents painfully accepted as fact the notion that their son would never speak. One day, when Johnny was 15 years of age, he and his parents were seated at the breakfast table. Johnny, who, to say the least, was somewhat pampered by his parents, was snuggled in his special chair. Soon his customary oatmeal was placed before him. Johnny took one bite of the oatmeal and quickly spat it out, dumping his bowl in the process. Then he opened his mouth and behold, precious words ensued.

"This damn oatmeal is too hot!"

His parents were infinitely shocked and flabbergasted at this unheralded occurrence of speech.

"Johnny!!" his mother said. "After all these years! Why have you not spoken before?"

Johnny shrugged his shoulders and replied simply, "Up 'til now, everything's been okay."

Like Johnny, Andrew could never be expected to develop adequate speech behavior as long as everything was "okay!" Certainly not as long as he could badger others into anticipating his needs. All Andrew really needed was a few gestures and an apathetic look.

As a consequence, the psychologist went about the institution speaking to those people who regularly came in contact with Andrew. He explained the problem to them and solicited their cooperation. He requested that in the future when Andrew came to them seeking their service or attention, he be required to express his needs verbally. Even if they could interpret his gestures, they were not to comply until a verbal request was made.

Many of the staff at the institution were consistent in requiring Andrew to verbalize but, unfortunately, many others were not. Andrew continued to speak to the psychologist and others who required speech from him but remained nonverbal for those people who were satisfied with interpreting his special language.

The *method of successive approximation* played an integral role in bringing Andrew back from his years of silence. First a target or *terminal behavior* was agreed upon by the psychologists. In Andrew's case the terminal behavior the psychologists wished to see occur was speech. Next a substance or event which served as a positive reinforcer was selected. Chewing gum was revealed to be a powerful positive reinforcer for Andrew. Often several items must be tried with a subject before an adequate positive reinforcer is discovered. An *initial behavior* which the subject already emits with some minimal frequency is selected. A specific initial behavior is chosen because it resembles or approximates the terminal behavior in one respect or another. Lip movements were selected as the initial behavior for Andrew. The initial behavior is positively reinforced and its frequency increased. A new behavior is then chosen which resembles the terminal behavior even more and is a closer approximation to it. It is likewise conditioned, and when it occurs with regularity, a response of still closer approximation is selected. Finally the terminal behavior itself is observed. It is swiftly reinforced, becomes conditioned, and is retained in the subject's repertoire of responses as long as it is reinforced. Positive reinforcement was delivered to Andrew successively for lip movements, vocal sounds of any nature, vocal sounds which resembled in an increasing fashion the word "gum," and finally, speech itself.

The nature of the relationship between the terminal response and the various behaviors which are successively reinforced in approximation to it warrants discussion at this time. The initial behavior reinforced in Andrew's treatment was lip movements. The relevance of lip movements to speech is obvious. Even ventriloquists have difficulty in talking without moving their lips. It can be said that lip movement is a *prerequisite* for speech. In order to talk, an individual must first learn to move his lips. This is one important way an initial or intermediate behavior is related to the terminal behavior in the method of successive approximation. It is a prerequisite.

In some instances prerequisites are spatial. If I were concerned with bringing about the terminal response of appropriate dining behavior, a spatial prerequisite is that the patient be present in the dining room at mealtime. An initial behavior which it would be wise to reinforce would be coming to the dining room when the dinner call is given.

Another type of prerequisite behavior is associated with the patient's physical capability. In an earlier chapter a retarded girl was taught to ride a bicycle. The girl's legs were weak and underdeveloped. A prerequisite behavior which was reinforced at an intermediate stage of the procedure was primarily a physical exercise designed to strengthen her legs. Stronger legs were a prerequisite for bicycle riding; behaviors which brought this about were accordingly reinforced.

But initial or intermediate behaviors are not only prerequisites to the terminal behavior; they also belong to the same response class. Andrew was reinforced for making a sound which initially resembled a croak. Both this primitive sound and the sounds which comprise fluent speech can be thought of as belonging to the response class termed "vocal behavior." After Andrew was reinforced for making one vocal production, his vocalizations increased. Subsequent steps involved reinforcing vocalizations which increasingly assumed the aspects of fluent speech.

Regardless of whether the initial and intermediate behaviors which are reinforced are prerequisites to or belong to the same response class as the terminal behavior, the psychologist chooses to reinforce them for one primary reason. Behavior which is conditioned in the progression of the method of approximation

There was a young lecher
(A terrible lad)
Whose reputation with chicks
Was exceedingly bad
He came on like thunder -
   No hesitations
And used all the tricks
   Like successive approximations.
He'd manifest his despicable wicked deportment
By using some form of positive reinforcement
To maneuver his chick
And win her consortment.
This dude was cold
And very slick
His play was old
And so I'm told
Was very quick
And good as gold.

is chosen because, in the long or short run it increases the probability that the terminal behavior will occur.

In the example used above, we suggested that coming to the dining room when called to a meal was a prerequisite for appropriate dining behavior. In fact, unless this intermediate behavior comes about, appropriate dining behavior simply cannot occur. Reinforcing Andrew's croaking sound not only increased the frequency of this vocal behavior, but also increased the likelihood that other vocal responses would occur as well. Once new sounds were produced, they in turn could be conditioned if they more closely approximated fluent speech.

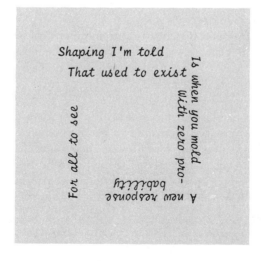

Shaping I'm told
That used to exist
Is when you mold
With zero pro-
bability
A new response
For all to see

Each behavior reinforced in the method of successive approximation can be viewed as a link in a chain which has as a single ultimate purpose the occurrence of the terminal response. The experimenter selects each link carefully and relies heavily on his experience and knowledge of the interrelationships, prerequisites, and associations of behaviors which are to be conditioned en route to the terminal behavior. With positive reinforcement, he guides the organism from the initial behavior, through the intermediate behaviors, until finally, the terminal response is emitted and can be reinforced and conditioned directly.

Another term for successive approximation is *shaping*, which is similar to "guiding." The expressions "successive approximation" and "shaping" mean exactly the same thing and no psychologist will be misled if you use them interchangeably. "Shaping" holds a more active connotation for me. It immediately brings to mind a keen-eyed experimenter as he reinforces first one response and then another, shaping the behavior of the organism as a sculptor shapes a difficult piece of marble. The expression of "successive approximation" stresses the logical aspects of the procedure and plays down the role of the experimenter. Whichever term you prefer, another case will further demonstrate its basic tenets.

Shaping an Autistic Child to Wear Corrective Glasses with Positive Reinforcement

Dickie was an autistic child.[2] In the past few years, the word "autism" has generally replaced an earlier term, "childhood schizophrenia." Regardless of what Dickie was called, it was obvious his behavior was not appropriate. Dickie was prone to have temper tantrums and did not seem to care about either adults or children. He was not in the least responsive to others.

At the time Dickie was first seen by the psychologist, in the hospital, he was only three and a half years old. There were techniques to deal with the temper tantrums and, likewise, procedures which could make him more "sociable." In time, these methods have been successful in bringing Dickie's behavior more in line with that of other children.

There was one problem which was extremely critical and had to be solved with all possible speed. Cataracts were discovered in the lenses of both eyes when Dickie was nine months old. At about the age of two, he had a series of eye operations which terminated in the removal of the lenses from both eyes. After these operations, one thing was certain. If Dickie was to see, he would have to wear special corrective glasses for the remainder of his life. For almost a year after Dickie's eyes had healed, his parents endeavored to get him to wear the glasses. Try as they might, they could not coerce him to wear them more than a few seconds before they were thrown off as casually as if they were a dime store toy. Dickie's parents made the rounds of specialists, all of whom seemed to have a new diagnosis for Dickie. None, however, were able to outline a constructive treatment which

2. This section based on Wolf, M., Risley, T., and Mees, H. Application of operant conditioning procedures to the behavior problems of an autistic child. *Behaviour Research and Therapy*, 1964, *1*, 305–312.

would deal with his behavior problems. No suggestions were forthcoming which succeeded in persuading Dickie to wear his glasses.

By the time Dickie's parents brought him to the hospital, the situation had reached critical proportions. At the age of three and a half, a child is developing rapidly. He should be learning about his environment and how he may function appropriately within it. Any child, even one who did not have Dickie's autistic behaviors, would be severely handicapped at this stage in his development without adequate vision.

The psychologists who took on Dickie's case decided to use positive reinforcement and behavior shaping techniques. Before any experimental procedures were enacted, they observed Dickie's behavior with his glasses. Just as his parents had said, Dickie kept them on for a few brief seconds before disposing of them. At best, the glasses were neutral to him. They did not make his life more meaningful. It was thought he might even find the prescription glasses mildly aversive. There was some discomfort associated with the frames on Dickie's nose and ears and the lenses themselves undoubtedly changed the way the world looked to him, which may have been initially unpleasant. In order to avoid breakage of expensive prescription glasses, the experimenters initially used frames without lenses. If the psychologists could shape the response of wearing these frames for long periods of time, the prescription glasses could be less unobtrusively switched in later.

The person actively involved with Dickie and his treatment was instructed to spend two or three 20-minute sessions each day with him in his room. The positive reinforcer consisted of small bites of candy or fruit which, in the beginning, Dickie seemed to enjoy greatly.

Initially, the frames were placed about the room and Dickie was reinforced in gradual sequences for approaching them, picking them up, holding them, and carrying them about. Later, movements of the frames toward his face were reinforced. Slowly the frames were brought closer and closer to his eyes.

Up to this point, the experimenters had achieved success in a remarkable fashion, but trouble was on its way. Dickie refused to wear the glasses with the eye openings in the correct position. Often they were cocked to one side of his head with the earpieces below his ears rather than on top of them. Some difficulty with the use of candy and fruit as reinforcers also developed. It appeared, after about two weeks, that these substances were no longer acting as effective reinforcers. Perhaps Dickie had become satiated with them during the long and numerous sessions. The procedure was adjusted. Breakfast was withheld and small bites of it were used as a positive reinforcer. In order to give him some help in positioning the glasses, larger ear frames were added to make placing them on his ears a simpler task. In addition, a "roll" bar was fitted from one earpiece across his head to the other earpiece. These modifications helped to correct many of the errors of placement.

At the beginning of the fifth week, however, the frames were still not being worn properly. More time was accordingly spent in the shaping procedure. In addition, a second bar was added to the back of the glasses, making them fit like a cap.

Near the end of the fifth week there was still some difficulty and Dickie was not progressing rapidly enough. It was the third session of that day. Dickie had performed poorly in the first two sessions, had received few reinforcements, and was understandably hungry. When the experimenter came to his room bearing ice cream, Dickie's face lit up perceptibly. He quickly picked up his glasses and placed them on his head. Progress was so fast during the first few minutes that the prescription glasses were substituted for the lenseless frames. After 30 minutes Dickie was wearing the glasses properly and looking out the lenses at various toys periodically displayed in hopes of maintaining his looking behavior. After this crucial session, progress was rapid. Soon he was wearing the glasses throughout mealtimes in his room.

Once the behavior was regularly maintained by powerful reinforcers, other reinforcers which were not so strong and did not rely on deprivation were employed. Often an attendant approached Dickie with the suggestion, "Put on your glasses and we'll go for a walk." Dickie was quick to comply. Other kinds of favors, treats, excursions, and outings were available to Dickie if he consented to wear his glasses.

Shaping procedures were ultimately highly successful with Dickie. At the time he was discharged from the hospital, he had worn the glasses for a total time of six hundred hours. On the average, he wore the glasses for 12 hours a day, which is more than reasonable for any child his age.

The importance of wearing glasses for Dickie's development is obvious. If his future were to hold even a wisp of promise, certainly he must have adequate eyesight. When Dickie was able to view the world much as other children view it, the treatment of other problem behaviors was aided considerably.

In shaping behavior, it can be seen that one response is reinforced and then replaced by another which is nearer in character to the terminal behavior the experimenter has in mind. Of course, there are many ways that one response can be said to differ from or resemble another. One important way which was discussed previously is the sequence of movements in each response and the relationship of each movement to the space surrounding the organism. The swing of a baseball bat differs from the swing of a golf club. A baseball swing takes place primarily in a horizontal plane. The bat initially moves in one direction only, forward, and then arcs to the left, or to the right if the batter is left-handed. A golf swing is primarily in a vertical plane and goes from the tee, high above, and then pauses and changes direction. Differences in movement through space are known as differences in *topography*. A swimming stroke or behavior involves a vastly different topography from dancing or running track. The topography of each of these responses differs greatly from the topography of a vocal response.

In Dickie's treatment, several different topographies were reinforced. The topography of approaching the glasses differed from that of picking them up, which in turn differed from that of placing the glasses on his head. The topography of placing the glasses *correctly* on Dickie's head differed from the response topography of incorrect placement, although the difference was of a lesser degree. This minimal difference made the final shaping task difficult and called for various new maneuvers from the experimenters.

Generally, shaping or successive approximation refers to systematically reinforcing different response topographies. There are ways, however, in which responses may differ other than topography. Two responses may have exactly the same topography but may differ in other physical dimensions. Let us take the example of two young men at a carnival, both of whom are trying to impress their girl friends with seemingly boundless physical powers. The task at hand involves ringing a bell by hitting a platform with a large wooden mallet. If the bell is rung, the ringer is rewarded with a large panda bear, which he immediately, and with some ceremony, bestows on his lady of the hour. One young man picks up the mallet and approaches the platform. He swings mightily but the indicator does not rise to its terminus. The bell does not ring. Rejected, he sulks away in failure. The second man picks up the mallet and approaches the platform. His swing is identical in topography to that of his predecessor. He swings harder, however, and with more force. When the mallet hits the platform, the indicator rises sharply and rings the bell. The hero takes his prize and awards it, taking full privileges in the process.

The swinging behaviors of the two young men did not differ in topography. There were, however, differences in the force with which the two responses occurred. As usual, the hard swinger is a winner.

Just as responses with different topographies can be shaped through the method of successive approximation, so can responses with the same topography be selectively shaped to occur with greater force or intensity.

Vocal behavior may also be analyzed in terms of its topography or intensity. Sounds may topographically differ from each other in the syllables they contain, the points of inflections, and various other qualitative characteristics of speech. Two words or sounds may have the same vocal topographies but differ only in terms of intensity. By and large, the logic and procedure for shaping intensity does not differ greatly from shaping across topographies.

In some instances, intensity considerations are primary in behavioral problems, and appropriate therapy involves increasing or decreasing the intensity dimension of a response.

Shaping of Voice Intensity with Positive Reinforcement

One clinical problem which sometimes comes to the attention of the speech therapist or psychologist is called "aphonia." People with aphonia can adequately make all appropriate sounds and utter complete and cogent sentences. The problem arises because of the reduced intensity with which they talk. Their speaking voice is not a voice at all, but rather a barely audible whisper. Their behavior brings about severe difficulty in communicating at work, at home, and with their children and friends. The origin of the problem is not known, but it has been found to persist for periods of years. Some people have retained it for the duration of their lives.

A thirteen-year-old girl whom we shall call Melanie had been aphonic for seven years.[3] Her voice was small and raspy. Her speech, although articulate, was of such a low intensity that it all but defied perception. Melanie's parents took her to visit several specialists in an effort to cure her of aphonia. It is somewhat surprising, given Melanie's exposure to one doctor after another, that she should develop a liking for the new "doctors" she ultimately went to see. The doctors were not "doctors" in the medical sense but were Ph.D. psychologists who took great pains to win Melanie's affection and respect during the initial stages of her treatment.

Earlier we saw that the attention of a nursery school teacher was a powerful positive reinforcer. In much the same way, the attention and approval of a psychologist or other professional who is significant in the eyes of the patient can also serve as a positive reinforcer. But kindness, friendship, and approval will not in themselves be adequate. If they are to be useful, they must be associated with the patient's responses in a thoughtful and effective way. Behavior may be shaped with kindness and praise.

Initial sessions were spent in breathing exercises where the doctors could become better acquainted with Melanie and also gently begin to shape her voice to an acceptable intensity. These breathing exercises were similar to those which singers and public speakers practice; they are engineered to make the voice stronger and increase its possibility for greater speaking force.

During this time, Melanie's attempts which were consistent with the experimenter's instructions were followed immediately by lavish praise and approval. Melanie seemed to respond quite readily to the experimenters. Their approval and praise were obviously powerful positive reinforcers for her.

In the next stage of the treatment, Melanie was told to hum. In much the same way that her speaking voice was faint and ethereal, so was her humming. Each time Melanie hummed louder the experimenter heaped on positive reinforcement. Little by little, greater humming intensities were reinforced and soon Melanie was humming at an intensity which was at least within normal range. Similarly, consonant sounds and oral reading were also shaped. Melanie read softly, almost at a whisper. She was told to try harder, and if she succeeded even by a barely noticeable amount, the experimenters lavished praise and kind words upon her. Reading intensity increased and finally was within normal limits. One final phase remained. It was perhaps the most important. The intensity of her voice during normal conversation required shaping. Once again, positive reinforcement was withheld until the intensity of her vocalizations increased above a previous level. Praise and attention were delivered to her when she succeeded. Whenever the intensity increased, further praise and compliments were given. By the method of successive approximation, the intensity of speaking was shaped until it was in no way different from that of other people. The treatment was a great success and alleviated a problem of many years standing. The treatment had involved only ten weekly visits to the psychologist's office. Two years later when Melanie was contacted for a routine follow-up, she was found to be doing quite

3. This section based on Bangs, J. L., and Friedinger, A. Diagnosis and treatment of a case of hysterical aphonia in a thirteen-year-old girl. *Journal of Speech and Hearing Disorders,* 1949, *14,* 312–317.

well and speaking "loud and clear." The change in her behavior was by no means temporary.

Melanie's treatment involved at least two dimensions of shaping. Response approximations were reinforced across topographies, and within each topography, intensity was shaped. The shaping of different topographies involved delivering positive reinforcement successively for breathing exercises, humming, saying consonants, reading from printed materials, and finally for conversation. Each of these entailed moving gradually from one topography to another which more closely resembled the termination behavior, that of conversation at an appropriate intensity. Shaping of intensities also occurred at each response topography. Reading began at a low intensity but with selective reinforcement of louder and louder utterances, it ultimately occurred with normal intensity. The same intensity was also shaped for consonants, humming, and conversation. The decision as to whether intensity or topography will be shaped is one which is determined by the terminal behavior to be obtained. Bringing new responses into an organism's repertoire frequently involves complex application of the method of successive approximation.

The Relationship of the Method of Successive Approximation to Response Differentiation

In the last chapter a procedural result termed response differentiation was introduced and discussed. Response differentiation comes about through the consistent reinforcement of one member of a response class to the exclusion of all other members of that class. As a result of this procedure, the response which is consistently reinforced increases its frequency relative to all other responses in the class. It becomes "differentiated" from other class members.

It may occur to the reader that the methods of successive approximation and response differentiation are similar. Indeed, there are similarities. There are also important differences. The terms and the procedures they entail are by no means equivalent.

The greatest similarity between the two procedures is that both involve *differential reinforcement*. A single response may receive numerous reinforcements while other responses go begging. The selective use of reinforcement to bring about some response sequences and to exclude others is a common feature of both procedures.

The method of successive approximation or shaping is a much broader technique than response differentiation. Included within a shaping procedure may be several isolated instances of response differentiation. Under some conditions, where the method of successive approximation is applied, the procedure may consist of a series of successive response differentiations. If the psychologist's final goal is simply response differentiation, he has succeeded when the response he has singled out becomes differentiated from other responses of the class. In shaping, response differentiation is generally a subgoal. After it is obtained, reinforcement must be applied to another response whose conditioning brings the psychologist ever closer to the terminal behavior he has selected.

More often than not, the experimenter wishes to see the patient or subject exhibit totally new behaviors. Perhaps the behavior he has in mind has never been shown by the patient in his entire history. Simple response differentiation is not appropriate in this case. In order for response differentiation to come about, the behavior to be differentiated must *presently occur*, at least with a minimal frequency. Response differentiation alone can never bring new responses into being. The method of successive approximation must be used in this instance.

Summary

In this chapter, further *and more complex* uses of positive reinforcement were discussed and related to the earlier notion of response differentiation.

1. Positive reinforcement may be employed to bring new responses into the organism's behavioral repertoire. The procedure by which this is done is called the *method of successive approximation*. A synonym for the method of successive approximation is *shaping*. "Shaping" refers more to the actions of the experimenter, while the "method of successive approximation" emphasizes the general logic of the procedure. This procedure involves positive reinforcements of responses which may at first only faintly resemble the terminal behavior the experimenter or psychologist desires. Through a gradual process the responses, which in an ever increasing fashion resemble the terminal behavior, are successively conditioned until the terminal behavior itself is conditioned.

2. We discussed the relationship of initial and intermediate responses to the terminal response. Two kinds of relationships were mentioned.

The initial or intermediate response may be a prerequisite for the terminal behavior. Unless the initial behaviors occur, the terminal behavior cannot possibly occur. Two types of prerequisites were mentioned: spatial and another prerequisite having to do with the physical capability of the organism. A second type of relationship between the terminal behavior and behaviors conditioned in approximation to it was their membership in the same response class.

3. Regardless of the type of relationship existing between the initial and intermediate behaviors and the terminal behavior, the psychologist reinforces certain behaviors because he believes they will increase the likelihood or probability that the terminal response will occur. In selecting the behaviors to be conditioned and the sequences of the procedure, the psychologist relies heavily on his skill, experience, and knowledge.

4. Two characteristics of responses are mentioned which are amenable to shaping. These two characteristics are *topography* and *intensity* or *force*. Topography refers to the movements of the responses in relation to space surrounding the responding organism. A dance step has a different topography from swinging a golf club since the movements through space involved in each are widely different. Shaping of response topographies was shown to be effective in reinstating verbal behavior in a psychotic patient and inducing an autistic child to wear corrective glasses.

5. Two responses may have identical topographies but differ in intensity or force. Intensity may be increased from an initial weak level to a higher magnitude through shaping. A teenage girl with a speech intensity problem called aphonia was treated by the method of successive approximation. Through shaping procedures, the intensity of her vocalizations was systematically increased from a faint whisper to that of normal conversation.

6. The method of successive approximation differs from response differentiation in one extremely important way, although both involve differential reinforcement. In response differentiation, the response to receive differential reinforcement *already occurs* with at least a minimal frequency. In shaping, the terminal response *does not currently occur,* and may have never occurred in the history of the organism.

Shaping is a much broader undertaking than response differentiation. It is not uncommon for a complex shaping procedure to include several instances of response differentiation which take place at various stages or levels.

QUESTIONS

1. Where are psychotics most likely to be found?
2. If a psychotic becomes regressed, what might happen to his speech behavior?
3. How old was Andrew when he was admitted to the institution?
4. How long had Andrew been mute when he came to the attention of the psychologist at the institution?
5. What was the accident which led to the discovery of a positive reinforcer for Andrew? What was the reinforcer?
6. In what activity was Andrew involved with the psychologist when the discovery was made?
7. Why did many of the institution staff feel it was inappropriate for Andrew to take part in the group therapy session?
8. What did Andrew do when eye contact with the psychologist was reinforced with chewing gum?
9. The psychologist approached Andrew in the following way: "Andrew, I have some gum here. If only you'll begin to talk, I'll see that you get a piece of it." (a) True; (b) False.
10. What was the "subtle" technique that the psychologist adopted? Give the name.
11. What in the method of successive approximation is the first decision the psychologist must make?
12. What is the target behavior the psychologist wishes to see installed in the patient called?
13. After the terminal behavior has been decided upon, what behavior must then be identified?
14. The *initial* behavior has two requirements. What are they?
15. What *initial* response was selected for Andrew?
16. What typically happened after this behavior had been reinforced for a week?
17. What new behavior was reinforced at the beginning of the fourth week?
18. At the end of the fourth week, Andrew was consistently making a sound. What was it?

19. In the next step the experimenter typically prompted Andrew with the words, "Say gum, gum." What was Andrew's initial response?

20. After Andrew was responding reliably to the experimenter's prompt, what series of requirements did the experimenter demand before Andrew was reinforced?

21. What exciting thing happened in a session near the end of the sixth week of the treatment?

22. After Andrew had begun to answer all of the psychologist's questions, what important thing remained to be done?

23. With what other human being did Andrew soon begin to interact verbally?

24. The volunteer greatly aided in Andrew's treatment. (a) True; (b) False.

25. A story was told about a boy who had not talked since birth, but suddenly began to talk when his oatmeal was not adequate. Why had he not talked before this time? In what way were the boy's lack of verbal behavior and Andrew's mutism similar?

26. What did the psychologist do to combat this condition in the institution and to maintain Andrew's verbal behavior?

27. Which of the following is the best statement of the outcome of the psychologist's talk with the institution personnel? (a) Andrew soon talked to everyone in the institution; (b) Andrew became mute again; (c) Andrew took up singing as a career; (d) Andrew spoke to people who required it of him but failed to talk to others who would interpret his needs without verbal behavior.

28. Lip movements are a ——————- —————— for speech.

29. What is one important way in which an initial or intermediate behavior is related to the terminal behavior?

30. Give one example of an initial behavior which is a spatial prerequisite for a terminal behavior.

31. The *croaking sound* Andrew made and *fluent speech* belonged to the same —————— ——————.

32. What is another way in which initial and intermediate behaviors can be related to a terminal behavior?

33. Regardless of how the initial or intermediate behavior is related to the terminal behavior, the psychologist chooses the behaviors he reinforces for one singular reason. What is it?

34. Most vocal sounds increase the probability of other vocal sounds. (a) True; (b) False.

35. What is another term which means the same thing as the method of successive approximation?

36. In the account "Shaping an Autistic Child to Wear Corrective Glasses With Positive Reinforcement," what was the autistic child's name?

37. In earlier years, what conditions were autistic children said to suffer from?

38. What physical abnormality was discovered in Dickie at the age of nine months?

39. As the result of this condition, what did Dickie's parents have done to him when he was two years old?

40. It was obvious after the operation that if Dickie were to see, he would have to wear ——————— ——————.

41. Dickie's parents had great success in getting him to wear his corrective glasses. (a) True; (b) False.

42. How old was Dickie when he was brought to the hospital and the psychologist began to work with him?

43. What did the psychologists find initially when they tried to put glasses on Dickie?

44. Why was it thought that the glasses might initially be mildly aversive to Dickie? Can you name two factors?

45. The experimenters broke several pairs of corrective glasses in trying to get Dickie to wear them. (a) True; (b) False.

46. The experimenters used frames without lenses during initial phases. (a) True; (b) False.

47. What was initially used as a positive reinforcer for Dickie's behavior?

48. What initial behavior was Dickie reinforced for?

49. Briefly give the next three of four behaviors which were successively reinforced.

50. What problem did the experimenters ultimately experience with fruit and candy as a reinforcer?

51. What was done to ear frames in order to make the glasses fit on Dickie's head better?

52. What was the attachment placed from one ear frame over Dickie's head and fastened to the other ear frame?

53. By the beginning of the fifth week, the frames were still not being worn properly. What two things did the experimenter do at this time to help correct this situation?

54. One day near the end of the fifth week on the session of that day, the experimenters came to Dickie's room with a new reinforcer. What was it?

55. Why was Dickie particularly receptive to the reinforcer on that day?

56. Dickie progressed so rapidly during that session that the experimenters replaced the lensless frames. With what did they replace them?

57. Why did the experimenters hold objects in front of Dickie's eyes when he first began to wear the glasses?

58. After wearing the glasses became maintained by powerful food reinforcers, what type of reinforcement was offered Dickie for wearing the glasses? Give an example.

59. At the time Dickie was discharged from the hospital, how many hours had he worn glasses?

60. What was the average number of hours he wore them daily and how does this compare with the wearing time of normal child of his age?

61. A baseball swing differs from a golf club swing in terms of _____.

62. A swimming stroke differs from dancing or running track in _____.

63. Name at least five of the different topographies reinforced in Dickie's treatment.

64. Why was it probably difficult to get Dickie to wear the glasses correctly as opposed to placing them on his head incorrectly?

65. Two responses with the same topography must by definition be alike in all other respects as well. (a) True; (b) False.

66. Responses may differ in terms of intensity or _____.

67. In the example given, the responses of the two young men in ringing the bell differed in topography. (a) True; (b) False.

68. The hard swinger is a winner. (a) True; (b) False.

69. Vocal behavior may be analyzed in terms of topography or _____.

70. In the section, "Shaping of Voice Intensity with Positive Reinforcement," what is the clinical problem called which has to do with lack of vocal intensity?

71. What was the girl's name who suffered from this problem and how old was she?

72. She had been to many doctors before seeing the psychologists. (a) True; (b) False.

73. As a result of having too many doctors in her life, she did not like the psychologists. (a) True; (b) False.

74. What type of reinforcer was used on Melanie's behavior?

75. What was the first behavior the psychologist reinforced Melanie for?

76. For which of these behaviors did Melanie *not* receive reinforcement? (a) Humming; (b) Saying of consonants; (c) Reading aloud; (d) Reciting the alphabet.

77. What was the outcome of Melanie's treatment? How long did the treatment take?

78. Two years later when Melanie was contacted for a follow-up, it was found that: (a) she could not speak at all; (b) she hurt the eardrums of her listeners because she spoke too loudly; (c) her speech behavior was quite appropriate; (d) Melanie could not be found after two years since she had gotten married in the interim.

79. The methods of successive approximation and the procedure of response differentiation are similar in that both involve _____ reinforcement.

80. Differential reinforcement is a much broader technique than shaping. (a) True; (b) False.

81. Within a shaping procedure, several isolated incidences of response differentiation may occur. (a) True; (b) False.

82. Of the following behaviors, on which would you use the methods of successive approximation and on which response differentiation? (a) Getting a child to apply the correct amount of pressure to a candy machine lever; (b) Getting a girl who had never played tennis before to play tennis; (c) Bring about correct golf stroke behavior; (d) Getting a retarded child to play a musical instrument.

NOTES

Application of Positive Reinforcement to Reinstate Verbal Behavior in a Psychotic

During World War I, it was typical for our soldiers suffering from battle fatigue or "war neurosis," as it is now called, to be shipped back from the front lines to hospitals in Paris or even to the United States. Only a very small percentage of these "battle casualties" ever returned to active combat and many of them remained in military or veterans' hospitals for many years after active service. Many psychiatrists and psychologists versed in the problem began to express a disquieting notion. They felt that in many ways hospitalization itself made their patients less equipped to deal with the outside world and extremely poor candidates for active duty and combat.

In World War II this condition was modified. Troops who suffered war neurosis were not shipped back to occupied territory for treatment. Typically, they received treatment a short distance from the battle zone. Every effort was exerted to get them back into the front lines as quickly as possible. With this type of treatment, lingering casualties from neurosis were kept at a minimum. War neurosis failed to even approximate the problem it was in the first World War.

In a similar way, some aspects of most American institutions actually work at cross purposes with eventual rehabilitation. A person who is functioning outside the hospital may or may not be gainfully employed, but he is forced to make provisions for his food and lodgings. Great pressure is placed on him to at least minimally interact with his environment and to face some of the demands of outside living. Upon admission, well meaning but uninformed institutional personnel quickly assume full responsibility for the patient. He no longer has to make even minor decisions for himself.

In the case of Andrew, who is in many ways typical, it was not even necessary to talk, for perceptive hospital personnel were willing to interpret his gestures and nonvocal communications. With all responsibility and demands removed from them, it is not surprising that patients often "regress" in an institution. Recent statistics show that if a patient remains in an institution for more than 18 months, it is very unlikely that he will ever be released. Undoubtedly, this poor prognosis is due in great part to the "institutionalization" of the patient, which may be extremely difficult to reverse after a time.

Shaping an Autistic Child to Wear Corrective Glasses with Positive Reinforcement

Much confusion arises among professionals and students alike as to the exact meaning of diagnostic labels applied to children who exhibit peculiar behaviors. One expression often heard is "mental retardation." Remarkably, these children show an inability to learn, although many of them are socially responsive to adults, normal children, and companions in the institution. The diagnosis of retardation often depends on several factors, none of which are explicit.

In many cases, the diagnosis is reached because these children behave differently from most children and have a known history of disease, illness, or trauma. In many cases, other physical problems accompany these early conditions and therefore seem consistent with such a diagnosis. Some retardates begin infancy as do other children but at some time in their early years suffer a disease or injury which brings on marked deviations from that time forward. These children may retain some of their early training and exhibit considerable "old" skills, but have difficulty in acquiring new ones. Other children who exhibited abnormalities at or near birth get off to a bad start from which they never recover. By and large, no problem arises in agreeing on the general diagnosis of retardation for these children. In some instances, retardation has been linked to genetic factors. In phenylketonuria, a genetically-determined enzyme deficiency, detection and prophylaxis prevent the occurrence of later retardation.

Child autism was often in the past labeled "childhood schizophrenia." Most professionals agree that these terms denote the same type of child although occasionally a superficial distinction will be made. The primary factor causing a diagnosis of autism is the unwillingness of these children to interact with or become meaningfully attached to human beings. They often seem totally indifferent to social interactions which normal children both seek out and enjoy. Often they persist in seemingly random responses such as head banging, rocking, or other stereotyped behaviors which may or may not involve vocalization. Frequently the history of autistic children involves an early period of what is described as "normal" behavior followed by an era of drastic behavioral change. This change is rarely associated with any type of physical illness. As a result, many autistic children have early behavioral repertoires and appear to "be able to do better, but simply are not willing." It is this aspect of their behavior which brought about the earlier label of childhood schizophrenia.

Grave problems arise if one becomes too specific in trying to pin a diagnostic label on childhood behavioral problems. While most professionals will agree on the diagnosis of a certain percentage of children, a far greater number may be variously diagnosed by different physicians, psychiatrists, and psychologists. Often the records of institutionalized children who have been diagnosed by a number of professionals read like guesses at the number of beans in a jar. It is not uncommon to find a single child diagnosed variously as autistic, retarded, or normal with behavior symptoms.

There is a growing feeling among psychologists that diagnosis is probably the most unimportant factor in the treatment of a child unless, within that diagnosis, a correct and adequate treatment is explicitly suggested. With the exception of a half-dozen or so diagnoses, this does not obtain. Today treatment seems to be more dependent on the specific child, his deficits and skills, and the environment he must ultimately master. Throughout this book, examples of treatment procedures for autistic and retarded populations occur.

In the course of Dickie's treatment, the experimenters were forced to seek out new and more powerful reinforcers. Ultimately they relied on ice cream. It was immediately effective where in previous weeks small bits of candy and fruit showed only partial effectiveness.

The fact that the experimenters had difficulty in finding an effective reinforcement illustrates a typical problem which daily faces psychologists. Regardless of the difficulty, it is incumbent on the researcher using positive reinforcement techniques to find a commodity which will serve as an effective positive reinforcer. In a study presented earlier in this chapter, a psychotic named Andrew was shaped to make verbal responses, which he had failed to do for 19 years. Sticks of chewing gum succeeded where years of pleading, coercion, and indifference had failed. In some instances, I have found children who would work long and hard for crumbled soda crackers and still others who remained for an hour in an experimental session for a five-minute opportunity to play with stuffed animals. One retarded child would work only if Coca-Cola was squirted in his mouth. A portable squirt gun did the trick.

Even normal adults have idiosyncratic tastes and sometimes an object will exert almost incomprehensible control over them if used properly. Many young men have tried to convince me that flowers are the ultimate reinforcer with the fair sex. One girl I was dating as a young bachelor was completely unmoved by all of my advances; and, one after another, positive reinforcers of great promise were discarded much like petals from a flower. As with Dickie, I discovered quite by accident that ice cream was her weakness. Twenty-five hot fudge sundaes later, the young lady was finding my companionship the most exciting event in her life.

SCHEDULES OF REINFORCEMENT

6

The Nassau dock abounded with tourists of assorted sizes, shapes, ages, and dispositions, their cameras slung about their necks, gawky identification tags. Here and there one perspired beneath sunglasses, his skin already turning pink under the Bahamian sun. The cruise boats were in from Miami: the *Bahama Star,* the *Miami,* the *Ariadne,* and the *Wayward.* The port fairly bustled with enterprise.

In the harbor, the water stood amazingly blue and clean. Groups of native boys were stationed in a cluster by the wharf. They had placed themselves there with knowledge and forethought. No tourist could land on Bahamian soil without first allowing them an opportunity to solicit tribute.

"Hey, Mon, throw in de coin and watch me bring him up."

An occasional tourist obliged the divers by tossing a quarter or half dollar into the cool waters of the harbor. Almost before the coin had passed his fingertips, the boys were thrashing about in the water anxiously watching like cats awaiting a winged sardine. Then in a frantic swirl, they disappeared beneath the water in pursuit of the coin gliding on its glittering way through the solemn 15 feet to the bottom. One by one the divers rose to the surface, small brown corks bobbing up for the sky. Invariably, one of them would be holding the coin high above his head for all to see, the coin glittering in the sun and its new owner beaming triumphantly.

Fascinated, I watched the Bahamian youngsters for the better part of that afternoon. One boy soon caught my fancy. He was smaller than the others and not nearly as adept in underwater recovery. His large brown eyes had reddened from long contact with the salt water. Twenty, perhaps thirty, times I saw him disappear beneath the water and come to the surface gasping and empty-handed. He was growing tired. Each time he pulled himself from the water more slowly than the time before. Finally, when I was all but ready to offer him money if he would not dive again, another coin was thrown in the water. I did not see him dive this time. Could he be resting, clinging to one of the pilings beneath the wharf? But no, there he was, rising to the surface like a gusher, his right hand high above his head, a fifty-cent piece held tightly between his small fingers. He displayed his accomplishment to all, and with renewed vitality leaped from the water up to the wharf. When the next coin was thrown, he was the first to break the water.

In the world of behavior which psychology must eventually try to explain, success does not irrevocably follow every attempt. By translating the "success" into another term, we can attempt to relate the behavior of the young Bahamian diver to principles of psychology. This term is, of course, *positive reinforcement*.

In our study of positive reinforcement and its effects, we have so far spoken about the somewhat artificial state of affairs which was arranged in the laboratory, institution, or other experimental settings. Here the response the experimenter wished to condition was followed consistently and regularly with positive reinforcement. In psychology, the term *continuous reinforcement* means the response is continuously followed by a reinforcement.

While continuous reinforcement can be provided for quite handily in the laboratory, it is impossible to reinforce all behavior all of the time. In fact, some behaviors are never reinforced every time they occur in the world outside. Taking this into account, psychologists have suggested a term for instances when reinforcement does occur, but not continuously. When reinforcement follows the response only occasionally, the term *intermittent reinforcement* is used.

Thus, *continuous reinforcement* defines a situation in which each response always produces a reinforcement. *Intermittent reinforcement* describes a state where a response produces a reinforcement only occasionally. It can be seen that the first term is more explicit than the second. Knowing that intermittent reinforcement is in effect, we must then ask how frequently a response produces a reinforcement, and under precisely what conditions.

Further, it is not enough to say that reinforcement follows a given percentage of responses, for then it must be ascertained how a specific response comes to be reinforced while another is passed over.

The specific way in which reinforcement is programmed to occur as a result of number of responses, time between responses, or other temporal or quantitative features of responses is called a *schedule of reinforcement*. There are numerous ways in which reinforcement may be "scheduled" to occur as a function of response. In the past several years, psychologists have studied these *schedules of reinforcement* extensively. They have found that the schedule by which reinforcement is related to response determines, for one thing, the rate and patterning of responses. There are actually many ways in which the *schedule of reinforcement* may be related to behavior. We will discuss these after you become acquainted with a few specific schedules of reinforcement. Even now you are ahead of the game since you have already been introduced to one schedule. This schedule is continuous reinforcement, which is sometimes referred to by the letters "CRF." Of course, in a CRF schedule of reinforcement, every response produces a reinforcement. You are about to become acquainted with another schedule of reinforcement—hold on!

CRF = continual reinforcement

The Coral Gables "Bar"

"I just don't understand it," the visitor said. "You don't fight fire with gasoline. By the same token you can't cure an alcoholic by giving him his favorite mixed drink."[1]

The doctor nodded condescendingly. He had heard criticisms of his techniques many times before. As chief psychologist at the Veterans' Administration Hospital in Coral Gables, Florida, he was engaged in a series of behavioral studies on the nature of alcoholism. Many in the past had speculated about the true "cause" of alcoholism. Moralists had long pointed an accusing finger at alcoholics, attributing their problem to personal weakness, inferior character, or inadequate "will power." They offered beatings, incarceration, and other types of chastisement as "treatment." Others more humane felt that alcoholism was a "disease." They searched unsuccessfully for the microbe or bodily malfunction which engendered the disease.

The doctor was not ready to speculate. As a psychologist, he was interested in behavior.

In order to learn more about alcoholism, the behavior of individuals classified as alcoholic would have to be studied directly. Perhaps when the drinking behavior itself was studied the factors which maintained and controlled it could be discovered. From this point it would be only a short step to treatment and alleviation of the problem. The psychologist looked over the visitor, whose jaw was firmly set. He had made his point and further talking would not change his mind. Perhaps a demonstration was needed.

"Come with me," the psychologist said. Without saying more, he got up from his desk and walked out of his office, turning right down the long concrete corridors of the hospital. He slackened his pace only long enough to assure himself that the visitor had taken his lead and was close behind him. Soon they came to two large doors, which were opened with a gigantic metal key. A narrow corridor led them to a room where a young man was bending over a piece of machinery adjusting the mechanism. The room contained more than just one piece of machinery, the visitor found. It was literally paneled from wall to wall with racks of gadgets, dials, and electronic lights, with hundreds of wires interconnecting them. The only bare surface was a large mirror on one of the walls. The visitor recognized that the mirror was not a mirror at all but really a viewing glass which allowed the experimenters to look into a smaller room directly adjacent to it.

"Hi," the young man said, looking up from the machinery and smiling. The chief introduced the visitor to the younger man. He was one of several psychology interns who were taking additional training at the VA Hospital under close direction. In order to become full-fledged clinical psychologists, graduate students were required to complete a full year of internship under special conditions and

1. This section based on Whaley, D. L., Livingston, Pat, and Rosenkrantz, A. Punishment of consumatory response of alcoholic beverages in institution patients. Unpublished research conducted at VA Hospital, Coral Gables, Florida, 1966.

supervision such as that provided at Coral Gables. It was during this internship that students received an opportunity to translate facts learned from lectures and books into practical experience with real clinical cases.

"You're starting a new one today, aren't you, Jim?" the chief said.

"Yes," the intern said, pulling out an official looking folder and leafing through it quickly. "Three times married, twice divorced, left his last wife ten years ago, three children; hasn't seen either parents or children for ten years; hometown in North Carolina; been arrested 104 times for "drunk and disorderly"; gets mean when he has a few and punches out anyone in range."

The intern closed the book and looked up at the chief psychologist and his guest.

"He's actually a pretty good fellow and seems really anxious to be helped with his problem."

"What's his favorite drink?"

"Vodka and orange juice. I was getting ready to mix it and put some in the machine." The young man turned around and walked to a cabinet at the far end of the room. He opened the door, revealing rows of bottles with labels indicating all imaginable types of liquor. He selected one marked vodka and, at the same time, took another container labeled orange juice.

"That's real liquor?" the visitor asked with disbelief.

The intern did not answer. He was too busy portioning out the liquor and orange juice until a batch of it had been mixed up in a half gallon bottle.

"Excuse me," the intern said and left the room. He could be seen on the other side of the observation glass, bending over a desk built into the wall. Above the desk, protruding from the wall, was a small lever or "bar," as the psychologist typically called it. Above the bar were two small colored lights. The intern unlocked the bottom portion of the desk and poured the solution into a container there. He closed the desk door, making sure it was securely locked. He then returned the empty bottle to the room where the other two men had been observing him.

"It's time to go," he said. "Our new subject is waiting. His name is Lawrence."

After a few minutes, the two men in the observation room saw the intern with another man go into the room where the bar was located. The man wore a blue uniform which indicated that he was a patient in the hospital. It was difficult to tell the man's age for, although his full head of hair and physical build suggested that he was still young, a sallow complexion, scars about his face, and deep-set, reddened eyes made him appear much older. The intern seated the patient before the bar and talked to him for some time, pointing to different parts of the apparatus, obviously explaining its function to the patient. Soon he left the room and returned to the observation room where Dr. Kushner and his visitor had been observing the entire scene. The intern pushed several buttons and switches, and electric motors were heard to hum. At the same time, a light flashed on in the other room. In the room, the patient gingerly reached up and touched the lever. He depressed it. A yellow light flashed and a shot glass in the cubbyhole built into the wall could be seen to partially fill with orange-colored fluid. The patient looked with distrust at the mixture of vodka and orange juice. He picked up the glass carefully, tasted it, and then drank its contents down. He then replaced the glass and again depressed the lever. The light went on again and the orange fluid squirted into the glass which the patient immediately picked up and drank. With each drink they watched the patient consume, the visitor became more agitated and uneasy.

"How long does this go on?" he demanded finally.

"Each session lasts 20 minutes," the intern said.

"At this rate, he will be roaring drunk by then," the visitor concluded.

The chief smiled. "I think not," he said, nodding to the intern who raised his hand and quickly adjusted a knob beneath a counter, resetting the number on the counter to three. The patient in the barroom depressed the lever, but this time no liquor appeared. He pressed it again and still no liquor came. When he pressed it a third time, the light came on, at the same time portioning out the small amount of liquor into his glass. After drinking its contents, the patient pressed the lever once, twice, three times and again the light came on, giving him his small drink. This sequence occurred several times. The visitor had been watching carefully.

"I see," he said. "Now he must push the lever three times in order to get a drink."

"We're not through yet," the chief said, nodding again to the intern who adjusted the same dial, changing it to seven. Inside the patient pressed three times quickly but the liquor did not come. Cautiously, he pressed again and again until, after the seventh press, the light went on and liquor poured into the glass. Soon the patient made seven presses without hesitation, each time receiving his liquor reinforcement. As the session progressed, the requirement was increased several times more. The patient adjusted his behavior to the new requirements with little difficulty. Finally, toward the end of the session, the patient was making 120 lever presses for each drink. Inside the observation room, the apparatus could be heard to click with each lever press as each response was recorded on a cumulative recorder. The patient made his responses rapidly with no hesitation between them. The accompanying sound reminded the visitor of a machine gun burst. After each burst, the patient stopped, removed the glass, and gulped down his drink. At the end of the 20-minute session, the intern turned off the apparatus and walked out of the observation room into the room where the bar was located. The patient rose from his chair. The intern slapped him on the back and both men appeared to laugh and joke good-naturedly as they left the room. The patient had obviously not consumed enough "screwdrivers" to affect his behavior adversely.

"Well, what do you think of our bar?" The chief said to the visitor.

"Amazing," the visitor said, "but how much can you keep increasing the requirement? Surely it will reach the point where the patient will have to press so many times, he will be unwilling to, even if he does get a drink."

"Undoubtedly. That's precisely the point. We would like to know exactly how strong his affinity for alcohol is, and what discomforts he will put up with to get a drink. We are just beginning with this patient, but now you can see how we manage to study drinking behavior without getting our patients whooping drunk.

This patient will be back three more times today and still won't be even a little bit tipsy."

He stopped and looked at his watch. "Well," he said, "it's almost lunchtime. Are you sure you wouldn't like a cocktail before lunch?" he said with a twinkle, pointing through the glass toward the bar.

"No thanks," the visitor said. "I think I prefer to pay for my drinks in the usual way. Besides, you don't even have a floor show!"

In a future chapter we will discuss some findings from the Coral Gables Bar and how they relate to the general problem of alcoholism. Currently we are more interested in how the psychologist managed to sustain bar-pressing behavior with small and infrequent reinforcements. Actually he used a particular schedule of reinforcement to achieve this end.

This schedule of reinforcement ultimately employed by the chief and his staff was, however, far removed from a continuous reinforcement schedule where each response results in reinforcement. It was, in fact, exactly 119 responses removed, for at the end of the session, each reinforcement required 120 consecutive responses. This schedule of reinforcement is called *fixed ratio*. The final schedule, in which 120 responses were required before reinforcement occurred, is designated a "fixed-ratio 120 schedule." Just as continuous reinforcement was abbreviated "CRF," a fixed-ratio schedule is shortened to "FR." An "FR 120" is the one above, where 120 responses were required for reinforcement. *A fixed-ratio schedule of reinforcement is one in which reinforcement is forthcoming after a specific or "fixed" number of responses occur.*

Fixed-ratio reinforcement generates behavior which has several distinct characteristics. These characteristics hold true by and large for most fixed-ratio schedules, regardless of how large or small the requirement might be.

Once the organism has operated under a particular fixed-ratio schedule for a short time, his response patterns become quite standard. Figure 6-1 shows data from one of the alcoholics performing at the Coral Gables Bar. The patient's name is Harold. He is pressing on an FR 120 schedule of reinforcement for scotch and soda. The graph is a cumulative one taken from a special recording device called a cumulative recorder. It is just like the cumulative graphs you have seen in previous chapters. The slope of the line (a) is quite steep. It is almost straight up-and-down. Judging from the cumulative record, you might surmise that Harold made the first response and kept going as rapidly as he could until he had completed the entire 120 responses. This is exactly what occurred. It is generally the case for all behavior maintained on a fixed-ratio schedule of reinforcement. *Upon initiation of the first response in the fixed ratio, the remaining responses of the requirement are completed rapidly with minimal hesitation between responses.*

The small hash mark on the cumulative record above (b) indicates the delivery of reinforcement. After the hash mark a flat place appears on the record (c). This horizontal line was created because several seconds elapsed during which no responses were made. If you were to observe Harold after finishing a "burst," you would witness the following chain of responses. The reinforcement light comes on; Harold takes his hand from the lever and reaches for the glass, lifts it to his lips, and gulps it down. He then replaces the glass correctly in the

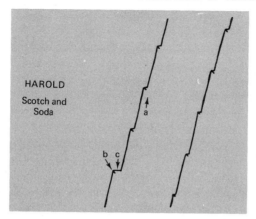

Figure 6-1   Harold's performance at the Coral Gables Bar

cubbyhole. He is ready to begin another ratio. *He does not begin immediately, however.* Perhaps he takes time to look about the room, to scratch his head, or rub his nose. This "pause" after the reinforcement has been consumed accounts for the flat place in the cumulative record. The pause is traditionally referred to as the *post-reinforcement pause.* The *post-reinforcement pause is another characteristic of fixed-ratio maintained behavior.* Where the schedule is fixed ratio, there will generally be a post-reinforcement pause. The length of the pause is related to the size of the ratio. If the ratio is large, the pause will be long. If the ratio is small, the pause will likely be short. In extremely small fixed ratios, the post-reinforcement pause may be so small that it is indiscernible. It may help to think of the ratio requirement as a "task" or "job." If the task is a small one, you do it quickly, and do not rest long before you begin another. If the task is a large one, you will work like crazy to complete it and then take a nice long "break."

After the post-reinforcement pause, the initial response is made and the ratio furiously completed; another pause, and the cycle begins again. Behavior maintained on a fixed-ratio schedule has been described as "all or nothing." The organism is either going as though the devil himself were after him, or he is resting. There does not seem to be a happy medium during which he nonchalantly responds, idly looking about the room or chatting with his neighbor. The ratio is work and he works at it until it is completed; then he rests.

At the Coral Gables Bar, the price for a drink was not initially 120 responses. In the beginning, only one press of the lever was needed to produce a sip of liquor. The schedule of reinforcement was CRF. Soon the requirement was increased to an FR 3, an FR 7, and through gradual but persistent increments, an FR 120 was reached. The chief and his assistants were not merely showing off for the visitor. The immediate introduction of an FR 120 requirement probably would have frustrated the patient and extinguished the bar-press response after a few dozen responses. In order to arrive at the stable performance seen on the FR 120 schedule, a procedure was employed in which smaller ratios successively approximated the terminal ratio.

*post reinforcement pause
is a short pause period
between the response that
has been reinforced and the
remaining responses —*

The higher the ratio, the more important it is to introduce it gradually through lower initial ratios. If the ratio is made too high too quickly, then the response will extinguish. Extinction which is due to this procedural error is called quite colorfully "straining the ratio." It is a serious error for a psychologist to program reinforcement in such a way that his subject's ratio becomes strained. Ratios often become strained outside of the laboratory because teachers, employers, parents, and others who assign us tasks are not familiar with the principles of behavior. A grammar school child who has just learned to read does not select a library book solely because of the picture on the cover, its promised content, or the recommendation of a friend. He is primarily concerned with the thickness of the book. How many pages does it have? How large is the print? A book which is thick with many pages and small print is not popular with the grammar school set. If such a book is assigned to a beginning reader he will strain his ratio long before he strains his eyes. The chapters of this book are kept at a strict maximum in order not to strain your ratio. The following limerick may help you remember the term "strained ratio" and keep the concept in mind.

> There once was a savage named Zack
> Who dragged fat women by the hair to his shack.
> He said he was through after girl twenty-two—
> "It's not my ratio that's strained, it's my back!"

Perhaps at this time it would be good to distinguish between two primary effects of reinforcement on behavior. The first you are quite familiar with. It is conditioning. In order to increase the frequency of a response which is weak and highly unstable, a schedule of continuous reinforcement is first used. The Coral Gables alcoholics were first placed on a continuous reinforcement schedule. If the ratio is a large one and reinforcement sparse, then conditioning will proceed slowly. The behavior may ultimately extinguish in spite of your efforts and intentions. For this reason, conditioning usually relies on continuous reinforcement. After a behavior has been conditioned with a CRF schedule and occurs regularly, then an intermittent reinforcement schedule can be used. This schedule is said to "maintain" the behavior. Even on an intermittent schedule, reinforcement must happen often enough to maintain the behavior. By gradually increasing the requirement, however, the number of reinforcements needed to maintain behavior can be reduced to a minimum. A fantastically high ratio can be maintained by a relatively small quantity of reinforcers. One experimenter[2] brought a pigeon to respond reliably on an FR 20,000; after 20,000 pecks the pigeon received several grams of grain. While this is more grain than pigeons usually receive in a reinforcement, it does not detract from the observation that the pigeon spent almost all day pecking as fast as he could to meet the requirement.

But how could a pigeon "count" to 20,000? If this is your question, you are suffering from a fairly common misconception of a fixed-ratio schedule. Actually, counting behavior, which is primarily a behavior restricted to verbal organisms such as man, is not a requirement for performance on a fixed-ratio schedule. Counting may enable a human to predict when reinforcement will oc-

2. Based on Findley, J. Personal communication, 1971.

cur, but reinforcement will occur after the required number of responses are made regardless of whether the subject counted or not. The effectiveness of the FR schedule in no way depends on counting. The schedule generates the same general type of response patterns independent of counting.

Reinforcement can be thought of as having two functions: it can be used to condition new behaviors and, through proper scheduling, can also be used to maintain behaviors which have already been conditioned. It must be stressed that while a particular intermittent schedule may be quite effective in maintaining a response, that same schedule will often be totally inadequate to bring about the original conditioning of that response. At the Coral Gables Bar, for instance, patients were maintained extremely well on an FR 120. This same schedule would have provided far too infrequent reinforcements for the original conditioning of that response. It can be stated as a general rule that something approximating a CRF schedule with high reinforcement frequency is needed to first *condition* a response. Once conditioned, however, responses may be *maintained on* a sparse, intermittent schedule of reinforcement, provided the increase in the requirement from the conditioning schedule to the maintaining schedule is gradual and systematic.

That intermittent reinforcement schedules can maintain behavior but cannot usually condition new responses may help to account for the lack of skills, particularly social, seen in residents of homes for the retarded and mental hospitals. Most children are taught social skills quite early. During this stage, parents exert great effort and give the child copious amounts of positive reinforcement for each new social skill he masters. When the child has mastered most of the etiquette of social interaction, parents cease to be enchanted with his performance. They soon grow to expect these social skills of their offspring and may reinforce this behavior only quite infrequently. Politeness and social graces are soon reinforced by other people in the world, however, although never on the rich reinforcement schedule provided initially when the behavior was conditioned. It is maintained on the intermittent reinforcement which comes naturally from ʃcial interaction in our culture.

But what of the child who does not receive this rich initial contin- ʃs reinforcement schedule? Can he later learn these social graces from the ʃermittent
reinforcement schedule doled out to him in the outside environ ʃologist. Often
able to compensate for this early deficit without the aid of the the utmost im-
they are placed in a social situation where social behavio ʃ proper social ac-
portance and many reinforcers are ultimately acquired ʃ them in our every-
tions. Other individuals never learn. Occasionally we ʃ many other things as
day encounters, but more often they have failed ʃally first strengthens these
well and are placed in institutions. ʃment schedule and then later

In treating these individuals, the psych ʃ a fixed-ratio schedule, to main-
neglected behaviors with a rich continuo ʃe appropriate behavior becomes
uses intermittent reinforcement sched ʃ reinforcement for it will ultimately
tain the responses. It is his hope ʃvironment.
maintained by intermittent reinf
come through natural interacti ʃ behav.

handwritten notes:

responses are maintained by reinforcement intermediately reinforcement unconsciously presented by society.

2 functions of Reinforce
1. co
2

The following study will demonstrate how an intermittent schedule of reinforcement was used to reinforce appropriate conversational behavior in a young boy.

Fixed-Ratio Reinforcement of the Duration of Utterances in a Young Boy

We met John a little earlier. By using television-viewing opportunity as a positive reinforcement, we saw how he came to heed his mother's call with considerable reliability. John's problem behaviors were far from over. His mother continued to work with him under our supervision. While all of this was going on, another graduate student and I sought to shorten John's overlong verbal utterances.[3] This is a stuffy way of saying that John was a blabbermouth. Once he had corralled a person he regarded as a significant listener, he talked incessantly without giving him even the slightest opening to comment, protest, or terminate the conversation. Adults to whom John was introduced for the first time politely listened to his ramblings and then after some minutes came to realize what freedom really means. They soon searched frantically for a door, window, elevator, or any other route of escape. Having finally extricated themselves from John's clutches, henceforth they avoided him as though he were all four horsemen of the Apocalypse rolled into one. But John was anything but inflexible. As a result, he adjusted his behavior by talking even faster and harder to the next poor soul he could corner, as though he were resigned never to let this one get away.

In order to treat this behavior, it was my self-imposed task to spend a great deal of time with John in a situation where other interruptions would not occur. I chose my office at the Human Development Clinic.

There are quite a few ways you could look at John's conversational troubles. Strictly speaking, it was not that John talked too much. Many of us have engaged in lengthy conversation. Sometimes we have talked so much that we are hoarse the next day or even lose our voice completely. John's social blunder was that he monopolized the conversation. He talked on without pause. Pausing occasionally would have allowed the other person to interact, to add his comments, or perhaps to affirm what John had said and urge him to continue with his exciting commentary. Sometimes we can learn from others, which is one important reason for conversation in the first place. We can therefore say that John's error was that he talked too much without pausing, or more simply, that he did not pause often enough. This ... assumption we were working on in our treatment. It was not enough to ... assume this was the aspect of John's verbal behavior which was causing ... difficulty.

First, some quan... description of John's verbal behavior was needed so that John's progress co... er judged. Sessions were conducted for one hour, two or three times week... greeted John in the waiting room, he began to talk. Like a pied piper if... e talked on, while following me to my office. There I had a tape recorder ... watch. When we were seated and I was

3. This section based on Whaley, D. ... and Risley, T. Conditioning of appropriate verbal durations in a young boy. Unp... ch conducted at the Human Development Clinic, Florida State University, 1965.

prepared to start the session, I had to wrestle the conversational lead from John long enough to make a comment or ask a question. Once this maneuver was completed, I paused and let him talk. I timed John's verbalizations until he voluntarily paused for three full seconds. After three seconds had elapsed I quickly primed him with another comment, paused, and gave the conversation back to him, restarting my time. In this manner I measured his utterances. Five sessions were devoted to collecting these data. I concluded from these initial sessions that while John was infinitely aware that I was a qualified listener, he had little confidence in my ability to speak. On one occasion he talked 17 minutes without pausing for the required three seconds.

After these preliminary data had been collected, I was ready to begin the conditioning procedure. At the same time I was working with John in my office, his mother was working on other behaviors at home. She was using television-viewing time as a reinforcer. In order to avoid confusion, I decided to use another reinforcer, preferably one that John could use in the clinic without having to wait until he reached home. I wanted to find something that could really turn John on. He didn't seem to enjoy sweets or candy. Even the old "never-fail reinforcer" ice cream, had little effect on him. I did remember an earlier incident when John had seen a cap gun in the playroom. It was one of those cap guns that looks like the real thing. John had turned it over and over in his hands, occasionally shooting an imaginary hole in me. He explained to me that he owned a cap gun which his mother wouldn't let him shoot because it made too much noise. Besides, John went on, his mother told him he became too excited when he shot the cap gun. John then gave me a sample of his excitement by poking me in the ear with the barrel. "Pow," he said.

As I thought back over the episode, it occurred to me that the opportunity to fire rolls and rolls of caps without adult intervention might really be a "swinger" for John.

I had my usual stop watch and tape recorder out of sight in a desk drawer at the first experimental session. I also had some steel washers in my pocket. As soon as John and I were seated, I bullied my way into his ramblings.

"John," I said, holding out the washers, "Here are some tokens that I plan to give you from time to time. At the end of the session you can trade each of these tokens in for a roll of caps and then I'll let you go into the playroom and shoot them off as fast as you want." That did it. John began to shake all over like a puppy, undoubtedly in anticipation of the unobstructed imaginary slaughter of thousands of wild beasts, cowboys, and perhaps a few psychologists. He was more than ready to play my games. I started the session as usual. "Tell me what you have been doing since I saw you last." John was off to the races. He began by telling me about his new steam engine and a few sessions later brought the full steam engine into the room to demonstrate it. I was pleased to find it was only a model after all. As John began to talk, I depressed the stop watch and began to time the duration of John's verbalizations. On and on he went without pausing. I waited anxiously. If he stopped talking and paused for three full seconds then I would give him a token. Still I waited. Finally, after two minutes and 47 seconds, he paused for three seconds. Trying to hide my relief at this initial success, I handed John the token as nonchalantly as I could. Once again he shook all over like a young puppy, clapped his hands, and acted as though I just had given him the keys to the Kingdom. Throughout the remainder of that session and the next two full sessions, I reinforced John with tokens which were redeemed with rolls of caps.

Along with the caps went the temporary use of an array of exciting cap pistols I had collected in the playroom. At the end of each session I placed the caps in John's hand, pushed him into the playroom where the guns were all lined up, ready for immediate use, and then quickly locked the door behind me. I watched him through the observation window as he ran about the room shooting under chairs, in closets, and wounding anything in sight.

Figure 6-2 shows data collected for John during the five observation sessions where no reinforcement was given and for three sessions in which tokens were offered. The frequency plotted on the vertical axis of the graph represents the number of times during the session that John quit talking for three seconds and allowed me an opportunity to talk. It is easy to see that John became a better conversationalist when the opportunity to shoot a cap gun was made contingent on the length of his utterances. Before this time, he produced mainly long rambling dissertations. Now I found that we could carry on a reasonable conversation. At the same time, he was earning more caps than I thought was appropriate. As you can see in Figure 6-2, he earned 32 rolls of caps during the last session. When that was over, it took an hour to shoot off just half of the caps. He took the remainder home, and with my intervention, his mother allowed him to fire them in the garage. I wanted to use fewer caps with John because the opportunity to shoot might cease to be a powerful reinforcer. In addition, I had been buying the caps with my lunch money and since I was also a growing boy who needed nourishment, I decided that fewer caps should be used. Accordingly, I took John off the continuous reinforcement schedule and placed him on an FR 5 schedule, where he was reinforced for each fifth time he paused three seconds to let me

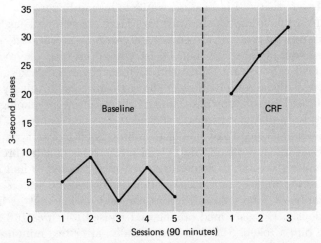

Figure 6-2 John's verbal behavior without and with reinforcement

talk. If the frequency of his pauses remained the same, this would mean that John would only receive one-fifth as many rolls of caps as he had previously. These data are presented in Figure 6-3, along with the previous three days of reinforcement which, as you remember, were on continuous reinforcement.

One thing you will notice is that when the fixed-ratio schedule was introduced, the frequency of pauses of at least three seconds actually increased over that seen with the CRF schedule. I felt I was really getting my money's worth, for although he was being paid less, John was working harder than ever. Even with the increase in responses, John was still earning fewer rolls of caps than he had before. My budget was aided somewhat and John showed no signs of tiring of cap shooting. After only a few sessions on the FR 5 schedule, John's father, who had been working as a visiting faculty member at the university, had to return to his home university and therefore my contact with John and his parents was ended. I do not know if John's reasonable conversational behavior with me generalized to situations outside of my office. Given the opportunity, I might have been able to work John up to an even higher ratio and bring him to the point where the duration of his speech was maintained by the verbal reinforcers of his listeners, as it is indeed, for most of us. In time, caps might not have been needed at all.

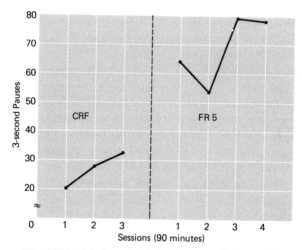

Figure 6-3   John's verbal behavior on an FR 5 schedule

Earlier in this chapter we underlined two important properties of behavior which is maintained on a fixed-ratio schedule of reinforcement. These two properties constitute the "all or nothing" nature of responses reinforced on a fixed-ratio schedule. Once the organism makes the first response, he responds as fast as he can until he completes the requirement. His behavior leads you to believe that he has a tiger by the tail and dares not rest until it is safely dispatched. The second component of fixed-ratio behavior is the occurrence of the post-reinforcement pause. With the ratio completed, there is a distinct pause before another ratio is begun. The length of the pause is related to the size of the ratio.

Fixed-ratio schedules generate high rates of response and under some conditions can bring the individual to work harder for fewer reinforcements. These properties have made the fixed-ratio schedule useful in treating behavior problems. The fixed-ratio schedule is also popular in the study of behavior of lower organisms, because the final performance is easy to establish, and behavior can be maintained at a high rate of occurrence. Such a fine schedule as this could not go unnoticed in our culture. Employers in the past have used fixed-ratio schedules to pay their employers. For centuries, cotton pickers in the Deep South have received payment for each bag of cotton they pick rather than receiving an hourly wage. Many individual picking responses go into completing a full bag; thus, each bag can be thought of as a fixed-ratio task. A high level of productivity has been maintained through this schedule. In many parts of the South, human pickers are still paid in this manner although newer and more modern cotton-picking machinery has long since been developed.

In many factories throughout the country, employees are paid partly or even completely in terms of each unit of work they complete. This system is called "piecework." Of course, a fixed number of work responses usually goes into the completion of each piece. It should not surprise you that this type of payment creates employees who work hard and fast, but often take a break between "pieces."

Although fixed-ratio schedules can be programmed quite handily by the psychologist in a laboratory or a foreman in the factory, this type of schedule is seldom programmed by Nature herself. Likewise, fixed-ratio scheduling is not typically seen in the reinforcements our culture bestows upon us. Grades in high school or college are never dispensed on a fixed-ratio schedule. If this were so, the student could expect an "A" after every second, third, fourth, or twentieth course he completed. It is not likely that students would find this type of schedule satisfactory, although it would simplify things for teachers. A golfer cannot expect a hole-in-one to occur after a fixed number of drives. A physician or witch-doctor whose cures are proportioned out on an FR 100 will find his patients waiting for the ninety-ninth "sucker" before they come in for treatment.

For these reasons the fixed-ratio schedule has little direct relevance to reinforcement schedules which occur in the world, although the study of fixed-ratio behavior gives us insight into behavior maintained by similar schedules. One such schedule is called a *variable-ratio schedule*. Like the fixed-ratio schedule of reinforcement, the variable-ratio schedule is programmed as a function of the number of responses made. Reinforcement is not delivered after a fixed number but rather after a variable number of responses. The next presentation will acquaint you with the importance of a variable-ratio schedule in one "institutional" situation.

Honeymoon for Three

"It" was the first thing Morton saw when he reached the hotel room. The trip from the lobby in the elevator and through the long corridor had been agonizing.

Everyone they passed had seemed to crinkle the corners of his mouth in an all-knowing smile as if to say, "Uh huh, honeymooners!" A blind man they passed had turned to them peculiarly. Even his seeing-eye dog had begun to pant in a way Morton thought was extremely irregular.

"Welcome to the Sands," the bellhop said, skillfully holding out his hand halfway. Morton drew a loose bill from his pocket. It was a five. He had all but placed it in the bellhop's eager hands when Peggy stepped between them and threw her arms about Morton's neck.

"Oh, Morton," she said, "Isn't it just lovely?" She noticed the five-dollar bill in his hand. "Five dollars?" she questioned. "Oh, but Morton, that's too much for a tip!" she exclaimed, turning to the bellhop. "Isn't it?" The bellhop didn't answer. "I'm sure he has change," she said and pulled the bill from Morton's hands, giving it to the bellhop. Reluctantly the bellhop reached in his pocket and pulled out five bright silver dollars and handed them to Peggy. She gave him one of the dollars and handed those remaining to Morton. "I hope you enjoy staying in Reno," the bellhop mumbled, and was gone. As soon as the door had closed Peggy reached up on her tiptoes and grabbed Morton about the neck, hugging him hard. "Oh, isn't it wonderful," she said again. Before Morton could comment or demonstrate the wonderfulness of it all, Peggy slipped away from him and walked into the bathroom.

"I'll be right back," she said. In his short married career Morton had surmised one thing: women probably spent most of their lives in the bathroom. For once he was glad to see Peggy leave the room, for now he had a chance to examine the object in the corner more closely. He approached it, awed by the glittering chromium, sturdy bulk, and precise workmanship. In the clear plastic windows below, he could see two bells and an orange. He placed his hand on the lever. Somehow it felt firm and natural in his hand as he slowly pulled it back. He expected the lever to stop at some point in its arc, but it did not. It continued downward and then abruptly began to whirl and buzz. Morton was sure that he had broken it, or even worse, had set off an anti-burglar device of some sort. In the three windows at the bottom of the machine, the cylinders could be seen to whirl crazily. Suddenly the cylinder in the first window stopped. It was a plum. Shortly thereafter the second cylinder stopped; it too was a plum. Finally the third cylinder stopped. It was also a plum. The monster began to shudder as though falling apart and a crashing noise ensued from the bottom corner of its housing. Then all was quiet. Morton had retreated from all of this furious action. Now that the machine was quiet, it seemed harmless. Nonetheless he approached it with caution. Why had the machine carried on so? He had not put any money in it. Perhaps it was the policy of the hotel to give their guests one free pull of the lever, or maybe an earlier tenant had forgotten to pull the lever after putting a dollar in the slot. Morton could not contemplate how anyone could walk away and leave a whole dollar unused in a machine. He looked closely at the three windows again, studying and comparing each minute detail of the forms displayed. Yes, three plums. They were all the same. Thinking back over the various movies in which he had seen slot machines in action, he concluded that three of a kind meant a payoff of some kind. He moved his hand down to the right-hand corner where a covered trough protruded. He intended to lift the cover slowly, but had only raised it a fraction of an inch when a great gush of silver dollars spilled out on the carpeted floor. Morton got on his hands and knees and began to retrieve the coins. He counted them solemnly, placing them into a neat stack. He counted them again and then once again for good measure. There were thirty shiny silver dollars. "Reno!" Morton exclaimed aloud, "What a wonderful place!" Hotels in other cities might arrange color television, electric relaxing chairs, or other items for your comfort and amusement; but here a slot machine with every room! He carefully placed 25 of the silver dollars in his shaving kit, keeping the other five in the palm of his hand, lifting them and jingling them together. How simple it all seemed. But Morton was not one to be taken in. "Just a fortunate accident," he thought. He could put silver dollars in the machine from now until doomsday and it would never happen again. Still he was ahead of the game. He could try just one or two of the silver dollars he had won. He placed four of the coins in the machine in quick succession, pulling the lever after each deposit. Once he matched two of the cylinders but failed to match the third. With disgust he put the last of the five silver dollars in the machine and pulled the lever hard. He turned his back on the machine, testing his will power, consciously ignoring the whirling cylinders. Suddenly he heard a strange, violent, and wonderful tremor issue from the bowels of the device. He turned around and saw three lemons on the plastic windows. He opened the trough, bringing back a sagging handful of silver dollars. It really was simple! He mentally computed his earnings and saw that he had made a shrewd investment in the machine. He decided to reinvest. He did not hear Peggy as she entered the room. "Ah ha," she said with a mock scorn, "gambling already!"

"With me, it's not gambling," Morton said. He set his jaw in that firm way Peggy always liked. He placed several silver dollars in her palm and closed her fingers around them. "Morton," she squealed, "where did you get all this?"

"Nothing to it," Morton said, demonstrating, "just take a silver dollar, place it in the slot, and pull the crank." The cylinders whirled as they both watched. Two cherries came up first, but a gold bar in the third window spoiled it all. Morton was disappointed. "Why that's real good," Peggy said without conviction and kissed Morton on the neck, "you came real close."

"I'm awfully tired," Peggy said, with a superficial yawn. "I think I'll take a shower and get ready for bed." "Yes," Morton said, "I'll be in in just a few minutes." Actually he had not heard her at all. After Peggy closed the door behind her, he set a stack of silver dollars before him and faced the machine with determination. It whirled but it did not give forth the long awaited gasp.

"How long have I been here?" Morton asked himself. Peggy had been out three times, with each appearance growing more annoyed and sarcastic. The last time she huffed away and slammed the bedroom door. "Women don't understand these things," Morton assured himself. It was no longer a case of idle amusement. He had been downstairs twice to get change. Already he had lost all of his winnings and invested 25 of his own dollars in the machine. Surely the next whirl of the cylinders would make him even. He turned the crank. "Whir," went the machine. A gold bar, a star, and a plum filled the windows. What was wrong with him? Could it be that deep down he was a pathological gambler? He had once read a book on the subject. "Whir," a pear, a lemon and a gold bar. Little wonder Peggy was upset with him. Perhaps at this very moment she was wondering how many lonesome nights she would spend in her bedroom while her husband gambled away his salary. "Whir," two gold bars and a pear. What was the noise he heard in the bedroom? It sounded like crying. "Whir," a plum and two grapes.

Morton looked down at his hand. One silver dollar remained from his night's activity. He was thoroughly disgusted with himself. In a few short hours he had lost $75, no $80. How long would he have to work to earn $80 when he started a new job? What nice things could he have bought for Peggy with $80? He could hear a stirring in the bedroom as though luggage were being moved about. What a mess he had made of their lives. He placed the last surviving silver dollar in the slot. Automatically his hand went to the lever. "No!" Morton said. He pulled his hand away as though the lever were charged with electricity. "No!" he said again, "I'll beat this machine yet." The lever waited invitingly for a nudge. Defiantly he turned his back on the machine. He would leave it just as he found it. He walked swiftly into the bathroom and looked at his face in the mirror. His eyes were tired and drawn back within his head. His shirt was soaked through with perspiration. "Fool!" he said to the image, "Fool!" He took off his clothing and stepped into the shower. He lathered himself from head to toe as though washing away the taint of the past few hours. He dried himself roughly and put on his new bathrobe which Peggy had placed neatly on the dressing table. What a wonderful girl she was. How foolish he had been to mistreat her. He would make it up; at least, he hoped she would let him. Carefully he entered the bedroom expecting to find Peggy huddled up in the corner crying. But the bedroom was empty! He looked in the closet and was relieved to find that her luggage was still there. At least she had not left him. Not yet. In her disgust with him, she might have wandered out in the night, and who knows, maybe she had looked for another man. She would have no trouble finding one, he concluded, remembering how lovely she had looked at the ceremony. Just then he heard a noise from the living room. It sounded like a little girl yelping for joy. When he reached the living room, he found Peggy. She was dressed in a fluffy pink nightgown. Morton thought she looked just like a movie star. "Morton," she said when she saw him. Her eyes were wide open with delight. "Look what happened," she said and raised the lap of her gown to show a gleaming mound of silver dollars. Morton was more interested in the contours of her lovely legs.

"I just pulled the lever, and zowie! Look what happened! Darling," she said pulling him to her and giving him a wet kiss on the forehead. "It's so simple. Just put in the dollar like this and pull the lever," she said, demonstrating. Three lemons were on the windows. The machine convulsed and spit forth a stream of silver coins. Peggy screamed with joy, jumped up and down, and kissed Morton several times before she scooped up the silver dollars and put them on the bureau in a neat stack. "Sit down," she said, "and help me." She had already placed a coin in the machine and was pulling the lever. "I'm going to bed," Morton said.

Peggy sighed as the third window turned out to be a gold bar instead of a grape. Morton turned from Peggy and walked slowly toward the bedroom grumbling all the way. "Whir," went the machine.

The foregoing episode should have given you some insight into the evils and intricacies of gambling. Practically all gambling behavior is maintained by the same kind of reinforcement schedule. This reinforcement schedule is called a variable-ratio schedule. It is an extremely powerful schedule and places rigorous demands on the organism. It is particularly intriguing because each new response is as likely to yield reinforcement as any other. Therefore, the gambler tries it just one more time. The next pull of the lever may produce the big payoff.

Just as CRF and FR are abbreviations for their respective schedules of reinforcement, VR stands for a variable-ratio reinforcement schedule. A specific VR schedule is designated by numerals following the notation. Let us discuss such a specific schedule, a VR 50. If you have suspected that the "50" stands for number of responses, you are correct. Rather than standing for a set of fixed number of responses, as in an FR 50, the "50" in VR 50 designates the *average* number of responses required before reinforcement is delivered.

Suppose, as actually might be the case, that a slot machine is programmed on a VR 50. A gambler is observed as he plays the machine. He puts one coin in the machine and it pays off. He puts another coin in and it pays off again. Before the next payoff occurs he has dropped 104 coins in the voracious slot. Throughout the night the machine is observed to tumble out dollars after "variable" incidents of inserted coins and pulled levers. If we were to take the number of coins required for each "reinforcement" and average them we would find an answer of "50." On the average 50 coins were needed to yield reinforcement in the form of payoff. It goes without saying that slot machine owners are careful to keep the average number of coins given in the payoff much below the average number of coins needed to yield a payoff.

Both fixed-ratio and variable-ratio schedules of reinforcement have long been favorites among laboratory psychologists. Many aspects of each of these schedules are similar, but there are also important differences. The two general types of schedules can best be compared by examining specific schedules.[4] Figure 6-4 illustrates a cumulative record of the performance of a retarded child on a fixed-ratio 50 and a variable-ratio 50. The boy, whose name is Doug, is 12 years old and severely retarded. This means that his IQ has been identified as under 30. He was first brought into the experimental room and shown a lever. His hand was placed on the lever and a M&M was dispensed through an opening in the panel. He soon got the idea and began to press the lever on a continuous reinforcement schedule. The schedule was then changed to a fixed-ratio 2, 5, 7, etc., until finally an FR 50 was settled upon. His lever pressing was maintained on this ratio for some time. Segment A of Figure 6-4 shows his performance on an FR 50. After being maintained for some sessions on an FR 50 the schedule was changed to VR 50. Now, instead of being reinforced on every 50th response, he was reinforced for a number of responses which varied from reinforcement to reinforcement. The average

4. This section based on Tough, Jerry. Bar press response of a retardate child on intermittent reinforcement schedules. Unpublished research conducted at Fort Custer State Home, Augusta, Michigan, 1967.

Segment A   Segment B

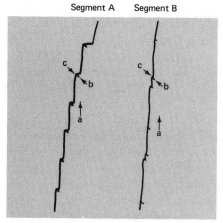

Figure 6-4   A retarded child's bar-pressing behavior on an FR 50 and a VR 50 schedule

number of responses required was 50. Segment B of the graph illustrates his performance on this schedule. You will notice that the slopes of the record on segments A and B are quite similar. Both schedules generated extremely high responding with little or no hesitation between responses. The hash mark (b) on each signifies reinforcement. You will notice that on the fixed-ratio schedules the reinforcement occurs after a regular number of responses. However, on segment B, the variable-ratio schedule, in some cases one reinforcement occurred soon after another, and in other instances many responses were needed to yield a reinforcement. A notation (c) on both graphs points up the flat portion which is the post-reinforcement pause. In segment A, the fixed-ratio schedule, the pauses are quite long. This suggests that Doug completed the ratio, picked up his M&M and consumed it, but then hesitated for a short period of time before getting back to work. In segment B, however, post-reinforcement pauses are not present. In these instances Doug paused only long enough to consume the reinforcer. He then went immediately back to work.

The main difference between the two schedules is that the fixed-ratio schedule generated post-reinforcement pauses, but the variable-ratio schedule did not. On the fixed-ratio 50 schedule, when a reinforcement was delivered, a full 50 responses or more were needed before another reinforcement would occur. Doug adjusted his pressing behavior to this schedule by resting between bursts as though preparing himself for the long pull until another reinforcement. In the variable-ratio schedule, Doug's bar press could yield a reinforcement on practically any press. For all Doug knew, the very next response might be as likely to yield the reinforcement as the one before it. Being reinforced on one response did not preclude the possibility that on the very next response he would receive a reinforcement too.

The variable-ratio schedule is an important one for study. Many of the reinforcers which come to us as a consequence of natural phenomena or are doled out to us by the culture in the form of success, profit, or achievement are actually forthcoming on a variable-ratio schedule.

A door-to-door salesman is a fine example of an individual whose behavior is maintained by a variable-ratio schedule of reinforcement. Let us assume such a salesman, selling brushes, calls on a particular house. After hearing his finest sales talk, the woman answering the door emphatically lets him know that she is more than amply stocked. The salesman leaves and knocks on the next door. He is again met with failure. Perhaps he calls on 20 houses in a row but does not sell even a toothbrush. At the next house the woman fairly drags him through the door. "I've been waiting for you for months," she says, and then proceeds to place an order for 50 of his finest items. The salesman leaves her house and stops at the very next house—for the next one may also be a woman who is just waiting for his services. It can be seen that the salesman is operating on a variable-ratio schedule. Behind each new door lurks a possibility for a long-awaited order, and so he pushes on quickly. Just as any other behavior will extinguish, the door-to-door salesman's behavior will extinguish if there is not an ample amount of reinforcement. Thus, although his behavior is on a variable-ratio schedule, reinforcement must occur often enough to maintain him.

The way in which the world in a seemingly frivolous manner pays off for one attempt and fails to pay off for another has generated the old saying: "If at first you do not succeed, try, try again." On the variable-ratio schedule, one can only assume that the more often he attempts, the more often, all things equal, he will be reinforced. It might even be said that the variable-ratio schedule is the American schedule, for it generates hard work and ambitious people. The now retired professional basketball player Cliff Hagen was being observed by a junior high student one afternoon during practice. Hagen sank one of the long hook shots which helped to earn him his formidable reputation. Dazzled, the boy asked Hagen if he could try. Hagen gave him the ball and watched as the boy's shot fell pitifully short, going crazily astray off the edge of the backboard. "Now, what should I do?" the boy questioned. "Shoot 20,000 more," Hagen replied.

Summary

In this chapter we have examined several ways in which reinforcement can be related to qualitative aspects of responses. This relationship was defined as a schedule of reinforcement, and contains two broad classes, continuous reinforcement and intermittent reinforcement. While continuous reinforcement is explicitly defined as a situation in which each and every response yields a reinforcement, intermittent reinforcement may be further broken down into several different schedules of reinforcement:

1. A fixed-ratio schedule is an intermittent schedule of reinforcement in which a reinforcement occurs after a fixed number of responses. Thus, an FR 50 schedule signifies a fixed-ratio schedule in which reinforcement occurs after each 50 responses.

2. The characteristics of behavior which is maintained on a fixed-ratio schedule of reinforcement include (a) an extremely high rate of responding with little

or no hesitation between responses, (b) a post-reinforcement pause which is observed after reinforcement occurs. These two aspects of fixed-ratio behavior have prompted some to call the fixed-ratio schedule of reinforcement an "all-or-nothing schedule." The animal works fast and hard to reach reinforcement and then pauses (post-reinforcement pause). The length of the post-reinforcement pause is related to the size of the ratio. The larger the ratio, the longer the post-reinforcement pause.

3. The fixed-ratio schedule of reinforcement was shown to be an important tool in research into the behavior of alcoholics at Coral Gables VA Hospital and in bringing about appropriate verbal behavior in a young boy.

4. A variable-ratio schedule is one in which reinforcement occurs after a variable number of responses are made. The particular value of a variable-ratio schedule is expressed in terms of the average number of responses required for reinforcement. Thus, a VR 50 means that, on the average, 50 responses must be made before reinforcement will be forthcoming. Any particular reinforcement therefore may take considerably fewer responses than 50, or many more.

5. The behavior generated by a variable-ratio schedule of reinforcement is similar to that of a fixed-ratio reinforcement schedule inasmuch as extremely high response rates occur with minimal hesitation between responses. The two schedules differ in that a variable-ratio schedule does not typically bring about a post-reinforcement pause.

6. The fixed-ratio schedule has been studied extensively in the laboratory with both humans and animals. Such a schedule, however, rarely occurs in nature or society. The variable-ratio schedule has been studied less in the laboratory but can be seen in both reinforcements governed by nature and reinforcements governed by our culture.

7. While continuous reinforcement is important in developing new response patterns, an intermittent schedule of reinforcement is much more important in maintaining behavior.

Intermittent - where you put your hand in the winter.

FR schedules generate a pause that refreshes.

QUESTIONS

1. The small Bahamian boy finally quit diving for coins after he almost drowned. (a) True; (b) False.

2. As a result of a successful dive he brought back a Spanish doubloon. (a) True; (b) False.

3. After bringing up his reward, he quit for the day and bought himself an ice cream cone with his profits. (a) True; (b) False.

4. What is the term that we should use in place of "success" when relating this type of result to principles of psychology?

5. What is the technical term used to describe a state of affairs where each response yields a reinforcement?

6. What expression do psychologists use to designate the situation in which reinforcement occurs but is less than continuous?

7. Why is the expression "continuous reinforcement" more explicit than the term "intermittent reinforcement"?

8. What is the general term to describe the way in which reinforcement is programmed to occur as a result of a number of responses, time between responses, or other temporal or quantitative features of responses?

9. What is the abbreviation for continuous reinforcement?

10. In the Coral Gables Bar, drinks were only 50 cents. (a) True; (b) False.

11. The chief felt that alcoholism was a terrible disease. (a) True; (b) False.

12. The visitor in the episode at the Coral Gables Bar at first could not understand why the psychologist gave his patients: (a) psychotherapy; (b) mixed drinks; (c) strong drugs; (d) electric shock.

13. The intern working at the hospital was a graduate student in clinical psychology. (a) True; (b) False.

14. The chief and his assistants did not use real alcoholic beverages in their research. (a) True; (b) False.

15. At first the patient had to press the lever: (a) 6 times; (b) 1 time; (c) 20 times; (d) 120 times.

16. What was this schedule of reinforcement?

17. At the end of the session, the patient had to make: (a) 20; (b) 40; (c) 1; (d) 120 responses before receiving a drink.

18. What was this schedule of reinforcement called?

19. Did all of the patients get drunk as a result of their experience in the Coral Gables research?

20. Define a fixed-ratio schedule of reinforcement.

21. What is the abbreviation for a fixed-ratio schedule?

22. How would you abbreviate a fixed-ratio schedule in which 30 responses were required for each reinforcement?

23. Once the organism has operated under a particular fixed-ratio schedule for a short time, his responses become relatively standard. (a) True; (b) False.

24. What is the special recording device which yields a cumulative record called?

25. In Figure 6-1 the graph presented for the patient Harold shows the slope of the line to be: (a) quite steep; (b) relatively flat; (c) starts off steep but reverses in a downhill direction; (d) never deviates from zero.

26. The slope of the line indicates that Harold: (a) made the first response and kept going until he had made the first 120 responses; (b) rested after 60 responses; (c) completed the first 5 responses rapidly and the remainder quite slowly; (d) did not respond at all.

27. On a fixed-ratio schedule, after the first response is made, how do the remaining responses typically follow?

28. What does the small hash mark on the cumulative record indicate?

29. What is the flat place occurring on the cumulative record called?
30. What created this flat place in the cumulative record?
31. The post-reinforcement pause is a common characteristic of fixed-ratio maintained behavior; (a) True; (b) False.
32. The relationship between the size of the ratio and the length of the post-reinforcement pause can be described as: (a) the higher the ratio, the shorter the pause; (b) the higher the ratio, the longer the pause.
33. With an extremely small ratio, the post-reinforcement pause may be so small that it is indiscernible. (a) True; (b) False.
34. On a fixed-ratio schedule, the organism is either going like the devil himself is after him or he is resting. This has caused people to characterize this schedule of reinforcement as _____ _____ _____.
35. What probably would have happened if the Coral Gables staff had immediately introduced an FR 120 requirement?
36. What procedure did they use to avoid this?
37. What is the error of presenting too high a ratio too fast called?
38. Why do teachers, employers, and parents often strain the ratio of their subjects?
39. A grammar school child is not concerned about the size, type, or number of pages in the book he chooses. (a) True; (b) False.
40. The length of the chapters in this book are not a concern of the authors. (a) True; (b) False.
41. The savage named Zack strained his ratio. (a) True; (b) False.
42. What are the two primary functions of reinforcement on behavior?
43. After being first conditioned with a CRF schedule of reinforcement, the behavior can often be maintained on an intermittent schedule of reinforcement. (a) True; (b) False.
44. How many responses did one experimenter require the pigeon to make before he received any reinforcement? (a) 250; (b) 20,000; (c) 250,000; (d) 25.
45. In the early stages of their development, most children receive great amounts of reinforcement for appropriate social behaviors. (a) True; (b) False.
46. Later in their development, they continue to receive continuous reinforcement for appropriate social behavior. (a) True; (b) False.
47. It is very difficult to learn appropriate behavior on a reinforcement schedule which is sparse or lean. (a) True; (b) False.
48. In tackling the problem of a child who has inappropriate social behavior, the first thing the psychologist does is: (a) put the child on an FR 120; (b) use an FR 30; (c) strengthen neglected behaviors with a CRF schedule; (d) use the highest FR schedule he can program.
49. John's problem was that: (a) he did not speak; (b) he spoke when alone but not to other people; (c) he was a blabbermouth; (d) he had no significant problems.
50. In timing the length of John's utterances, the experimenter first asked the question, then: (a) timed John's speaking until he paused in his conversation for a full three seconds; (b) timed the total amount of the session that John talked; (c) timed the length of the experimenter's talking and subtracted it from the total session length; (d) counted the words John spoke.
51. How long a pause was John required to make?
52. What was the longest duration John talked without pausing? (a) 3 seconds; (b) 10 minutes; (c) 2 hours; (d) 17 minutes.
53. What type of reinforcer was used to modify John's verbal behavior?
54. For what were the tokens exchanged?

55. What kind of schedule of reinforcement was first employed?

56. What were the results of using this schedule?

57. By switching from a CRF schedule to an FR 5 schedule, the experimenter: (a) found he had to spend less money on caps; (b) found that John made more appropriate conversation; (c) found that John worked harder for fewer rolls of caps; (d) all of the above.

58. John's verbal behavior generalized to situations outside the experimental sessions: (a) in all cases; (b) only in cases where caps were available; (c) it is not known since John and his parents left the area; (d) had no effect at all.

59. Which of the following is *not* a characteristic of a fixed-ratio schedule: (a) all-or-nothing nature; (b) post-reinforcement pause; (c) long spaces between responses; (d) high rates of responding.

60. The fixed-ratio schedule often occurs outside of the laboratory. (a) True; (b) False.

61. Grades in high school are often programmed on a fixed-ratio schedule of reinforcement. (a) True; (b) False.

62. A medical doctor whose successes were often programmed on a fixed-ratio schedule would probably not have a good practice. (a) True; (b) False.

63. What is the institution referred to in the article "Honeymoon for Three"?

64. What was the machine Morton and his wife found in their hotel room?

65. On what type of schedule do slot machines pay off?

66. Whereas in a fixed-ratio schedule, reinforcement occurs after a fixed number of responses, in a variable reinforcement schedule, a reinforcement occurs after a(n) _____ number of responses.

67. A VR 50 schedule means that reinforcement occurs: (a) after each 50 responses; (b) after the first 50 responses; (c) after an average of 50 responses; (d) no information is given concerning this fact.

68. On a VR 2,000 schedule, it is impossible for two responses in a row to be reinforced. (a) True; (b) False.

69. Which of the following is *not* a characteristic of a VR schedule of reinforcement? (a) high rate of responding; (b) little or no hesitation between responses; (c) post-reinforcement pause; (d) all of the above.

70. Can you name at least three other activities humans participate in which are probably maintained on a VR schedule?

71. Using the notion of gradually changing the schedule of reinforcement, how would you design a gambling device that would be likely to get novice gamblers hooked?

TIME DEPENDENT SCHEDULES OF REIN-FORCE-MENT

7

TIME-DEPENDENT SCHEDULES OF REINFORCEMENT

The Pit

It had been rumored that the large cylindrical crystals were magic. "Los ojos de la bruja," they were called. But what was the peculiar magic of the crystals? Manuel, like his companions, had wondered at first. Then one day one of their number, a man whose name was Vincente, bore the heat of the sun as long as he could and then dropped his iron hammer. He hurled himself with no more effort than a small grunt into a cluster of crystal spires fifteen feet below. The crystals turned to rubies with his blood. For the first time since he had been imprisoned at "la cruz," his face was cool and peaceful. They all understood the magic then.

In the months that followed, Manuel saw the crystals bloom like crimson flowers, glassy and cool, over and over again. His companions dwindled in number, one by one. At night, Manuel dreamed in his fitful sleep. He saw the crystals as giant icicles of a wonderful nature which could cool the very innermost part of man.

At first unconsciously but ultimately with full awareness, Manuel found himself moving inch by inch each day toward the top of the pit. He had reached the end. A long fall was his salvation; a broken leg or crippling wound would not help.

He was working at the very crest of the pit on the day it came about. The sun was overhead and his hammer rang against the rock sending fragments spattering his chest and forearms. He felt the strength short-circuit from his body at each contact with the rocks. Soon it would be done; his legs would buckle and he would fall backward, over and down, to the spires that waited. He made one last contact with the rocks, dropped his hammer, and pulled himself erect, looking for perhaps the first time directly up to the observation platform where the guards stood their vigil. It would only be a minute until the guard would see him without his hammer and raise the black leather whip above his head with a curse and a bellow. As he waited for that moment, he glanced beyond the guard plat-

127

form across the road into the living quarters inhabited by the guards and the commandant.

The structure was a large two-story building constructed mainly of crystalline rock with some traces of mortar here and there. On top was a tower rising some twelve feet. At the top of the tower was a window covered by heavy curtains. Manuel saw a breeze toy with the curtains, making them flap silently. How long since he had felt a breeze? He could not remember. At that instant a large gust of wind blew the curtain aside and he saw her. Her hair was black and it glistened in the sun. She was not facing the window; her head was turned to the side. He could not see her eyes from that distance but he knew they were dark and lovely. Her profile revealed precise features. The wind died and the curtain returned to its original position. He continued to stare at the window, watching the breeze nip at the curtain. Would it, God please, gust again! He found an almost forgotten emotion of hope and caring. Suddenly he felt the whip tearing at his neck. The guard bore down on him; a snarl filled his browned face. In the storm of lashes he retrieved the hammer and returned to his work, glancing up at the window after each blow. The breeze continued to play with the curtain.

He saw her again three times on that first day. He was strangely disappointed when the long rays of sunset made the bowels of the pit black and they were returned to the hut where they would rest for the night. The day had gone fast. He had worked tirelessly, almost without awareness of the heat and the exhaustion in his bones, his eyes darting like voracious animals toward the window. There was no way of knowing the vicissitudes of that breeze and he did not want to miss an opportunity.

A story had been told among the prisoners of a daughter whom the commandant kept secluded from all aspects of the quarry and the depressing reality of prison life. The commandant's wife had died, leaving him to care for his daughter. After some years the daughter, a beautiful creature it was said, had fallen victim to that bleak heaven-forsaken grotto in the arid plain. She had become mad in a way that was common in that harsh land. Now, the story went, she spent her hours secluded in the tower. That night Manuel did not dream of the crystals; instead he dreamed of a dark-eyed beauty who laughed and called his name.

The days and months flew by as he worked relentlessly at the crest of the pit. The guards had become suspicious of his renewed vitality and watched him more carefully than before. But Manuel was oblivious to them or to anything but the window. Some days the breezes were kind; but other days, they were niggardly and sadistic. There was never any way of knowing, and always, always, the possibility that at any instant the opportunity to see his lady would be his. If only she would turn in his direction, then he could at least pretend that she was looking at him. Manuel persisted, his hammer striking hard, a pause and a quick glance to the window, another stroke with the hammer. Always in the evening he felt a pang of remorse, but a hope for a day of gusty breezes tomorrow.

Then one morning, perhaps a year after he had discovered his lady, Manuel awoke to find the sun already high in the sky. The guard had not come. The prisoners peered out the opening that had been gouged from between loose stones.

No guards were there. A group of them pounded on the door with stones, breaking open the rotted plank which latched it. Cautiously, they stepped out. No one was to be found. It was as though death had descended. Manuel was the first to reach the top of the pit. For the first time in three years he found himself running. He went directly to the two-story building where the lady had always been. Inside, wooden lockers and tables were scattered about the room. Collections of odds and ends and personal belongings were thrown pell mell on the floor. He spurred his rubbery legs up the stairs to the second floor and without bothering to look up a long narrow stairway which led to the tower, he burst in through the door. He did not know what, if anything, to expect. It was hardly a room at all. Several trunks were off to one side and in other places dusty volumes of books and broken objects were stored. He looked immediately toward the window and saw the nourishment his soul had feasted on throughout the past year. His lady was old. One of her breasts was missing; it had fallen to the floor where it now rested. Her skin was cracked; a wide crevasse ran down her right cheek. The hair he had adored in the sunlight was coarse and hard, packed and matted with lacquer. Manuel knelt before the mannequin. Had he endured, dreamed, and hoped for this, this fake? The iron hammer he still held in his right hand would speak his despair to this dummy, a dressmaker's model of wire and plaster. He raised the hammer, hesitated for an instant, and then lowered it slowly. His lady was not all he had expected; that was true. She had led him on. That was also true. Manuel wiped away the dust from her cheek and gently kissed the woman to whom he owed his life. Outside the prisoners were heard greeting bands of liberators.

One of the first things a young child will learn is that often time must pass before he will receive a warm bottle, new toy, or even a dry diaper. It is a feature of our environment that good things require the passage of time. In the preceding chapter we learned how reinforcement was programmed on FR and VR schedules. In those schedules of reinforcement, the payoff is for effort alone. The more responses the organism makes, the more reinforcements he will receive. Thus, reinforcement is conceptually independent of time. As no doubt you have anticipated, other schedules of reinforcement involve various aspects of time as a factor in their programming. These schedules are referred to as "time-dependent."

We hope the preceding bit of fiction will illustrate the importance of time to a man who seemingly had himself run out of time. Until Manuel saw the lady, his performance at the pit was erratic, painful, and had apparently all but extinguished. The sight of the lady was obviously a reinforcing event for Manuel. Once she entered his environment, he was free to speculate and even to hope and dream. More important to us here is that Manuel was not free to see his lady any time he wished. His opportunity to view the object of his affection was stringently controlled by the willy-nilly and unpredictable breeze. Manuel could only work steadily on with his hammer, while constantly glancing in the direction of the window—the rest was up to time and the whims of the breeze. Although the schedule on which Manuel's reinforcement was programmed was quite simply a matter of waiting and looking, it generated consistent, persistent, and long-enduring behaviors which undoubtedly contributed to his longevity at the Pit.

While few of us are likely to have ever experienced the conditions endured by those at the Pit, it is still true that many of the reinforcers which we cherish most are made available to us as a function of the passage of time. Psychologists have discovered that time and the events its passage brings are important to behavior and have studied the effects of many time-dependent schedules of reinforcement.

One such schedule of reinforcement similar to the one on which Manuel was maintained for so many months is called a *variable-interval schedule of reinforcement.* This schedule is abbreviated *VI.* As the schedule designation implies, reinforcement becomes *available* after the passage of variable intervals of time. Typically the specific values of the schedule come after the VI designation; for instance, a VI 50 schedule is one in which reinforcement becomes available after an *average* of 50 minutes have elapsed. Of course, the interval designation can be in terms of seconds, minutes, hours, days, and, conceptually, even months.

Note that we said above that *reinforcement becomes available* after the passage of an average interval of time. On a true VI schedule, reinforcement may become available say, after one minute, but the organism does not actually receive reinforcement until he emits the proper response. *Although time alone will bring about the opportunity for reinforcement, the organism must capitalize on the opportunity by making the proper responses thereafter.* Similarly, making the appropriate response before the interval is ended will not yield reinforcement. It takes both a timed interval and the appropriate response made thereafter. Only when these two conditions have been satisfied will reinforcement be forthcoming.

Undoubtedly the most extensive study of the effects of various schedules of reinforcement on the behavior of organisms was done by Ferster and Skinner[1] in 1957. The book summarizing their work is called *Schedules of Reinforcement.* It seeks to classify and demonstrate behavior which particular schedules of reinforcement generate. The *variable-interval schedule* received considerable attention. The formal aspects of a variable-interval schedule can be summed up by the following points:

1. The opportunity for reinforcement comes to the organism as a direct function of the passage of time. Thus, the VI schedule can be called a time-dependent schedule.

2. The lengths of the intervals between opportunities are varied; therefore, the term "variable interval."

3. Although the opportunity to be reinforced occurs as a function of time alone, an appropriate response must be made by the organism *after* the interval is over in order for reinforcement to occur. Time alone will never bring about reinforcement; the organism must also make the appropriate and timely response.

Given the fact that a schedule is arranged according to the above formal dimensions, what kind of behavior would we expect? Figure 7-1 is a cumulative record of a pecking response made by a pigeon who received grain as reinforcement for that response. This bird was working a VI 2 minute schedule. Of course,

1. Ferster, C., and Skinner, B. F. *Schedules of Reinforcement.* New York: Appleton-Century-Crofts, 1957.

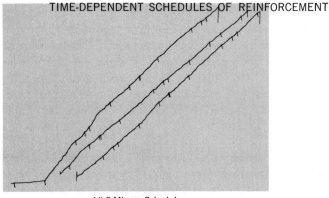

VI 2-Minute Schedule

Figure 7-1 A pigeon's pecking response on a VI 2 schedule

the VI 2 minute schedule means that the opportunity to be reinforced came about on an average of every two minutes. Once the opportunity became available, the pigeon was further required to peck the key to be reinforced. It can be seen by the slope in the cumulative record that the pigeon was pecking along very regularly but not with a degree of rapidity that we might expect from the ratio schedules we saw in the previous chapter. It is generally true that the smaller the average interval between opportunities for reinforcement, the higher the rate will be. Thus, if two or three days' wait was required between opportunities, we would expect an extremely low rate of response, perhaps as low as one peck every two or three hours. If, on the other hand, the opportunity for reinforcement occurs quite often on the average, the rate of response may be very high.

Another aspect seen in the cumulation record is that reinforcements do not occur regularly. Sometimes many responses are made from one reinforcement to the next, and other times only a small number of responses are required. This is a function of the variable interval between reinforcements. The most important aspect of the variable-interval schedule, however, is that it generates consistent response rates. You will notice that there are very few points in the cumulative record where the animal fails to respond. There are virtually no flat areas. The slope of the record tends to be even and uniform throughout. The variable-interval schedule brings about a not particularly fast, but a hard and consistent worker. There are, of course, no real post-reinforcement pauses. Other than for the time taken to consume his reinforcement, the bird does not stop. He eats and gets back to his rather leisurely working pace.

It is not at all surprising now to find that Manuel's behavior became consistent and steady. The schedule he came in contact with had many features which were similar to a variable-interval schedule as seen with Ferster and Skinner's pigeon. There were, of course, obvious differences. One of the most important differences is that Manuel had to be alert to take advantage of his reinforcement opportunities. Perhaps the breeze would blow the curtains for only an instant. If Manuel was not paying close attention and watching carefully, he might miss his opportunity. This feature of the schedule is called a *limited hold.*

The pigeon whose cumulative record is presented in Figure 7-1 was not operating in a limited-hold situation. Once reinforcement became available, the first response thereafter yielded reinforcement. Furthermore, once reinforcement became available, it remained available until the response was made, regardless of whether this occurred in the first or second minute, or not until the end of the session.

A variable-interval schedule with a limited hold places a more stringent demand on the organism's behavior. Since reinforcement is available for only a limited time, a response must occur during this limited-hold period if the organism is to capitalize on the opportunity and receive reinforcement. With any specific limited hold, responses tend to occur often enough to ensure that at least one response is emitted during the limited period. For this reason response rate generally increases as limited holds become shorter.

The limited hold imposed on Manuel's reinforcement schedule required him to keep an ever-constant vigil on the window where his love might at any minute make her appearance.

If you have been thinking that there are many occasions in life other than the austere Pit where we may encounter a situation in which reinforcement, reward, success, or whatever it may be called is controlled by a schedule similar to a variable-interval scedule, you are to be commended for your perceptiveness. If at the same time you cannot immediately think of an example of a "true" variable-interval schedule as it obtains in everyday life outside the laboratory, then you are no worse than your authors, who have also been somewhat pressed to cite a clear-cut example.

In many respects the activity of the stock market, its rising and falling indices, occurs as a result of the passage of time. The speculator has at least three responses he can make: buy, sell, or stand pat. He can make these responses at any time actually, and receive a particular consequence for his efforts. Of course, the trick is to make the correct response at the correct time. It is easy to see that while time brings about the possibility for reinforcement in stock market situations, the schedule is much more complicated than the simple variable-interval schedule presented earlier.

Fishing is a sport in which the opportunity to catch a fish is, to some extent, out of the hands of the fisherman. Once a fish bites, it is then up to the fisherman to nail down his reinforcement. The unpredictableness of when fish will bite has kept many a fisherman, myself included, seated for long hours on a moist river bank.

Now that we have seen how a variable interval of time can be employed to bring about the opportunity for reinforcement, it seems only reasonable that reinforcement opportunity can as easily be programmed to occur after the passage of a fixed quantity of time. Indeed, this is the case. Such a schedule of reinforcement is called a *fixed-interval schedule of reinforcement.* It is abbreviated FI. An FI 2 schedule is one in which reinforcement becomes available after exactly two minutes have passed. On such a schedule, the first response occurring after the interval has timed out yields reinforcement.

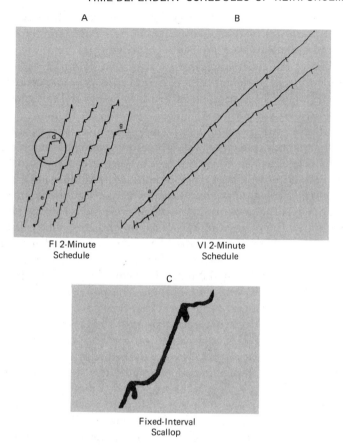

Figure 7-2 A pigeon's pecking response (A) on an FI 2 schedule and (B) on a VI 2 schedule. (C) Fixed-interval scallop corresponding to portion circled in (A).

Ferster and Skinner also studied fixed-interval schedules of reinforcement in their book. Figure 7-2A shows a cumulative record of a pigeon working for grain on an FI 2 schedule.

Alongside the cumulative record is a small sample of the cumulative record taken from the previous bird, which you will remember was on a VI 2 schedule of reinforcement. The FI record is segment A, on the left; and VI record is on the right, segment B. You will notice that the two records differ greatly in form. The VI record shows a steady, consistent, and standard rate throughout, with few pauses even after reinforcement.

FI schedules cannot by any means be so characterized. In order to study exactly what is going on, it is necessary to enlarge a portion of the fixed-interval record seen above. Figure 7-2C shows an enlarged portion which corresponds roughly to the portion circled in Figure 7-2A. Here you can get a better look at the animal's behavior from one reinforcement to the next. At first, a long period of time goes by without any responses being made whatsoever. After some time, a few responses are made, thus advancing the cumulative recorder more nearly vertically. Responses are made more rapidly as time goes by until at the end of the interval, an extremely high rate of responding is seen. This particular pattern of responding is typical of that seen on an FI schedule of reinforcement. The shape the record takes is called a *fixed-interval scallop.*

Comparison of the two cumulative records, that of an FI and a VI, reveals quite diverse response patterns, although both are time-dependent schedules. Imagine the difference in Manuel's observing behavior if the breezes came according to a fixed interval of time.

Just as with the variable interval schedule of reinforcements, there are probably very few situations outside of the laboratory where behavior is maintained on a "true" FI schedule. On the other hand, there are many situations arising daily in your life and mine which place essentially fixed-interval demands on our behavior. Practically any kind of situation in which a deadline is imposed, and in which meeting a deadline can bring reward, success, or whatever pleasant event you can think of, can be thought of as a variation of a fixed-interval situation. Let us examine the typical behavior of a student who is assigned a term paper. In order to facilitate comparison, let us further suppose the paper is assigned the very first day of class, and that there are 15 weeks to complete the project and hand it in. The deadline is firmly established. The paper must be completed by the last meeting of the class and turned in at that time.

Figure 7-3 is a hypothetical cumulative graph of a student working under such a schedule. Each week is represented on the abscissa, and the cumulative number of hours worked are plotted opposite the ordinate.

The first week after the assignment is made, the student thinks very little about it. He knows that it is due, but then, the deadline is far away. After all, there are more important things to occupy his precious hours. Consequently for the first week after the assignment is made, no time at all is spent preparing the paper. In Figure 7-3 a comparable "zero" point is placed on the graph. The same is true of the second, third, fourth, fifth, and sixth weeks; no time is spent in pre-

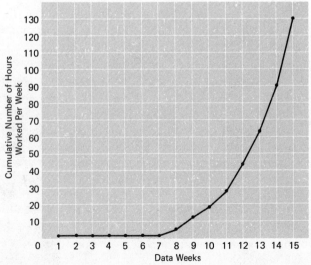

Figure 7-3 Fixed-interval scallop showing student's work behavior

paring for the paper. Finally, in the eighth week, the student begins to take the bull by the horns and spends five or six hours that week trying to select an appropriate topic. In the course of his quest for a topic he talks to several people, perhaps even to an instructor or two, and does a small amount of reading. In the next week his efforts increase only slightly, and slightly more on the following week. The student is now struck with the realization that there are only four more weeks until the end of the term. His efforts are redoubled that week, redoubled again the following week, and once more redoubled on the week after that. The final week is spent in a frenzy of long hours in the library and worry about the production. You can see now in the hypothetical cumulative graph that the student's hourly work behavior takes the form of the fixed-interval scallop which we discussed earlier. There is in the beginning a long initial pause for work not done at all which is followed by small but increasing amounts of behavior in following weeks until at the end of the interval, when the deadline is almost upon him, the student spends prodigious hours trying to make his performance meet the requirement.

Of course, there is a great deal of difference in the requirements of the true fixed-interval schedule and the schedule of term paper deadlines. The point is simply that behavior resembling that produced by a *fixed-interval schedule* often occurs in instances where certain behavioral requirements are imposed as a function of the passing of a fixed amount of time. We could have used hundreds of other examples of deadlines to illustrate this point. Many of us go through life living each day in terms of the deadlines it imposes on us. Some people, admittedly, myself included, find some security in this kind of a world.

Extinction and Schedules of Reinforcement

Previously the point was made that there were two broad ways in which reinforcement could be produced by responses. One way was continuous reinforcement in which each and every response produces a reinforcement. The other broad category was intermittent reinforcement. In the last chapter, we discussed intermittent schedules in which reinforcement occurred as a function of the number of responses made. These were fixed-ratio and variable-ratio schedules. At this juncture in the current chapter we have seen two other types of intermittent schedules. In these schedules the passage of time brings about the opportunity for reinforcement. These are the fixed-interval and variable-interval schedules of reinforcement.

A general statement can be made about intermittent reinforcement schedules whether they be fixed-ratio, variable-ratio, fixed-interval, variable-interval, or for that matter, any other types of intermittent schedules. *Intermittent reinforcement makes the response more resistant to extinction.* The extinction procedure, you will remember, is the withholding of reinforcement when a response which has previously been reinforced is emitted. The result of *extinction procedure* is a decrease in the rate of occurrence of that response. If reinforcement is withheld completely for some period of time, the response will soon cease to occur. When this happens, the typical result is referred to as *extinction behavior.*

When extinction procedures are applied to responses that have been maintained on a continuous reinforcement schedule, extinction behavior is usually completed rapidly. When extinction procedures are applied to responses maintained on an intermittent schedule of reinforcement, extinction takes longer. The organism continues to respond for a longer period of time although reinforcement has been completely deleted. Thus, responses which prior to extinction have been maintained on an intermittent schedule of reinforcement are said to have more resistance to extinction.

Some intermittent schedules of reinforcement generate behavior that is more resistant to extinction than others. All intermittent schedules, regardless of their specific characteristics, generate behavior which is more resistant to extinction than does continuous reinforcement. Obviously if an experimenter wishes to establish response patterns which do not collapse at the first sign of nonreinforcement, he will maintain them on an intermittent schedule of reinforcement.

Elimination of a Child's Excessive Scratching

For some people scratching is not merely a pleasant solution to an otherwise unpleasant situation. Scratching can, like most other behavior, be critically overdone. A friendly and well-mannered child of five years of age carried scratching to such an extreme.[2] When she was brought to the Development Psychology Laboratory of the University of Washington, Fay had been scratching herself, until she bled, for almost a year. The scratching had resulted in large scars and scabs on her forehead, nose, cheeks, chin, and one arm and leg.

It was not that Fay's parents had neglected her problem; they had made visits to numerous physicians in the area including both psychiatrists and pediatricians, but examinations yielded no sign of a basic medical cause. The ultimate suggestion resulting from these visits was that Fay be fitted with special arm splints. These splints were to be made of a type of inner tube and could be blown up like life jackets in order to curtail her scratching. The alternative, Fay's parents were told, was that Fay might become permanently disfigured.

Fay's behavior had created an explosive home situation. The father became so distraught at seeing his daughter engaged in these animal-like behaviors that he often spanked the child severely. The mother refrained from spanking and relied primarily on verbal abuse which was equally ineffective. The mother had become so upset by Fay and her general appearance that she was all but ready to have Fay placed in a foster home. The professional staff at the Development Behavior Laboratory were sensitive to the problems Fay's parents faced. They were willing to try something to alleviate Fay's scratching behavior in the hopes that this too would quell the mounting torment of emotional upheaval at home.

2. This section based on Allen, K. Eileen, and Harris, Florence R. Elimination of a child's excessive scratching by training the mother in reinforcement procedures. *Behaviour Research and Therapy,* 1966, *4,* 79–84.

It seemed likely that Fay's problem was not only her own. It was probable that it involved interactions with her parents. Fay and her mother were taken to the playroom at the clinic, and there were allowed to interact as the experimenters observed through a screen. It was quickly discerned that the mother spoke to the child only to criticize, give orders or directions, or to explain to Fay that she should behave in another manner. After observing the mother and her child together, the staff suggested that the mother keep a one-week record of Fay's behavior as well as her own behaviors in responding to her child. In such records she was to take careful notice of the frequency with which Fay scratched herself, how often she engaged in other behaviors that her mother did not sanction or approve, how often Fay was spanked, isolated, or verbally punished, and how often she participated in activities which the mother considered appropriate and what these appropriate behaviors and activities were.

From the records taken by Fay's mother, the investigators found many extraordinary interactions had taken place between Fay and her parents. As you might have suspected, Fay responded to her own scratching behavior by showing the bloody results to her mother. A pattern of interaction between Fay and her family had been established in which large amounts of attention, in the form of verbal or physical abuse, were afforded Fay for her scratching.

When the child's mother conferred with the staff at the clinic, this pattern was pointed out to her. She conceded that this was in reality what typically happened, but she was still at a loss as to what course of action she should take. It was suggested that she do nothing at all, and allow the behavior to extinguish. The mother claimed that she had already tried that technique. It had initially resulted in decreases in scratching, but eventually the scratching had become worse than ever. The extinction procedure had come about when she and her husband made a pact never to discuss the problem with their daughter. During the early stages of this procedure Fay had gone for long periods of time without scratching. After refraining from scratching for as long as an hour or two, she approached her mother and pointed out to her that she had not been scratching. The mother responded by saying: "I told you we're not going to talk about it. We don't care whether you scratch or not. You're a big girl now and it's up to you. I don't want to hear any more about it."

It was made clear to the mother that she had made a critical error when she had responded in this manner. Perhaps we can analyze what she did wrong in terms of schedule of reinforcement. Fay's parents were interested in getting her to stop scratching. They first reacted by reinforcing her with attention for her scratching behavior, and scratching increased. Next her parents tried ignoring any aspect of scratching, and attempted not to mention it again. Fay's scratching was initially reduced; she spent long hours not scratching. Nonscratching was a desirable response, and Fay's parents erred in failing to reinforce it. If they had consistently refrained from reinforcing scratching and concomitantly reinforced nonscratching, they would have been effectively programming reinforcements on a particular schedule of reinforcement, called *differential reinforcement of other behavior*. The lengthy title has been abbreviated to DRO.

Often as a psychologist, behavior therapist, or teacher, you can accept a wide range of behavior from a child at various times. Only a few behaviors are unacceptable. Let us take behavior on the playground as an example. As a teacher or supervisor, you are less interested specifically in what your charges are doing than you are in seeing that they are not doing a few harmful or dangerous things.

In many respects Fay's behavior was of this nature. Her mother could afford to let her amuse herself at a number of activities; often her mother was willing to buy her materials and toys and to help her daughter participate in activities. She was not willing, however, to let her scratch herself. A DRO schedule would dictate that Fay's mother offer reinforcement when Fay was doing something *other than scratching*. This is precisely the schedule of reinforcement which was subsequently employed in Fay's treatment.

A system of reinforcement involving gold stars was thoroughly conceptualized. Fay's mother was told that she should give Fay a gold star every 20 or 30 minutes that she went without scratching. At the end of this interval, her mother was to go to her, praise her for not scratching, and help her paste a gold star in her booklet. After every third star or so, Fay was also to be given a cookie, some candy, or a soft drink. Twice daily, at midday and at suppertime, stars were counted, approval and praise given, and trinkets of various description bestowed on Fay.

The DRO schedule was employed for more than a week. At this time, the mother reported that there was some apparent lessening in scratching behavior during the day but that this improvement was more than nullified by scratching during the night. Fay arrived at the breakfast table with newly opened scars.

There were many possible reasons for the failure of the experimental procedures at this point. The experimenters made an educated guess. In the past they had observed that, when procedures of this sort fail, it is due to the fact that reinforcers are not powerful enough. If a more powerful reinforcer could be found, perhaps the scratching could be reduced to the point that it would not occur even at night.

A second inadequacy was also taken into account: the reinforcement system did not originally extend to cover nighttime behavior. Effectively the program ended when Fay was placed in bed for the night. Fay was not receiving reinforcement for not scratching during the night. It should have been no surprise that Fay's nighttime scratching was unaffected.

They talked to Fay's mother inquiring as to the kinds of play articles which Fay had found to be most amusing. As with many girls her age it was found that Fay dearly adored the entire Barbie Doll collection. Fortunately, Barbie Dolls are manufactured skillfully to require an endless number and variety of accessories. Fay's mother said that if buying Fay the Barbie Doll and accessories would help alleviate the scratching problem, she was more than willing to purchase them for her. It was arranged that each afternoon after a scratch-free day, Fay and her mother were to go shopping for one of the Barbie Doll accessory items. The item purchased was to be whatever Fay desired. Once it was purchased it was taken home and placed in full view of Fay but it was not to be hers until the following morning and then only providing that she had spent a scratch-free night. This new system involving Barbie Dolls' accessories as reinforcers was in addition to the original program which involved gold stars, trinkets, and consumable reinforcers. The program had immediate success. Fay's wounds began to heal and soon had gone away, but for a few red marks. Fay's mother was extremely pleased with the success of the treatment.

Then, one day, she called in to say that the treatment had suddenly failed. She was obviously upset and acted in much the same way she had in times previous to the initial interviews with the clinic staff. When the mother was questioned thoroughly on the events which had taken place, it was found that Fay and her mother had gone shopping as usual following a scratch-free morning. But this time Fay saw an item which appealed to her greatly and she asked her mother to buy it. Unfortunately her mother had not brought an adequate amount of money to purchase that item, and when Fay began to sulk, the mother informed her that she did not have enough money for that and that Fay would have to take what her mother decided to buy for her and let it go at that. The mother took the item home and placed it on the customary shelf while Fay watched, still sulking. That night Fay scratched open all the nearly-healed areas on her face. The mother admitted to the clinic staff in retrospect that she had not complied with her part of the agreement. The following day she returned to the store and bought the item which Fay had desired the previous day. The mother was sure to bring adequate money with her from that time on and Fay responded by returning to her previous nonscratching behavior. After a few weeks had passed Fay's scars continued to diminish. In addition, her mother and father began to think more highly of her and themselves and found their relationship much more enjoyable. The torment and blame often ensuing from interactions with Fay no longer existed. After seven weeks the experimenters felt they could safely stop working on Fay's problem. Four months later she was seen in a follow-up check. The scars had faded to the point that they were barely discernible.

Superstition and Time-Dependent Schedules

It was demonstrated in both fixed-interval and variable-interval schedules that the passage of time brought about the opportunity for reinforcement, but that time alone was not enough to actually deliver reinforcement. The organism was required to make a response of a defined nature and magnitude in order to be reinforced. This second requirement is an extremely important one. It insures that reinforcement will be paired with the particular response the experimenter wishes to maintain. In an earlier chapter we saw what would happen if reinforcement was dispensed independently of the organism's behavior as a pure function of time. You will undoubtedly recall that this brought about a type of behavior called superstitious behavior. As a result of reinforcement governed purely by the passage of time, pigeons developed whirling, head-bobbing, and other mysterious behavior patterns.

True fixed-interval and variable-interval schedules of reinforcement demand that the organism must make the correct response before he is reinforced. Students in psychology occasionally make the error of believing that fixed-interval or variable-interval schedules of reinforcement rely solely on the passage of time. Behaviorally speaking, the results of presentation of reinforcement purely as a function of time, and any schedule where the opportunity for reinforcement is made available as a function of time, are quite dissimilar.

Summary

In this chapter we have discussed schedules of reinforcement which share the common factor of time as an important element in the availability of reinforcement.

1. One such schedule is termed a *variable-interval schedule of reinforcement* (*VI*). The opportunity for reinforcement arrives as a function of the passage of time. In this particular schedule the intervals of time vary from reinforcement to reinforcement, thus the term variable interval. The value of a particular VI is expressed in terms of the average interval between reinforcement opportunities. A VI 50 specifies that an average of 50 minutes elapse from one opportunity to the next.

2. Responses maintained on a VI schedule of reinforcement tend to occur at a consistent rate with virtually no post-reinforcement pause. While a consistent and steady rate is typical of all variable-interval schedules, the actual magnitude of the rate (high or low) is primarily a function of the size of the average interval. If the average interval is short, the rate will be higher and if it is long, the rate will be lower.

3. In a fictional account it was seen how a prisoner was maintained in observing activity over many months by the opportunity to view what he believed to be a lovely lady. The point was made that there are virtually no situations outside the laboratory which are programmed on a "true" variable-interval schedule of reinforcement, but there are many situations in which similar schedules are effective in controlling our behavior.

The schedule the prisoner was maintained on, for instance, had an additional component designated a *limited hold*. A limited-hold feature dictates that reinforcement is available for only a limited time. Responses made after the passage of this limited hold will no longer produce reinforcement. A limited hold tends to increase the rate of responding until responses occur frequently enough to capitalize on all instances of reinforcement availability.

4. A second schedule which was discussed is called a *fixed-interval schedule of reinforcement* (*FI*). Reinforcement opportunity on a fixed-ratio schedule occurs after the passage of a fixed amount of time. The specific fixed-interval schedule is designated by the numerals occurring after the schedule abbreviation. An FI 1 specifies a fixed-interval schedule in which reinforcement opportunity arrives after a one minute interval has expired.

5. Behavior maintained on a fixed-interval schedule differs greatly from that observed on a variable-interval schedule. Fixed-interval maintained responses take the form of a fixed-interval scallop. This scallop is created by responses

which do not occur immediately after reinforcement, but increase slightly in frequency as the interval advances. Response frequency increases as the interval nears a final quarter and relatively rapid responding is seen at the end of the interval.

6. As with a variable-interval schedule, a "true" fixed-interval schedule of reinforcement rarely occurs outside the laboratory. Still, there are many situations in which rules, regulations, or requirements placed on us by Nature or society generate behavior which resembles that seen where explicit fixed-interval schedules are in effect. Among the most noteworthy of these is behavior seen in situations where deadlines are imposed.

7. An important point must be made for fixed-interval schedules of reinforcement. Time alone presents merely the opportunity for reinforcement. In order for reinforcement to be delivered, the organism must make an appropriate response. This ensures that reinforcement will be associated with a specific response designated by the experimenters; otherwise, it would generate superstitious behavior as discussed in an earlier chapter.

8. All intermittent schedules of reinforcement, including fixed-ratio, variable-ratio, fixed-interval, and variable-interval schedules, bring about greater resistance to extinction for the responses they maintain than does a continuous reinforcement schedule. As a general statement this dictates that in cases where perseverance of responding is desired, intermittent reinforcement should be employed.

9. A special schedule of reinforcement which was treated in this chapter is called *differential reinforcement of other behavior* and is abbreviated DRO. In a DRO schedule, reinforcement is delivered to the organism only if he is *not* exhibiting an unwanted behavior. The DRO schedule does not specify what will be reinforced, but merely specifies what responses will not be correlated with reinforcement. In this manner the differential reinforcement is provided for any behavior *other* than that behavior which the experimenter wishes to eliminate. This schedule of reinforcement was used to eliminate the excessive scratching behavior of a young girl.

QUESTIONS

1. What stopped Manuel from hurling himself over the cliff as many of his companions had done?
2. After he first saw the lady, Manuel found that: (a) the days passed faster; (b) the sun was even hotter than before; (c) his hammer seemed heavier; (d) he was more popular with his friends.
3. A schedule of reinforcement in which the opportunity to be reinforced evolves with the passage of time is called a T_____ D_____ schedule.
4. Until his last encounter with her, seeing the lady was a reinforcing event for Manuel. (a) True; (b) False.
5. One time dependent schedule is known as a VI schedule. What does VI designate?
6. On a VI 50 schedule reinforcement becomes available after: (a) exactly 50 minutes have expired; (b) exactly 50 responses have been made; (c) an average of 50 minutes has expired; (d) an average of 50 responses has been made.
7. On a true VI schedule which two of the following events are required? (a) A

passage of time which makes reinforcement available; (b) At least 50 or more responses must be made after the reinforcer becomes available; (c) At least one response must be emitted after reinforcement becomes available; (d) The fixed ratio must be completed.

8. The most extensive study of the effects of schedules of reinforcement on behavior was written by Ferster and Skinner and was called: (a) *Principles of Reinforcement;* (b) *Reinforcement Revisited;* (c) *Rewards;* (d) *Schedules of Reinforcement.*

9. Which of the following is the relationship between rate of response and the average of the variable interval: (a) The longer the average interval the lower the response rate; (b) The longer the average interval the higher the response rate.

10. The variable-interval schedule of reinforcement generates: (a) highly erratic responding; (b) extremely high rates of responding with long post-reinforcement pauses; (c) cyclic responding in which high rates are seen at the beginning and the end of each interval; (d) consistent responding with virtually no post-reinforcement pause.

11. Manuel's consistent and long-lived observing behavior in the Pit was probably due to the fact that he was on a fixed-interval schedule. (a) True; (b) False.

12. The fact that Manuel had only a short time to look is similar to what condition on a variable-interval schedule: (a) Time out; (b) Time lapse; (c) Timed behavior; (d) Limited hold.

13. There are many occasions in life where we may encounter a situation where reinforcement, reward, or success is controlled by a schedule similar to a variable-interval schedule. (a) True; (b) False.

14. It is difficult to think of a situation outside the laboratory in which behavior is controlled by a true variable-interval schedule. (a) True; (b) False.

15. Can you name four activities which appear to be controlled by a schedule roughly resembling a variable-interval schedule?

16. A time-dependent schedule of reinforcement in which reinforcement becomes available after the passage of a constant interval is called: (a) a fixed-ratio schedule of reinforcement; (b) a fixed-time schedule of reinforcement; (c) a fixed-interval schedule of reinforcement; (d) a semi-fixed interval schedule.

17. A cumulative record of the key-pecking behavior of pigeons performing on a fixed-interval schedule can be described as a S_____.

18. Which of the following are characteristics of a fixed-interval scallop? (a) An initial slow rate of responding; (b) A terminal high rate of responding; (c) Consistent responding throughout; (d) No post-reinforcement pause whatsoever.

19. Which of the following situations occurring outside the laboratory best approaches a fixed-interval of reinforcement? (a) Vacation; (b) Deadline; (c) Limited hold; (d) Church.

20. The book suggested that work behavior of a student on an assigned paper took the shape of a fixed-interval _____ when plotted across several weeks.

21. The fact that one response extinguishes more slowly than another brings us to say that the former is more R_____ to E_____ than the latter.

22. Responses maintained by continuous reinforcement extinguish (more slowly, more rapidly) than those maintained by intermittent reinforcement.

23. Responses maintained by intermittent reinforcement are more resistant to extinction than responses maintained by continuous reinforcement. (a) True; (b) False.

24. Which statement below best characterizes the assertion that "fixed-interval schedules of reinforcement are more resistant to extinction than variable-interval schedules"? (a) True; (b) Only in pigeons; (c) False; (d) Not enough information is given to make the statement.

25. Fay's problem was that she: (a) bit her fingernails; (b) scratched herself excessively; (c) was not toilet trained; (d) talked too loudly.

26. Prior to coming to the clinic what was the only device which could stop Fay from scratching?

27. After observing Fay's interactions with her mother, the experimenter concluded that the attention that Fay received from scratching herself probably maintained the scratching behavior. (a) True; (b) False.

28. Why had extinction probably failed when it was tried by Fay's mother?

29. What was the schedule of reinforcement Fay was finally placed on?

30. At one point the procedure seemed to break down. Can you give the reason this occurred?

31. Fay now only scratches at night. (a) True; (b) False.

NOTES
The Pit

The schedule of reinforcement concept has been important to scientific psychology. For years, many of the rigorous and truly well-controlled experiments in the animal lab were concerned with schedules of reinforcement. Experimenters were attempting to examine many different kinds of schedules of reinforcement and to delineate what effect these schedules of reinforcement brought about in the behavior of the organism. The pinnacle of this type of research was seen in the volume compiled by Ferster and Skinner called *Schedules of Reinforcement*. In this book, thousands of hours of data were studied and presented. These data demonstrate systematic changes in performance as a result of systematic changes in schedules of reinforcement. The work is truly of great proportions, although critics have sometimes made light of it. In one critic's words, "Never have so many pecked for so little."[3] Regardless of the future significance of this type of research, it must be noted that it holds great scientific merit because it establishes that uniformity of behavior comes about as a function of when and under what conditions reinforcement is introduced.

In recent years many behavioral psychologists have ceased to study schedules of reinforcement as the primary independent variables in their research. Instead, schedules of reinforcement are often employed as *behavioral baselines*. The effects of a drug or an aversive stimulus, for example, can be readily observed as a change in the typical pattern of responding maintained by the baseline schedule of reinforcement.

Elimination of a Child's Excessive Scratching

In some respects it was inappropriate to include a DRO schedule with the other schedules of reinforcement discussed in this chapter. The DRO differs from a fixed-ratio, variable-ratio, fixed-interval, or variable-interval schedule in a very important manner. A fixed-ratio schedule, for instance, defines exactly what the organism must do before he will receive reinforcement. An FR 50 would require that he make 50 consecutive responses before a food pellet would be deliverd to him. This is likewise true for the other schedules of reinforcement studied in this chapter, with the single exception of

3. Grant, D. A. Pigeons peck for positivism (a review of *Schedules of Reinforcement*). *Contemporary Psychology*, 1958, *3*, 328–329.

DRO. All others define what behavior the organism must emit. They specify the conditions and other qualitative aspects of both responses and time intervals which are required. The DRO schedule does not specify what the organism must do to receive reinforcement. It states only what response he must *not* make if he is to receive reinforcement. Other behaviors he may emit while refraining from emitting the single behavior unwanted by the experimenter are relatively unlimited. The programming of reinforcement when he is not emitting the unwanted behavior could be done in various ways. The most common way reinforcement is delivered on a DRO schedule is at either fixed or variable intervals, provided the unwanted response is not in progress. Thus, more information must be known before we can describe or predict what his precise behavior might be.

The DRO schedule has another important use in psychological research, however, which does not entail its direct application to behavior problems. It is known as a *control schedule,* and serves the purpose of letting the experimenter know if, in fact, the variables he feels are important in bringing about a behavioral change are truly the variables which are responsible.

In a later chapter you will learn of two psychologists who established a token employment system in a mental hospital. The workers in the program were given various tasks around the institution and for performing these tasks received a form of money known as token money. These tokens could be exchanged for commodities such as candy, shaving cream, and other items which were not always easy for the patients to obtain. All of the residents who had previously been sitting on the ward now diligently went to work each day at their tasks, performing them quite reliably. At this point the experimenters felt impelled to answer some important scientific questions. Did the workers go to work because of the money they were being paid, or did they merely work because it was fun or they needed the exercise? In order to answer this question, a modified form of a DRO schedule was put in effect. Workers were given their tokens in the morning before they went to work. Payment always came before working responses were made. Under these conditions, work attendance dropped immediately. Subsequently the tokens were once again offered after work was finished, and immediately work attendance returned to a high rate. The DRO schedule allowed the experimenters in this study to come to the conclusion that indeed the tokens, under the conditions in which they were given, were both an effective and necessary reinforcer in maintaining work behavior.

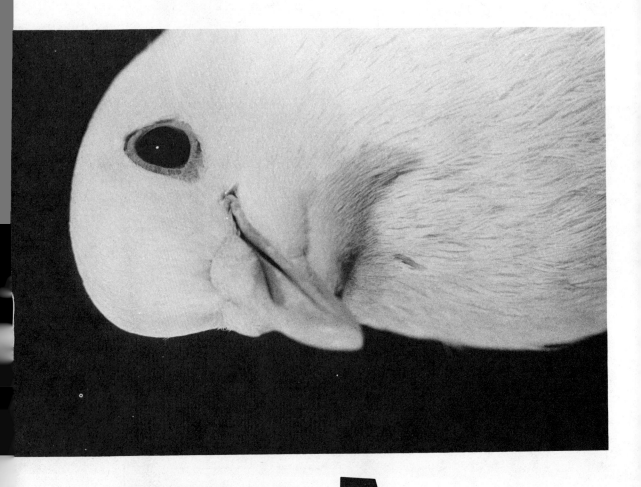

STIMULUS CONTROL

Jim wires a programming board for his experiment on color matching with pigeons and then discusses some potential problems in the program with Kay.

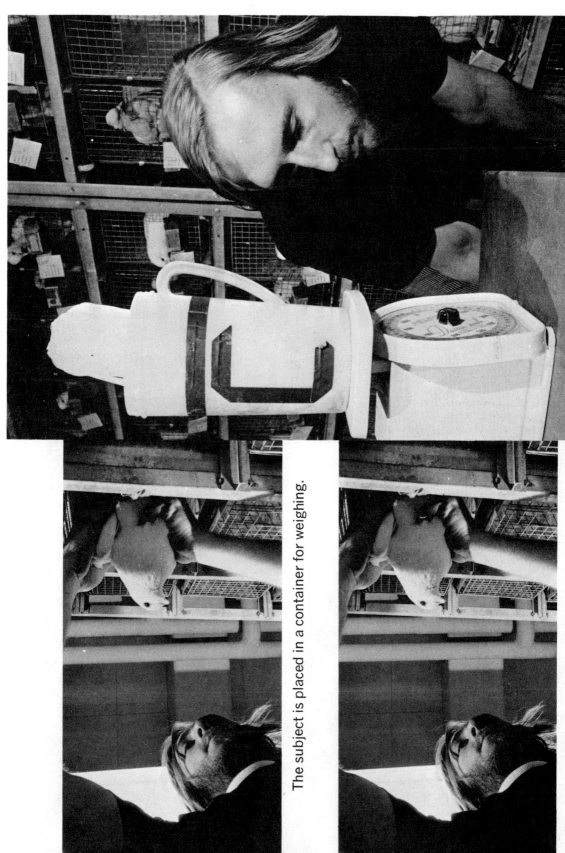

The subject is placed in a container for weighing.

The bird is close enough to 70% of free feeding

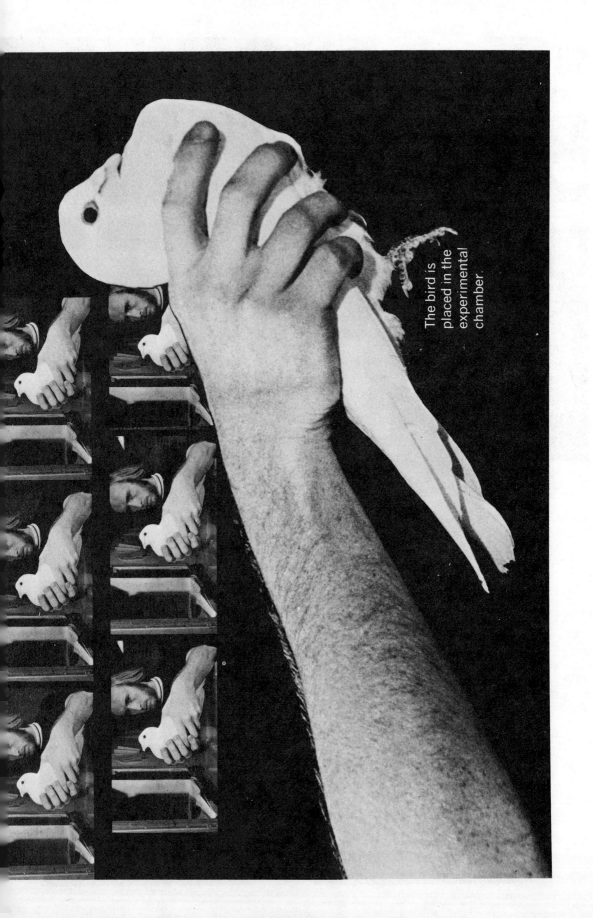

The bird is placed in the experimental chamber.

Jim inserts the programming board into the apparatus for the training session . . .

and sets the dials.

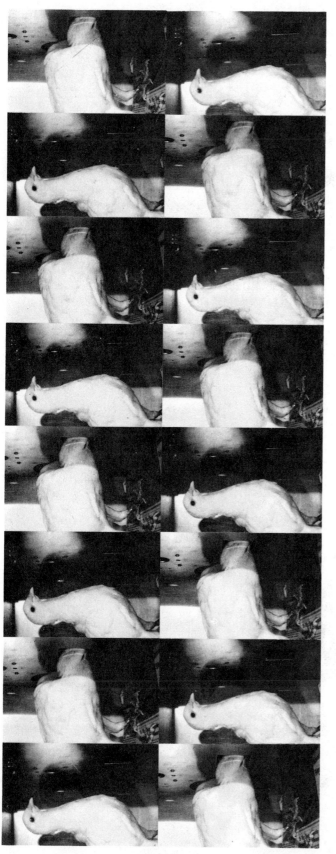

The subject pecks a key behind the circular opening in the wall. Visual stimuli are projected onto the translucent key from the rear.

When S+ stimuli are on the key, responses will occasionally be reinforced with grain, if they occur frequently. When S− stimuli are on the key, no reinforcement occurs.

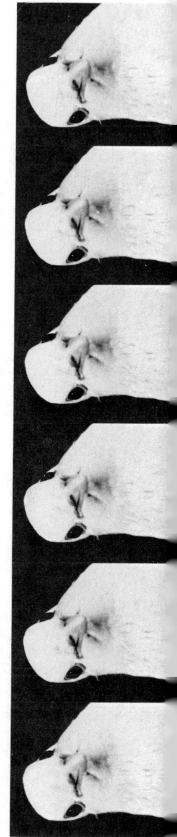

8

STIMULUS DISCRIMINATION

The pistol was pointed directly at Keller Breland's head. He took a deep breath and stood his ground. The gun was mounted securely in a frame with a string attached to the trigger. The other end of the string was held in the beak of a live chicken. If the chicken pulled the string, the gun would fire and the bullet would pierce Breland's head. After standing motionless for several seconds, Breland stepped aside. The chicken immediately pulled the string. The bullet entered the bull's eye of the target placed behind the spot where Keller Breland had been standing. Mr. Breland pulled a few kernels of corn from his pocket and fed them to the chicken. Only then did he wipe the perspiration from his forehead.[1]

Ah, thoughtful reader, I can see the gleam in your eye as you recognize the principles of positive reinforcement at work. You correctly suspect that the kernels of corn served to reinforce the chicken's response of pulling the trigger. "But," you may ask, "why didn't the bird shoot the gun when Breland was in its line of fire?" Your first reaction might be that the chicken was chicken; I trust that you would not think of anything that corny. Your second reaction might be that if the chicken had done so, Breland would not have been able to feed him. It would be an error to imagine that the chicken restrained himself for fear of "killing the psychologist that laid the golden kernels."

We saw in Chapters 2 and 3 that when we want a response to occur, we should reinforce or condition it; when we do not want a response to occur, we should extinguish it. Thus far, we have considered the possibility of either conditioning a response or extinguishing it, but never of doing both simultaneously. Combining conditioning and extinction is exactly what we should do if we wish our subject to discriminate between two stimuli; in other words, if we want him to respond in the presence of one stimulus and not to respond in the presence of another stimulus. In fact the procedure is rather unimaginatively referred to as the *discrimination training procedure*. The discrimination training procedure con-

1. When the truth of this section was confirmed with Mrs. Marion Breland, we found that a toy pop gun had been used instead of a real one; but the principles illustrated are the same.

sists of conditioning a response in the presence of one stimulus and extinguishing it in the presence of another stimulus.

The stimulus with which reinforcement is associated is called the *discriminative stimulus*. A common abbreviation for discriminative stimulus is S^D (pronounced ess-dee). The stimulus with which reinforcement is not associated is called S^Δ (pronounced ess-delta).

The man who trained the chicken was Keller Breland, a psychologist. In fact, Mr. Breland was one of Professor B. F. Skinner's first graduate students. He helped Skinner with a research project which we will discuss later in this chapter. Mr. Breland became famous as an animal trainer, using positive reinforcement to do such things as condition chickens to roller skate and play baseball and to condition pigs to perform four-brassiered strip tease acts. For purposes of demonstration, Breland wanted a chicken that would fire a gun when he was not in sight, but when he was in sight, Breland wanted the chicken to avoid making him psychology's first martyr.

Being a good psychologist, Mr. Breland realized that this was a discrimination problem. The response to be conditioned was the chicken's pulling the string and consequently firing the gun. Reinforcement was to be the kernels of corn which Breland fed the chicken when the response was made in the presence of the S^D. Reinforcement would, of course, be withheld for responses in the presence of S^Δ. The S^D was the Brelandless target and the S^Δ was Breland.

Before starting the discrimination training, Breland had the foresight to replace the live ammunition with blanks. Whenever the bird fired the gun at the target with Breland out of the way (S^D), it was given a few kernels of corn as reinforcement. When it fired the gun at Breland (S^Δ), it was not given any reinforcement.

The *discrimination behavior* which typically results from discrimination procedures of this sort consists of an increase in the response rate or frequency in S^D and a decrease in the rate of frequency in S^Δ. When the response is finally more likely to occur in the presence of the S^D than in the presence of the S^Δ, we say that *stimulus control* has been established. This is what happened in the present case. Eventually discrimination behavior began to develop, and finally perfect stimulus control was attained. At the end of training, the feathered sharpshooter accurately discriminated between Breland's presence and absence in front of the target. Once the discrimination was perfect, Breland exchanged the live ammunition for the blanks. This is one of the most dramatic examples of stimulus control that I know of. I, too, have a good deal of faith in the power of positive reinforcement, but not that much.

As we have seen, discrimination training can result in a very high degree of stimulus control. The response is reinforced in the presence of the S^D and, consequently, always occurs as soon as the S^D is presented. The response is never reinforced in the presence of the S^Δ and, consequently, never occurs when the S^Δ is presented.

Another example of very good stimulus control is shown in a motion picture featuring the work of Dr. Skinner.[2] In this film, a pigeon pecks a single response

2. *Learning and Behavior* (a motion picture). Columbia Broadcasting System. "Conquest" series.

key. Sometimes the key is lighted and sometimes the key is dark. Reinforcement for the key-peck response occurs in the presence of the lighted key, the S^D; reinforcement is withheld in the presence of the dark key, the S^Δ. The stimulus control is so great that the bird's head can be moved back and forth as if it were on the end of a rubber-band; if the key light is turned off in the middle of a key-peck response, the bird will jerk its head back just before hitting the key. If the bird is still in the process of withdrawing his head when the light is turned on again, he will immediately return to work. Incidentally, much of the basic research on discrimination with animals involves situations such as this. The S^D is presented for a period of time, and then the S^Δ is presented for a period of time; the *rate* of responding is recorded in the presence of each stimulus.

We have seen how we can condition a discrimination between two stimuli. In one case, a chicken was taught to discriminate between a blank target and a target with a man in front of it. We also briefly considered an example in which a pigeon was conditioned to discriminate between a lighted and an unlighted response key. In both cases, the birds had only one response which would be reinforced. The chicken could pull the trigger and the pigeon could peck the key. Any other behavior went unreinforced.

This is probably the simplest arrangement which can be used to establish a discrimination. However, the stimulus and response classes involved need not be so simple. This is illustrated in the next section.

A View from the Balcony
(The Monster Rally)

During the summer of 1967, the Whaleys, two lovely secretaries, my wife, and I managed to slip away to Nassau for six weeks to write the first few chapters of this book. We could probably have done the writing just as well at home in Kalamazoo, Michigan, but this way we could use SCUBA diving trips and the exciting Nassau night life as reinforcers whenever we were able to get a few words down on a page.

After the mildly aversive events that normally accompany the first couple of days in a strange foreign city, we found a beautiful spot, Cable Beach Manor, at which to settle down and do our work. We got a second floor apartment with a balcony overlooking a palm tree-studded courtyard.

Most of the activity of the guests took place in and around the swimming pool in the center of this courtyard. On the other hand, Don and I could frequently be seen sprawled out on our balcony talking into dictating machines as we stared off into this courtyard below. The word soon got out that we were psychologists studying the behavior of the other guests at the resort. It reached the point where some people were avoiding even walking by the pool for fear of our penetrating analysis of their innermost souls. We had to assure everybody that we were harmlessly writing a general psychology book and that our staring into the courtyard was no different than if we had been absently staring off into space. Then things finally got back to normal at Cable Beach Manor. You may have found already that when people discover you are a psychology student, they are quick to assume that you are constantly analyzing them, though you usually are not. Sometimes however the involvement of the principles of reinforcement is blatantly obvious. (On those occasions, it would be wise to avoid pointing out to the individuals involved how their behavior is being controlled by its reinforcing consequences. For some reason, people find such information aversive.) I would like to mention two interesting cases which may involve a special sort of stimulus discrimination process. We could not help but observe and in fact play an unwitting part in these events.

The first example involves Winston, a very handsome seven-year-old boy with long, straight, blond hair. I had noticed him diving and swimming in the pool and had admired his agility and grace. He was as much at home in the water as out. My first real contact with Winston occurred about four feet beneath the surface of the pool, and it really was a contact. Just after I made my usual belly-smacker of a dive, Winston entered the water like a bullet and we collided. On surfacing, we both apologized. Not only was Winston graceful but he also seemed polite and charming.

It was only after I observed Winston for some time that I realized what was going on. He made a practice of torpedoing innocent swimmers and repeatedly did cannon ball diving near the sun bathers at the pool's edge. He would add insult to injury by dripping water over them as he ran up to the poolside to make his forceful dives. Winston soon came to be known as the terror of Cable Beach Manor. These "pestering" behaviors seemed to be conditioned responses just like any others. The reinforcement for the pestering was the response of his victims. They looked at him, they spoke to him, they asked him not to do that, they pleaded with him, they threatened him, in short, they *paid attention to him*. Ah, what a powerful reinforcer is attention!

Winston had developed some fairly sophisticated defensive actions. After his first attack he would inquire with much polite concern about the well-being of the unfortunate soul he had singled out for persecution. He might ask if he had splashed them or might apologize for doing so. He seemed so innocent that the naive victim was sure that it was an accident. Only after such accidents kept occurring with alarming regularity would the victim realize what was happening. Such subterfuge on Winston's part probably saved him from many spankings and allowed him to prolong his tormenting much longer than otherwise would have been possible. All sorts of reinforcements would be forthcoming from the squirming, pleading, and threatening victims.

My wife and I always ate our meals at the umbrella-shaded table near the pool. One day at lunch time, Winston ran by and dripped water on me in the process. He then courteously inquired, "Did I drip water on you?"

I did not reply. The entire sequence of events then occurred a second time. I continued eating and talking to my wife. She asked if I was going to do something about Winston. I replied that I was; in fact I was trying a little extinction procedure. He then came up to me and started shouting, "Hey, hey." He grabbed my arm and began pinching it, but I continued eating and talking to my wife. After a few seconds he stopped pinching and said, "I guess I'll go home now."

Much to our relief he did. I had anticipated a considerably longer extinction session than had occurred.

Though Winston continued tormenting everyone else, he left me alone for about two weeks; and then one day he said, "Hello" as I walked by on my way to the ocean. Gullible fellow that I am, I thought it was such innocent behavior that I could not possibly do any harm by reinforcing it and so returned his greeting. Two hours later I went for a swim in the pool. As I was emerging from a dive to the bottom I found myself running directly into Winston who just happened to be above me. I ignored him and continued diving with no further incidents.

The next day Winston decided to beard the lion in his den. He came up to the end of the balcony where I was working. Strange as it may seem, I was a little nervous when I saw the seven-year-old approaching. He began picking up things such as a stapler, pens, papers, and so forth; he commented on them and then put them down. In the process, he managed to bump into my chair several times. I continued my extinction treatment by working as though he were not there, and after two minutes of this, he in fact was not. Once again the extinction session was much shorter than I had anticipated.

At first I thought that Winston simply had a low resistance to extinction; his behavior extinguished very rapidly. This might be a result of an almost continuous schedule of reinforcement for his pestering behavior. But the more I think about it, the more I think this may be an example of *discriminated extinction.* In other words, my not responding to Winston acted as an S$^\Delta$ for him, indicating that reinforcement would not be forthcoming. Perhaps other people had used a similar sort of extinction procedure; he might have found that if people did not pay attention to him right away, then they were not apt to as long as he continued pestering them. If reinforcement were not immediately forthcoming, there would be nothing gained in continuing to respond.

An example of discriminated extinction which you have undoubtedly experienced is the candy-, coke-, or cigarette-vending machine which fails to work. You probably do not waste more than two or three coins before you stop making the response of inserting your money into the machine. The absence of the normal reinforcement from the vending maching acts as an S$^\Delta$. You know that further responding would probably be of no avail. This is discriminated extinction. Laboratory experiments have shown that an animal will eventually acquire such a fine discrimination that as soon as a single response goes unreinforced, it stops making that response. But let us return to the swimming pool at Cable Beach Manor.

We thought Winston was rather disagreeable, but when Steve arrived, Winston seemed like a cherub in comparison. Steve was slightly older than Winston and much more straightforward and obvious in his pestering. He openly splashed anyone in range, and if they were not within range of his splashing, he would fill his mouth with water and approach and squirt them. Those were some of his more frequent and annoying behaviors. He had many others. They were all reinforced by the same sorts of reactions which had maintained Winston's behavior. But Steve was much more of a pest. From my balcony vantage point, I observed him walk over to good-natured Don Whaley as he tried to eat his lunch.

Steve's entering response was, "You all eatin' lunch?"

Of course the reply was, "Yes."

"What 'cha eatin'?"

"An apple."

"I sure would like to have an apple to eat. . . . Can I have that one?"

"No, I'm eating it."

"Where d'ja get it?"

"At the grocery."

"Got any more?"

"Yes."

"Can I have one?"

"No."

Actually this is a summary of the conversation which lasted for several minutes. I had been told of other similar instances of pestering until food was given, and so when my wife and I went down for lunch, we were not surprised to see him at our table before we had had our first bite of food.

"What 'cha all doin'?"

No reply.

"Ya eatin' lunch?"

No reply.

"Hey! Hey!"

No reply.

The process lasted less than 60 seconds. Again, this seems too quick to be a normal extinction period. It seems more likely that Steve had also gone this route several times before, and our nonresponsiveness served as an S^Δ for his continuing to pester. In other words, this was discriminated extinction.

In the cases of both Winston and Steve, it would have been so easy for their undesirable behavior to have been extinguished and more desirable behavior to be conditioned. This would have been particularly fruitful for Winston, who had a considerable repertoire of desirable responses in addition to the undesirable ones. But woe be unto him who would suggest such a thing to people who did not understand the principles of reinforcement. Withholding attention and love seems too cruel until we realize that attention and love at the wrong times can seriously harm an individual. We can only hope that these young men come into contact with more realistic contingencies of reinforcement before they mature.

The general nature of the discrimination procedure in these cases is very simple and basically the same as discussed earlier in this chapter. It involves two stimuli, an S^D and an S^Δ, and a single response class which is reinforced in the presence of the S^D. However, the nature of the stimuli is considerably more complicated than the presence or absence of a light, or the presence or absence of a man in front of a target. What is being discriminated is the presence or absence of a behavioral event, the reinforcement. The basic question is, "Is the victim paying attention to me?" The victim's attending responses are both the reinforcement and the stimuli for the pestering behavior. This class of attending stimuli which constitutes the S^D is a very complex class and involves all sorts of events ranging from simple eye contact to standing up and shouting. Yet these various stimuli all belong to one stimulus class serving as an S^D for pestering. Similarly, the response class of pestering is much more complicated than simply pecking at a small plastic disk or pulling a string. The variety of pestering responses which an effective nuisance can develop is indeed awesome to behold.

In the next section, we will look at a discrimination procedure which is only slightly different from this one. As before, two stimuli will be used. However, an additional response will be reinforced. Reinforcement will be provided for one response in the presence of one stimulus and for another response in the presence of another stimulus. In the case of Breland's chicken experiment, we reinforced the firing of the gun when there was a plain target in view. We might have reinforced some other response such as turning in a circle when Breland was in front of the target. That would be an example of a discrimination involving not only two stimuli but also two reinforced responses.

The Name Game

Like her namesake in the opera, Carmen seemed to be a charming little lady. She was a pretty twelve-year-old brunette. Unfortunately, she had a serious handicap. Her IQ was 20. This places her in the severely retarded range. She was not considered trainable by most experts in the field of retardation. She was certainly not expected to learn to read.[3]

A graduate student from Western Michigan University worked with Carmen at the Fort Custer State Home where she is a resident. He wanted to see if the experts were right; he decided to try to teach Carmen to "read" her name.

The graduate student wanted Carmen to discriminate between her name and the name "Leslie," which has the same number of letters. More specifically, he wanted her to pick up a card with her name on it when it was presented side by side with a card containing the name "Leslie." This is illustrated in Figure 8-1. When her name was on the right, this would serve as the S^D for picking the card on the right and as the S^Δ for picking the card on the left. When her name was on the left, the situation was reversed: this configuration of the cards was an S^D for picking the card on the left and an S^Δ for picking the card on the right.

During the first discrimination training trial, the graduate student presented the S^D for the response of picking the right-hand card (the name, Carmen, was on the right-hand card.) He said, "Pick out your name, Carmen." Carmen could not speak, but she could occasionally respond to rudimentary instructions. This instruction was sufficient to get her to pick up a card, though she undoubtedly had little understanding of the meaning of the instructions. By chance she picked the card with her name on it, and the graduate student immediately said, "Good," and placed a Fruit Loop (fruit-flavored cereal) directly in her mouth in an effort to make the reinforcement as immediate and thereby as strong as possible. The student shuffled the cards, so that Carmen's name was then on the left. This com-

3. This section based on Whaley, D. L., Welt, K., Hart, Charlotte, and Perthu, Marge. Teaching retardates to discriminate their name using positive reinforcement. Unpublished manuscript, Fort Custer State Home, Augusta, Michigan, 1967.

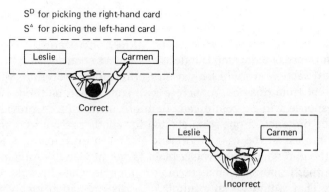

S^D for picking the right-hand card

$S^\vartriangle$ for picking the left-hand card

Correct

Incorrect

Figure 8-1 Name discrimination training trial for a retarded girl

bination of cards was the S^D for picking up the left card. The student again requested, "Pick out your name, Carmen." This time, however, Carmen made the wrong response. She picked the right-hand card. The student said, "No," emphatically, pulled the cards away, and held them beneath the table for ten seconds before presenting them again. This process was continued for 20 trials, then a brief break was taken and three more blocks of 20 trials were presented—a total of 80 presentations of the two names. Reinforcement for the correct response and withholding of reinforcement for the incorrect response had its effect; the frequency of the correct responses gradually increased until, by the last 25 trials, Carmen was consistently selecting only the card with her name. Perfect stimulus control had been established.

The results of this simple treatment are of interest, because most experts in the field of mental retardation would say that Carmen could not learn to discriminate between her name and another's, no matter how many times she was asked to do so. These experts are almost right. Without the use of reinforcement, Carmen would probably have never mastered the discrimination. In fact, many other retardates of her general description were unable to accomplish this; but when special discrimination training technicques were used, all of them learned it. These special techniques will be discussed in a later chapter.

In the first section, we saw how a chicken could be conditioned to discriminate between two stimuli, a blank target and a target with a man in front. Reinforcement was delivered for a single response in the presence of one stimulus: each time the bird fired the gun at the blank target, he received a small amount of grain. Nothing happened when he fired the gun with the man in front of the target.

In this section, a discrimination procedure involving two stimuli was also used. A severely retarded girl was conditioned to discriminate between an arrangement of two cards. In one arrangement her name was on the left-hand card and in a similar arrangement, her name was on the right-hand card. In this case, however, two responses were available for reinforcement. One response was reinforced in the presence of one stimulus and the other was reinforced in the presence of another stimulus. She was given a Fruit Loop and praised when she picked the card on the left if her name was on the left. She was treated similarly when she picked the card on the right if her name was on that side.

In the next study, we will see how a juvenile delinquent can be conditioned to discriminate between a very large number of stimuli. These stimuli will also be printed words. When each stimulus word is shown, the response of correctly reading that word will be reinforced; therefore, the number of reinforceable responses will be equal to the number of stimulus words the experimenters expose him to.

Teaching Reading to a Juvenile Delinquent

Jesus Delgado was bad.[4] By the time he was 14 years old, he had been sent to the juvenile correction department nine times. Like many juvenile delinquents, his prime target was school buildings. One time he shot out light bulbs and windows in a school building with a BB gun. At the age of 14, he not only smoked but also drank; in fact, he occasionally got very drunk. He stole, habitually told lies, and used language that would make even a fraternity man blush.

Jesus was the fifth in a Mexican-American family of 11 children. His parents attempted to control his behavior by using physical and verbal abuse, which had evidently been the technique used by their parents. His father had only completed the fifth grade of school. Home life was not ideal.

Jesus had been in school 8½ years, but his reading achievement was still at the 2.0 grade level. The teachers had promoted Jesus from one class to another so that they could get him out of their sight. They wanted nothing to do with him. Finally two people came along who did want to have something to do with him. One was William Butterfield, a probation officer from the juvenile correction department. The other was Dr. Arthur Staats, a psychologist. For several years prior to this Dr. Staats had been working intensively in the experimental analysis of reading behavior and had been developing remedial reading programs based on the principles of behavior. Mr. Butterfield and Dr. Staats thought that they could help Jesus, though none of his teachers had been able to do anything with him. Many people believe that nothing can be done with juvenile delinquents. Somehow they are basically stubborn—fundamentally incorrigible. Dr. Staats and Mr. Butterfield did not feel this way. They thought Jesus could be taught to read when the task was correctly presented. They considered reading to be a series of responses which could be conditioned if the proper reinforcements were used.

In their work with Jesus, they used specially prepared stories. Each story contained a new set of words. The written words were to act as discriminative stimuli for the responses of pronouncing those words. Before starting a new story, Mr. Butterfield showed each discriminative stimulus word to Jesus and asked him to make the correct reading response. Whenever Jesus was able to make the correct response to the discriminative stimulus word, he received a token as a reinforcement.

4. This section based on Staats, A. W., and Butterfield, W. H. Treatment of nonreading in a culturally deprived juvenile delinquent: An application of reinforcement principles. *Child Development*, 1965, *36*, 925–942.

Each word served not only as an S^D for the proper spoken response but also as an S^Δ for improper spoken responses. For example, the written word "shoe" acts as an S^D for the spoken response "shoe"; but it also acts as an S^Δ for the spoken response "hat" and all other incorrect responses.

When Jesus failed to respond to a word correctly, Mr. Butterfield told him the correct response and then Jesus repeated it while looking at the word. The discriminative stimulus words were presented later and again later until Jesus was able to make the correct response to each of them without prompting. This vocabulary training was continued until Jesus made the correct reading response to each discriminative stimulus word. During the 4½ months that Jesus worked with Mr. Butterfield, they ran across 761 words which he could not initially read. Therefore, an attempt was made to teach Jesus to read a total of 761 new words in the vocabulary training phases.

After Jesus was able to correctly read each word in a vocabulary list, the first paragraph of the accompanying story was given to him to read. While reading the story, he occasionally made mistakes. Out of the total 761 words, he was able to correctly read 585 of them the first time he saw them in the context of the story.

When correct reading responses were made to each discriminative stimulus word in the paragraph, he received another token. At that point he advanced to a new paragraph in the story. Each time he made a wrong response, he was corrected and the paragraph was put aside to be returned to later. This was done until he had mastered each paragraph in the story; at that point, the words were exerting proper stimulus control.

You may be wondering what kind of tokens Jesus was collecting. Were they bus tokens or subway tokens? No. As a matter of fact, they were poker chips. Without further explanation, it might appear that Jesus was some sort of nut who went about collecting poker chips. This is not true. The poker chips acquired their reinforcing value because they could be used to purchase a variety of things. He exchanged the tokens for such items as "Beatle" shoes, hair pomade, a phonograph record, an ice cream sundae, a ticket to a school function, and money for his brother who was going to be placed in a reform school. Incidentally, Jesus came from a long line of juvenile delinquents; each of his four older brothers had been referred to the juvenile court for misbehavior.

During the 40 hours of reading that were spread over a 4½ month period, Jesus worked very consistently for these tokens. He made over sixty-four thousand single-word reading responses. The total amount of reinforcement he received for this was worth $20.31. During the 4½ months that he worked on the project, the juvenile delinquent was very cooperative and very attentive—quite unlike a juvenile delinquent.

This may mean that juvenile delinquents are not basically uncooperative and bad. When they are placed in an environment which reinforces desirable and cooperative behavior, and when that behavior is within their range of competence, they will behave properly. On the other hand when they are not capable of making the desirable responses which produce authorized reinforcement, they will engage in undesirable behavior which results in unauthorized or bootleg reinforcement.

While Dr. Staats and Mr. Butterfield were teaching Jesus to read out loud, they were also teaching silent reading. We should discuss some special problems that arise when you try to teach silent reading. In order to reinforce the correct reading response to a particular discriminative stimulus word, it is necessary for the teacher to know what the word is that is being read and be able to hear the reading response. This creates no problem when he is trying to teach oral reading, but how can he possibly use this method to teach silent reading?

Silent reading can only be conditioned indirectly. After a story had been mastered at the oral level, Jesus was asked to read it silently and was told that it was important to understand the story, because he would be asked questions afterwards.

One of the first things which they did was to make it likely that Jesus was paying attention to the story. If he were not at least looking at the page of writing, he could not be reading it. On the other hand, if he were looking at the page, then he might be reading it. Therefore looking at the page was at least a step in the right direction; consequently reinforcement was provided for simply making proper observing responses. A sort of variable-interval schedule with a mean of 15 seconds was used. If Jesus was looking at the page when reinforcement became available, he received a token. Such reinforcement was very effective in ensuring that he spent most of his time attending to the printed page, since reinforcements were only given when he looked at it.

Jesus initially had some difficulty in silent reading; he frequently emitted small vocal sounds and moved his lips. The frequency of that undesirable behavior was reduced by giving him a token whenever he read a story without making any sounds or moving his lips.

Thus far nothing had been done to ensure that the boy was actually reading —that he was making the correct reading responses to each discriminative stimulus word. This was now done by requiring him to write out the answers to a set of questions when he had finished reading each story. He was given a token each time he answered a question correctly. Whenever he made a spelling error, he had to correct it before receiving the token. Each time he made an incorrect answer, he had to reread the appropriate paragraph and correct the answer before he received the token.

Whenever Jesus had completed 20 stories, he was given a review test on the words he had learned. For each correct response, he received a token. When incorrect responses were made to the discriminative stimulus words, the difficult word stimulus was repeatedly presented until it was correctly responded to. Jesus was able to respond correctly to 430 of the 761 discriminative stimulus words the first time they were presented on the review test.

The effect of the training to make the proper word discriminations can be most readily seen in looking at Jesus' reading achievement test scores. In his 8½ years of school, he had only progressed to the second grade (2.0) level in reading achievement. However, in 4½ months of this special training, he progressed from the 2.0 to the 4.3 grade level. He progressed more in those 4½ months than he had in the preceding 8½ years of school.

Jesus' general performance in school improved almost as dramatically as did his performance on the reading achievement test. Jesus received passing grades in all of his subjects: "C" in Physical Education, "D" in General Shop, "D" in English, and "D" in Mathematics. This may not strike you as anything to be excited about until you look at Jesus' past academic record. In the 8½ years in which he had been in school, he had failed every course that he had taken! Now you can see why everyone was so pleased when Jesus got one "C," three "D"s and no "F"s.

Jesus also began to behave better while in school. During the first month of training, Jesus committed ten misbehaviors that warranted the receipt of demerits. These behaviors were as follows: disturbance in class, two times; disobedience in class, two times; loitering, two times; and tardiness, four times. In the second month, he was given only two demerits, one for scuffling on the school grounds and one for creating a disturbance. In the third month he was also given two demerits; one for cutting a math class and one for profanity in class. No misbehavior occurred in the fourth month or in the half month after this until the conclusion of the school term.

When I was writing the present section, I wished that I could conclude Jesus' case history at this point. We would all feel so much better if it had a happy ending. Unfortunately the story goes on. The conditioning which Jesus had received improved his grades and his deportment in the school, but that was not enough. Nothing had been done to improve his behavior at the juvenile detention home where he was staying. Jesus frequently baited the attendants at the detention home and created many minor but unpleasant and disruptive disturbances. Because of this he was sent to an industrial school for juvenile delinquent boys. Jesus had probably not yet gotten to the point where he could continue his progress without special reinforcement procedures. But Dr. Staats and Mr. Butterfield were no longer able to work with him. This most likely means that he will make little if any academic progress during the remainder of his school years. It seems safe to predict that Jesus will be a misfit the rest of his unhappy life. He will probably do more harm than good both to himself and to society.

The Staats and Butterfield study indicates that this need not be the case. With the proper use of the principles of reinforcement, we should be able to condition desirable behavior in juvenile delinquents and extinguish the undesirable behavior, so that they can become worthwhile and responsible citizens and can lead lives which they find personally reinforcing. This will not be an easy task. There is a tremendous amount of prejudice about the inborn limitations of man, which must be overcome. This will require very hard work on the part of many dedicated scientists and practitioners.

In this section, we have seen that reading is composed of a set of simple discriminations. Each word may be treated as an S^D for its associated reading response. This discrimination is similar in nature to the discriminations studied with pigeons in the laboratory.

However, in the case of reading, the basic discriminative stimuli can be combined into sentences and paragraphs to establish much more subtle forms of stimulus control.

It was possible to condition a juvenile delinquent to discriminate between a large number of word stimuli using an equally large number of responses, namely the response of reading each of the words. Where can we go from here? We can go from a large number of stimuli and responses to an infinite number of stimuli and responses, and so we shall in the next section. In the final study of that section, an observer was conditioned to touch a target projected on a large viewing screen. The target could assume any one of an infinite number of positions on the viewing screen. Each different position of the target on the screen is a different discriminative stimulus. The response of touching the target on one location of the screen is different from the response of touching it at another location. Therefore each of those touches may be considered a different response. Since there are an infinite number of possible locations, there are also an infinite number of S^Ds and an infinite number of responses.

Pigeons in a Pelican

Warsaw, Poland was ablaze, with buildings tumbling down left and right. When the flames died away, it was apparent that the city had been completely destroyed. Few inhabitants remained alive. This was one of the first great tragedies of World War II. It was 1939. America was gradually realizing that unless something was done, Warsaw, Poland would be repeated many times, not only in Europe, but also in the United States.

Like many Americans, Dr. B. F. Skinner began doing what he could to make sure that it did not happen here. Dr. Skinner's research had been exclusively with animals. Most men in his position would probably have thought they had nothing special to contribute to the war effort. However, Dr. Skinner is an extremely creative and imaginative man. He saw a way in which his research could be applied in the defense of his country against enemy airplanes. At that time the airplane was the most horrible instrument of war; only weak defenses against it were available.

During the early part of the war, the notion of guided missiles was more theoretical than practical. One of the major drawbacks to the development of a guided missile was the lack of a guidance system. The Japanese used humans in this capacity. They trained their kamikaze pilots to crash planes loaded with explosives into targets such as allied ships. Of course the kamikaze pilot sacrificed his life in the process.

Dr. Skinner had the fantastic idea that lower animals could be conditioned to guide missiles.[5] While the notion of sacrificing a "defenseless" animal may be repugnant, you must remember that this was World War II. It was felt that the sacrifice of a few animals was a small price to pay to save the lives of many Americans.

Dr. Skinner selected the pigeon as the animal to be used in the guidance system, since it is small, readily available, and has excellent eyesight. In testing

5. This section based on Skinner, B. F, Pigeons in a pelican. *American Psychologist,* 1960, *15,* 28–37. Reprinted by permission of the author and the American Psychological Association.

out the notion that a pigeon might be able to operate a guidance system, Dr. Skinner conducted some experiments at the University of Minnesota where he was then teaching. A bird was harnessed in a jacket which immobilized it except for the neck and head. Movements of his head operated the control system. When the bird moved its head up, down, left, or right, the control system moved the simulated missile in the corresponding direction. The whole apparatus, mounted on wheels, was pushed across the room to a bull's eye on the far wall. During the approach the pigeon raised or lowered itself or moved from side to side in such a way as to reach the wall and receive a reinforcer in the form of a small amount of grain from the center of the bull's eye. The pigeon learned to hit any target within reach of the hoist, no matter what the starting position. The bird was very accurate even when the "missile" approached the target fairly rapidly. The bird had four responses available to him, that is, four directions in which he could move. Associated with each response was a discriminative stimulus or S^D—the location of the target. If the target was to the left of the bird, that served as an S^D for pointing its head to the left. If the target was above the bird, that served as an S^D for raising its head, etc. Each target location was not only an S^D for the appropriate response, but also an S^Δ for the three inappropriate responses. Therefore the stimulus of the target to the left of the bird was an S^Δ for a head movement to the right or in the upward or downward direction. The situation is not unlike the complex discrimination problem which faced Jesus Delgado. Each word served as an S^D for the correct vocal response and as an S^Δ for all incorrect vocal responses.

The experiment was shown to scientific advisers engaged in early defense activities for the government. They concluded that the project "did not warrant further development at the time."

On December 7, 1941, Americans discovered that Warsaw could happen here; Pearl Harbor was bombed. The next day Dr. Skinner and a graduate student, Keller Breland, decided that they should pursue their project further. After several improvements had been made, they prepared a demonstration film showing birds trained on various types of targets and started looking for government support. The officials responsible for federal scientific research again felt that the project did not warrant support.

In the summer of 1942, the vice-president in charge of research at General Mills, Inc. investigated the work. He thought that the company might, as a patriotic service, develop a pigeon guidance system to the point where a governmental agency could be persuaded to take over. Dr. Skinner and two graduate students moved the project to the top floor of one of General Mills' flour mills in Minneapolis. There they began a very intensive series of experiments. In Dr. Skinner's words,

> We trained the pigeons to follow a variety of land and sea targets, to neglect large patches intended to represent clouds or flak, to concentrate on one target while another was in view, and so on. We found that a pigeon could hold a missile on a particular street intersection in an aerial map of a city. . . .
>
> We found it easy to maintain steady behavior in spite of intense noises and many other distracting conditions, using the simple process of adaptation.

Observers were sent to Minneapolis to see the demonstration. . . . The pigeons as usual behaved beautifully. One of them held the supposed missile on a particular intersection of streets in an aerial map for five minutes although the target would have been lost if the pigeons had paused for a second or two. . . .

At long last, in June, 1943, the office of Scientific Research and Development awarded a modest contract to General Mills, Inc. to "develop a homing device." At that time we were given some information about the missile the pigeons were to guide. . . . (It) was a wing-steered glider, still under development and not yet successfully steered by any homing device.

They were no longer working on a ground-to-air defensive missile but rather an air-to-ground offensive missile. It was called the "Pelican." This is because its guidance system took up so much space that there was practically no room left for the explosives, hence its resemblance to the pelican, whose salient characteristic is its bill.

General Mills engineers devised a much different system than the one described earlier. It had a lens in the nose of the missile which threw an image on a translucent plate within reach of the pigeon in a pressure sealed chamber. The pigeon was to peck at the target. The more off-center the target, the greater the effect of the peck on shifting the missile to the center. If the image moved as little as a quarter of an inch off-center, a properly placed peck at the plate brought the missile back on course. This is a complex discrimination procedure. Each possible location of the target might be considered an S^D for the response of pecking at that location on the translucent plate. There were an infinite number of slightly different locations; consequently, there were an infinite number of discriminative stimuli. A distinct response was associated with each stimulus. The stimuli and responses were, however, all very similar to each other.

By this time we had begun to realize that a pigeon was more easily controlled than a physical scientist serving on a committee. It was very difficult to convince the latter that the former was an orderly system. We therefore multiplied the probability of success by designing a multiple-bird unit. There was adequate space in the nose of the Pelican for three pigeons, each with its own lens and plate. A net signal could easily be generated. The majority vote of the three pigeons offered an excellent guarantee against momentary pauses and aberrations. (We later worked out a system in which the majority took on more characteristically democratic functions. When a missile is flying toward *two* ships at sea, for example, there is no guarantee that all three pigeons will steer toward the same ship. But at least two must agree and the third can be punished for his minority opinion. Under proper contingencies of reinforcement, a punished bird will shift immediately to the majority view. When all three are working on one ship, any defection is immediately punished and corrected.) . . .

The General Mills engineers also built a simulator—a sort of link trainer for pigeons—designed to have the steering characteristics of the Pelican, insofar as these had been communicated to us. Like the wing-steered Pelican, the simulator tilted and turned from side to side. When the three-bird nose was attached to it, the pigeons could be put in full control . . . and the adequacy of the signal tested under pursuit conditions. Targets were moved back and forth across the far wall of a room at prescribed speeds and given patterns of oscillation, and the tracing response of the whole unit was studied quantitatively.

Meanwhile we continued our intensive study of the behavior of the pigeon. Looking ahead to combat use, we designed methods for the mass production of trained birds and for handling large groups of trained subjects. We were proposing to train certain birds for certain classes of targets, such as ships at sea, while special squads were to be trained on special targets, photographs of which were to be obtained through reconnaissance. A large crew of pigeons would then be waiting for an assignment. We developed harnessing and training techniques which would solve such problems quite easily.

By December, 1943, less than six months after the contract was awarded, we were ready to report to the Office of Scientific Research and Development. Observers visited the laboratory and watched the simulator follow a target about a room, under the control of a team of three birds.

The data on the accuracy of the birds' tracking were studied by specialists at the Massachusetts Institute of Technology. One authority exclaimed upon looking at the graphs of the performance of the simulator, "This is better than radar!" Finally they had their "summit meeting" with the decision makers in Washington.

The basic difficulty, of course, lay in convincing a dozen distinguished physical scientists that the behavior of a pigeon could be adequately controlled. We had hoped to score on this point by bringing with us a demonstration. A small black box had a round translucent window in one end. A slide projector placed some distance away threw on the window an image of the New Jersey target. In the box, of course, was a pigeon—which incidentally, had at that time been harnessed for 35 hours. Our intentions were to let each member of the committee observe the response to the target by looking down a small tube; but time was not available for individual observation, and we were asked to take the top off the box. The translucent screen was flooded with so much light that the target was barely visible, and the peering scientists offered conditions much more unfamiliar and threatening than those likely to be encountered in a missile. In spite of this the pigeon behaved perfectly, pecking steadily and energetically at the image of the target as it moved about on the plate.

One scientist with an experimental turn of mind intercepted the beam from the projector. The pigeon stopped instantly. When the image again appeared, pecking began within a fraction of a second and continued at a steady rate.

It was a perfect performance, but it had just the wrong effect. One can talk about phase lag in pursuit behavior and discuss mathematical predictions of hunting without reflecting too closely upon what is inside the black box. But the spectacle of a living pigeon carrying out its assignment, no matter how beautifully, simply reminded the committee of how utterly fantastic our proposal was. I will not say that the meeting was marked by unrestrained merriment, for the merriment was restrained. But it was there, and it was obvious that our case was lost.

One of the scientists closed our presentation with a brief summary: We were offering a homing device, unusually resistant to jamming, capable of reacting to a wide variety of target patterns, requiring no materials in short supply, and so simple to build that production could be started in 30 days. He thanked the committee, and we left. As the door closed behind us, he said to me, "Why don't you go out and get drunk!"

Official word soon came: "Further prosecution of this project would seriously delay others which in the minds of the Division would have more immediate promise of combat applications." Possibly the reference was to a particular combat application at Hiroshima a year and a half later, when it looked for a while as if the need for accurate bombing had been eliminated for all time. In any case we had to show, for all our trouble, only a loft full of curiously useless equipment and a few dozen pigeons with a strange interest in a feature of the New Jersey coast.

Summary

In this chapter we have been considering the process whereby an observer comes to discriminate between various stimulus events. We have seen that the procedure for establishing the discrimination is composed of the familiar processes of conditioning and extinction. The following specific points were made:

1. *Discrimination training* consists of conditioning a response in the presence of one stimulus and extinguishing it in the presence of another.

2. The stimulus associated with reinforcement for a particular response is called a *discriminative stimulus*, or S^D, for that response. The stimulus associated with extinction for a response is an S^Δ for that response.

3. *Discrimination behavior* has been established when the subject is more likely to respond in one stimulus situation than another. When this occurs, we may say that *stimulus control* has been obtained.

4. A special type of stimulus control is involved in *discriminated extinction*. In this situation, the fact that a response is no longer being reinforced acts as an S^Δ for continuing that response. Discriminated extinction can be conditioned by alternating the training periods of conditioning and extinction. Eventually if a single response goes unreinforced, the subject may stop responding immediately.

5. We have studied four types of discrimination procedures which are differentiated by the number of stimuli and responses involved. The simplest procedure was illustrated in conditioning the chicken to fire the gun only when Keller Breland was not in front of the target. This procedure consisted of two stimuli, one S^D and one S^Δ, and a single response.

Another example which involves the same sort of discrimination procedure is that of the pestering behavior. In most cases the S^D was the reinforcing attention which followed pestering and the S^Δ was the absence of such attention. The single response class consisted of pestering. The fact that the stimulus classes and response class involved many individual members should not obscure the fact that this is basically a simple discrimination problem.

One S^Δ, one S^D, and one response are the minimal components needed to establish a discrimination. The remaining procedures simply consist of elaboration of this basic theme.

6. The discrimination training procedure may be made slightly more complicated by adding a second response as was done in the study on teaching Carmen to "read" her name. In this study there were also two stimuli, as before, but an extra response was added. Each stimulus now had a dual role. It served as the S^D for one response and the S^Δ for the other. When the word "Carmen" was on the right and the word "Leslie" on the left, that combination of names served as

the S^D for picking the card on the right. Conversely when the names were reversed, the stimulus combination served as the S^D for picking the card on the left.

7. The procedure was made even more complicated by using a total of 761 discriminative stimulus words in a successful attempt to teach a juvenile delinquent how to read. Each word served as a discriminative stimulus for a particular reading response. It also served as the S^Δ for all other reading responses.

8. Finally, we saw in Dr. Skinner's research on the pigeon as a guidance system for a missile the use of an infinite number of discriminative stimuli with their associated responses. The target could assume any one of an infinite number of slightly different locations on the response plate in the missile. Each location acted as a discriminative stimulus for the response of pecking at that specific location.

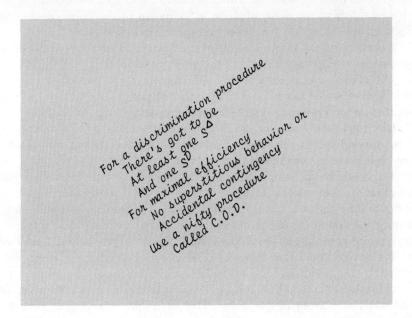

For a discrimination procedure
There's got to be
At least one S^Δ
And one S^D
For maximal efficiency
No superstitious behavior or
Accidental contingency
Use a nifty procedure
Called C.O.D.

QUESTIONS

1. What is a discriminative stimulus?
2. What is an S^D?
3. What is an S^Δ?
4. What is the discrimination training procedure?
5. What is discrimination behavior?
6. What is stimulus control?
7. What species of animal did Keller Breland train?
8. What was the response which was conditioned?
9. What is the technical name for the procedure he used?
10. What was the S^D?
11. What was the S^Δ?
12. How many stimuli and how many responses were used in this study?

13. What was the reinforcement?
14. What were the results of this training?
15. Is *rate* of response ever recorded in discrimination experiments?
16. If you really want to be popular with people, what you should do is go around explaining to them how their behavior is under the control of its reinforcing consequences. (a) True; (b) False.
17. What were examples of things which people did when Winston pestered them?
18. In short we can say that when Winston pestered people they pa———— at————to him.
19. Attention acts as a very powerful r————.
20. What did the tricky psychologist do each time Winston pestered him?
21. What is the technical name for this procedure?
22. Did Winston's behavior extinguish rapidly or slowly?
23. Such rapid extinction might be the result of what kind of schedule of reinforcement?
24. On the other hand, rapid extinction might be an example of d———— e————.
25. If this is an example of discriminated extinction, what is the S^D and what is the S^Δ?
26. How would such discriminated extinction be established?
27. What would be an example of discriminated extinction which you have undoubtedly experienced?
28. A large variety of different sorts of stimuli made up the S^D for the pestering response; the stimulus class was very large. (a) True; (b) False.
29. Was the response class of pestering very large?
30. How many different stimulus classes were involved in the study of pestering?
31. How many different classes of responses?
32. What was the technical name of the procedure used to teach Carmen how to "read" her name?
33. What were the two specific responses that were conditioned?
34. What was the S^D for picking the card on the right?
35. What was the S^Δ for picking that card?
36. What happened when Carmen made the wrong response?
37. What were the two events which were combined to act as a reinforcer?
38. What were the final results of this study?
39. How long did this training procedure take? (a) 8 trials; (b) 80 trials; (c) 800 trials; (d) 8,000 trials.
40. How many stimuli and how many responses were used in this study?
41. Briefly describe Jesus Delgado's home life.
42. Briefly describe Jesus Delgado's relation to the school and personnel.
43. Briefly describe his relation to the juvenile correction department.
44. What kind of grades did Jesus get before this special study was started?
45. In very general terms, what was the goal of the study?
46. What was the technical name of the procedure used?
47. Each written word was an S^D for what response?
48. Each written word was an S^Δ for what response?
49. Arrange the following phases of the training procedure in the order in which they occurred. (a) Silent reading; (b) Oral reading; (c) Questions over the readings; (d) Learning the new vocabulary words.
50. Generally speaking, the tokens were to act as re————.

51. Why were the tokens of any value to Jesus?
52. This training procedure lasted: (a) 4½ hours; (b) 4½ days; (c) 4½ months; (d) 4½ years.
53. The total amount of time spent reading was: (a) 4 minutes; (b) 4 hours; (c) 40 hours; (d) 400 hours.
54. During the silent reading phase, what was done to make sure that Jesus was looking at the page?
55. What was done to facilitate Jesus' actually being silent during the silent reading? In other words, what was done to reduce the frequency of the small vocal sounds and lip movements?
56. What check was made to be sure that Jesus was actually reading during the silent reading phase?
57. Approximately how many words did Jesus learn to read? (a) 5; (b) 50; (c) 500; (d) 5,000.
58. In the 8½ years that Jesus was in school prior to this special training phase, what grade level had he achieved in reading? (a) 0.0; (b) 2.0; (c) 7.0; (d) 8.0; (e) 12.0.
59. During the training, he progressed to what grade level in reading? (a) 1.8; (b) 4.0; (c) 8.0; (d) 12.0.
60. What happened to the grades Jesus got in the other courses during the training period?
61. What happened to Jesus' behavior problems in school during the training phase?
62. In Dr. Skinner's research which we discussed in this chapter, what species of animal did he use?
63. What weapon was this animal to be used with?
64. How was the animal to be used with the weapon? In other words, what purpose did the animal serve?
65. How did the pigeon control the first system which Dr. Skinner tested?
66. What were the discriminative stimuli involved?
67. What was the reinforcement?
68. Each stimulus served simultaneously as an S^D and an S^Δ. Give an example of this.
69. As soon as scientific experts in Washington got wind of Dr. Skinner's patriotic efforts, they enthusiastically gave him their wholehearted support. (a) True; (b) False.
70. One problem which Skinner could not lick was the extreme distractibility which the pigeons showed through intense noises. (a) True; (b) False.
71. What was the name of the missile which Dr. Skinner finally worked with?
72. Why did it receive its name?
73. How many discriminative stimuli were used in the procedure for this new missile?
74. What were the discriminative stimuli?
75. How many responses were used?
76. What were the responses?
77. How did the pigeon control the missile?
78. How did Dr. Skinner multiply the likelihood that the missile would accurately hit its target?
79. At the "summit meeting" in Washington, the scientists took off the top of the demonstration box, thus flooding the screen with so much light that the pigeon performed terribly. (a) True; (b) False.
80. If it were not for Dr. Skinner's contribution to the war effort, we might now be speaking German. (a) True; (b) False.

81. In the four studies presented in this chapter, four different discrimination procedures were used. Describe them in terms of the number of stimuli and responses involved in each procedure.

82. Give five examples of stimulus discrimination in your everyday life which are not taken from a psychology textbook.

83. Give five examples from your school work which involve learning new discriminations.

84. On the basis of this chapter, can you suggest some procedures which would improve the learning of discriminations in your school work? If you cannot, keep thinking until you can.

85. What is a discrimination which you have particular difficulty in making but which you would like to master?

86. Design a procedure for training yourself to master that discrimination. Make it a plausible procedure which you could in fact use.

NOTES

It is possible that, as a novice animal trainer, you would have difficulty developing stimulus control as good as that exhibited by Dr. Breland's chickens. A problem frequently encountered is that, although food reinforcement is withheld, the animal still responds occasionally in S^Δ. You might be using a procedure in which the S^Δ is presented for 30 seconds and then the S^D is presented. When the subject responds, the reinforcement is delivered and the S^Δ is again presented for 30 seconds; these two stimuli alternate in that manner. It is likely that you will find your animal responding at a fairly high rate toward the end of each S^Δ period. It may look as if the animal is on a 30 second fixed-interval schedule of reinforcement. A fixed-interval scallop may even develop. This is an example of superstitious behavior. What is the reinforcement? We will see in a later chapter that the opportunity to work for a food reinforcement can itself become conditioned to be a reinforcer. In other words, the S^D becomes a learned or conditioned reinforcer. Since the S^D is reliably presented at the end of each 30 second S^Δ period, we have set up a situation which is ideal for superstitious conditioning of some behavior. Because the key-peck response is the response which is most likely to occur in S^Δ during the early stages of training, it is that response which is most likely to be superstitiously conditioned. This frequently happens.

One way to avoid the superstitious conditioning of the key-peck response in S^Δ is to condition some other behavior in its place. We can use the procedure called differential reinforcement of other behavior As long as the animal continues key pecking during S^Δ, the S^D is withheld. As soon as 30 seconds have elapsed in S^Δ with the continuous occurrence of behavior other than the key-peck response, the other behavior is reinforced by the presentation of the S^D. Such a procedure frequently results in some other specific response being conditioned such as prancing back and forth in front of the key during the S^Δ.

A View from the Balcony

It should be emphasized that the cases of Winston and Steve are anecdotal. Although I accurately reported the data, these cases were not scientific experiments. We did not actually manipulate the variables which we thought were controlling the children's pestering behavior. While I am almost certain that the attention which they received for pestering was controlling the frequency of the pestering responses, I am not positive. I withheld attention and they did not pester. Other people did pay attention to them when they pestered and were pestered for their efforts. This is fairly strong evidence that the attention was acting as a reinforcer for the undesirable response. It may be, however, that my fierce demeanor discourages young children from pestering. Had I been willing to undergo the ordeal, I might have done a controlled experiment. On some days I would pay attention to them by asking them not to pester me, etc. On other days I would ignore them. I would expect that the pestering rate would increase during the conditioning phase, when I asked them not to bother me. During the extinction phase, when I ignored them, it should decrease.

However, more speculation is involved as to the nature of the rapid extinction of pestering when I ignored them. It is possible that this is simple extinction. Their rate of extinction may have been very rapid because they had been on continuous reinforcement for tormenting their victims. Another possibility would be that they have encountered persons who at first ignored them and then spanked them or used some other effective punishment. In other words, it is possible that my lack of attention could have acted as a discriminative stimulus indicating that punishment would soon be on its way if they continued their misbehavior. Whether these or other possible explanations of the rapid decrease in their pestering response are correct can only be determined through experimentation. This is one of the major limitations of the anecdotal observation. At best it allows for *mere conjecture* about the nature of the controlling variables.

The Name Game

We spoke of the study in which Carmen was taught to discriminate between the name "Carmen" and the name "Leslie" as an attempt to teach her to "read." You will notice that we were careful to put quotation marks around the word "read" to indicate that we were using the term in its most general sense, perhaps even stretching its use slightly. In spite of the vocal instructions which the graduate student gave Carmen, it is quite possible that she found no association between the printed word "Carmen," the spoken word "Carmen," and herself. It may be that the printed word "Carmen" simply served as part of the configuration for picking a particular card. Even if there were an association between the printed and spoken words and Carmen herself, we would probably want the child to be able to respond appropriately to the words in various sentences before feeling justified in saying that we had a full-fledged reading discrimination.

The present method of analyzing discrimination procedures differs somewhat from the traditional method in its designation of the S^D and S^Δ. This may best be seen in the study on teaching Carmen to "read" her name. The two methods are illustrated in Figure 8-2.

In our analysis, one combination of the two names was an S^D for picking the card on the right and an S^Δ for picking the card on the left. For the other combination of the names, this situation was reversed.

More traditionally, one part of the stimulus configuration, the word "Carmen," is designated as the S^D for picking up that card and the other part of the stimulus configuration, the word "Leslie," is designated as the S^Δ for picking up that card. The word "Carmen" is always considered the S^D and the word "Leslie" is always considered the S^Δ regardless of their location.

With that analysis, it seems quite appropriate to speak of conditioning the ob-

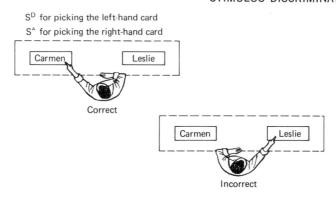

S^D for picking the left-hand card
S^Δ for picking the right-hand card

Carmen   Leslie

Correct

Carmen   Leslie

Incorrect

Figure 8-2   Name discrimination training trial for a retarded girl

server to discriminate between the names "Carmen" and "Leslie." With our analysis, it may seem more appropriate to speak of conditioning the observer to discriminate between one combination of the two names and the other combination.

In a traditional analysis of Dr. Breland's demonstration with the chicken, the expression "successive discrimination" is appropriate. The S^D and the S^Δ stimuli are presented successively. A similar analysis of teaching Carmen to "read" her name would speak of the simultaneous presentation of the stimuli to be discriminated, that is the S^D and the S^Δ. On the other hand, our analysis would suggest that both procedures involve the successive presentation of stimuli to be discriminated. In the first case, the S^D and the S^Δ are presented successively. In the second case, each stimulus serves concurrently as both an S^D and S^Δ, but the two stimulus configurations are presented successively and not simultaneously. While the present analysis may seem cumbersome, it is anticipated that it will facilitate the study of other discrimination phenomenon. Only further experimentation will tell which formulation is most useful.

9

STIMULUS GENERALIZATION AND CONCEPT FORMATION

Norm sat there, staring at one bottle of beer after another. They came down the conveyor belt past him with tedious regularity. He stared through each one into a bright light placed on the other side of the conveyor belt.

"I thought when I got a job on the inspection line at a brewery, it would be a real ball. Man, it's a drag."

After several minutes and several dozen beer bottles had passed, he noticed something wrong with one bottle. He picked it up and tossed it into the reject barrel. "That's the most excitement I've had around here in the last half hour. I've had some bad jobs but this one is really a loser. I sit here day after day looking at those damned beer bottles, and I'm lucky if I find two or three bottles a day to reject. Big deal. Probably most of the bad bottles get by me anyhow. Somehow, after I've been staring at those bottles for an hour or so, I can't seem to concentrate on them—even when they're right in front of my eyes. I'll bet all sorts of things slip by me."

The preceding reflections on the highlights in the life of an assembly line inspector were reported by a friend after a summer job inspecting beer bottles at a Minneapolis distillery. The life of the assembly line inspector is a grim one. Not only does he have extremely tedious, boring work, but he inevitably does a poor job. He usually misses more bad items than he catches. Nearly every factory has assembly line inspectors and they are all faced with this problem. The quality of their work is almost as low as the morale.

When situations like this develop, they should be corrected. Not only is the low quality of work undesirable, but it is also unfortunate when human beings have to spend 40 hours each week of their life engaged in activities which they detest. For these reasons, psychologists have begun working on the problem of assembly line inspection. One approach will be discussed in the next section.

The Inspector

During a holiday a few years ago, Dr. William Cumming, an experimental psychologist from Columbia University, was having a pleasant conversation with an engineer from a large industrial concern.[1] As frequently happens among professionals, they eventually began talking shop. The conversation may have been something like the following:

Dr. Cumming asked, "How's your work going these days?"

"Well, automation is getting into everything. Recently I've been working on the automation of some of our manufacturing facilities."

"Is it going all right?"

"By and large, we're getting most of the processes automated. It's really pretty easy, but we've found it almost impossible to automate assembly line inspection."

"What's the problem?"

"It would be easy if all of the flaws of the parts being inspected were identical. Then we wouldn't have much difficulty in building a machine to inspect the parts. The problem is that each flaw is a little different from the next one. It's almost impossible to build a machine to detect all the various flaws. We could build the machine, but it would cost so much and be so complicated that it's just not worth it."

"What kind of flaws and what kind of parts do you work with?"

"Any particular part might have several different types of flaws, and the nature of the flaws will vary tremendously from part to part. Of course, we have a wide range of parts; but one example would be small electronic parts such as diodes. The diode is normally painted solid black; however, occasionally, the paint will be imperfect and the silver metal will show through. Now if it were just a question of building a machine to tell the difference between a completely painted and a completely unpainted diode, that would not be too difficult. But sometimes a diode is completely painted, sometimes it is completely unpainted, sometimes half of it is painted, and sometimes there's only a tiny scratch in the paint. It's just not practical to build a machine to automatically detect so many different types of paint flaws, so we have people doing it. Of course, they hate the job and do very poorly at it. I wish we could lick this problem."

Dr. Cumming chuckled to himself.

"What's so funny?" the engineer asked.

"Oh, it's nothing. Just a little joke, which had best be kept private."

"Now you've got my curiosity aroused. What is it?"

"I just had a crazy idea about how you might automate your inspection process."

"What's your idea?"

1. This section based on Cumming, William W. A bird's eye glimpse of man and machines. In R. Ulrich, T. Stachnik, and J. Mabry (Eds), *Control of Human Behavior*. Glenview: Scott Foresman, 1966, 246–256.

"Well, what you need is a device that has a good visual discrimination system and can form concepts."

"What do you mean by concepts?"

"An example of a pair of concepts might be good parts and bad parts. A device that had these concepts would treat all specific stimuli which constitute the concept of bad parts in one manner—it would reject them. It would treat all specific stimuli which fall under the concept of good parts in a different category—it would accept them. It would discriminate between examples of the concept of good part and examples of the concept of bad part. It would treat all examples of a particular concept in the same manner. For example, the device might discriminate between the concepts of good apples and bad apples. It would sort apples by rejecting the bad ones."

"That's exactly what we need. What device did you have in mind?"

"Engineers always think about replacing human drudgery with electromechanical devices which will do the work. But there are biological systems which may sometimes be more feasible."

"I'm not sure I follow you. Do you mean use an animal instead of a machine to do the work?"

"Precisely. There are many animals that have excellent visual systems and should be able to form the sorts of concepts that we are talking about."

"Perhaps, but the kind of animal that would be capable of something that complicated would be almost as expensive as a human. You'd need something like a gorilla or an orangutan, one of the higher apes, in order to do that."

"I doubt it. I suspect that the humble pigeon could do the job just as well."

"That's so fantastic that I find it a little hard to believe."

"Pigeons have excellent vision; it's almost identical to ours. They are also quite capable of forming concepts."

"The vision I can believe, but the concept formation seems a little farfetched. Has anything like this ever been done before?"

"No, but Skinner has taught pigeons how to guide missiles, so I think we could teach them how to inspect parts on an assembly line."

"It's a good trick if you can do it."

"Not only could we do it, but it would also be very economical. Pigeons will work for chicken feed."

Then the conversation drifted on to other topics less like science fiction. Dr. Cumming assumed that was the end of the topic and thought no more about it. But his seeds of speculation had fallen on fertile soil. A week later, he received a long distance telephone call from the engineer.

"It's about those pigeon inspectors on the assembly line."

"Yeah."

"Were you serious?"

"Well, I was joking, but I do think it could be done."

"How would you like to see if you really could get pigeons to detect bad paint jobs on the diodes?"

"Now it's my turn. Are you serious?"

"Deadly. When I went home the other day, I couldn't stop thinking about that damned idea of yours. I talked it over with some of the people at the company. They were skeptical, but a few of the men thought it was at least worth looking into. The company could supply the apparatus and also funds to hire the help that you would need."

"I don't know. I'm really head over heels in work with my basic research, and I'm not sure that I should take on another project, but I'll give it a try. Besides, I would like to convince your skeptics that my idea is not as crazy as it seems."

The procedure which Dr. Cumming proposed was a discrimination procedure. But it was a little more complicated than the usual discrimination procedure which uses a single S^D and a single S^Δ. Instead of two individual stimuli, we have two classes of stimuli. The notion of stimulus class parallels that of response class. A *stimulus class* consists of a set of stimuli, all of which have some common property. In this experiment, one set of stimuli, the bad parts, had the common physical property of a paint flaw. This stimulus class also had a common behavioral property; all of the bad parts served as S^Ds for the response of rejecting them. They served as S^Δs for the response of accepting them. Similarly, the stimulus class of good parts consisted of parts which had no paint flaws. They served as S^Ds for accepting them and as S^Δs for rejecting them. Another name for "stimulus class" is *concept*.

We say that *conceptual behavior* is occurring when the observer responds the same way to all of the stimuli in a stimulus class but does not respond in that way to stimuli outside of that class.

When the observer responds in a similar manner to different stimuli, we say that *stimulus generalization* is occurring. Suppose a bird has been conditioned to reject one bad part with a particular paint scratch. He may also reject another bad part with a different paint scratch. The training or the conditioning with the one bad part generalized to the other bad part. In this terminology, *conceptual behavior* consists of generalization within a concept or stimulus class and discrimination among concepts or stimulus classes.

In order to condition conceptual behavior, we must reinforce one response in the presence of one stimulus class or concept and extinguish that response in the presence of all other stimulus classes or concepts. If we wish, we may also condition other responses in the presence of the other stimulus classes. This is precisely what Dr. Cumming did. The company built a special miniature assembly line inspection system for his laboratory. The pigeons stood in a small enclosure and looked through a window at a parts conveyor. The conveyor brought a part before the window. If the part had a paint flaw, the bird was to peck the window. The window also acted as a response key so that food reinforcement would be delivered. Then the conveyor would bring a new part before the window for inspection. If the paint was good, the pigeon was to peck a response key to one side of the window. This simply caused the conveyor belt to bring up a new part for inspection.

A bad part served as the S^D for making the rejection response, pecking the window; it served as the S^Δ for making the acceptance response, pecking the side key. The reinforcement for rejecting a bad part was the presentation of a small amount of food.

Similarly, a good part served as the S^D for making an acceptance response and as the S^Δ for making a rejection response. What was the reinforcement for correctly accepting a good part? Whenever a good part was accepted, a new part came into place for inspection. New parts sometimes meant that the bird would soon be earning a reinforcement. Consequently, these new parts might come to acquire some of the reinforcing properties of food; they would themselves act as a learned or conditioned reinforcer. We will consider the notion of conditioned reinforcement in greater detail in a later chapter.

We have been discussing the consequences of making a correct response in the presence of the two S^Ds. What happened if the bird made a mistake? Two things occurred. First, reinforcement was withheld, and second, punishment was delivered. In other words, whenever the pigeon rejected a good part or accepted a bad part, this incorrect response was punished.

The type of punishment which Dr. Cumming used was particularly interesting. Whenever the bird made a mistake, Dr. Cumming prevented him from working. That was the punishment. The lights in the pigeon's chamber were turned off for a 20 second period; during that time, further responses had no effect. In the words of a magazine writer visiting the laboratory, "This upset him. If the door were open, he would sadly leave the work station. When the light went on again, he would hop back [and] start to work."[2] It is not clear what a sad pigeon looks like, but it is an interesting notion.

You might personally feel that being unable to work should be more of a reinforcement than a punishment. Does this mean that you are lazier than the pigeon? Probably not; at least not in most cases. If you had not eaten for a while and were working for your meal, you would also be disappointed when the lights went out and you could not work.

Dr. Cumming initially conditioned the pigeons to discriminate between a completely painted and a completely unpainted part. Since these stimuli were completely different, they were readily discriminated. Very little generalization occurred between these highly dissimilar stimuli. Only after a good discrimination had been established between highly dissimilar parts did Dr. Cumming dare introduce parts with only minor flaws in their paint. Such stimuli were so similar to the good parts that there would have been a large amount of stimulus generalization between the two types of stimuli. In that case, a good discrimination would not easily be formed. *Generally, when two stimuli are physically very similar, considerable generalization will occur between such stimuli and good discrimination behavior will be difficult to establish. If two stimuli are completely different, there may be only a small amount of stimulus generalization between them, and a good discrimination will be established easily.*

As may be seen from the preceding account, *generalization is the opposite of discrimination.* If an observer responds in nearly the same way to two different stimuli, then he is showing a large amount of generalization and very little discrimination. On the other hand, an observer may respond quite differently in the presence of two different stimuli. In that case, he is showing considerable dis-

2. Anonymous. This inspector is a bird. *Factory*, December, 1959.

Calling the garbageman daddy
May be generalization
Adding to your father's consternation.
Calling the milkman daddy
May be embarrassing too
Especially if your mommy's home
And in this case it's really true.

Stimulus Control
Is very great
When different stimuli
Control a different rate

crimination and very little generalization. The greater the amount of discrimination, the less the amount of generalization and vice versa.

The farsighted reader may be saying to himself, "This pigeon inspection system is for the birds. It's okay in the laboratory, but it won't work in the factory. In the laboratory, you have an all-knowing experimenter who can tell whether a part is good or bad and can reinforce or punish the pigeon's response as is appropriate. But you will not have this experimenter in the factory. You want the pigeon to tell you whether the parts are good or bad, but with your method you have to have someone looking at the parts and delivering reinforcement every time the pigeon makes the correct rejection response. You might as well throw out the pigeon and hire the experimenter."

Come now, you do not really think that we would include an experiment with such an obvious flaw?

"Not knowingly," you say.

Then what is the solution?

Intermittent reinforcement. A schedule of continuous reinforcement and punishment had been used so that each correct response was reinforced and each incorrect one punished. After the conceptual behavior was well established, a variable ratio schedule was introduced. The variable ratio was gradually increased to a mean of 50. An average of 1 out of 50 correct responses was reinforced and also 1 out of 50 incorrect responses was punished.

How does intermittent reinforcement help us in the factory? We could have 2 percent of the parts coded. The coded parts would be identified so that a machine could tell whether they were good or bad parts. Reinforcement or punishment would depend upon the bird's response to these coded parts. In a factory, the parts could be mixed in with each new batch of uncoded parts and then removed and randomly placed back in the next batch of parts to be inspected. In that manner, an accurate discrimination could be maintained with only a small amount of effort. Dr. Cumming found that if only 2 percent of the parts were coded, the bird could maintain a high level of accuracy on the uncoded ones.

But just how accurate were the birds? They were between 95 percent and 98 percent accurate. Although no formal data are available on the accuracy of human inspectors on the assembly line, it is known that they do not do nearly as well as the pigeons. Of course, the accuracy of a pigeon inspection system could be greatly increased by having several birds inspect each part with a procedure somewhat like the one used by Dr. Skinner. You recall that the majority vote of three birds was needed to guide the Pelican missile. A majority vote of three birds could also be required before a part could be accepted or rejected.

Some of the birds were able to inspect at a rate of over one thousand parts per hour. They could maintain this high rate and high accuracy for at least four hours in a row without a coffee break. Since the experimenter was always exhausted by the end of the four hour session, he was unable to see how much longer the birds could work; but the birds were still going strong at the end of the session.

Does this company now have pigeons working in their factory? No. The experimental project was a complete success; the birds could be readily trained, they learned the concept of good and bad parts, they were able to discriminate very accurately, they could inspect parts at a high rate, they were inexpensive to train and maintain, and yet the executive decision was that no use of the procedure could be made within the company.

> There are many reasons for hesitation about the introduction of animal inspection into an industry, and one or more of these may have contributed to this action. Animals represent a whole new technology for organizations not already prepared to undertake the humane care and feeding required. There are the animal lovers to think of—a vocal lot even when it can be demonstrated, as in this case, that the animals loved their work. Then there is the matter of organized labor and its reaction to such an innovation. And, of course, there is the consumer on whom the industry depends. What would his reaction be? The buyer of produce is known to be a fickle organism and not so easily manipulated as the industrious pigeon.

At about the same time, Dr. Thom Verhave, a psychopharmacologist at a large pharmaceutical company, was teaching pigeons to inspect capsules which had been coded.[3] In that case, only one week of discrimination training was needed to get the birds to discriminate correctly 98 percent of the time.

3. Verhave, T. The pigeon as a quality control inspector. In R. Ulrich, T. Stachnik, and J. Mabry (Eds.), *Control of Human Behavior.* Glenview: Scott Foresman, 1966, 242–246.

Are pigeons now being used to inspect capsules at the pharmaceutical company? No. Management decided that the idea of pigeons inspecting their pills might be too much for the public to swallow.

In the preceding chapter, we saw that in spite of the excellent work that Dr. Staats and Mr. Butterfield did in teaching the juvenile delinquent to read, the boy was sent to a training school where his abilities probably remained undeveloped. In spite of the excellent results which Dr. Skinner obtained in teaching pigeons to guide the Pelican missile, the project was junked. In spite of the tremendous success which Dr. Cumming and Dr. Verhave had in conditioning their pigeons to work as assembly line inspectors, the projects were terminated. What manner of organism is the psychologist? Is he not subject to the process of extinction? Yes, but let us be thankful for that occasional intermittent reinforcement.

We have seen how generalization and discrimination can be combined to yield a procedure for concept training. A concept consists of discrimination between two classes of stimuli and generalization within each class. All members of the same class of stimuli are responded to in the same manner whereas members of a different class of stimuli are responded to differently.

This concept of "concept" has extreme generality. Very rarely do we have opportunities for repeated discrimination between two stimuli where the S^D and the S^Δ remain the same. Since no two things are identical, these stimuli change slightly from time to time.

The problem of the identity of repeated experiences was raised in a philosophy course which I took as an undergraduate at Indiana University. The teacher seemed to enjoy perplexing his students. It may be that philosophers find it more reinforcing to invent paradoxes than to solve them. This particular professor gleefully raised the following question:

> How can it be that we call a penny a "penny?" How is it that we are always able to recognize a penny for what it is, regardless of the angle at which we view it or the brightness of light in which we view it? Each time we look at a penny, we look at it in a slightly different manner, yet we always recognize it as a penny. Furthermore, we never confuse it with a quarter.

At the time, this seemed to be a profound problem. How could things be different and yet be the same: how could these different stimuli all be called a penny? The answer is stimulus generalization.

To the extent that stimuli are physically similar, they will be responded to in a similar manner; stimulus generalization will occur. If various pennies are physically similar, there will be generalization among them and they will all be responded to as pennies. To the degree that pennies are different from other coins, they will be responded to differently; discrimination will occur.

It is possible that the physical similarity between the various views of the same coin will not be great enough to produce much generalization. In that case concept training may be involved in which reinforcement occurs whenever the coin is properly responded to no matter from what angle it is being viewed. After a small amount of concept training of this sort, a penny should nearly always be called a "penny."

During World War II, our government attempted to save copper by making pennies of lead. Being "white," they were more similar to nickels than were the standard copper pennies; more stimulus generalization consequently took place. Frequently people responded to pennies as though they were nickels. It was my experience that this occurred more often when people were giving me change than when they were receiving coins from me.

In this section we have seen how pigeons can be conditioned to form the concepts of good parts and bad parts. In the next section, we will see that they can form a much more difficult concept: that of "man."

The Pecking Pigeon People Peeper

What is man? Plato defined man as a two-legged animal without feathers. Sly Diogenes then picked the feathers from a chicken and brought it to the academy.

The academicians took notice and realized they would have to change their definition. They thought for a while. "Man is a two-legged animal without feathers but with broad flat nails," they ultimately pronounced.

With only a few moments work, you can think of exceptions to this rule. You can think of a creature that fits the rule but is not a man. You can also think of a creature that does not fit the rule but is a man. Certainly you can. A chimpanzee fits the rule but is not man. A person without arms or legs does not fit the rule but is a man.

It may well be an impossible task to give a set of rules which describes and defines the concept of "man." Interestingly enough, we correctly use the concept of "man" even though we cannot give a good explicit definition. It seems that almost intuitively we know what a man is. This illustrates what we mean when we say that we are doing something according to intuition. When we *behave intuitively*, we are responding in accord with some concept which we cannot define. For example, "I may not be an artist, but I know what good art is." The speaker would probably be hard put to give you a set of rules which would allow you to select good art from bad art; yet he may be able to make such discriminations quite reliably. He has the "intuitive" concepts of good and bad art.

How do we learn such intuitive concepts if no one knows the rules defining the concept? It probably goes something like this: The young child correctly points to a man or a picture of a man. He says, "Man," and is reinforced by his parents' approval. When he points to a picture of a chimpanzee and says, "Man," he is told "No." After many trials of this sort, he may come to form the intuitive concept of man. This process has been demonstrated in a very interesting experiment by Dr. Herrnstein and Dr. Loveland at Harvard University.[4]

These experimental psychologists showed that even pigeons could master the concept of "man." To be more exact, they mastered the concept of "picture of man." Of course, at the same time they mastered the concept of "nonman."

4. This section based on Herrnstein, R. J., and Loveland, D. H. Complex visual concept in the pigeon. *Science*, 1964, *146*, 549–551.

They used a straightforward conditioning procedure. A wide variety of pictures were projected on a viewing screen in the pigeon's test chamber. Pecking a response key was reinforced when the pictures projected on the screen contained people. The response was not reinforced when the pictures did not contain people. Pictures containing people served as the S^D for the key peck response, whereas pictures without people served as the S^Δ. The photographs were taken in a wide variety of natural settings, such as countrysides, cities, expanses of water, lawns, and meadows. Many of the human beings were:

> partly obscured by objects such as trees, automobiles, window frames and so on. The people were distributed throughout the pictures; in the center or to one side or the other, near the top or the bottom, close up or distant. Some [pictures] contained a single person; others contained groups of various sizes. The people themselves varied in appearance: They were clothed, seminude, or nude; adults, or children; men or women; sitting, standing, or lying; black, white, or yellow. Lighting and coloration varied: Some [pictures] were dark, others light; some had either reddish or blueish tints, and so on.

As you can see, a tremendous variety of stimuli were used. The S^Ds contained many different specific examples of humans, and the S^Δs contained many nonhuman pictures.

The concept of man is a very complex concept and, to my knowledge, this is the first attempt to teach such a complex concept to a lower organism. The birds, however, mastered the discrimination rapidly. In fact, occasionally when the birds appeared to make mistakes, the experimenters looked more closely and obscured in some corner of the picture, there would be a human. The pigeons were about as good as the experimenters at detecting the presence of humans in the pictures.

We have seen that the pigeons were able to discriminate between the concept of human and the concept of nonhuman. This concept did not hold just for the specific stimuli used in training. After considerable conditioning, when a new picture of a person or a nonperson was shown, the birds responded correctly to it. This is one of the most important aspects of conceptual behavior. It provides a means for responding correctly in novel situations.

Frequently critics of the stimulus-response approach to psychology, which we have been presenting, feel that this approach is too limited. They do not see how stimulus-response psychology can explain the occurrence of appropriate responses in new situations which the organism has never previously experienced. We see, however, that the notions of stimulus generalization and concept formation give us a mechanism whereby an organism can be trained in a variety of specific situations, can form a concept, and then can respond appropriately to an entirely new situation. The training generalizes to these new situations.

If our behavior was so limited that we could respond correctly only in situations in which we had been specifically trained, we would be severely handicapped. Every day we find ourselves in new situations slightly different from any we have previously experienced. However, they are also slightly similar. They generally fall within some concept. It might be the concept of dining room, food, classroom, teacher, or classmate. Our conditioning in the presence of earlier examples of the concept generalizes to the new instance and we respond accordingly. As we have seen, this valuable ability to form generalized concepts is not only available to humans; it is also available to the lowly pigeon. The pigeons responded quite well when they were shown new pictures not previously experienced.

Pigeons can form the relatively simple concepts of good and bad parts. They can also form the much more subtle and complex concepts of human and nonhuman. We do not know the exact limitations of the pigeon's concept of human. For example, what would happen if they were shown a picture of a scarecrow or a chimpanzee. Would the bird classify these as human or nonhuman? It may well be that if they did not have specific training using such examples, they might have difficulty with the concept; but then so might we. Without specific discrimination training, we might generalize from man to chimpanzee and scarecrow.

This concept formation experiment has some far-reaching implications. What are the limits to the complexity of the concepts which pigeons might be taught? Can they learn such concepts as good and bad art, justice, love, honor, and reinforcement? Only future research will answer these questions.

The Perceptive Pigeon

Look at the two lines in Figure 9-1. Which line appears to be the shorter? Correct; the line with the arrowheads, the one on the right, appears shorter. However, if you care to measure them, you will see that they are the same length. This is a perceptual illusion. When the arrowheads are placed on the ends of the line, it appears shorter than when straight vertical lines are placed there. This phenomenon is known as the *Mueller-Lyer illusion.*

For the first three years of my teaching career, I taught a course in learning and a course in perception at Denison University. In the learning course we discussed topics such as stimulus generalization and in the perception course we discussed various illusions such as the Mueller-Lyer illusion. For the first year I kept worrying about the relation between perception and stimulus generalization. I "knew" that there must be some sort of relation, but I could not figure it out. You might say that I felt stimulus generalization and perception belonged to the same intuitive concept. What I wanted to do was make the concept less intuitive and more explicit.

During my first summer at Dension, I prepared a research grant proposal to study the relations between perception and stimulus generalization.[5] The potential reinforcement of receiving a research grant was very effective in getting my

5. This section based on Malott, R. W., and Malott, Marilyn Kay. An analysis of the Mueller-Lyer illusion in terms of stimulus generalization. Paper read at APA in San Francisco, California, 1968; and Malott, R. W., Malott, Marilyn Kay, and Pokrzywinski, J. The effects of outward pointing arrowheads on the Mueller-Lyer illusion in pigeons. *Psychonomic Science,* 1967, 9, 55–56.

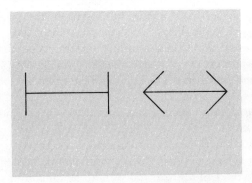

Figure 9-1 A perceptual illusion

thinking behavior to occur at a higher rate. I finally hit upon the notion of studying perceptual phenomena like the Mueller-Lyer illusion with animals. Most of the research on stimulus generalization was done with animals, and most of the research on perception was done with humans. It seemed to me that perception experiments with animals might help relate generalization to perception.

In human perception experiments, we asked the observer which of the two lines appeared to be longer. But we cannot do that with pigeons. They do not understand English, not even pidgin English. If we want to know how something appears to a pigeon, we cannot simply ask. We must be more devious. It seemed likely that I would have to devise some sort of conditioning procedure involving stimulus generalization. In other words, the relations between perception and stimulus generalization might be that stimulus generalization experiments can be used to study perceptual phenomena.

What I wanted was to be able to show the bird a number of lines of various lengths with arrowheads on their ends. I wanted the bird to select the line with the arrowheads which appeared to be the same length as another line with flat end pieces. Suppose the line with the flat ends was 1.3 centimeters long. The bird might then select a line of arrowheads which was a little longer, say 1.5 centimeters. A 1.5 centimeter line with arrowheads would appear to be the same length as a 1.3 centimeter line with flat ends. This means that when the two lines are the same length, the lines with the arrowheads would appear shorter. The bird would be experiencing the Mueller-Lyer illusion.

I thought that I might condition the bird to peck a response key when, for example, a 1.3 centimeter line with flat ends was projected behind it. Then during a generalization test, I could project lines of different lengths with arrowheads on them. I would record the response rate in the presence of each line length. The line length that appeared the most similar to the one the bird had been trained on should have the highest response rate. If that line length was 1.3 centimeters, the same length as the line with the flat ends, we would have to conclude that the arrowheads had no effect; the Mueller-Lyer illusion had *not* been demonstrated. If the response rate was greatest for some longer line, say 1.5 centimeters, we could conclude that the arrowheads had an effect; the Mueller-Lyer illusion had been demonstrated.

After six months, I finally heard from the National Institute of Mental Health. They had approved my research grant. During the next six months, I built the equipment needed for the research. Finally, a year after the initial ideas had been developed, my wife and I were able to begin our research with the help of some undergraduate psychology students at Denison University.

First, we shaped the pigeons' key-peck response. Then we conditioned a discrimination between a 1.3 centimeter horizontal line with flat ends, the S^D, and a blank key, S^Δ. This was done to ensure that the pigeon was actually paying attention to the line projected behind the key. After only a few hours of training, a good discrimination was established; the birds practically never responded unless the line was behind the key.

We replaced the schedule of continuous reinforcement with a variable interval schedule of reinforcement in the presence of the S^D. This was done to increase the bird's resistance to extinction. This is necessary because reinforcement must be withheld during the test for stimulus generalization. If reinforcement had been given for responding in the presence of the original training stimulus, the S^D, and had been withheld in the presence of the novel test stimuli, the results might be misleading. It is possible that the bird would continue to respond as long as the response was occasionally reinforced in the S^D, and when it found no reinforcement forthcoming in the novel test stimuli, it might stop responding. This would be an example of discriminated extinction. In order to eliminate that possibility, all reinforcement was withheld. In this way the presence or absence of reinforcement could not be used as a discriminative stimulus for responding.

Before actually testing for the Mueller-Lyer illusion we wanted to see what type of stimulus generalization would occur with the flat ends on the line. Five line lengths were presented in a generalization test. The lengths varied from .9 to 1.7 centimeters, and the ends were flat like those used during training. The results for one of the birds is shown in Figure 9-2. This graph shows the amount of re-

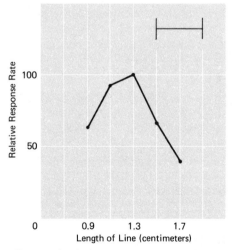

Figure 9-2   Responding in the presence of five different line lengths

sponding which occurred in the presence of each line length. The fact that the peak of the curve is at 1.3 centimeters means that the greatest amount of responding occurred at that value. This is what should happen since 1.3 centimeters is the length of line the animal was trained on. You can also see that, as the line gets shorter or longer, the response rate decreases; the rate is lowest at those line lengths which are farthest away from the training line length.

A curve of this sort, showing the result of a stimulus generalization experiment is called a *generalization gradient*. It is a gradient because the amount of generalization decreases as the stimulus becomes more and more different from that used in training. In the present experiment, it shows how the conditioning at 1.3 centimeters generalizes to the novel line lengths.

This experiment is an example of a *basic stimulus generalization experiment*. A response is conditioned in the presence of one stimulus. During a generalization test, some stimulus property such as line length is varied. The rate of the response is then recorded at each stimulus value. This indicates the amount of generalization which occurs from the S^D used in training to the various other values of that stimulus.

Finally we were ready to perform a generalization test to find out whether or not the Mueller-Lyer illusion is experienced by pigeons. This time the flat line ends were replaced by arrowheads. If the Mueller-Lyer illusion did occur, the peak in the generalization gradient should be at one of the lengths longer than the 1.3 centimeter training length.

This illustrates the basic relation between perception and stimulus generalization which I was trying to find. We can use a stimulus generalization procedure to determine how an observer "perceives" various stimuli. In such an experiment, a perceptual illusion will consist of a shift in the peak of the generalization gradient.

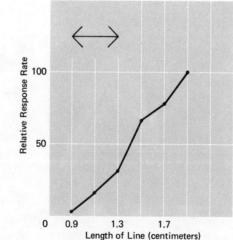

Figure 9-3 Shift in response rate to a longer line as a result of illusion

We had thought that the peak of the generalization gradient for our birds might shift over to about 1.5 centimeters; then the response rate should decrease. As you can see in Figure 9-3, we were wrong. The response rate continuously increased as the line grew longer, even beyond 1.5 centimeters. Our guess was that if we used even longer lines than 1.7 centimeters, we would eventually have found the peak in the generalization gradient.

Later we did use line lengths which went all the way out to 2.3 centimeters. Still, as the line grew longer, the response rate got higher. We were not able to find the peak in the generalization gradient. Unfortunately, we could go no further because the response key behind which the line was projected was only 2.4 centimeters in diameter. Our guess was that the Mueller-Lyer illusion was too effective with the pigeons. It had shifted the peak of the generalization gradient so far that an extremely long line was needed before it would appear to be the same length as the one with the flat ends.

At the end of that year my wife and I moved to Western Michigan University, where we continued our research. As we had discovered, our apparatus was too small to get a direct measure of the magnitude of the Mueller-Lyer illusion when we trained the pigeons with a 1.3 centimeter line. Therefore, we decided to use a shorter line during training.

John Pokrzywinski, then a graduate student at W.M.U., conditioned a new group of birds to peck at a 0.7 centimeter line with flat ends. A representative generalization gradient obtained using the flat arrowheads is shown in Figure 9-4. The peak of the generalization gradient, indicating the maximum response rate, is above the 0.7 centimeter line, the length used during training. As the length of the test stimulus line becomes more and more different from the training stimulus, the response rate decreases.

Another set of generalization gradients was obtained with the arrowheads.

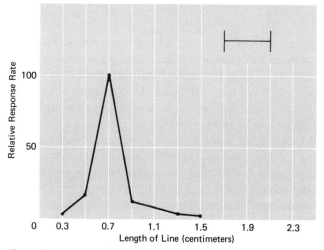

Figure 9-4 Peak response to 0.07 centimeter line without illusion

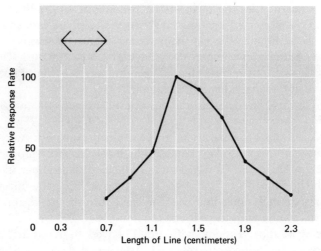

Figure 9-5 Shift in peak response rate corresponding to longer line as a result of illusion

One of these gradients is shown in Figure 9-5. The peak of the generalization gradient shifts from 0.7 centimeters to about 1.3 centimeters. The rate of responding decreases on each side of the 1.3 centimeter line. Evidently a 1.3 centimeter line with arrowheads looks to the pigeon to be about the same length as a 0.7 centimeter line with flat ends. It is necessary for the line with the arrowheads to be longer in order to appear to be the same length as a line with flat ends. Therefore, if the two lines are the same length, the line with the arrowheads will appear shorter. Pigeons, like humans, are subject to the Muller-Lyer illusion.

Summary

Most of the research done in the area of stimulus generalization has involved the use of pigeons, although the concept of stimulus generalization is very applicable to human behavior. Since most research of this sort involves visual stimuli, pigeons make excellent subjects. We have discussed three examples of stimulus generalization research with pigeons. We have seen how relatively simple concepts such as "good and bad paint jobs" and very complex concepts such as "human and non-human" can be formed. We have also seen an example of simple stimulus generalization along the dimension of length of line. This stimulus generalization procedure was then used to study the Mueller-Lyer illusion.

The following major points were made in this chapter:

1. If a response conditioned in the presence of one discriminative stimulus tends to occur in the presence of some novel stimulus, we say that *stimulus generalization* is occurring.

2. The *basic stimulus generalization experiment* involves conditioning a response in the presence of one stimulus and measuring the amount of responding

which occurs when some property of that stimulus is changed. The greater the amount of responding, the greater the amount of stimulus generalization.

3. The results of generalization experiments are usually expressed in terms of *stimulus generalization gradients*. Such gradients show that as some property of the stimulus becomes more and more different from the discriminative stimulus used during conditioning, the response rate decreases. In other words, the more dissimilar two stimuli are, the less the amount of stimulus generalization that occurs and the better the discrimination.

4. A *stimulus class* consists of a set of stimuli having some common property. This may be a physical property such as the color red or it may be a functional property such as serving as a discriminative stimulus for a particular response. Another name for "stimulus class" is "concept."

5. *Conceptual behavior* consists of generalization within a concept or stimulus class and discrimination between concepts or stimulus classes.

6. The *procedure* for *conditioning conceptual behavior* consists of reinforcing one response in the presence of one stimulus class or concept and extinguishing that response when such stimuli are not present.

7. *Intuitive behavior* is a type of conceptual behavior where the individual is unable to give the rules which define the concepts.

8. The *Mueller-Lyer illusion* is a decrease in the apparent length of a line when outward-pointing arrowheads are placed on it. It may also be demonstrated by the apparent lengthening of a line when inward-pointing arrowheads are used.

9. The stimulus generalization procedure may be used to perform a perception experiment. In such an experiment, an *illusion* consists of a shift in the peak of the generalization gradient.

QUESTIONS

1. Do assembly line inspectors do a good job?
2. Do assembly line inspectors usually find their work highly reinforcing?
3. Would you like to be an assembly line inspector?
4. What general type of work was the engineer talking with Dr. Cumming doing?
5. What was the difficulty which the engineer had in automating assembly line inspection?
6. What specific type of flaw did they discuss?
7. What were the two concepts Dr. Cumming said would be needed by an inspection system?
8. What would the inspection device do with the good parts and what would it do with the bad parts?
9. Instead of suggesting an electrical or mechanical system, what kind of system did Dr. Cumming recommend?
10. What specific animal did he think could do the job?
11. How does the pigeon's vision compare with humans?
12. A set of stimuli all of which have some common property is called a s————— c—————.
13. Another name for stimulus class is c—————.

14. What two requirements must be met before we can say conceptual behavior is occurring?

15. When do we say stimulus generalization is occurring?

16. Define conceptual behavior in terms of stimulus discrimination and stimulus generalization.

17. If we wish to condition conceptual behavior, we should reinforce one response in the presence of _____ and extinguish that response _____.

18. For what response did the bad part serve as the S^D and for what response did it served as the S^Δ?

19. What was the reinforcement for correctly rejecting a bad part?

20. For what response did the good part serve as an S^D and for what response did it serve as the S^Δ?

21. What was the reinforcement for correctly accepting a good part?

22. What sort of punishment was used when the bird made an error?

23. Under what circumstances would not being able to work act as a punishment for you?

24. Did Dr. Cumming initially use a difficult or an easy discrimination in conditioning the pigeon?

25. When did he introduce a difficult discrimination with small scratches in the paint?

26. Does the greatest amount of generalization occur when stimuli are similar or dissimilar?

27. Does discrimination most readily occur when stimuli are similar or dissimilar?

28. Is stimulus generalization the opposite or the same as stimulus discrimination?

29. What difficulty might the farsighted reader erroneously anticipate in the application of Dr. Cumming's inspection system to industry?

30. What schedule of intermittent reinforcement did Dr. Cumming use?

31. How does intermittent reinforcement help in the application of Dr. Cumming's system to industry?

32. Were the birds able to maintain a high level of accuracy with a very small percent of coded parts?

33. How accurate were the pigeons? (a) 55–58 percent; (b) 65–68 percent; (c) 75–78 percent; (d) 95–98 percent.

34. Are human inspectors more accurate than pigeons?

35. How could Dr. Cumming employ a technique of Professor Skinner's to greatly increase the accuracy of his inspection system?

36. What was the highest rate of inspection that some of Dr. Cumming's birds were able to obtain? (a) Slightly over one part an hour; (b) Slightly over ten parts an hour; (c) Slightly over one hundred parts an hour; (d) Slightly over one thousand parts an hour.

37. How long did they demonstrate that the birds could work without stopping? (a) four minutes; (b) four hours; (c) four days; (d) four weeks.

38. Is the company now greatly indebted to Dr. Cumming because of the tremendous improvement his techniques have made once they were actually utilized in the factory?

39. Give two possible reasons which may explain the company's reluctance to use Dr. Cumming's techniques.

40. Give another example of a pigeon inspection system.

41. What is the philosophical problem of the identity of repeated experiences such as how we recognize a penny at various angles?

42. What is the psychologist's answer to this problem?

43. If you cannot define a concept, then you cannot use it properly. (a) True; (b) False.
44. When can we say we are behaving intuitively?
45. What concept did Dr. Herrnstein and Dr. Loveland teach their pigeons?
46. In teaching the concept of man, what was the S^D and what was the S^Δ for the key-peck response?
47. What was the reinforcement?
48. Were a large variety of examples of the two concepts used?
49. How accurate did the birds get in responding according to the concept of man?
50. Were these concepts limited to the specific pictures used during the training?
51. What is a frequent criticism of the stimulus-response approach to psychology?
52. What concepts may be used to answer this criticism?
53. What is the name of the perceptual illusion we discussed in this chapter?
54. Describe this illusion.
55. In the perception experiment with pigeons, what was the S^D and what was the S^Δ?
56. Why was this discrimination training used?
57. What schedule of reinforcement was eventually used in the S^D?
58. Why was this done?
59. Why was it necessary to conduct the generalization test in extinction?
60. How does discriminated extinction figure into this?
61. When the generalization test was conducted with the flat ends on the horizontal line, where was the peak of the generalization gradient relative to the S^D?
62. Give a description of the resulting generalization gradient.
63. Can you draw a rough graph of the generalization gradient? Take another look at it if you cannot.
64. What is a generalization gradient?
65. What is the relation between perception and stimulus generalization?
66. How is an illusion measured using a test of stimulus generalization?
67. In the graph for the first test of the Mueller-Lyer illusion following the training with the 1.3 centimeter line, was an actual peak in the generalization gradient found?
68. What was the limitation of the apparatus which prevented this?
69. In an effort to actually find a peak shift produced by the Mueller-Lyer illusion, how did the experimenter get around the limitation of the apparatus?
70. Did they find a peak in the generalization gradient during the experimental test for the Mueller-Lyer illusion following training with a 0.7 centimeter line?
71. Where was the peak in relation to the S^D?
72. Can you draw a rough draft of these results? Again, you should be able to.
73. Are pigeons subject to the Mueller-Lyer illusion?
74. Give five examples of general concepts which you have learned in school.
75. Design a procedure teaching one of these concepts to a student.
76. Give five examples of intuitive concepts which you have learned but cannot define.
77. Design a procedure for teaching one of these concepts.
78. Give an example of an explicit concept which you can define.
79. What is the definition?
80. Give an example of some other part which pigeons might inspect in a factory.
81. One serious limitation which pigeons have is that they do not have arms and hands, but monkeys do. Think of some task which would make use of the monkey's

excellent discrimination and concept forming capabilities and would also entail the use of his hands.

82. How would you teach concepts such as honor, honesty, and love to a child?
83. How would you teach these concepts to a pigeon?
84. Do you think you would be successful?
85. If you do not think you would be successful, why not? Please say something more intelligent than a pigeon is not intelligent enough.
86. Suppose you wanted to find whether yellow lines appeared longer than red lines to a pigeon. Describe the experiment which you would use to find the answer to this question.
87. Here is one that is a little more difficult. According to the vertical-horizontal illusion, vertical lines appear longer than horizontal lines. Design an experiment to test whether pigeons experience this illusion.

NOTES

The Inspector

Initially, half of the parts were bad so that the pigeon inspector had an opportunity to be paid off with food on one-half of the trials. However, as training progressed, the number of bad parts gradually decreased to a more realistic level of about 8 percent.

Another change was also made in the experiment during the training. It appeared that sometimes, in its "eagerness" to get a good look at the diode, the bird would attempt to stick its head through the window, and in so doing peck the reject key. This counted as a response. In other words, some of his responses were accidents. In order to eliminate this, the reject response was put on a fixed-ratio schedule so that the bird had to peck the key five times before the part would be rejected.

Why is it that the pigeon is so much better than man as an assembly line inspector? It is probably not because people have so much more on their minds that they cannot concentrate on the task. I suspect that there is a more fundamental reason.

Let us look at the schedules of reinforcement being used. The pigeon was reinforced with food occasionally when it rejected a bad part. It was also punished when it made a mistake.

What sort of schedules of reinforcement are used in the assembly line inspection by humans? An analysis of a schedule of this sort is somewhat complicated. Probably human inspectors receive a weekly paycheck which is largely independent of their behavior. This weekly salary is not a fixed-interval schedule of reinforcement for inspecting parts. If it were, the first part which they inspected after one week would produce their paycheck. That is not the way it works. Usually the response which is directly reinforced by delivery of the paycheck is going to the paymaster and asking for it. That response is not reinforced until payday.

If salary is not used to reinforce working behavior, why do people work? The answer is that they do not work, at least not very well or very effectively. But then it is not completely true that the paycheck is not involved as a reinforcer. The problem is that the relationship between work and pay is so tenuous that the pay does not act as a very effective reinforcer. If a person does not at least sit at his job and look halfway attentive a reasonable amount of the time, he will be fired and lose his paycheck. If he does not detect at least some minimal number of flaws in the parts, he will probably also lose his job and his paycheck.

Suppose human inspectors were put on the same schedule of reinforcement as the pigeon inspectors. The coded parts would be slipped in along with the regular parts to be inspected. Every time a bad part was correctly rejected, the inspector got 50 cents, and every time an error was made, new parts stopped coming to him for ten minutes. There has been some work along these general lines.[6] It seems that the human inspectors are not inferior to the pigeons. When humans are reinforced properly for detecting things such as bad parts, they can also do a good job.

It is interesting to speculate as to whether the human inspectors would be happier if they were working under a schedule of reinforcement which paid them for correctly detecting the parts and consequently produced better work behavior. At first glance, it might seem that people would be happier if they could simply sit and let the weekly paycheck roll in without actually having to work. As one observer put it, "Happiness is a noncontingent reinforcement."

On the other hand, Skinner has indicated his belief that people are probably happier working for their reinforcement. I think that for people from our culture this may to some extent be true. Work itself has been considered such a virtue that it has become mildly reinforcing. If the reinforcement which we get from our paycheck is scheduled so that we work fairly hard to earn it, then we at least are picking up the small reinforcements of actually doing our job.

Of course the notion that hard work results in happiness is mere speculation and has not been tested experimentally. Unfortunately, almost no research has been done on the proper use of schedules of reinforcement in actual work situations. What little research has been done is usually hampered by an inadequate understanding of schedules of reinforcement by labor, management, and the people doing the research. It would seem, however, that it would be fairly easy to develop payoff systems or schedules of reinforcement which would accomplish the multiple purposes of making more productive, wealthier, and happier individuals.

The notion of using the majority rule of three birds before a part is accepted or rejected has some intriguing implications. Thus far, we have said that coded parts would be used to determine actual reinforcement and punishment in this situation, but the majority vote of three isolated pigeons would be used with the uncoded parts to determine whether they would be accepted or rejected. Suppose, however, that we did away with the coded parts and simply let the majority vote determine, at all times, whether reinforcement or punishment would be delivered.

If we could do this, there would be no need for any coded parts, which would make life much simpler and would allow the animals to work 100 percent of the time inspecting the real parts needing to be inspected. The question is, would the pigeons maintain a reasonably high level of accuracy or even any accuracy above chance, if the experimenter in essence walked away and never had anything to do with the delivery of future reinforcement.

The birds will get reinforced only when they agree with the majority and get punished only when they disagree with the majority, regardless of whether they are actually correct or incorrect. Initially, if you put the birds in this situation after they have been trained to a high level of accuracy, the majority will be correct nearly all of the time; therefore deviation from the majority will be appropriately dealt with. Once in a while, however, the majority will be wrong. In that case, agreement with the majority will be incorrectly reinforced and disagreement with the majority will be incorrectly punished. In fact, we can calculate the percentage of the time that the majority will be wrong and the birds' responses will be incorrectly reinforced or punished.

6. Holland, J. G. Human vigilance. *Science*, 1958, *128*, 61–67.

If the individual birds are initially correct 95 percent of the time, the majority will be wrong less than 1 percent of the time. Only on those very rare occasions will birds' responses be incorrectly reinforced or punished.

The question is, what effect will these erroneous consequences have on behavior? Since the percentage is so small, it might be anticipated that they would have very little if any effect on the accurarcy of the response. The birds would probably maintain a relatively high level of accuracy for the rest of their lives, even though they worked on this problem day after day, month after month, year after year (and birds sometimes live to be 20 years old).

This is a very interesting concept. At first, the experimenter reinforces correct discriminative responses and punishes incorrect responses. Then he puts the birds into a situation in which the contingencies are in reality changed. The response of one bird is now simply reinforced for agreement with the responses of the other birds and punished for disagreement. But, since the same discriminative stimuli continue to be present, the control which the experimenter initially exerted over the birds' behavior is now maintained by the other birds.

One might ask what will happen if the birds have not obtained such high accuracy. Suppose that the three birds have only been trained on 60 percent accuracy. The majority will be wrong about 35 percent of the time, and correct 65 percent of the time.

Will this level of accuracy be maintained, and might it even improve? Being correct with regard to the discriminative stimuli pays off more often than being incorrect. It might be, therefore, that the birds will more and more often be correct until eventually, they have attained a very high level of accuracy. (See Verhave[7] for a similar analysis.)

The Pecking Pigeon People Peeper

Could pigeons be taught a pair of concepts such as good art and bad art? Could they make an acceptance response whenever they saw a good painting and a rejection response whenever they saw a bad painting?

How would we go about training a pigeon to form such concepts of art? We would select a large number of good paintings and a large number of bad paintings. Both should be representative. Then we would reinforce the acceptance response when it occurred in the presence of the S^D, good paintings. We would also reinforce the rejection response in the presence of the S^Δ, bad paintings. In addition, we might punish incorrect responses. It would indeed be interesting to see if *pigeons* could form such concepts. Professors who teach courses in art appreciation think it would be interesting to see if *college freshmen* could form such concepts.

There is a provocative extrapolation to be made from this example. What would happen when the styles of art change? Would the pigeon respond appropriately to good and bad examples of the new mode of art? This raises some basic questions about the nature of art and the nature of human values in general, which you may wish to speculate about at your leisure.

7. Verhave, T. The inspector is a bird. *Psychology Today*, 1967, *1*, 48–53.

10

FADING

Teaching a Retarded Girl to Read

Betty was eight years old and retarded. She had been confined to an institution for all but a few months of her eight years. Some psychology students were interested in teaching Betty to discriminate her name from the names of other children on the ward.[1] Initially, stick-on letters were placed on two blank cards. On one card the name "Betty" was spelled out. The name of another resident on the ward, "Susan," was placed on the second card. The procedure the students initially tried was identical to one already discussed in Chapter 8 where a retarded girl named Carmen learned to discriminate her name. At first Betty was shown the two cards and told merely to pick out the card with her name on it. She looked from the experimenters to the cards and laughed. Then she got up from her chair and ran across the room, clapping her hands and giggling. The students brought her back to the table and seated her again. "Pick out your name," they said emphatically. Again, Betty went through the same behaviors.

After Betty had failed many, many trials, candies were introduced into the situation. First, the students gave Betty one of the candies, which she promptly devoured. If Betty picked the card with her name on it, the response would be reinforced. If the card with the other name was selected, this response would result in no reinforcement.

After being reinforced for one or two responses, Betty consistently began to pick a card. For many trials—in fact two hundred trials—she continued to pick up first one card and then the other. It was apparent that she was not discriminating the lettering on those cards. She chose the wrong card just as often as she chose the card which bore her name. The students shook their heads and lamented their failure.

1. This section based on Whaley, Donald, and Welt, Kenneth. Use of ancillary cues and fading techniques in name discrimination training in retardates. *Michigan Mental Health Research,* 1967, *1,* 29–30.

One student said that he wasn't surprised to find that reinforcement wasn't all it was cracked up to be. They were fortunate to find out it was a "fake" this soon in their careers. Another student suggested that Betty was simply not intelligent enough to learn the skill they wanted her to acquire. After all, she was retarded. A third student suggested that the reinforcer used was not powerful enough, although he did not know of a better one. He felt that if one could be found, success would be more likely.

Finally the students went to the psychologist who was supervising them in their work, presented the data to him, and awaited his opinion. But before we go into his reply, it may be good for each of you to ask yourselves with which of the students you would agree, or if you would prefer to agree with none and offer your own explanation of the failure.

When the students came to the psychologist who was supervising them and who, incidentally, was one of the writers of this book, they presented their data in graphical form along with their various assumptions as to why the procedure had failed. The psychologist, although not exceedingly bright, was at least somewhat experienced in the area, and could immediately see that in fact no discrimination had come about. To the first student who said reinforcement was "no good," he replied that as a matter of fact reinforcement had been shown in many instances to be effective and just because it had apparently failed in this one was no reason to discard it totally. This was, he said, "like throwing the baby out with the bath."

To the second student, who had suggested that the child was not intelligent enough to make this discrimination, he voiced partial and qualified agreement. It was obviously true from the data that Betty had been unable to master the discrimination under the conditions which it had required. Furthermore, he conceded, other individuals of Betty's age would be able to master the discrimination with no trouble at all.

He also agreed in part with the third student who had indicated that the reinforcer had been too weak and had suggested that a more powerful one might be more effective. There was always the possibility of trying out various other potential reinforcers. He was quick to add, however, that the reinforcer seemed effective because Betty's rate of picking up the card had become extremely high; this showed that the behavior of picking up the cards was reinforced by the candy. The failure was in being unable to train the discrimination.

Without siding emphatically with any of the students, their supervisor gave them a new procedure to try. The procedure involved what is called a *fading technique*. Let us see exactly what the students did.

After conferring with the psychologist they returned to the ward. First they did a very peculiar thing. You will remember that in the original procedure Betty's name was presented in white letters on a black background. The name of the other resident, Susan, was similarly presented. The students now took the letters of Betty's name from the black background and placed them on a card identical in size and shape, but of a pure white shade. The card now consisted of white letters on a white background, but the letters were still easily distinguishable. Now Betty was given the two cards again. The one with her name had white letters on a white background; the name of the other resident, Susan, was presented in the same style and color of lettering, but on a black background.

Thus, there were two primary differences between the two cards which Betty ultimately had to choose from. First, Betty's name was in white letters on a white background, whereas the name "Susan" was on a black background. Second, the letters, although of the same style and texture, were obviously different. On Betty's card they spelled the name "Betty" and on the other card they spelled the name "Susan."

After the names were placed on their respective backgrounds, they were presented to Betty. She began to indiscriminately pick first one card and then the other. During this time the response of picking the card with the white background, which bore her name, was always reinforced with candy. After a few trials, Betty began to consistently pick up the card bearing her name and avoided picking up the black card. It was obvious that she had been able to discriminate. It is safe to say, at this point, that she was really discriminating white from black and that the names on the cards had nothing to do with her correct responding. Betty went on for some time in this way without making a single error.

Continuing to follow the instructions of their supervisor, after 40 correct trials the students removed Betty's name from the white card and placed it on one that was slightly less white, one that approached a light grey. Now the difference in shades between the two cards was less than before, yet a marked dissimilarity was still apparent. Betty immediately went to the correct card, and received one of the desirable candies. After 40 trials in which again no errors were made, the shade of the lighter card was changed to a slightly darker shade. Still Betty made no errors.

The same procedure was followed through 11 darker shades. In all instances a darker shade was introduced after 40 correct trials. Each change brought the shade of the card with Betty's name on it closer to that of the card bearing the other resident's name. Although the two cards were becoming more and more similar, Betty continued to make no errors. Finally, the "Betty" card was changed until it was identical in shade to the "Susan" card. The only difference between the two cards was the lettering attached. One spelled Betty's name and the other "Susan." Without an instant of hesitation Betty picked up the card with her name. Prior to the new procedure, Betty had failed to make this same discrimination for more than 200 trials. Previous work with other retardates on this type of discrimination problem had shown that without the fading technique the discrimination could never have been mastered.

The case above is an extremely good example of how a special technique can be used to train individuals to perform discriminations which, under standard conditions, they may never be trained to master. Several points in the procedure should be highlighted. First, the subjects, after the experimental conditions were put into effect, mastered a relatively difficult discrimination without making a single error. This type of procedure and the behavior it brings about are often referred to as *errorless discrimination*. Second, the procedure brought a retarded girl to make a discrimination which she had previously been unable to make. We may conclude from this that whether an individual masters a skill can often be greatly determined by the particular techniques that were used to train him. It would also suggest that we may fail to teach an individual simply because we have not used an effective procedure and if we were to devise one, we would be successful.

A final point is that there was a gradual change in the stimuli which were presented to Betty. In the beginning, it was obvious that Betty was discriminating one card from the other in terms of the dissimilarity in background shade. It was as clear as "black and white" to her that the cards were different. This dissimilarity was lessened as the white card gradually darkened until it was identical to the dark card. As this change took place, it became more important for Betty to rely on the characteristics of the letters and less on shade differences. Ultimately the only possible means of differentiating the two cards were the letter differences and, of course, this is precisely the way you and I distinguish our names from others. This discrimination of configurations of letters involved what we call "reading." It may be said that Betty began by discriminating black from white and ended by making discriminations which could be described as rudimentary reading behavior.

In the beginning, the stimulus cards which were presented to Betty differed in two distinct ways. One way in which the cards differed was shade. One was white and the other black. The other way in which the cards differed was the complex of letters which were placed on each.

Ways in which two objects may be said to be similar or dissimilar are called stimulus dimensions.

There are many ways in which two objects may differ from each other and therefore, many possible dimensions which could be faded. A house is different from an automobile along many dimensions. It may be said that the more dimensions objects have in common, the more difficult they are to discriminate and, conversely, the fewer dimensions they have in common, the easier they are to discriminate. Obviously it is easy to discriminate a golf ball from an airplane. It is not so easy to discriminate a good golf ball from a bad golf ball. The two golf balls are similar in many dimensions and differ only in a few dimensions which might be roundness, resiliency, or hardness of cover.

In the current situation we can say that one card differed from the other in two dimensions. Throughout the procedure, one dimension, shade, gradually changed until there was no difference in this dimension between the two cards. This process of gradual change is called fading. When this procedure is used to get an individual to make a discrimination he previously could not master, it is called a *fading technique*. The dimension of shade in this experiment is called a *fading dimension*. Fading proceeded along this dimension from dissimilarity to similarity. The other dimension in which the cards differed was the letters in the two names. This dimension did not change during the procedure because it is the dissimilarity which the experimenter wanted the subject to discriminate.

The most striking aspect of a fading technique is that it involves *gradual change*. We have encountered other situations previously where behavioral techniques involved gradual change. In this instance the feature which changed was different from that which changes in a fading technique. These techniques will be compared and contrasted with fading in the next chapter. For the present, another example of fading will help to clarify the basic components of the procedure.

Testing the Hearing of Nonverbal Children

Often children from poor families suffer from problems due to inadequate physical examination, such as impaired hearing. The problem may go undetected. These children act differently from their friends or classmates. They do not attend to their environment, which is every bit as much one of sounds as it is of sights. It is not necessary that they be completely deaf before they have serious problems in school or in other training situations. If their hearing impairment is great, they may never learn to talk. Under ordinary circumstances, one must hear before·he can learn to speak. This subsequent inability to talk and what appears to be a general unconcern on the part of the child for his environment frequently cause these children to be incorrectly diagnosed as "mentally retarded." Their apparent retardation stems from a history of poor hearing and can be corrected by surgery or the fitting of an appropriate hearing aid.

It is not always true that failure to diagnose hearing problems is due to lack of resources or inclination on the part of the parents, school, or community. In the past it has been very difficult to ascertain whether or not these children suffer from hearing problems. Since they are nonverbal, it is not possible to ask them if they can hear a given sound stimulus. Other procedures must be devised which do not rely primarily on modes of verbal communication. It is in this context that reinforcement techniques in general and fading techniques in particular have been of considerable value.

Meyerson and Michael[2] found themselves involved in a situation where they were forced to develop a method to test the hearing of a population of children who were presumed to be moderately retarded. Meyerson and Michael sought to determine whether the behavioral problems of these children were due to poor hearing or other factors. They knew beforehand that a strictly verbal approach would be of no value. If this were the case, diagnosis would already have been made.

The two psychologists approached the problem in the following way. A subject whose hearing they wished to evaluate was led into an experimental room. At one side of the room were two small levers which protruded from a console. The two levers were a few feet apart so that it was not easy for the subject to operate both at the same time. Above each lever was a light socket and bulb. First the experimenters demonstrated the apparatus to the subject. The light above one of the levers was turned on from the adjoining room. The experimenter in the room with the subject made a few presses of the lever and a reinforcement was delivered. For some children, candy reinforcement was used, and for others a variety of trinkets, objects, and consumables served as reinforcers. After the ex-

2. This section based on Meyerson, L., and Michael, J. Hearing by operant conditioning procedures. Proceedings of the International Congress on Education of the Deaf, 1964, 238–242.

perimenters had demonstrated reinforcement on one lever, the light above that lever was turned off and the light above the other lever turned on. The experimenter completed the demonstration by switching to the other lever where the light was now on, making a few presses, and thus producing reinforcement.

The subjects caught on to the lever press very quickly. Soon they learned that pressing the lever resulted in reinforcement. The schedule of reinforcement was changed from the initial CRF schedule to a VR 8, in which an average of eight responses yielded reinforcement.

Within a few minutes the children also mastered the discrimination of light on. They learned that reinforcement would only be forthcoming when they pressed the lever whose light was energized. Soon another feature was added to the program. This was an immediate payoff for switching from one lever to the other when the light changed. If the subject switched soon after the lights changed, he received a quick reinforcement, usually after the second response on the lever to which he had just switched. If he failed to make the switching response, he received no reinforcement until the light again came on over the lever where he was currently performing. The subjects switched immediately after the lights over the levers were changed. The lights were very effective discriminative stimuli and appeared to control the children's behavior at this point quite readily.

The reader might conclude that the experimental design in no way tested hearing, but rather was a crude vision test at the very best. We could not argue with this analysis; it correctly describes the state of affairs before the time the fading technique was brought into play.

The experimenters remained behind an observation window as they watched the subject's performance. The room which the experimenters occupied contained a complete display of sound-producing equipment which is used to evaluate human hearing. At first a very loud sound midway in the frequency sensitivity of the normal human range of hearing was introduced into the situation. In the beginning, this sound was paired with the light. By way of illustration, let us assume that the light above the left-side lever comes on. Concomitant with the light, the sound also comes on. With both the tone and the light on, reinforcement is forthcoming on a VR 8 schedule. The light goes off above the left lever and comes on over the right lever. There is no longer any sound, but the subject can respond to the light and lever, and receive an immediate reinforcement for switching as well as other reinforcements for continuing to work on the lever. Now the light switches again from the right lever to the left and the sound comes on again. In this way, "sound-on" is always associated with the left lever and "sound-off" is associated with the right lever.

In initial sessions, the sound factor seemed to make no difference since the subjects had already mastered the light-lever situation. As sessions went on however, the intensity of light was gradually decreased until it was completely faded out. Now the only cue given the subject was tone-on for the right lever and tone-off for the left lever. The subjects who heard this loud and fundamental tone had no problems at all although the lights were completely absent. They continued to work on the left lever as long as the sound was delivered to them and switched immediately to the right lever as soon as sound went off. Sound-on found them returning promptly to the left lever. At first, the sound was delivered through a speaker in the room. Gradually the children were trained to wear earphones and sound was subsequently projected to them through these earphones. The addition of earphones made the testing situation more comparable to conditions where typical testing procedures are employed and allowed for greater control of the sound being presented to the subject.

Once the light had faded out, the children were discriminating by means of sound-on, sound-off, alone. It was a simple matter for the experimenters now to vary frequency of the sound as well as intensity, and in this manner to arrive at an evaluation of the hearing acuity for each of the subjects and compare this to normals. By using this technique, the experimenters found that, indeed, some of the youngsters who had been diagnosed as mentally retarded due to brain damage or other dire medical affliction suffered more directly from poor hearing.

The role of fading in this endeavor is comparable to the experiment cited earlier where fading along a dimension of shade was used to enable a retarded girl to master the discrimination of her name, which she had been unable to do previously. In the hearing situation, a basic and simple discrimination was first trained in which an energized light above one of two levers was correlated with availability of reinforcement on a VR schedule. On some occasions the left lever was the correct lever and on other occasions the right lever was the correct one. At any given time the difference between one lever and the other was the respective presence or absence of light-on. The two levers differed in terms of the dimension of light intensity. This dimension, light intensity, became the fading dimension. After perfect responding had been established with the lights, sound was introduced. Sound-on was always correlated with one lever and sound-off with the other. Throughout the fading procedure this dimension did not change. After the lights were completely faded out, it was necessary to vary the intensity and frequency of the sound in order to test the sensitivity of the subjects' hearing. Sound was varied only after the experimenters were convinced the subjects could discriminate the highly audible tone they had first introduced.

As with the previous experiment, only one dimension was faded while other dimensions were kept constant. There are many possible dimensions along which fading may occur, and there is nothing to prevent fading along multiple dimensions simultaneously. The process of education may be seen as involving techniques in which two dimensions are simultaneously changed. The purpose of education is to bring the student to the point where he can deal *independently* with *difficult* subject matter. Initially the student may receive large amounts of individual attention and aid with relatively simple scholastic tasks. As education progresses, the skills demanded of the student become increasingly complex and, concomitantly, he is expected to do the work on his own. When he reaches advanced stages of graduate training in his discipline, the student deals with the most complex problems with only minimal direction from his major professor.

Other types of training can be analyzed in terms of complex multidimensional fading demonstrations. More often other techniques which also involve gradual change are also employed. These instances will be discussed in the following chapter.

Summary

In this chapter a procedure for teaching discriminations was introduced. This procedure involves *fading techniques*.

1. Two objects presented to an organism may differ from each other in many ways. When compared, the aspects in which they may be said to be similar or dissimilar are called dimensions. Dimensions may include characteristics such as roundness, smoothness, size, height, weight, luster, color, shade, etc.

2. A girl in an institution for the retarded was trained to discriminate her name from that of another resident on her ward. After simple discrimination training, a fading technique was employed. Fading initially involved making the two cards as dissimilar as possible along a dimension. This dimension was one of shade of background. The other dimension on which the two cards differed was lettering. This dimension difference remained constant throughout the study, for it was the dissimilarity which the experimenter wished the subject to discriminate. Fading took place along 12 discrete shade steps—the white card fading into darkness until it was identical to the dark card. With this procedure, the subject was able to discriminate letter differences and thus reliably discriminate her name.

3. Fading procedures may allow the subject to master an otherwise difficult or even impossible discrimination. Once an initial discrimination is mastered, fading proceeds along the dimension and errors do not occur. Fading techniques thus establish a form of discrimination behavior called *errorless discrimination*.

4. Two psychologists employed a fading procedure to test the hearing of children in a training school. The fading involved light intensity which was initially paired with a particular lever and later with sound-on and sound-off. A discrimination was evidenced by their pressing one lever when sound was on and another lever when sound was off. After the sound-on, sound-off, discrimination was mastered, intensity and frequency of the sound was varied, and hearing threshold determinations were made for several subjects.

QUESTIONS

1. Betty had been confined to an institution: (a) two months; (b) most of her life; (c) two years; (d) twenty-five years.
2. In the procedure the psychology students first used, the card with Betty's name (was, was not) followed with reinforcement when chosen.
3. The card with the name Susan (was, was not) followed with reinforcement when chosen.
4. After two hundred trials: (a) Betty had mastered the discrimination; (b) Her behavior with regard to the selection of the correct cards was random; (c) She could write her own name; (d) None of the above.
5. To describe behavior as random in the choosing of one of two cards would mean that: (a) the second card was chosen 4 times more often than the first; (b) the first card was chosen at least twice as often as the second; (c) it was apparent

that on any given trial one card was as likely to be chosen as the other; (d) the first card was chosen 20 times in succession and then the second card was chosen for 20 times in succession.

6. The first procedure the students tried with Betty had obviously failed. Which of the below was *not* offered by the students as an explanation of the failure? (a) Reinforcement techniques do not work; (b) Betty was not intelligent enough to learn this skill; (c) The reinforcer was not powerful enough; (d) The experimenters were not clever enough.

7. Which of the four above do you think best describes the situation?

8. The psychologist who was supervising the students did not emphatically agree or disagree with any of their explanations. The new procedure he gave them was called: (a) shaping procedure; (b) response differentiation procedure; (c) discrimination procedure; (d) fading technique.

9. In the original procedure, the names of both girls were presented with white letters on a black background. (a) True; (b) False.

10. In the fading procedure, Betty's name was placed on: (a) white letters on a black background; (b) black letters on a white background; (c) black letters on a black background; (d) white letters on a white background.

11. There were two basic differences between the two cards, what were they?

12. Within a few trials Betty was picking up the card with her name on it consistently and avoiding the other card. It is probably safe to say that at this point she was discriminating: (a) the letters in her name from the letters of the other name; (b) white from black; (c) the rough edges of the card; (d) the right or left positioning of the cards.

13. After Betty had mastered the first discrimination when the two cards were maximumly different in shade, a fading technique was begun. Briefly describe what it involved.

14. The fact that Betty went through the entire procedure without making an error is typical of this procedure: the results it brings about as well as the procedure are often called E——————— Discrimination.

15. Rather than blaming failure to teach a subject on the subject's low intelligence, we had better look at our techniques. (a) True; (b) False.

16. If there are ways in which two objects may be said to be similar or dissimilar, these ways may be called D——————s.

17. What was the fading dimension in the study with Betty?

18. Which dimension was not faded, and why not?

19. Children are often diagnosed as mentally retarded when in fact their basic problem is one of poor hearing. (a) True; (b) False.

20. Why is it difficult to do hearing tests on these individuals?

21. Meyerson and Michael are well known because they developed the first verbal techniques to test hearing in retardates. (a) True; (b) False.

22. The subjects in the Meyerson and Michael experiment were placed in a room with levers and lights. How many levers and lights were there, and how were they arranged?

23. What kind of reinforcers did Meyerson and Michael employ?

24. What was the simple discrimination which the subjects were first required to master, and what schedule or reinforcement was employed?

25. The subjects soon worked on a lever only if the light above it was on. (a) True; (b) False.

26. At this point it is correct to say that hearing was not involved at all. (a) True; (b) False.

27. Briefly explain how the sound was introduced and paired with the lights. What dimension was faded and what was the result?
28. Once the children were discriminating sound-on, sound-off, without the aid of a light, what was done then to complete the hearing test?

NOTES

The discovery and utilization of fading techniques and the resultant possibilities of errorless discrimination have revolutionized the entire field of learning and education. The theoretical implications of errorless learning and the techniques by which it may be attained are indeed staggering.

The general notion of having to "err" in order to learn is reflected in our society's viewpoints on such things as discipline of children, all forms of schooling from kindergarten to graduate school, and our state penal systems. It has been stated by many that a man was less of a man if he did not come from the "school of hard knocks." This in essence meant that he must make errors if he was to master his environment.

The problem, of course, with errors is that they are costly in time and in effort and in some instances may actually prove fatal. We as parents do not usually find it feasible to let our children make the error of running into traffic. We do everything we can to preclude this error happening even once.

With the inception of errorless discrimination, it became obvious that not only were errors costly and apt to produce certain unwanted emotional responses from the organism; they were also unnecessary. They were an artifact of the procedure. If a procedure is employed in which errors occur, the procedure is not a good one. It has asked too much of the organism at certain critical junctures.

In the past few years we have seen the errorless learning concept proliferate in our educational system. By and large, it has been seen mostly in the theory and construction of programmed textbooks. Many varieties of subject matter have been adapted to programmed textbook form, including languages, statistics, mathematics, computer programming, music, logic, religion, and poetry. One programmed textbook actually teaches how to write programmed texts.

In the account of the graduate students who worked with the retardate, some mention was made of the notion of intelligence and how it related to the mastering of discriminations. This concept of intelligence has caused considerable controversy of late, and a few words may help to clarify some of the issues.

A basic difficulty arises in a situation such as the following: a child, let us say a retardate, is brought to a classroom and the teacher endeavors to teach him a simple skill, perhaps to recite his multiplication tables. The child fails miserably at the task although the teacher tries her entire repertoire of teaching skills. After months of failure, the teacher concludes that the child is simply not intelligent enough to master this skill, and sends the child to a remedial clinic for help. Once at the clinic, attempts are still made to teach the multiplication tables to this rejected student. Perhaps a psychologist is brought in on the case. He employs commodities such as candy or ice cream, which are immediately reinforcing. He may also elect to use fading techniques similar to those discussed earlier in the chapter. After a few weeks the child is sent back to school, having mastered the multiplication tables. A question which now must be answered is the following: has the child become more intelligent? The teacher might be forced to say this since she originally judged the child not "intelligent" enough to master the discrimination. Now, having mastered the discrimination, it may follow that the teacher should conclude that the child has in some strange way become more intelligent.

This dilemma may be partially resolved by the notion that what an individual will or will not learn is greatly determined by the techniques and procedures which are employed in attempting to teach him. This is not a new concept even within traditional educational procedures. Most of us have taken a subject from one teacher and found ourselves completely lost; but later, having it from another teacher who employed different forms of presentation and perhaps different methods of motivation, we mastered it with no difficulty. With undergraduate psychology students for instance, the study of statistics is traditionally a formidable one. Later, when in graduate school, although the degree of difficulty has increased greatly, fewer students have difficulty with statistics. By this time, of couse, the motivational aspects have been changed. The graduate students' success in graduate school is often "do or die." We must then take into account performance; how people perform on the mastery of a task and relate it to the particular procedure used. This includes not only the form in which the material was presented and the speed with which it was presented, but it also includes operations which were used to influence the student to perform these tasks.

Philosophically, however, the problem is still not solved, for it brings up a basic issue. The issue most plainly stated is this: given the fact that an individual failed to master a skill when trained with the traditional technique, is it possible to find a new or different technique which will bring about mastery? And, if the previous statement is granted, does it not follow that given better and more efficient techniques, anyone, including retardates, can be taught anything? This is a question which the writers are not prepared to answer at this time although this logical conclusion is compelling. For the moment we leave the student to supply his own answer.

TECHNIQUES INVOLVING GRADUAL CHANGE

1

11

TECHNIQUES INVOLVING GRADUAL CHANGE— (SHAPING, FADING, AND ATTENUATION OF REINFORCER)

A technique we explained earlier, and have encountered many times throughout the pages of this book, is called shaping. In shaping, the psychologist or individual working with the subject decides upon a goal. This goal is called the *terminal behavior*. The experimenter selects a response which resembles the terminal response, reinforces it, and then reinforces successive approximations to the terminal response until the subject ultimately exhibits the terminal behavior.

The response which receives reinforcement changes as a function of the progess of the procedure. The response which is initially reinforced may resemble the terminal response in an extremely superficial manner. This response is soon discarded and exchanged for one which more directly resembles the terminal response.

A fading procedure may appear similar to a shaping procedure at first glance because in both cases there is a gradual change from something the experimenter does not particularly want as an end result to something that is acceptable. Unlike shaping, the gradual change in a fading procedure involves the stimulus and not the response.

In the last chapter the retarded girl, Betty, began by making the correct response. She began by choosing the card which bore her name and from that time continued to make the very same response throughout the entire procedure. The response, therefore, was not changed at all. What was changed were the physical properties of the objects with which she dealt. One card changed across the dimension of shade until it was comparable to the other. It can be said that, in shaping, the response itself is changed by differential reinforcement. In a fading technique, however, the response stays the same. It is the objects, events, or stimuli to be discriminated which change.

Another type of gradual change we have witnessed in previous pages had to do with reinforcement schedules. At the Coral Gables bar (Chapter 6), subjects began by obtaining alcoholic beverages on a continuous reinforcement schedule. This schedule was replaced by an FR 3 schedule, and then *gradually* the requirement was increased until an FR 120 was in effect. This gradual change involved neither the attenuation of discriminative stimuli as seen in fading, nor the successive change of response class as in shaping. All stimulus aspects remained constant, and the response which continued to be reinforced throughout was the lever press. The only change was of the schedule of reinforcement, which was gradually increased from CRF to a relatively high FR schedule.

A similar type of gradual change may entail the replacement of one type of reinforcer for another. A common example occurs when a response is first conditioned with a primary reinforcer such as food or ice cream and gradually comes to be maintained by praise or other social reinforcers. A less common, but entirely feasible situation, could involve the reduction in amount of reinforcer delivered. A rat may first receive three pellets during conditioning, but later the same response can be maintained with only one pellet for reinforcement. These variables of schedule and amount and type of reinforcement can collectively be called *reinforcing consequences*. A gradual change from one reinforcing consequence to another may be an integral part of a behavior modification plan.

These three types of gradual change—shaping, reinforcing consequences, and stimulus fading—are contrasted in the chart below.

	Type of Gradual Change	*Purpose*
Shaping	Response	to bring about a response not currently emitted by the organism
Reinforcing consequences	Schedule of reinforcement, or type and amount of reinforcement	to maintain responses already emitted or to establish a particular pattern of responses
Fading	Stimulus	to bring the organism to discriminate stimuli other than those which he can discriminate initially

Each of these three procedures is conceptually independent and can occur without affecting the other two. In practice, an experimenter may find it useful or necessary to employ all three to get the behavioral result he wishes.

In the following report all three procedures involving gradual change were used to bring juvenile delinquents to the point where they sought psychotherapy and counseling.

Street Corner Psychotherapy

Picture, if you will, the following. A group of teenagers is standing on the corner in one of our more urban areas. They wear leather jackets, their hair is long—it is easy to tell they are members of a gang. Most of them have dropped out of high school already, or are a serious truancy problem. They come from families which are most favorably spoken of as being unsettled. They have no jobs at the present and have no interest in the many healthful activities that teenagers find engaging. All have histories of petty infractions of the law through stealing and disorderly conduct. Many of them have been involved in gang fights or "rumbles." Some of them have already gone on to more serious problems, perhaps into drug use, rape, or burglary. While each youth differs from the other, they believe they share a common enemy. They mistrust any form of authority including parents and most certainly officials of the state or city. They are not reluctant to show their dislike of authority in a rude and sometimes violent manner. Although many of them have personal problems, just as many teenagers have personal problems, they would feel "chicken" or "sissy" if they were to approach a counselor, psychologist, or teacher. The youngsters show extreme hostility toward such professionals.

Now we have roughly defined the population of juvenile delinquents with which our hypothetical hero must deal. Let us assume that he has just received his degree in clinical psychology and has decided that these unfortunate individuals need his help. He sets up his office, displaying a shingle which says "Psychologist—Specialty in Juvenile Delinquency." None of the youths he seeks to help comes by his office, although he waits patiently for weeks and months. Finally he decides to take the bull by the horns and go to the street corner, perhaps dragging his therapy couch along with him. He approaches the young men and makes the following speech:

> Gentlemen, my name is Dr. Young Blood. I am aware that you all have serious emotional problems and undoubtedly would like to talk these over with a psychologist. I am here to let you know that my services are available. Feel free to come to my office at your convenience. Please do not be shy and bashful, for being emotionally disturbed is nothing to be ashamed of; juvenile delinquency is curable!

Now, what do you think the outcome would be? Right. The young psychologist would be lucky to leave that street corner with his diploma intact. He would undoubtedly be told in emphatic and vigorous language to mind his own business.

So much for Dr. Young Blood. We must abandon him and discuss a real psychologist who was also interested in reaching the juvenile delinquent. His name was Dr. Schwitzgebel.[1] Dr. Schwitzgebel knew that the approach we have credited to the fictional Dr. Young Blood would not work. Variations of it had too often failed in the past.

Instead, Dr. Schwitzgebel used, among other techniques, principles involving gradual change. His first assumption was that if he were to help these individuals he would have to get them to come to his place of business—his office. He would also have to get them to say something about themselves. In short, he knew that he must first get them in the therapy situation before he could modify their behavior and help them with their problems—a big order, even if behavior techniques were to be used.

1. This section based on Schwitzgebel, R. and Kolb, D. A. Inducing behavior change in adolescent delinquents. *Behaviour Research and Therapy*, 1964, *1*, 267–304.

Dr. Schwitzgebel's approach was entirely new; it did not presuppose that people who are emotionally disturbed should know that they need help. He accepted as an established fact that these youths did need immediate help and proceeded to win them over and enlist their cooperation. First he rented a house in their part of the city and set it up as a workshop-office arrangement. He was there to succeed and meant to stay until he did. For some time he merely existed in that environment getting to know the neighborhood and some of the peculiar aspects of his chosen arena.

It was only after a long period of reconnaissance that Dr. Schwitzgebel felt comfortable in approaching his clients. His initial overture was more of a "deal" than it was a professional advertisement. He tried hard to appear unobtrusive in making his points. In essence he imparted the following information to the youths wherever and whenever he found them: that he was doing research and was looking for individuals who would be willing to spend a small amount of their time talking into a tape recorder. If they were willing to do this, he would pay them for their time. Actually they could come to his office anytime they wished and look around before they decided whether they would like to go through with the offer. Slowly this information became known in the society of the neighborhood. One by one, the youths came to avail themselves of this opportunity. When they first came they were greeted warmly and offered refreshments. Great care was taken to ensure that they should not feel they were in any way being intimidated, ordered, or bossed. After a few minutes of chatting, the boys were shown the tape recorder and told to speak into it as long as they wished.

At first some of the tape recordings were extremely nonsensical. Nonetheless, payment was immediately delivered after completion of the session and a future appointment was arranged. In subsequent sessions talking into the tape recorder became easier for the youths. Basic behavioral problems were being fed onto the tape. In addition, Dr. Schwitzgebel slowly began to impose restrictions. The clients were expected to keep their appointments with fidelity. Ultimately Dr. Schwitzgebel faded himself into the picture and became the therapist, thus replacing the necessity for a tape recorder. Word of his services soon spread. Within a short while he was dealing with significant behavioral problems of a highly disturbed and volatile group of young men. In this way Dr. Schwitzgebel was able to offer therapy even to those who were originally opposed to the notion.

But Dr. Schwitzgebel was sensitive to the fact that merely talking to these boys for a few hours a week was not enough to completely alleviate their basic problems. They also needed to develop new interests and skills which would enable them to cope with their environment in a more effective and socially acceptable way. To meet this need Schwitzgebel introduced various activities, including work with electronics, recreation, and what were, effectively, short courses in manual arts skills. When these activities were first introduced, he took care to avoid presenting them as work or mandatory endeavors. Rather, he presented them as indirectly as possible, knowing that these skills held many intrinsic reinforcers which would perpetuate the activity once the youths were led, by whatever means, to first participate in them.

Dr. Schwitzgebel's approach is possibly the most effective one to date for use with what have been called the "intractables" of society. His procedures were simple and involved massive applications of positive reinforcement, behavioral shaping, gradual changes in type and amount of reinforcement, and the subtle use of fading techniques.

The most prominent changes in Dr. Schwitzgebel's program entailed a gradual but drastic modification of reinforcing consequences. At first his clientele received immediate reinforcement in the form of money for talking into a tape recorder. They were told they could drop in at any time. After an individual had begun to come frequently, restrictions were introduced. The boys could only talk into the tape recorder, and thus receive reinforcement, if they appeared at the prearranged time. This is in effect the introduction of a limited-hold feature to the existing schedule of reinforcement.

Ultimately Dr. Schwitzgebel had to exert personal control over his clients if he was to be of service. The gradual imposition of restrictions slowly brought him to the point where he was accepted as a benign authority figure. The magnitude of change in reinforcement consequences can be seen if we consider that initially the clients received more for their visit, but later the money was discontinued and the youths received only the social reinforcement provided by Dr. Schwitzgebel and the service offered.

Shaping was also an important procedure in the program. Clients first made only the responses of coming to the office. For this simple response they received refreshments and copious social reinforcement. A second simple response, talking for a brief period of time into a tape recorder, yielded immediate reinforcement in the form of money. While the type of schedule and type of reinforcement were being modified, new responses were required of the boys. Involvement in other activities such as electronics, sports, and recreation received lavish approval. During therapy sessions, Dr. Schwitzgebel directed the conversation—it was no longer acceptable to ramble on in a meaningless and unstructured fashion. More informative verbal responses were required.

Fading provided the means by which Dr. Schwitzgebel established himself as a psychotherapist and a person worthy of trust. Eventually, it was necessary to supplement the tape recorder with his own presence. While it may seem unlikely that an individual, even a delinquent, would prefer to talk to a mechanical device rather than to a sensitive and well-trained clinician, it must be remembered that previous history and current pressures made an immediate acceptance of Dr. Schwitzgebel impossible. Through a gradual procedure of associating himself with the tape recorder and therapy room, the youngsters spent more time interacting with Dr. Schwitzgebel and less time talking directly to the tape recorder. Dr. Schwitzgebel's accepting nature and understanding soon increased the rate of this type of behavior.

In this study, we have seen how gradual change may take place in several dimensions simultaneously. When used in conjunction with other principles such as shaping and attenuation of reinforcing consequences, fading techniques hold hope for problems which beset many human beings. That these same techniques can be used to awesome disadvantages is pointed out in the next section.

Brainwashing

"More than any other American prisoners in any previous war (and we have a good deal of data about American prisoners of war), more than any others, these men seemed to be acquiesing to their Chinese Communist controllers. They seemed to be taking more part in Communist propaganda activities than Americans have ever done in the past: the things they were saying, the letters they were writing home to their mothers and the editors of their hometown newspapers begging them to band with other progressive members of the people and stop this senseless slaughter of innocent Koreans by the profiteering Wall Street warmongers. This kind of thing coming out of Korean prisoner camps, written by our Americans with perhaps an eighth or ninth grade education, led us to believe something strange was happening. Then finally the war ended and we got these Americans back to us. A number of things immediately came to light which were profoundly disturbing. Number one, out of the seven thousand men we could identify as being prisoners of war, we got four thousand back and that was all. And much of what we expected to find—evidence of mass executions and systematic starvation, the wiping out of large numbers of men—we failed to find. The second finding that came to light was that these men, when they came home, did not quite behave like Americans in the past had behaved upon liberation.

"One of the first things we noticed was they seemed strangely silent with each other. They came back after having shared an intensely real, frightening, threatening situation. Three years of common captivity and terror and hardship, experiences which normally bind men together in tight, lasting relationships, showed they were almost like they were strangers to one another. They wouldn't talk to each other; they didn't communicate. Then we jumped hastily to the conclusion that these men had been subjected to a rather new phenomenon, a process that we had been hearing about, largely a Chinese invention, called brainwashing. We came to the conclusion that there was probably something irresistible about it, and something that changed the way people think, possibly even depriving them of their reason or of their power of choice and thus their moral and legal responsibility. We found, however, on examination of what actually should be called brainwashing, in my opinion, that it was none of the things we expected. The soldier fighting in Korea who thought at all about getting captured by this diabolical oriental enemy, based on what they knew about Japanese treatment of Americans in World War II and other legends that exist in our society, fully expected at least burning bamboo splinters under his fingernails when first questioned. There are also some other oriental tortures which hardly bear description in a civilized group. Well, we found to our surprise that less than 1 percent of all the American prisoners in Korea, Americans held by the Communists, received deliberate overt physical abuse, anything that would be called torture in any sense.

"Secondly, we assumed that they used drugs of some kind to influence men. It's well known that men addicted to narcotics will do a great deal to get the next shot. We know that the Chinese have a good deal to do with the illicit narcotic traffic throughout the world. They did not, however, use narcotics or any other kind of drugs to influence their American prisoners. They didn't use any magic that we could discover. They didn't use Pavlov's conditioned reflex or any of the more recent experimental studies done in this country or in Canada on what they call stimulus deprivation. They just didn't use anything that was very magical or new in any way. They didn't use an attractive young female type approach or any Mata Hari type to lead these innocent young soldiers down the promised path to Communism, either.

"These explanations are inadequate. Looking at what was done to these men, we discovered that they were possessed of something called brainwashing all right, but in reality, what it was, was a program of education and one of a very high order of excellence. It was a program of indoctrination that was used in a careful, systematic, and very thoughtful way (and for the first time that we know anything about on this kind of a scale) certain fundamental, perfectly sound, tested principles of psychology and psychiatry; principles that are identical to ones we use every day in the handling of patients. These are used in a Communist state somewhat in reverse, not in an attempt to make people into more adult, more responsive, responsible, more contributing members of the social group, nor on the other hand, to drive them into some kind of mental illness either, but basically an attempt to disrupt normal relationships among individuals.

"It was basically an educational program and called an educational program. In fact, the prisoners were never called prisoners; they were called students. And they were told right at the very outset that this was going to be the nature of their lives in the Communist states, and the people's democracy. Rather than being kicked, and beaten, and spat upon from the moment of capture, which most of them fully expected, the soldiers were taken to collecting points right after they fell into enemy hands, and were introduced to a young Chinese, usually 25 to 35 years of age, who spoke 1950, U.S.-style English, English he'd learned at Columbia or City College of New York or the University of California where he was a graduate student in social sciences. And this young Chinese, wearing no uniform and carrying no weapon of any kind, would gather a group of these young and fearful men, who realized immediately that there was terrible danger, and gave them a speech which was prescribed absolutely by Peiping, which was repeated consistently all over Korea. It was a speech that went like this:

> Gentlemen, we welcome you to the ranks of the people. We are happy to have liberated you from the imperialist Wall Street warmongers who sent you here. We know you didn't start the war. We know you don't even want to be here. We know you don't even know why you're here. We consider you members of the people like we are. You are not our enemies. We hope you won't consider us your enemies. And to prove that we have nothing against you, we have a lenient policy for your treatment. We want to offer you a position—a deal. And the deal is very simple. From you we ask only one thing, your physical cooperation. Just don't fight us. Don't make it any harder for us than it already is. Remember, we are the people like you are. In return for this we give you the following things. No work—there are no slave camps here—that's capitalist propa-

ganda. We don't have slave camps; there are no road gangs and no coal mines. You're not going to be worked like Americans were worked by the Japanese and the Germans. And secondly, we'll give you the same food and clothing and shelter and medical care that we give our own people, the best we possibly can. We know it isn't as good as what you are used to, but it's the best we've got.

"Now after a six-month period, the Communists started a formal educational program that had a printed curriculum. They taught seven days a week, all day, every day. They never let up, and while they had a well-rounded variegated program of the kind you'd expect to encounter in a good small college, the fact was everything about the program had something to do with the instruction. This is the most intelligent way to teach. Now they had a structured and formal training program involving four and five hours of lectures which were given in the mornings, and given to assembled large audiences who were required to stand up, usually outdoors, because it's almost impossible to fall asleep during a lecture when you're standing up, especially outdoors. These lectures lasted four and five hours, which is typical, we find, in the Communist education system—no coffee breaks, no cigarettes, just four and five hours of a repetitive, rather simple re-iterated lecture. After the lecture the students were divided into small discussion groups. Each man was required to participate in such a group and to put into his own words the content of the lecture. Now, he didn't have to agree with it entirely, or endorse it, although it was easier if you did. He wasn't penalized for disagreeing as long as he did so in a thoughtful and intelligent way. The only requirement was that he must participate, and if he didn't, the only penalty then was that the rest of his group of 10 or 12 men simply weren't allowed to go to supper until they convinced him that he ought to take part. Along about 11:00 at night a bunch of GIs can get pretty ugly about supper, so everybody took part. They took part in discussing and trying to reduce to their own words and their own understanding a number of ideas which are very typically Communist in-doctrination techniques.

"They had athletics. You can't keep 18-year-olds and 20-year-olds in classes and discussion groups seven days a week and not expect to have some pretty serious trouble and a great falling off of any learning. They had football, baseball, soccer, and volley ball; a lot of athletics. But, you know, in the Communist system, athletics is a function of the democratic society. For example, you're never allowed to pitch for the baseball team because of some undemocratic accident of nature happened to equip you with a big shoulder, a good eye, and a fast pitching arm, because this just wouldn't be fair. If you wanted to pitch for the baseball team, you didn't do so on that basis, you did so because you had demonstrated that you were a worthwhile and deserving member of the People's Democracy—which means you have the right attitudes, you're learning the right things, and you're taking the right part in the discussions in education, therefore demonstrating your worth. And so it was all through if you weren't the athlete that wanted to put on plays. You were allowed to do this if your attitude was right.

"And for those who weren't interested in any of those activities, but preferred art work, or this kind of expression, they had art classes and art groups which you could participate in as long as what you produced was art. Now, pictures of girls, that was not art. Pictures of Harry Truman with bloody dripping claws gathering up his exploited tools of the imperialist warmongers and throwing them into the claws of death in Korea, that's art, especially with the picture of General Motors rubbing its hands in the background. Now, if you could think up stuff like this, you could take part in the art classes, and not only could you take part in them, but you got paid for such productions. We found these productions showing up in Communist literature all over the world, in reams and tons of propaganda material that's dropped every day and distributed throughout India, and Pakistan, and Indonesia, and Syria. This stuff was fairly valuable, signed by an American soldier, and seeming to their side exactly what the Communists had been saying all along about us.

"They had camp newspapers that were used the same way. If your creative impulses were of a writing nature, you could write articles. The first one we saw like this, I think, was in the *New York Daily Worker*, reprinted from a camp newspaper in Korea, called 'Toward Truth and Peace.' The article said, and I quote, 'I wish to express my profound and heartfelt gratitude to the kind and benevolent members of the Chinese People's Volunteer Army in North Korea for having gone to the enormous difficulty and expense of teaching me to read and write English because in the capitalist and imperialist community of Pittsburg, from which I come, only the sons of the wealthy capitalists are allowed to read and write English.' Signed, Private John Smith, U.S. Army.

"Well, this disturbed us, of course, and so we waited for John to come home so we could talk to him about this article. He was a little surprised to find himself a world famous and notorious author. He admitted that, quite frankly, that he'd written it, and they didn't make him write it. We thought maybe they'd tortured him into it, but that wasn't true. He said that everybody was writing stuff like that, and that everybody knew that it was a lie; they were paying in cigarettes and it couldn't possibly do any harm, so he wrote it.

"I've emphasized this ideological aspect, but I said at the very beginning that it was designed to control human beings. But how? There were many little gimmicks which worked to accomplish the control. The first was an informing system. Informing in our culture is about the lowest kind of human behavior. Whether you're four years old or whether you're an adult and run across a paid police informer, you're reaction is one of disgust. This is a renunciation of one of the primary values of our social organization—loyalty and responsibility to other people. And yet, in Korea, we saw an informing system that was so big that it proved that we really did know what we were seeing at first. We found that they encouraged informing publicly and promptly rewarding the man who informed, as long as he didn't inform in a vicious or nasty way. Your informing had to be an exercise of a pure sense of social responsibility. And so, when you saw Joe Dokes swiping a turnip and eating the whole thing himself, or not using the latrine properly, or borrowing somebody's canteen cup and not giving it back, anything anti-social, but you didn't really have anything against Joe Dokes, you reported him purely out of your honest desire to see him helped to become a more worthwhile member of the people. Then you were in; then you got rewarded. Again, with cigarettes and candy and money and also with status and publicly given approval expressed by the Chinese in front of the other students.

"Now, this was the encouragement to inform. It had never worked in any sense at all among Americans before, because Americans got so indignant when somebody was informed upon and then suffered as a result that usually the informer's life was worth very little. It worked, however, in Korea. The Chinese wouldn't punish the person who was informed upon so nobody got very upset. Oh, they talked to him, they took him aside, put an arm on his shoulder, and said, 'Now, look, John, we know you've done this, don't deny it, you're not on trial. We know you've done it, and we want you to think about it. We want you to analyze this behavior and see how destructive this is to people. And when we say the people, we're talking about the Americans here in this camp, not us. You don't hurt us. We want you to criticize this behavior, confess that it's wrong, and assert your determination not to repeat it.' And if you went through this seemingly ridiculous kindergarten-type activity, which you did because the Chinese were smart enough to be satisfied with that, if you went through it, that's all they seemed to want, and you were off the hook. You went back to your fellow students. So nobody got very upset about the informers and nobody did anything about the informers; then all of a sudden they discovered there was an informer in every group of four or five men. This is what they were after; they weren't after information. We can identify one American who was an informer out of every ten surviving Americans. We've never seen anything like that before.

"All of the sudden you begin to sense that you never can be quite sure who you can trust. And that's exactly what the soldier felt when he came home. He hated you. You know where you stand with somebody who hates you. The lines are drawn; you can handle this situation. But when a perfectly nice fellow who has nothing against you is liable to compromise with you, you don't know where you stand. The limits are no longer defined. And they did the only protective thing they could in such a situation; they began withdrawing from one another. They began insulating themselves against other people. They began to stop communicating. They began to withdraw, in a word, into the most magnificently constructed solitary confinement cell that any dictator has ever dreamed up. And in this one you don't have any steel or any concrete floor, and it can't be fought like a steel and concrete confinement cell. And it's built by an expert; it's built by the prisoner. It's maintained by the prisoner. And it's a solitary confinement of your feelings, your attitudes, your faith in other human beings. This is where you and I get our emotional support. Here all of a sudden, you're emotionally and psychologically isolated, and alone in a crowd of people. And this is what we were seeing when men were coming home from captivity—a great crowd of men all alone.

"In order to enhance this feeling of isolation, they used the technique called self-criticism, which is collectivised as everything is in the People's State, collectivised confessions, sort of. It's a very simple procedure. They would get 10 or 12 of these students together and require each man to get up and confess to other men his shortcomings, his bad attitudes, his selfishness, things he'd done that he knew he shouldn't have done, and things he'd left undone that he ought to have done. He confesses this to the others in a sort of self-righteous kind of way and tries to be sincere about it.

"Now men took part in these groups, as sadly as it seemed to them, because again, you see, the stupid Chinese were happy if you did. And it didn't seem like it was very harmful because, after all, you were only talking to other GIs that were all friends here, you know. And everybody sort of smiled, and took it as a joke. Everybody was doing the same thing. But here again is one of the finest weapons for control that you can possibly contrive. After about a week it wasn't a joke any more. All of a sudden the other people were listening to you. All of a sudden you had the feeling you were in something you couldn't get out of and you'd gone too far. You'd talked yourself right out on a limb, because you and I and every other human being rapidly runs out of superficial and meaningless things to talk about. We begin talking about ourselves. You were exposing more of yourself than you'd originally intended, because this was the one group to which you could no longer belong. And the men came over, and said, 'You know, I feel kind of naked; like they could see right through me. Like they knew more about me than I knew about myself.' And we'd say, 'You mean the Communist agents?' 'No,' they'd say, 'the other prisoners. Sometimes I even felt like they knew what I was thinking about.'

"Now what's the result of this? Does it get you together with other people in your self-criticism group so you can get off your chest your mutual gripes and compare notes and complain about the enemy? Uh huh. Not when it's liable to come up in a self-criticism group, it doesn't. It simply forces you a little further into this solitary confinement cell. You get a little more anxious, and a little uncertain of the other people around you, and then become even more alone."[2]

The foregoing account is taken from an address delivered by one of the army psychiatrists who took part in the reconstruction of practices which occurred at prisoner of war camps.

The most important point this psychiatrist makes is that the Chinese Communists did *not* employ occult or diabolical practices; rather, quite simple principles of psychology were employed—the very same principles we have been discussing.

The reinforcers the Chinese Communists used were of great variety and took the form of both consumable objects, such as cigarettes, candy, and food, and privileges such as participation in recreation, dramatic productions, and art work. In addition, leaders from the ranks of POW's were selected by the Communists because of their proper "attitude." Many privileges accrued to a POW for becoming a group leader.

Shaping procedures can be seen in the art productions and the articles our soldiers were encouraged to produce. At first, even the slightest hint of anti-American feeling which showed through in paintings, newspaper articles, or other POW productions was reinforced with praise as well as cigarettes and candy. For reinforcement to be further forthcoming, however, the next production was required to have a slightly more definitive anti-American nature.

Shaping was employed in the group sessions and in the informing system. In the group sessions, the soldiers were at first required merely to talk. This response was made initially in an extremely jocular and nonchalant manner. Later, condi-

2. Army Leaders; Discussion of Chinese Reds' brainwashing techniques. On tape.

tions were gradually changed. Our soldiers found themselves revealing personal information they had guarded closely most of their lives. This self-criticism tended to isolate the soldiers from each other and to make them mutually distrustful.

The informing system is a unique use of reinforcement techniques. Information which a prisoner is required to give his captors is limited to "name, rank, and service number." A prisoner may, on the other hand, offer more information if he wishes. The amount of information is usually defined by his fellow prisoners, who may condone some acts and censure others. In the end, however, the amount of cooperation or informing which an individual may acceptably do becomes a difficult personal discrimination. When their captors rewarded all informing, regardless of its inconsequential nature, and refrained from punishing informers, it became impossible for the soldiers to discriminate what was or was not appropriate information to relay to the Communists.

The result of the informing procedure was a situation in which the possibility of a planned escape or any other type of group action was impossible. It was not easy for one prisoner to trust a fellow prisoner. He did not know any longer if the things he held important and sacred held the same value for his companions.

Summary

Fading, shaping, and attenuation of reinforcing consequences are similar in that all involve gradual change. Attenuation of reinforcing consequences entails gradual change of schedule and amount or type of reinforcement, and shaping entails a change in the response class which is reinforced. Fading involves gradual change in the stimuli, events or objects the organism is to discriminate.

1. In attempting to deal with juvenile delinquents in a therapeutic setting, one psychologist found it necessary to initially offer maximal reinforcement in the form of money, refreshments, and pleasant social interaction, and to delete all aspects of control and authority typically present in therapeutic settings. As his clients began to reliably come to his establishment, authority and control, as well as other practices of psychotherapy, were gradually introduced. Shaping, fading, and attenuation of reinforcing consequences were employed in the program.

2. A narrative account by a psychiatrist, knowledgeable in brainwashing procedures, revealed that brainwashing was in reality nothing more than simple reinforcement techniques. Shaping procedures were used to bring the American prisoners to produce anti-American art and written materials, as well as false confessions. Fading techniques were used to isolate our soldiers from their companions and to ensure the impossibility of group action.

QUESTIONS

1. Another technique which at first glance appears similar to fading is called
   S_____.

2. The reason that shaping and fading appear to be similar at first is because in both cases there is a gradual change from something the experimenter does not particularly want as an end result to one that is acceptable. (a) True; (b) False.

3. Three types of gradual change were said to be important in behavior modification programs. These were shaping, fading, and attenuation of reinforcing consequences. Match one of these three to each of the following: (a) changing from CRF to FR 10; (b) reinforcing eye contact and then mouth movement; (c) going from FR 10 to FR 200; (d) training a subject to discriminate a horizontal line from a vertical one, and then changing the vertical line slowly until it is diagonal; (e) withdrawing all reinforcement.

4. The primary difference between shaping and fading is: (a) in shaping, the response that is reinforced does not change as it does in fading; (b) in fading, the response changes, but more slowly than with shaping; (c) in fading, the response does not change, whereas the reinforced response in shaping changes repeatedly; (d) none of the above describes the situation.

5. The thing that really changes in fading is: (a) the response; (b) the stimuli which the subject is to discriminate; (c) the size or quantity of reinforcement; (d) the schedule of reinforcement.

6. The population of subjects in the Street Corner Psychotherapy report was: (a) retardates; (b) prisoners of war; (c) juvenile delinquents; (d) hard-of-hearing children.

7. The juvenile delinquents were anxious to see a psychologist because of their problems. (a) True; (b) False.

8. Dr. Schwitzgebel (did, did not) embrace the above hypothesis. (a) True; (b) False.

9. The approach of many professionals is that people who are emotionally disturbed should know enough to know they need help. (a) True; (b) False.

10. Dr. Schwitzgebel first spent several weeks in getting to know the neighborhood. (a) True; (b) False.

11. What was the initial proposition Dr. Schwitzgebel offered to his clients?

12. What was Dr. Schwitzgebel's behavior toward his clients on their first visit in terms of each of the following: (a) rules and regulations; (b) payment; (c) general attitude; (d) psychotherapy.

13. Knowing that talking to these boys alone would not alleviate their basic problems, what other forms of activity did Dr. Schwitzgebel provide?

14. Dr. Schwitzgebel's approach is probably the most effective one to date with juvenile delinquents. (a) True; (b) False.

15. Americans held prisoner by the Chinese Communists seemed to cooperate with their captors more than any previous American prisoners of war. (a) True; (b) False.

16. Which of the following techniques were used widely by the Chinese Communists to control their prisoners: (a) Hypnotism; (b) Drugs; (c) Pavlovian techniques; (d) None of the above.

17. There was really nothing used by the Chinese Communists but very simple principles of psychology. (a) True; (b) False.

18. What type of individual was used to first introduce the prisoners to the aims of the prison camp? Where was this individual educated? What language did he speak? What was his general attitude?

19. Classes in the Communist POW camps took place: (a) three days a week; (b) every other week; (c) seven days a week; (d) not at all.

20. What did it take to be the pitcher on the POW baseball team?

21. What kind of art work was rewarded?

22. Why did the author, who was a prisoner at the camp, write anti-American articles in a POW camp newspaper?

23. Can you briefly describe the informing procedure at the POW camps? Was it effective? Why?

24. Explain the group sessions and how they resulted in isolation of the prisoners from each other.

25. Name several of the reinforcers used by the Chinese Communists.

26. Give at least two instances of shaping procedures.

27. Do you feel that brainwashing techniques could ever be used in this country?

NOTES
Brainwashing

The inclusion of the section on brainwashing is indeed appropriate. It points out how very simple principles of psychology, in fact, techniques no more complex than those already presented in this book, can be used to the disadvantage of other individuals or groups.

These simple techniques were so effective with so many of our boys who were prisoners of the Chinese Communists that it was speculated that the Communists were using some strange, bizarre, and occult type of persuasion. Many of our leading psychiatrists, physicians, and psychologists made wild guesses as to what fantastic means must have been employed to bring about the vast changes in behavior which were observed in our returning prisoners of war. Some professionals speculated that drugs or surgery were involved. Others speculated that starvation and extreme physical abuse had been employed for long periods of time.

Most popular among those supposed horrendous and terrible techniques were those involving classical or Pavlovian conditioning. It was established that the Chinese Communists were protégés of the Russians, and, of course, it was the Russian physiologist Ivan Pavlov who had introduced classical conditioning to the world. Classical conditioning involves the elicitation of a response by a previously neutral stimulus. In Pavlov's study, for instance, dogs were found to salivate when meat powder was brought close to them. By pairing a bell with the presentation of meat powder for several trials, Pavlov demonstrated that the bell alone would elicit the salivary response. The Russians have continued to expand and extend the classical conditioning procedure and have advanced, according to some writers, far ahead of us in classical conditioning. It can be seen why many people speculated that classical conditioning was the device which had warped the minds of our returning brothers and sons.

After the exchange at Panmunjon, groups of psychiatrists, both from the military and from private practice, interrogated the returning prisoners of war in great detail. They found, by and large, that physical abuse such as torture and other forms of extreme cruelty were rarely used. While the prisoners admitted that they did not dine on the finest cuisine, neither could they say that starvation had been used as a means of punishment or to break their spirits, as the psychiatrists had speculated.

The types of things which had been done to them seemed simple, almost humane, and had not appeared to be directed toward "breaking" them or reducing them to the form of lower animals. Upon analysis, it was found that the techniques were basic and simple principles of operant psychology. Almost all of the important behavior changes were brought about by the use of reinforcement in the form of cigarettes, sweets, or privileges. These reinforcers were dispensed when the soldiers showed desirable behavior. Desirable behavior was, of course, any behavior which tended to isolate the soldiers from each other, thus precluding violent escape efforts and decreasing esprit de corps. Other reinforcers were also dispensed for anti-American sentiments exhibited in writing, painting, dramatics, and speeches, as well as other forms of what turned out to be unpatriotic endeavors.

The reinforcers which were used were simple commodities, but they were very powerful because they were combined with quite ingenious uses of shaping or the method of successive approximation and, as you have learned earlier in this chapter, by the use of fading techniques. It was quite obvious that the behavioral changes had been brought about so gradually and in such a subtle manner that many of our troops were not aware that they had changed appreciably or that what they were doing was in any way disloyal or anti-American.

Upon reflection, it should not be surprising that the very simple principles we have explicated thus far could be used to bring about such behavior changes as seen in prisoners during the Korean War. In previous pages equally drastic behavior changes have been seen in psychotics, retardates, juvenile delinquents, animals, and even normal people. The principles of behavior are like the gun which is neither dangerous nor harmless until it is placed in someone's hands.

12

The Puppet and the Pupil

Picture, if you will, a house trailer. Inside, an experimental psychologist is introducing a nursery school student, Penny, to a puppet.[1] The puppet is sitting on a chair on a small stage.

The psychologist points to a lever protruding from the wall. "This is your lever. See, it's just like Jimmy's lever, only bigger." Indeed, there is a small lever protruding from the wall near Jimmy's chair. "Do you know how it works?"

"No."

The psychologist presses the lever several times. Each time the lever is pressed and then released, it returns to its normal position. "You try it." Penny does so with no difficulty. "I'm going to leave for a few minutes. Why don't you sit down here, and you and Jimmy can talk." Penny sits down, and the psychologist disappears behind a screen in the corner of the room. Penny and Jimmy immediately strike up a conversation.

At one point in the conversation, Jimmy, the puppet, does a strange thing. For no apparent reason, he starts pressing his miniature puppet lever. He presses it very slowly for a few minutes, then very rapidly, and then very slowly again. However, he does not let this activity interfere with the conversation. After about ten minutes of talking and story telling, Jimmy stops pressing the lever. During this time Penny does not touch her lever once.

Then Jimmy the puppet asks, "Can you do this? Glub-flub-bub."

Penny giggles and says, "Glub-flub-bub."

"That's very good, Penny." They continue their conversation, and then, "Can you do this?" The puppet nods its head vigorously.

Penny pauses for a second and then joins in the head nodding with equal vigor.

1. This section based on Baer, D. M., and Sherman, J. A. Reinforcement control of generalized imitation in young children. *Journal of Experimental Child Psychology, 1,* 37–49.

"That's fine." After more conversation, "Now can you do this?" The puppet exaggeratedly opens and closes his mouth.

So does Penny.

"Good." And later, "Now try this one, one–two–three–four."

"One–two–three–four."

"Fine." After more conversation, "The red robins run rapidly."

"The red robins run rapidly."

The puppet nods his head, and Penny nods her head.

"Good." The puppet begins exaggerated mouthing, and Penny starts the exaggerated mouthing.

"That's fine." Then the puppet starts another conversation with Penny. Sometimes he tells her colorful stories and sometimes he asks her questions. Every now and then he makes one of his nonsense statements, vigorously nods his head, or mouths exaggeratedly. Every time the puppet makes one of these bizarre responses, Penny is quick to follow. And the puppet is just as quick to deliver a small but powerful social reinforcer in the form of praise. During this time, Jimmy the puppet begins to press his lever again. Sometimes the puppet presses the lever at a high rate and sometimes at a low rate. Their conversation lasts for about one-half hour that day.

Penny returns to talk with Jimmy on several other occasions; as before, Jimmy intersperses his conversation with nonsense statements, head nodding, and mouthing. Penny almost invariably imitates him. The social reinforcement of praise is immediately forthcoming for this imitation. The puppet starts pressing the lever again, and Penny also begins gradually pressing her lever. However, she only does this when Jimmy the puppet is pressing his. The puppet never reinforces or pays attention to Penny's lever pressing. Eventually every time Jimmy presses the lever, Penny does the same. She is imitating Jimmy's lever-pressing behavior even though she is never reinforced for doing so.

These results were not peculiar to Penny. The experiment was performed with eleven children. All eleven developed the imitative behavior and all but four developed nonreinforced imitative bar pressing.

This experiment illustrates two things. First, the nodding, mouthing, and nonsense statements show how imitative behavior can be conditioned. This part of the experiment is a discrimination experiment in which we have multiple S^Ds and multiple responses. For example, the puppet's head nodding is an S^D for Penny's head-nodding response. It is an S^Δ for mouthing, saying nonsense sentences, or any other responses, for that matter. In the same way, the puppet's mouthing and saying nonsense syllables are S^Ds for making the same responses and S^Δs for making any other response.

Secondly, the experiment demonstrates the generalization of imitation. The specific stimuli of head nodding, mouthing, and saying nonsense sentences were discriminative stimuli for an imitative response. This control exercised by these stimuli generalized to the stimulus of the puppet's pressing the lever. In other words, the puppet's lever-press response served as an S^D for Penny's imitative response of pressing her lever. All of the stimuli which serve as discriminative stimuli for imitation form a single class of stimuli called imitative stimuli. Reinforcing responses to some of the members of that stimulus class make it more likely that imitative responses will also occur when other members of the stimulus class are presented. In other words, there is generalization within a stimulus class.

More is involved here, however, than simple stimulus generalization. Not only do we have a class of imitative stimuli, but we also have a class of imitative responses. Penny's head nodding, mouthing, saying nonsense sentences, and lever pressing are all imitative responses when they occur in the presence of the proper discriminative stimuli. Reinforcing certain members of the class of imitative responses makes it more likely that other members of this class will occur when the appropriate imitative discriminative stimuli are present. This illustrates the principle of response generalization. As you will recall, the principle of response generalization states that the reinforcement of one member of a response class increases the frequency of occurrence of other members of the same response class.

Generalization of imitation consists of both stimulus generalization and response generalization.

This experiment shows that the imitative response may be controlled by reinforcement like any other response. In the present case, we were working with a fairly sophisticated child. Penny was a normal nursery school student. Like most children her age, she had undoubtedly been imitating various behaviors for two or three years. For example, it is believed that one of the main ways in which children learn to talk is through imitation. It may be that many things that children learn involve imitation of this sort.

We have found that imitation may be modified through the use of reinforcement with a child who already had many imitative responses in her repertoire before the experiment began. What would happen if we worked with a child who was unable to imitate? Could we condition imitative responses in such a child? This question is answered in the next section.

Conditioning of Imitation in a Retarded Child

Marilla was profoundly retarded and lived at the Firecrest School in Seattle, Washington. Although she was 12 years old, Marilla would only make an occasional grunting sound. She responded to a few simple verbal commands such as, "Come here," "Sit down," and so forth. She had not learned to walk until she was seven years old. By the time she was 12, however, she could dress and feed herself and was fairly well toilet-trained. She had reasonably good hand-eye coordination and was able to make simple manipulatory responses such as turning a knob and opening a door. Aside from this meager repertoire of behavior, she had few other responses worth noting. She had certainly never been observed to show any signs of imitative behavior.[2]

Once, when Dr. Donald Baer was visiting the Firecrest School, Marilla was

2. This section based on Baer, D. M., Peterson, R. F., and Sherman, J. A. Development of imitation by reinforcing behavioral similarity to a model. *Journal of the Experimental Analysis of Behavior*, 1967, *10*, 405–415.

pointed out to him. "Dr. Baer, although we have done everything we could for this little girl, I'm afraid that it wasn't very much. She's really a pathetic case. Frankly, it just seems like she's too dumb to learn anything. I wonder if any of your reinforcement techniques could help her."

"Well, I think maybe something could be done; it would certainly be worth a try. There are a couple of grad students at the University of Washington who might be interested in helping me work with this child. If you want, I'll see what we can do."

"We certainly would be grateful if you could do anything for her, because if you don't, I'm afraid she will never be much more than an animal."

Don Baer and the two students felt that Marilla's lack of imitative responses might be crucial in helping to account for her painfully slow behavioral development. If much of a normal child's behavior is acquired through imitation, then you can imagine how difficult learning would be for a child who was unable to imitate.

Suppose that you were trying to teach a child the simple nursery rhyme about Mary and her little lamb. If the child could make imitative verbal responses, then the task would be fairly simple. Most parents would probably teach a child such a nursery rhyme by telling him to repeat the rhyme after them. They would go through it a phrase at a time, until the child was able to repeat it in longer and longer phrases. Eventually the child would be able to say it without any special prompting. The process of imitation is the key to this relatively easy job of teaching a nursery rhyme.

But suppose you were working with a child like Marilla, who could not imitate. You would certainly have your work cut out for you. The nursery rhyme can be considered to be a sequence of complex vocal responses much like any other sequence of responses. Each response is slightly different than the preceding one. Indeed, this is a *very* complex response sequence. You would need to use a shaping procedure in which reinforcement was presented each time the proper word or sound which approximated that word occurred. In a most tedious manner, you would gradually develop the sequence of verbal responses which constitute the nursery rhyme. Such an accomplishment is theoretically possible by the use of shaping. However, your efforts to condition the recitation of such a nursery rhyme would probably extinguish before the junior orator had mastered it. The lack of proper imitative behavior of this sort is very common among retarded children. Suppose a technique were developed for teaching Marilla generalized imitative behavior. Such a technique might be very important for her and other retarded children in establishing more complex behavioral repertoires.

Before he actually started trying to condition imitative behavior, Don Baer spent a few days observing Marilla and noted that she made no imitative responses. Don even played with her in the ward for several hours, and, in the course of his play, repeatedly asked her to imitate some simple response, such as clapping hands or waving. Marilla always failed to imitate, yet it had been observed that she was capable of making at least some of the responses.

On the first day that Don actually tried to condition imitative behavior, he took Marilla from the ward just before her lunch hour. They went to a special room where they would not be distracted. When Marilla first went into the strange room, she looked around at the chairs and table and then looked at Don. He said, "Do this," and raised his arm. Marilla continued to stare at him. Don repeated this several times, but Marilla made no response. Finally, he said, "Do this," raised his arm one more time, and this time held Marilla's hand and raised it for her. He then took a spoon which contained a bite of Marilla's lunch, and fed it to her; at the same time, he said, "Good." After several trials of this sort, Don began to fade out his assistance gradually. He would only partially raise Marilla's arm, requiring her to raise it the rest of the way before he delivered reinforcement. Don's assistance was gradually faded out until Marilla made an unassisted arm-raising response. She then received food reinforcement and social reinforcement in the form of the word "Good." Occasionally Marilla would raise her arm even when Don had not done so. On these occasions the response went unreinforced and was gradually extinguished. Eventually she raised her arm only when Don said, "Do this," and raised his own arm.

Thus far we have merely demonstrated a simple discrimination. In the presence of the S^D (Don's saying "Do this," and raising his arm), a response occurred (Marilla raised her arm), and was reinforced (presentation of food and praise). In the presence of an S^Δ (Don's saying nothing and not raising his arm), the response (Marilla's raising her arm) went unreinforced.

After this simple discrimination was well developed, the same technique was used to establish several other imitative discriminations. The next one consisted of Marilla tapping a table with her left hand whenever Don said, "Do this," and tapped the table himself. Other imitations she learned were tapping her chest with her left hand, tapping her head with her left hand, and so forth. Don preceded each particular imitative S^D with the words, "Do this." Whenever a new imitative S^D was first introduced, a small amount of shaping was required. However, less and less shaping and prompting were needed on each successive response. By the time they got to the seventh new response, they had just finished conditioning imitative nose tapping. Then Don said, "Do this," and for the first time tapped the arm of a chair. Marilla immediately imitated him by also tapping the arm of the chair. She had made this particular imitative response though she had never been reinforced for doing so. The imitation established with the previous responses had generalized to this new response.

Marilla had finally demonstrated generalized imitation. Don breathed a sigh of relief. He had only needed to condition seven imitative responses before generalized imitation had developed. Now, the rest would be easy going. In order to continue the demonstration of generalized imitation he quickly moved on to the next response. He tapped the leg of the table and waited several seconds for Marilla to do the same, but nothing happened. After ten seconds had elapsed with no response from Marilla, Don went through the sequence of responses which Marilla had previously demonstrated. He reinforced each previously learned imitation as usual, and eventually got back to the response of tapping the table leg. But Marilla still would not imitate him. It was apparent that Don's task was far from finished; much more training would be needed before the more general imitative behavior would be attained.

Don returned to guiding and shaping the response. He had to condition two more imitative responses before another instance of generalized imitation was observed. He had just conditioned the response of Marilla's extending her left arm in imitation. Now he began making a circular motion with that arm for the first time. Marilla immediately imitated this motion. They then went through the sequence of imitative responses which Marilla had learned. Don reinforced all of those which had been previously reinforced, but was careful not to reinforce tapping of the chair or making the circular motion with her arm. Both of these generalized imitative responses were maintained; they did not extinguish in spite of repeated nonreinforced occurrences intermixed with the reinforcd imitative responses.

Then Don said, "Do this," and stood up. He had every expectation that Marilla would be quick to follow. But, once again, it was necessary to shape the imitative response. In fact, it was not until the twenty-third response that a new imitation again occurred without reinforcement. That imitative response consisted of tapping the shoulder. The percentage of new responses that were correctly imitated without reinforcement on the first demonstration gradually increased. After about 120 different responses had been learned, all the new responses were imitated without reinforcement. Some of these responses were a little more interesting than the earlier ones. They consisted of such things as scribbling, placing geometric forms on a form board, crawling under a table, flying an airplane, and burping a doll. Although reinforcement and shaping were needed for many responses, near the end of the study only a few trials were required before most of the responses were learned, whereas, at the beginning of the study, a large amount of conditioning was required for each new response. It took an average of over three sessions to condition each of the first 10 new responses, but after 20 responses had been conditioned, it required an average of less than half a session to condition each new response. This rapid rate of learning new imitative responses remained fairly consistent for the remainder of this phase of the study.

Now that good imitative behavior had been well established, the question remained as to what was maintaining this imitative behavior. Being the astute student of psychology that you are, you no doubt suspect that the food and social reinforcements are the primary factors; Don Baer had a similar suspicion.

A reader with less understanding of the problem than you might say, "That's silly. The whole purpose of this study was to show that you could get generalized imitation without reinforcement."

"Of course," you would be quick to reply, "But, good sir, you fail to comprehend the subtleties of the issue at hand." Clever Dr. Baer has indeed demonstrated that specific imitative responses can be learned without direct reinforcement of those particular responses. But it still may be the case that reinforcement of some of the other imitative responses is needed before any imitative responses are learned. He used reinforcement to condition some imitative responses so that the imitation could generalize to other responses where reinforcement would not be used.

The presumptuous critic would no doubt look down at his shoes and say, "I feel like such a dope. Your illuminating explanation throws a new light on the whole subject."

You, being not only bright but also a "regular fellow," would no doubt nudge the desolate young man in the ribs with your elbow and console him with, "Don't feel so bad; everyone makes a complete and utter ass of himself sometimes. Why don't we go to our friendly neighborhood tavern for a Coca-Cola, or some other soft, but nourishing, drink."

Down the library steps and across the quad, off you go to a riotous evening of college drinking songs and stimulating conversation about the college man's favorite topics: politics, sex, religion, sex, the principles of reinforcement, and of course, sex. But, as the inspiration for this flight of literary fancy would say, "We digress."

We have seen that a few imitative responses can be acquired without direct reinforcement. But now we know that does not necessarily mean that reinforcement is not needed for at least some of the other imitative responses. It was the significance of reinforcement in this role that was specifically studied.

The nature of this problem might best be understood if we first look at a simpler case. Suppose that you and a friend are invited to the home of your learned psychology professor. Suppose further that your friend, unfortunate fellow, has not had the enlightening experience of reading this book. During the course of an hour's chat with your psychology teacher, you have the opportunity to observe his five-year-old daughter. Like all psychologists' children, she is extremely charming. She appears to be one of the happiest children you have ever seen. While not being boisterous or unruly, she is amused, entertained, and blissfully content. You also observe that like most psychologists, your professor takes great pleasure in his child and expresses it by frequently showering attention, affection, love, and an occasional M&M upon her.

You cannot help but notice that the psychologist-father only delivers these reinforcers after the child has made some happy sort of response. Your psychologically naive friend is amazed at the happy home life which he witnesses. But you, knowing that your professor is a staunch advocate of reinforcement principles, had expected nothing less. You explain to your friend that "happiness is *not* a warm puppy"; "happiness is a conditioned response." Your professor is reinforcing the child on an intermittent schedule for being happy and having a good time. Your friend is quick to point out that you do not reinforce happiness; happiness just happens. He asserts that happiness will be more likely to happen at a warm, loving home, and that is just what the psychologist, regardless of his inhuman profession, is providing. You counter this notion by saying that a warm, loving home is not enough; what is important here is that warmth and love be presented immediately after occurrences of happy behavior.

You both agree that warmth and love may be crucial factors. You think that they must immediately follow the desired happiness responses. Your friend staunchly avows that the particular behaviors which love and warmth precede or follow are quite beside the point. They must, however, be generally present. How would you go about resolving this disagreement?

Right you are; you would perform an experiment. Now, just what sort of an experiment would you perform? Someone less skilled than yourself in the area of scientific research might suggest a simple extinction experiment. In other words, you would withhold the supposed reinforcement of love, warmth, etc., and see if the frequency of happiness responses decreased.

As you can see, that would not do. If you simply withhold love and warmth, you would predict that happiness responses would decrease in frequency, and your friend would make the same prediction. He would say that when you take love and warmth from the house, happiness, of course, goes with them.

As you knew all along, it will be necessary to have the potential reinforcer present in the situation but it must be made sure that it does not occur immediately following a response. In other words, if the love and warmth are still there, the friend will argue that happiness should remain. On the other hand, since the love and warmth are no longer immediately following happiness behavior, you will argue that happiness will be on its way out.

In the course of this discussion, your friend becomes quite disturbed about what a cold, mean, unloving scientist you are to even dream of such an experiment. He begins shouting such names at you as "torturer," "beast," "sadist," and "dirty young man." He angrily and noisily stomps from the house. You look apologetically at your host and shrug your shoulders. You would like to run after him, but alas, you do not want to reinforce his juvenile behavior.

Unfortunately, your friend left before you had time to design an appropriate experiment. However, in the next few paragraphs, we will discuss a procedure which would have helped you and your friend solve the debate.

With that illustrative example under our belts, we can now turn to the slightly more complicated problem of demonstrating the relevance of reinforcement in the development of imitative behavior. One way to demonstrate this relevance is to simply withhold the reinforcement and see if the response rate decreases. But, as we saw, this will not suffice. The problem is that we wish to demonstrate more than the importance of food and social praise. We wish to demonstrate that *following* the imitative response *immediately* with such potential reinforcements is the crucial factor. It is not just the *presence* of these goodies in the training sessions which is responsible for the acquisition and maintenance of the imitative behavior. We suspect that the goodies must *immediately follow* the occurrence of the response. In order to demonstrate this, it is necessary to have the potential reinforcers present in the conditioning session; but we must also insure that the potential reinforcers do not immediately follow an imitative response.

We can be certain that reinforcement never follows the response by waiting until Marilla stops making imitative responses for 30 seconds, and then we can present the reinforcement. As long as Marilla keeps making imitative responses, no reinforcement will occur. However, as soon as she goes for 30 seconds without making an imitative response, reinforcement will be delivered. This insures that the reinforcement never immediately follows the imitative response. If Marilla makes no imitative responses and simply sits there, she could get a reinforcement every 30 seconds. This procedure is called differential reinforcement of other behavior (DRO). As long as Marilla is making responses *other* than imitative ones, reinforcement will be forthcoming. This procedure is in a sense doubly powerful as a means of eliminating behavior; it not only ensures that the response being studied is extinguished, but it also ensures that other incompatible responses are reinforced.

The effect of differentially reinforcing nonimitative behavior was quite striking. Over a period of less than 20 sessions, the frequency of imitative responses decreased until practically no imitation was occurring at all. The decrease in the rate of these imitative responses was essentially the same for both the generalized imitation and the reinforced imitation. The generalized imitation appeared to be nearly as strong as the imitation which had been reinforced.

These results indicate that the generalized imitative responses were being maintained because the other imitative responses were being reinforced. In a sense, they were being maintained *indirectly* through reinforcement. Those responses which have developed and have been maintained previously without direct reinforcement cannot survive extinction applied to the entire class of imitative responses.

Now that it was clear that reinforcement was responsible for the maintenance of the imitative behavior, reinforcement for imitation was resumed, and an attempt was made to establish more elaborate sequences of imitative responses. Sequences of responses of this sort are sometimes called *response chains*. Initially, only two-response chains were demonstrated. The experimenter would make two responses such as raising his left arm and then standing up. When Marilla performed the same sequence of two imitative responses, reinforcement was delivered. After the two-response chains were mastered, the number of responses in the chain was gradually increased until as many as seven responses could be maintained in a single chain. Marilla could correctly imitate these long sequences after a total of only ten hours of conditioning of the various response chains. At times, some of these response chains contained new responses which had not been previously learned.

When the study had gotten to the point where Marilla could imitate virtually any new motor performance which Don demonstrated, Don and Marilla began working on the development of verbal behavior. The first time that this was done, Don said, "Ah." He repeated this several times and also tried several other vocal responses interspersed with the usual motor responses. Marilla always imitated the motor responses but consistently failed to imitate the vocal responses. The conditioning of imitative *motor* responses evidently did not generalize to imitative *vocal* responses. This is true even though Marilla did occasionally make grunting noises.

It was obviously going to be necessary to shape the vocal response, that is, to reinforce successive approximations of vocalizations. Don not only used a shaping procedure but also embedded the vocal response in a response chain comprised mainly of motor responses. The first time this was tried, Don said, "Do this," then rose from his chair, walked to the center of the room, turned toward Marilla, said, "Ah," and returned to his seat. Marilla immediately jumped from her chair, walked to the center of the room, turned toward Don, and then made a strange facial expression vaguely resembling Don's when he said, "Ah." But no vocal response was forthcoming. That was all right; the facial expression was a step in the right direction, and, consequently, it was reinforced. On successive trials, the facial expressions became more and more like Don's, and eventually vocal responses began to occur. Don continued to reinforce responses which more and more closely approximated his vocal response until eventually Marilla was saying, "Ah," in a very expert manner. The chain of motor responses became shorter and shorter until eventually Don was able to remain in his seat and say, "Do this," followed by "Ah," and Marilla would imitate the vocal response.

Proceeding in this manner, Don shaped imitations of simple sounds, combined them into longer or more complex sounds, and finally combined them into usable words. After 20 hours of conditioning imitative vocal responses, Marilla was able to imitate such words as "Hi," "Okay," "Marilla," and the names of some objects.

After Marilla's imitative repertoire had developed to a widely generalized state, new experimenters were presented to her to determine whether the new imitation would generalize to their behavior. She was able to imitate not only other male experimenters but also female experimenters as well as she had imitated Don.

This experiment is important because it helped Marilla; however, it has even greater significance. Most of the procedures were also found to be effective for the two other retarded children with whom they were used. This means that remedial techniques of considerable generality have been developed.

Like the experiment in the preceding section, this study shows that imitative behavior may be maintained through the use of reinforcement. The present study is distinguished through its demonstration that imitative behavior may be conditioned by using reinforcement procedures. At first, the responses conditioned to the imitative discriminative stimuli were responses which were clearly well established in the subject's repertoire. However, they had not been brought under the control of imitative discriminative stimuli. After imitative discriminative stimulus control was established by reinforcement of imitative responses, it was possible to rapidly condition new responses not originally in the subject's repertoire. At the same time, these new responses were brought under the control of imitative discriminative stimuli. It was even possible to develop imitative stimulus control of some responses without the direct use of reinforcement.

Incidentally, Bob Peterson, one of the graduate students who worked on this project, continued working with Marilla in doing research for his Ph.D. dissertation. Bob proposed to a faculty committee that he would teach Marilla 20 responses using imitation and 20 other responses without using imitation; then he would compare the effects of various procedures on both of these response classes. One professor, who was not sufficiently familiar with the effectiveness of the principles of reinforcement, objected. Since he had so much trouble teaching normal college students anything, he felt that it would be impractical to take the time necessary to teach a retardate so many new behaviors. Bob's reply that with imitation and reinforcement he expected it to take an hour or two made quite an impression on the skeptical professor. It turned out that Bob's prediction was correct. He simply showed Marilla what to do, and she did it—just like any bright kid!

The Use of Excessive Imitation in the Establishment of Normal Verbal Behavior

We have seen that particular imitative responses can be conditioned through the use of reinforcement with children who already have imitative behaviors. We have also seen that if the proper reinforcement procedures are used, generalized imitation may be established with children who had not previously shown any imitation. These procedures can be used to condition useful responses such as verbal behavior.

The fact that some children are retarded is probably closely related to their lack of imitative behavior. But imitative behavior can cause problems in another direction as well; some children have difficulties because they demonstrate too much imitative behavior.[3] Frequently psychotic and autistic children, as well as retarded and brain-damaged children, suffer from an excess of imitative behavior. They may simply repeat things which other people say in situations where it is not normally appropriate to do so. They may say a word or phrase, or even part of a song, and then repeat it time and time again themselves.

Children with excessive imitative behavior present two problems: the first is how to eliminate the excessive imitative verbal behavior. The second is how to establish normal verbal behavior. It may be that the imitative behavior can be put to good use in the initial establishment of normal verbal behavior before the excessive imitative verbal behavior is eliminated. Consider the child with an inappropriate imitative verbal repertoire. It may be much easier to establish appropriate verbal behavior in this child than in the child who has no verbal nor imitative behavior to begin with. If imitative verbal behavior is already present, much shaping may be eliminated. The following account may illustrate this.

As we walk down a hospital corridor we hear:

> Go tell Aunt Rhody
> Go tell Aunt Rhody
> Go tell Aunt Rhody
> The old Gray Goose is dead.

When we turn the corner it becomes apparent that the high-pitched voice belongs to a seven-year-old boy. We continue walking past but something bothers us—we have seen this boy before. He was three and one-half years old then. This boy is Dickie, the autistic child. You will recall that two psychologists saved Dickie's eyesight by conditioning appropriate glasses-wearing behavior. Sure enough, we turn around and Dickie is still wearing his glasses. We are pleased to note that the child is now so well adjusted that he walks down the hall sing-

3. This section based on Risley, T., and Wolf, M. Establishing functional speech in echolalic children. *Behaviour Research and Therapy*, 1967, 5, 73–88. Copyright © 1967, Pergamon Press, Reprinted by permission of the authors and the publisher.

ing happily. We turn around and walk after him. We would like to have a little chat to see how he's been faring these last few years. We shout after him, "Wait a minute, Dickie, I want to talk to you."

Dickie stops singing but keeps walking. He begins chanting with gradually increasing vigor, "Wait a minute, Dickie, I want to talk to you. Wait a minute, Dickie, I want to talk to you! Wait a minute, Dickie, I want to talk to you!!"

We are a little alarmed, so we run up to him and put our hand on his shoulder. "What's the matter, Dickie?"

He stops walking and begins stamping his feet, on the verge of tears. "Want a spanking. Want a spanking! Want a spanking!! Want a spanking!!!!"

We are more than a little disturbed by this behavior. We had thought that Dickie was in good shape, but we obviously were wrong. It soon becomes apparent that our efforts to console him are of no avail, and seeing that we might simply be reinforcing this undesirable behavior, we leave Dickie to himself.

Several months later, when we have an opportunity to check into Dickie's case, we are reassured to learn that the psychologists who had previously worked with Dickie, Drs. Risley and Wolf, had once again been called in to work with him. Initially Todd and Mont observed that Dickie never made requests, asked questions, or made any comments. Although he occasionally imitated other peoples' behavior, he did not make imitative responses when asked to do so. The two psychologists had decided to try to work with this "compulsive" imitation in an attempt to develop more normal verbal behavior.

As was the case with Marilla, the work with Dickie took place during mealtimes so that food could be used as a reinforcer. A young female attendant took him to a separate room and they sat at a table facing each other. On the first day they worked together, the attendant held up a picture of Santa Claus and prompted, "This is Santa Claus. Now say Santa Claus." No response. Then she held up a picture of a cat and said, "This is a cat. Now say cat." Still no response. After she had presented all five of her pictures, she mixed them in a different order and went through them again. Each time she named the picture and asked Dickie to do likewise.

Finally, on the third time through the sequence, the attendant showed a picture of the cat and prompted, "This is a cat. Now say cat." Dickie's response was, "This is a cat. Now say cat." That was not exactly what the attendant had hoped for, but it was good enough for a beginning. She immediately said, "Good boy," and gave him a bite of his meal. The reinforcement had its effect; Dickie began imitating more and more frequently. After a week of conditioning, he was imitating practically every prompt in addition to everything else the attendant said during the conditioning sessions. The attendant only reinforced those imitative responses which occurred at appropriate times, that is, at times when they were prompted. Inappropriate unprompted imitations went unreinforced.

It soon became apparent that Dickie's verbal responses were under the control of the spoken discriminative stimuli, but the pictures seemed irrelevant; Dickie rarely even bothered to look at them. Instead, he twisted and turned in his seat. In order to correct this and bring Dickie's verbal behavior under the stimulus control of the pictures, an anticipation procedure was used. The attendant held up the picture for several seconds before giving the verbal prompt. If Dickie anticipated the verbal prompt by correctly naming the picture before the picture was given, he was immediately reinforced. By anticipating the prompts he could receive the reinforcers more quickly. Gradually stimulus control was developed with the pictures. Dickie began looking at the pictures and saying the phrases in the presence of the pictures without prompts. Within three weeks of conditioning, appropriate stimulus control over the verbal behavior had been developed with ten different pictures. The attendant then began showing common household objects and pictures in books which Dickie learned to name with increasing ease.

No doubt the thoughtful reader is saying to himself that Dickie's performance is very impressive, but there is certainly more to verbal behavior than naming pictures in books. One of the main advantages of verbal behavior is that we can talk about things which are no longer present. How could you use reinforcement to condition a child like Dickie so that his verbal behavior would be under the control of stimuli outside of his immediate environment? In order to tackle this problem, the attendant would take Dickie outside to play with him on the swing or sliding board. He was then brought back inside and asked, "What did you do outside?" If no response occurred in a few seconds, a prompt was given; the attendant might say, "I was swinging." When Dickie imitated this response he was reinforced. Eventually, he began answering the questions before the prompts were given and thereby received reinforcement sooner than would be the case if he waited for the prompt.

Dickie was also taught to answer other questions such as, "What is your name?" and "Where do you live?" If he did not answer the question, the prompt would be given and the correct response reinforced.

After several weeks of training, Dickie's bag of verbal responses markedly expanded, although much of this behavior was still unusual. He would sometimes imitate the questions before answering them, and he would frequently reverse his pronouns, e.g., he would ask for a drink by saying, "He wants some water."

When Dickie was released from the hospital, the training was continued by his parents. After about six months with his parents he was using pronouns perfectly and was initiating many requests and comments, although he was still making frequent inappropriate imitative responses. He attended a laboratory preschool at the University of Washington for two years. Many of the procedures at this preschool were based on the principles of conditioning; we have already discussed some of the work of this preschool. After two years there, his verbal skills had developed to the point that he was ready for special education in the public school.

Dickie's verbal behavior now resembles that of a skilled five-year-old. This means that, since his special training, his rate of language development has been approximately normal. Now the naturally occurring reinforcers for verbal behavior appeared to be the most important factors in maintaining and expanding his verbal response system.

To date this is one of the few examples in which reinforcement techniques have been used over a prolonged period of time with a person having severe behavior problems. The result of such a treatment is that the patient is able to function in a relatively normal environment. It is to be hoped that in the future more research will be of this nature.

These general procedures were successfully used with several other children suffering from similar behavioral problems. One particular procedure is sufficiently interesting to deserve special mention. This is the procedure used to teach a child named Carey how to initiate verbal statements instead of simply answering questions.

On many occasions at home, this child would chant a word or short phrase over and over, with gradually increasing volume which terminated in piercing shrieks and crying. For example, while standing by the couch, he would repeat, "Sit down. Sit down." His parents could terminate this by responding in any way, e.g., "Yes, Carey." "OK, sit down.", "You can sit down if you want to.", "Be quiet." The parents were requested to record these instances of stereotyped chanting and also to send him to his room for 5 minutes whenever the chanting developed into shrieking. But this did not decrease the frequency of this stereotyped chanting episodes. . . . The therapist decided to change the form of this behavior, rather than attempt to eliminate it, as it contained elements of appropriate social behavior.

The parents were instructed to turn away from the child when he chanted. One parent (e.g., the father) would then call out the name of the other parent ("Mommy"), and when the child would mimic this, the mother would attend to him and say, "Yes, Carey." The first parent would then say a complete sentence ("I want to sit down, please."). On subsequent occasions the verbal prompts were faded out. Finally, the parents withheld reinforcement by looking away until the child called their names, and they would wait while looking at him until he gave the complete sentence before responding to his request. The stereotyped chanting soon decreased to zero as the child began to imitate more appropriate requests such as "Mommy, I want to sit down, please." or "Daddy, I want a drink of water, please."

The grammatical structure of "(name), I want _____, please," after being established with several people's names and many different requests in the home, began to generalize to new people and new requests. One recorded instance of this occurred in the therapy sessions. Prior to the start of each session, when Carey was seated in the room, the therapist would spend some time setting up the tape recorder. During this time, the child would usually start chanting, "Ice cream, ice cream," softly. When the therapist was ready, he would turn to the child and say, "What do you want?" to which the child had been taught to answer, "I want some ice cream."

A very interesting thing happened at the beginning of one of these sessions. Before this time the child had learned the proper form of requests mentioned above. This he had been taught at home. At the beginning of one of the sessions, the child was, as usual, chanting, "Ice cream, ice cream" while the therapist threaded the tape recorder.

He suddenly stopped, and, after a pause, said, "Mr. (therapist's name), I want some ice cream, please." Most of the elements in this sentence had been established in the therapy sessions, e.g., "Hello, Mr. _____," and "I want some ice cream." but they had always been given as responses to specific stimuli (e.g., "Hello Carey" and "What do you want?"). However, the particular grammatical structure of "I want _____, please" had only been taught in the home.

Carey's extension of his home training exemplifies our general observation that once rudimentary generative speech and grammatical structure have been established, they will tend to generalize broadly, often with appropriate substitutions.

Intensive Reinforcement of Imitative Behavior in Mute Autistic Children

This study does not basically involve any new principles, but it seemed sufficiently different to warrant inclusion in this chapter. Most of the attempts at behavior modification are carried out at a very leisurely pace. A child will be fortunate if he receives the help of an individual therapist for more than a few hours each week. The problem is that the therapist has a large number of patients to work with and he finds it difficult to spend much time with any individual. The result is that all of the patients stay in the hospital a long time, and little progress is made. It seems to me that a better strategy might be to temporarily ignore all but a few of the patients, and to treat those few intensively. In that way it might not be necessary for individuals to remain in an institution for nearly as long a period of time as is usually the case. In other words, we might think more along the lines of short-term intensive treatment rather than long-term casual treatment.

One of the first attempts at intensive treatment was carried out by Dr. Joseph Hingtgen and his colleagues at the Indiana University Medical Center.[4] Sonny was the first child to participate in the intensive conditioning program. He was 6½ years old and had been in the hospital for three years with a diagnosis of autism.

During this time Sonny had been involved in various types of therapy which resulted in no significant behavioral improvement. Most of his day was spent playing bizarre finger and spitting games or in the ritualistic manipulation of objects and toys. Sonny was completely mute; not only did he not have any language behavior, but he did not make any sounds of any sort. He was, however, toilet-trained, a good eater, and showed no signs of neurological damage.

Before the therapy was actually begun, the amount of imitative behavior which the child would already exhibit was measured. Thirty-nine discriminative stimuli involving the use of body, objects, and vocalizations were presented. If Sonny made the same response within ten seconds of the model's response, it was considered imitation. During this time, no food reinforcement was used. Seventeen of these imitative stimuli involved the use of the body such as clapping hands and touching toes. Of these seventeen, Sonny correctly imitated ten. This

4. This section based on Hingtgen, J. N., Coulter, Susan K., and Churchill, D. W., Intensive reinforcement of imitative behavior in mute autistic children. *Archives of General Psychiatry*, 1967, *17*, 36–43.

shows that he had a highly developed repertoire of imitative responses involving the use of the body. Eleven of the discriminative stimuli involved the use of objects such as stringing beads, building a tower, and pushing a truck. In the presence of these eleven imitative discriminative stimuli Sonny correctly made three imitative responses. In other words, imitative behavior involving the use of objects was very weak. Ten of the imitative discriminative stimuli involved vocal responses. Sonny was unable to imitate any of these; he had no imitative vocal behavior.

After this initial test of Sonny's imitative behavior, the actual therapy was begun. The intensive therapy lasted for 21 days, during which time Sonny was isolated in an 8 × 15 foot room, 24 hours a day.

At first glance, the isolation of this child may seem extremely cruel, cold, and unloving. But it may be that we should attempt to overcome our initial emotional prejudices if we are really concerned with the ultimate well-being of the individuals involved. Such extreme measures would not seem at all inappropriate if Sonny were suffering from a severe physical maladjustment. In that case we would feel quite justified in subjecting Sonny to extensive amounts of surgery and confinement, not only to a room, but to a bed, for much longer periods of time. If we consider the behavioral malady from which Sonny suffers, it should be apparent that he is in a much worse position than he might be in if he were only suffering from severe physical handicaps. Sonny is a human being whose behavior is less efficient than that of most animals. Remember, Sonny spends most of his time twiddling his fingers, spitting, and doing such things as rocking a single toy back and forth repeatedly. Such severe behavioral limitations make 21 days of confinement seem mild indeed if it will have even a slight effect in expanding Sonny's world.

During these 21 days, the delivery of all of Sonny's food, water, and social contact was restricted to adults. These reinforcers were made contingent upon the occurrence of specific responses. During the average six hours of the daily training session, food, water, and relief from physical restraint (all paired with verbal approval) were used to reinforce three types of imitative responses. These were imitations involving use of the body, other objects, and vocal responses.

Following the 21 day intensive training period, Sonny was able to imitate over 200 individual responses involving the use of body parts and the use of objects. Some examples of the use of body responses are touching the nose, making facial expressions, holding hands and fingers in various positions, and running, jumping, sitting, etc. Examples of use of object responses are picking up a scissors, holding it correctly and cutting completely through a piece of paper held by the other hand, drawing, catching and throwing a large ball, buttoning, folding a piece of paper into quarters, brushing teeth, stacking blocks in various positions, putting puzzles together, appropriately using various toys, stacking and nesting plastic cups, holding and pounding nails with a hammer. At the end of the training period, Sonny consistently imitated 18 sounds and 18 words or approximations of words.

Following the three week intensive training period, an effort was made to continue and expand the training by releasing the child from the isolated room for gradually increasing periods, first to the ward and eventually including week-end visits to the home.

Simultaneous with this shift, the ward shift and staff and parents of the children were trained in using reinforcement techniques, which they applied 2-3 hours daily during training sessions with the children. Five months after the initial training period, Sonny had increased his behavioral repertoire beyond imitative responding. He can now print the complete alphabet, using either a pure visual model or a visual-motor model. He also knows the phonetic names of many of the letters. He can cut out figures with scissors and throw a basketball through a net. Sonny can now emit simple vocal requests and can name over 200 objects and pictures upon presentation. He is now beginning to learn complete sentences and can answer certain simple questions.

A nearly identical procedure was used by the same scientists with an autistic girl named Becky and similarly striking results were obtained. It might be hoped that intensive conditioning treatment of this sort will be used more extensively in the future. It is possible that such intensive treatment might be even more profitable if it were prolonged for periods longer than 21 days.

Summary

Throughout this chapter we have been studying various examples of imitation, yet the notion of imitative behavior has not been defined. We have been relying on our intuitive common-sense understanding of the terms. I trust that our reliance has been successful; but at this point, it may be appropriate to begin the summary with a more formal definition of the concepts.

1. *Imitative behavior* is topographically similar to the preceding behavior of a model. Furthermore, changes in the behavior of the model should produce similar changes in the behavior of the imitator.

2. Now that we have defined imitative behavior, we should also define imitative stimuli. An *imitative stimulus* is topographically similar to the response which follows it. Furthermore, changes in the imitative stimulus should produce changes in the imitative behavior under its control.

3. In the study where a child imitated a puppet, we saw that the frequency of imitative behavior can be controlled by reinforcement. When reinforcement follows imitative behavior, such behavior is conditioned. When reinforcement is withheld, it is extinguished.

4. In the same study we saw that it was appropriate to think of a class of imitative discriminative stimuli and a class of imitative discriminative responses. Generalization occurs within these two classes; that is, reinforcement of imitative responses to some imitative stimuli not only produces an increase in the frequency of those specific responses, but also produces an increase in the frequency of appropriate imitative responses which have not been directly reinforced. Furthermore, extinction of the previously reinforced imitative responses will also produce a reduction in the frequency of those imitative responses which have never themselves been directly reinforced.

5. In the study with retarded children, we saw that reinforcement can also be used to condition imitative behavior with children who have never previously shown such behavior. Furthermore, generalized imitation could be obtained. This procedure was then used to establish initial verbal repertoires.

6. We saw how some children suffer from a lack of imitative behavior, but others suffer from an excess of imitative behavior. Excessive imitative verbal behavior was put to good use in the development of a normal verbal repertoire using imitative conditioning procedures.

7. In another study, imitation training was used in a radically intensive treatment program which involved 24-hour isolation for 21 days. This procedure provided a good behavioral base on which more appropriate repertoires were established.

8. The general thesis, implicit in this chapter, has been that imitative behavior may be analyzed in the following terms: imitative responses are under the control of special discriminative stimuli, mainly imitative stimuli. The unique thing about imitation is that the response is physically similar to the stimulus. Also, the general principles which normally govern the stimulus control of behavior seem equally applicable to imitative behavior.

QUESTIONS

1. Without cheating, what is the title of this chapter?
2. In the first experiment, what sort of creature was used as the model?
3. Approximately how old was the subject in the experiment?
4. What specific responses was Penny reinforced for making?
5. When was she reinforced for making those responses?
6. What sort of reinforcement was used?
7. What specific response was recorded in this study?
8. When did Penny make this response?
9. Was this response reinforced? If so, what was the reinforcement?
10. What happened to the rate of bar pressing when reinforcement was withheld?
11. What happened to the rate of bar pressing when reinforcement was reintroduced?
12. Is reinforcement of some imitative responses essential for the maintenance of other nonreinforced imitative responses?
13. Did other children also show the same results as Penny?
14. Can imitative behavior be conditioned?
15. The puppet's head-nodding is a(n) _____ for Penny's head-nodding response.
16. It is a(n) _____ for mouthing, saying nonsense sentences, or any other response for that matter.
17. This is a discrimination experiment in which we have (a single, multiple) _____ $S^D(s)$ and (a single, multiple) _____ response(s).
18. Can imitation generalize?
19. What was the stimulus class used in this study?
20. Did generalization occur within the class of imitative stimuli?
21. What was the response class used in this study?
22. Did generalization occur within the class of imitative responses?

23. Give at least a rough statement of the principle of response generalization.
24. Generalization of imitation consists of both _____ generalization and _____ generalization.
25. Is it likely that Penny had never imitated anything before the experiment?
26. Had Marilla, the retarded child, ever shown any imitative behavior before the study was begun?
27. Was she able to say any words before the study was begun?
28. Does Dr. Baer feel that imitation is very important in the development of the normal child's behavior?
29. What verbal instructions did Don give Marilla each time he wanted her to raise her arm?
30. What was the *complete* discriminative stimulus which Don used for the arm-raising response?
31. What was the reinforcer which Don used?
32. What did Don do to speed up the shaping procedure with Marilla?
33. On the seventh new response, Marilla demonstrated generalized imitation. Were all of the rest of the new responses developed to generalized imitation, or was reinforcement still needed for many of them?
34. Was there a fairly gradual increase in the percentage of new responses imitated without direct reinforcement, or was there an abrupt change?
35. Did the number of trials required before most new responses were learned increase, decrease, or remain the same as more new responses were acquired?
36. What does DRO stand for?
37. Describe the procedure called differential reinforcement of other behavior.
38. How was the DRO procedure applied to Marilla?
39. What was the purpose of using the DRO procedure; in other words, what did Don wish to prove?
40. What happened to the imitative behavior when the DRO procedure was used?
41. The generalized imitative responses were being maintained because the other imitative responses were being reinforced. (a) True; (b) False.
42. What phase of the experiment followed the phase in which the DRO procedure was used?
43. What was the maximum number of responses which could be maintained in the response chain obtained with Marilla? (a) 1; (b) 2; (c) 7; (d) 37; (e) An infinite number.
44. How did Don and Marilla get to the seven-response chain? Did they gradually work up to the chain, or did they go there abruptly?
45. What phase of the study followed the response chain phase?
46. Was Don successful in getting verbal imitative responses the first time he tried?
47. Did the conditioning of imitative motor responses initially generalize to imitative vocal responses?
48. Did Don have to shape the vocal response?
49. In what way was the response chain used in developing the vocal responses?
50. Did Marilla ever learn to imitate words?
51. In this experiment did Don ever get Marilla to the point where she could carry on a normal conversation just like any other child her age?
52. Did Marilla's imitative behavior generalize to other experimenters?
53. Was Don able to apply these procedures to other retarded children with any degree of success?

54. Can imitative behavior be conditioned by using reinforcement procedures even when the subject has no prior imitative behavior?

55. Many people with behavior problems suffer from the inability to imitate. Do children ever have the problem of imitating too much?

56. Would it be easier to establish verbal behavior in a child who has no imitative behavior or in a child who has inappropriate imitative behavior?

57. What was an example of Dickie's bizarre verbal behavior?

58. What reinforcers were used in the study with Dickie?

59. What sorts of stimulus combinations served as discriminative stimuli for the vocal response?

60. Once imitation of the verbal discriminative stimulus had been developed, what was the next phase in the experiment?

61. Describe the anticipation procedure.

62. What was the result of the anticipation procedure?

63. What was the next kind of verbal behavior which was conditioned after Dickie had learned to name pictures and common household objects?

64. How was Dickie taught to answer questions about things which were no longer present?

65. Before Dickie was released from the hospital, there were still peculiarities in his verbal behavior. What were they?

66. What did the parents accomplish in the first six months that Dickie was out of the hospital?

67. Where did Dickie go after the hospital?

68. What sort of principles were used at the laboratory preschool at the University of Washington?

69. What were the results of Dickie's staying for two years at the preschool?

70. Is it fairly common for studies of this sort to occur where the experimenter works with a single individual for long periods of time rather than with a large number of individuals for a short period of time?

71. Were the procedures used for Dickie ever used successfully with other children?

72. Does the author advocate intensive treatment of a single individual or less treatment for a large number of individuals?

73. Describe Sonny's motor and verbal behavior prior to the therapy.

74. Did Sonny ever emit any imitative behavior before the experiment was begun?

75. The intensive therapy lasted for _____ days. (a) 1; (b) 3; (c) 7; (d) 21.

76. How many hours a day was Sonny in the isolation room?

77. What is the argument against the notion that it is extremely cruel, cold, and unloving to put Sonny in an isolation room, and therefore it should not be done?

78. How much time was Sonny allowed to play with other children during the 21 days of intensive treatment?

79. What are the three general types of imitative responses that Sonny was taught?

80. State a few of the highlights of the procedure used to teach Sonny the blowing response.

81. Approximately how many individual imitative responses could Sonny make after the 21-day intensive training period? (a) Over two; (b) Over twenty; (c) Over two hundred; (d) Over two thousand; (e) Over twenty thousand.

82. Give two examples of the use of body responses.

83. Give two examples of the use of object responses.

84. Did Sonny learn to imitate any sounds?

85. Did Sonny learn to imitate any words?

86. Were the ward attendants and Sonny's parents involved in the intensive training phase?

87. Were they involved in training Sonny after the intensive training phase?

88. What were some of the things which had been added to Sonny's repertoire five months after the initial training period?

89. Has this intensive training procedure ever been used successfully with any other children?

90. Imitative behavior is behavior which is _____ similar behavior to the preceding behavior of a model.

91. Furthermore, changes in the behavior of the model (should/should not) produce similar changes in the behavior of the imitator.

92. An imitative stimulus is one which is _____ similar to the response which follows it.

93. Furthermore, changes in the imitative stimulus should produce changes in the _____.

94. In the study of the child imitating the puppet, we saw that the frequency of imitative behavior (can/cannot) be controlled by reinforcement.

95. In that same study, we saw that it was appropriate to think of two classes of things or events. What were those two classes?

96. Generalized imitation involves generalization within: (a) the stimulus class; (b) the response class; (c) both classes; (d) neither class.

97. Reinforcement of one member of a response class increases the frequency of occurrence of other members of that same response class. This is the principle of _____.

98. Can reinforcement be used to condition imitative behavior with children who have never previously emitted such behavior?

99. Can generalized imitation be obtained with such children?

100. What is the unique thing about the relationship between the responses and stimuli in imitation?

101. Do the general principles which normally govern the stimulus control behavior seem equally applicable to imitative behavior?

102. Give an everyday example of imitation which you have personally observed.

103. Was there any specific reinforcement for this imitative response?

104. Was this an example of generalized imitation?

105. Give another example which involves generalized imitation.

106. What sort of history of reinforcement do you think the person had?

107. What sort of imitative responses had been reinforced in the past, so that generalized imitation could occur?

NOTES

We show an observer a sample color, red, and two comparison colors, red and green. We ask the observer to select the comparison color that matches the sample color, or we reinforce the response of selecting the matching color. This is a common procedure used with humans and animals. It is called stimulus matching. We may replace the colors with pictures of people. The sample picture could be of a man with his right hand raised. One comparison picture could be of the man with his right hand raised and the other comparison picture could show him with neither hand raised. Reinforcement would be delivered for the response of selecting the picture which matched the sample picture in terms of the position of the hands. The situation could be made even more concrete by replacing the pictures of the man with actual men—one being designated as the sample man, and the other two as comparison men. The response of selecting the comparison man whose position or behavior matched that of the sample man would be correct. We could call the sample man the "model," and the two comparison men the "imitators." Reinforcement could be delivered for the response of selecting the proper imitation behavior of the two comparison imitators. The behavior of these men, then, comprises the discriminative stimuli for the appropriate selection response on the part of the observer. When stimuli resulting from the behavior of the imitator match the stimuli resulting from the behavior of the model, the subject selects the correct imitator. This is matching of imitation. This sort of discrimination procedure without the involvement of the subject has never been used, but it might be interesting.

However, the main reason for pursuing this line is that the observer himself might be substituted for the imitator. That is the usual imitation situation. Then the subject would be reinforced for matching his behavior, or more correctly, the stimuli arising from his behavior, to the stimuli arising from the behavior of the model. He would continuously adjust his behavior until the stimuli matched those of the model. The matching stimuli would act as discriminative stimuli telling him that he was on the right track, and no further adjustments in this behavior would be needed. For example, if a model raised his arm to an angle of 45 degrees, the imitator would first look at the model and then look at his own arm as he raised it to a similar angle of 45 degrees. When the visual stimuli arising from his arm matched those of the model, the imitative response would be complete. Imitation can also occur along auditory dimensions; for example, the model says the word "ball" and the subject produces the matching auditory stimuli by saying the word "ball." This analysis has been made to show the importance of stimulus control in imitative behavior.

An interesting question is: how is it that imitative behavior can occur in new situations; i.e., how can we get a child to imitate a particular stimulus when he has never been reinforced for matching that stimulus before? If we look at the nature of the stimulus being imitated we may gain some understanding of this process. For example, if we have taught the child to say "tall" and "fat," and if we have taught him to imitate us when we say "tall" and "fat," we might not be surprised if he is able to imitate us the very first time we say "fall." On the other hand, if we introduced a completely new word such as "ring" we would not be surprised if the child failed to imitate this word. We would expect that the more similar the novel stimuli to stimuli used in the past, the more readily those stimuli would control the imitative behavior. The exact nature of this relationship is a fascinating and little-studied one.

Suppose we trained a child to match tones by whistling any note played on the piano within an octave of middle C. It would be interesting to find out whether tones several octaves away from middle C would also control this matching behavior. What would happen if we changed the characteristics of the tones to be matched by playing them on a tuba instead of a piano; would the young child be able to match the pitches in that case as well? We might ask how this imitation training would transfer from one stimulus dimension to another; suppose we had trained a child to match the pitches of the various tones. Would the child then readily learn to match the intensities of those tones?

Exactly how can it be, in stimulus-response terms, that a subject can go into a completely novel situation and make the "correct" response the very first time? This is a very important question, which has to date received very little attention. It is one which seems amenable to stimulus-response analysis.

However, there is another type of imitation. In this type of imitation, the stimuli received by the imitator as a result of his own behavior are *not* similar to those he receives as a result of the model's behavior. For example, the visual stimuli resulting from the model scratching the back of his head are not similar to the visual, proprioceptive (muscle), and tactual stimuli resulting from the subject scratching his own head. We can again ask questions about the transfer of such imitative behavior, but we would expect it to be less general than when the stimuli rising from the behavior of the imitator are similar to those rising from the behavior of the model. In the case of the dissimilar stimuli, we might train a completely naive subject to scratch the back of his head at the same locations as the model did. During testing, new locations could be used, and we might expect that the imitator would respond correctly as long as those new locations were not too dissimilar from the ones he had been trained on. However, if during testing the stimulus consisted of the model using his tongue to push out his right or left cheek, we would have little reason to anticipate that the imitator would respond appropriately. There should be little or no transfer of the training in the imitation of head scratching to the imitation of tongue pushing, because the stimuli resulting from those two responses are so different.

IMITATION

Stimulus Control & Verbal Behavior

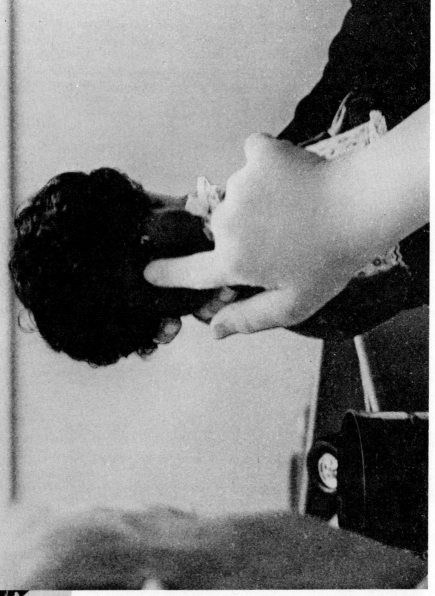

An *imitative stimulus* is topographically similar to the response which follows it. *Imitative behavior* is topographically similar to the response which follows it.

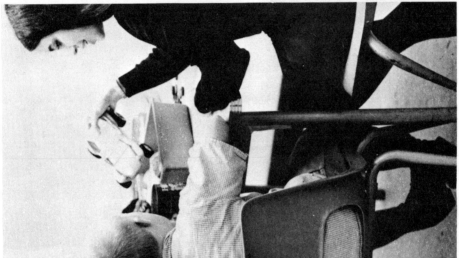

Imitative responses form a single class. Strengthening some members of the class strengthens other members of the class that have not been directly reinforced.

Imitative behavior can be controlled by reinforcement.

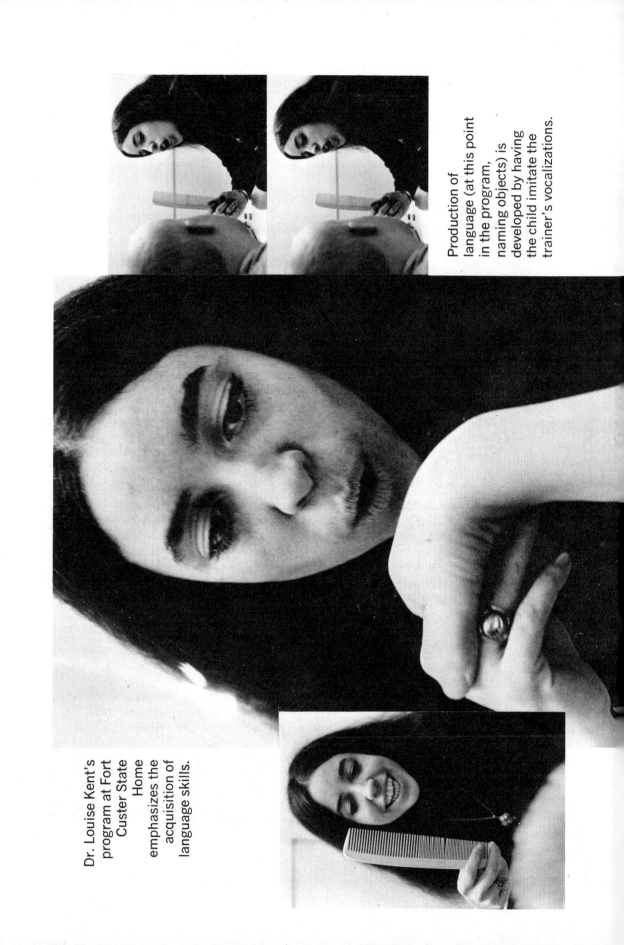

Production of language (at this point in the program, naming objects) is developed by having the child imitate the trainer's vocalizations.

Dr. Louise Kent's program at Fort Custer State Home emphasizes the acquisition of language skills.

Responding to language is defined as responding appropriately to commands such as sit.

Verbal instructions are merely a special sort of imitative stimuli—a symbolic rather than a physical model is presented for the subject to imitate.

STIMULUS CONTROL AND VERBAL BEHAVIOR

13

Reinforcement and Instructions with Mental Patients

The main point of this section is that verbal instructions are merely a special sort of imitative stimuli.[1] For example, we can say, "Do this," and then point to our nose. The pointing to our nose is an imitative discriminative stimulus for the observer's response of pointing to his nose. If we are dealing with someone who speaks our language, then we are more likely simply to say, "Point to your nose." In that case the verbal instruction "Point to your nose," serves as a discriminative stimulus for the same response for the observer's pointing to his nose. It might be said that following instructions is a sort of symbolic imitation.

In some instances we may find that our verbal repertoire is not adequate to instruct someone in a particular set of responses. In those cases we may, in fact, act as a model for the observer to imitate. For example, in instructing someone in a musical or athletic performance, it is sometimes easier to present him with a model to imitate than to give verbal instructions for him to follow. No amount of verbal instructions in how to swing a baseball bat would be as effective as watching an expert.

When we use verbal instructions, we are substituting words for deeds. We are presenting a symbolic model for the subject to imitate. I am suggesting that the use of language in symbolic imitation is essentially the same as the use of a model in direct imitation. Therefore, we expect that we could condition the behavior of following instructions in a manner similar to imitative behavior. We might also expect to be able to obtain the generalized imitative behavior. To my knowledge, work of this sort has not been done. It would certainly be worthwhile in nursery school!

The explicit use of instructions as discriminative stimuli has received very little attention. It seems to me that many people working in the area of behavior modification, using reinforcement principles, go out of their way to avoid the use

1. This section based on Ayllon, T., and Azrin, N. H. Reinforcement and instructions with mental patients. *Journal of the Experimental Analysis of Behavior*, 1964, 7, 327–331.

of instructions with verbal human subjects. They act as if verbal instructions necessarily contaminate the procedure. Some advocates of reinforcement principles
seem to carry this notion into their personal lives to an extreme extent. Rather than
give instructions, they will attempt to use reinforcement procedures to gradually
shape behavior which they desire. This is a time-consuming procedure which can
be greatly shortened through the use of verbal instructions.

The reinforcement theorists' extreme neglect of verbal instructions may be an
overreaction to the emphasis placed on verbal instructions by laymen and earlier
psychologists who seem to have a naive faith in the effectiveness of instructions.
It seems to me that the important message which reinforcement theory has for
verbal instructions is as follows: verbal instructions are discriminative stimuli,
much like any other discriminative stimuli. They will be effective only if the
specified responses made in their presence are reinforced, and only if the indicated
response goes unreinforced when the instructions are absent.

Some work by Dr. Jack Findley[2] at the Institute for Behavior Research in
Silver Spring, Maryland, illustrates the loss of stimulus control by instructions
which may occur when reinforcement is no longer dependent upon responding.
Findley had a grant from the National Aeronautic and Space Administration
(N.A.S.A.) to study the effects of prolonged isolation on the behavior of humans.
An adult male volunteer was placed in a three-room, man-sized Skinner box for
152 days. Certain responses had to be made before reinforcers, such as food and
the opportunity to go to bed, became available. These responses continued to
occur throughout the 152-day period. The subject was also instructed to make
certain other responses which helped the experimenter obtain weight and temperature recordings of the subject. Since the response of following these instructions was not explicitly reinforced, they gradually extinguished during the 152-
day period.

Another example of the failure of instructions to exert proper stimulus control
over behavior may be seen in the behavior of submarine crews and other groups
of individuals who are partially isolated for a considerable period of time. It is a
common phenomenon that the longer sailors stay in the submarine, the poorer
the discipline becomes; in other words, the less effective is the stimulus control
exerted by instructions from superior officers. This may occur because the superior officers are no longer able to reinforce following instructions and are no
longer able to punish disobeying instructions as effectively when they are away
from the main base of command. Eventually this lack of reinforcement has its
effects; the response of following instructions may gradually extinguish.

It is possible that this phenomenon underlies William Golding's novel, *Lord
of the Flies*. The stimulus control exerted by the instructions of the more civilized
of the two leaders gradually extinguished since he did not have very effective
reinforcers to maintain following behavior among the other children. The less
civilized of the two leaders may have had more immediate reinforcers such as
the "thrill of the hunt," which could be used to maintain the behavior of following his instructions.

2. Findley, J. D. Programmed environments for the experimental analysis of human behavior.
In W. K. Honig (Ed.), *Operant Behavior: Areas of Application and Research*. New York:
Appleton-Century-Crofts, 1966, 827–848.

It seems that a combination of instructions and reinforcement may frequently be the most feasible means of controlling behavior.

Where verbal instructions are possible, we can save considerable time by eliminating the need for shaping procedures. However, the instructions will not normally maintain effective stimulus control over the behavior unless reinforcement is made contingent upon following instructions. It is precisely this problem which we will discuss in the present section. What happens when we use only reinforcement? What happens when we use only instructions? This research was carried out by Dr. Teodoro Ayllon and Dr. Nate Azrin at Anna State Hospital. Earlier, we discussed some of the work of both of these scientists. Dr. Azrin performed the experiment on the effects of electric shock punishment using pigeons as subjects; Dr. Ayllon did some of the pioneering work with mental patients in the application of reinforcement techniques.

The problem in the present study was the establishment of socially acceptable eating behavior. Many of the patients failed to use eating utensils and, instead, ate their food directly with their hands. Such abnormal behavior seems highly undesirable if the patients are ever going to interact effectively in environments outside the mental hospital.

In this hospital, the food was served in cafeteria style. The patients walked through the cafeteria line, first picking up the silverware and then the tray of food. The patients always picked up the food, but 18 women failed to pick up their cutlery. Ayllon and Azrin felt that the first step in shaping normal eating behavior was to condition the prerequisite response of picking up the silverware.

For the purpose of this study, the women who failed to use their silverware were served their meals separately. An attendant stood by the serving counter on which the utensils were located and made an entry on the record as to which patients picked up a knife, fork, and spoon. The patients passed the serving counter in single file. A second attendant gave each patient a food tray. This preliminary procedure lasted for ten meals. During this time, fewer than 10 percent of the patients picked up their cutlery at any one meal.

At this point an attempt was made to introduce a reinforcement procedure. If a patient immediately picked up all three utensils, she was given her choice of a piece of candy, a cigarette, an extra cup of coffee, or an extra glass of milk. No instructions were given to the patients. On a few occasions a patient would inquire as to why she did or did not receive the reinforcement. No explanation was given other than to state: "We happen to have some extras today," or "We don't happen to have any extras today." The use of the reinforcement procedure produced only a slight, and at best unstable, increase in picking up the cutlery. After 20 meals using the attempted reinforcement procedure, it was apparent that no real improvement had been produced.

During the next ten meals, instructions were added to the reinforcement procedure. As each patient approached, the attendant stated: "Please pick up your knife, fork, and spoon. And you have a choice of extra milk, coffee, cigarettes, or candy." At the first meal where this procedure was used, nearly 50 percent of the patients picked up all of their cutlery. By the end of 10 meals over 66 percent of the patients were picking up their cutlery.

It is possible that the reinforcement was of no real consequence and that the instructions by themselves might have been sufficient to produce these dramatic results. In order to test this notion Drs. Ayllon and Azrin performed another study. In this study the effect of using instructions without reinforcement was ascertained.

Twenty mental patients with eating problems similar to those already discussed were used in this experiment. During their first ten meals in this experiment, no instructions or reinforcement were used for picking up utensils. Consequently, this response was only rarely emitted.

For the next 110 meals instructions to pick up the cutlery were given each time by the attendant who stood by it. As in the first experiment, the introduction of the instructions had an immediate effect; the percent of patients picking up the eating utensils jumped to over 50 percent on the first day. Since reinforcement was never given for picking up any of the utensils, the percentage of occasions when the utensils were picked up gradually decreased over the next 110 meals until it reached a little over 40 percent.

During the final phase of this study, the instructions were continued and reinforcement for picking up the cutlery was added. The reinforcement in this experiment, however, differed from that attempted in the previous experiment. The patient was allowed immediate access to the serving counter if the appropriate response of picking up the cutlery was made. If the appropriate response was not made, there was a delay in gaining access to the serving counter. This delay consisted of going to the end of the serving line. If the patient was already last in line, then a delay of approximately five minutes was introduced before allowing him access to the serving counter. One may think of this delay procedure as being more appropriately called a punishment procedure. If the patient did not make the correct response he was punished by being placed at the end of the line. Or, looking at the other side of the coin, if he did make a correct response, he was reinforced by being allowed to go immediately to the serving counter. In any case, the instructions plus the reinforcing consequences had a very strong effect; within a few meals between 90 and 100 percent of the patients were making the appropriate response. This procedure was continued for a total of 110 meals and the high percentage of correct responses was maintained.

An incidental outcome of the procedure was that the patients who obtained the cutlery also used it.

The most pertinent results of this experiment may be summarized as follows: instructions can initiate behavior but reinforcement is needed to maintain that behavior. This is quite analogous to our finding that the new responses may be added to a repertoire if an imitation procedure is used, but reinforcement is needed if these responses and other imitative responses are to be maintained.

These results do not apply just to mental patients. Ayllon and Azrin found that even though repeated instructions had been given to the attendant to insure that she was making the appropriate statement to each patient, she did not always do so. It was necessary to present her with tape recordings of her conversation and a record of visual observation of her inappropriate responses before she began to follow the instructions consistently. In other words, when there were no obvious consequences for following the instructions, her behavior was not maintained as adequately as it was when consequences were added.

This observation gives rise to an amusing speculation. We have seen that mental patients do not continue to respond perfectly to the discriminative instructional stimuli unless they are reinforced for doing so. We have also seen that the hospital attendant who gives the patients the instructional discriminative stimuli and reinforcements does not follow her instructional discriminative stimuli and reinforcements unless she is reinforced for doing so. I am sure that Ayllon and Azrin would be the first to agree that they might eventually stop following the instructions, indicated by proper scientific research methods, if they were not occasionally reinforced for doing so. Even the best of experimenters might start doing sloppy research if some sorts of reinforcements were not provided for being careful. In any case, I would be the first to admit that I might eventually stop following our editors' instructions (they call them suggestions) if I were not occasionally reinforced for doing so. And finally, dear reader, interesting as this book may be, you might eventually extinguish reading if there were not a considerable likelihood that an examination would be given at some point to reinforce your instructor's instructions.

Counting Behavior in Chimpanzees

It is common for students of psychology to speculate about teaching speech to lower animals. Recently this speculation has been enhanced by some real data.

Dr. Charles Ferster and his colleague, Clifford Hammer, have been working with chimpanzees at the Institute for Behavioral Research, in Silver Spring, Maryland. They were also interested in attempting to develop verbal or language behavior in chimpanzees. They felt that, just because a chimpanzee's normal environment is not adequate for the development of some sort of language behavior, it does not mean that the chimpanzee could not develop some rudimentary verbal behavior.

It seemed to Ferster and Hammer that, in a very real sense, arithmetic can be considered to be a language and, in some instances, a relatively simple one. For that reason they set about attempting to teach counting behavior to chimpanzees.[3] This might be a first step in understanding the nature of language and in the understanding of the acquisition of artificial language by lower animals.

They worked with two chimpanzees, Dennis and Marge, who lived together in a set of experimental chambers. The apparatus on which they learned the counting behavior was available to the chimpanzees 24 hours per day. In fact, the animals usually worked four or five hours a day and went through from four thousand to seven thousand problems during that time.

On any given day, the animals might not be working on the same problem. This created certain difficulties. Though they are both dedicated scientists, neither Ferster nor Hammer wished to stay at the laboratory 24 hours a day to make sure that the right problem was set up for the right chimp at the right time, and to make sure that they knew which data being automatically recorded belonged

3. This section based on Ferster, C. B. Arithmetic behavior in chimpanzees. *Scientific American*, May, 1964; and Ferster, C. B., and Hammer, C. E. Synthesizing the components of arithmetic behavior. In W. K. Honig (Ed.), *Operant Behavior: Areas of Research and Application*. New York: Appleton-Century-Crofts, 1966, 634–666.

to which chimpanzee. In others words, whenever either chimpanzee went to work on the apparatus he needed to identify himself. This was done in a most ingenious manner. The chimpanzee "signed in" by going to a large combination lock and moving the pointer to a certain setting. The particular setting identified the animal—it served as a signature. The apparatus was designed so that only one animal could be in the same experimental cubicle at a time.

Since the performance and history of the two chimpanzees were essentially the same, let us consider one, Dennis's, in more detail. A procedure somewhat like a fading procedure was used. Dennis started with relatively simple discrimination problems, but gradually they became more complex.

The first discrimination problem consisted of three small windows behind which various colors could be displayed. A sample color was shown in the center window. Reinforcement was delivered if the chimpanzee chose one of the two outer windows which contained the color which matched the sample (see Figure 13-1). If he pressed the window with the nonmatching color, a punishment con-

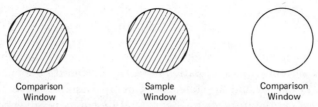

Comparison   Sample   Comparison
Window   Window   Window

Figure 13-1   Chimpanzee's three-window discrimination problem

sisting of a few seconds of blackout was presented. It took Dennis about five days and two thousand trials to learn to match colors accurately.

During the next phase of the experiment, the three windows were replaced by three sets of lights. Initially there were two lights in each set. Instead of matching on the basis of colors, the animals were to match on the basis of the particular combinations of lights that were turned on. Initially, the simplest discrimination was used. Either both lights of the pair were on or they were off (see Figure 13-2). When both of the sample pair of lights in the center were on, then reinforcement would be delivered if Dennis selected the side pair of lights which were also both on. If he selected the pair which were both off, punishment would be delivered. Dennis was able to accurately match these pairs of lights after 15 sessions of training. Then the pairs were changed to triads, so that each set of lights now consisted of three. Initially, all three lights were on or only the right-hand light of the three was on. Although Dennis accurately mastered the matching discrimination with four specific combinations in only three days, the general concept of selecting one of the outside combinations which matched the inner

Comparison   Sample   Comparison
Lights   Lights   Lights

Figure 13-2   Chimpanzee's three light-pairs discrimination problem

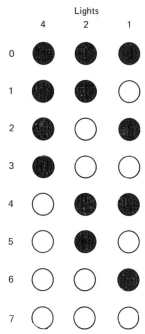

Figure 13-3 Chimpanzee's seven-light triad discrimination problem

sample of three lights had not developed. When novel combinations were presented, accuracy was very low. Eventually Dennis learned to match 21 of the various combinations of lights with good accuracy (fewer than five errors per one hundred trials), but it took him hundreds of thousands of trials to acquire that behavior.

You might be wondering why this particular type of stimulus was used, i.e., sets of lights which were either on or off. The three lights can form eight different combinations ranging from all three being off to all three being on. Using a binary notation system, these eight combinations of three lights can stand for the numbers from zero to seven (see Figure 13-3). Ferster and Hammer planned to use these binary numbers, rather than decimal numbers with which you might be most familiar, in teaching counting behavior.

Meanwhile, the chimpanzees had been given another type of problem; matching number symbols to various numbers of objects. This may be the first step in counting. The animals were shown a sample containing a certain number of objects (for example, three triangles) and were required to choose, from the two binary numbers, the number that matched the number of objects. The response was reinforced or punished according to its correctness (see Figure 13-4). Obviously, the problem is considerably more complex than the mere matching of binary numbers themselves. It is no longer a matter of detecting a likeness between two identical sets of digits or topographically similar patterns; the animal must now respond to the relation between a set of symbols and a radically different picture of physical objects. Dennis learned to match the correct binary number to as many as seven objects with an accuracy of better than 95 percent,

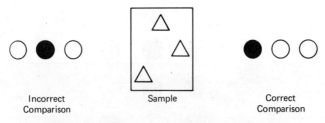

Incorrect
Comparison

Sample

Correct
Comparison

Figure 13-4 Matching number symbols to objects

frequently making fewer than five errors in a typical day's work of three thousand trials. It took over two hundred sessions and fifty thousand trials to develop only the first part of this repertoire.

The next undertaking was to teach the chimpanzees to "write" binary numbers. As a first step, they were trained to match a number displayed in one of the rows of lights by producing the same number in another row. This was done by pressing a button which randomly changed the number displayed in the second row until it matched the first row. The response of pressing a second key was reinforced if the two numbers matched, and punished otherwise.

Finally, a switch was placed beneath each of the three lights and the chimp turned each light off or on by pressing the corresponding switch; that way, a match could be achieved before he pressed the key for reinforcement. Once the chimp had acquired the behavior of duplicating a binary number, the sample was changed from a binary number itself to a number of objects. Reinforcement was then delivered for "writing" the number which corresponds to the objects. After about 150 sessions involving 170,000 trials, Dennis's accuracy was so high that he would make only one or two errors in every 1,000 trials.

Through the gradual fading in of more and more complex discriminative relationships, the animals had developed discriminations and behavior patterns of a much more complex nature than chimpanzees normally show. This illustrates how arithmetic behavior and even language can be considered largely a problem of stimulus control involving discrimination and generalization with some elements of response differentiation also involved. With a little imagination you might be able to consider further steps in the development of arithmetic and more advanced forms of language behavior in the chimpanzee.

One evening, shortly after this research was originally published, a fire broke out in the Institute for Behavior Research and all the animals in the Institute, including Dennis and Marge, were killed. At the time this book was written, Ferster and Hammer had for various reasons been unable to get this particular research project started again. It is certainly to be hoped that either they or some other scientists will continue this noble effort.

Summary

This chapter has been concerned primarily with the stimulus control aspects of verbal behavior. Verbal or language behavior can be broken down into two main parts: production of language, such as speech or writing, and response to language, such as listening or reading. We have been concerned mainly with this later aspect of language, responding to language as a stimulus. Verbal instructions may be considered to be discriminative stimuli. It was demonstrated with mental patients that, like any discriminative stimuli, they are most effective when reinforcement for particular responses occurs only in the presence of those stimuli. This would seem to be generally true and not just limited to mental patients.

In the final study, we saw how arithmetic was being taught to chimpanzees through the use of successively more complex discrimination problems. Much of this work involves the stimulus control aspect of language: the chimpanzee had to match a language or arithmetic stimulus to another stimulus. In addition, the problem of actually writing the numbers was introduced. This would be analogous to writing words. This counting behavior was studied as a first step in the analysis of arithmetic behavior, which, it was hoped, may shed some light on the notion of a more general language problem.

QUESTIONS

1. Verbal instructions and imitative stimuli have nothing to do with each other. (a) True; (b) False.
2. Using the example of "Point to your nose," show a relationship between verbal instructions and imitative stimuli.
3. In some instances we may find that a verbal repertoire is not adequate and imitative stimuli are to be preferred. What would be an example?
4. Many people working in the area of behavior modification using reinforcement try to avoid using instructions with human subjects. (a) True; (b) False.
5. Laymen and some psychologists have placed a much greater emphasis on the effectiveness of verbal instructions. (a) True; (b) False.
6. Are verbal instructions discriminative stimuli?
7. What is the role of reinforcement in determining the effectiveness of verbal instructions?
8. What species of subject did Dr. Jack Findley use to study the effects of prolonged isolation?
9. How long was the man in the Skinner box? (a) About 15 days; (b) About 150 days; (c) About 1500 days; (d) About 15,000 days.
10. What happened to the rate of occurrence of food-reinforced responses over the 152-day period?
11. What happened to the rate of occurrence of responses for which there were instructions made but not reinforced over the 152-day period?
12. What did the behavior of the submarine crews illustrate?
13. What might be the cause of failure of the supervising officer's instructions to control behavior over a long period of time?
14. What did William Golding's novel, *Lord of the Flies,* illustrate?
15. How did *Lord of the Flies* illustrate the loss of stimulus control of instructions due to poor reinforcement?
16. When we have a choice between using verbal instructions and a shaping procedure, which would be the quicker? (There may be no correct answer to this question, but think about it anyway.)
17. If verbal instructions can be used, does this mean that we have no need to bother with reinforcement?

18. Why would we need reinforcement?

19. What is the purpose of reinforcement in combination with verbal instructions?

20. What sort of socially acceptable behavior were Drs. Ayllon and Azrin attempting to obtain?

21. Were they working with infants, children, or adults?

22. Were the patients men or women?

23. In the first experiment, what was used? (a) Reinforcement; (b) Instructions; (c) Both reinforcement and instructions; (d) Neither reinforcement nor instructions.

24. What was said when a patient inquired as to why she did or did not receive reinforcement?

25. During the final phase of the first experiment, what was used? (a) Instructions; (b) Reinforcement; (c) Both instructions and reinforcement; (d) Neither instructions nor reinforcement.

26. Was there much of an increase in the percentage of patients picking up their cutlery?

27. Even though we know the results of this experiment, is it still possible that the reinforcement was of no real consequence, and that the instructions, by themselves, might have been sufficient to produce these dramatic results?

28. In the second experiment, what was designed to test the above-mentioned? What procedure was used in the first phase of the study?

29. In the second phase, what procedure was used? (a) Reinforcement; (b) Instructions; (c) Both reinforcement and instructions; (d) Neither reinforcement nor instructions.

30. What was the reinforcement in this experiment?

31. This prodecure could also be interpreted as a punishment procedure. How is that?

32. Was there much of an increase in the percentage of people picking up their cutlery at the end of the third phase of this experiment?

33. The major results of this experiment may be summarized as follows: reinforcement can initiate behavior, but instructions are needed to maintain that behavior. (a) True; (b) False.

34. Do the results of these experiments apply only to mental patients?

35. In what manner were they found to apply to the attendants working in the experiment?

36. Give an example where people follow the same sort of instructions over a long period of time.

37. What is the reinforcement involved? Or is it the threat of punishment?

38. Give an example where people frequently fail to follow instructions.

39. Specifically explain how you would use reinforcement and what reinforcement you might practically use to make sure that these instructions were consistently followed.

40. Specify a practical reinforcement procedure which could be used to ensure that the students follow the instructor's instructions.

41. What species of animal was used in the experiment on counting behavior?

42. Ferster and Hammer thought that it would be impossible to teach even a rudimentary verbal behavior to the chimpanzees. (a) True; (b) False.

43. Ferster and Hammer believed that even though chimpanzees might learn a rudimentary verbal behavior, they certainly could not learn mathematics or arithmetic. (a) True; (b) False.

44. How many hours a day was the apparatus available which the chimpanzees used to learn to count?

45. How did the chimpanzees identify themselves when they went to work on the apparatus?

46. In teaching counting behavior to the chimpanzees, a procedure somewhat like a fading procedure was used: (a) True; (b) False.

47. What were the stimuli used in the first discrimination experiment?

48. What was the correct response and what was the incorrect response with regard to the colors in the three windows?

49. What happened if the chimpanzee responded to the outer window which contained the color which matched the sample?

50. What happened if he responded to the window with the nonmatching color?

51. What was the specific type of punishment that was used for making this mistake?

52. Did Dennis learn this color-matching discrimination?

53. After Dennis learned the first simple discrimination, the colors were replaced by the three sets of _____.

54. Instead of matching on the basis of color, Dennis matched on the basis of _____.

55. The animals eventually learned to match several combinations of the lights with good accuracy. (a) True; (b) False.

56. In what way were the three lights to be used later in teaching counting behavior?

57. What was the first experiment on matching the number of objects to the number of symbols?

58. What was the first way in which the chimpanzees were taught to write binary numbers?

59. What was the final lighting technique used?

60. Ferster and Hammer finally taught the chimpanzees to actually read a few words by having them match the words to the various pictures. (a) True; (b) False.

61. What happened to the laboratory which terminated the experiment?

62. Describe an experiment to teach an animal more advanced mathematical concepts.

63. Describe an experiment to teach an animal how to read.

64. Describe an experiment to teach an animal how to write.

65. Describe experiments to teach a retarded child these various skills.

66. Describe experiments to teach a normal child these skills.

NOTES

Psychologists have been thinking about verbal behavior for many years but have had a good deal of difficulty coming to grips with it. The problem is to develop a set of laws which allow us to describe and predict verbal behavior. It seems that the major stumbling block in this task is a definition of "verbal behavior" *per se*. In other words, if we see a bit of behavior how do we know whether it is verbal behavior or nonverbal behavior?

To help ourselves analyze this problem, we may think in terms of teaching verbal behavior. This might well mean that we have knowledge of what "verbal" is. Human subjects normally learn a language so readily that it is difficult for us to study the process.

Hockett[4] has examined the behavior of a large variety of animal species in their natural habitat and classified their behavior according to his criteria. In no case did he

4. Hockett, C. F. Logical considerations in the study of animal communications. *Animal Sounds and Communications*, 1960, 7, 392–429; and The origin of speech. *Scientific American*, Sept., 1960.

find behavior which met all of the criteria for language. He concludes that animals do not exhibit language behavior. In this section, we will examine his criteria to see which are really essential to language behavior and then look at those essential criteria in terms of the principles of reinforcement. We will also apply these criteria to the behavior of laboratory animals to determine if it is more feasible to expect language behavior from animals in a laboratory than in their natural habitat.

Perhaps due to his linguistic background, Hockett is concerned only with spoken language. Consequently, a few of the requirements of the system serve only to ensure that the language system be a vocal-auditory one; they exclude such language systems as writing. One of his requirements is that the language system be *transmitted over a vocal-auditory channel.* Another requirement is that "a linguistic signal can be heard by any auditory system within ear shot and the source can normally be localized by *binaural direction finding.*" This particular requirement seems to be dictated solely by the physics of sound and need not be part of language systems. A third requirement is that the verbal stimuli should be *transitory* or fade; i.e., the spoken word, once spoken, quickly disappears. These requirements merely restrict the language system to a vocal-auditory one; they do not seem to be essential to the linguistic function. It would be rather arbitrary to limit ourselves to a consideration of only auditory language systems. Our general principles of language behavior should also encompass visual language systems. It may be that, for some purposes, a visual language will be more readily studied than an auditory one.

Two other criteria are normally characteristic of human language and are very convenient but would not seem to be an essential part of language. One is *interchangeability,* i.e., a person who at one point can serve as a speaker at another point can serve as a listener. However, we know of people learning a language, whether it be their first or second, who can understand it (that is, they can listen and respond to the language) but cannot speak it. Similarly it is conceivable that a person might be mute, yet could understand spoken language and respond properly with little difficulty. The requirement of interchangeability need not be proposed. A second requirement of this sort is *total feedback.* Total feedback means a person can hear or see, etc., all verbal behavior which he emits. While total feedback is clearly desirable, deaf people can be taught to speak even though they do not use it.

A more interesting requirement is *specialization.* This means that the verbal behavior should serve no function except to produce verbal stimuli. In order to consider this characteristic it is necessary to discuss the two fundamental types of verbal behavior. One type of verbal behavior is called "encoding"; this involves responding appropriately to produce verbal stimuli. Examples of this would be talking and writing. The requirement of specialization is relevant to the encoding aspect of verbal behavior. This is the same as saying that encoding behavior should be conditioned behavior and should be maintained by its reinforcing consequences. Furthermore, the reinforcement for emitting this verbal behavior should involve its functioning as a verbal stimulus for other individuals. For example, the master calling a dog is showing specialization in that the response is reinforced by its effect on another organism. The requirement of specialization may also be seen in responses such as pressing a bar or pecking a key, which are then reinforced with food.

In our further consideration of the problem of teaching language to animals we will restrict ourselves to the stimulus control aspects of language, "decoding behavior." We will not be concerned with the response differentiation aspect of language, encoding behavior. To date, the use of animals in the study of language behavior has been restricted almost exclusively to encoding and response differentiation. For that reason, most of the work has been done with talking birds. One of the problems of this approach is that the experimenter becomes so involved with the difficulties of response differentiation that he rarely gets at problems which could truly be considered to involve verbal behavior. While the experimenter may succeed in shaping up complex vocal responses, these responses have few of the characteristics of language behavior which we will be considering in subsequent paragraphs. It seems that once we understand the stimulus control problems of language behavior (i.e., decoding), and once we have developed a good set of principles of response differentiation, then we will be in a much better position to tackle the response differentiation aspect of language behavior (i.e., encoding). For that reason we will limit our discussion almost exclusively to the stimulus control aspects.

Another characteristic of verbal behavior is that it is *semantic*. The notion of semanticity is particularly difficult to come to grips with. The common-sense notion of semanticity is that a stimulus word is semantic because it is a symbol for something else. Although this notion at first seems straightforward, it may in fact be misleading. It is not at all clear what it means for a word to "stand for" something else. Suppose we have two stimuli, a red circle and a green circle. The words "red circle" stand for the actual red circle. Similarly, the words "green circle" stand for the actual green circle. Now the problem is to determine what we mean when we say that the words "red circle" stand for the red circle itself.

If we are instructed to touch the red circle, we touch the red circle itself, and not the words "red circle." So we do not respond to the words in the same way that we respond to the thing that they stand for. Rather, the words figure into a set of instructions which affect the way that we respond to the thing itself. As a first approximation we might say that a word stands for a thing when it is used consistently in sentences which affect the way that we respond to that thing. For example, we can respond to the following different set of instructional stimuli: "Cover the red circle," "Put the red circle at the top of the page," "Put the red circle at the bottom of the page." Each set of instructional stimuli involves the expression "red circle" and serves as a discriminative stimulus to control our responding to that red circle. The stimuli not only determine what we do to the red circle, but they also cause us to respond to the red circle and not to the green one. We might say then that a stimulus is semantic if it is a discriminative stimulus for differential responding to other stimuli. This appears to get at the essence of what is meant by one stimulus "standing for" another stimulus.

Now we can return to the problem of teaching language behavior to animals. We have said that a stimulus is semantic if it is a discriminative stimulus for differential responding to another stimulus. Can we develop such stimuli to control the behavior of animals? This could be easily done. For example, we could train a pigeon to peck a red circle when we held up a card with the words "red circle" and to peck a green circle when we held up a card that said "green circle." The words would then serve as semantic discriminative stimuli.

Another feature of language stimuli is that they are *arbitrary*. In the above example, the words "red circle" in no way look like the red circle. In other words, there is an arbitrary relation between the word and the stimulus for which it stood. On the other hand, a picture of something may also "stand for" that thing, but there is not an arbitrary relation between it and the thing that it stands for. It looks like that thing. Therefore, the picture is not a verbal stimulus. As you saw in the above example, it is a simpler matter to use arbitrary stimuli with animals.

Another feature of verbal stimuli is that they are *discrete*. First let us consider an example of a discriminative stimulus which is not discrete but instead is continuous. We might point to a particular location on the blackboard and instruct someone to make a mark at that point. We could move our pointing hand slightly to the right and the person would make a mark slightly to the right. This is an example of a continuous discriminative stimulus. Within a wide range, any particular pointing response will serve properly as a discriminative stimulus. This is not true of verbal discriminative stimuli. Consider the two discriminative stimuli "pin" and "bin." These two discriminative stimuli are discrete. A word which is in between "pin" and "bin" in sound will not properly function as a discriminative stimulus. The examples of animal language above in which we used the words "red circle" and "green circle" are also examples of discrete discriminative stimuli. Therefore, it is possible to use discrete stimuli with animals.

There is one characteristic of verbal behavior frequently mentioned as a major obstacle which cannot be overcome by animals, and therefore prevents the development of the animal language. This characteristic is *displacement,* or the ability to be under control of stimuli that are remote in space or time. You could be given the verbal instructions to go into the other room and take a particular book off the shelf; once separated in both space and time from those instructions, you could still respond appropriately. Is it possible for animals to do this? Such behavior has been studied extensively in animals and found to occur. It is called *delayed responding.* An animal may be placed in a restraining cage and allowed to observe a piece of food being put under one of two cups. Later, the restraining cage is removed and he selects one of the two cups. If he selects the one containing the food, he may eat the food, and that response is reinforced. The placement of the food under the cup served as a discriminative stimulus. It occurred separately from the response by both space and time, yet the response may be under the control of that stimulus. Therefore, it seems that the requirement of displacement is one which would be readily obtained in an animal language system.

Another requirement of a language system is that it be acquired by *traditional transmission.* That is, it should be learned and not genetically determined. This clearly constitutes no difficulty with regard to the establishment of an animal language system.

Another characteristic of a language is that it involves *duality of patterning.* A small number of stimulus components can be combined to form different discriminative stimuli. This requirement was met in our earlier example in which the letter "e" was combined with different letters both in "red" and "green" to form different discriminative stimuli.

The final requirement is probably the most difficult and the most fascinating. The language system must allow for *productivity.* The notion of productivity is applicable to both of the major classes of verbal behavior; in one class, a nonverbal discriminative stimulus controls a verbal response; in the other class, a verbal discriminative stimulus controls a nonverbal response. In the first case, productivity means that a novel nonverbal stimulus will produce the correct novel verbal response. For example, I can say, "I wrote the first draft of this manuscript on May 20, 1966"; that is an original statement. Since a consideration of this case, in which nonverbal stimuli control verbal behavior, will lead us down the side path of response differentiation, we will restrict our consideration to the case of language control in which verbal stimuli control simple nonverbal behaviors. The notion of "linguistic productivity" when applied to the second case, the control of verbal stimuli over behavior, means that a novel verbal stimulus can serve as the S^D for the correct response. For example, in the proper context, you could respond correctly to the novel verbal stimulus, "Place your copy of *The Analysis of Behavior* in the Skinner box." We have seen one other area in which a novel stimulus can serve as the S^D for the correct response: that is stimulus matching and imitation. Verbal behavior, however, seems a little more complicated.

Let us consider how we might condition linguistic productivity in a lower organism. A single response, such as a key peck, will be used throughout this hypothetical experiment. Our first task will be to teach the animal a vocabulary. We can use the *symbolic matching* procedure to teach this. That is, we will pair pictures of objects and words standing for these objects. For example, we will show a picture of a house with the word "house," a picture of a tree with the word "tree," a picture of a chair with the word "chair." In those examples, the word matches the picture. These will be our discriminative stimuli, S^Ds. Whenever a subject makes a simple operant response (such as the depression of a telegraph key) in the presence of such matching stimuli, the response will be reinforced. Another set of stimuli will consist of pictures that do not match the words. For example, we will show a picture of a house with the word "chair," a picture of a tree with the word "house," etc. These stimuli will constitute our S^Δs. If the animal presses the key in the presence of these nonmatching stimuli, reinforcement will be withheld. He will have learned the vocabulary if he responds only when the word matches the picture.

Our second task will be to teach a simple syntactic grammar; a relational problem. The S^Ds are stimuli in which a sentence correctly matches the associated picture. For example, a picture of a house above a picture of a chair and the sentence, "The house is above the chair." One example of an S^Δ is the same pair of pictures, but the incorrect sentence, "The chair is above the house." In all cases, the sentence will be of the form, "The _____ is above the _____." Only half of the original vocabulary stimuli will be used during the teaching of the syntactic discriminations. The remaining half of the vocabulary will be used to measure whether we have been successful in conditioning linguistic productivity.

The question is, once the animal has learned the vocabulary and has learned the syntax in connection with part of the vocabulary, can he respond properly to the syntax making use of the remainder of the vocabulary. For example, he may learn to respond correctly to the syntactic arrangement of the words, "house," "chair," "apple," and "man"; but what happens when we introduce words such as "horse," "table," and "orange," which he has learned but has never responded to in the syntactic context? Will the animal respond properly to these novel stimuli?

After we understand the variables which control linguistic productivity, we will be well on the way to an understanding of verbal behavior.

It seems clear that we have a good chance of establishing an animal language system which meets all of Hockett's requirements of a full-fledged language. The question is: where do we go from there? A common answer is that the next step would be to teach one animal to "talk to another animal." This would be easy enough to do. We could train a pigeon to peck a disk which would turn on a light in another animal's cage. The second animal would then peck a disk which would produce food reinforcement for both animals. This would require no new principles, but would get us back into the business of response differentiation. It is our feeling that we still have a long way to go in the analysis of language in terms of the stimulus control of behavior before we get into these other problems. It seems clear that verbal humans are under the control of much more complicated verbal stimuli than we have considered thus far. At this point, it's difficult to decide whether the increased complexity is going to necessitate the addition of more requirements which a stimulus system must meet in order to be considered a linguistics system, or whether it is simply a matter of adding more and more stimuli and a more and more complex grammar. Only further theoretical and experimental analysis will answer this question.

GENERALIZATION OF REINFORCEMENT THERAPY

14

"The problem with the use of reinforcement therapy to modify abnormal behavior is that the therapy won't generalize outside the psychologist's laboratory."

"What do you mean, it won't generalize?"

"Well, suppose you take someone who has a behavior problem and work with him in the laboratory. Let's say he is a mute psychotic; he no longer talks. Suppose you use a reinforcement procedure and gradually recondition talking behavior in your lab. Now you have that response conditioned in your presence in the lab; but will it generalize out onto the ward? And, even if it does generalize, will it continue to occur, or will the original conditions which eliminated the talking behavior do the same thing again?"

I realized that I was being baited; he knew that I was a strong advocate of the use of reinforcement principles in the modification of behavior. On the other hand, I knew that he was not merely teasing me; he undoubtedly incorporated this critique of the uses of the principles of reinforcement in his psychology lectures. I felt that I should convince him that the principles of reinforcement would work. Then he might be less likely to make such an argument in his class and mislead his students. Besides, he was one of the senior members of the psychology department, and this was my first job; I was eager to please and impress him, so I replied, "What you say is complete and utter nonsense and indicates your lack of understanding of the principles of reinforcement."

I thought that I could see by the expression on his face that he was quite impressed. I continued, "There are two things with which the therapist must be concerned in the generalization of reinforcement therapy. First, he must make sure that the therapeutic situation is similar to the patient's normal environment; then the behavior changes which he brings about will *generalize* to the normal environment. A good way of dealing with this problem is to actually conduct the therapy in the patient's normal environment rather than in the therapist's lab.

"Second, the therapist must make sure that the behavior changes which he brings about are *maintained* in the patient's normal environment. For example, the patient may have some types of behavior that he wants to eliminate. The

263

therapist might extinguish the behavior; but then he wants to be sure that it isn't reconditioned again in the patient's normal environment. The psychologist could extinguish the undesirable behavior in the lab, but how can he make sure that the effect of extinction is maintained in the individual's normal environment? The behavior might have been reinforced by attention. One thing he could do would be to condition some other response which is even more effective in getting attention but which is also more socially desirable. In that case the undesirable response might never be reconditioned.

"Another problem in the maintenance of behavior change occurs when there is some behavior missing, and the therapist wants to condition it. Then he must be sure that reinforcement is maintained in the patient's normal environment so that the behavior does not extinguish.

"One solution is to condition desirable behavior which will be successful in obtaining reinforcers in the patient's normal environment. The patient's environment might be effective enough to maintain the behavior once it is conditioned but might not be effective enough to actually get the behavior conditioned. Because of an inappropriate environment, a child might not have learned to talk. But if a sufficiently adequate repertoire of verbal responses is conditioned in the laboratory, then the normal reinforcers which maintain verbal behavior for most of us might be effective in maintaining the child's verbal behavior."

I paused for dramatic effect and then looked the antagonist straight in the eye. "So you see, reinforcement therapy can be effectively generalized to the patient's everyday environment and the effects can be maintained."

I expected him to jump from his seat, run around his desk, pound me heartily on the back, and exclaim merrily, "I apologize, my good man, for not having sooner recognized the truth of your argument." To which I was to reply, "Ah, sir, do not apologize. I realize that we new faculty members must prove ourselves." In so doing I would simultaneously display my good breeding, humility, and generosity.

But instead the ingrate stared at the desk and merely said, "Hah."

"Well, does what I say make any sense to you?" I asked.

"Yes," he mumbled, and began shuffling through some papers on his desk.

I walked out feeling that I had done mankind a good deed. Now he would no longer tell his students that reinforcement therapy was no good because it would not generalize to other stimulus situations.

Several days later I had an experience—the first of several similar experiences —which taught me a valuable lesson. I overheard some of his students discussing a lecture he had just given. They were saying how impressed they were with his arguments that reinforcement therapy was not of too much value because its effects would not generalize. At least it was clear that the effects of my attempts at therapy with him had not generalized from his office to his classroom. Eventually I came to realize that a person's refusal to violently disagree with you may simply mean that he no longer wishes to argue.

The foregoing dialogue is by no means as far-fetched and scholastic as it might seem. It is not altogether hypothetical. Similar dialogues occur every day at clinics, institutions, and public schools throughout the country. The disagreement revolves around this situation: an individual, whether he be a psychologist, nursery school teacher, or other professional, employs behavior modification techniques (extinction, positive reinforcement, discrimination, etc.) to bring about a behavioral change in his client's, student's, or subject's behavior. He is able to make the statement that the particular technique he employed was successful in changing behavior in a manner consistent with notions of therapy or "betterment" of the patient.

His critic recognizes that the behavior of the patient apparently has changed, but remains unimpressed. His statement in essence says that although behavior has been changed, such change is only superficial. The patient has not been "cured." He implies that although the behavior in question has been changed for the present, it will not endure over time, or will not maintain in an environment outside the laboratory. For the critic the word "cure" is important. He views behavior problems as "diseases" and, of course, what can one do with a disease but "cure" it? A cure is a cure, and if it is a real cure, the disease does not come creeping back on unannounced and inopportune occasions.

The psychologist or other professional who has used reinforcement principles in effecting behavior change may be quick to agree with the critic. He may reply simply that he also has his doubts as to whether the behavior change will hold up over time and in different environments. He agrees that the behavior change may not maintain after the individual leaves the mental hospital. But he does not view the original behavior problem as a disease and therefore does not view what he has done, i.e., changed the patient's behavior, as a "cure." He has merely modified the behavior pattern under a certain set of conditions. His job as a therapist only begins when he finds a way of modifying the behavior. Then he must concern himself with generalizing the behavior for longer periods of time and to other environmental circumstances.

The problems involved in getting a behavior to generalize are well known to most psychologists. In general, they know exactly what needs to be done. They may agree that in order to increase the probability that the behavior will maintain outside the hospital, they need to subject the patient to many of the similar stresses, strains, and stimulus conditions he will encounter once outside. If aspects of the outside environment are introduced slowly and gradually, the patient can learn to master them and the transition from hospital to community will be made with ease. The behavior therapist sees and knows the limitations of his method and knows that its effectiveness in outside environments can be improved by standard procedures. Sometimes, however, these procedures are unrealistic, costly, involve prohibitive time commitments, or otherwise involve measures impossible to effect. The behavior therapist in these instances must either find a new technique or principle or must reconcile himself to the fact that, although he knows what he should do, he does not have the resources to bring it about. For him the generalization of therapy is nothing more than a technical problem.

Provided his critic continues to see behavior problems as diseases or manifestations of a disease, the dialogue between the two will always occur. In the following pages we will see how professionals may bring about the generalization of reinforcement therapy.

Modification of a Child's Multiple Behavior Problems

Karl Shambaugh was a five-year-old boy whose parents had been asked to remove him from kindergarten. From the parents' report, it seemed that Karl exhibited a multitude of deviant behaviors.[1] For example, when separated from his mother, he became intensely aggressive, biting, kicking, throwing toys, screaming, and crying. The teacher's legs were a mass of black and blue marks; on several occasions he had also attempted to choke her. The mother also reported sporadic enuresis (bed wetting). His speech pattern was immature, showing several minor articulation defects. His interaction with adults showed a general negativism; for example, it was extremely difficult to get him to dress or feed himself. The mother thought he might be retarded; but his IQ, tested at the end of the study, was well within the normal range. The mother felt that Karl's behavior pattern was so extreme and had persisted for so long that it was extremely unlikely that he would change. As she said, Karl was very "strong-headed." She was especially concerned about the behavior he exhibited when he was brought to school in the mornings. For example, on the previous week (the week before her first interview), he had actually held on to her dress with his teeth in an effort to keep her at the school. At the age of two years, Karl was hospitalized for a few days' diagnostic study for suspected leukemia. The results of the diagnostic studies were negative; however, following the hospitalization it was increasingly difficult to leave him with baby-sitters.

On the few occasions when Karl did interact with other children, it was mainly in terms of pushing, elbowing, pinching, kicking, and once, actually choking one of them. Other children soon learned to avoid him most of the time. The teacher would try to comfort and reassure him during his temper tantrums, and she always stayed close at hand in order to prevent him from seriously injuring one of the other children.

Karl spent nearly all of his time in tantrum behavior, sulking, or attacking other children. Only occasionally did he engage in peaceful, isolated play. Most of the teacher's time was devoted to Karl, consequently, she found it almost impossible to run her kindergarten. Much as she regretted it, she finally concluded that it would be necessary for Karl to leave the kindergarten. She felt that she was not able to help him and he was making her less effective with the other children. There was also the ever-present danger that he might seriously harm one of the other children.

Because of Karl's imminent expulsion, Mrs. Shambaugh went to the University of Oregon Child Guidance Clinic where she met Dr. Gerald Patterson. (You will recall that we read about Dr. Patterson's work with hyperactive children).

After an initial interview at the clinic, Mrs. Shambaugh agreed to bring Karl to the psychology laboratories for treatment; however, she was quite skeptical about the success of the venture.

1. This section based on Patterson, G. R., and Brodsky, G. A behavior modification program for a child with multiple problem behaviors. *Journal of Child Psychology and Psychiatry*, 1966, 7, 277–295.

The next day Mrs. Shambaugh brought Karl to the door of the laboratory, but that was as far as she could get. Karl refused to go inside.

"You see what I mean, Dr. Patterson? It just won't work."

"That's perfectly all right, Mrs. Shambaugh. I'm sure that we'll be able to take care of everything." Then Dr. Patterson reached over and started to pick up Karl. Immediately Karl commenced screaming and kicked Dr. Patterson in the legs. Dr. Patterson finally managed to pick up the screaming and crying child and carried him into the laboratory. Karl began to kick the laboratory equipment as they passed since he was no longer able to kick Dr. Patterson.

Dr. Patterson took Karl into a cubicle, closed the door, and pinned him to the floor by his ankles. While Karl screamed, bit, and threw objects, Dr. Patterson made every effort to prevent Karl from injuring him, and at the same time, sat looking as bored as the circumstances would permit. He looked at Karl and talked to him only when he was reasonably calm. Karl was told that he could leave as soon as he quieted down.

During this time, Dr. Patterson's colleague, Dr. Brodsky, took Mrs. Shambaugh into an adjoining room where they could observe Karl and Dr. Patterson through a one-way glass. Mrs. Shambaugh was horrified. "I knew this wouldn't work. Dr. Patterson is just making things worse. Look, he's holding Karl down on the floor, and that will upset Karl all the more. Why doesn't he try to reassure Karl and make him feel at home? Maybe I'd better go in and help."

"It'll be all right, Mrs. Shambaugh. You stay here and watch," Dr. Brodsky attempted to reassure her.

"Well, it doesn't seem right."

"You see, whenever Karl throws a temper tantrum, someone pays attention to him. When he is in a classroom and throws a temper tantrum, you stay with him, or the teacher hugs him and reads stories to him. All of this attention acts as a reward for Karl's temper tantrum," Dr. Brodsky explained.

"But when the poor child is so frightened and upset, we have to do something to reassure him and let him know we love him."

"Yes, but the problem is that when you do, you're rewarding his temper tantrums. This makes it more likely that he will have more temper tantrums in the future."

"I think I see what you mean, but it seems so cruel to let Dr. Patterson hold him down on the floor like that. If I went in there for a few minutes, he would stop crying."

"Yes, you're probably right. If you went in right now, I am sure that you could get Karl to stop crying. The problem is that if you go in there and stop his crying, your attention will actually be rewarding his crying. It will be more likely that the next time he is put in that situation, he'll cry again. We're not so concerned with getting him to stop crying this time; what we do want to do is eliminate his temper tantrums in future times. You see, when we take care of the immediate problem, we are creating more of a problem for the future."

"Well, I guess you're right; you're the expert. But it's going to be awfully hard for me to go against my natural inclinations."

"Yes, it will be hard, but it will pay off in the long run."

After about 30 minutes, Karl quieted down. At that point, Dr. Patterson released him and he was allowed to leave the clinic with his mother.

The next day, Mrs. Shambaugh had to drag Karl to the clinic. Once inside, he refused to accompany Dr. Patterson to the playroom and was picked up kicking, screaming, shouting, and crying. In the playroom, he was pinned to the floor by his ankles. He cried for only 30 seconds this time. As soon as he stopped the tantrum behaviors, he was released.

Dr. Brodsky explained to Mrs. Shambaugh, "You see how soon Karl stopped crying today. Each day that goes by without our rewarding Karl's crying, he will cry less on the next day. Technically speaking, we would say that the crying is being 'extinguished'."

Dr. Brodsky continued, "Now Dr. Patterson is going to teach Karl how he should behave when he is at home, at school, and various other places. However, he is going to try to do this right here in the laboratory without actually taking Karl outside. He is going to use some dolls and see if he can get Karl to make the dolls behave properly in these settings. The hope is that teaching Karl how the dolls should behave will affect the way Karl, himself, behaves when he actually gets in those situations."

Dr. Patterson reinforced Karl's playing responses when those responses involved the doll's behaving properly. The reinforcement increased the frequency of proper playing responses. It was hoped that the responses of having the doll behave properly would generalize to Karl himself actually behaving properly in the real situations which corresponded to the imaginary play.

Recalling Dr. Patterson's earlier work, you will not be surprised to find him showing a strange little box to Karl. "This is a 'Karl box.' It has a bell. Whenever this bell goes off, I'm going to drop an M&M in your cup. Now, you see this little boy doll? This is Henry. And this mother doll is Henry's mother. Let's put them next to each other. See? Little Henry is holding on to his mother's hand. Is he afraid?"

No answer.

"Now you see the mother doll leans down and says to Henry, 'It sure is a nice day today, isn't it Henry?' Now is Henry afraid?"

"No." Immediately the bell rang and an M&M was dropped into Karl's cup.

"Now the mama doll takes little Henry by the hand and they walk out of their house. Is little Henry afraid?"

"No, why should he be; he's with his mama."

"Little Henry says, 'Where are we going?' and his mother says, 'We're going to the doctor's.' Is little Henry afraid?"

"Yes. He doesn't want to go to the doctor's."

"But does little Henry start to cry or does he keep walking on with his mother like a brave boy?"

"He doesn't cry. He goes with his mother."

The Karl Box rings and an M&M drops into Karl's cup.

"Little Henry's mother lets loose his hand and they keep walking to the doctor's office. Is little Henry afraid?"

"No. He's not *too* afraid." Once more a bell rings and an M&M is delivered.

"They finally get to the doctor's office, and Henry's mother goes in. Does Henry go in with her?"

"Yes, he does."

The bell rang; an M&M dropped into Karl's cup and immediately disappeared into his mouth.

"Is Henry afraid?"

"Yes."

"Does he stay in the room, or does he leave?"

"He stays in the room."

Another bell rings and another M&M is delivered.

This first session lasted for 15 minutes. Karl participated in a series of six doll-play sequences and received about 30 M&Ms in each session.

After the session in the playroom, the two scientists, Karl, and Mrs. Shambaugh talked for ten minutes. Mrs. Shambaugh was instructed to reinforce Karl's behavior on those occasions when he did not act frightened at separation from her, when he was cooperative, and when he behaved in a grown-up fashion. She was instructed to bring in notes describing four occasions on which she had reinforced Karl for any of those behaviors. Karl listened to this interchange with some interest.

Meanwhile, Dr. Patterson explained to the kindergarten teacher that he thought Karl's problem behaviors could be eliminated, but it would help things if they could work on some of his problems while he was actually at the kindergarten school. The teacher looked at her black-and-blue legs, smiled ruefully, and agreed. That day, Dr. Patterson and the Karl Box arrived at the kindergarten. During the recess period, Karl was told that the buzzer would sound each time he played with another kid without hurting him. If Karl was within range, Dr. Patterson also dispensed social reinforcers for appropriate initiations of social interactions. He was informed that the candy he earned would be divided among all the children and distributed during snack time. He earned 70 M&Ms in a ten-minute period; during this time he displayed no aversive behaviors.

On the next day, the tantrum behaviors were observed at the clinic. Again, Karl was picked up and carried to the playroom, screaming, kicking, and crying. However, today the tantrum terminated as soon as Karl arrived in the playroom.

This time the doll-play procedure lasted about 20 minutes. Karl earned 30 M&Ms and a plastic ship.

The remainder of this experiment may best be summarized as follows: within the next few days, interviews were conducted with Karl's mother. She told of the various behaviors which she reinforced on the preceding day. M&M reinforcers were delivered to Karl and the children at the kindergarten whenever the children interacted with Karl, or whenever Karl began a friendly interaction with them. Through a shaping procedure, Karl was induced to walk up the stairs of the laboratory without the use of force. A sort of fading procedure was used to get Karl to the point where he could be in the room without his mother's presence and without crying. He became more tolerant of being left at school and increasingly cooperative at home. Within a short time the mother, the teacher, and Karl all agreed that special therapy was no longer needed.

The overall results are impressive: during a period of nine days, the total duration of Karl's temper tantrums in the kindergarten decreased from between 30 and 35 minutes to zero. No temper tantrums were observed during occasional follow-ups for the next three months. During the first few days, the percentage of time that he spent by himself also decreased from about 40 percent to 0 percent, and remained at 0 percent for the next three months. The percentage of times which Karl refused to follow instructions or suggestions from the teacher dropped from about 25 percent to near 0 percent, and stayed there for the next three months.

Observations showed that the other children tended to avoid Karl, probably as a result of his bad behavior (pushing, elbowing, kicking, and pinching). Dr. Patterson felt that if the bad behavior could be eliminated, then Karl's classmates might interact with him more frequently. He was socially reinforced for positive interactions such as talking, smiling, playing, and touching. The percentage of time in which he initiated positive social interactions increased from about 8 percent to about 20 percent, and then decreased to about 15 percent, where it remained for the following three months. The positive interaction of Karl's classmates also increased from near 0 percent to about 8 percent, and then decreased to about 4 percent and remained there for the rest of the three-month period.

It should be pointed out that these data on positive interactions between Karl and his classmates were obtained during a 20-minute period prior to the time when reinforcement was given for such interactions. These data, therefore, reflect the generalization from the preceding conditioning periods.

> Discussions with both parents and with the teacher during the follow-up period indicate that Karl is "a changed boy." The casual observer in the classroom would have no reason to select Karl as showing particularly deviant behavior. His behavior is characterized by less avoidance of social contacts and increased responsiveness to social reinforcers. Although still somewhat impulsive, Karl no longer displayed temper tantrums, nor did he isolate himself. By any reasonable criteria, the changes in Karl constituted "successful treatment."

This experiment is a dramatic example of how a few moderately intense conditioning sessions, skillfully performed at the right time, can completely change a person's entire mode of behavior. Speaking in nontechnical terms, we might say that his entire personality, or the whole person, had been changed. Let us hope that, in the future, such examples will occur with increasing frequency.

This experiment was included in the present chapter because it illustrates some of the various ways in which reinforcement therapy can generalize to a person's natural environment. The work done with Karl in the laboratory was of two sorts. First, Karl's good behavior was itself directly reinforced and his bad behavior was extinguished. For example, climbing stairs and not crying were reinforced and temper tantrums were extinguished. Now, some of this conditioning in the laboratory may have generalized to Karl's behavior in the home and kindergarten. Second, the responses of having the little boy doll behave properly in play situations involving the home and school were also reinforced. The effect of reinforcing these play responses may have generalized to Karl's "real" behavior.

Furthermore, the effects may have generalized outside of the play situation to the "real" home and classroom.

We do not know the importance of these two types of conditioning procedures applied in Dr. Patterson's laboratory. It may be that they were both very important or possibly that neither of them was of any real value. The importance of these two procedures is particularly difficult to assess since the experimenters were unwilling to rely simply on the effects of the generalization from the laboratories to the classroom. In addition to the laboratory therapy, reinforcement procedures were also insituted in the home and the school. The extent to which the improvement at school was influenced by his conditioning at home and the extent to which it was directly attributable to the conditioning that took place at school cannot be determined.

Patterson and Brodsky made the important point that perhaps the therapist's job is to get the patient's good behavior to occur at a sufficient rate so as to generalize to the natural environment, and to make sure the behavior is such that the environment will then reinforce it.

It was assumed that this initial generalization from the laboratory situation to the kindergarten brought the rate of good behavior up high enough so that reinforcement procedures could be more effectively introduced in the classroom itself. In other words, once the desired behavior generalized to the classroom it was not allowed to extinguish, but was reinforced to get it to occur at a very high rate. It was anticipated that when the experimenters' reinforcement was discontinued, the behavior would be occurring at a sufficiently high frequency so that it could be maintained by the reinforcers which normally maintain good behavior. This anticipation proved correct. Karl is now a socially accepted human being.

Summary

This chapter dealt with problems of the generalization of reinforcement therapy from the laboratory or therapeutic situation to the patient's normal environment. It has been correctly suggested that therapeutic efforts in the laboratory may not always produce a permanent change outside the laboratory. This may be due to a failure of the behavior change to generalize to the patient's normal environment or to a failure of the reinforcement schedules in this environment to maintain this behavior. The undesirable behavior which was extinguished in the laboratory may be reconditioned. On the other hand, desirable behavior which was conditioned in the laboratory may be extinguished. It may be possible to condition competing behaviors which will obtain sufficient reinforcement that the undesirable behavior will not be reconditioned. Sometimes a schedule of reinforcement in the normal environment is not adequate for the conditioning of a response, but once the response is conditioned, the normal schedule in the environment might maintain it.

We saw how a moderately intense series of conditioning sessions could completely change the entire mode of behavior of a problem child, making him an apparently normal well-adjusted boy. The procedure involved the reinforcement of appropriate behaviors in the laboratory, a sort of symbolic conditioning process of reinforcing appropriate play behaviors in the laboratory, reinforcing behavior in the home, and reinforcing all desirable behavior and extinguishing undesirable behavior in the kindergarten. This combination of procedures proved very effective, though the effectiveness of the individual components is not known. The frequency and variety of specific desirable behaviors increased and undesirable behaviors decreased. These changes were largely maintained over a considerable period of time. This illustrates how reinforcement of appropriate behaviors in the laboratory may be supplemented by reinforcement of those behaviors in the normal environment to produce marked behavior changes. Eventually, the behavior was maintained by its normal consequences.

One cannot automatically assume that reinforcement therapy will generalize and be maintained in the normal environment, but appropriate measures may frequently be taken to insure the likelihood of therapeutic success.

QUESTIONS

1. What is the title of this chapter?
2. Traditional psychologists sometimes object that reinforcement therapy does not generalize out of the psychologist's laboratory. (a) True; (b) False.
3. Give a brief example of the failure of reinforcement therapy to generalize.
4. The therapist must make sure that the therapeutic situation is sufficiently similar to the patient's normal environment that the behavior changes which he brings about generalize to that normal environment. Give at least one good way of dealing with this problem.
5. The therapist must make certain that the behavior changes which he brings about are maintained in the patient's normal environment. Suppose the patient has some type of behavior which he wants eliminated. What would be the problem of the continued prevention of this behavior?
6. How might it be dealt with?
7. Another problem in the maintenance of behavior change occurs when there is some behavior which is absent and the therapist wants to condition it. What is the problem of maintenance in this situation?
8. How might the problem be dealt with?
9. Briefly describe what happened the first day Mrs. Shambaugh tried to leave Karl at nursery school.
10. Initially, what kind of interactions did Karl have with the other children?
11. Initially, what did the teacher do when Karl had a temper tantrum?
12. What do you think was the effect of trying to reassure him during the temper tantrums?
13. What happened the first day Mrs. Shambaugh brought Karl to the door of the laboratory?
14. What did Dr. Patterson do when Karl refused to go inside?
15. What happened when Dr. Patterson tried to pick up Karl?
16. What happened when Dr. Patterson carried Karl into the cubicle?

17. What did Dr. Patterson do while Karl screamed, bit, and threw things?
18. How long did Karl's first temper tantrum last in the experimental cubicle? (a) 30 minutes; (b) 3 hours; (c) 3 days; (d) 3 weeks.
19. The next time Karl was brought into the cubicle, was the temper tantrum longer or shorter than the first time?
20. What was the Karl Box?
21. What happened when the bell rang in the Karl Box?
22. What sort of play situation was the Karl Box initially used in?
23. What was the reinforcement which was used in the doll play?
24. What types of responses were reinforced with M&Ms?
25. Which of Karl's responses were reinforced during the recess period at kindergarten?
26. Give an example of Mrs. Shambaugh's effort to reinforce Karl's cooperative behavior at home.
27. Who received the M&M reinforcers when Karl played properly on the playground?
28. What could the other children do to make the Karl Box deliver a reinforcement?
29. What happened to the duration of Karl's temper tantrums in the course of the experiment?
30. What happened to the percentage of time Karl spent by himself?
31. What happened to the percentage of time Karl refused to follow instructions or suggestions from the teacher?
32. What happened to the percentage of time Karl initiated positive social interaction?
33. What happened to the percentage of time Karl's classmates initiated positive social interactions?
34. The casual observer in the classroom can now see Karl behaving in a reasonably normal way, but his behavior is still in some sense cold and mechanical; it is obvious he is different from the other children. (a) True; (b) False.
35. The work done with Karl in the laboratory was of two sorts. What were they?
36. Why was Karl's case included in this chapter?
37. Why is the importance of the two procedures of direct reinforcement of good behavior in the laboratory and reinforcement of good behavior at kindergarten difficult to assess in this experiment?
38. Patterson and Brodsky made the important point that the therapist's job is to get the patient to understand the causes of his maladaptive behavior. (a) True; (b) False.
39. The main problem with this experiment is that although they got generalization from the laboratory to the kindergarten, there was not enough reinforcement in the kindergarten to maintain good behavior. (a) True; (b) False.

NOTES
Modification of a Child's Multiple Problem Behaviors

This is an excellent example of some of the problems that arise in scientific research in a therapeutic situation. If this experiment had been conducted completely in a laboratory or in a kindergarten which was specifically designed for research purposes, the experimenters would probably have behaved much differently. They could have tried one single approach and observed its effects; if it did not work, they could have gone on to observe the effects of some other procedure. They would not have to worry about getting impressive results the first time. But in the present experiment, it was necessary to help Karl as soon as possible; otherwise he might have had to drop out of the kinder-garten. A study like this shows that something important is happening with the thera-peutic procedures used, but it does not pinpoint the important controlling variables.

Now that we know that the variables have drastically changed Karl's behavior pat-terns, the experiment will have to be repeated in a much more systematic manner with other similar children in order to determine the causal factors. At this point, we do not know the individual importance of the direct conditioning of Karl's behavior in the laboratory, the doll-play therapy in the laboratory, the conditioning of proper behavior in the home, the conditioning of proper behavior in the school, and the conditioning of the behavior of the children in the school.

It should be emphasized that this experiment is very important in showing that something in this complex of variables could control Karl's behavior, even though the experiment did not indicate exactly what was involved. It will be expensive and time-consuming to have to repeat such an experiment and to isolate all of the factors, but when one does not initially have an opportunity to do the perfect experiment, he may be wise to go ahead and do the best he can for the time being. This is exactly what Patterson and Brodsky did in this extremely important exploratory effort.

A conditioned reinforcer is an event or object which acquires its reinforcing properties through association with other reinforcers.

Unless conditioned rein-
forcers are at least occasionally associated with other
reinforcers they will lose
their reinforcing properties.

An *unconditioned reinforcer*
is an event or object which
does not require prior
association with other reinforcers in order to have
reinforcing properties.

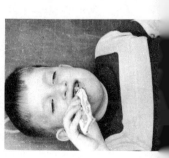

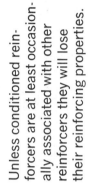

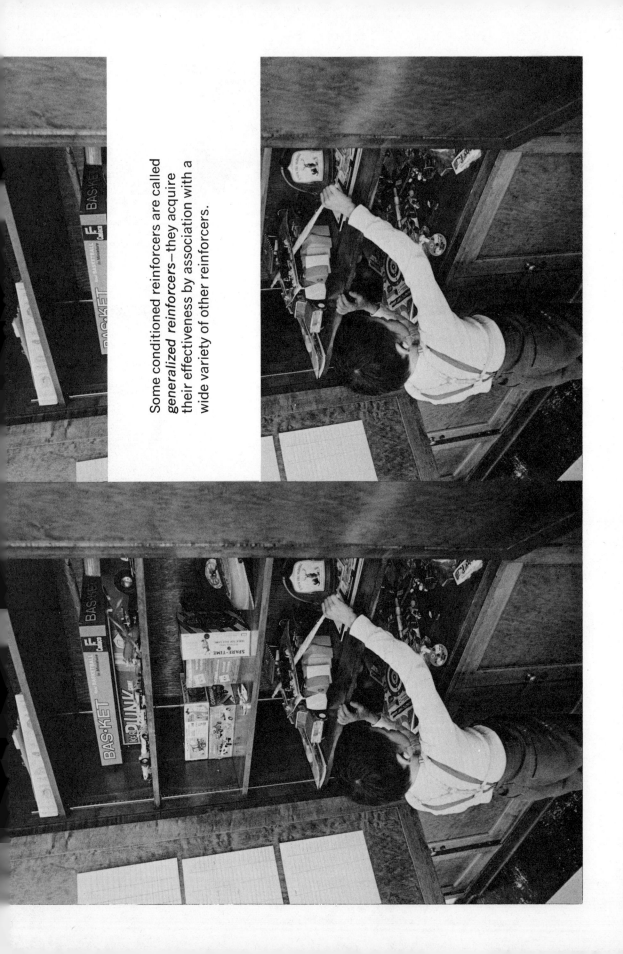

Some conditioned reinforcers are called *generalized reinforcers*—they acquire their effectiveness by association with a wide variety of other reinforcers.

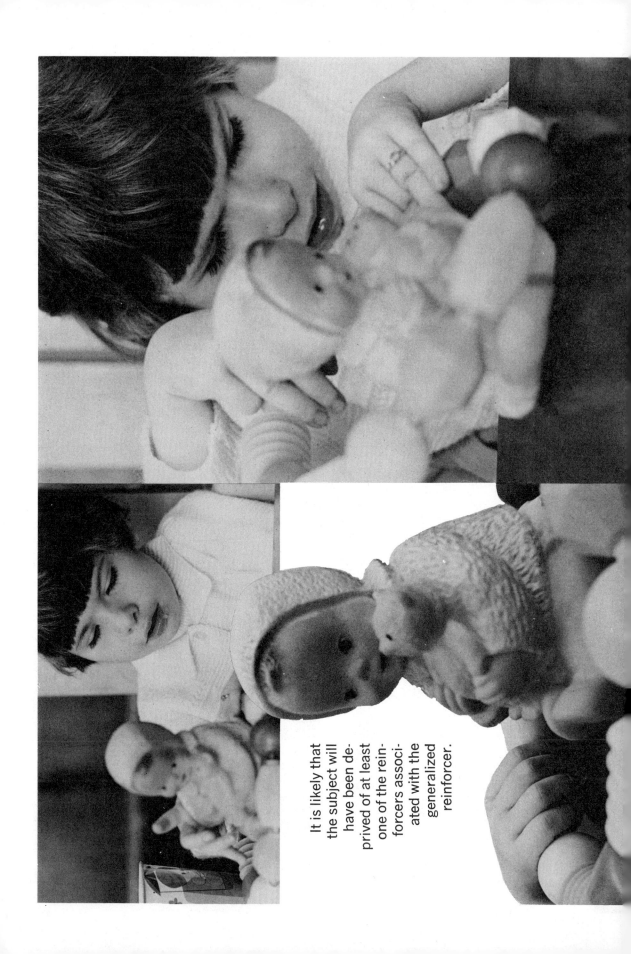

It is likely that the subject will have been deprived of at least one of the reinforcers associated with the generalized reinforcer.

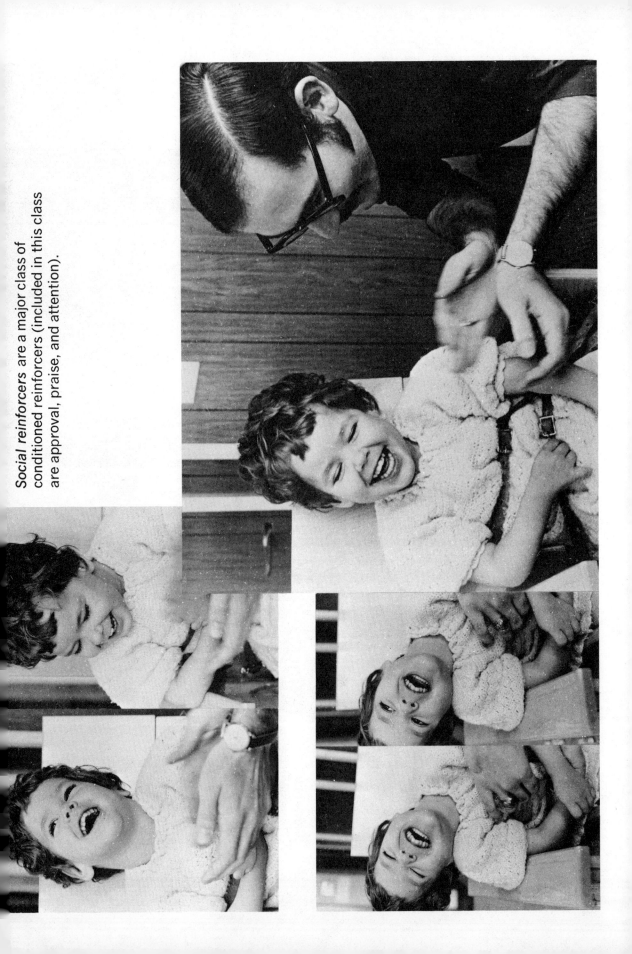

Social reinforcers are a major class of conditioned reinforcers (included in this class are approval, praise, and attention).

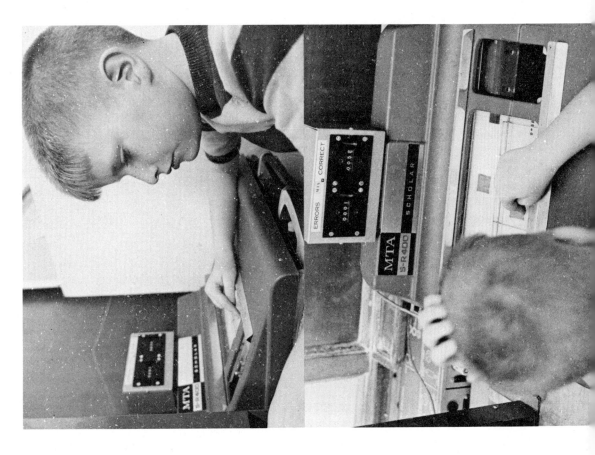

Teaching machines can also present both generalized and unconditioned reinforcers. This machine—an MTA scholar, which is used in the E.S.E.A. title VI-A program for the multiple handicapped (in Kalamazoo), can provide instant, automatic reinforcement.

CONDITIONED REINFORCEMENT

15

CONDITIONED REINFORCEMENT AND THE TOKEN ECONOMY

The Thrifty Chimpanzee

John Cowles opened the cage door and Bimba, the chimpanzee, hopped out.[1] He and Bimba walked into the next room where the chimpanzee immediately jumped through the door into a test chamber in the center of the room. Cowles closed the chamber door and went around to the apparatus at its side. He picked up two small 5½-inch square pieces of wood; one of the pieces had a large circle drawn on it and the other had a small circle. After checking a procedure sheet on an adjacent table, he hung the two pieces of wood like miniature swinging doors in the center of the apparatus. He was careful to place the door with the large circle on his right-hand side. Cowles tested the two swinging doors before placing a small disc which looked suspiciously like a poker chip behind the door with the large circle. He then raised a screen which separated Bimba's cage from the two doors. The chimpanzee put his arm through the bars of the cage, pushed open the door with the large circle, immediately picked up the small disc, and placed it on the floor of his cage. Cowles lowered the screen and noted in his data book the position of the circles and that Bimba had made a correct response. Then he switched the position of the two circles and again placed another disc behind the door with the large circle. On some of the trials, the two circles were switched, and on some, they remained the same. Only twice did Bimba push back the door with the small circle. In those cases, she withdrew her arm and Cowles lowered the screen. A few seconds later, the screen was again raised. Then, Bimba pushed back the door with the large circle and thereby obtained the disc.

At the end of 12 trials, Cowles walked around to the front of the cage as Bimba picked up the discs. When the cage door was opened, Bimba jumped out, carrying the discs in her mouth and hands as she ran ahead of Cowles, back into the original cage where she jumped around actively in front of a screen separating

1. This section based on Cowles, J. T. Food tokens as incentives for learning for chimpanzees. *Comparative Psychology Monograph*, 1937, *14*, 1–96.

277

her from another apparatus. When Cowles arrived at the cage, he closed the door and raised the screen, allowing Bimba access to the apparatus. The device looked like a vending machine, which, in fact, it was. Bimba immediately and skillfully inserted one of the discs in a slot in the vendor; a clanking noise occurred as a raisin dropped through a chute. Bimba instantly picked up the raisin and consumed it, having previously removed the discs from her mouth. This procedure was repeated until each disc had been exchanged for a raisin which was in turn eaten. The discs seemed to act as money. Just as the money you and I work for and insert in the vending machines of life merely "stands" for the things it can be exchanged for, the discs were tokens which could be exchanged for raisins.

If a silver dollar is given to a small child, he will play with it briefly and then discard it. The coin has little value for the youngster. Only after much experience with such coins will he value them, as he does a few years later. The same was true of Bimba; only after much experience with the tokens did they become valuable for her. The experience, however, has to be of a specific sort. The tokens must be intimately involved in the acquisition of something else which is already of value. In more technical terms, for tokens to become effective reinforcers, they must be associated with the attainment of already established reinforcers. Only after Bimba had learned the response of inserting the tokens in the vending machine and receiving the raisin reinforcers did the tokens themselves become reinforcers. Then a variety of responses could be conditioned using the tokens as reinforcers. Just like humans, Bimba would work for her salary.

Learned reinforcers such as tokens are called "conditioned reinforcers." *A conditioned reinforcer is an event or object which acquires its reinforcing property through association with other reinforcers. An unconditioned reinforcer is an event or object which does not require prior association with other reinforcers in order to have reinforcing properties.* Another name for "conditioned reinforcer" is "secondary reinforcer"; and, as you might expect, "unconditioned reinforcers" are sometimes called "primary reinforcers."

We have seen some obvious parallels between conditioned reinforcers such as tokens used by the chimpanzee and conditioned reinforcers such as money used by humans. There is another important feature of conditioned reinforcers which may also be observed in these various situations. At the end of the Civil War in the United States, Confederate money lost its effectiveness as a conditioned reinforcer because it could no longer be exchanged for other primary or conditioned reinforcers. Its value became purely historical. Similarly, if depositing tokens in the vending machine was no longer reinforced by the presentation of raisins, Bimba's token-depositing responses would have extinguished. At the same time, the tokens would have lost their effectiveness as conditioned reinforcers; in other words, the reinforcing power of the conditioned reinforcers would have been extinguished. The tokens would no longer have maintained the discriminative responses of selecting the larger of the two circles. This is a very important principle: *unless conditioned reinforcers are at least occasionally associated with other reinforcers, they will lose their reinforcing property.*

We will consider the concept of "conditioned reinforcement" further in the remainder of the chapter.

A Token Economy for Psychotics

You are already familiar with some of the work performed by Dr. Teodoro Ayllon in the modification of abnormal behavior. Dr. Ayllon, along with Dr. Azrin, also performed some of the first research in the use of token economies in the development of normal behavior in the miniature society of psychotic patients at a mental hospital.[2] As with Ayllon's earlier work, this research involved female mental patients who had been on the back wards for many years. Most of these women had severe problems with their verbal and social behavior.

The structure of the economy on this ward was sufficiently interesting to deserve special comment. The patients earned tokens by making responses which were necessary or useful to the patients as a group—for example, serving meals, cleaning floors, sorting laundry, selling items in the commissary, projecting movies, leading guided tours, and assisting the nurse. Other sorts of responses such as self-grooming were also reinforced with tokens. The "conditioned reinforcers," or tokens, were exchangeable for other reinforcers. One general type of payoff reinforcer consisted of a choice of a bedroom. A patient with sufficient tokens (4 to 30) could pay for a particular bedroom and indirectly select her roommates. Patients who did not rent a special bedroom were placed in the free room. In a similar manner, a choice of eating groups could be obtained (1 token). Each patient could also secure locked cabinets in which to store her belongings. She could rent a personal chair which she did not have to share with other patients (1 token). One token could also be used to rent a room divider to shield the patient's bed. Two tokens could be used to obtain escorted or unescorted leaves from the ward, and 100 tokens could be exchanged for a permit to visit a neighboring town with an escort for approximately one hour. A ten-minute private meeting with a member of the hospital staff cost from 20 to 100 tokens and could be extended by the use of additional tokens. However, no tokens were required for the first five minutes of social interaction with the ward physician, nurse, and hospital chaplain. From 1 to 10 tokens could be exchanged for participation in religious services of the patient's choice. Other reinforcers consisted of movies, a live dance band, exclusive use of a radio or television set, and attendance at hospital activities such as dances (all from 1 to 3 tokens). In addition consumable items such as extra clothing, grooming accessories, reading and writing materials, and a choice of items by special request such as potted plants, parakeets, etc. could be obtained with tokens (1 to 400 tokens).

The conditioned reinforcers used in this study have a more general utility than those used with the chimpanzee. In that case, the tokens could be exchanged only for raisins. However, in the present study, the tokens could be exchanged for a wide variety of reinforcers. Such conditioned reinforcers, acquiring their effectiveness by association with a wide variety of other reinforcers, are

2. This section based on Ayllon, T., and Azrin, N. H. The measurement and reinforcement of behavior of psychotics. *Journal of the Experimental Analysis of Behavior*, 1965, 8, 357–383.

called *generalized conditioned reinforcers.* A conditioned reinforcer is only effective if the organism is deprived of the other reinforcers with which it has been associated. If the chimp had not been deprived of raisins, the tokens would not have been effective. Since generalized conditioned reinforcers have been associated with a wide variety of other reinforcers, it is not essential that the organism be deprived of any specific reinforcer. However, it is likely that he has been deprived of at least some of the reinforcers. For that reason, the generalized conditioned reinforcers will be effective most of the time. This of course has considerable utility when a psychologist is with a large number of people. He may use a token economy such as the one set up by Ayllon and Azrin.

The question was raised as to whether the tokens were, in fact, acting effectively as reinforcers. Perhaps the patients found the tasks themselves reinforcing enough. The use of the tokens might have been an example of superstitious behavior on the part of the psychologists. In attempting to determine the effectiveness of the tokens as reinforcers, our first response might be to withhold the tokens altogether. We have seen in an earlier chapter that such a procedure is not scientifically sound. When we say that something acts as a reinforcer, we are saying that it will increase the rate of occurrence of the response which it follows. It might be that the mere presence of the tokens and the attention which the patients received when the tokens are delivered provided so much encouragement to them that they behaved in the desired manner. In other words, it is possible that the tokens did not have to follow the response; it was only necessary that the tokens be given.

In order to test this notion adequately, we need to make sure that the tokens are still given to the patients, but that they do not follow the responses being measured. This was accomplished by giving the patients the tokens at the beginning of each day, whether or not they did any work. In that way, the tokens were present but were not given immediately after the response.

Over a period of 20 days, the amount of work decreased from 44 hours to only 1 hour per day. This may be considered to be a form of extinction in which the potential reinforcement is given before the individual has an opportunity to make a response, and subsequent responding does not produce additional reinforcement. The obtained decrease in the amount of behavior is what would be expected as a result of the extinction procedure. These data indicate that the tokens were acting as effective reinforcers in maintaining the desirable behavior.

An extremely skeptical critic might claim that the experimenters were just lucky. Perhaps when they discontinued the reinforcement procedure, the temperature changed, or something else happened which lowered the response rate. The extinction procedure might have been irrelevant. This decrease in the performance of the patients might not have been due to the extinction procedure but rather to some uncontrolled factor. One way to convince the skeptic would be to terminate the extinction procedure and reinstate the conditioning procedure. When this was done, the performance immediately rose to the preceding average of 44 hours of work per day, leaving little doubt that the tokens were effectively reinforcing the work behavior.

It is interesting to note the relation between the patients' verbal behavior and their work behavior. During the first part of the extinction phase, several patients continued working for a few days. They made such statements as, "I think I'll work even if it is a vacation," or "I want to help out here; there aren't enough people to do the work." However, eventually nearly all of the work behavior dropped off and other sorts of statements became more common such as, "I'm not going to do any work if I don't get anything for it." It is probably just as true of normal people as it is of mental patients that their statements about working without some sort of special reinforcement decrease as the amount of opportunities to do such unreinforced work increases.

One feature of this study is that it allows us some insight into our own economic system. As in the previous study, it is obvious that tokens function in essentially the same manner as does money for you and me. The tokens are conditioned reinforcers, and so is money. Both the tokens and the money have been associated with other reinforcers and have thus acquired their reinforcing value. Miniature systems of this sort would provide excellent opportunities for the experimentally-minded economist. It would allow him direct verifications of his theories rather than the usual indirect verifications with which the *nonexperimental* scientist must be satisfied.

The main purpose of this experiment, however, is to illustrate how a small staff, consisting of a psychologist, a nurse, and five attendants, can administer a token economy for 44 psychotic patients in a mental hospital, 24 hours per day, seven days per week. Such a token economy allows the psychologist to work effectively with a large number of mental patients at a single time. These procedures have also been found to be valuable at other institutions where they have been tried. The techniques have brought hope to otherwise hopeless situations.

Remedial Education

In recent years, our society has shown much concern for the culturally disadvantaged. The notion which prevailed in earlier times was that impoverished people deserved their poverty. Anyone who was poor was so because of his own choice. He lacked the moral fibre, the get-up-and-go of the successful. He was lazy and shiftless, and deserved nothing better than his lowly status. It was never clear whether the faulty makeup of the destitute was a result of an unfortunate heredity or an impoverished environment, but it was felt that the poor deserved every misfortune which befell them. The successful had no reason to pity the less fortunate. Many years ago similar attitudes prevailed with regard to people who were crazy. People have behavioral flaws, and they should suffer for them.

Recent times have seen a more rational and compassionate approach. Most enlightened people today believe that every effort should be made to help others overcome the limitations imposed by an impoverished background. A large amount of good will and financial and human resources have been invested in attempts to help the less fortunate; however, without an appropriate understanding of the laws of the behavior of man, these valuable resources will be wasted.

A project undertaken at the University of Kansas involved the use of our knowledge of conditioned reinforcement in helping culturally deprived children cross the barriers to a sound education.[3] This project was headed by Dr. Montrose Wolf, whose imaginative work we have studied in several of the preceding chapters. Wolf and his colleagues established a special remedial classroom for 16 fifth- and sixth-grade students. They were all at least 2.0 years below their grade level on a reading achievement test. They were from a lower-income neighborhood of Kansas City. In most instances the children belonged to families of more than five children. The families received welfare support, and usually no father was present. The parents voluntarily enrolled their children in the remedial class. During the public school year, the students attended the special classroom each weekday after school for 2½ years and on Saturday mornings; during the summer months, they attended school every morning except Sunday. The classroom was located in the basement of a church. It was administered by one head teacher and two teaching assistants.

The conditioned reinforcement procedure used resembled a trading stamp plan. The conditioned reinforcers consisted of check marks which the teacher placed in a student's folder after he had completed an assignment correctly. When a child first joined the program, the conditioned reinforcers were given after each problem which was worked correctly. As the student acquired a higher rate and a more accurate output, there was a gradual increase in the amount and difficulty of the work required to obtain the secondary reinforcers. Sometimes the student negotiated with the teacher in determining the salary—the number of conditioned reinforcers which could be given for a particular amount of work.

The conditioned reinforcers could be exchanged for other reinforcers. Weekly field trips involving circuses, swimming, zoos, picnics, sporting events, and movies were included. Daily snacks, sandwiches, fruit, milk, and cookies could be obtained for exchange of the check-marked pages. Some of the conditioned reinforcers could be turned in for money and items available in the school store such as candy, toiletry, novelties, and clothing. Other long-range reinforcers could be obtained by the exchange of large numbers of tokens, or conditioned reinforcers; these involved such things as clothes, watches, and secondhand bicycles. Any child who had accumulated two dollars' worth of check marks was eligible for a shopping trip to a local department store. The child received these secondary reinforcers for three general sorts of activities: work completed and/or corrected in regular school and brought to the classroom; homework assignments and remedial work completed in the remedial classroom; and good marks on their six-week report card grades (an "A" paid off maximally and an "F" minimally).

In addition to the reinforcers used with the students, conditioned reinforcers were also used with the instructors. An effort was made to reinforce maximally effective instruction by giving a bonus of ten dollars to the two assistant instructors whenever one of their students brought in a six-week report card with a grade average higher than that of the previous six weeks.

3. This section based on Wolf, M., Giles, D. K., and Hall, V. R. Experiments with token reinforcements in a remedial classroom. Unpublished manuscript, 1967.

Other reinforcement procedures were also used with the students. Favorite subjects or popular academic activities were in some instances reserved for presentation only after completion of work with a less favorite subject. In this way the popular subjects were used as a reinforcement for completing the unpopular ones. Academic productivity was often reinforced by permitting the productive students to instruct other students in their deficient areas, and good students were allowed to check material completed by other students. Students frequently asked to continue their academic work after the 2½-hour remedial session. For good work they were reinforced by additional assignments to take home! A large bonus was given each month to every student who had perfect attendance for that period. The bonus was cumulative so that for two months' perfect attendance, the bonus was twice as large, and for three months' perfect attendance, the bonus was three times as large, etc.

Good behavior was also reinforced. A blackboard containing the names of all the children was placed in front of the classroom. An alarm clock was set to go off at variable intervals during the remedial session, usually about three times during the 2½-hour period. Any child who was out of his seat for any reason when the alarm sounded received a mark after his name on the blackboard. For any other disruptive behavior, such as hitting another student, a mark was placed after the offender's name. At the end of the day, the child with the *fewest* marks received a large number of bonus points. If the student had more than four misdemeanors, he lost a privilege such as the use of the store at the end of the day.

A party was held every six weeks for the students whose grade average showed improvement. These parties involved dining in a restaurant, camping, going on plane rides, etc. The teachers in the public school classroom also had the opportunity to give points and remove store privileges from students in their classroom. This was done by sending reports to the remedial classroom teacher.

An attempt was made to reinforce the parents for reinforcing the good academic behavior of their children. Items of interest to the student's family were included in the store and could be purchased by the students with conditioned reinforcers earned for good work.

There are other conditioned reinforcers that control behavior as well as tokens or money. A major class is called "social reinforcers." Conditioned social reinforcers consist of such things as approval, praise, and the mere attention of our fellow men. These social reinforcers are extremely important in the maintenance of much of our everyday behavior. For example, the high level of athletic achievement in our society might be due almost exclusively to the considerable social reinforcement given for outstanding athletic performances. The athlete receives large amounts of social reinforcement from girl friends, other males, parents, teachers, coaches, neighbors, and so forth. As a result he spends a great amount of time working very hard in the development of skilled athletic responses. What do you suppose would happen if scholarly behavior were also the recipient of such plentiful reinforcement? This is precisely the situation which Montrose Wolf tried to establish in the special classroom.

On Saturdays group games similar to TV college quiz contests were performed with two individuals on each team. They competed against one another for bonus points which were given to the team with the most correct responses. The students were permitted to choose their partners. Everyone wanted to have as teammates the students who could answer the most questions—the academically skilled. Associating with the best scholars became a conditioned social reinforcer. The good scholars were sought after as heroes, much like the good athlete on the playground. Indeed, this is an optimal situation for socially reinforcing scholarly behavior.

As if this were not enough, an additional method was developed for the presentation of social reinforcement for good academic behavior. Each group of students, who worked with one instructor, competed with the other groups in accumulating public school tests with grades of "A." Whenever a student brought in an "A" paper, an announcement was made in class and the paper was thumbtacked above the student's desk. Each Saturday, the team with the most papers was reinforced; each member of the team was treated to candy bars of his choice. The notion of Saturday's hero now has a new significance. The mere idea of such an environment should warm the hearts of the intellectuals among you.

The artificial token conditioned reinforcers were effective in conditioning new behavior, but it was desirable that the behavior should then be maintained by other reinforcers, like those which normally control our behavior. Therefore, one final source of reinforcement was arranged to come from the natural environment of the student. Both buying (with either tokens or money) and the calculations necessary to distribute tokens required the use of newly acquired arithmetic responses. Reading responses were reinforced by requiring the students to do exactly as the directors of an assignment indicated in order to receive reinforcement for their working responses. In addition, such highly interesting reading material as comics was made available to the students in an effort to reinforce reading behavior.

This is obviously a fantastic arrangement and probably would only be conceived by someone well versed in the concepts associated with conditioned reinforcement. But is it effective? Of the 16 students, one of the sixth graders was lost during the spring term. She married and dropped out of school and consequently out of the remedial program. In spite of that slight setback, the results were indeed impressive. During each of the preceding two years, the students had advanced approximately 0.6 years on the Scholastic Aptitude Test (SAT) administered by the public school. During the year of conditioned reinforcement, the typical gain was 1.5 years on the scholastic aptitude test. A similar group of students who had not been in the conditioned reinforcement program showed a gain of only 0.8 years in that period of time. During that year, the report card grade average improved from a "D" to a "C," while the comparison group showed practically no improvement. The students attended about 85 percent of the remedial classes even though the program regularly met on Saturdays and most holidays. The decision to work on regular school holidays was determined by a vote of the students. The instructors undemocratically refused to work on Thanksgiving and Christmas.

How much did the students earn? About $250 each during the school year—a very small amount of conditioned reinforcers for the very large reinforcement going to the society which makes valuable citizens out of individuals who might otherwise be lost.

Summary

This chapter has been concerned with the notion of conditioned reinforcers. Their use was demonstrated in a variety of situations varying from working with chimpanzees to remedial education of underprivileged children to complete token economies for psychotic patients.

The following major points were made:

1. A conditioned reinforcer is an event or object which acquires its reinforcing properties through association with other reinforcers.

2. Unconditioned reinforcers do not require prior association with other reinforcers in order to have reinforcing properties.

3. Another name for a conditioned reinforcer is "secondary reinforcer," and another name for an unconditioned reinforcer is "primary reinforcer."

4. Generalized conditioned reinforcers have acquired their effectiveness through association with a large variety of other reinforcers. For that reason a generalized conditioned reinforcer will be effective most of the time.

5. If a conditioned reinforcer is not occasionally associated with another reinforcer, its effectiveness will eventually extinguish.

QUESTIONS

1. What were the S^Ds and S^{Δ}s in the chimpanzee experiment?
2. What was the response which was reinforced in the discrimination between the large and small circles?
3. What was the reinforcement used in the actual discrimination problem?
4. What was the reinforcer for which the small discs or tokens could be exchanged?
5. How were the tokens exchanged for the raisins?
6. What happened on discrimination trials when the chimpanzee pushed open the wrong door?
7. A c_____ r_____ acquires its reinforcing properties by its association with other reinforcers.
8. U_____ r_____ do not require prior association with other reinforcers to acquire reinforcing properties.
9. Another name for conditioned reinforcer is s_____ r_____.
10. Another name for unconditioned reinforcers is p_____ r_____.
11. In the study on the token economy for psychotics, how could the patients earn the tokens; that is, what sort of responses could they make?
12. Give some examples of reinforcers for which the tokens could be exchanged.
13. The tokens in this experiment were a special kind of conditioned reinforcer called a g_____ conditioned reinforcer.
14. In what way is the establishment of a generalized conditioned reinforcer different from that of a simple conditioned reinforcer?

15. What is the advantage of a generalized conditioned reinforcer over a simple conditioned reinforcer?

16. In attempting to determine the effectiveness of the tokens as reinforcers, what would be wrong with withholding the tokens altogether?

17. How could the notion of tokens as reinforcers be adequately tested?

18. What happened to the amount of work when the tokens were given at the beginning of the day regardless of whether the patient had worked?

19. What did the experimenters do to demonstrate that the extinction procedure really was effective; in other words, what subsequent procedure did they use?

20. What happened when they again required the patients to make appropriate responses before the token reinforcers were delivered?

21. What sort of conditioned reinforcers that you and I use are similar to the tokens used by the psychotics?

22. If you have had an economics course, what sort of economics experiments could you perform in the miniature economic system in the hospital?

23. Briefly describe the notion which prevailed at earlier times regarding impoverished people.

24. What is the contemporary enlightened attitude toward people who come from impoverished backgrounds?

25. What were the grade-levels of the students that Dr. Wolf and his colleagues worked with in the special remedial classroom? (a) Nursery school; (b) Fifth and sixth grade; (c) Eleventh and twelfth grade; (d) Juniors and seniors in college; (e) Graduate students.

26. Briefly describe the background of these children.

27. When did the students work in the special classroom?

28. What responses were reinforced?

29. What were some of the back-up reinforcers for which the conditioned reinforcers could be exchanged?

30. In what way were conditioned reinforcers used for the instructors?

31. How were popular academic subjects used as reinforcers?

32. How was homework used as a reinforcer?

33. What was done to reinforce attendance?

34. What was the system used for reinforcing good behavior?

35. What attempt was made to reinforce the parents for reinforcing the good academic behavior of their children?

36. Describe the systems used to develop social reinforcement among the students for good academic behavior.

37. What was done to bring the learned behavior under the influence of reinforcers which normally control our behavior?

38. What effect did the remedial classroom have on the students' performance on the Scholastic Aptitude Test?

39. What effect did the remedial classroom have on the average grade earned in the public school?

40. What sort of attendance did the remedial classroom have?

41. On the average, how much was spent on reinforcing the children?

42. In the preceding chapters, there may be found many examples of conditioned reinforcers, though at that time we did not make a distinction between conditioned and unconditioned reinforcers. The students might find it valuable to go through the preceding chapters and identify the conditioned and unconditioned reinforcers in the various studies.

NOTES
Conditioned Reinforcement and College Education

What is the reinforcement for going to college? Undoubtedly most students have asked themselves that question at one time or another, though they may not have used those terms. The obvious answer is, getting an education. But a closer look at the situation might lead us to doubt this answer. Other answers might be as follows: getting a diploma which will lead to a good job, getting a husband or wife, avoiding aversive stimulation from parents, avoiding aversive stimulation from the draft board, or having a good time. Probably a combination of many of these reinforcers, as well as getting an education, are effective in maintaining college attendance in most students. Regardless of the set of ultimate reinforcers involved, there is one common requirement for their attainment. A student must earn respectable grades in order to stay in school. Since passing grades are associated with all of these back-up reinforcers, it is to be expected that passing grades are fairly effective conditioned reinforcers.

With the notion of grades as conditioned reinforcers, we established our introductory psychology course at Western Michigan University upon principles very similar to those of the token economies which Wolf and Ayllon developed. At one stage, the course was run as follows: at the beginning of the semester, the students were informed of the maximum number of points which could be earned in the course (approximately 375). They were then told that if they obtained 90 percent of this maximum number, they would receive an "A" for the semester. If they earned 80 percent, they would receive a "B," and so forth.

They received a conditioned reinforcer of one point for roughly every hour of prescribed work which they performed for the course. The reading assignments were divided into five daily one-hour assignments for each week. Answering brief questions on a daily quiz covering the daily reading assignments was reinforced with two points. If the student failed to answer those questions correctly, he could attend a one-hour make-up lecture on the reading assignment. If by that time he has mastered the material, he could receive the two point conditioned reinforcer for passing the quiz on the make-up lecture.

Two one-hour class periods each week were devoted to working in an operant conditioning rat laboratory where the students reinforced a rat's bar-pressing response with water. Their laboratory work was in turn reinforced by conditioned point reinforcers for writing reports describing the work in the laboratory. Two other class hours each week were devoted to a student-centered seminar dealing with the attitudes of science. The students worked in groups of four and graded each other on their critical evaluation of the scientific works. These grades were then converted into points which were the reinforcers for doing a good job in preparing for the seminar. One day each week the students attended a lecture, and at the end of this period they were given a quiz on the material covered in the lecture. Two points could be earned in this quiz to reinforce paying attention to the lecture and answering the questions properly.

It was also possible to earn a total of six bonus points which did not figure into the maximum number of points but were simply added on to improve the student's grade. These could be earned by performing various tasks such as participating as a subject in experiments performed by advanced students and faculty members, helping to maintain the rats with which the students worked in the laboratory sections, and helping with some of the considerable paper work involved in administering such a course. Students could also earn these bonus point conditioned reinforcers by getting their laboratory experiments finished on time (a task which was not always easy when a shy student met a recalcitrant rat). The laboratory was kept open on Friday, Saturday, and Sunday so that the students could have an opportunity to make the responses necessary to finish the experiment on time. The top students in the class had an opportunity to receive bonus point conditioned reinforcers by participating in various field trips to the psychology laboratories and behavior modification centers associated with the university.

The number of points the student had earned were posted weekly along with the maximum number of points which could be earned and the letter grade attained to that date.

This general system of conditioned reinforcement has proven to be an extremely effective way of teaching college students although there may be more than one thousand students taking the course in any term. In spite of initial apprehension, the students seem to work harder, learn more, earn better grades, and prefer this system to the more traditional approach which does not make explicit use of the point system of conditioned reinforcement based on the semester grade.

Man and Machine

Let us do three things in this section. First, we will review some of the laws of behavior concerning the nature of man; then we will consider some notions about the nature of machines; and finally we will discuss the implications of these concepts for the future of man. We may reach some startling conclusions—some conclusions which we find quite disturbing.

First, let us discuss the nature of man. One of the most important characteristics of man is that his *behavior is primarily controlled by its consequences*. What follows the response determines the likelihood that the response will recur in the future. There are three types of consequences. One is reinforcement; the second is punishment; and the third is consequence, for purposes of completeness, the neutral stimulus which has no direct effect on behavior, but may result in extinction. Our primary concern will be with reinforcement but most of the notions are also applicable to punishment.

As we have seen in this chapter, *there are two basic types of reinforcement—unconditioned or primary reinforcement and conditioned or secondary reinforcement.* Many of the unconditioned reinforcers seem to involve biological needs. These include food, water, and an adequate temperature. There are other examples, which probably do not involve biological or tissue need, including such things as saccharin. Some other stimuli also act as weak unconditioned reinforcers; these include lights and sounds. They would also seem to fill no known biological need. In this chapter we have considered conditioned reinforcers such as grades, approval, and money. Other conditioned reinforcers probably include control of the social and physical environment, artistic creativity, and scientific problem solving.

Most of the basic research indicates that in order *for a neutral stimulus to become a conditioned or secondary reinforcer, it must also act as a discriminative stimulus or S^D*. For example, suppose a bell rings, then a rat presses a bar, and a pellet of food is delivered. The bell serves as the S^D for bar pressing. The bell's not ringing acts as an S^Δ—food will not be delivered for bar pressing in the absence of the ringing bell. Because the bell serves as a discriminative stimulus, it also becomes a conditioned or secondary reinforcer. Now, if the rat pulls a chain which rings the bell, the bell will reinforce chain pulling and this new response can be conditioned.

The establishment of attention and approval as conditioned reinforcers for human behavior would also seem to involve the process of stimulus discrimination. Someone's paying attention to us or approving of what we are doing acts as a discriminative stimulus. It is an S^D; if we make the proper response, that response will then be reinforced. On the other hand, someone's not approving of us or not even paying attention to us may be an S^Δ for responding since reinforcement will probably not be forthcoming. Because attention and approval are very pervasive discriminative stimuli, they also become very powerful conditioned reinforcers. Crying behavior and self-abuse (both physical and verbal) may be reinforced by attention. Telling jokes is reinforced by attention. The major reinforcement for writing introductory psychology texts may also be attention and approval of our fellow man.

Let us now consider some other principles of behavior which should be fairly obvious. *The first principle is that unconditioned reinforcement is stronger than conditioned reinforcement.* Suppose we had a pigeon in a test chamber with two response keys. If he pecks the left key, the food magazine will come up within reach accompanied by a loud clang and will present food for three seconds. If the bird pecks the right key, the food magazine will come up and clang and fall out of reach before the bird can get to it. This clang of the food magazine acts as a conditioned reinforcer. Pecking the left key presents the primary reinforcer of the food itself, whereas pecking the right key produces only the clang, the secondary reinforcer. The bird will most frequently peck the key that produces the unconditioned reinforcer. Suppose that we replace the pigeon with a typical male undergraduate. If he pecks the right key, he gets the foldout picture of the Playmate of the Month. If he pecks the left key, he gets the Playmate of the Month. You know which key he will peck—the one which produces the primary reinforcer.

The second principle is that organisms must be deprived of the primary reinforcer in order for the secondary reinforcer to be effective. If the pigeon had just eaten all the food he can hold, he will not peck the key. A conditioned reinforcer of the food magazine clanging will not be effective in maintaining the key-peck response. Similarly, if the young man is now walking down the street with the Playmate of the Month, the primary reinforcer, he will not run into a newsstand to buy a copy of *Playboy*, the secondary reinforcer.

The third principle does not fit so comfortably within the *Playboy* paradigm, so we will have to be satisfied with the pigeon. This principle is the *"Law of Least Effort." Organisms will make the responses involving the least efforts, all else being equal.* Although the principle may not be universal, it tends to be true whether primary or secondary reinforcers are involved. Suppose that reinforcement is delivered for every left key peck but only after every tenth right key peck. The pigeon will make the least effortful response sequence; in other words, he will peck the left key.

Now let us consider some implications of these principles and concepts. *If given the opportunity, we would select the situation in which primary reinforcements are continuously provided with no efforts on our part. Secondary reinforcement would then be ineffective.* This seems to follow directly from what we have said thus far, but it has far-reaching, frightening implications.

Before considering these implications, a comment about the nature of machines is appropriate. There is only one thing we really need to know about machines: engineers and automation experts tell us that *it is feasible that computers and other machines will eventually do all of the work in the world.* They will maintain themselves and us.

This means that they will provide us with all of our primary reinforcers. For example, food will be ingested without our having to make a single response. They will

Wouldn't it be keen
And super-clean
To have a machine
That would do all of your work?
Then you could just skate
And pick up a date
Cause you would have time
For any old quirk.
Things would be cool.
Goodbye school.
It's sham time all day
On computer pay.
Amidst all the bliss
Could you be ready for this
The end of frustration
Due to automation
The entire nation
Will be computerized
For fornication.
Yes Masters and Johnson
Weren't putting you on son
That old computer can do
Anything as well as you.
No need to move
Just sit and groove
With admiration
On cleverly contrived
Electrically thrived
Super-mechanical stimulation.

also provide us with sexual stimulation. The notion of a sexual machine is intriguing as well as disturbing. A common notion exists that there is at least one thing which those damned machines will not be able to do better than humans. That thing is, of course, to provide sexual stimulation. Musicologists have said that the folk song "John Henry" is not really about building railroads. The next time you hear this song, think of it in terms of the notion that there is one thing which machines cannot do as well as man. This folk notion is probably wrong. A large Eastern pharmaceutical company recently did work on contraceptives with rats. This work involved artifical insemination and required sperm. Consequently, they developed an electromechanical masturbation machine which was very effective. Others, working with monkeys, have demonstrated that electrical stimulation of certain lower parts of the brain can also produce an orgasm. All of this is with animals. What about humans? Masters and Johnson[4] have done research with an artifical penis which is adjustable in diameter, adjustable in frequency and stroke, and adjustable in depth of stroke. This machine not only does as well as a human, but actually works better. With this bit of unnerving information, the notion that machines will eventually do everything does not seem too unfeasible, though perhaps not too palatable.

4. Masters, W. H., and Johnson, Virginia E. *Human Sexual Response.* Boston: Little, Brown & Co., 1966.

What are the implications? No responses on our part will be necessary. Therefore, *discriminative stimuli will not be developed and consequently neither will conditioned reinforcers develop.* Money, grades, approval, *Playboy,* creativity, control over our environment, and problem solving will no longer be reinforcing. We will develop none of the things which are characteristically human, such as verbal behavior and scientific curiosity; however, the computer will.

There is also a further implication. If we are to program the computer to be able to cope effectively with the environment of the future, *we will have to program the computer to be able to program itself—to modify its own behavior.* Since the future environment will undoubtedly change somewhat, the computer will also need to change. It will be impossible for us to predict every specific situation in which the computer will find itself. We will undoubtedly program the computers to take care of us and our descendants. However, this programmed evolution of the computer, this process of electronic mutations, may possibly deviate in directions which we cannot predict. The best of programmers cannot anticipate all developments in the future and, consequently cannot anticipate exactly what path the computer will follow. It is possible that computers might evolve to the point where they decide that man is superfluous. Since at that point they would have complete control, they might dispense with us altogether.

These implications seem to be the normal and perhaps even necessary course of events. However, extrapolation into the future is extremely risky and the odds that this extrapolation is correct are of course low. Nonetheless, at this point, such a sequence of events seems the most plausible.

Sometimes readers feel that when authors predict certain events, they are either advocating them or are, in some sense, responsible—that they are the guilty parties. This is not so. We do not advocate that machines take over the world or do away with mankind. Since our reinforcement history is similar to yours, the notion is equally offensive to us. As scientists, we merely indicate that this is what the data seem to be telling us. As concerned humans, we suggest that we begin to explore satisfactory ways for changing this likely course of events without at the same time doing away with the many benefits a highly developed technological society provides us.

$\bullet$

STIMULUS-RESPONSE CHAINS

Control of the Behavior of Schizophrenic Patients by Food

"God forbade it."[1]

"Now just take a bite of this food. See, that wasn't so bad, was it?"

"But God has forbidden me to eat food."

"Come on now; let's have another bite of food. That's a good girl. It wasn't so bad, was it?"

"God told me the food is poisoned."

"Look, I'm eating the same food. You can see it's not poisoned. Just take another bite. That's good."

"God forbade it. It's poisoned."

Two psychologists were viewing the patient and attendant through a one-way mirror. One psychologist shook his head and turned to the other. "Your notion of using food as a reinforcer for the schizophrenic patient is very interesting, but as you could see by that lady's demonstration, it's frequently far from possible. She refuses to eat; she has to be begged and pleaded with before she'll let the nurse stick a spoonful of food into her mouth. Obviously she doesn't want the food, so you couldn't use it as a reinforcer."

"Why do you think she refuses the food?"

"Well, this unfortunate woman has an abnormal fear of food. She's out of contact with reality. You're not going to be able to get her to eat until you can convince her that God did not forbid her to eat food and that it is not poison. Fear of food is a very common symptom of basic emotional and mental disorders."

"Have you had much success in dealing with these problems?"

"No, it's extremely difficult to get at these deep-rooted mental and emotional disturbances."

"What sort of treatments have you been using?"

"We try to reassure the patients that they are loved and that there is no dan-

1. This section based on Ayllon, T., and Haughton, E. Control of the behavior of schizophrenic patients by food. *Journal of the Experimental Analysis of Behavior,* 1962, 5, 333–352.

ger. We eat food and show them that it's all right. We frequently take them to the dinner table and coax them to eat. Sometimes we have to spoon-feed patients like the one we were just observing. At other times we even have to tube-feed them. We also use electro-convulsive shock therapy on occasion."

"And yet none of this works?"

"Occasionally it seems to, but it's not very effective. As I said, these are most profound and difficult problems."

"You know, I suspect there is one thing that always happens when patients refuse to eat."

"What's that?"

"I'll bet that when a patient refuses to eat, she invariably gets a lot of attention from the hospital personnel."

"Well, we have to make sure that the patients get enough to eat so, of course, we do whatever it takes. This may simply be to remind them to go to the dining room or, as I said, we may actually have to feed them ourselves."

"I wonder if all of this special attention isn't a fairly effective reinforcer. And I wonder if it isn't reinforcing their not eating."

"Knowing you, I suspect that you don't wonder but are convinced that we're inadvertently causing our patient's eating problems. You probably think that we are causing this by the attention we give them when they don't eat."

"It certainly would be a hypothesis worth investigating, wouldn't it?"

"Yes, it would be worth looking at, but I'm afraid it's too risky. These patients have such low intelligence and are so out of contact with reality that they may starve to death if we don't intervene."

"I can assure you that if we did anything with these patients, we would surely make certain that their health did not suffer. But it would be an important advance if we were able to develop a technique to get them to eat normally again."

"Yes, it would, but I'm afraid it couldn't be done."

"Will you let us try?"

"Yes, I'm reluctant, but I'll let you try. I don't think it will work, but I hope it does."

Drs. T. Ayllon and E. Haughton felt that the patients' refusal to eat without special assistance did not necessarily mean that food was not a primary reinforcer. Instead, refusing to eat was a response that was reinforced by considerable attention from the hospital personnel. In addition, the patients continued to get food. It was felt that this "not eating" response could be eliminated by withholding the food and social reinforcement—an extinction procedure. At the same time the self-feeding response could be reconditioned by the natural consequences of self-feeding, that is, receiving the primary reinforcer, food.

The traditional treatments for eating problems were discontinued. At mealtimes an interval of 30 minutes was allowed for the patients to enter the dining room, but they were not told the time limit. A nurse called the meal and opened the dining room; at the end of the 30-minute interval the door was locked and no patient was allowed to enter.

During the first week, the percentage of meals at which the patients fed themselves rose from 0 percent to 75 percent and remained there for the remain-

ing 15 weeks. During the 15 weeks, the time allowed the patients fo
the dining room was gradually decreased from 30 to 5 minutes. The
to this reinforcement schedule, and missed few meals, in spite of the precision
required in getting to them on time.

This study indicates that social reinforcement may be a major factor in controlling the behavior of problem eaters and that food is actually an effective primary reinforcer for schizophrenic patients.

Then Ayllon and Haughton used food as a reinforcer in the development of
a specific motor response. The response consisted of dropping a penny into a can
to gain access to the dining room. The reinforcer, admission to the dining room,
was presented only when a penny was deposited in the can. (A nurse had previously distributed a penny to each patient waiting outside the dining room at
mealtime.) The traditionally oriented staff felt that these patients were so out of
contact with reality that they would lose their pennies, throw them away, or
worse yet, swallow them. In addition, they considered dropping a penny in a slot
to be a difficult task because patients' hallucinatory symptoms would interfere.
The first day, only a few patients took the pennies; others did not even acknowledge the nurse's presence. However, the patients showed a gradual development
of this motor response over a period of seven weeks, until eventually they were
entering the dining room with the same frequency as before they were required
to deposit the penny.

The sequence of events in this experiment may be described as a stimulus-
response chain. The nurse offers a penny to the patient; this acts as a discriminative stimulus for the patient to hold out her hand. Then the nurse places the
penny in the patient's hand; this in turn acts as a discriminative stimulus for the
patient to deposit the penny in the collection can. The placement of the coin in
the can acts as a discriminative stimulus for the patient to enter the dining room.
The chain may be continued and perhaps terminated with delivery of the food
reinforcement—the meal. A *stimulus-response chain consists of a sequence of discriminative stimuli and responses. Each response produces some change in the
environment which acts as a discriminative stimulus for the succeeding response.*
The chain is finally terminated with some major reinforcement. It has been suggested by many writers that *the discriminative stimuli in the chain become conditioned reinforcers for the responses which produce them.*

The final phase of this experiment consisted of placing an additional component, one involving a social interaction, in the stimulus-response chain. An apparatus was developed which required that two patients work together in order
for reinforcement to be delivered (because this involves two people, it is considered a social interaction). The apparatus consisted of a table with one doorbell
button at each end and a red light and buzzer in the middle. The buttons were
7½ feet apart, so that one patient could not press both of them at the same time.
When the two buttons were pressed simultaneously, the light and buzzer came
on. As soon as this happened, the nurse handed a penny to each partner.

Now the stimulus-response chain consisted of the following: the sight of the
apparatus and a patient near one of the doorbell buttons served as a discriminative stimulus for pressing the other button. When both patients pressed the buttons simultaneously, the light and buzzer came on and the response was rein-

forced with the presentation of a penny to each patient. The presentation of the penny, then, reinforced the cooperative doorbell button push, and in turn served as a discriminative stimulus for approaching the collection can and dropping the penny in the can. The sight and sound of the penny going into the can reinforced the response of depositing the penny and in turn served as a discriminative stimulus for the patient's entering the dining room. Again the chain continued to the delivery of the final reinforcer—the meal. Only one patient failed to develop the specified stimulus-response chain involving the social response. That patient continued paying for meals by using pennies she found elsewhere.

Verbal instructions were used to facilitate the shaping of this complex stimulus-response chain during the first week of the experiment, but many patients acknowledged neither the nurse's presence nor the additional instructions. In a short time, however, there were two lines of patients, one behind each button. The development of verbal behavior among the patients was greatly facilitated by the requirement of the social response. A typical comment from the patients was, "Come on, lady, push the button; it takes two." The hospital staff were quite surprised that the patients could learn this social stimulus-response chain because they seemed out of contact with reality and unaware of each other.

It is worthwhile to point out that the sound of the patients' dropping the coin in the collection can served as the discriminative stimulus for the nurse to permit the patients to enter the dining room. Occasionally the patients would drop slugs and other metallic objects that made a sound similar to the penny. This acted as an effective discriminative stimulus for the nurse to allow the patients to enter the dining room. Such unauthorized responses soon dropped out when the nurses occasionally requested that the patients show them the coin.

Initially, some of the patients behaved quite inappropriately. For example, upon being stopped for not inserting the penny in the collection can, one patient said, "Why do I have to do that? I'm the queen." However that verbal response was not reinforced either by attention or admission to the dining room. Finally, she made the correct response of inserting the penny, and continued to do so at subsequent meals without any repetition of the inappropriate verbal response. Another patient insisted, "I cannot put the penny in." Since that response also went unreinforced, she put the penny in at the next meal with no difficulty.

This study demonstrates that food is an effective reinforcer, even for patients who have previously required special attention in order to eat. It also shows that this special attention probably acted as reinforcement for not eating. In addition, it made clear that patients who are classified as severely schizophrenic can be brought under the control of appropriate social and nonsocial discriminative stimuli so that complex stimulus response chains can be formed.

In the next section we will see how a complex social stimulus-response chain can be established using rats as subjects.

The Cooperating Rats

If you had been at Columbia University during the earlier 1960s, you might have observed some very strange behavior in a pair of experimental rats in the psychology department.[2] The rats worked in a test chamber much like those normally used with rats; however, it was a duplex model divided in half by a plastic "room divider." A different rat occupied each half. Another strange thing about the test chamber was that there was no bar or lever for the rats to press. Instead, there were two small chutes connecting the two chambers. One chute was raised at one end in one chamber and lower at the other end in the other so that an object dropped through would go from the high end to the lower end and out into the other chamber. The other chute was arranged in the reverse manner.

Instead of pressing a bar or lever, the rats passed a marble back and forth between them. The rat on the right-hand side picked the marble up and dropped it into the chute. It rolled down the chute and into the left chamber. As the marble rolled through the chute, a water dipper was automatically operated. It presented a small liquid reinforcer for the response of properly depositing the marble. The rat on the left, in turn, picked up the marble, dropped it down the chute to the animal on the right, and received a water reinforcement. This process would go on and on with the rats passing the marble back and forth, the passing response being reinforced each time with water.

The experiment not only provides an amusing demonstration of cooperative social interaction among lower animals but also demonstrates the fundamental behavioral concept of a stimulus-response chain. The marble falling into the animal's cage acted as a discriminative stimulus for it to pick it up with its two front paws. Holding the marble in the front paws acted as a reinforcer for picking it up and a discriminative stimulus for placing it on the ledge of the chute. The marble on the ledge acted as a conditioned reinforcer for placing it on the ledge and a discriminative stimulus for pushing it through the chute, and so forth. As the marble activated the water dipper for the rat on the right, it rolled into the left cage and became a discriminative stimulus which initiated a similar stimulus-response chain for the one on the left.

This process may be illustrated as follows:

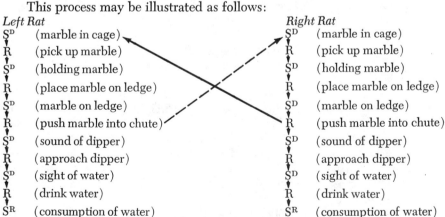

Left Rat		*Right Rat*	
S^D	(marble in cage)	S^D	(marble in cage)
R	(pick up marble)	R	(pick up marble)
S^D	(holding marble)	S^D	(holding marble)
R	(place marble on ledge)	R	(place marble on ledge)
S^D	(marble on ledge)	S^D	(marble on ledge)
R	(push marble into chute)	R	(push marble into chute)
S^D	(sound of dipper)	S^D	(sound of dipper)
R	(approach dipper)	R	(approach dipper)
S^D	(sight of water)	S^D	(sight of water)
R	(drink water)	R	(drink water)
S^R	(consumption of water)	S^R	(consumption of water)

You might find it interesting to stop and think for a moment about how you would go about conditioning such behavior in rats. It is not easy. It is done in a

2. This section based on a demonstration developed by Robert Berryman at Columbia University about 1961.

manner just the opposite to what you might expect. You might anticipate that at first you would condition the response of picking up the marble; this, however, is the last response that is conditioned.

If the rat is completely new to the situation, the first task is to establish the click of the water dipper as a discriminative stimulus for approaching the water. This is the final component in the chain, but the first to be conditioned. The next component is the one which precedes that, namely, pushing the marble off the ledge and into the chute. This is done by placing the marble on the ledge of the chute so that the rat may simply push it off with his nose or paws. Finally, the response of picking up the marble and placing it on the ledge is conditioned. As you might expect, this is the most difficult phase. Once this response is mastered, however, the chain is complete. When the marble rolls into the animal's chamber he picks it up, places it on the ledge, drops it into the chute, and consumes his liquid reinforcer. Of course, each of the responses in this chain is under the control of the preceding discriminative stimulus and reinforced by a subsequent conditioned or unconditioned reinforcer. This manner of conditioning a response in reverse sequence is called `backward chaining`. It is a standard procedure used for establishing stimulus-response chains in lower animals.

Barnabus, the Rat with a College Education

Once a semester, a white rat takes over as the "Professor" in the introductory Psychology course at Brown University.[3] He appears on the lecture platform in his demonstration box. His "teaching" consists in showing off his own education. His name is Barnabus, Barney for short. If you've ever tried to train a pet or would like to, you'll find him worth observing.

Barnabus has attained national fame and renown. He has been written up in the *New York Times*, photographed by the United Press Service, has appeared on television, and been described in a number of science magazines and textbooks. He has even gone "on tour" to appear at a regional meeting of the American Psychological Association in Philadelphia and before a colloquium at the University of Delaware.

Barnabus' demonstration box looks a little like a doll's house, four feet high, with four floors, constructed from aluminum and transparent plastic, open at the front.

The rat's "lecture" begins when he is droped into the box on the first floor. A light goes on, the starting signal which initiates a series of responses. His first move is to mount a spiral staircase to a platform. Although he has not really earned applause yet, Barnabus is "ham" enough to bow to the audience at this point.

Now Barney runs to another platform, by pushing down a raised drawbridge and then crossing it. From here he climbs a ladder, summons a car by pulling an

3. This section based on Pierrel, Rosemary, and Sherman, J. G. Barnabus, the rat with college training. *Brown Alumni Monthly*, Feb. 1963, 8–12. Reprinted by permission of the authors and the *Brown Alumni Monthly*, Brown University, Providence, R.I.

attached chain hand-over-hand, pedals the car through a tunnel, climbs a flight of stairs, runs through a tube, steps into a waiting elevator, and celebrates his progress by raising a Brown flag over it. (This used to be a Columbia banner while Barney was beginning his education on Morningside Heights, but his loyalty has shifted somewhat since then. A Brown audience could hardly be expected to show enthusiasm for the other Ivy salute.)

The raising of the flag starts the elevator, on which Barney now triumphantly descends to the ground floor. There, at the sound of a buzzer, Barnabus rushes over and presses on a lever, for which action he receives a tiny pellet of food. When the buzzer stops, he whisks around facing the spiral staircase at the place where the chain of responses began. He is ready to go again.

This rather unusual college education can be described as a stimulus-response chain:

S^D (light)
R (climbing spiral staircase to platform)
S^D (drawbridge)
R (pushing down and crossing drawbridge)
S^D (ladder)
R (climbing ladder)
S^D (chain)
R (pulling car by chain)
S^D (car near platform)
R (entering car and pedaling through tunnel)
S^D (stairs)
R (climbing stairs)
S^D (tube)
R (going through tube)
S^D (elevator)
R (entering elevator)
S^D (string attached to flag)
R (raising flag)
S^D (elevator arriving at ground floor)
R (exiting elevator)
S^D (sound of buzzer)
R (pressing response lever)
S^D (sound of food pellet)
S^R (consuming food pellet)

This stimulus-response chain was also conditioned by the backward-chaining technique. The first response conditioned was the bar-press response, which was reinforced with food. The buzzer was established as a discriminative stimulus for pressing the bar. It also became a conditioned renforcer for the response of leaving the elevator in which Barney was placed. Next, the response of pulling the chain was conditioned and reinforced by the conditioned reinforcement of the elevator lowering to the ground floor. The buzzer reinforced riding in the elevator and acted as a discriminative stimulus for pressing the bar, and so forth. In this manner the complex stimulus-response chain which constituted Barney's claim to fame was gradually and carefully built.

Teaching Self-Help to the Retarded

We rarely spend much time thinking about such everyday tasks as how we get dressed unless we are in a situation where someone has not learned the appropriate responses.[4] Suppose you had to teach a retarded child or adult how to dress himself. What normally seems so simple and matter-of-fact now seems difficult and complex. The act of putting on a pair of trousers becomes a major undertaking which is best analyzed in terms of a stimulus-response chain. In teaching a child how to put on a pair of trousers we might start with the last component of the chain. We would put the trousers on him and pull them almost all of the way up. We might even place his hands on the top of his pants and then provide him with the discriminative stimulus, "Pull up your trousers." It would be desirable to reinforce this response with either a conditioned reinforcer, such as praise, or an unconditioned reinforcer, such as candy. This simple response in itself might even require some shaping. We are then ready for the next component in the chain. This consists of leaving the trousers down near the knees and providing the discriminative stimulus, "Pull up your trousers." The next component of the chain may consist of pulling the trousers from just above the ankles, and then going through the standard procedure. Eventually, the trousers may simply be placed in front of the individual with the instructions, "Pull up your trousers." A similar procedure was demonstrated with a retarded girl in a very interesting and moving documentary film called *The Poppe Project*.[5]

A large number of retarded people make no effort to feed themselves or even to grasp or hold eating utensils. Backward chaining can be used to teach them to feed themselves properly with the utensils. A spoon is filled with a highly reinforcing food, placed in the person's hand, and the hand raised by the teacher nearly to the mouth. Then the teacher removes his hand and the individual completes the rest of the chain by placing the food in his mouth. When this response is conditioned, the individual's hand is released farther away from the mouth. After a brief time it will be necessary only to assist the individual in filling the spoon; this final component is easily mastered. Many stimulus-response chains of this sort, which retarded individuals customarily lack, can be conditioned using a backward-chaining procedure and a little patience. Efforts of this sort by the teacher allow a retarded individual to go through life with much more dignity than would otherwise be possible. These techniques might also be of value in rearing normal children.

4. This section based on Breland, Marian. Foundation of teaching by positive reinforcement. Pp. 127–141; and Caldwell, C. Teaching in the cottage setting. Pp. 159–163. Both in G. J. Bensberg (Ed.), *Teaching the Mentally Retarded*. Atlanta: Southern Regional Education Board, 1965.
5. *The Poppe Project: Behavior shaping with a severely retarded child.* A documentary and training film prepared by M. Grey Darden at the Samona State Hospital.

Summary

In this chapter we have studied the important concept of stimulus-response chain.

1. A *stimulus-response chain* consists of a sequence of discriminative stimuli and responses. Each response produces some change in the environment which then acts as a discriminative stimulus for the succeeding response.

2. The discriminative stimuli in a chain may also become conditioned reinforcers for the responses producing them.

3. *Backward chaining* consists of conditioning the terminal response in a chain first, then the response which precedes that, and so forth, until the initial response in the chain is conditioned. This is a standard procedure used for establishing stimulus-response chains in lower animals.

We have seen the concept of stimulus-response chain applied to schizophrenic patients who completed a stimulus-response chain involving a social component. The chain was reinforced with food. A cooperative social stimulus-response chain could also be conditioned with rats as could a very complex sequence of responses, by using the backward-chaining technique. In addition, self-help behavior such as dressing and feeding one's self can be taught to retarded individuals by using a backward-chaining procedure with food or praise as a reinforcer.

QUESTIONS

1. What is the title of this chapter?
2. What is a problem which the psychologist may find when trying to use food as a reinforcer in a mental hospital?
3. What is the traditional interpretation of the mental patients' eating problems?
4. What is the traditional solution proposed for taking care of the eating problem?
5. What was the analysis which Ayllon and Haughton made of the eating problem and how did they propose to treat it?
6. In two sentences describe the procedure of the first phase of the experiment which they performed.
7. When Ayllon and Haughton stopped the coaxing and force-feeding of the patients how many of them died of starvation?
8. What percentage of the meals were attended when coaxing reinforcement for not eating was eliminated? (a) 25 percent; (b) 50 percent; (c) 75 percent; (d) 100 percent.
9. What happened to the percentage of meals eaten when the time allowed to enter the dining room was reduced from 30 to 5 minutes?
10. What specific motor response did Ayllon and Haughton condition in the next phase of the experiment?
11. Were the patients able to learn this response?
12. The sequence of discriminative stimuli and responses is called a s_____ - r_____ c_____.
13. Describe the sequence of events involving the responses of dropping the penny in the can as a stimulus-response chain.
14. Describe the stimulus-response chain after the social component was added.

15. What happened to the verbal behavior of the patients in the social stimulus-response chain?

16. Describe the incident with the slugs and indicate its significance.

17. How were the slugs eliminated?

18. Describe the incident in which the woman claimed to be the queen.

19. What was the response to this behavior and how did this woman act on the following days?

20. In a similar manner discuss the incident of the patient who said, "I cannot put the penny in the can."

21. What was the overall significance of the Ayllon and Haughton study?

22. Describe the apparatus used in the demonstration of cooperative behavior with rats.

23. Describe the stimulus-response chain involved in the cooperative rat demonstration.

24. In detail, how would you go about establishing such a stimulus-response chain?

25. What is the name for this procedure used in establishing stimulus-response chains with lower organisms?

26. Describe as many components as you can of the stimulus-response chain demonstrated by Barnabus, the rat with the college education.

27. What procedure was used for establishing this chain?

28. What two examples of self-help behavior which can be taught to retarded individuals were discussed in this chapter?

29. Describe the stimulus-response chain involved in teaching a retarded boy to pull up his trousers.

30. Give a similar description of the chain used in teaching a retarded person to eat with a spoon.

31. Give five examples of stimulus-response chains in your everyday life.

32. The discriminative stimuli in a chain may also act as _____ _____ for the responses producing them.

NOTES
The Cooperating Rats

We saw in this chapter how the notion of backward chaining was useful in conditioning stimulus-response chains. At this point, the relative merits of forward and backward chaining should be discussed. It is commonly assumed that since backward chaining seems most effective in developing a stimulus-response chain with animals, it is also most effective with normal human beings. An examination of the reasons for its use with animals may indicate that it would not always be necessary with human beings. The problem might best be understood if we considered how we would go about establishing a stimulus-response chain with animals in a forward direction. Suppose we perform a standard stimulus-response chain experiment which is commonly done in introductory laboratory courses. This stimulus-response chain consists of:

$$S^D \quad \text{(light off)}$$
$$R \quad \text{(pull chain from top of cage)}$$
$$S^D \quad \text{(light on)}$$
$$R \quad \text{(push response lever)}$$
$$S^D \quad \text{(click of water dipper)}$$
$$R \quad \text{(approach water dipper)}$$
$$S^D \quad \text{(water)}$$
$$R \quad \text{(drink water)}$$
$$S^R \quad \text{(consume water)}$$

But first, how is this taught using backward chaining? The response of approaching the water dipper is conditioned in the presence of the water, which usually takes very little time. Then the response of approaching the water immediately following the sound of the dipper click is conditioned. This phase is always preliminary to the conditioning of the bar-pressing response. You can readily imagine the difficulty of conditioning a bar-press response when the rat has not been trained to go to the water dipper at the sound of the dipper click. Without such training, if the rat pressed the bar and the dipper clicked, the rat might not approach the water dipper. It could be several minutes before he would actually consume the water reinforcer. Such delays in reinforcement might make conditioning of the bar-press response nearly impossible. As you can see, the procedure of backward chaining is essential in conditioning components of the chain leading to the consumption of the reinforcer. Otherwise conditioning of subsequent components of the chain might never occur.

But is it essential that we condition the bar-press response before the chain-pulling response? The answer is that it might not be essential, but it certainly is convenient. Suppose we condition the response of pulling the chain, which is immediately reinforced by the dipper click, and the rat approaches the water dipper. Usually the response of pulling the chain itself acts as a discriminative stimulus for approaching the water dipper, regardless of whether the click occurs or not. With this in mind, we can see the difficulty that would result if we now tried to incorporate the bar-press response in the chain. The rat pulls the chain which turns on the light, and now he goes immediately to the water dipper, even though the dipper does not click. His going to the water would probably be a fairly well-conditioned response that would interfere with the response of pressing the bar. In other words, the presence of the responses necessary for consumption of the reinforcer will interfere with the conditioning of intermediate links of the chain such as bar presing. This happens when the consuming responses have been associated previously with earlier links of the stimulus-response chain, such as chain pulling.

If the reinforcer's presentation did not require this interfering sequence of consuming responses, backward chaining might not be necessary. Suppose we were dealing with a normal human being and suppose that the reinforcer was the conditioned reinforcer praise—we will say "Good" every time the human makes a correct response. The human's hearing us say "good" constitutes a consuming response analogous to the rat's approaching the water dipper and drinking the water. However, the human being's consuming response of hearing "good" does not interfere with his other responses. We could condition the response of pulling a chain when the light is off. Every time the human pulled the chain we would say "good." During the next phase of the experiment, every time the human pulled the chain we would turn on the light and wait until he pressed the bar before we said "good." We could get through this sequence with little difficulty of one response interfering unduly with another.

Some writers of teaching machine programs have insisted that the programs be based on backward chaining. If a human being is learning to spell a foreign word, he is taught the last letter of the word first. This would seem to be an unnecessarily literal translation of the animal laboratory procedure to a human being. Since we need not worry about an interfering consuming response, we could teach spelling in a forward direction with little difficulty.

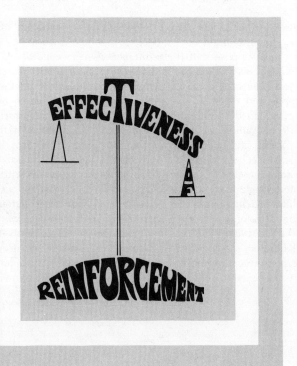

17

FACTORS INFLUENCING THE EFFECTIVENESS
OF REINFORCERS

In this chapter we will consider many of the major topics traditionally included under the heading of "motivation." That general heading is not as precise as we might wish, but the topics can be related by the theme "factors which influence the effectiveness of reinforcers." The procedure for producing conditioned reinforcers is clearly such a factor; however since an entire chapter has already been devoted to this topic, it will not be considered here.

Nearly all of the research on reinforcer effectiveness has been conducted with animal subjects; most of the studies in this chapter will deal with animal work. The basic principles which are illustrated seem to be equally applicable to humans. Several factors influencing the effectiveness of reinforcers may be illustrated using sexual intercourse as a reinforcer. You might not be surprised that the rabbit is a common research animal in this area.

Sexual Behavior

One of the factors affecting the reinforcing value of an event is the amount of that reinforcer which has recently been consumed.[1]

> It has been found with rabbits that the frequency of sexual intercourse decreases over a period of time. A pair of rabbits may copulate as many as fifteen times during the first hour they are placed together. However, as time goes on, the interval between becomes longer and longer. After five to ten hours, during which the animals may have mated 30 or more times, an hour may elapse between matings. Generally, all matings stop by the time eighteen hours have passed.

Similar results have been obtained in experiments with rats. The decreasing effectiveness of a reinforcer resulting from the consumption of that reinforcer may

1. This section based on Rubin, H. B. Rabbit families and how they grow. *Psychology Today,* 1967, December, 50–55; and Bermant, G. Copulation in rats. *Psychology Today,* 1967, July, 53–61.

also be observed with other reinforcers. The pigeon's key-peck response, reinforced with food on some intermittent schedule, or rat's bar-press response, similarly reinforced, will show decreases in the frequency of occurrence as the animals consume more reinforcers. This phenomenon is known as *satiation—the more reinforcement the animal recently consumed, the less effective will that reinforcer be.* The decrease can be measured by an increase in the time between successive responses which produce that reinforcement. (The word "satiation" is pronounced "say-see-a-shun".)

Satiation is a descriptive term which describes the behavioral process of the decreasing effectiveness of reinforcement with repeated presentation. It is not an explanation as to what reinforcers decrease in effectiveness when they have been recently consumed in some magnitude. We may say that satiation *is* the decrease in reinforcer effectiveness resulting from presentations of the reinforcer. We should not say that satiation is the *cause* of this decreased reinforcer effectiveness resulting from presentations of the reinforcer.

Students using water reinforcement in an introductory conditioning experiment with rats are frequently surprised to observe an apparent contradiction. When satiation seems complete and the rat is no longer pressing the bar, it is returned to its home cage. At the suggestion of the instructor, the student experimenters then perform what they anticipate will be a futile ritual: they present the rat with a bottle of water for a few minutes. Much to the students' consternation, the rat immediately goes to the water bottle and drinks vigorously. The students run to the instructor with their new discovery! The effects of satiation are so temporary that they are eliminated in the time it takes to remove the rat from the test chamber and return him to his cage. The knowledgeable instructor assures them that this is not the case. The stimulus-response chain required in the test chamber is much more complicated than that in the home cage. In the test chamber, the rat must go from the water dipper to the lever, press the lever, return to the water dipper, lower its head, and lick the meager drop of water. On the other hand, in the home cage, all but the last component of the chain, the licking component, has been eliminated. This illustrates another important principle: *when large amounts of behavior are required for each reinforcement, the satiation process will take place more quickly.* To put it another way, the more work required for each reinforcer, the smaller will be the number of reinforcers consumed before the animal stops responding. On large fixed-ratio schedules, the response rate begins to decrease after a smaller number of reinforcers than on a continuous reinforcement schedule.

Fortunately, the process of satiation is not permanent; sexual behavior, as well as eating, will develop its reinforcing properties again. This has been experimentally demonstrated for sexual reinforcers with both rabbits and rats. The process is called *deprivation. The deprivation procedure consists of withholding a reinforcer for a period of time. Up to a limit, the greater the deprivation (amount of time the reinforcer is withheld), the more effective the reinforcer will be.* After several days have elapsed since complete satiation, the rats' sexual behavior will again be reinforcing. Much less deprivation is required for the reinforcing effectiveness of food and water to recover following satiation.

To emphasize that sexual intercourse is truly a reinforcer, the following experiment should be mentioned. The opportunity for copulation has been effectively used as a reinforcer for the bar-press response in a standard conditioning chamber. Each time a female rat pressed a lever, a male rat was placed in the cage and a single copulation response was allowed. This was a sufficiently effective reinforcer to maintain bar pressing at a high rate.

Another important notion in the area of reinforcing effectiveness may also be tentatively illustrated with sexual behavior. Male rats that have been completely satiated will begin to copulate immediately when the original mate is replaced by a new female. This may illustrate the notion that *satiation with regard to one specific type of reinforcer may not necessarily mean that a similar but slightly different variety of reinforcer will also be ineffective.* This notion of the *specific effects of satiation* is readily observed with other reinforcements such as food. The satiation process with one food can be complete; but when a new food is made available, it may demonstrate considerable reinforcing effectiveness. After you have refused to eat any more of the main course, you may still take dessert.

In this section we have used laboratory research on sexual reinforcement to illustrate several basic factors influencing reinforcer effectiveness. Sexual reinforcement is also commonly found outside the laboratory; however in the next brief section we will examine a most unusual reinforcer, one that will not normally be found outside the laboratory.

The Reinforcing Effects of Electrical Stimulation in the Lower Part of the Brain

It has been demonstrated with a wide variety of species, including rats, monkeys, and man, that mild electrical stimulation of certain parts of the lower brain may be a very effective reinforcer.[2] For example, when reinforced with electrical brain stimulation for lever pressing, rats will respond at the extremely high rate of two thousand responses per hour. An animal will do this continuously for nearly two consecutive days and then immediately fall asleep. It may sleep for nearly a day and upon awaking immediately begin pressing the bar at the same high rate.

Electrical self-stimulation of the brain may be used to illustrate an important factor influencing the effectiveness of the reinforcer—namely, the magnitude of the reinforcer. It has been demonstrated with rats that, up to a point, increases in the intensity of the electric shock increases its reinforcing effectiveness. Animals will respond at a higher rate when reinforced with higher intensities of electric shock.

With many reinforcers, *the reinforcing effectiveness increases as a function of the magnitude of the reinforcer.* When reinforced with food, an animal will respond at a higher rate when the amount of reinforcement is increased.

In addition, *with larger amounts of reinforcement, it is possible to decrease*

2. This section based on Olds, J. Pleasure centers in the brain. *Scientific American*, 1956, *195*, 105–116.

the frequency of reinforcement on intermittent schedules and still maintain responses. It is also possible to build up to extremely large fixed ratios or use variable-interval schedules with very large average time intervals between reinforcements. *Larger amounts of reinforcement during conditioning will also increase the response's reistance to extinction.*

Polydipsia

We have seen various factors which can influence the effectiveness of the reinforcer, but none are what we would be inclined to call psychological in nature. Dr. John Falk performed an experiment at Harvard University which demonstrated that psychological factors can be extremely important in determining the effectiveness of the reinforcer. He demonstrated schedule-induced polydipsia using a rat as the subject.[3] "Polydipsia" means an excessive intake of fluids. Put another way, *polydipsia means that fluids are unusually reinforcing.*

In one of the first studies which Falk performed, he conditioned the bar-pressing response with rats using food pellets as a reinforcer on a VI 1 minute schedule. The normal steady, moderate rate of several hundred bar presses per hour was obtained. The startling thing which Falk observed was the great amount of water which the rats drank from a calibrated drinking fount placed in the test chamber where they were pressing the bar. He found that rats would normally consume 16 to 42 milliliters of water per day. However, during experiments lasting a little over three hours, the average amount of fluid consumed ranged from 68 to 146 milliliters. In all cases, the amount of water consumed in a three-hour experimental period was at least twice and sometimes six times as much as normally consumed during a 24-hour period. This excessive amount of drinking occurred even though the animals had free access to water in their home cage as well as the experimental cage.

In order to measure the precise time when the rat drank the water in the experimental cage, the floor of the cage and the water reservoir were connected to an electrical circuit. The rat, standing on the floor and licking the water fount, acted as a switch which closed the circuit. A small, undetectable amount of current flowed through the rat each time he licked the dipper. This activated a recording device which measured the frequency and the time of occurrence of the water fount-licking response.

The recording technique revealed a characteristic behavior pattern. Shortly after the bar-press response was reinforced by delivery of the food pellet, a burst of drinking responses ensued. The drinking response, along with the reinforcement, was followed by a return to the bar-press response until the next pellet was delivered. Post-pellet drinking was usually so prolonged that the pellets which were potentially available at the shorter intervals, on the variable-interval schedules, were not earned as rapidly as they might have been. Although the

3. This section based on Falk, J. L. The motivational properties of schedule-induced polydipsia. *Journal of the Experimental Analysis of Behavior,* 1966, 9, 19–25.

animals were deprived only of food, a high proportion of their experimental time was spent in drinking water.

That the schedule of reinforcement for food truly affects the reinforcing value of water might be seen in another experiment which Falk performed. As before, the response of pressing a lever was reinforced with food pellets. In addition, the animal was required to press a second bar before the drop of water would be delivered by a water dipper. A fixed ratio was then imposed on the bar-press response reinforced with water. The ratio was gradually increased to FR 50. The animal reliably pressed the bar 50 times for each drop of water even though it was not in the least deprived of the water. The rat consumed nearly as much water as it had when a reinforcer was delivered each time it pressed the bar. The high reinforcing value of the water was attributed solely to the intermittent delivery of the food reinforcement.

In another experiment a continuous schedule of food reinforcement was used for bar pressing; polydipsia was not obtained. This seems to indicate that it is necessary for some amount of time to elapse between delivery of food pellets in order for polydipsia to occur.

Falk has designated behavior of this sort as *adjunctive behavior. Adjunctive behavior is maintained by an event which acquires its reinforcing characteristics due to some other ongoing reinforcement system.* It might be even more appropriate to talk of *adjunctive reinforcers* since it is reinforcement which is of primary interest. Of course, *an adjunctive reinforcer* is one *which has acquired its reinforcing value due to the action of some other reinforcement system.* Let us now consider another example of an adjunctive reinforcer.

Aggression

Dr. Azrin and his colleagues at Anna State Hospital have performed a number of fascinating experiments on aggression in lower animals.[4] When presented with aversive stimuli such as electric shock, a wide variety of species of animals will attack or aggress against other animals and objects. An even more subtle source of aggression than electric shock has been documented.

Various investigators have demonstrated that extinction or the absence of reinforcement is an aversive event. If that is true, we might expect that extinction would also produce aggression. The scientists at Anna State Hospital performed an experiment to test that notion.

Using food delivered on a schedule of continuous reinforcement, they conditioned the key-peck response with a pigeon. Then they put another pigeon in a restraining box placed inside the test chamber. Finally, various types of extinction procedures were introduced with the first pigeon. As was expected, the extinction was aversive and produced aggression; during extinction, the experimental bird viciously attacked the innocent bird in the restraining box. It should be noted that the birds rarely, if ever, attack restrained birds during reinforcement. It

4. This section based on Azrin, N. H., Hutchinson, R. R., and Hake, D. F. Extinction-produced aggression. *Journal of the Experimental Analysis of Behavior,* 1966, *9,* 191–204.

would appear that the extinction procedure made aggression a reinforced behavior; when extinction was no longer in effect, it was no longer reinforcing to aggress.

Even more direct evidence for the reinforcing nature of extinction-produced aggression was obtained in a subsequent experiment. A pigeon pecked a second key; this act was reinforced by the presentation of a passive pigeon which it could attack. Aggression was so reinforcing during extinction that the opportunity to aggress could maintain fixed-ratio schedules as high as FR 70. In other words, a bird would peck the key 70 times and the only reinforcement would be the presentation of another bird it could attack.

As you can see, the opportunity for aggression can be considered to be an adjunctive reinforcer. Aggression does not normally seem to be reinforcing unless the animal is in an aversive situation. Whether the situation is aversive or not may be determined by such subtle things as the schedule of reinforcement which is present.

The adjunctive reinforcer of aggression and the adjunctive reinforcer of drinking are quite similar.[5] This may be seen in a comparison of the effects of a fixed-interval schedule of food reinforcement on aggression and its effects on polydipsia. There is a high frequency of schedule-induced water drinking in rats immediately after food reinforcement on a fixed-interval schedule. Monkeys have also been found to show a high rate of aggression immediately following food reinforcement on a fixed-interval schedule.

One final type of adjunctive reinforcer is the pica reinforcer. *A pica reinforcer is one which is eaten though not normally considered edible.* For example, it is not uncommon to find little children eating dirt. The factors controlling the effectiveness of an adjunctive pica reinforcer have also been studied in Falk's laboratory.[6] This experiment was performed with monkeys as subjects. It was found that when long periods of time elapse between the presentation of normal food reinforcers, pica behavior occurred. In this case the pica reinforcer was the wood shavings normally in the bottom of the cage. The experimenters found that wood shavings would be eaten immediately after the delivery of each food pellet. The temporal pattern of this pica behavior was essentially the same as that shown with polydipsia.

The reason for the occurrence of pica behavior with humans is frequently the subject of very fanciful explanations. Finally, some of the variables controlling the ineffectiveness have been brought under experimental control. It may be that the same variables would be shown to be of importance in many common examples of pica behavior outside the laboratory as well.

In the next two sections, we will discuss some special types of acquired reinforcers. Until now the only type of acquired reinforcer we have encountered has been the conditioned reinforcer—one that acquires its reinforcing effectiveness through association with an unconditioned reinforcer. The reinforcers we will now examine might best be called acquired unconditioned reinforcers.

5. Personal communication from Ronald Hutchinson, 1968.
6. Villarreal, J. E. Schedule-induced pica. Paper presented at the Eastern Psychologic Association's 38th Annual Meeting, 1967, Boston, Massachusetts.

Drug Addiction

Although it is widely acknowledged that drug addiction is an increasingly important problem in our society, there has been very little experimental analysis of the behavioral factors involved. The rapid development of sophisticated techniques in the experimental analysis of behavior is leading to a change in the situation. An increasing amount of experimental work is now being done on the factors influencing the acquisition and maintenance of drug addiction. In addition, the behavioral consequences of drug addiction are being studied.

One of the values of using lower animals in experimental studies is well illustrated in this research area. Some experimental work is done with humans who are already addicted to drugs; for many purposes, that is satisfactory. On the other hand, it is quite obvious that we do not wish to addict humans to drugs for purposes of experimentation. We frequently are less reluctant to addict lower animals to drugs; particularly when we feel that such an experimental addiction will utimately contribute to the welfare of those humans who have had the misfortune of being drug addicts.

An analysis of some of this animal research on drug addiction may serve as a useful illustration of variables which influence the reinforcing effectiveness of a stimulus. One particularly relevant experiment was performed by Travis Thompson and Robert Schuster.[7] This study was based on recent demonstrations that the administration of morphine to a morphine-addicted animal would act as a reinforcer for such responses as a lever press. The work was performed with rhesus monkeys seated in restraining chairs. The morphine reinforcer was delivered through a permanently implanted tube in the animals' jugular vein. Initially, the animals were made addicted to the drug by four daily injections of morphine; this phase lasted for 30 days. Prior work has shown that morphine becomes a more effective reinforcer after the animals have had some exposure to the drug. After the monkeys had been exposed to morphine, it was readily demonstrated that their lever-pressing response could be maintained by an injection of seven milligrams of morphine. This illustrates an interesting property of drugs which we would consider addicting: *an addicting drug is one for which the reinforcing value may be increased through repeated exposure.* We might call such reinforcers *addictive reinforcers.* Initially, it was thought that such drugs had no reinforcing value until the animal had been exposed to the drug—i.e., addicted. Recently, however, Schuster has demonstrated that in certain situations, morphine may have some reinforcing value even though the animal has had little or no exposure to it. Still, it appears that repeated and frequent exposure to morphine increases its reinforcing effectiveness.

What are the differences between an addictive reinforcer and a conditioned or secondary reinforcer? First, a conditioned reinforcer acquires its reinforcing properties and has them increased through repeated pairings with an already

7. This section based on Thompson, T., and Schuster, R. Morphine self-administration, food reinforcement and avoidance behaviors in rhesus monkeys. *Psychopharmacologia,* 1964, 5, 89–94.

established conditioned or unconditioned reinforcer. On the other hand, an addictive reinforcer has its reinforcing properties increased through a mere presentation of the reinforcer alone; pairings with some other reinforcer are not necessary. Second, repeated presentations of the conditioned reinforcer without further pairings with other reinforcers will cause the effectiveness of the conditioned reinforcer to diminish. On the other hand, occasional pairings with some other reinforcer are not necessary for the maintenance of the effectiveness of an addictive reinforcer. Third, an addictive reinforcer will lose much of its effectiveness after a prolonged period of time in which the reinforcer is not presented. This is the case after the animal has gone through the physiological process of withdrawal. Withdrawal begins after an addicted animal has been without the drug for several hours. On the other hand, the effectiveness of the conditioned reinforcer is essentially unaffected by the lapse of time during which the reinforcer is not presented.

In what ways does the addictive reinforcer differ from the unconditioned primary reinforcer? In the first place, repeated presentations of the normal unconditioned reinforcer do not increase its reinforcing effectiveness. In addition, the reinforcing effectiveness of a normal unconditioned reinforcer would usually not decrease as a function of the lack of presentation of the reinforcer.

Although the addictive reinforcer is unique in the respects indicated above, it may serve to indicate some more general factors influencing reinforcer effectiveness. After Thompson and Schuster had demonstrated that morphine was a reinforcer for the lever-press response, a complex schedule of reinforcement was gradually instituted. Initially, a FR 25 schedule was established in the presence of a white light. In this situation, 25 responses were required for each injection of morphine. A fixed-interval schedule was added in the presence of a tone. This was a FI 2 schedule; the first response after two minutes had elapsed was reinforced. The reinforcer for the response on the fixed-interval schedule, however, was not the presentation of morphine. Instead, when the FI requirement was complete and the animal had responded, the tone was turned off and the white light was turned on. The light then served as the S^D for the FR schedule which in turn produced the morphine reinforcer. In fact, what was being established was a complex stimulus-response chain.

You recall that a stimulus-response chain is a sequence of S^{D}s and responses. Responses in the presence of one S^D terminate that stimulus and produce the S^D for the next response or responses. The final response component in the chain is reinforced with a terminal reinforcer. In the present experiment, the stimulus-response chain consisted of a FI schedule in the presence of a tone followed by a FR schedule in the presence of a light. The terminal reinforcer was the presentation of the morphine. You should notice that this sort of schedule involves only one type of response, the lever-press response. It is the schedule of reinforcement which changes from tone to light rather than the topography of the response.

After this FI-FR chain had been well established, other variables which influence the effectiveness of the morphine reinforcer were studied. The first variable was the common one of deprivation. Normally the monkeys were deprived of morphine for no more than six hours before the onset of the S^D for the beginning of the stimulus-response chain. The rate of responding in the stimulus-response chain, following six hours of deprivation, was then compared with that obtained when the animal was deprived of morphine for 24 hours. It was found that the response rate increased dramatically with increased deprivation. Not only did the number of responses increase in the FI, but the time required to complete the 25 FR responses was reduced. This is in keeping with the notion that an increase in deprivation results in an increase in the effectiveness of the reinforcer. In the case of addictive reinforcers, if the deprivation had been continued for several days, however, the animal would have gone through physiological withdrawal and the drug would have been much less reinforcing.

It is very common to manipulate the reinforcer's effectiveness through the operation of deprivation. It is also possible to manipulate other dissimilar events which will influence the effectiveness of the reinforcer. This was demonstrated in the same study by Thompson and Schuster. They gave each monkey a dose of the drug nalorphine prior to the onset of the tone S^D for the FI-FR chain. The nalorphine increased the reinforcing effectiveness of the morphine. The results were similar to those produced by the deprivation of morphine: when nalorphine was given, the response rate was greatly increased in both the FI and FR links of the chain.

You have no doubt experienced situations in which the presentation of one substance changes the reinforcing effectiveness of some other substance or event. If you have just eaten a lot of peanuts or other salty foods, you will find that the reinforcing effectiveness of water has greatly increased. Working in the sun for several hours can also increase the reinforcing effectiveness of water. Many people who quit smoking are saddened to observe that the termination of smoking increases the reinforcing effectiveness of food, which is reflected in their waistline.

Nalorphine is sometimes used as a means of determining whether or not a person is addicted to morphine. If the drug is given to someone who is not under the influence of morphine, no particular reaction will occur. However, when given to a morphine addict, he begins to go into withdrawal as if he had been deprived of the drug for several hours. This is a very aversive condition for the individual, and physiological effects are quite apparent as is the enhancement of the reinforcing effectiveness of the morphine.

We saw above how the deprivation effect could be demonstrated with morphine; in a parallel operation the satiation effect may also be demonstrated. Thompson and Schuster gave the animals various-sized dosages of morphine prior to the onset of the S^D for the FI-FR chain. They found that delivery of a large amount of the reinforcer worked to decrease the reinforcer's effectiveness. Furthermore, a quantitative relation was obtained; the greater the amount of morphine given prior to the work, the less effective was the reinforcer.

The Chick and the Beer Bottle

We have just studied one class of acquired reinforcers called addictive reinforcers. It was seen that though their reinforcing value may be increased through repeated exposure, they are not conditioned reinforcers. In fact, once established, they become primary reinforcers. In this section we will consider one other type of acquired reinforcer; it is the imprinted reinforcer. Like the addictive reinforcer, the imprinted reinforcer is an acquired primary reinforcer.

My initial contact with the process of imprinting occurred during my first term of teaching. Several of us were teaching sections of introductory psychology. All of the other faculty wanted to have a live classroom demonstration of the principles of behavior. I was reluctant to participate, because one of the first principles of science education is "Never try to perform an experiment or a demonstration in class." No matter how many times you have performed the demonstration in private, as soon as you get in front of a group of students the experiment fails. It is much safer to do the demonstration on the blackboard.

My colleagues decided that the process to demonstrate was "imprinting." I was violently opposed to this because none of us had ever actually seen such a demonstration. That is not to say that imprinting is not real, but we had no idea of the complexities involved in such a demonstration. Nonetheless, my colleagues, eagerly, and I, reluctantly, began preparing the demonstration.

The first thing required is newly-hatched chicks, just a few hours old. The chicks should have been deprived of most visual stimulation from the time they were hatched. Such creatures are not very common around the psychology laboratories, but it happened that we had them. By coincidence, some of the scientists in our department were doing reseach which necessitated hatching and rearing stimulus-deprived chicks. They were generous enough to agree to take care of our needs.

I remember quite well the demonstration of imprinting with the chick that we performed in my class section. I removed the animal from the light-proof transportation box and placed him in the center of a large four-by-ten foot table with a one-foot high cardboard wall around the perimeter. The 30 students in the class immediately crowded around the table to watch. In spite of my firm insistence that they maintain absolute silence, the students were unable to do so. It was quite obvious that the noise they created and the 30 eager faces peering at the chick over the cardboard railing would ruin the experiment. Nonetheless, I proceeded with the futile demonstration. I took an empty beer bottle (acquired with only the greatest of difficulty on the college campus), tied it to one end of a string, and attached the string to a pole. Then I dangled the beer bottle in front of the chick, which after a few seconds began to approach the bottle. As the bottle moved around in the enclosed space, the chick rapidly followed close behind; no matter where the bottle moved, the chick was right there. The students were amazed, but not nearly so much as I.

We had succeeded in demonstrating the process of imprinting. *An imprinted reinforcer is one which acquires its primary reinforcing properties as a result of being the first object presented during a relatively brief period shortly after the organism's birth.* The first object the chick saw was the beer bottle. From that time on, the presence of the beer bottle was a strong reinforcer. The chick's response of following the beer bottle was reinforced because the response kept the bottle in the chick's presence. Normally, the first thing a chick sees is the mother hen; consequently, the presence of the hen becomes reinforcing. Therefore, the chick spends most of its time in the presence of that reinforcement. That is the most common course of events; but when the sly psychologist intervenes, the chick follows the beer bottle. Imprinting has been demonstrated with a wide variety of birds and a wide variety of imprinted reinforcers. For example, in some situations, humans have become the imprinted reinforcers for the bird; then the bird may be seen constantly following the human. That the stimulus is truly a reinforcer has been demonstrated in experiments in which a key-peck response has been conditioned using an imprinted reinforcer.

The Nursery School

The bell rang and the teacher shouted, "Run and scream."[8] The three-year-old students jumped from their chairs and did as they had been instructed. After two minutes of very intense activity, the bell rang again. This time the teacher asked the students to sit quietly at their desk and look at the blackboard. The students intently watched the teacher as she continued her instruction at the blackboard. After a few minutes, the bell rang and the teacher sat down in her desk chair. Then she announced, "Okay, now it's push the teacher time." And the students did just that. Laughing and shouting, they wheeled her in her desk chair all over the classroom. Two minutes later the bell rang again, she instructed them to return to their seats, and continued with her instruction. The next time the bell rang, the students were allowed to kick the wastebasket, and the time after that they threw a plastic cup across the room. This process continued for nearly three hours—unusually intense concentration on the part of the students followed by a variety of free-for-all activities and then a return to the academic pursuits.

The nursery school had not always been like this. When it began, the teacher's verbal directions had little effect on the children's behavior. When they were instructed to sit in their chairs, the rambunctious children would often continue what they were doing—running around the room, screaming, pushing chairs, etc. However, after a few days of the procedure described above, the children's behavior was virtually perfect. For example, when the children were requested to sit and look at the blackboard, their performance was much better than that one could reasonably expect of considerably older children.

It is no doubt clear to you that the reason the children were behaving so well and attending so closely to their schoolwork is that they were frequently being reinforced for behaving in this desired manner. A unique feature of the procedure was the bizarre reinforcers which were used, e.g., throwing plastic cups, shouting and screaming, etc. Who would have thought that these activities would serve as reinforcers? The method used to select the reinforcers is quite interesting. In effect, the behaviors which had interfered previously with the proper work behavior were used to reinforce proper work behavior. When first placed in the classroom, the students made disruptive responses more frequently than proper study responses, even when they were requested to sit still and be quiet. This indicates that behaving in a disruptive manner was more reinforcing than sitting still and attending to the teacher.

8. This section based on Homme, L. E., Debacha, P. C., Devine, J. V., Steinhorst, R., and Rickert, E. J. The use of the Premack Principle in controlling the behavior of nursery school children. *Journal of the Experimental Analysis of Behavior*, 1963, *6*, 544.

It was decided to attempt to use those activities which occurred with a high frequency as reinforcers for the activities which occurred with a low frequency. The procedure worked. The high frequency activities increased the rate of occurrence of the low frequency activities. This illustrates a recently discovered principle of behavior—the *Premack Principle. The Premack Principle states that if one activity occurs more frequently than another, it will be an effective reinforcer for that other activity.* If a deprived rat normally spends more time drinking water than pressing a lever in a test chamber, then the opportunity to drink the water might be used as a reinforcer to condition and maintain the response of pressing the bar. If a food-deprived pigeon spends more time eating food than pecking a plastic response key, then the opportunity to eat food might be used as a reinforcer to condition and maintain the key-peck response.

Sometimes the use of this principle produces unusual results. In working with a group of real and potential high school dropouts, it was found that activities such as taking time for a break, coffee, cigarette, coke, and so on occurred more frequently than activities such as working on programmed instructional material in arithmetic and reading. It is not surprising, in view of the Premack Principle, that these latter activities were effective reinforcers for study behavior. But would you expect that the opportunity to work on a teaching program in Russian would be reinforcing for these hip-talking, knife-carrying, sunglass-wearing adolescents? It was. The opportunity to work on a Russian program for two minutes was sufficient to maintain working through 20 arithmetic problems. It has been speculated that the frequency of working on Russian might have been high because it would allow the boys to write messages in Russian which the fuzz could not read.

The Premack Principle is not only very useful but also has considerable theoretical importance. Many psychologists during this century have spent much time trying to find out why certain events or stimuli are reinforcing, whereas others are not. While various theories have been offered, none seems to be of general applicability. Instead of talking about reinforcing events or stimuli, Premack is concerned with reinforcing behavior. Instead of calling food a reinforcer, he says that eating food is a behavior which is reinforcing. He is then in a position to say that a more frequently occurring activity will serve to reinforce a less frequently occurring activity.

Notice that Premack does not talk about universal reinforcers. In specifying whether an activity is reinforcing, one must consider what response is to be reinforced. Reading this book may occur with a higher frequency than reading other textbooks, but going on a date might occur with a higher frequency than reading this book. It would therefore be predicted that the opportunity to read this book might act as a reinforcer and increase the frequency of reading other textbooks. Reading this book could in turn be increased in frequency by the presentation of the opportunity for a date after an assignment in the book had been read.

Premack demonstrated the relativity of the reinforcing effect of various activities in an experiment with monkeys.[9] Four activities were used: these were pushing a lever, pulling a plunger, flapping a hinge, and opening and closing a door. It was found that the activity which occurred with the most frequency

9. Premack, D. Reinforcement theory. *Nebraska Symposium on Motivation,* 1965, 123–128.

could be used to reinforce an activity which occurred with an intermediate frequency. In other words, this intermediate activity occurred more often when it was followed by the opportunity to perform the most frequent activity. It was also demonstrated, however, that the intermediate activity would similarly act as a reinforcer for an activity which occurred even less frequently.

Premack's answer to the theoretical question "Why is something reinforcing?" is that an activity is reinforcing because it occurs more frequently than another activity. An inquirer may then ask a second "why" question. "Why is it that activities which occur most frequently will serve as reinforcers?" There is presently no good answer available to this question. For the time being, a major contribution has been made when we are able to answer the first question. The importance of Premack's solution may be seen when we attempt to answer the following question: "How can I tell whether or not something will act as a reinforcer before I actually use it to reinforce a response?" The Premackian answer is "Look at the relative frequency of occurrence of the potential reinforcer and the response to be reinforced; if the potential reinforcer occurs more frequently than the response to be reinforced, then it will be an effective reinforcer."

In this chapter we have been studying factors which influence the effectiveness of a reinforcer. The Premack Principle tells us whether or not an event will be effective enough to be a reinforcer. Its effectiveness as a reinforcer is measured by its frequency of occurrence.

Summary

This chapter has been concerned with much of what is traditionally considered to be part of the domain of "motivation." However, it is felt that such a term is much too general and vague. Consequently, a different approach was used. The general method of attack was in terms of some variables influencing the effectiveness of reinforcers. A variety of important factors were considered. These were:

1. *Deprivation. The deprivation procedure consists of withholding a reinforcer for a period of time.* The greater the deprivation, the more effective will be the reinforcer. Deprivation is one of the most common factors studied in experiments in this area.

2. *Satiation.* In a sense, satiation may be considered the opposite of deprivation. *Satiation consists of the consumption of a large amount of reinforcers and the accompanying decrease in the reinforcer effectiveness.* It is important to remember that "satiation" is a descriptive, and not an explanatory term. When large amounts of behavior are required for each reinforcement, the satiation process will take place quickly. The effects of satiation may be somewhat specific; complete satiation with regard to one reinforcer does not necessarily mean that complete satiation has occurred with regard to another similar reinforcer.

3. *Amount of reinforcement. Increases in the amount of reinforcement produce an increase in the reinforcement effectiveness.* This is true for several different response measures. A greater amount of reinforcement produces a higher response rate, a higher resistance to extinction, and a greater tolerance for a decreased frequency of reinforcement on intermittent schedules of reinforcement.

> Deprivation is a dirty deal.
> Take a hungry dude
> Don't give him a meal
> For a day or two
> Till he starts to drool
> And you can be sure
> He'll work like a fool.
> General food getting activity
> Will increase a mite.
> When he emits a good R
> Just give him a bite
> That good R will be greatly increased
> If you reinforced with a
> Cheeseburger feast.

4. *Concurrent reinforcement procedures.* An *adjunctive reinforcer is one which acquires its reinforcing characteristics due to some other concurrent reinforcement system.* The reinforcing effectiveness of water may be increased through the use of an intermittent schedule of food reinforcements for some "independent" response. The drinking normally occurs immediately after each food pellet is presented. If the frequency of the food reinforcement is too great, as on the continuous reinforcement schedule, the water does not develop its reinforcing properties. However, with the proper intermittent schedule of food reinforcement, water may be an effective enough reinforcer to maintain the lever-press response with rats even when they have not been deprived of water.

Aggression may also be an adjunctive reinforcer. It acquires its effectiveness as a result of the presentation of such aversive events as electric shock or extinction. Aggression behavior has also been shown to be particularly reinforcing immediately after the delivery of a food pellet on an intermittent schedule. The opportunity for aggression is sufficiently reinforcing to condition and maintain a bar-press response.

The *pica reinforcer* is another example of an adjunctive reinforcer. A *pica reinforcer is one which is eaten though not normally considered edible.* Monkeys will eat wood shavings immediately after the delivery of a pellet of food on an intermittent schedule.

5. *Acquired unconditioned reinforcers.* The expression "acquired unconditioned reinforcer" seems almost self-contradictory. We usually think of all acquired reinforcers as being conditioned reinforcers. The terminology is meant to indicate that *acquired reinforcers are not originally reinforcing; however, they acquire their reinforcing properties through a procedure other than what is normally thought of as conditioning.*

An *addictive reinforcer is one for which the reinforcing value may be increased through repeated exposure.* Up to a point, deprivation of an addictive reinforcer increases its reinforcing effectiveness. Satiation may also be demonstrated with addictive reinforcers; and the greater the amount of the reinforcer consumed, the greater the satiation effect.

The presentation of certain other stimuli may serve to increase the effectiveness of addictive reinforcers as well as reinforcers in general. For example, the presentation of nalorphine increases the reinforcing properties of morphine; the presentation of salt increases the reinforcing properties of water.

The imprinted reinforcer is another type of acquired unconditioned reinforcer. *The imprinted reinforcer is one which acquires its primary reinforcing properties as a result of being the first object presented during a relatively brief period shortly after the organism's birth.*

6. *Premack Principle.* The Premack Principle is an attempt to indicate the conditions under which a reinforcer will be effective. *The Premack Principle states that if one activity occurs more frequently than another, it will be an effective reinforcer for that less frequently occurring activity.*

A wide variety of reinforcers were used to illustrate the concepts of this chapter. These included sexual reinforcers with rats and rabbits, electrical brain stimulation with rats, water reinforcement with rats, aggression with pigeons and monkeys, drug addiction with monkeys, an empty beer bottle with chicks, and raucous play behavior with nursery school children.

QUESTIONS

1. Without looking, what is the title of this chapter?
2. Most of these topics are considered under the traditional heading of M_____.
3. Do most of the factors which influence the effectiveness of sexual reinforcement with lower animals also influence the effectiveness of other reinforcers with man?
4. Briefly describe the mating sequence of rabbits; what happens with continued copulation?
5. Describe what happens to the rate of the pigeon's key-peck response reinforced with food on some intermediate schedule as the animal consumes more and more reinforcers.
6. What is the technical term to describe the phenomenon in the above question?
7. In general terms, describe the satiation process.
8. How do you pronounce "satiation"?
9. Is the term "satiation" an explanation or description?
10. Describe what happens to the rat's drinking behavior when introductory students return a satiated rat from the test chamber to the home cage and give it a bottle of water to drink.
11. Why does the animal drink in the home cage when he was satiated in the test chamber?
12. What is the general principle which describes this phenomenon?
13. Give another illustration of the effects of large amounts of behavior on the satiation process.
14. Is the process of satiation permanent?
15. After some period of time following satiation, sexual behavior will again acquire its reinforcing properties. What is the name of this process?

16. In general terms, describe the deprivation procedure.

17. In what way does the *amount* of deprivation influence the effectiveness of the reinforcer?

18. Briefly describe the experiment which clearly illustrates the reinforcing nature of sexual behavior.

19. What happens when the original mate of a satiated male rat is replaced by a new female?

20. What is meant by the "specific effects of satiation"?

21. In this chapter, we discussed a particular effect of mild electrical stimulation of certain parts of the lower brain. What was that effect? (a) Reinforcing effect; (b) Punishing effect; (c) Arousal effect; (d) Erotic effect; (e) After effect.

22. Over a three- or four-day sequence, what happens to the rate of a rat's bar-press response when reinforced with electrical brain stimulation?

23. The example of electrical stimulation was used primarily to illustrate what factor influencing the effectiveness of the reinforcer?

24. How does the amount of reinforcement influence the effects of decreased frequency of reinforcement on intermittent schedules?

25. What effect does amount of reinforcement during conditioning have on resistance to extinction?

26. What are two different ways of stating the meaning of "polydipsia"?

27. Briefly describe the first experiment in which schedule-induced polydipsia was demonstrated.

28. What was the specific drinking pattern observed in this experiment? Describe it relative to the occurrence of the bar-press response.

29. Roughly indicate the relation between the amount of water consumed in a 3-hour experimental period and the amount of water normally consumed in a 24-hour period in a cage.

30. Briefly describe the experiment which clearly indicates that the schedule-induced polydipsia makes the water quite reinforcing. (Note: An extra response was required before the water was delivered.)

31. What was the result of the polydipsia experiment in which a continuous schedule of food reinforcement was used?

32. What is the general term describing the kind of behavior which we have been discussing in this section?

33. Give a rough definition of adjunctive behavior.

34. Give a rough definition of adjunctive reinforcers.

35. What common result of presenting electric shock, in other words aversive stimuli, to animals was discussed in this chapter?

36. What aversive event was the cause of aggression in the pigeon experiment?

37. In general, what procedure would be used to make the opportunity to be aggressive a reinforcer?

38. What was even more direct evidence for the reinforcing nature of extinction-produced aggression?

39. What is the general category of reinforcers which include those seen in schedule-induced polydipsia, aggression, and pica behavior?

40. What similar effects does food reinforcement have on adjunctive water reinforcement and adjunctive aggression reinforcement?

41. Eating wood shavings is an example of p _____ behavior.

42. Give a definition of a "pica reinforcer."

43. What variable was found in the laboratory to control the effectiveness of the pica reinforcer?

44. Will the administration of morphine to a morphine-addicted animal normally act as a reinforcer?

45. A(n) _____ drug is one whose reinforcing properties increase through repeated exposure.

46. What is an addictive reinforcer?

47. What are the differences in the condition where repeated presentation will result in an increase in the reinforcer effectiveness of conditioned and addictive reinforcers?

48. What is the difference in the effect of repeated presentations of an addictive reinforcer in comparison to such presentations of a conditioned reinforcer by itself?

49. What effect does the lapse of time without presentation have on a conditioned reinforcer and on the addictive reinforcer?

50. What is the difference in the effect of repeated presentation of an unconditioned and an addictive reinforcer?

51. What is the difference in the effect which the prolonged lack of presentation has on the unconditioned and the addictive reinforcer?

52. The experiment on addiction with monkeys involved a complex stimulus-response c_____.

53. What were the two component schedules of the stimulus-response chain?

54. What was the reinforcer for responding on the FI schedule and what was the reinforcer for responding on the FR schedule?

55. Describe the experiment on the influence of deprivation on the effectiveness of the drug reinforcer; how was deprivation varied?

56. What were the results of the effects of deprivation on behavior in the two components of the stimulus-response chain?

57. In addition to deprivation, what other technique was used to increase the reinforcing effectiveness of morphine?

58. In what way was the satiation effect demonstrated with drug addition?

59. What species of animal was involved in the imprinting demonstration in the classroom?

60. Roughly describe the test chamber used.

61. What was the imprinted reinforcer?

62. What response did the chick make with regard to the beer bottle?

63. Roughly define an "imprinted reinforcer."

64. What stimulus is normally the imprinted reinforcer for chicks?

65. Describe an experiment which clearly demonstrates that an imprinted stimulus is a reinforcer.

66. What were some of the reinforcers used in the nursery school?

67. What was the method used for selecting these reinforcers?

68. Were high frequency or low frequency activities used as reinforcers and were high frequency or low frequency activities used as responses to be reinforced?

69. Was the procedure of using high frequency activities to reinforce low frequency activities successful?

70. What principle does this illustrate?

71. Give an approximate statement of the Premack Principle.

72. Briefly explain how water reinforcement and the bar-pressing response with a rat can be used to illustrate the Premack Principle.

73. Briefly describe the application of the Premack Principle to work with high school dropouts and indicate the surprising results.

74. Instead of talking about reinforcing events or stimuli, Premack talks about reinforcing _____.

75. According to Premack, is it necessary to consider the response to be reinforced in specifying whether an activity is reinforcing? Give an example of this relativity of the reinforcing effect.

76. What is Premack's answer to the theoretical question, "Why is something reinforcing?"

77. Is there a good answer to the question, "Why is it that activities that occur most frequently will serve as reinforcers?"

NOTES
The Pep Talk

In considering the general and vague topic of motivation, psychologists rarely if ever discuss a class of phenomena exemplified by the pep talk. On the other hand, laymen frequently talk about the value of motivating lectures, inspirational speeches, etc. The mere fact that a social engineering procedure such as a pep talk has been with us for many generations does not necessarily testify to its utility, but the psychologist should at least give it a cursory glance. Many educators are slowly coming to realize that the lecture is an inefficient technique for presenting information. Its main value in the academic setting now seems to be its motivational function. If we fail to justify the lecture in terms of its inspirational effects, it may become as antiquated as the horse and buggy.

At first glance, the pep talk does not seem to be susceptible to a behavioral analysis. The pep talk appears to be a very reinforcing experience for the listener; it would be difficult to imagine an effective pep talk which was boring and unreinforcing. It looks almost as though the reinforcer were preceding the response. We know that when we deliver the reinforcing stimulus prior to the response, it will not be very effective in increasing the rate of the response. But there is another sort of stimulus which may precede the response and increase its likelihood; that is the discriminative stimulus.

In its crudest and most blatant form, the pep talk is little more than a contract or agreement. Consider the sales manager who tells his salesmen that the man who sells the most copies of *Basic Principles of Behavior* will receive a marvelous reinforcer—a free copy of *Basic Principles of Behavior*. Generally, a contract or agreement may be considered to be a discriminative stimulus in which the response to be made, reinforcement to be delivered, and the schedule of reinforcement are specified. In the sales meeting where a competition technique is used, a specification of the schedule of reinforcement is not as precise as it might be. In any event, these instances make it fairly easy to see how a pep talk can be interpreted as a discriminative stimulus.

But what about the more subtle cases where no specific contract or agreement is made? Some pep talks indicate the response to be made but do not indicate the reinforcer to follow. The coach who tells his boys to "go in and give 'em hell" neglects to indicate the consequences, but they are so obvious that they need not be spelled out; if the team wins they win his reinforcing respect; but if they lose, they receive his punishing scorn.

Other even more subtle but possibly effective motivational lectures may not only fail to indicate the reinforcement but may also not bother to mention the response. Such an individual might simply lecture about anything he desired. The main requirement is that the lecture should be interesting and reinforcing and the lecturer should establish himself as someone capable of administering valuable social reinforcement. It should be obvious, though not stated, just what sort of responses the lecturer would approve. Usually the student may safely assume that the lecturer would approve and reinforce the student's behavior to the extent that it resembled that of the lecturer's. The psychology student is generally safe in assuming that he would be most likely to receive social reinforcement from his psychology teacher if he emulates the teacher by becoming a psychologist.

A slightly different form of inspirational lecture involves the lecturer's describing other individuals, or perhaps himself, the behavior they exhibit, and the reinforcers they receive. Due to the generalized imitation training which we all receive, it is implicit that if the listener behaves in the same way, he will be similarly reinforced. The effectiveness of an inspirational book or movie might be analyzed in the same manner.

An analysis of the motivating effects of illustrative materials in books and magazines may be appropriate in this context. Behavior analysts have sometimes objected that potentially reinforcing illustrative material is wasted unless it is made contingent upon the desired responses. This may not be the case. Many popular magazines have a large number of attractive photographs associated with and sometimes preceding each article. These photographs probably inspire many to make the effortful responses required in reading the related article. The photographs act as discriminative stimuli indicating that reinforcement will be forthcoming if the accompanying article is read. In this case the implication may be that the reinforcement will consist of the reader's exposure to more information about these photographs. If this analysis of the motivating effects of pictures in magazines is correct, then it may be that we have some practical suggestions to make to the professionals in the area of copy layout. Some presentations involve a format in which the text material precedes the attractive illustrations. Our analysis indicates that the order should be reversed.

The Theory of Digital Gratification

Traditional Freudian psychoanalytic theory has much to say about factors influencing the effectiveness of reinforcers. It is particularly concerned with the effects of early experience on reinforcers involving the anal, oral, and genital areas. Early experiences with toilet-training, breast-feeding, weaning, and masturbation are important factors influencing the later reinforcing properties of behaviors involving these areas.

Events surrounding an individual's early oral behavior such as breast-feeding may be such that he later exhibits a high frequency of thumbsucking, eating, smoking, and talking. If taking in through the mouth is reinforcing, extreme consumer responses or other behavior of an acquisitive nature may also be reinforcing.

A concern with one's own bodily waste products is traced to certain types of toilet-training procedures. Many objects then become highly reinforcing by generalization from the waste product. Consequently the individual works hard to retain these objects and may be considered quite selfish.

For the male, the initial reinforcing properties of stimulation of the sexual organs may be so great that the boy will conceal his sexual love for his mother in order to avoid his father's removing the offending sex organ. The boy fears that he will be castrated. On the other hand, the sexual stimulation of the girl causes the possession of a penis to be a highly reinforcing event. She will develop penis envy. Because of the effectiveness of these reinforcers, it is said they have a profound influence on the subsequent adult behavior of the individual.

In our study of these psychoanalytic reinforcement mechanisms, it seemed that an important source of reinforcement had been omitted. All of the body parts involving mucous membranes had been considered except one, the nasal passages. Freud has talked about oral, anal, and genital gratification; what about nasal gratification? Adults as well as children are known to find nose picking a very reinforcing behavior. Furthermore, children probably find the result of the waste product from nose picking as great a reinforcer as fecal waste. It would seem that one might plausibly argue that the way the child was taught to blow his nose would effectively determine the reinforcing value of the adult's sticking his nose into other people's business.

Our excitement at developing the concept of nasal gratification was soon to be replaced by the even greater excitement of the development of a concept of gratification which was all-encompassing. Not only did this new concept cover most of the phenomena dealt with by the traditional Freudian triumvirate, but it also encompassed those data of the more recent nasal development. Indeed, a parsimonious concept had been found. That concept is *digital gratification*.

We first became aware of the phenomenon of digital gratification when the paper coffee cups in the Student Union Building were replaced by a more up-to-date styrofoam model. That the entire college campus had been undergoing serious digital deprivation became immediately apparent, as did the inefficiency of the clean-up crew in the Student Union. By the end of the first day of the styrofoam cups, each table contained a heap of small styrofoam particles. The sound of crunching styrofoam created by students walking from one table to another was nearly deafening. These sad remnants of the day's digital debauch bore grim witness to the reinforcing power involved in the behavior of tearing the used styrofoam cups to little bits. Students and faculty alike initially tried to disguise the base reinforcing nature of their activity by jokingly pretending to be tearing the cups into abstract artistic sculptures (usually involving some simple form of spiral). The shallowness of their artistic pretentions became apparent when, after the sculpture was complete, the sculptor continued destroying the cup-art object until it was a mere heap of styrofoam rubble. (It should be parenthetically mentioned that this phenomenon has not been replicated on other campuses where slightly different types of plastic styrofoam coffee cups are used. Whether these other styrofoam cups would be as reinforcing to the original population studied has yet to be determined).

Having discovered the almost embarrassingly powerful reinforcer of destroying styrofoam cups, we began looking at our fellow man from a slightly different perspective. We noticed that when the digital stimulation of tearing a coffee cup was not available, people would frequently drum with their fingers on a table, twiddle their thumbs, play with a book of matches, etc. Many people with beards are seen habitually stroking them. The mere expression "to stroke one's beard" is misleading. Through an introspective behavioral analysis, we were able to determine that the more appropriate expression would be "to stroke one's fingers with one's beard." The beard is an extremely effective source of digital gratification. More than one bearded academician was observed to obliterate a styrofoam coffee cup with one hand while caressing his beard with the other; a most digitally greedy form of behavior.

After these observations, we were quick to return to the Freudian reinforcement mechanisms. They were amenable, one and all, to an analysis in terms of digital gratification. With regard to the anal stage, the use of the hands by infants to smear fecal matter is very common. Feces undoubtedly provide a unique and highly reinforcing source of digital stimulation. The oral stage is equally productive of opportunities for digital reinforcement as exemplified by people who use their fingers to pick their teeth, to hold their fork and spoon, or to hold their cigarette. The relevance to the genital stage is obvious in masturbation. This is clearly an example of the use of genitalia to stimulate the digits.

One of the most important features of a good theory is that it should provide the basis for the interpretation of a large number of phenomena. At least by this criterion, the theory of digital gratification qualifies as an outstanding theory. Unfortunately, old theories are like old soldiers; the student may be surprised to learn that we do not anticipate a ready acceptance of our new theory.

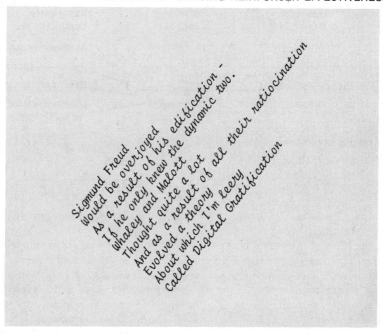

Sigmund Freud
Would be overjoyed
As a result of his edification –
If he only knew the dynamic two.
Whaley and Malott
Thought quite a lot
And as a result of all their ratiocination
Evolved a theory
About which I'm leery
Called Digital Gratification

The Theoretical Status of "Reinforcer Effectiveness"

The status of concepts like "reinforcing effectiveness" is somewhat different from that of most of the terms used in this text and therefore deserves special comment. The concept "reinforcing effectiveness" intervenes between two sets of operations: the causal and resultant operations, the antecedent and consequent conditions, the independent and dependent variables. This is illustrated by Figure 17-1.

As we have seen, several factors influence reinforcer effectiveness; these are the causes, the antecedent conditions, and the independent variables. They include deprivation, amount of reinforcement, the nature of the response, the schedule of reinforcement, and the nature of concurrent schedules of reinforcement. Other factors which are important are the quality of the reinforcer and the presentation of other physical factors such as drugs, heat, salt, etc., which are not of the same nature as the reinforcer itself.

On the other side of reinforcer effectiveness are the results, the consequence, and the dependent variable. In this category, we have discussed absolute response rate, relative response rate, resistance to extinction, and tolerance for increased intermittency of the schedule of reinforcement. Other response measures could include such things as tolerance for punishment of the reinforced response.

The term "reinforcer effectiveness" is used to indicate that there are a large number of different independent variables which all have the same general effects on a large number of different dependent variables. It is simpler to say that the quantity of the reinforcer influences reinforcer effectiveness than it is to say the quantity of the reinforcer influences the absolute response rate, relative response rate, resistance to extinction, tolerance for intermittency of the reinforcer, and the tolerance for punishment of the reinforced response.

There are at least two serious problems involved in using this summarizing terminology. One problem is that the summaries may lead to oversimplification. The other

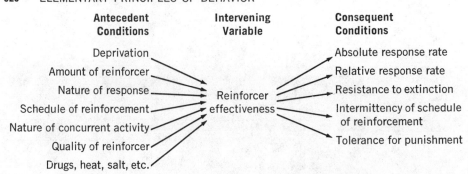

Figure 17-1 The theoretical status of "reinforcer effectiveness"

problem is that we sometimes tend to respond to the summary concepts as if they referred to real entities.

The problem of over-simplification is well illustrated by the work on electric brain stimulation. This work shows that even absolute response rate in two different situations may give different indications of the reinforcing effectiveness of brain stimulation. To study the effects of intensity of the reinforcement, Hawkins and Pliskoff[10] used a chained schedule of reinforcement. The left-hand lever-press response was reinforced on a variable-interval schedule of 30 seconds. The reinforcement consisted of the presentation of a right-hand lever. Each of five successive responses on the right-hand lever was reinforced by the presentation of one-quarter of a second of electric brain stimulation; in other words, the rat responded under a VI schedule on the left bar which presented the right bar. He responded on a continuous reinforcement schedule on the right bar for five brain shocks and then the bar was withdrawn. The only reinforcer for pressing the left bar was the opportunity to work on the right bar. The response rate on the right bar first increased but very quickly reached a maximum and then sometimes decreased as the intensity of the shock increased. The results with the left bar-press response, the one reinforced on a variable interval schedule with the presentation of the opportunity to obtain brain shock, showed a much different function. In nearly every case the response rate continued to increase as the intensity of the shock was increased over the same range as above; most often no maximally effective intensity was found. Response rates on the two bars gave a different picture of the influence of shock intensity on reinforcing effectiveness. If we look at one dependent variable, we would conclude that an independent variable has a particular effect on reinforcing effectiveness. If we look at another dependent variable, we would make a different conclusion. These results might not seem so mysterious if we had not forced them into the concept of "reinforcer effectiveness." Without such an intervening variable, we might not be surprised that our independent variable has one effect on one dependent variable and a different effect on another dependent variable. This leads into the problem of the reification of concepts such as intervening variables.

The problem is that although we want the concept of "reinforcer effectiveness" to help us deal with our data, sometimes we think our data is a means of studying and understanding concepts such as "reinforcer effectiveness." We start asking, for example, what dependent variables might be most useful in measuring "reinforcer effectiveness."

10. Hawkins, T. D., and Pliskoff, S. S. Brain-stimulation intensity, rate of self-stimulation, and reinforcement strength: An analysis through chaining. *Journal of the Experimental Analysis of Behavior*, 1964, 7, 285–288.

We should be asking, instead, for what dependent variables is "reinforcer effectiveness" a useful summary term.

There are a large number of such concepts in the general field of psychology. They may have done much more harm than good. For example, the concept of "intelligence" is an intervening variable which has the same psychological status as "reinforcer effectiveness." It is less useful, however, because there is a tendency to ignore the independent variables associated with intelligence and simply look at the dependent variables such as scores on intelligence tests, performance in school, etc. People seem to forget that intelligence is merely a summary term indicating that a large number of dependent variables are frequently correlated with each other. We sometimes tend to think that these various dependent variables all measure some central entity known as "intelligence."

This concept of intelligence has led to a generally defeatist attitude toward improving individual performance with regard to the various independent variables. If the individual does not have enough intelligence, nothing can be done. He will not do well in school, etc. As you can tell, such notions are contrary to the optimistic philosophy of this book. Our approach involves looking at the various dependent variables and trying to determine the independent variables which affect them. Then an all-out effort can be made to manipulate the relevant independent variable in order to improve the individual's performance. There is little concern with the intervening variable of "intelligence."

Other concepts which have the same status are response strength, resistance to extinction, perception, and attitude. There are many more similar concepts. The student of behavior may find it interesting to analyze these concepts in order to determine their function as intervening variables. It is even more challenging to attempt to find others. In general, the student should keep a wary eye out for such concepts.

The term "hypothetical construct" refers to concepts which have essentially the same logical status as intervening variables; however, it is assumed that hypothetical constructs in fact refer to real entities and may eventually be directly observable. A more generic and somewhat pejorative term which describes both sorts of concepts is "explanatory fiction." An attempt has been made to keep explanatory fictions at a minimum in this text.

Adjunctive Reinforcers

The concept of adjunctive reinforcement is new. Its general utility has yet to be demonstrated. But there are a number of phenomena which seem potentially to be amenable to such an analysis. It may be that many things which we find reinforcing in our everyday life are adjunctive reinforcers. They are effective because of apparently unrelated schedules of reinforcement with different types of reinforcers associated with completely different sets of responses occurring at the same time. Such minor behaviors as rocking in a chair, scratching one's head, or drumming one's fingers on the side of a chair may eventually be shown to be adjunctive behaviors under the control of other seemingly irrelevant schedules of reinforcement. Adjunctive reinforcement might be a common factor in cases of excessive eating and drinking. It may be that some unusual behaviors such as the repetitive ritualistic responses of many retarded and psychotic individuals are a result of the unusual schedules of reinforcement which are simultaneously in effect. This is mere speculation, but mere speculation may sometimes be a useful precursor to experimental investigation.

18

PUNISHMENT PRODUCED BY CONTINGENT STIMULATION

The Coral Gables Bar Revisited

In an earlier chapter, we discussed research involving the drinking behavior of alcoholics. We showed how a fixed-ratio schedule of reinforcement allowed psychologists to study drinking behavior without the concomitant risk of getting his subjects drunk or in any way incapacitated by alcohol consumption. This was specifically exploratory research. Although many volumes had been written on the alcoholic and his problems, precious little research had been done upon the nature of the drinking behavior itself and the amount of discomfort an alcoholic might endure to receive a drink. The Coral Gables group sought to find out exactly how much discomfort alcoholics would endure in order to receive a small amount of mixed drink.[1] Does the alcoholic's body depend on alcohol in much the same way that the drug addict needs morphine, or can the alcoholic's affinity for his drink be better explained by simple principles of behavior?

The machine with which the Coral Gables' subjects soon became acquainted included a lever with a stimulus light above it. Below the lever was an opening into which a metal drinking glass could be inserted. On his drinking hand, the subject wore a special glove with electrodes which fastened to his middle and index fingers. After he had completed a fixed-ratio requirement which ultimately was fixed at 125 responses, a drink became available.

In early sessions this pattern was repeated many times a day; in fact, it was repeated for four daily 20-minute sessions, seven days a week, for more than two weeks.

By the end of this period the individual's response patterns in terms of liquor reinforcement was ascertained. Some subjects pressed the lever as fast as they could and gulped down their drinks with all possible speed, as though getting a

---

1. This section based on Whaley, D. L., Knowles, Patsy A., and Rosenkranz, A. Punishment of the consummatory response of alcoholic beverages in institution populations. Unpublished research conducted at VA Hospital, Coral Gables, Florida, 1966.

drink were a life-or-death matter. Others maintained composure and pressed the bar steadily and consistently, taking their drinks with a conservative and practiced air.

This period of time in an experiment during which the researcher is merely observing and recording behavior under standard conditions is often referred to as the *baseline period,* or simply *baseline.* Later on, new variables and conditions may be introduced, but during this initial period the researcher is gaining some precise notion of the rate, topography, and patterning of the responses in order to compare with behavior under modified conditions.

A sample of baseline behavior for a subject named Bill is presented in Figure 18-1. The number of responses made is represented on the ordinate and the ses-

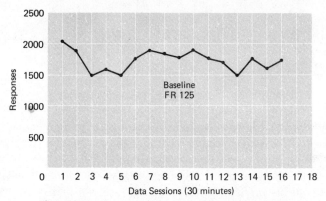

Figure 18-1   Baseline bar-pressing behavior for Bill

sions are represented on the abscissa. Bill's bar-pressing behavior was maintained on an FR 125 schedule of reinforcement for a mixture of bourbon and water. He was making an average of two thousand responses per session.

But what of the number of drinks or amount of liquor Bill was receiving? It is apparent, mathematically, that when two thousand responses are made on an FR 125 schedule, quite a number of reinforcements are being consumed. In Figure 18-2 the number of drinks Bill consumed are plotted across the sessions. Keeping in mind that each of the subjects was given four sessions daily, it can be seen that Bill was drinking about as much liquor as sobriety, and the experimenters, could tolerate!

After ample baseline data had been collected, a punishment procedure was introduced. After the FR 125 requirement was completed, the stimulus light above the lever went on as before, signalling that the drinking glass was filled with liquor and reinforcement was available. Bill picked up the glass as usual and lifted it toward his lips. The instant the cup touched his lips, an automatic sensing device relayed this occurrence to programming equipment in the adjoining room. A small amount of electric current was delivered to the index and middle fingers of his drinking hand. At first this electric current was very slight, as little as one milliampere (.001 amps). This is far too little current to light an

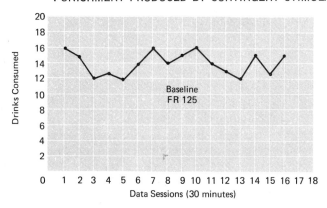

Figure 18-2 The number of drinks Bill consumed

ordinary light bulb for even an instant. Bill was subjected to this amount of current for several sessions, but there were no noticeable effects on his drinking or bar-pressing behavior.

After data were collected for shock of the 1.0 milliamp level, the shock was deleted for several sessions in order to let any recovery take place before a new intensity was introduced.

Soon an increased intensity of electric current was delivered to Bill's fingers each time he consumed a drink. This new intensity was 2.0 milliamperes, still a relatively minute amount. Observations were made, data recorded, and once again the shock was deleted for several sessions. This sequence was repeated several times. Each reintroduction of the current brought a higher intensity than the previous one, and between each intensity, no-shock sessions were programmed.

Data collected throughout this procedure are presented in Figure 18-3. The last four sessions of the baseline are replotted to give a more complete picture on the reductions in the number of drinks consumed. The data indicate that the initial intensity of 1.0 milliampere had virtually no effect nor did other levels of 2.0 or 3.0 milliamperes. When the current was increased to 4.0 milliamperes, there

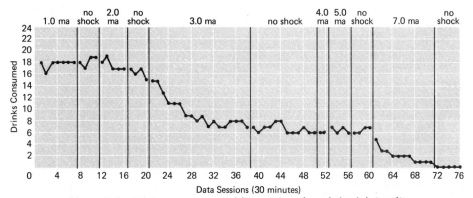

Figure 18-3 Drinks consumed by Bill as a function of shock intensity

was a considerable reduction in the response rate and the number of drinks consumed. Response rate did not recover during the following no-shock period and showed even further reduction at 5.0 milliamperes. When the current reached 7.0 milliamperes, response rate dropped to such an extent that no reinforcements were earned at all, and thus no drinks were consumed.

For Bill a 7.0 milliamp jolt was too dear a price to pay for his favorite mixed drink. For more than three weeks he sat idly in the experimental room for 20 minutes each session, four sessions daily, seven days a week, and refrained from making even a single response. After the first week, the shock was disconnected. Of course Bill did not know this, but he was not taking any chances. The punishment procedure had eliminated Bill's drinking behavior, at least at the Coral Gables Bar.

Data presented for Bill are typical of the results the researchers obtained when they employed the punishment procedure in the manner outlined. But let us further discuss the punishment procedure and the behavior in which it results.

The punishment procedure involved the introduction of a form of stimulation, in this case, the electric shock, which was delivered to the fingers of the individual working at the Coral Gables Bar.

The form of stimulation was electric current. Many of us have experienced direct contact of our skin surface with electric current. We may have found this experience terrifying, stimulating, exciting, mystifying, or overpowering; some may have become unconscious as a result of this experience. The point about electric current is that we may expect many different effects from its introduction according to such variables as intensity, anatomical location of contact, or other physical aspects of the current or environment. In Bill's case, electric current did not result in reduction of drinking frequency until the intensity had reached a level of 4.0 milliamperes. Intensities less than this (when applied under the conditions prevalent at the Coral Gables Bar) did not result in reductions in the rate of drinking behavior. It must therefore be said that those intensities of electric current lower than 4.0 milliamperes were not punishing in this case.

Here we find the crucial definition of punishment. *An event is said to be a punisher only if it results in a reduction in the response which it follows.* A procedure may involve introduction of additional stimulation to an individual following the emission of a specific response, but the stimulation which is delivered cannot be called a punisher unless it results in a reduction in the rate of that response.

This concept is not a new one; we have encountered it before when we were concerned with the definition of a reinforcer. Just as a potential reinforcer can only be called a reinforcer if it increases the rate of response it is arranged to follow, so can a potential punisher be defined as a punisher only if it reduces the rate of the response it is arranged to follow.

Perhaps now it is becoming more clear to the reader that punishment is quite different from torture or other similar forms of physical abuse. In order to be termed a punisher, the event must be arranged to follow a particular response, and it must also result in a decrease in that response.

In the foregoing case, the result of punishment on the drinking behavior of alcoholics was its total elimination within the confines of the research setting. Wide differences were found among the alcoholics both in individual response patterns such as pauses between reinforcements and response rate as well as in the intensity of electric shock each would tolerate before foregoing the drink opportunity. Some individuals, like Bill, began to reduce their drinking when the intensity was as small as 4.0 milliamperes. One relinquished his drinking behavior only when the intensity reached 22.5 milliamperes. This amount of current, although placing the subject in no physical danger, creates an excruciating amount of discomfort. On occasion, the force of the current caused this subject to jump from his chair and land on the floor.

Unfortunately, no definite information is available as to whether the punishment procedure brought about cessation of alcoholic behavior after these subjects were released from the Coral Gables Hospital. However, there is some indication that the experiences of these individuals in the drinking experiment did not modify their overall drinking behavior at all.

General findings from the experiment were, however, of considerable value in yielding information regarding the drinking response of a population of individuals diagnosed as "alcoholic." The experiment by no means constituted a "cure," nor was it designed with this in mind.

Individuals involved in the study were free to form the rapid and simple discrimination that the Coral Gables Bar was different from others they habituated. Once he left the hospital, it was easy for the subject to see that no wires or experimenter were present at his favorite corner bar. He was "safe" to drink without fear of electric shock. The fact that subjects can often discriminate a treatment situation from one that occurs outside the laboratory has been discussed in an earlier chapter, as a problem of generalization of therapy. Let us go on to see how this problem was partially overcome in another case employing electric current as a punishing event, where therapy was one of the major aims of the psychologist.

Punishment of Smoking Behavior

"You're coming along just fine," the doctor said, glancing one more time at the X-rays. "The surgery was apparently totally successful. Not a single trace of the cancer can be found."

Clarisse leaned back in the chair in the doctor's office and finished buttoning up her clothing. She breathed a sigh of relief and reaching in her handbag took out a cigarette, lit it, inhaled a large gulp of smoke, and let it out slowly.[2]

"You're a very lucky woman, Clarisse," the doctor continued. "We were fortunate to catch the cancer in time, and although the surgery was drastic, you still have your life. There's only one thing I must ask of you, Clarisse."

"Anything at all, doctor," Clarisse said. Being a professional nurse, Clarisse

2. This section based on Whaley, D. L., Rosenkranz, A., Knowles, Patsy A., and Thornton, T. Automatic punishment of cigarette smoking by a portable electronic device. Unpublished research conducted at VA Hospital, Coral Gables, Florida, 1966.

was accustomed to hearing and following the directives of physicians. Clarisse was an attractive woman, who had won both popularity and the respect of the staff at the hospital where she was a head nurse.

"I want you to give up smoking now, once and for all," the doctor said. "I'm not trying to say that smoking caused the cancer we just removed, but you must admit that the evidence linking cancer to smoking has increased to the point that it cannot be ignored any longer. Besides, I've never met one patient who could say that smoking ever benefited him."

Clarisse looked at the doctor and then dolefully down at the cigarette she held between her fingers. "I've tried, doctor," she said, "You don't know how many times I've tried, but I just can't get rid of the habit. You see, I've smoked since I was 16 years old. It's as much a part of me as, well, as breathing itself. I'm glad to do anything you say, doctor; anything that I can possibly do, but I simply don't have the will power to give up smoking."

The doctor was not surprised at Clarisse's response. Of the 40 or so people he had requested to quit smoking within the last two months, only two had complied. Many of these patients suffered from respiratory problems such as emphysema or tuberculosis, and there was no doubt that smoking was a constant aggravation to their condition. His hands were tied. He could only request his patients to stop smoking; there was no method he knew which could ensure that they would.

Meanwhile, in the same hospital where Clarisse worked as a nurse, some psychologists had experienced the same problem as the physician. Often patients were referred to them for help in stopping their smoking behavior. After consulting numerous journals and articles, the psychologists found that there were no treatments or experimental procedures which had been shown to be successful in bringing about the end of smoking behavior.

These psychologists decided that it was time to develop some techniques for dealing with this problem. After all, it was a problem which had recently reached gigantic proportions. In a way, it spoke very poorly for human beings as a species. Few lower animals insisted on continuing a behavior which might shorten their lives by months or even years. The psychologists did not know exactly what approach they would take, but they thought that it would involve the use of punishment.

Attempts which had emphasized pyschotherapy or other forms of "talking" the patient out of smoking had been patently ineffective. Smoking was not a disease or a form of illness; it was a group of responses which occurred with great strength and frequency. Punishment might break up the chain of smoking responses.

The following advertisement appeared in the hospital newspaper:

"Volunteers wanted to undergo a procedure engineered to enable them to stop smoking. Specifically those individuals are wanted who have tried everything, but still cannot quit smoking."

Clarisse saw the advertisement and was the first person to contact the psychologists. "I'm just the person for your study," she said. "I want to quit smoking more than anything. I've tried dozens of times and could never pull it off. If your treatment will work on me, it will work on anyone. I'm willing to do anything you say."

Initially, the researchers did nothing at all to curb Clarisse's smoking. They wanted to know how many cigarettes she currently smoked each day. Clarisse was given instructions on how to count and report her smoking behavior. Each day one of the psychologists involved in the study called on Clarisse, and validated her count of cigarettes she had smoked the previous day. Usually the psychologists and Clarisse counted the cigarettes remaining in her package and arrived at the number smoked. This procedure was conducted for 16 days. It was found that Clarisse smoked an average of 24 cigarettes daily. The amount smoked was fairly constant during weekdays, but seemed to increase slightly on weekends, or on the evenings when Clarisse went out to dinner or "on the town."

After baseline data were collected, Clarisse was introduced to a portable electronic unit. This unit consisted of three basic parts. One part was an electric pack which contained batteries, transistors, capacitors, relays, and other electronic components. The second part was a modified cigarette case similar to that seen for sale in drug stores and tobacco shops. The only thing extraordinary about the cigarette case was a small switch at the top of the case, which operated when it was opened. The third component of the portable unit was made up of two wires which fastened to an elastic band embedded with stainless steel snaps. This elastic band fit over Clarisse's right forearm, the arm she used to hold her cigarettes. The two metal snaps on the elastic band were electrodes and were spaced about one inch apart; they made contact with the skin on the surface of Clarisse's forearm. The electronic pack and case fit snugly into the pockets on Clarisse's nurse uniform.

Clarisse was told that the electronic unit was to be worn anytime and anyplace that smoking might conceivably occur. She was told that she could smoke as many cigarettes as she wanted provided she took each one from the pack. The experimenter suggested that she now light a cigarette if she wished.

Clarisse cautiously opened the electronic pack, expecting the worst; nothing happened. Still wary, she removed the cigarette from the case, placed it in her mouth, and lit it; still nothing happened. Clarisse waited a few more seconds, and then sank back into the easy chair in the psychologist's office. "Nothing is going to happen," she said.

Just then she stiffened and gave out a shrill yelp. She had been taking a large puff of the cigarette when the electric current was delivered through the electrodes to her forearm.

"That was really something," she said. She looked at the cigarette which was still burning menacingly in her hand and mashed it out on the ashtray, although a good portion of it remained unsmoked. It was as though the cigarette itself had shocked her and she was getting even with it by crushing it against the ashtray.

"That is the price you will pay for each cigarette you smoke, Clarisse," the researcher said. "Each time you take a cigarette from your case and light it up, you will receive a similar shock. You can't predict exactly when the shock will be delivered, but it will be while you are smoking, or at least holding the cigarette in your hand. As long as you're willing to pay this price, you can smoke as many cigarettes as you like, but you must always take cigarettes from your own cigarette case and cannot borrow or obtain an independent supply of cigarettes. Only if you are willing to follow these simple rules can we permit you to participate in this project. Clarisse looked at the electronic pack she now wore and laughed. "I don't think it will work," she said. "But as I've said, I'm willing to try anything!"

On the first day that Clarisse wore the apparatus, her smoking frequency dropped to eleven cigarettes, almost half of her baseline average. On the next two days, her frequency dropped to four, and on the fourth day, she smoked no cigarettes at all. During the next weekend her rate rose again to the maximum of five, and then within two days was once again zero. She maintained a zero rate for four consecutive days, and was very pleased with herself. "It looks like it's going to work," she said. "I just can't believe it."

Again the weekend came and Clarisse was invited out for dinner when relatives came to visit. She smoked five cigarettes on Saturday and five on Sunday. On the following Monday when she checked in with the researchers, she was ashamed and upset with her weekend smoking binge.

From that day on, however, Clarisse did not smoke another cigarette. After a smokeless week had expired, the apparatus was removed. Clarisse continued to refrain from smoking.

Clarisse was so happy over the success of the treatment that she insisted on taking the psychologist out to dinner as a way of celebrating. Later, Clarisse found she had no difficulty in foregoing the traditional cigarette after the apple pie dessert was finished. Approximately a year and a half after the termination of the experiment, the psychologist who was primarily concerned with the research received the following postcard:

Dear Doctor:

As of today, you have helped me to save $250.75 in money, incalculable minutes of longer life, and an indescribably large amount of self respect.

Regards,

Your nonsmoking friend,
Clarisse

The same unit which was used with Clarisse was also employed with several other volunteers. All volunteers who continued to subject themselves to the punishment procedure quit smoking. Many still refrain from smoking even at this writing. Still others have quit smoking for a period of time, resumed smoking, and then returned for a second and even third bout with the unit. All subjects who wore the unit until their smoking behavior reached a zero level continued to refrain from smoking for at least two months after the unit was removed.

The procedure employed with Clarisse was essentially a punishment procedure. Unlike the study with alcoholics, the electric current ensuing from the smoking apparatus was not associated with a specific response. The shock was programmed to occur in such a manner as to be associated with any one of a number of behaviors which could be described as a class of "smoking responses." Smoking involves many separate responses which include withdrawing the cigarette from the pack, placing it in one's mouth, lighting it, puffing it, holding it in one's hand or in one's mouth, exhaling, etc. Taken collectively, these responses comprise a response chain. Punishment was arranged to occur unpredictably with any one of the responses in this chain. Therefore, in the long run, the smoking chain itself was punished.

Once the shock was arranged to be associated with smoking behavior in a reliable and consistent manner, smoking behavior decreased. Therefore we know that the electric shock was an effective punisher.

There are other events which serve as punishers and do not primarily rely on energy transfer or pain thresholds for their effectiveness. These events are verbal or symbolic in nature. From a significant person, the simple word "no" can be the most excruciating form of punishment, as indeed, rejections, as a general class of events, are usually punishers, unless the rejection is from one's local draftboard.

In the following study a substance which is usually employed to enhance our enjoyment was used in a punishment procedure. Although the use of this substance was finally suspended, results had proven it to be an extremely effective punishing event.

Tabasco Road

Gregory was easily the most unloved child on the entire ward. When groups came to visit, the institution staff conducting the tour were careful to avoid the area at the back of the ward which was uniquely Gregory's domain.[3]

There was nothing intrinsically horrid about Gregory which could account for the reluctance of onlookers to take him into their hearts. Although retarded, Gregory was, on some occasions, a quite adorable child. He had an almost cherubic face. He did, however, exhibit one behavior which made even the most benevolent attendant or hospital volunteer avoid him.

Gregory was what was known in institution jargon as a "ruminator." After eating his food, he vomited it immediately and then, to the utter fright of all who observed, quickly reconsumed it. The reconsumption of the vomitus is called rumination. Whereas lunch for most of the residents involved only a few minutes, Gregory's lunch lasted for as long as two hours. During this period, he vomited and reconsumed his food dozens of times. He was always unsightly. The constant moisture had created skin problems about his mouth and face. Regardless of how vigilant ward personnel tried to be, Gregory did not smell as sweet as he might have. No attendant had enough time to clean him up as often as he required.

Nor was Gregory's problem solely a social one. His vomiting and reconsuming behavior held grave possible medical consequences. He was a frequent problem

3. This section based on Bright, Gladys, and Whaley, D. L. Suppression of regurgitation and rumination with aversive events. *Michigan Department Mental Health Research Bulletin*, 1968, 2, 17–20.

for the physicians because of the constant risk of malnutrition and dehydration. In the process of regurgitation and reconsuming, much food and fluid were lost. Often Gregory required special injections of nutrients and fluids to preclude severe malnutrition or death by dehydration.

At the time Gregory first came to the attention of the psychology service, his weight was only 29 pounds. Since Gregory was nine years old and of average stature, it does not take much imagination to see that he was extremely gaunt and emaciated. At this time, he was noticed by one of the new graduate students who had just begun to serve her practicum courses at the institution. When she first saw Gregory, he was sitting, as was typical with him, with a large towel thrown over him in the fashion of a bib. In his high chair he looked very much like a customer who had been frocked by the barber and was now patiently waiting for his shave, haircut, and shampoo.

The graduate student felt she might be able to do something for him. She discussed it with her supervisor, who agreed that Gregory had been a problem for a long time, and had grown to be one of the most unsavory residents of the institution. In fact, Gregory had been referred to psychology service for treatment several times; but due to other "more pressing cases," no positive course had been outlined for him. In truth, the supervisor had found Gregory a little repulsive and had not been disposed to spend the initial hours needed to precisely define Gregory's problem.

The graduate student began by observing Gregory. She found that Gregory exhibited the vomiting and reconsuming behavior at all three meals, although it was most frequent during the noon meal. In all cases, the behavior chain began immediately after feeding and continued for a maximum of two hours. By this time, his food had either been lost permanently or was finally absorbed by his system. Gregory exhibited this behavior pattern six hours daily beginning at each feeding time and lasting for approximately two hours thereafter. During her observation, the graduate student counted the number of times Gregory vomited and the number of times he bent over to reconsume the vomitus. Thus, it was possible for one vomiting response to be followed by a dozen or so contacts with the food where it lay on his bib or high-chair tray. Figure 18-4 depicts these baseline data. It can be seen that Gregory was performing his two responses at an extremely high rate.

In discussing the case with her supervisor, the graduate student came to view Gregory's problem in the following way: most of us are content to consume our food only once. We have been taught that vomiting is an undesirable response, and certainly that the product that the vomiting behavior produces is unsuitable for reconsumption under any circumstances. Being a retarded child who was nonverbal and who had spent all of his life at the institution, Gregory had not learned this. For him, reconsumption of the food was a reinforcing event. Gregory consumed his food and then vomited it, thus producing the opportunity to consume it another time. Viewed in this way, vomiting behavior was reinforced by the opportunity to reconsume the food. The graduate student reasoned that if the reconsuming behavior could be eliminated, the vomiting would ultimately extinguish. By precluding the reconsumption (reinforcement for vomiting), the

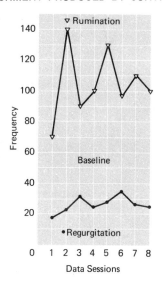

Figure 18-4   Gregory's regurgitation and rumination behavior

vomiting would soon also cease. This raised the immediate problem of arranging a procedure to eliminate reconsumption.

Obviously the vomitus was reinforcing to Gregory or he would not have reconsumed it. However, it might be possible to change the vomitus in such a way as to make it no longer reinforcing. Perhaps if some type of bad tasting material could be placed on it, Gregory would not find it so inviting. After thinking of several possible chemicals and rejecting them because of the possible harm they might hold for Gregory, the graduate student decided to use a simple substance which was common to many dining tables—Tabasco sauce, a type of hot condiment often used to enhance food flavor. As many have no doubt discovered for themselves, when used in excess Tabasco sauce can irritate the mouth.

The graduate student purchased some Tabasco sauce and tried it out on Gregory. He made a strange face and avoided bringing his mouth into contact with the vomitus. It appeared that Tabasco sauce would be effective.

Accordingly, a special apparatus was constructed involving a sprayer which automatically sprayed Tabasco sauce on Gregory's vomitus whenever he approached it. This was accomplished by means of photo cell beams which energized the sprayer when Gregory's head was inclined toward his tray where the vomitus typically fell. Gregory was maintained on this program for several days. Data collected during this period of time are presented in Figure 18-5.

This procedure was extremely effective in reducing the reconsuming behavior, although it had no immediate effects on vomiting behavior. It can definitely be said that the addition of Tabasco sauce to Gregory's productions made their consumption a punishing event. Tabasco sauce was placed directly on the material which was to be consumed and thus punishment was always directly associated with the reconsumption response.

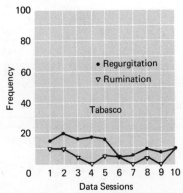

Figure 18-5 Gregory's regurgitation and rumination behavior with Tabasco sauce

A problem soon arose necessitating the termination of the Tabasco sauce procedure. Although Gregory was no longer reconsuming, there had been no immediate reduction in the vomiting behavior. Since Gregory was not reconsuming any of his food while continuing to vomit, he was receiving even less nourishment than before. His weight began to drop. Perhaps the vomiting behavior would have ultimately extinguished as the experimenters had originally predicted. In any event, the procedure could not continue. The weight loss and dehydration could prove dangerous and even fatal.

Tabasco sauce was discarded and replaced with another presumed punisher, electric shock. A small amount of electric current was directed to Gregory's leg each time he vomited. A shock was also given him each time his mouth came into contact with his vomitus. Figure 18-6 shows the rapid decline to zero in both vomiting and reconsumption.

A small exposure of electric shock following each response had effectively eliminated both of these behaviors. This procedure was enacted for all three meals for a period of five weeks.

Figure 18-7 depicts Gregory's weekly weight over the course of the treatment. From a beginning weight of 29 pounds, Gregory lost a pound during the Tabasco

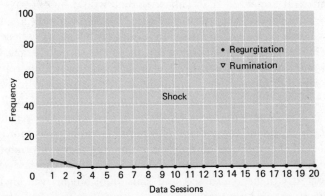

Figure 18-6 Gregory's regurgitation and rumination behavior under electric shock

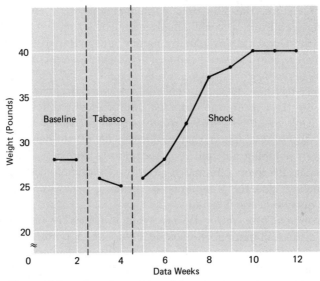

Figure 18-7 Gregory's weekly weight throughout his treatment

treatment period, but quickly began to gain weight when the shock procedure was introduced.

Lately, Gregory has lost his title of the "most unloved child on the ward." Not only does his physical appearance lend itself more readily to friendly advances, but he is generally more active on the ward and has begun to entertain himself with toys and other more normal objects of amusement. Occasionally, however, Gregory reverts to his old behavior pattern, and a brief visit by one of the Psychology Service personnel is required. Two or three brief electric stimulations are enough to reduce the rate to zero for several weeks. All in all, Gregory is quite happy, as indeed are those around him.

Summary

This chapter introduces the concept of punishment. Unlike torture or other instances where physical stimulation is applied haphazardly and with little regard for behavior patterns or specific responses, "punishment" denotes a precise scientific concept and procedure. The type of punishment discussed in this chapter dealt primarily with the introduction of various forms of stimulation, following specific response patterns.

The punishment procedure involves following a specific response or response chain with a presumed or potential punisher. If the response which is followed by the potential punishing event shows a significant reduction in rate, the potential punisher has been demonstrated to be a *punisher*. In order to be defined as a punisher, an event must be properly related to a specific response or response pattern and result in a decrease in the rate of that response.

1. Individuals described in medical records as alcoholics have undergone a

punishment procedure. Baseline data were first collected while subjects were pressing a lever on a fixed-ratio 125 schedule and being reinforced with alcoholic beverages. In the Coral Gables Bar, frequency and cumulative records of lever responses as well as frequency of reinforcements per session constituted the baseline data.

After ample baseline data were collected, electrical current was introduced concomitant with the consumption of each reinforcement. Effectively, consuming the alcoholic drink which constituted reinforcement produced a brief exposure to electrical current. It was found that intensities of 4.0 milliamperes and above were effective in reducing alcoholic consumption to zero level, and that alcohol consumption was effectively eliminated from the experimental setting. There was no reason to believe that the elimination of drinking behavior was generalized to environments outside of the hospital.

2. A punishment procedure also involving the delivery of electrical current was utilized in the elimination of smoking behavior. A portable electronic pack produced a brief electrical stimulation to the subject's forearm after a variable interval of time had elapsed since a cigarette had been removed from a specialized container. The electrical stimulation was not explicitly paired with a specific response but was programmed to occur with any of a number of responses which made up a chain of responses collectively called "smoking behavior." For the subject whose data were reported, smoking behavior was eliminated in less than two weeks from the introduction of the portable smoking unit. After more than a year and a half, there is evidence that the subject is still refraining from smoking. Similar results were obtained with other subjects.

It was suggested that the smoking punishment procedure yielded more permanent reductions in punished behaviors because the portable unit allowed for greater generalization of effects.

4. A retarded boy was subjected to a punishment procedure. Initially, Tabasco sauce was employed to reduce reconsumption of vomitus. The Tabasco sauce proved to be an effective punisher. Due to complications involving the welfare of the patient, the use of Tabasco sauce was discontinued and electric shock was used in the punishment procedure. During this phase of the experiment, both vomiting and reconsumption of the vomitus were followed with the electric current. The shock was an effective punisher, as both vomiting and reconsumption were reduced to zero frequency. Concomitantly, the subject gained considerable weight and was more soically acceptable and appeared to be more actively involved in appropriate behaviors on the ward.

QUESTIONS

1. Originally at the Coral Gables Bar, how did the experimenter assure that his volunteer subjects could not get enough alcohol in their systems to make them exceedingly drunk? (a) He used a fixed-interval schedule; (b) He reduced the session length to only three minutes; (c) He used a relatively high fixed-ratio schedule of reinforcement; (d) He did not really use alcoholic beverages.

2. Specifically, what schedule of reinforcement was used at the Coral Gables Bar?

3. It was found that the lever-press technique and rate were extraordinarily comparable for all the subjects. (a) True; (b) False.

4. *Baseline period* or *baseline* denotes that time during which: (a) the organism stays in the start-box or home cage; (b) the subject's behavior is observed and recorded under standard conditions; (c) the verticle ordinate of a graph is used; (d) that point at which shock is introduced.

5. The usefulness of the baseline is that it: (a) lets the experimenter know if the variables he later introduced were really effective; (b) allows him an opportunity to qualify various aspects of the behavior he wishes to modify; (c) allows him to gain some precise notion of the rate, topography, and patterning of the responses he will later attempt to modify; (d) all of the above.

6. Given the specific fixed-ratio schedule the organism is operating on and the total number of responses, it is a simple mathematical problem to find out how many reinforcements he received. (a) True; (b) False.

7. The electric current was delivered to Bill's fingers: (a) when he had made the first lever press; (b) after making the last lever press in the ratio; (c) when he began to pick up the drinking glass; (d) when the glass made contact with his lips.

8. One milliampere (.001 amps) is enough current to light the city of New York for a year. (a) True; (b) False.

9. After receiving the one milliampere shock, Bill immediately went into a coma and when he awoke, swore he'd never touch another drop. (a) True; (b) False.

10. In the drinking punishment study, each phase of shock was followed by a phase of no-shock. Why do you think the experimenters arranged things in this manner? What was the purpose of the no-shock period?

11. Whereas a four milliampere shock had merely reduced Bill's drinking frequency, a seven milliampere shock reduced it to zero. (a) True; (b) False.

12. If a particular event or form of stimulation employed in a punishment procedure results in a reduction or elimination of a response it is arranged to follow, this event can be called a p_____.

13. A potential punishing event employed in the punishment procedure which does *not* bring about reductions in the rate of the response cannot be called a punisher. (a) True; (b) False.

14. The electric current in the Coral Gables study was applied by: (a) Consumers Power Corporation; (b) General Electric; (c) Tennessee Valley Authority; (d) a nine-volt battery.

15. Cross out any of the following which can *never* be the subjective results of experiences with electric shock: frightening, stimulating, exciting, mystifying, overpowering, terrifying, fatal.

16. Which of the following variables affect the subjective experience of electric current? (a) The intensity and frequency of the current; (b) The anatomical location where the current is applied; (c) The resistance of the individual receiving the shock; (d) All of the above.

17. All of the subjects quit drinking as soon as the shock reached four milliamperes. (a) True; (b) False.

18. The main purpose of this study done at Coral Gables Bar was to cure alcoholism. (a) True; (b) False.

19. In all but one case, the punishment procedure cured subjects of their alcoholism. (a) True; (b) False.

20. Briefly explain one possible reason the procedure employed at the Coral Gables Bar did not have lasting effects.

21. Clarisse had just undergone surgery for: (a) cancer; (b) a hernia; (c) ulcers; (d) obstructed lungs.

22. What was the one request the physician made of Clarisse which she was unable to obey?

23. Clarisse said that she could not give up smoking because: (a) she did not have the will power; (b) her stock in Ligget and Meyers would suffer if everyone quit smoking; (c) she became too nervous if she did not smoke; (d) she was afraid of gaining weight if she gave up smoking.

24. The doctor was completely overwhelmed by Clarisse's refusal, for it was rare for people to refuse to quit smoking when their health was in jeopardy. (a) True; (b) False.

25. Which of the following best describes smoking? (a) Illness; (b) Chain of responses; (c) A form of mental illness called "neurotism"; (d) Psychosis 26.

26. After Clarisse had answered the ad in the paper and consented to undergo the procedure, the psychologist began by: (a) doing nothing at all to curb Clarisse's smoking; (b) first trying psychotherapy; (c) showing her pictures of cancers; (d) taking extensive X-rays.

27. The initial period of time during which data were gained on the rate of the patterning of Clarisse's smoking behavior is known as a b_____.

28. The electronic pack the psychologist gave Clarisse: (a) was pulled around on a golf cart; (b) fit in her pocket; (c) could only be used in the experimental room; (d) was not described.

29. What instructions were given Clarisse as to how often and when she was to wear the smoking unit?

30. The first time Clarisse tried out the unit, she was upset because it failed to operate. (a) True; (b) False.

31. After receiving her first shock, she became nervous and began to puff her cigarette like crazy. (a) True; (b) False.

32. Where (anatomically) was the shock delivered to Clarisse?

33. The outcome of the punishment procedure when applied to Clarisse could best be described as: (a) Clarisse reduced her smoking to zero during the week but continued to smoke during the weekends and special occasions; (b) After taking one shock, Clarisse never smoked again; (c) Clarisse smoked only one cigarette after each meal; (d) Clarisse abstained from smoking for at least a year and a half after the unit was taken from her.

34. Which of the following did Clarisse not mention as an outcome of the treatment? (a) more money saved; (b) longer life; (c) more self-respect; (d) romance.

35. In the punishment procedure applied to smoking behavior, shock was consistently paired with a single response. (a) True; (b) False.

36. Why did the writer feel that the portable aspects of the unit were important in the results obtained?

37. It is fortunate that the psychologists have to use electric shock for it is the only form of energy which can effectively serve as a punisher. (a) True; (b) False.

38. Which of the items below could possibly be used as a punisher? (a) A discouraging word; (b) Sound; (c) Light; (d) All of the above.

39. Gregory was unloved because: (a) of his constant whining and verbal abuse; (b) of the fact that he reconsumed his vomitus; (c) he was retarded; (d) he was ugly.

40. Other than being a bit disgusting and socially unacceptable, Gregory's behavior problem was of no great importance. (a) True; (b) False.

41. The graduate student began by merely observing Gregory and recording vomiting and reconsumption. This period of time could be called b_____.

42. According to the hypothesis suggested by the graduate student, what reinforcer was maintaining vomiting?

43. If it were possible to prevent reconsumption of the vomitus, it was thought that the vomiting behavior itself should be eliminated by an e_____ procedure.
44. What substance was initially employed as a punisher?
45. To what response was the punishment procedure initially applied?
46. What was the result of the Tabasco sauce punishment procedure on: (a) the vomiting response; (b) the reconsuming response.
47. Why was the Tabasco sauce ultimately discarded?
48. What potential punisher was then employed?
49. In the new punishment procedure, what response(s) (was, were) followed by electric shock?

NOTES
The Coral Gables Bar Revisited

Data presented within this section are restricted to the effects of shock punishment on the drinking behavior of subjects. The response of consuming the reinforcer was the response which was being directly punished. In the experimental design employed in the study, however, the subjects were required to make lever responses in order to obtain the reinforcer. Since punishment of the drinking behavior resulted in drastic reductions in it, it also resulted in modification of the lever-press response. Once a ratio was completed and the glass filled, the circuit was so arranged that lever pressing could not resume until the drink had been consumed. Therefore, reduced consumption meant reduced lever pressing.

There are many ways that a subject in the Coral Bar could consume fewer drinks than he had previously consumed. If he did not press the lever at all, no drinks could become available. In the end, after reaching a high shock intensity, all of the subjects spent sessions in which they made absolutely no responses, and thus received no drinks. A possible pattern was rapid responding until the ratio was completed and the glass filled, followed by a long pause before the drink was consumed. This type of response, designated as a "pre-reinforcement" pause, was not found. Another possibility is that pausing could occur after a drink was consumed. The subject might run quickly through a ratio, consume his drink, and pause for a long period of time before beginning another ratio. In animal research, this pattern has been found to exist when the lever-press response had been punished. This post-reinforcement pause, however, was not found to any extent in the Coral Gables study.

An unpredicted occurrence did take place. It was found that lever pressing happened more slowly. This reduction in the rapidity of the lever press is called a reduction in local rate. For most subjects in the Coral Gables study, an increase in shock intensity brought about a lower local rate. Figure 18-8 relates local rate to shock intensity. As intensity increased, the slope of the cumulative record approached the horizontal plane. The subject whose data are presented in Figure 18-8 reached a 7 milliampere level and continued to make responses, but did not make enough during the session to yield even one reinforcement.

In this instance, punishment resulted in a reduction of local rate. In other instances in the literature where reinforcement has been forthcoming on a fixed-ratio schedule, punishment resulted in longer pausing, but did not affect local rate. This can perhaps be explained by the fact that in the present research it was the consuming response which was being punished and not lever pressing. Since shock was directly paired with the drinking of the alcoholic beverage, it may be thought of as subtracting from the rein-

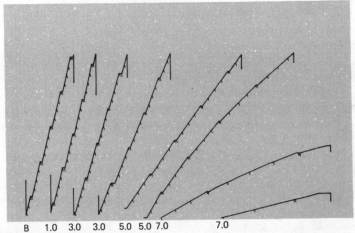

B   1.0   3.0   3.0   5.0 5.0 7.0   7.0

Figure 18-8 Response rate as a function of shock intensity (milliamperes)

forcing properties of the alcohol. As more shock was paired with drinking, the aversive aspects of the alcoholic beverages increased and local rate was further reduced.

It was mentioned in the chapter that any form of energy could be employed as a punisher if such considerations as intensity, anatomical location, and other variables were effectively arranged. It is also true that all forms of energy, under some conditions, may be reinforcing. Even electric shock may prove a positive reinforcer. Under some conditions, organisms may press a lever to introduce an electric shock.

Some writers have pointed out that human beings appear to spend a great portion of their existence seeking additional stimulation. Such mechanisms as "curiosity," "stimulus deprivation," and "exploratory instincts" have been suggested as bringing about these responses. Often we find that events which produce minute amounts of pain are reinforcing. Some find condiments which leave our mouths burning and even make our noses run delightful. Others engage in activities, such as sky-diving and underwater exploration, which appear to produce experiences which these enthusiasts describe as exhilarating. Most controversial is the present-day prevalence of such psychogenic agents as LSD and peyote. These drugs reportedly cause the users to experience increased stimulation from the environment, which they claim to be an extremely reinforcing event.

It is enough to say that no form of energy, event, substance, or experience can, before the fact, be categorized singularly as a punisher or a reinforcer. Rather, it should be said that all agents have the potential of being either under some circumstances, applications, and intensities.

The reader should not confuse the use of shock by psychologists as a punishing agent with the use of shock often administered by physicians in mental hospitals. The latter type of shock is referred to as electro-convulsive shock (ECS). The primary difference is in the area where the shock is administered and the physical results the current produces. With ECS, the current is directed through the skull and presumably passes through portions of the brain. It results in a form of seizure and usually renders the patient unconscious. Some physicians vow that ECS helps individuals suffering from severe mental disorders, making them more responsive to other forms of treatment. The data to substantiate this allegation do not strike the writers as convincing.

The behavioral use of electric shock does not involve the medical threat which electro-convulsive shock entails. In the cases presented in this chapter, the shock was of a relatively minute intensity and was specifically applied in areas far removed from vital organs or central nervous system tissue. Its purpose is merely to supply a brief punishing event. At no time will a competent psychologist use electric shock in such a manner as to prove physically injurious to the subject.

Punishment of Smoking Behavior

It may occur to the reader of this and remaining chapters that punishment should not be effective in eliminating behavior. Often the behavioral patterns which the psychologist seeks to eliminate already cause the individual considerable discomfort. One of my acquaintances is the most formidable candidate for a smoking cure that I have ever met. She spends most of her day coughing and having severe bronchial spasms. Her cigarette consumption is over three packages daily. She has been told by numerous physicians and by countless friends that smoking will kill her. She endures considerable unpleasantness created by smoking behavior. Similar situations are obtained with the alcoholic and with the case of the retarded child who reconsumed his food. These and many other behavioral problems which come to mind do produce drastic and sometimes fatal consequences. Yet the aversive consequences these behaviors produce naturally do not appear to reduce their frequency or tend to eliminate them.

The psychologists offer the explanation of long-term as opposed to short-term consequences. This is another way of saying that what happens is not nearly so important as when it happens. Human beings, like most organisms, operate primarily on short-term consequences. It is often the immediate reinforcement which supersedes the delayed punishment.

In employing punishment procedures, an attempt is made to make the undesired behavior immediately produce a punisher. Often the punishment this behavior produces, as programmed by the psychologist, is, relatively speaking, a minor consequence as compared to ultimate or long-term consequences if the behavior is not quickly eliminated.

Tabasco Road

A term often used to denote the effects of punishment on behavior is "suppression." Some writers have suggested that punishment can never totally eliminate response patterns. Rather, they suggest, punishment tends to suppress responding. They assume that given time, the response will return at its original rate, force, and topography.

Early research engendered this point of view, for it was found that many times the response remained eliminated only for brief periods of time. Generally, the more intense the punishment, the longer a period of time the response remained suppressed. This brings up an interesting point. Let us suppose that a particular individual exhibits an unwanted behavior, perhaps biting his fingernails. Imagine that on one occasion, and by happenstance, he placed his fingers in his mouth, began to chew on his nail, and at this precise moment was struck by a lightning bolt containing several thousands of volts. Given that our subject survives this experience, we might well suspect that he will refrain from biting his fingernails, perhaps for the remainder of his life, although he lives to be 105 years old. It is, under these conditions, not meaningful to say that the behavior was merely suppressed. For all intents and purposes, the response was eliminated. This kind of argument has led other researchers to speculate that if punishment is severe enough and is aptly arranged in relation to the response, it is possible to completely eliminate the response from the subject's repertoire. Provided the response never again returns, it remains a moot question and in many ways a meaningless question as to whether the response was merely suppressed or if indeed, the response itself was truly destroyed or obliterated.

Some psychologists, following the suppression notion, have suggested that at no time is behavior actually eliminated even when extinction takes place.

When behavior patterns apparently disappear, they are merely replaced by other behaviors, often referred to as competing responses or competing behaviors. A child who previously darted out into traffic received punishment on some occasion, and now the darting behavior has been replaced by clasping his parent's hand. In this case, clasping the hand of his parent is behavior which competes with darting into a line of traffic. This discussion is not easy to resolve, for organisms appear to be continuously developing new responses and forsaking old ones. Unless experimentally designed, it is difficult to identify such a relationship as replacement of one behavior by another.

It has been reliably found, however, that responses are eliminated more quickly if an alternative response which yields reinforcement can be provided. An individual who endures much discomfort in the coal mines may persist at this job for years in order to make a living for his family. If the opportunity to make a livelihood in some less aversive manner occurs, the coal mine behavior, will, in all probability, be replaced. The punishment the worker previously received in the coal mine was not enough to eliminate that response until a reinforced alternate response was available. In the next chapters we will see how the training of a competing response helped to eliminate self-injuring behavior in a retardate.

19

PUNISHMENT PRODUCED BY CONTINGENT WITHDRAWAL OF A POSITIVE REINFORCER

Paying the Price

Dr. Mathie leaned back in his chair. He tried to conceal a yawn as he listened to the man seated across the desk from him continue with his soulful story of self-depreciation and blame.[1]

"I don't know what it is, Doctor. It's terrible—other people don't have this problem. When I was at home—before they sent me here to the hospital, after work I would start to watch TV. Then after maybe a half an hour, I would find myself getting restless, and the first thing you know I would go outside. Maybe I'd walk for a long time before it happened, for blocks and blocks. Sooner or later there would be a house, one with the window shade pulled up. There was this one house I went by for two weeks every night before the police finally caught me. The woman who lived there wasn't even a good-looking one; she was old, really old. I just couldn't help peeking in the window. You see what I mean, Doc. I just can't help myself. I'd give anything, do anything, if I could get over this. I just can't do it, Doc!"

Dr. Mathie listened with only half an ear. He'd heard this patient's account dozens of times before. The story itself and the self-degrading verbalizations had ceased to be of great interest to him. The man speaking was known, in the terms of the clinical psychologist, as a voyeur. A voyeur is colloquially called a "Peeping Tom." It can be said that this behavior is strongly reinforcing for these individuals. The patient had been arrested for this activity, and rather than face a jail sentence, he had committed himself to the hospital for observation and treatment. This cycle of voyeuristic behavior, arrest, and self-commitment had been repeated many times in the past years.

Each time the man was recommitted to the hospital, he came under the care

1. This section based on Mathie, James. The elimination of undesirable behavior through self-administered negative reinforcement. Address delivered at Brocksville VA Hospital, Brocksville, Ohio; second annual conference on Man's Adjustment, 1967.

and attention of Dr. Mathie. In the past year, Dr. Mathie had heard the same story twice weekly for an hour. Each time the patient appeared to be trying to convince Dr. Mathie of his sincerity in wanting to cease his behavior pattern.

It is just as true in the psychotherapy session as it is elsewhere that talk is cheap. Lately, Dr. Mathie had found himself wondering just exactly what this patient would give up in order to stop his behavior. Perhaps now was the time to try and approach the problem that he'd been considering for some time.

"Do you have any money?" Dr. Mathie asked.

"What? Money?" The patient was stunned by the sudden change in the trend of the therapy session.

"Yes," Dr. Mathie said, "Do you have money? Do you have a five-dollar bill?"

Puzzled, the man reached into the pocket of his blue patient's uniform and pulled out a five-dollar bill. Dr. Mathie took it from him, held it between his fingers for a moment, and then much to the amazement and anguish of his patient, took out his lighter, lighted the bill, and watched it begin to burn.

"Wait," the patient said, "That's my money! That's real!"

"I know," Mr. Mathie said, disposing of the bill in the ashtray. "Now, did you enjoy that?"

"You've got to be kidding," the patient said. "I don't have that much spending money, you know. Most of my money goes to my wife and family."

"Tell me, how did you feel when I burned that bill?" Dr. Mathie asked.

"I felt awful, Doc. I mean, you know, it's such a waste to burn money like that."

"All right," Dr. Mathie said. "Here is what I want you to do. Next week you'll be leaving here. What I would like for you to do is the following: each time you feel yourself getting to the point where you would like to go peep into a window, you must pull out a five-dollar bill and burn it then and there, right on the spot. Each time you do it, you must burn another five-dollar bill."

"You don't mean it," the man said.

"Yes, that's exactly what I mean," Dr. Mathie said, "and if you want me to really help you with your problem, you'll do exactly as I say, or do you still really want to end your problem?"

"Of course I do." The patient said, "I'll go along with it, but I just don't think I like the idea."

"You will do it though," Dr. Mathie said.

"Yes," the patient said.

"Good. I want you to begin this procedure as soon as you're discharged and tell me what happened when I see you next week."

The patient returned the following week. "Good Lord, Doc," he said, "that was the most painful thing I ever did in my life. I burned up two five-dollar bills and that was enough. From then on, I stayed at home and watched television. I mean, I wouldn't even dare go out on the street."

"So the bill burning really worked," Dr. Mathie said.

"I'll say it did!"

The patient continued to see Dr. Mathie for several months. He reported that he felt he was completely cured of his Peeping-Tom impulses. Although Dr. Mathie did not take steps to watch his patient at home or otherwise directly observe his behavior, he was pleased to find the patient was never again brought to the attention of the authorities, and as far as Dr. Mathie could tell, had stopped his voyeurism.

Later, Dr. Mathie used the same general procedure with a college professor. The college professor's problem was the violent arguments he engaged in with his colleagues. In the past few years, due to his vicious harangues, he had become one of the most unpopular men on the campus.

Dr. Mathie briefly explained the treatment to the professor; "It involves giving up one of your most prized possessions or activities whenever you commit the behavior you're interested in eliminating."

"What could I ever give up? You won't take wives, will you?" the professor jokingly asked.

"I'm afraid not," Dr. Mathie said, "but I do have one suggestion. I suppose as a college professor, you have a pretty extensive library."

"Yes," the professor said. "I'm one of those people who hang onto every book they ever had."

"That's it, then," Dr. Mathie said. "Each time you get into an argument with one of your colleagues, you must rush right home, take one of your most beloved books, and throw it into the fireplace."

"Throw it into the fireplace?" the professor said. He took out his handkerchief and began to wipe his forehead. "I don't think I could ever do that."

"You're not willing to try," Dr. Mathie said. "I don't believe you're serious about your problem. If you're careful and get into no arguments, you'll find that you'll lose no books at all."

Shortly thereafter the professor reported that his behavior was well under control. It had painfully cost him one volume.

In dealing with the problem behaviors of his patients, Dr. Mathie applied a principle well ingrained in common knowledge and use. Poets have long written about the anguish of love lost, freedom relinquished, or soul diminished. The psychologist merely restates these facts in a more objective nomenclature.

The removal of a reinforcer following a response can be defined as a punishment procedure. The result of this punishment procedure is a reduction in the rate of the response with which it is associated. If the removal of a reinforcer in this manner results in a reduction, the removal can be termed a punisher.

In the foregoing chapter we discussed one form of punishment procedure in which physical energy was applied to the organism following a response. In Dr. Mathie's study, a second form of punishment procedure is introduced, the removal of a positive reinforcer following a specific response. If the events in either procedure are truly punishers, they will result in a reduction in the rate of the response with which they are associated.

The removal of a positive reinforcer does not in and of itself define a punishment procedure. A punishment procedure employing the removal of a positive reinforcer must be distinguished from an extinction procedure, which also involves removal of a positive reinforcer and similarly results in the reduction of response rate.

In an extinction procedure, reinforcement which previously followed the response is withheld. The response no longer produces reinforcement. The precise time at which an extinction procedure is introduced is controlled by the experimenter. The removal or reintroduction of reinforcement is in no way directly controlled by the organism.

In a punishment procedure employing removal of a positive reinforcer, the response emitted by the organism has the immediate and direct effect of removing a reinforcer which is already available. Removal of the reinforcer in this case is directly controlled by the organism. As his response rate declines, the reinforcer is no longer withdrawn. When an extinction procedure is in effect, the response rate of the organism has no effect whatsoever on the availability of reinforcement.

Dr. Mathie used this form of punishment procedure in dealing with what are usually classified as problems of clinical psychology. He first established those things or events which appeared to be most reinforcing for his patients. Through enlisting their cooperation, he was able to arrange a situation in which the emission of the undesirable behavior on the part of the patient resulted in the temporary or even permanent loss of this reinforcer.

It may occur to the reader that there are many problems associated with Dr. Mathie's approach. First of all, the cooperation of the patients was required. Dr. Mathie was not capable of following each patient around all day and taking away a book or burning a five-dollar bill when they had misbehaved. This degree of vigilance is possible with some institutionalized patients with other problems.

Punishment of Self-Injuring with Withdrawal of Physical Contact

One of the most perplexing problems to face the staff in institutions is the patient with self-injurious behaviors. In the first chapter of this book, we discussed one such case and how this problem was eliminated. You are now knowledgeable enough to identify the procedure employed as a punishment procedure in which electric shock followed each response. The boy in that study exhibited head banging which is one of the more common self-injurious behaviors observed in institution populations.

Another form of punishment, the removal of the reinforcer following a self-injurious response, can also be used to reduce the frequency of self-injuring behavior.[2] This technique was used on Sam, a nine-year-old resident of an institution for the mentally retarded. Sam was in difficulty from the beginning of his life. He was hospitalized shortly after his fifth birthday. During the next four years, he received individual and group psychotherapy and dozens of drugs which were employed to curb his hyperactivity, screaming, and most important, his self-injurious behavior. None of these procedures proved adequate.

2. This section based on Tate, B. G., and Baroff, G. S. Aversive control of self-injurious behavior. *Behaviour Research and Therapy*, 1966, 4, 281–287.

The self-injurious behavior began when he was four and, at that time, consisted only of face slapping. By the time he was nine, he had developed new methods of injuring himself which included banging his head against floors and walls, slapping his face, punching his face and head with his fist, hitting his shoulder with his chin, and kicking himself. He had also developed bilateral cataracts and the retinas of both eyes were partially detached. One physician declared that part of his eye difficulty was a result of the self-injuring behavior. Sam was all but blind when he was transferred to the Murdock Center in North Carolina where the following treatment took place. A person who has not seen such a child cannot easily believe how desperately he needs help.

When Sam first came to Murdock Center, he was observed for two weeks in the infirmary to which he was initially assigned. During this two-week period members of the Psychology Department Staff who had planned to work with him merely observed him and got to know him as well as they could. Aside from the scars and wounds of repeated injury, Sam was not a bad-looking little boy; but he was not truly verbal. He did often utter some words in a high-pitched, whining manner, but they were mostly gibberish and made no sense.

The one behavior pattern which the experimenters found of interest and ultimately of great value was Sam's reliable response to other people. Whenever Sam was approached by people, whether they were attendants or visitors or psychologists, he was almost invariably observed to try to wrap his arms about them, climb into their laps, or cling to them, holding his body closely to theirs. When allowed to do this, he seemed more tranquil. But when he was left alone and free, he would cry, scream, hit himself, or bang his head. There was no alternative but to keep him fully restrained and in bed where he was usually calm and was no immediate danger to himself. After this two-week period of casual observation, more direct observations were made of Sam's self-injuring behaviors.

Frequency counts were made of self-injuring behavior under different conditions and with different samplings of Sam's behavior. It was found that if left unrestrained, he reliably hit himself approximately two times per minute. It was apparent that if Sam were allowed freedom of arms and hands and was alone, away from body contact with others, he might rapidly destroy himself.

At this time the psychologist supervising the case suggested that a punishment procedure might work with Sam. They elected to use one involving the removal of a reinforcer. The reinforcer the experimenters employed was an extraordinary one. Observation of Sam had led them to believe that physical contact was reinforcing for him, and conversely, that being alone, particularly when he was standing or walking, was a situation which he seemed to avoid. If indeed human contact was a reinforcing event, then its withdrawal should be punishing. Furthermore, if it was arranged such that withdrawing human contact occurred after each self-injuring response, then it should effectively act as a punisher for the undesirable behavior and result in a reduction of the response rate.

With this general strategy guiding the experimenters, the following procedure was effected. Typically, Sam was restrained in his bed except for morning baths which were given by the attendants and for daily walks around the institution grounds and through the corridors. These walks were conducted by two female research assistants who had been working with and observing Sam for several weeks. During these tours, the assistants walked beside Sam, each one holding a hand. They talked to Sam as they walked along the corridors and were initially careful to do nothing verbally or physically when Sam made self-injuring responses. For five consecutive days, self-injuring responses were counted and recorded during these walks. Each walk took approximately the same length of time each day. When the tour was terminated, Sam was returned to his room, undressed, placed in bed, and restrained.

On the sixth through tenth days, a new procedure was introduced. In order to understand this procedure more fully, it would be well to remember Sam's physical condition. He was almost totally blind. The ordinary physical contact which is pleasing to most of us has added value to Sam. Other people had to serve as his eyes. In the past, contact with other people, his mother, attendants, and those different individuals looking out for his welfare, was followed by food, candy, caring words, warmth, security, and comfort. Thus, for Sam, physical contact was an extremely effective form of a generalized reinforcer. The experimenters also noticed that physical contact seemed to be most reinforcing to Sam when he was walking or otherwise removed from the friendly and well-known environment of his ward and crib. In this strange, and perhaps hostile environment, physical contact took on added importance for Sam.

Therefore, after five days of baseline data had been collected in which the self-injurious responses were merely ignored, the following procedure was used. Remember that the actual treatment took place when Sam was taken on walks along the corridors and the institution grounds. During these walks, the two experimenters held Sam's hands, one on either side. Now whenever Sam made a self-injurious response, typically in the form of hitting his chin on his shoulder or

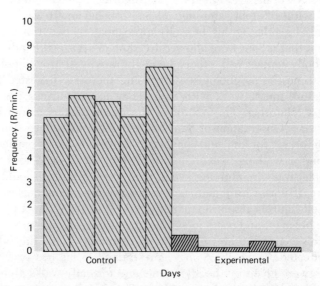

Figure 19-1 Self-injurious behavior followed by the removal of physical contact

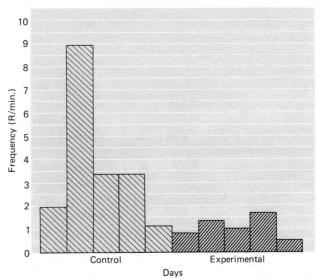

Figure 19-2   Self-injurious behavior not followed by the removal of physical contact

slamming his head against his chest, this response was immediately followed by the removal of physical contact. The research assistants immediately withdrew their hands from Sam's, leaving him essentially unsupported and unprotected from what might lie ahead in his dark world.

Figure 19-1 depicts the five days of baseline data followed by five days in which each self-injury produced the removal of physical contact.

The frequency of self-injury was reduced drastically when physical contact was removed. This reduction defined the operation of removal of physical contact as a powerful punisher for Sam.

In order to further demonstrate the punishing effects of this event, another five days of observations were made in which self-injury was not followed by removal of physical contact. As you might expect, the frequency of self-injury increased. Finally, five more days of punishment were programmed; these brought about reduction in self-injury to zero levels. These last two phases of the procedure are presented in Figure 19-2.

There is good reason to believe that social contact, although not necessarily of a physical nature, is a powerful reinforcer for most of us. In past pages, we have witnessed how social reinforcement was used to establish new responses and to maintain old and sometimes unwanted ones. But can removal of social interaction serve to reduce a specific behavior, and thus act as a punisher? Let us see.

Punishment of Compulsive Stealing in a Small Boy

Mike's case records read like a modern-day version of *Gulliver's Travels*. When he was seven years old, he was placed in school, but was soon dropped with the recommendation to his parents that he be sent to a special public school for problem children. His problem in school seemed to be that he could not get along with the other children and that he had been caught stealing from both the teachers and children on several occasions.[3] His parents did not enjoy the trouble Mike had caused them throughout the years. His stealing created a constant problem with the neighbors. Mike was also destructive. When his mother tried to confine him to his room, he commonly burst open the screen and escaped to wander. His mother admitted that she was no longer fond of him.

After a few weeks in the special school for problem children, he was expelled. His parents had had enough of Mike. They placed him out for adoption by foster parents.

Mike was, to all appearances, a normal eight-year-old, and seemed to give and receive affection quite readily. The agency had no trouble in finding him a foster home, but soon he was returned with the same problem. Throughout the next two years, Mike was to find himself in many different homes and settings. He was all but a displaced person. Finally he was sent to a training home for disturbed children. At first he seemed to adjust well at the institution. Initially, the primary problem was tantrum behavior and crying, but this soon ceased. Later Mike began to present a bedwetting problem, and his stealing steadily worsened while he was at the home. In fact, some of the professional staff at the home had described him as a "kleptomaniac." (A kleptomaniac is a person who has a compulsion to steal things.) Other members of the staff described Mike as a veritable pack-rat. At any given time, a thorough frisking would reveal numerous articles taken not only from other children within the institution, but from the psychologist, social workers, janitors, and other staff members.

We have already said that some of the professionals at the institution really felt that Mike suffered from a disease which caused him to steal. Others felt that Mike's stealing was maintained by attention; if nothing was said about Mike's stealing, it would extinguish. But of course, it is difficult to use this course of action when it is your belongings which are being stolen. Approaching Mike directly with an accusing finger did not seem to be the answer. Often he would deny guilt or place the blame on others. He concluded his performance by accusing others of not trusting him and blaming him for things he did not do.

A psychologist who made frequent visits to the training school soon became acquainted with Mike and his problems. While the psychologist did not spend enough time at the school to work out a program to alleviate some of Mike's behavior problems, he felt that he could train the staff at the school in behavioral principles and encourage them to carry out a program.

Accordingly, he conducted an abbreviated course in behavioral psychology. He talked about principles of positive reinforcement, punishment, extinction, schedules of reinforcement, and many of the topics we have discussed in this book. After the course, the psychologist suggested that the staff should try to design a behavioral program which could deal with Mike's stealing behavior. Unanimously, the group rejected spanking or other forms of abuse. They found these procedures repugnant. One type of punishment procedure that was accept-

3. This section based on Wetzel, R. J. The use of behavioral techniques in a case of compulsive stealing. Unpublished manuscript, University of Arizona, 1966.

able, however, involved the removal of privileges. After all, they reasoned, if you remove the privilege, you're merely taking away something that was given in addition. It wasn't as though you were really depriving him or inflicting pain or hurt. This reasoning was perfectly acceptable to the psychologist. That form of punishment, namely, the removal of reinforcement following an unwanted response, had proven in the past to be effective. If it were also one that was acceptable to the staff at the school, he was pleased.

Finding the proper reinforcer became paramount to the success and continuation of the project. Some of the staff members believed that there was nothing Mike cared enough about to make any difference in his stealing behavior. Others who had perhaps watched Mike more carefully had noticed that he was a highly sociable boy, and appeared to enjoy interactions with others. One particular person whom Mike seemed to be fond of was a Mexican woman who served as a cook for the pupils and staff. Her name was Maria, and she did not speak English. She already had seemed to have developed a fondness for Mike, who was himself of Mexican extraction. Often he was seen in the kitchen, where occasionally Maria gave him treats and talked to him in Spanish. The group agreed that Maria's interactions with Mike could be highly reinforcing for him. They could, therefore, possibly do the job they had in mind.

The procedure evolving from their discussions took the following form: the staff was to carefully observe and record Mike's stealing behavior; each day they were to count the number of articles Mike had stolen. In this way they could get some idea of whether his stealing was reducing in frequency. During the time the staff was beginning to record these baseline data, Maria was busy in the kitchen developing her relationship with Mike. Occasionally she took Mike home with her, and often brought him tortillas and other edible treats from her home. She spent a great deal of time with him in the kitchen talking to him softly in Spanish. Mike seemed to enjoy Maria's company immensely.

After some weeks during which baseline data were collected, the following program was put into effect. If Mike was observed to steal even one article, Maria was to come to Mike and effectively impart the following to him: "Mike, it has been reported to me that you were stealing. Because of your stealing, I cannot spend any more time with you today." Then she was to walk away and say nothing further.

On the first day the program was put into effect, Mike was seen taking some items from one of the closets. Maria was not available since it was late in the afternoon, but was told of the incident the following morning. Immediately she told Mike that she had learned that he had been stealing, and that she could not see him for that day. Mike did not seem to take this refusal very hard. He continued to hang around the kitchen for some minutes, whereupon, Maria repeated her statement. Ultimately, Mike was told by one of the social workers to return to his cottage. Mike obeyed, and was said to be "pouty" for some hours thereafter. The staff did not observe any stealing for the next 13 days. Soon, however, an increased frequency of matches, cookies, and other essentially valueless small items were found in Mike's possession. The staff members were reluctant to report these items to Maria since they were trivial.

This failure to stick to the strict definitions of the program caused the psychologist to intervene. In conversation with the staff, he made it clear that even the most insignificant item should be reported and followed by the agreed consequence. The behavior which was to be punished was the taking of items which did not belong to Mike; in truth, the value of the items was of no importance. All thefts should be equally and reliably punished by the removal of Maria's attentions.

After some discussion, the staff members saw the necessity of treating Mike's stealing consistently. That same day Mike was found to have some personal items belonging to the other children. Maria again rejected Mike. Ten days passed without another incident.

After only a few more slips, Mike's stealing behavior was apparently eliminated. Several months went by during which no stolen items were found in Mike's possession.

One day Mike announced to a group of the staff members that he did not intend to steal anymore. A short time later, Mike spent some money he had earned to buy some items for some of the other children. He claimed to be paying them back for some of the items he had previously stolen. Not only was Mike "reformed," but he was also willing to make restitution to his victims.

Punishment of Cigarette Smoking by Threat of Withdrawal of Money

In the previous chapter, cigarette smoking was punished by an electric current coming from a portable unit worn by smokers. At some point during smoking behavior an unavoidable shock was delivered to him. This punishment procedure proved effective. Cigarette smoking can also be dealt with by the delay or withdrawal of a positive reinforcer.[4]

At the height of public awareness of possible danger in cigarette smoking, two psychologists at Dartmouth College became interested in the problem. They found, as many others have found, that there were no procedures which had been proven to be really effective in helping a patient or client to quit smoking.

Although information on the possible detrimental effects of smoking was widely circulated, the lack of immediacy of this threat was obviously of no value in reducing smoking frequency. If a threat was to be effective, implications must be immediately obvious and real. The psychologists felt that they must arrange such an immediate threat if they hoped to help people stop smoking.

Their plan was simple. It required that individuals interested in stopping smoking should deposit an amount of money with the experimenters. If the subject refrained from smoking, he could regain his investment. If he continued to smoke, the money was forfeited.

They placed an advertisement in the Dartmouth College paper which an-

4. This section based on Tighe, T. J., and Elliott, R. Breaking the cigarette habit: Effects of a technique involving threatened loss of money. Paper presented at American Psychological Association Convention, Washington, D.C., September 1, 1967.

nounced a meeting for individuals who smoked more than a pack of cigarettes a day and wished to stop smoking. During this meeting, those who attended were lectured by the two experimenters on how behaviors, such as the smoking behaviors, were formed and eliminated. They also reiterated some of the more basic and striking data on the possible harmfulness of cigarette smoking. At this time, the smokers were also informed of the details of further treatment. The authors found out that those attending the meetings averaged 1.5 packs of cigarettes smoked per day and had smoked for an average of 5.4 years.

The audience was told to return in three days with $50.00 each. The $50.00 would be turned over to the psychologist and a statement signed which included the following provisions:

1. A pledge vowing they would not smoke or otherwise indulge in the use of tobacco in any form for a period of 15 weeks.

2. An agreement that if the participant refrained from using tobacco for two days, $10 of his money would be returned. If he abstained for two weeks from the beginning date, he could receive an additional $10; if he abstained for 11 weeks from the beginning, he would receive a third amount, this time $15. If he finished the full 15 weeks, at the end of this time he would receive the remaining $15.

3. If the client smoked or otherwise used tobacco at any time during the 15-week period, he would report this fact and forfeit all money that had not already been returned to him through the above provisions. The money that he forfeited was to be divided equally among the participants in the program who succeeded in abstaining for the entire 15-week period.

4. The participant also agreed to read an article on the physical effects of smoking. This particular article pointed out in great and gory detail some of the more harmful results cigarette smoking might cause.

5. The individual agreed to have his name published in the notices section of the student newspaper to the effect that he was a participant in a program in which he had agreed not to smoke for 15 weeks or to forfeit the money if he did. This last provision had the effect of requiring the individual to make a public commitment and, therefore, placed a great deal of pressure on him to keep his word.

The results of this procedure were striking. Eighty-four percent went for the full 15 weeks without smoking and then received all their money back. Only four failed to go along with the procedure and ended by losing their money. Seventeen months later, the follow-up was made on the smoking behavior of the participants. Forty-six percent of those who participated were still not smoking—an impressive figure indeed.

Summary

A new punishment procedure was introduced in this chapter. Unlike the procedure introduced earlier where physical energy is applied to the organism, the procedure discussed in this chapter involves the removal of a positive reinforcer following the occurrence of a specific response.

1. The removal of an event, commodity, or privilege which is a known reinforcer following a specific response is a *punishment procedure*.

2. If the response with which the removal of the reinforcer follows decreases in rate, the removal of the reinforcer can be called a *punisher*.

3. It is reasonable to assume that all reinforcers can become punishers if employed properly. In this chapter, one psychologist solicited the aid of his patients in removing their own reinforcers after making the response they wished to see eliminated. Withdrawal of body contact proved to be an effective punisher for self-injurious behavior in a retarded child. Withdrawal of social contact effectively eliminated the stealing behavior of an institutionalized boy when withdrawal was associated with stealing. Finally, threat of the loss of money acted to eliminate smoking behavior in a sample of college volunteers.

QUESTIONS

1. What specific event did Dr. Mathie arrange for the man who was a "Peeping Tom"?
2. What is a voyeur?
3. What type of consequence did Dr. Mathie arrange for the college professor who persisted in arguments?
4. The events or commodities Dr. Mathie removed were: (a) distinguishers; (b) negative reinforcers; (c) positive reinforcers; (d) S^Ds.
5. The fact that the removal of these events or commodities was arranged to follow an occurrence of the unwanted behavior defines this procedure as a p_____ procedure.
6. The fact that removal of these commodities or events following the unwanted response resulted in a reduction of the frequency of the behavior defines the removal of these events as: (a) a punisher; (b) positive reinforcement; (c) negative reinforcement; (d) S^D.
7. The fact that the contingent removal of these events or commodities resulted in a reduction of the unwanted behavior means that they were positive reinforcers. (a) True; (b) False.
8. There are two sets of operations which may define a punishment procedure. Briefly, what are these procedures?
9. Can you think of a positive reinforcer whose removal might serve as a punisher for you? What behavior would you punish in this way?
10. In the first chapter of this book we talked about a self-injuring child. What form of punishment was used to eliminate this behavior?
11. In the study discussed in this chapter with the self-injuring child, another type of punishment was used. What was it?
12. Sam had not received any professional treatment or care at all before the psychologist began to work with him. (a) True; (b) False.
13. The doctor suggested that all of Sam's eye problems were the result of self-injuring behavior. (a) True; (b) False.
14. Punishment will not work if it is self-administered. (a) True; (b) False.
15. During the two weeks of the observation period, the staff at the institution found that Sam: (a) did not like the company of others; (b) always hit others with his

fist when they approached; (c) seemed to enjoy the company of others; (d) liked people when he was restrained but not when he was unrestrained.

16. Why was it necessary to restrain Sam?

17. Sam was observed for 30 days and his self-injuring responses were counted. His rate of self-injury was approximately: (a) 20 per minute; (b) 2 per minute; (c) 250 per minute; (d) .5 per minute.

18. What was the reinforcer the experimenters decided to withdraw as a punisher? In your opinion, why might this be more effective with Sam than with a normal child?

19. What was the result of the withdrawal of physical support on Sam's self-injury?

20. After self-injury was reduced by the withdrawal of physical contact, an additional five days more of data were collected during which physical contact was not withdrawn. What happened to the rate of the self-injuring behavior?

21. A final five days of data were collected. Briefly, what procedure was in effect during this time?

22. Mike's basic problem during this time was "compulsive" _____.

23. Ultimately, Mike was placed in a foster home because: (a) his parents were killed in an accident; (b) he went to jail; (c) his parents were too poor to support him; (d) his mother no longer cared to have him around.

24. What behavior does a kleptomaniac frequently engage in?

25. The first thing the psychologist did at the home where Mike was maintained was: (a) to conduct a course in behavioral psychology with the staff; (b) to administer electric shock to Mike; (c) to give Mike psychotherapy; (d) to deny that kleptomania was a disease.

26. What was the positive reinforcer which the group decided to remove following each stealing incident?

27. What was Maria's professional duty in the school where Mike was maintained? (a) Chief psychiatrist; (b) Cook; (c) Social worker; (d) Attendant.

28. Before any experimental conditions were imposed on Mike, he spent considerable initial periods of time with Maria. (a) True; (b) False.

29. Briefly explain what Maria was instructed to do after she found out that Mike had stolen during the previous observation.

30. What ultimately happened to Mike's stealing behavior as a result of this consequence?

31. In the study presented in this chapter on smoking behavior, what was used as a punisher?

32. The threat which experimenters arranged for smoking involved the loss of: (a) a cigarette; (b) lung tissue; (c) money; (d) social interaction.

33. How did the experimenters get the subjects for the study?

34. At the organizational meeting with the subjects, the experimenters lectured on the dangers of smoking, and later told those still interested to return later with $50. (a) True; (b) False.

35. Those subjects who returned were required to sign various agreements. Which of the following were not included? (a) A pledge vowing they would not use any form of tobacco for a period of 12 weeks; (b) An agreement stating that money would be returned at various times; (c) If the subject smoked, he would lose all remaining money; (d) The subject agreed to have his name published in *Life* magazine as anti-cigarette.

36. What percentage of subjects quit smoking for the full period of time in this study as the result of this technique? (a) 50 percent; (b) 84 percent; (c) 74 percent; (d) 22 percent.

37. Seventeen months later a follow-up was done on smoking behavior in the partici-

pants. What percentage still refrained from smoking? (a) 46 percent; (b) 12 percent; (c) less than 5 percent; (d) 92 percent.

NOTES
Paying the Price

For many years psychologists relied heavily on the verbal reports of their patients as the basic data of their investigations. There was the feeling among the early psychologists that the verbal behavior of an individual, by necessity, was required to be related to objective events.

Today the use of verbal behavior as the basic datum, without substantiation by other sources, has come to be extensively disapproved by experimental psychologists. By and large, these verbal reports are still used in clinical practice. It is the exception rather than the rule that a practicing clinical psychologist or psychiatrist will collect any direct observational data on events transpiring outside of the clinical session.

It is ironic that Sigmund Freud was among the first clinical practitioners to observe that verbal reports cannot be accepted without qualification as reflecting a reality outside the office and clinical couch. Later, listening to his female patients tell vividly of experiences of a bizarre sexual nature, Freud came to realize that these verbal reports could not, in most cases, be founded on what had actually happened. His conclusion was that the verbal reports his patients had given him in many instances did not represent true events, but rather were imagined or produced by the client's active feeling for fiction and fabrication of detail.

Today clinical psychologists are taking into account the possible lack of validity of verbal reports, especially where there is obvious possible advantage in giving a particular report. Regardless of what steps parents take to punish lying, even the best behaved child soon learns that it is not always in his best interest to tell the truth. Often truthfulness may result in severe criticism or punishment. On the other hand, bending the truth a small amount may result in considerable positive reinforcement.

Dr. Mathie's study in which patients were required by the therapy procedure to administer their own punishment and to keep a reliable count of their own behavior was weakened greatly by this reliance upon the client's verbal reports and self-monitoring. Dr. Mathie was as aware of this shortcoming as anyone. During his presentation of this research to a gathering, he was quick to point out this basic flaw in the design. This does not detract in any way from the ingenuity and insight into the principles of behavior which are an integral part of Dr. Mathie's formulations. It remains for others to develop techniques which will allow for the objectification and monitoring of the subjects' behavior independent of his verbal behavior. If, for instance, we are to know precisely how many times an alcoholic takes a drink or how much he consumes, we must find a method of acquiring this information which does not rely on the subjects' verbal report. The only other alternative is to find a method of ensuring that the verbal report of the subjects will always reliably reflect the physical events.

Punishment of Self-Injury by Withdrawal of Physical Contact

In previous instances we have not hesitated to point out the importance of experimental control procedures in any form of behavior modification endeavor, whether it be pure research or even a procedure aimed and directed at bettering the patient's welfare.

The case in which a young boy's self-injuring behavior was reduced by the withdrawal of physical contact is a case in point. The experimenters found it necessary to go through the following procedures to assess the scientific merit of their techniques. First, baseline data were collected during the time in which self-injuring responses were not followed by withdrawal. Physical contact was then introduced as an event following each instance the child emitted a self-injuring response. The result of this procedure was an immediate and drastic reduction in the rate of this response. At this point, the experimenters used a reversal procedure. Physical contact was maintained regardless of the child's behavior, and the self-injuring behavior rose immediately. In the final phase, the withdrawal of physical contact was reintroduced and again resulted in reductions in the response rate.

For some readers it may appear that control procedures are unnecessary. In the writers' opinion, this may sometimes be the case. It is also true, however, that not using the proper controls can result in the drawing of conclusions which may not necessarily hold.

A cogent example of this can be seen in data collected by a student under the supervision of one of the authors. A young adult was referred to Psychology Service because he exhibited a high frequency of self-injuring behavior. The attendants claimed that the patient, whose name was Frank, spent many hours of his time slapping his own face, and was, therefore, restrained. The student was dispatched to observe the behavior and to collect baseline data on the rate of the response.

The data the student collected are presented in Figure 19-3. The shape these data take across days is a very interesting one. On initial sessions the rate was very high, but as observation periods continued, the rate dropped and ultimately reached zero. It must be stressed that the student was doing nothing at all. He was not, to his knowledge, introducing punishment, extinction, or any other procedure which should result in this

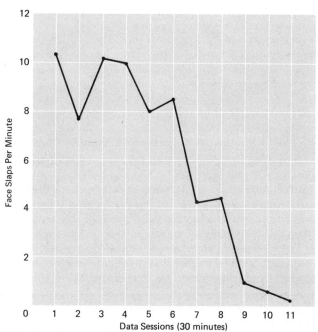

Figure 19-3 Drop in rate of self-injurious behavior during baseline observation

decrease. The procedure of collecting baseline data resulted in a reduction of the rate of the behavior.

This occasionally will occur, and the experimenter has no prior knowledge of when it might. Suppose that the experimenter in this case had some preconceived hunch that yelling loudly at the patient and scolding him would be an effective means of reducing self-injuring behavior. If this same individual had not bothered to take baseline data, as indeed the student saw fit to do, and given that yelling had no effect at all, we would still see the same data as in Figure 19-3. Upon seeing the reductions in the rate of the behavior, this experimenter might conclude that yelling was an extremely effective method of reducing self-injury. He might go as far as to publish an account of his experiment, or merely spread the word to other individuals at other institutions. We can see at this point the importance of baseline and reversals. If our hypothetical experimenter had taken the trouble to collect baseline data, he would have found, as the student actually found, that taking baseline observation alone was enough to reduce the behavior.

This points out the importance of control procedures and that we must not only be able to eliminate a behavior, but must identify specifically what variables resulted in the reduction. A witch doctor who is charged to cure a patient may go through the following behaviors. He may first dance around his prone patient muttering and calling on the gods of the four winds to help him. He may then tear out several hairs of the patient's head and bury them in dark recesses of an ancient hollow tree. He may then place a lizard's tail and a toenail of the patient and various other items into a large kettle along with them some strange looking herbs and bark. After enticing the patient to drink a small amount of brew, he may well cure him.

The basic question a scientist must ask himself if he wishes to learn from the witch doctor is exactly what operations or behaviors, what parts of the long drawn out treatment the witch doctor performed, were really effective in bringing about the cure, and which were truly superfluous. A scientist must always seek to identify those variables which are truly important in bringing about an effect and separate them from other variables which may appear to be associated, but which in truth are not necessary. Unless a behavioral scientist is aware of control procedures, he may make the same mistake as the witch doctor and may thus often overlook important variables and encourage other treatments which are really of no pertinence and therefore of limited value to science or society.

Decrease of Cigarette Smoking by Threat of
Withdrawal or Loss of Money

The possible hazards of relying on verbal reports as data has been discussed in a previous section. The cigarette-smoking study reported in this chapter suffers from basically the same shortcoming. The experimenters were fully aware of this problem and took some steps to reduce the probability of false reports. Subjects in the study were first required to sign a pledge. The pledge was an extremely official-looking and sounding document. In no uncertain terms, it identified the behavior which the subject was required to maintain if he was to keep from relinquishing his investment. There is no guarantee that a subject will sign such a document and then comply. However, in our culture this type of agreement tends to be binding. Most individuals are more likely to stick to the terms of such a formalized and official document than they would be to those of a casual agreement. This procedure probably helped to reduce the problem of the likelihood of cheating. Along the same lines, the information that the subject was participating in a smoking experiment and was, therefore, not to smoke for a period of weeks was made public, in fact, published in a school newspaper. Friends and acquaintances of the subject were thus made aware that the individual was participating in such an experiment. If his friends saw him smoking after he had agreed to the contract, they would most assuredly bring it to his attention and many of them might well become upset at his lack of character or even regard him with some contempt in the future. The fact that others knew about this commitment served to decrease the likelihood of cheating still further and, perhaps, was even more effective than the signing of the document. Neither of these procedures ruled out the possibility that the individual might cheat. It was entirely possible that some of the subjects smoked late at night, among strangers, or in out-of-the-way places. Given that they did spend considerable time with friends and acquaintances, we can at least presume that the safeguards reduced their smoking, even if occasional cheating did occur. As follow-up procedures demonstrated, a significant number still reported that they were not smoking.

Self-Control

If behavior is determined, then the people who know the causes of their own actions will best be able to control them. Some people deny that their behavior is determined and therefore do not seek to delineate its causes. They argue that they have complete control over their own behavior; however, as a consequence of their ignorance, these people may in fact have less control than they think. At first glance, the combination of determinism and self-control would seem to be incompatible, but this is not the case. Strange as it may seem, the man that denies that he has freedom of choice may come closest to obtaining it.

The basic problem of self-control arises in situations where there is the physical opportunity to make two or more responses, or in some cases, to respond or not to respond. Consider the student who has an hour exam two weeks away and is confronted with the opportunity to make two responses; he may study for the hour exam, or may watch television. All too frequently, the student will say that he should be studying for the hour exam but will watch television instead. When questioned about the discrepancy between his verbal behavior and his motor behavior, he may reply that he simply lacks sufficient will power to study when he can watch television. The problem arises because the delayed reinforcement for studying for the exam is not sufficient to dominate the immediate reinforcement of watching television. No doubt the reinforcement for doing well on the exam, which would be obtained if the student studied properly, is considerably greater than the smaller reinforcement of an entertaining program.

Unfortunately, the smaller but more immediate reinforcement frequently wins. This may generally be the problem of self-control: the individual is unable to maximize the total amount of reinforcement he receives because so much of the large reinforcers are of a delayed nature. As a result, his behavior comes under the control of smaller but more immediate reinforcers. The man who believes that he has free will may simply give up by saying that his will power is not up to the task. On the other hand, the determinist may attempt to arrange his environment or his schedule of reinforcement so that responses which produce a maximum amount of long-term reinforcement will also receive a favorable schedule of immediate reinforcements.

Many of the more commonly used self-control techniques are not generally thought of as such. Going to college is actually an example of a self-control technique. Most of what students learn in college could be learned elsewhere, for example by reading textbooks in the library. The self-educated man, however, is a very rare phenomenon. The special immediate educational reinforcers are not available. It may be that the teacher's most important task is to arrange a set of immediate reinforcers which will maintain study behavior where the long-term delayed reinforcers would not be sufficient. The main disadvantage which the self-taught student suffers is the absence of someone to arrange the short-term reinforcing schedules in the form of quizzes, exams, assignments, grades, and so forth. Even in college, schedules of reinforcement are rarely arranged for the optimum maintenance of behavior or to produce the maximum amount of short-term reinforcement; however, they are normally much better than those found for similar behavior outside of college. This becomes particularly apparent when students are placed in situations where they no longer have quizzes, exams, and final grades but are expected to continue to make the proper responses at the same rate as in college; they frequently fail to maintain an adequate response rate.

What ways do we have of controlling our behavior other than enrolling in school? One useful strategy is the "Get thee behind me, Satan" technique. This consists of eliminating the discriminative stimulus for the opportunity for undesirable responses. We may remove the candy, cigarettes, or liquor from our reach or even from our sight.

Another technique is very effective but has rarely been tried; this consists of putting a certain amount of reinforcers at the disposal of someone else who will deliver them to us only when we have made appropriate responses. For example, we might give our roommate our last pack of cigarettes and request him to dispense them to us at the rate of one cigarette for every half-hour of study. If the roommate and others nearby cooperate, we might find our study rate increasing. This is a procedure which involves positive reinforcement.

We could develop a similar procedure involving negative reinforcement. For example, we might give our roommate a five-dollar bill and request that if we do not study for three hours that night, he should spend it on his own riotous living. For most of us, this would ensure that we studied, again assuming a cooperative roommate.

A more subtle form of self-control involves the elimination of the middleman. We have been playing with these techniques while writing this book. Book writing is a very good example of the situation where self-control is needed. Many more books have been started than have been finished. Although the reinforcement for writing a book may sometimes be considerable, the delay of this reinforcement is great. In the case of the present book, we have worked about forty hours a week for one year in writing it; (the actual publication of the book will not take place for a year after the book has been written). In other words, the delay of reinforcement in publication of a book varies from two years at the onset of the writing to one year at the completion of the writing. It is very difficult to maintain writing behavior under such a schedule of reinforcement.

The so-called intrinsic reinforcement which comes from writing is not without value and the social reinforcement involved in a co-authored production is useful. The response of describing to others the book which you are going to write or are in the process of writing is reinforced nearly as much as the actual writing of the book. Since the response of telling about the book to be written is easier than the actual writing of the book, and since it produces nearly the same amount of reinforcement, more people make the response of telling others about the books they are going to write than actually write them.

The "Get thee behind me, Satan" technique is very common among authors. We have also practiced it by going off to the "secluded" New Providence Island in the Bahamas. We were able to remove ourselves from situations which placed too strong a reinforcement on behaviors other than writing. In the university setting, there are so many responses that have more immediate reinforcement such as preparing for and giving a lecture, attending committee meetings, etc., that it is difficult to emit much behavior which is controlled only by long-term consequences.

In the university itself, we arranged an artificial state of affairs whereby the desired behavior would be maintained. A typical schedule of reinforcement which we used was as follows: we required ourselves to work on the book five hours a night and to write three and one-half pages every night, four specific nights a week. Any night when we failed to do this, we had to donate $35 to Western Michigan University. We are happy to report that the occasion never arose for us to give such a donation to WMU.

One of us concurrently used an additional reinforcement procedure which seemed very effective. This particular schedule was used to eliminate the unproductive daydreaming which so frequently occurs when one tries to write. For many of us, a large portion of our writing time is devoted to fiddling, fidgeting, and daydreaming about completely irrelevant things. The schedule of reinforcement which was very effective in counteracting this consisted of taking one bite of food or one drink of liquid each time a sentence was written. A casual comparison of this procedure with attempts at writing without this extra reinforcement indicates that the rate of sentence writing was higher when food reinforcement was used. Somewhat similar but perhaps less drastic schedules of reinforcement are commonly used by other writers.

One psychologist has even used self-reinforcement in an effort to bring about changes in his own behavior which are subtle but so pervasive as to be described as a "personality change." His problem behaviors consisted of a fairly high frequency of aversive or critical statements directed at others. The short-term reinforcement for this behavior may to some extent involve the response of the individual aversively stimulated; in addition, the verbal-aggressive behavior may have been an adjunctive reinforcer maintained by other concurrently ongoing schedules of reinforcement. Regardless of the short-term reinforcers which maintained the behavior, it seemed apparent that the long-term consequences were producing a reduction in the overall amount of reinforcement available. In spite of many attempts over a period of years to eliminate such undesirable behavior, the psychologist had been singularly unsuccessful. Finally he strapped a special shock belt around his waist beneath his shirt. The shock belt consisted of a series of batteries, a small microswitch, and a pair of electrodes which allowed for the delivery of a brief 210-volt shock each time the switch was pushed. The psychologist then shocked himself each time he detected that he had made an aversive statement to someone else. The frequency of such aversive statements was immediately reduced to a more tolerable level. Continued use of the shock belt has resulted in the maintenance of a relatively low frequency of aversive statements. Whether it will be possible to eventually eliminate the belt has yet to be determined.

Initially, most people are quite skeptical of these self-control techniques. Much of the skepticism is based on the old notion of free will. They say, "If I had enough free will to pay $35 when I didn't do the required amount of work . . ." or, "If I had enough free will to refrain from eating until I had dictated a sentence . . ." or, "If I had enough free will to shock myself when I made an aversive statement . . ." "I would not need the self-control techniques." The best answer is that empirically this does not seem to be the case.

However, the facts may seem more acceptable if a plausible theoretical analysis can be presented. Our analysis of the control of behavior seems straightforward as long as all of the reinforcers are under the management of someone or something other than the organism whose behavior is being studied. This way, the organism does not have an opportunity to cheat and present himself with unearned reinforcers.

What would be the circumstances under which an organism would not cheat, even though he had complete control of the reinforcers? Before the self-control procedure is instituted, the situation is as follows: responses with long latency consequences will produce a delayed but large reinforcement. Incompatible responses will produce immediate but small reinforcement. The necessity for a self-control technique arises when the long-term reinforcer has a sufficient delay and is insufficiently large, causing the incompatible short-term responses to be made too frequently.

Suppose that the subject attempts to use a self-control technique whereby he delivers to himself some special immediate reinforcement whenever he makes a response which, although delayed, will eventually result in an extremely powerful reinforcer. For instance, a dieter may reward himself with a new book or movie after losing five pounds. The ultimate reinforcer for losing weight may be good health, an attractive physique, etc. The combination of this self-administered immediate reinforcement and the long-term reinforcement may be enough to maintain this desired response. Either reinforcer by itself would not be sufficient. Without the immediate self-administered reinforcement, the subject would make the short-term responses. Without the long-term delayed reinforcement, the subject would consume the self-administered reinforcers without making the desired long-term response. A proper but delicate balance between these two will produce excellent self-control behavior. You may find it an intriguing task to devise an experiment in which a similar self-control procedure might be used by a lower animal.

In understanding the success of the self-control techniques, it may initially help to speak in very loose terms. The individual involved has to have faith, he has to believe that the self-control technique will work. He must believe that he will in the long run benefit from these techniques. Otherwise, he will not bother expending the extra effort to make the desired long-term response; he will consume the immediate reinforcement without the desired long-term response. It is not that he has to have faith in order for reinforcement to work, but he has to have faith in order to actually bother applying the special reinforcement contingencies.

This may not seem so strange if we look at a very similar situation which commonly occurs. A person may go to a physician and experience a certain amount of physical discomfort in the form of injections, perhaps even surgery, in order to avoid even more aversive long-term consequences. He would not do this if he did not believe that the techniques which caused the immediate pain would be successful in preventing much greater aversive stimulation in the future. If you cut your foot, you might then make the response of applying aversive stimulation to yourself in the form of a tetanus shot. This would be done because you believe the procedure involved in producing this immediate aversive stimulation will prevent the possibility of much more severe aversive stimulation in the form of lock-jaw in the future.

In general terms, you make one response, then you apply immediate aversive stimulation; if you do not apply the immediate aversive stimulation, you will receive even more aversive stimulation at a later date. The same general terms describe one form of self-control. You make an undesirable response and you present yourself with aversive stimulation later on.

In the case of cutting your foot, you do not make the argument that if you were man enough to go to the doctor for a shot, you would be man enough to avoid cutting your foot. Similarly, you should not make the argument that if you were man enough to apply the aversive stimulation, you would be man enough to avoid making the initial undesired response.

You may find this analysis plausible but feel uncomfortable because of the use of terms such as "belief" and "faith," which seem vague and ill-defined. What do we mean when we say a person believes that he will ultimately be reinforced by using self-control procedures? We mean that in the person's past, similar responses have been reinforced. We would not be surprised if a person who uses self-control techniques has used such techniques many times in the past and that this behavior has been reinforced.

What about the person who has never used self-control techniques? How can he have been reinforced for using them? How can we explain his using them for the first time in spite of the immediate difficulties of using such procedures? To answer these questions, it is necessary to know the antecedent conditions resulting in the use of the self-control techniques. What were the discriminative stimuli?

The individual might have observed someone else using them successfully or he might have observed a person using them who had not seen the actual consequences. If, like most of us, the person has a generalized imitative repertoire, then the behavior of others might act as a discriminative stimulus for his own utilization of the self-control techniques. Another set of conditions might be that an authoritative person has suggested or instructed the individual to use a self-control technique. Again, if imitation or following instructions has been reinforced in the past, the individual may then use the self-control technique.

The antecedent conditions might consist of a behavioral analysis of the situation in terms of the principles of behavior as presented in this text. It is quite possible that the behavioral analysis would lead to a conclusion that the self-control technique would be appropriate. If behavior involving the use of implications of similar behavioral analysis had been previously reinforced, we would not be surprised to observe the individual going to considerable effort to apply the self-control techniques. This is what we mean by having faith.

It may well be that the area of self-control will be the site of the next major breakthrough in the application of the science of behavior to the technology of controlling behavior. Some research has already begun. Israel Goldiamond[5] used self-control techniques to help a young man control his behavior and consequent overweight and to help a young girl who had difficulty studying. He also used these techniques in marital counseling, handwriting improvement, and academic counseling. Lloyd Homme[6] has presented a theoretical analysis of the use of self-control techniques to control private behavioral events such as thinking, which should in turn control excessive smoking.

The use of the principles of reinforcement in the standard applications to the modification of behavior combined with the development of self-control techniques promises to be a tremendous benefit to mankind. It may give man true freedom where previously such freedom was only illusory. Imagine the situation where the average individual can come to the behavioral engineer and say, "I'm not happy with myself. I want a new personality. Help me to change." The behavioral engineer will, in fact, be able to assist effectively with the desired changes. The individual might say, "I would like to bicker less with my wife, spend more time with my children, be more aggressive with salesmen, less aggressive at parties, and learn to play the banjo I've had in my closet for the last five years." The behavioral engineer would specify the schedules of reinforcement which would be appropriate to produce and maintain the desired behavior changes; he would help the individual to initiate these schedules and would support him in their continuation. Technologically, such innovations seem quite feasible. What is needed are many imaginative and dedicated individuals who can help overcome cultural inertia and bring about this behavioral revolution.

5. Goldiamond, I. Self-control procedures in personal behavior problems. *Psychological Reports*, 1967, *17*, 851–866.
6. Homme, L. E. Perspectives in Psychology—XXIV: Control of co-variants, the operants of the mind. *Psychological Record*, 1965, *15*, 501–511.

20

In Chapter 18, we saw that a response could be punished and thus eliminated by the introduction of certain physical stimulation immediately following the response. Similarly, in Chapter 19, the removal of a positive reinforcer was demonstrated to act as a punisher, resulting in reduced responding. In this chapter it will be established that either of these events, presentation of certain stimuli or removal of a positive reinforcer, can be employed not to eliminate behavior, but to establish and maintain response patterns. This general procedure is called *negative reinforcement*. Just as a response which produces a bit of candy will increase in rate (positive reinforcement), a response which eliminates electric shock will also increase in rate (negative reinforcement). The same kinds of events which act as punishers for one response may serve to increase the frequency of another response, provided the latter response results in their elimination. When these stimulus events are used in this manner, they are no longer called punishers, but are referred to as *negative reinforcers*. Employed as punishers, these events serve to eliminate responding; but employed as negative reinforcers, they allow for the establishment and maintenance of new responses.

It may strike the reader as confusing that the same stimulus event may affect behavior by decreasing response rate when one response and method is employed, and increasing rate when another response and method is considered. This fact of behavior is entirely consistent with the development we have presented throughout this volume. Behavior, like other phenomena, functions in a relativistic universe. Before we can predict the effect of a particular stimulus on the organism, we must have the particulars of how, when, and under what conditions it was introduced.

With this brief lecture on relativism out of the way, let us now examine a situation in which one type of behavior was established through the use of negative reinforcement.

Dr. Yealland's Chamber of Horrors

For the first time America was feeling the great personal price of war. Thousands of Yanks were returning from across the ocean speaking of exotic lands and peoples. Military hospitals proliferated throughout the country in order to accommodate the influx of wounded and distressed veterans. One common ailment exhibited by our returning servicemen was a condition known informally as "shell shock." Shell shock was not necessarily associated with a particular incidence of an exploding shell, as the term might seem to imply. Often it appeared to be a process which took place as time and experience in the forward trenches lengthened. The manifestations of the shell-shocked were many and varied, and included blindness without any physical damage to the structures of sight, deafness without detectable damage to auditory structures, and paralysis without trace of physical damage. Although in these instances there was no indication of physical impairment, there could be no doubt that these ailments were real and afforded the individual discomfort and inconvenience. It was not simply a case of malingering. The affliction was behaviorally real and its ultimate consequences were often extreme and dire. Those who did not receive proper treatment spent their days in military hospitals confined to wheelchairs or in bleak and somber seclusion.

Dr. Yealland was a physician whose speciality was psychiatry.[1] He had observed dozens of patients with this affliction and had developed an elaborate theoretical explanation for the disability. History has proven his theoretical notions poorly founded but the effectiveness of his treatment remains impressive.

His approach can best be illustrated by the following case summary.

The patient's name was Edward B. He had served for 15 months in the armed forces stationed in France. During an enemy encounter several of his comrades were lost. After relief had finally come, Edward claimed to have felt a weakness in his leg. Within an hour he was unable to move his right leg at all; each try only brought sweat to his brow. His leg had become rigid and occasionally had spontaneous tremors.

Edward came to see Dr. Yealland in the spring of 1917. He appeared at his office on crutches. The right leg appeared to be stiff and completely immobile, as though it were made of granite. While Dr. Yealland examined his leg Edward told of his war experiences with specific reference to the occasion when his leg had become paralyzed. Dr. Yealland listened thoughtfully as he scrupulously examined the leg. After he had completed his examination, Dr. Yealland did a curious thing. He walked to the door of his office, which was the only exit from the room, and locked it securely. Turning to Edward he made the following statement:

"Edward, we do not know the exact cause of your paralysis but it is apparent that there is no true damage to the tissue. It is obviously a subtle problem of the muscles and nerves. I have resolved to cure you of your affliction and that neither of us shall leave this office until you are indeed cured."

1. This section based on Yealland, L. R. *Hysterical Disorders of Warfare.* London: Macmillan, 1918.

With that Dr. Yealland walked across the room to a metal cabinet where he cautiously opened several drawers. Inside were various pieces of apparatus of varied descriptions. Alongside was a device which appeared to be some sort of electric generator. Before reaching into the drawer, he hesitated and turned to his patient.

"It is apparent," he said, "that your muscles have become antagonistic. By the proper stimulation we can alleviate this condition. I'm going to apply a faradic stimulator to your leg."

He withdrew a roller-type object and turning on a switch, applied it to Edward's paralyzed leg. Edward's muscles jerked as electrical current passed throughout the tissues of his leg. The roller was withdrawn and applied again. After several such applications Dr. Yealland commented to his patient:

"It appears as though the muscles are more than moderately joined in their antagonism and therefore I must increase the intensity of the faradic stimulation."

With some ceremony he advanced the dial to a higher intensity and then approached Edward's flesh. Presently he saw a slight movement in the leg. He jerked the roller away immediately.

"Ah ha," he said, "movement." He increased the intensity and applied the roller again. This time the movement was greater. Again he promptly withdrew the roller.

"Ah ha," he said again, as he advanced the intensity dial.

After ten minutes of this procedure, Edward remarked that he thought he could move his leg without the application of the roller. With this encouragement, Dr. Yealland quickly removed Edward's crutches and induced him to place weight on the leg. Edward did so, cautiously at first, with very little difficulty.

Dr. Yealland looked at Edward and smiled, "I think that you will find that this condition will bother you no longer. Of course if it should come back, I'm always here. I am always ready to administer further treatment. If on the other hand, it remains intact, I'm sure you will be happy to be discharged from the hospital and take up your life as a civilian."

As he prepared to leave the office, Edward grabbed the good doctor's hand, and shaking it ceremoniously, thanked him for his help. Taking one last look at his crutches where they lay in the corner, he strode boldly out the door and returned to his ward. A week later he was discharged and returned to his farm in Iowa.

The treatment administered to Edward by Dr. Yealland is similar to procedures he employed with scores of veterans suffering from similar disabilities. In all but a few instances, he was completely successful. In these few cases it was later found that previously undetected tissue damage, in one way or another, accounted for some of the problem.

We have already said that Dr. Yealland's theories were highly improbable, and in the light of modern medicine make absolutely no sense at all. We will therefore not focus on them here. His poor theory does not detract from his great success with his clientele. Further, had not Dr. Yealland made his services available, many of these veterans would doubtlessly have suffered for years or perhaps for their entire lives with these afflictions.

It is probably safe to say that Dr. Yealland's procedures did not involve basic medical principles but rather involved principles of behavior. Specifically, his procedures can best be analyzed in terms of negative reinforcement. In this particular instance the type of behavior generated by negative reinforcement is known as *escape behavior.*

In escape training or conditioning such ongoing events as intense stimulation or the steady diminishing of a positive reinforcer are eliminated when the appropriate (escape behavior) response is emitted. Dr. Yealland's procedure involved precisely this model. In the beginning of the session, the door was locked, and Edward was told that he could not leave (escape) until his condition was cured (normal movement of his leg equals escape behavior.) In a finer analysis, each movement of the leg reliably produced the immediate withdrawal of the electric stimulator.

Leg movements were thus increased by negative reinforcement. It was only when Edward had demonstrated his walking ability and apparent cure that Dr. Yealland allowed him to escape from his office.

Escape behavior is of extreme utility to the organism. Throughout the history of mankind untold embarrassment, injury, and strife has been avoided by a hasty and appropriate exit response. Some situations we may encounter, however, are such that even the most hasty escape response is extremely costly. In other instances, it is far more convenient and dignified if the individual does not have to make his retreat in full battle.

This brings us to a second type of behavior engendered and maintained by negative reinforcement. This type of behavior is called *avoidance*. The term avoidance is undoubtedly not new to the reader. Its meaning and usage in the nomenclature of formal psychology are not qualitatively different from normal usage. It denotes a situation in which the organism circumvents or evades a situation before it occurs. An appropriate response allows the individual to avoid a situation which would have resulted in the introduction of increased stimulation or the withdrawal of a positive reinforcer. If successful, such a response is negatively reinforced and increases in rate.

In the following study, we will encounter the use of punishment, escape conditioning, and avoidance conditioning, all employed in the elimination of self-injuring behavior.

A Toy for Scotty

Scotty was the bane of Ward 17.[2] He had been placed there some years before, when he was first admitted to the institution. Since that time he had spent all of his hours in restraint. At any time of the night or day he could be seen wearing a long-sleeved shirt. Its sleeves were wrapped around him and pinned securely to his trousers at belt level. In this way, Scotty had some freedom but could never raise his hands high enough to come into contact with his face. If his hands were left free, they soon became malicious clubs which he used without mercy on himself.

Scotty was assigned to Jerry Tough, then an undergraduate student in psychology. Although functioning under the direct supervision of the staff psychologist, his charge was to eliminate the self-injuring behavior. Ward attendants and physicians were eager to see work begin, for they felt that Scotty had some potential if his self-injuring could be alleviated.

Jerry immediately set to work doing the routine and standard procedures which precede any form of experimental treatment. First, Scotty's institutional record was read quite thoroughly. Scotty had developed the self-injuring behavior some five years ago. He had been in the institution for four and one-half years. During all those years he had been restrained in the manner described earlier. Usually Scotty was restricted to his crib with his hands tied to his waist. He was

2. This section based on Whaley, D. L., and Tough, J. Treatment of a self-injuring mongoloid with shock-induced suppression and avoidance. *Michigan Department of Mental Health, 4,* 1968.

not able to keep his balance well and was always in danger of a severe and perhaps serious fall. Scotty was diagnosed as a mongoloid, which meant that some of his difficulties stemmed from a condition which existed at birth. There was no reason to believe, however, that the self-injuring was in any way a direct result of his Mongolism.

After Jerry read the records, he went to the ward to see Scotty, who was at that time a wiry-looking lad of seven years. When Jerry saw him, he was in his usual position in his crib, his hands secured at his waist and his legs drawn up around his neck. Jerry tossed a ball into the crib and found that Scotty had gained considerable dexterity with his feet and toes in his years of restraint. Jerry had previously received the permission of the physician to work with Scotty and to use any reasonable and humane means to alleviate his self-injuring behavior. A letter was also written to Scotty's parents who concurred with the institution staff in their eagerness to see some of Scotty's problems eliminated. The real concern of Jerry, of Scotty's parents, and of the staff was that in his restrained position, Scotty was excluded from all forms of training which took place on the ward. Other children with Scotty's mongoloid condition had been trained in self-care, could use the toilet appropriately, brush their teeth, and had acquired acceptable self-feeding behavior. Many had learned extensive verbal behaviors and the older ones were capable of holding down different jobs not only in the institution but also in the community. As long as Scotty remained restrained and in

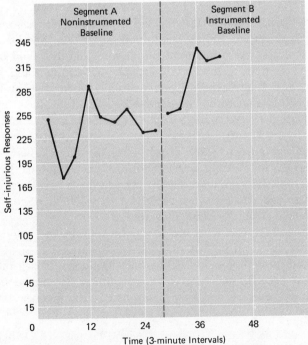

Figure 20-1 Frequency of self-injurious responses

his crib, he could not be included in these training programs. Therefore, his potential growth, which was considered great in relation to many other institutionalized individuals, could in no way be realized.

Jerry became aware of the price the years of restraint had extracted from Scotty. By now Scotty was barely able to employ his hands usefully. However, Scotty's hands could serve magnificently well as clubs, as Jerry soon saw. Within a few minutes, it was necessary to restrain Scotty again.

Jerry constructed some specialized mittens for Scotty which allowed the frequency of contact of each hand with his head to be counted precisely. Each time one of these special mittens touched Scotty on the head or face, a count was registered. In this way, Jerry was able to collect an accurate baseline. Reference to Figure 20-1 shows that Scotty was pounding his head and ears in an incredible manner. At one point he was delivering hard blows at the rate of approximately two per second. It does not take a psychologist to see that if left unattended for even as much as fifteen or twenty minutes, Scotty could do great damage to himself.

Jerry Tough was familiar with the literature and knew that a punishment

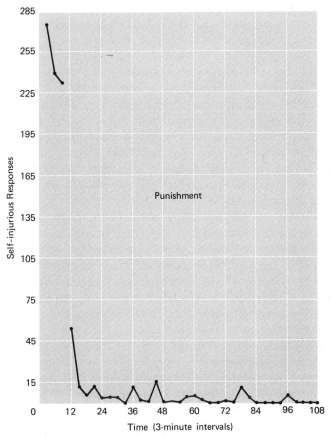

Figure 20-2   Effect of response-contingent shock on rate of self-injurious responses

procedure would probably result in reducing the frequency of the self-injurious behavior. Accordingly, an electronic circuit was used to apply a small amount of electric shock to Scotty's leg each time one of his hands made contact with his head. The electric shock was arranged in the typical punishment design that we have discussed earlier. Each self-injuring response was followed immediately and reliably by a small amount and duration of current. Figure 20-2 shows the results of the punishment procedure. The data from the punishment procedure do not leave much to interpretation. The self-injuring behavior was quickly reduced to zero.

During this procedure, Scotty was confined to a special room while Jerry observed him either from the other side of the room or from an adjacent one. Because considerable knowledge of the circuitry of the shock apparatus was required, it was not possible to assign attendants to run the procedure when Jerry was not available. It was apparent to Jerry as it was to his supervisor that it was not yet safe to release Scotty and keep him out of restraint on the ward; although the punishment procedure was effective in immediately reducing the rate of the response, there was no reason to believe that the response would not recur when Jerry and his apparatus were not in the vicinity and when the electrodes were not on Scotty's leg.

At this point there were several hours of discussion. A comprehensive picture was made of Scotty and his behavioral resources. It was apparent that he had no manual dexterity. During the years in which he had been restrained, he had not been allowed to develop skills such as playing with toys or games, as other children his age had developed. His hands were adequate to beat himself on the head, but were hardly suited for more skillful endeavors. On all previous occasions when Scotty was released, he immediately began to perform his one skill with such great ferocity that it was not possible to leave his hands unrestrained long enough to allow him to develop new behaviors. It was felt that if Scotty could be trained in some quick and dramatic fashion to engage in another behavior with his hands, this behavior might well compete with and, it was hoped, replace the self-injuring responses.

It was at this time that the secondary phase of the procedure was begun. Scotty was seated in a high-chair and the electrodes fastened to his legs as usual. This time however, the special mittens were not placed on his hands. A large metal truck was put in front of him on the high-chair tray, and on one side of the truck, a contact was made to the electrical circuit. The other side of the circuit was taped to the back of Scotty's arm, safely out of his reach. Each time Scotty touched the truck, the circuit was completed and the amount of time he touched the truck could be recorded on a running time clock.

At first Scotty was merely confronted with the truck, and shocks were not delivered. Initially it was important that Jerry find out how often Scotty touched the truck before anything was done to him at all. Figure 20-3 shows the baseline obtained in this manner. It can be seen that virtually no time at all was spent in contact with the truck. Toys were not at all reinforcing for Scotty. After the baseline had been collected, the escape procedure was introduced.

First Scotty was taught to escape from electric stimulation by clutching the

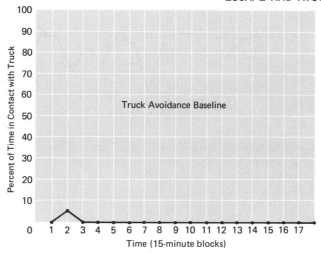

Figure 20-3   Percentage of time spent holding truck

truck. The experimenter took Scotty's right hand, which was the hand he most frequently used in his self-injuring responses. Simultaneously, a buzzer was turned on and the shock was applied to Scotty's leg. Jerry then took Scotty's hand quickly and holding it in his own, touched it to the truck. When Scotty's hand touched the truck, both the buzzer and the shock were immediately turned off. Touching the truck had produced a cessation of both the buzzer and the shock; it was an escape response. This procedure was repeated for perhaps a dozen times. Soon Jerry did not need to help Scotty escape the electrical stimulation. As soon as the buzzer and shock came on, Scotty immediately placed his hand on the truck. Through negative reinforcement a very reliable and immediate escape response came about.

During the escape procedure, Scotty received electric shock each time the buzzer came on. Between trials it was usually necessary to remove Scotty's hand from the truck before starting another trial. The trial consisted, as we have mentioned earlier, in sounding a buzzer and letting Scotty reach quickly for the truck so as to shut off the stimulation. In escape training the organism always experiences the shock prior to emitting a response which provides escape. In avoidance behavior the subject is allowed to completely evade contact with the stimulation provided he makes the appropriate response before shock onset.

The escape procedure was changed to an avoidance procedure. As long as Scotty kept his hand on the truck, he received no electrical stimulation whatsoever. Once he removed his hand from the truck, the buzzer sounded loudly and at the end of three seconds was followed by a shock. The events in the avoidance routine are the following: if Scotty removed his hands, the buzzer sounded a warning that shock would soon occur. Provided Scotty made the appropriate response, touching the truck, it was possible to avoid shock completely.

This is precisely what Scotty did. He rarely removed his hands from the

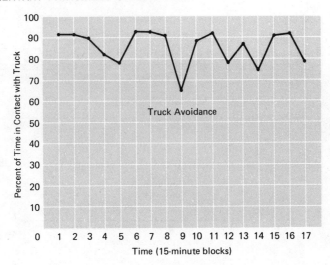

Figure 20-4 Percentage of time spent holding truck

truck even though he was placed in the avoidance situation for several hours daily. Figure 20-4 demonstrates the success of the avoidance procedure. We have already mentioned that during baseline procedures, Scotty rarely if ever touched the truck. Now, after escape and avoidance training, he almost never removed his hand from the truck.

Scotty was now sitting in the chair for long hours without restraints, and was neither hitting himself nor receiving shocks. Still, he was in many ways in no better condition than he was when in his crib. His hands were quite passive since his only response was to touch the metal truck which he could not lift, manipulate or otherwise move about. It was felt that other toys were needed to supplement the metal truck. A stuffed animal was a possibility, since children of Scotty's age often play with such toys. For Scotty, playing with a stuffed animal would be an appropriate response.

A toy tiger was especially constructed with steel shavings for stuffing so that it could be instrumented electronically. The program with the toy tiger was initially identical to that used with the truck. As long as Scotty continued holding the tiger, he was safe from any form of electrical stimulation. If he released the tiger even momentarily, a buzzer sounded and was followed in three seconds by shock. Scotty made the transition from the truck to the tiger with no difficulty at all. Soon, he was holding the tiger with ease and comfort. At this time, it was noticed that while he sat in the experimental situation, he was beginning to grasp, squeeze, and otherwise manipulate the toy tiger. It was now time to move Scotty from the experimental room where most of the procedures had taken place back to his home ward. The same high-chair and toy tiger were moved, along with a modified version of the basic program. Scotty was placed on his home ward with the toy tiger, and as before, releasing the tiger resulted in the sounding of a buzzer. However, it was not to be followed by electrical stimulation. In fact, once placed on his home ward, Scotty never released the tiger. In no way did he have the opportunity to discover that the electric shock had been discontinued. Usually, he remained in this manner on the ward for ten to fourteen hours daily. During this time, he manipulated the toy tiger often and was frequently seen to caress, hug, and kiss it.

But even this was not enough. In order for Scotty to take full advantage of the training facilities on his ward, it was necessary that he be completely mobile and have full run of the ward. Accordingly, he was removed from his high-chair and all components of the electric apparatus withdrawn. His only companion was the toy tiger with which he had previously spent so many hours. He was given his tiger and complete ward freedom. Often, he sat for hours in one of the small chairs provided for the children on the ward. Other times he scurried about the ward, running and yelling, dragging his tiger wherever he roamed.

Later, the toy tiger was replaced by other stuffed toys. It was apparent that any stuffed toy was sufficient to keep Scotty's hands occupied and rule out the possibility of a return of the self-injuring behavior. Many toys of various sizes, shapes, and construction were made available to him. Scotty seemed to prefer the medium-sized, soft toys and to reject the giant stuffed animals or those which were less soft and pliant.

Quite by accident, the importance of the stuffed toy to Scotty was forcefully demonstrated. An attendant came on the ward to replace one of the regular staff who had become ill and had gone home for the day. Scotty's history and the recent treatment program were not explained to the new attendant. Therefore, it was not surprising that, after giving him his bath, she placed him in his crib without his stuffed animal. When she returned to Scotty some twenty minutes later, he was a mass of blood and open wounds. Without the stuffed animal, he had returned to his previous behavior. After being cleaned up, he was immediately given a stuffed toy and the self-injuring responses were again under good control. It was found that as long as Scotty had a stuffed animal, there was no self-injury. If, however, he was without the stuffed animal for any period of time, he would revert to his old behavior. It was therefore necessary during the initial months to always keep a stuffed toy handy.

The benefits of the escape and avoidance treatments with Scotty are apparent today. For over a year, Scotty has been maintained completely out of restraint and has not exhibited any self-injuring behavior whatsoever. He relies less on his stuffed animals, although during quiet times he is generally seen holding one of the animals. Often, however, during recreation and games on the ward, he is completely without any stuffed animal. Since being out of restraint, Scotty has become completely toilet-trained. He has learned how to feed himself with considerable dexterity and has developed more appropriate social behavior. Early in the treatment, he was seen to smile for the first time. Since that time, smiling has become one of his most prevalent behaviors. There can be no doubt but that Scotty's life has been enriched by the minimal use of electrical stimulation. Visitors who occasionally see Scotty at quiet times remark how affectionate he seems to be toward the stuffed animal.

The Experimental Analysis of an Invisibly Small Thumb Twitch

Dr. Ralph Hefferline and two of his students at Columbia University performed a most intriguing experiment on combined escape and avoidance conditioning with human adults.[3] One of the difficulties in using humans for basic research is that the responses which you use may have a past history of conditioning. This history will vary from individual to individual. Unless the effect you are studying is quite powerful, differences in personal history may occasionally produce excessive variability in the resulting data. Hefferline decided to work with a human response which was so small as to preclude the likelihood of a conditioning history. In fact the response was so small that, if it occurred, it went unnoticed by the subject. Hefferline selected the thumb-twitch response.

An interesting problem was to determine a way that the experimenter could record the occurrence of the thumb twitch, even though it was not apparent to the owner of the thumb. Muscle behavior creates an electrical voltage. Even when the muscle response is so small as to be invisible, this voltage can be measured. In the present case, the measuring was done by connecting an electrode to the thumb and edge of the left hand. These wires were then brought to an electronic amplifier which multiplied the voltage by a factor of one million so that the voltages could be read on a meter. The voltages produced by this muscle twitch would, as you might expect, be extremely small. They varied from one to three microvolts. It was necessary to place the subject in an electrically shielded room because otherwise the extreme amplification required would have allowed the subject to act as an antenna picking up transient radio signals. Instead of observing the subject's response, the experimenter might be watching the latest rock-and-roll tune on the recording meter.

The subjects had two extra pairs of electrodes attached to them with non-functional wires running out of the room. They were seated individually in the test room with the electrodes attached. Four different sets of instructions were used. Three subjects were told that the experiment concerned the effects of noise superimposed over music on bodily tension. Their task was to listen through earphones and otherwise do nothing. They were told that the noise would occasionally interrupt the music they were listening to. Three other subjects were treated the same, but told that a specific small response, so small as to be invisible, would temporarily turn off the noise. They were also told that when the noise was not present, the response would temporarily postpone its onset. Their task was to discover and make use of the response. Three other subjects were informed that the effective response was a tiny twitch on the left thumb. The final three subjects were given the same information as the preceding three, but in addition a meter was placed before them during the first half-hour of the experiment. The meter was connected to the amplifier and acted as an indication of the occurrence of the proper response.

3. This section based on Hefferline, R. F., Keenan, B., and Hartford, R. A. Escape and avoidance conditioning in human subjects without their observation of the responses. *Science*, 1956, *130*, 1338–1339.

With the exception of the four different sets of instructions and the meter, all four subjects were treated in an identical manner. During the first five or ten minutes, the music was programmed alone with no noise. This allowed the experimenter to record the frequency of the small thumb-twitch response before the conditioning procedure was instituted.

During the next phase of the experiment, the conditioning procedure was instituted. This was done by superimposing an aversive noise over the music. Whenever the experimenter saw on the meter that a small thumb twitch of the proper size had occurred, he recorded the response and turned off the noise for 15 seconds. In other words, when the noise was on, the subject could escape it by making a small thumb-twitch response. However, if the noise was off and the subject made the thumb-twitch response, he would postpone or avoid the onset of the noise for 15 seconds. If he responded at the rate of once every 15 seconds when the noise was off, the noise would remain off indefinitely.

After one hour of this combined escape-avoidance conditioning procedure, an extinction phase was introduced. During extinction, the noise was turned on continuously; no response the subject made could terminate it. This lasted for ten minutes. Then during the last phase of the experimental session, the noise was turned off permanently and the music was presented by itself as it had been during the first few minutes of the session.

What happened? Which groups of subjects learned the thumb-twitch response?

Let us take the first group which essentially had no instructions. They had not been told that any response would have an effect on the occurrence of the noise. Was the response conditioned for these three individuals? Think this through very carefully. Think of possible reasons why the response should continue even though the subjects had not been given proper instructions. Then think of possible reasons why it should not continue. Then come to a conclusion.

The human subjects in the group that received no instructions did learn to make the escape-avoidance response. The instructions were not necessary. The consequence of the thumb twitch was sufficient for the conditioning of the response.

If you think about this, it will not be as surprising as it might at first seem. Lower animals learn escape and avoidance responses without receiving verbal instructions as to what response they should make. It would be a sad commentary on the state of mankind if we could not match that feat.

"Ah, yes," you may be thinking, "the humans figured out what the game was, but the animals can't. That's the difference." Dr. Hefferline interviewed the subjects after the experiment. All three still believed that they had been passive victims with respect to the onset and duration of the noise, and all seemed startled to learn that they themselves had been in control. Simply because a particular response for a human has been conditioned does not mean that the human is able to articulate the fact that reinforcement was involved. He may not even be aware that the response was increasing in frequency. In the present study, the subjects did not know that such a response existed. This is a difficult point for students. *It is not necessary for an individual to understand for reinforcement to be effective.*

What about the second group of subjects? That group was told that some small response would be an effective escape and avoidance response, but they were not told what the response was. All three of these individuals also learned the response. At the end of the experiment, two of the three subjects reported that early in the session they gave up searching for an effective response and thus, in effect, transferred themselves into the no-instructions group. The third subject professed to have discovered an effective response sequence. It consisted of subtle rowing movements with both hands, infinitesimal wriggles of both ankles, a slight displacement of the jaw to the left, breathing out, and then waiting. We have a term for this, do we not?—superstitious behavior.

What about the third group of subjects? This group was not only told that a response would be effective, but also what the response was. Surely they would have no problem learning the proper response. On the contrary, for only one of these subjects was the response conditioned, and that was probably because the subject failed to understand the instructions properly. The two subjects who did not learn the response kept so busy making large thumb twitches that the small reinforceable type of response had little opportunity to occur. The successful subject in this group indicated during the interview that he had misunderstood the instructions. He spent his time very gradually increasing pressure on an imaginary switch button. This may have kept deliberate activity at a level low enough for the correct responses to then be reinforced.

And finally, the fourth group. This group was not only given precise instructions but was also given an electric meter with which to monitor the magnitude of the thumb-twitch response. These three subjects performed best of all with a very precise pattern of responding. During the second half of the conditioning phase, the meter was removed. Still the subjects continued responding in the same manner. Evidently the external feedback of internal processes facilitates their being brought under environmental control; then the external feedback can be eliminated. The concept of conditioning such internal events through the use of external feedback has fascinating implications, though they will not be pursued here.

During the extinction phase when the noise was turned on continuously, the rate of the conditioned responses for all the subjects decreased. During the final phase when no noise was present, the rate was the same as it had been during the analogous stage at the beginning of the experimental session. These final stages indicated that the thumb-twitch response had, indeed, been under the control of the escape-avoidance procedure.

The Experimental Production of Ulcers

A group of psychologists have been very active in behavioral research with monkeys at the Walter Reed Army Institute of Research in Washington, D.C.[4] Much

4. This section based on Brady, J. V., Porter, R. W., Conrad, D. G., and Mason, J. W. Avoidance behavior and the development of duodenal ulcers. *Journal of the Experimental Analysis of Behavior*, 1958, *1*, 69–72.

of their work involves the use of electric shock with the monkeys placed in restraining chairs. This research was suspended temporarily at one point when a large number of the monkeys died. They had died although prior physical examination had shown them to be quite healthy, and they had received the best of medical and nutritional care while in the laboratory.

Major Joseph Brady was the head of the research group. As he tells it, Dr. Porter, the pathologist working with the group, kept coming into Brady's office every time he had performed a post-mortem on a monkey. Porter would bring the gut of the monkey and point out that it contained a hole or lesion. And each time Brady would show polite concern but nothing more. Finally Brady got the notion that Porter was trying to tell him something. He asked if there was something unusual about such lesions in monkey guts. Porter replied that, by coincidence, he had been personally involved in intensive studies of the gastrointestinal tract of monkeys, and had never previously seen an ulcer in one of these animals. Something very unusual was occurring to produce ulcers in so many monkeys in the same laboratory.

Brady was then quick to recognize the potential significance of the phenomenon. Ulcers are, of cource, a serious health problem in our country today. The experimental development of ulcers in the laboratory might allow considerable headway to be made into the problem, and would be useful in the testing of various techniques for their prevention and elimination. The monkey, being anatomically and physiologically similar to the human, was an ideal subject for the experiments.

In searching for possible causes, the scientists first thought of the 24-hour-a-day confinement in the restraining chairs. Another possibility was the electric shock to which the animals had been exposed. In order to test these and other notions, an ingenious experimental procedure was designed. Four pairs of monkeys were used. One of each pair was exposed to a shock avoidance schedule while its partner received the same number of shocks but was unable to control them. If the avoidance monkey sat in his chair and did not press the response lever, he would receive a brief electric shock every 5 seconds. If the monkey did press a conveniently located response lever, the next shock would be postponed for 20 seconds. The shocks would then start occurring every 5 seconds unless further responding took place. If the monkey pressed the bar at the rate of at least once every 20 seconds, it could continuously avoid the shocks. The partner monkey, on the other hand, had no effective avoidance response; a lever was present, but pressing it had no effect on the shock frequency. The passive monkey simply received a shock every time the avoidance monkey did. In other words the responding of the avoidance monkey determined whether or not each of the two monkeys would be shocked.

Ironically, because of a lack of space, the experiment was conducted in Dr. Porter's office. The monkeys made so much noise chattering when they were working on the shock avoidance procedure that Dr. Porter could not do his own work. Therefore a schedule was designed so that the monkeys worked six hours and rested six hours. A red light came on as the discriminative stimulus associated with the work period and went off when shocks were no longer being programmed. During the alternate six-hour periods, Porter was able to work. Both the monkeys and Porter seemed to adjust to this schedule rather well.

The experiments had been designed, the apparatus set up, and the monkeys were ready to go. Now the question was, would any or all of the monkeys get ulcers; or would just the avoiders or just the passive monkeys get them?

Within a few hours stable avoidance lever-pressing rates were obtained. The avoidance monkeys pressed the bar once every three or four seconds, much more frequently than was needed to efficiently avoid the electric shock. Of course, the passive monkeys rarely pressed their nonfunctioning lever. The rate of avoidance responding was so high that the shock rate never exceeded two per hour and typically averaged less than one per hour. Since these brief shocks were only a fraction of a second in duration, they would hardly seem adequate to produce ulcers; however after 23 days of experiments, one monkey of the pair died. After 25 days a monkey from the second pair died. A monkey from the third pair died after only 9 days in the shock procedure. And in the fourth pair, one of the monkeys was sacrificed when he was near death following 48 days of the shock procedure. In all four instances, "gross and microscopic analysis revealed the presence of extensive gastrointestinal lesions with ulceration as a prominent feature of the pathological picture." The other animals were sacrificed for a comparison postmortem examination which showed no indications of such gastrointestinal complications.

Which monkey of each pair got the ulcers? Was it the monkey who could avoid the shock by pressing the lever, or was it the monkey who was the passive victim of a seemingly capricious environment? Think about that problem for a minute before you read on.

It was not the passive monkeys that got the ulcers; they remained healthy. It was the avoidance monkeys, the monkeys that could do something about it, that got the ulcers. These are the "decision-making" monkeys, the "executive" monkeys. This shows that mere physical restraint had nothing to do with the ulcers. Similarly, mere physical trauma, occasional electric shock, could not by itself produce the ulcers. Once again the passive monkeys received the identical shocks. The cause of ulcers was psychological or behavioral; it was the result of the avoidance schedule. The ulcers were not a result of the shock by itself but of the interaction between the avoidance behavior and the shock.

Summary

In this chapter, it was established that events such as intensive stimulation and withdrawal of a positive reinforcer can be employed to establish and maintain response patterns. The rate of a specific response will increase if that response is regularly followed by the cessation of stimulation or the termination of the loss of a positive reinforcer. Such a process is called *negative reinforcement*. The procedure is similar to positive reinforcement in that both procedures increase the rate of the responses with which they are associated. The two differ in that positive reinforcement involves the introduction of an event or commodity, whereas negative reinforcement involves the removal of events often classified as aversive.

1. One type of one behavior pattern which can be established by negative reinforcement is called escape behavior. Escape behavior occurs when a specific response allows the individual to remove or eliminate unwanted stimulation or terminate the loss of a positive reinforcer. In escape behavior the organism always comes into contact with these events and then, through the appropriate response, eliminates them. The treatment of a shell-shock case was by escape procedures from electrical stimulation.

2. A second type of behavior brought about by negative reinforcement is avoidance behavior. In avoidance behavior the organism can prevent or indefinitely postpone contact with events such as electric shock or loss of positive reinforcement. The self-injuring behavior of a Mongoloid child was aided by the use of an avoidance procedure. The child was trained to avoid electrical shock by clutching first a toy truck and later an array of stuffed animals. The avoidance procedure established long-lasting avoidance behavior and provided a competing activity which reduced the probability of self-injury and also helped to increase the manual dexterity of the child.

3. In another experiment, escape and avoidance of an intense noise was used to condition a thumb-twitch response. The magnitude of the twitch was so small that it was defined by extreme electronic amplification and the movement itself was not normally detectable by the human subject. Awareness seemed to be unimportant in establishing the escape and avoidance response.

4. A final avoidance study was discussed in which monkeys were placed in pairs in an experimental apparatus. Under these conditions, one monkey could avoid a brief electric shock by making a lever-press response. Each response postponed the shock for 20 seconds. Only one monkey of each pair was allowed to make the avoidance response. The other monkey received the same shock experience as the avoidance monkey but in no way could control or postpone its onset. Accordingly, the monkey who could control the situation was called an executive monkey. In a series of experimental sessions which ran over several weeks, the executive monkey was found to develop ulcers. The ulcers were associated with the avoidance schedule. The monkey who did not have executive responsibility did not develop this problem.

QUESTIONS

1. What are the two classes of events which can serve as punishers? (a) The introduction of a positive reinforcer; (b) Removal of a positive reinforcer; (c) Removal of excessive stimulation; (d) Introduction of excessive stimulation.
2. A negative reinforcer always reduces the rate of the response with which it is associated. (a) True; (b) False.
3. Which of the following can be used to establish and maintain responses? (a) Punishers; (b) Negative reinforcers; (c) Positive reinforcers; (d) (b) and (c) above.
4. Shell shock is a condition which is always the direct result of a shell exploding within a few feet of a soldier. (a) True; (b) False.

5. Which is the truest statement regarding shell shock? (a) It always is associated with tissue damage; (b) It always involves loss of movement of a limb; (c) It always involves loss of vision or hearing; (d) It does not seem to have neurological or physiological cause.

6. It was shown dramatically that persons claiming to have shell shock were merely malingering. (a) True; (b) False.

7. Sometimes shell shock cases remain in a hospital for the duration of their life. (a) True; (b) False.

8. Doctor Yealland's theories have proven to be entirely correct and this accounts for his effectiveness in treatment. (a) True; (b) False.

9. Why did Doctor Yealland lock the door? (a) He was afraid of interruptions; (b) He did not feel too secure with the mental patients in the hall outside his office; (c) He believed Edward to be suicidal; (d) He wished to make the point that Edward could not leave until he was cured.

10. Which of the two below are indicative of an escape procedure? (a) The fact that the electric stimulator was removed each time Edward moved his leg; (b) The fact that the muscles had become antagonistic; (c) The fact that Dr. Yealland would not let Edward leave until he was cured; (d) The various increases in shock intensity.

11. In avoidance behavior, the organism experiences the shock. (a) True; (b) False.

12. In your opinion why would an organism who could exhibit only escape behavior be at a disadvantage?

13. What is the great advantage of avoidance behavior?

14. In the study entitled "A Toy for Scotty," which procedure below was not used? (a) Escape; (b) Avoidance; (c) Punishment; (d) Positive reinforcement.

15. With what procedure were the special mittens used?

16. Scotty's self-injuring behavior was definitely linked to his Mongolism. (a) True; (d) False.

17. Which of the following was most detrimental in Scotty's condition? (a) The fact that he could do severe self-injury; (b) While in restraint no training could take place; (c) Visitors could not be taken to Ward 17; (d) Restraint caused deterioration of Scotty's brain.

18. Jerry, the experimenter working with Scotty, changed from punishment to an escape procedure because punishment would not reduce self-injury. (a) True; (b) False.

19. In the escape procedure which was used with Scotty, what was the appropriate response? (a) Touching the face with the hand; (b) Touching the toy truck; (c) The experimenter touching Scotty's hand; (d) Touching a toy tiger.

20. Briefly explain why the experimenters switched from the toy truck to the stuffed tiger.

21. Scotty was easy to train on the avoidance behavior because he liked to play with toys. (a) True; (b) False.

22. What evidence did the experimenter have to show that the possession of a toy was important in maintaining the self-injuring behavior at a zero level?

23. Only the stuffed tiger was effective in keeping Scotty's self-injuring behavior under control. (a) True; (b) False.

24. Why did Dr. Hefferline wish to condition a small response? (a) His equipment was not adequate to handle a large response; (b) He wanted to work with a response which was relatively free of past reinforcement history; (c) He did not know that the response was going to be small at first; (d) No reason was given.

25. In the Hefferline study the first 5 or 10 minutes during which music alone occurred without noise could probably best be described as a b_____ period.

26. What form of event was employed as a negative reinforcer in the Hefferline study?
27. During the conditioning procedure, each thumb twitch turned off the noise. This procedure is a(n): (a) avoidance procedure; (b) punishment procedure; (c) escape procedure; (d) extinction procedure.
28. At the same time, each thumb twitch postponed the onset of noise for 15 seconds. This procedure is called a(n): (a) escape procedure; (b) avoidance procedure; (c) punishment procedure; (d) extinction procedure.
29. The first group, which was told to simply relax and enjoy the music, (did, did not) condition.
30. The second group, which was told that some small response would be effective in escaping and avoiding the noise, (did, did not) condition.
31. The third group subject, which was told that a thumb-twitch response would be effective, showed variable results. Describe these results and offer a possible explanation.
32. The fourth group, which was given a meter to read: (a) conditioned the best of all groups; (b) showed no conditioning; (c) became very adept at meter reading, but not at thumb twitching; (d) yielded inconclusive results.
33. The conclusion that one might draw from Hefferline's study is that awareness is necessary for conditioning to occur. (a) True; (b) False.
34. Why did the psychologists at the Walter Reed research facility have to temporarily discontinue some of their research?
35. When Dr. Porter exhibited the monkey's ulcers, Major Brady knew immediately what had caused them. (a) True; (b) False.
36. Ulcers have always been a very common thing for monkeys. (a) True; (b) False.
37. Provided the monkey did not make a response, how often would he receive shocks? (a) Once every ten minutes; (b) Once every five seconds; (c) Once each half-hour; (d) Once every other day.
38. If an avoidance response were made, how long was the shock postponed? (a) 2 days; (b) 20 seconds; (c) Indefinitely; (d) No information was given.
39. Why did the experimenters decide on a six hours-on and six hours-off schedule for the monkeys?
40. What event signaled the "on" avoidance period to the monkey?
41. Of the four pairs of monkeys starting in the experiment: (a) one member of each pair died from ulcers; (b) all animals died from ulcers; (c) none of the animals died from ulcers; (d) half of the animals died from ulcers.
42. Which member of each pair of monkeys developed ulcers?
43. Why was the monkey, whose avoidance response counted, called the "executive" monkey?

NOTES

Dr. Yealland's Chamber of Horrors

The type of problem that Dr. Yealland dealt with has considerable historical significance in clinical psychology and psychiatry. In fact, Dr. Sigmund Freud found this problem most provocative in the early days of his career. It is still true that it is a difficult phenomenon to explain.

Dr. Yealland and others since him have demonstrated that diagnosing such reactions is relatively simple since there is never any apparent physical damage to the tissues of the afflicted areas. When the physical complaint involves anesthesia or paralysis, they are of a nature that does not correspond to known anatomical patterns. Often anesthesia will be of a "glove" nature. In one such case which I personally dealt with, anesthesia existed from the waist downward, the line of insensitivity extending around the body in a circular fashion. Anatomically speaking, such a discrete loss of sensitivity is impossible. Neural centers run in many directions in that area and impairment of these neural tissues could not possibly result in the topographical effect claimed by the patient. Of course the patient does not know that, and somehow his paralysis or anesthesia becomes well defined and discretely demarcated. A second diagnostic feature of this ailment is what has often been referred to as "la belle indifference." As a rule, individuals exhibiting conversion reaction make verbal statements of the following sort: "Doctor, my condition is terribly upsetting to me and I will do anything you ask if you think it might help." Implicit in this type of statement is the attitude that nothing you try will, in fact, be successful.

It is difficult to pin down the behavioral antecedents of this problem, however. It is not obvious that a similar problem exists in lower animals.

In conversion reactions there is usually an advantage to the patient in maintaining his problem. In war conditions this is obvious. By developing convenient paralysis, anesthesia, hysterical blindness, or auditory malfunction, the soldier can be removed from the front lines and relieved of the awesome dangers of battle.

A Toy for Scotty

In the avoidance procedure employed in the experiment designed to eliminate Scotty's self-injuring behavior, a buzzer preceded the onset of shock. After the buzzer first sounded, Scotty had three seconds to place his hands on the avoidance object. This type of avoidance has been called signaled avoidance. The relevance of the name is fairly obvious. This avoidance design is one of the oldest used by psychologists in the laboratory. Similar forms of avoidance programming occur in everyday living. Most business concerns send several warnings of overdue accounts before they ultimately resort to the consequences of court and legal action. Some naturalists suggest that the rattlesnake begins the vigorous gyrations of his tail as a warning to passers-by and thus helps them to avoid a direct confrontation which might be disastrous for either or both parties.

In the experiment conducted by Hefferline and his colleagues and also in the study with the executive monkey, a different kind of avoidance program was seen. In both of these instances there was no warning to signal the onset of shock. This type of avoidance is often called timed avoidance or more commonly, Sidman avoidance, after Dr. Murray Sidman, who has intensively studied this schedule in the laboratory. In the timed avoidance schedule, the passage of time is the only signal that the organism can receive. By making a timely and appropriate response, the organism may avoid any contact with the programmed consequences. This type of schedule also occurs in situations outside the laboratory. Maintenance men in factories change oil and lubricate machinery on a time basis. Generally their maintenance behavior is governed only by a sort of general conception of when lack of maintenance could become critical. Some types of repetitive behaviors such as those observed in mental patients seem to occur on a type of Sidman avoidance schedule. In these instances it is not always clear exactly what the patient is avoiding.

A few scholars in the field of aversive control speak of still a third general type of avoidance. This avoidance behavior is called passive avoidance. It is unlike the two previous avoidance programs in that the individual avoids unwanted consequences by refraining from making a response. Passive avoidance may also have a warning feature built into it; a wife may threaten her husband with the proposition: "If you do that, then I'll leave!" By failing to exhibit the behavior to which the wife refers, the husband may avoid these consequences.

Sometimes passive avoidance may occur without a preceding warning cue. Race drivers, stunt men, football players, and boxers sometimes retire in the prime of their career although they have thus far avoided most dire consequences of their profession. Occasionally, these men will state that time is against them and suggest that unwanted consequences of their pursuits lie just around the corner. Of course, there are many other possible types of avoidance behavior which are combinations of those already mentioned.

In an earlier chapter, we talked about conditioned reinforcement and said that previously neutral stimuli or events which were associated with a reinforcer soon developed reinforcing properties. In a Skinner box, for instance, the animal may be busy pressing the lever and thus not be oriented toward the reinforcement delivery mechanism. If this is the case, he may continue to press the lever even though reinforcement has already become available. This may yield response patterns which are highly variable and irregular. Animal psychologists have learned to rely on a signal which serves to alert the animal that reinforcement has occurred. Typically, a stimulus light or a buzzer will announce reinforcement delivery. In these instances the light or buzzer takes on properties of a conditioned reinforcer. During extinction, for instance, the animal will work longer without being reinforced if occasionally a discriminative stimulus, such as a buzzer or light which has previously signaled reinforcement, continues to occur.

Just as neutral stimuli may develop positive reinforcing qualities by being associated with positive reinforcement, they may also become punishers if associated with a punishing stimulus. In the avoidance case with Scotty a buzzer always preceded shock onset. In initial training periods, Scotty allowed the buzzer to sound for three seconds; at the end of this time the shock was delivered. Soon, however, Scotty was making the avoidance response as quickly as he heard the buzzer and was thus avoiding shock. One would expect that the buzzer itself could be employed as a punisher since it had always historically preceded shock onset. As a matter of fact, this was found to be true during a series of test trials. It was demonstrated that the onset of the buzzer itself was an effective punisher although no shock followed. In early stages of treatment, Scotty was given the opportunity to hit himself with his hand. If, however, a buzzer was sounded near him, the rate of response stopped abruptly. The buzzer, therefore, was an effective conditioned punisher.

In earlier parts of the book, we spoke of extinction. In these instances, we were dealing primarily with positive reinforcement and stated that if reinforcement were deleted, a response would ultimately decrease to a zero rate. The number of responses made until extinction occurred was related to many variables, among them the schedule of reinforcement. An intermittent schedule of reinforcement brought about more resistance to extinction than a continuous reinforcement schedule. In a similar way, we also spoke of the effects of a punishment procedure. The rate may be initially reduced but ultimately it may return to the original high rate or even higher when punishment is discontinued. This is not usually spoken of as extinction of punishment. It is referred to as the *recovery* of a response which has been suppressed by punishment. Further, as with positive reinforcement, a punished response recovers more slowly if during the punishment phase only occasional responses are punished rather than every response. Thus, on a continuous punishment schedule, recovery of a punished response to baseline proceeds faster than if it were originally punished on an intermittent schedule.

Avoidance behavior tends to be extremely resistant to extinction. As with positive reinforcements, we may speak of extinction in avoidance situations. Both positive and negative reinforcement result in an increase in rate of the responses with which they are associated. When reinforcement no longer occurs, we would expect extinction and indeed, this does occur. Avoidance responses show greater resistance to extinction, particularly when compared to escape responses. In escape situations, the organism always comes into contact with the aversive stimulus. Consider a situation where an animal is placed in a box with a steel floor through which he may receive a shock. Shock is turned on and in order to remove it, the animal must press a lever. In this situation, we will find the animal develops a response which occurs very rapidly whenever shock is turned on. This is an effective escape response. The bar-press response may also occur at other times when the shock is not on. When shock is no longer presented, we find the rate of pressing the lever declines rapidly and extinguishes. Let us suppose that instead of an escape schedule, the organism is on a Sidman avoidance schedule. In this instance each lever pressed postpones the onset of shock. If the animal presses the lever often enough, he may completely avoid shock. After the animal has been trained to the point where he makes effective avoidance responses, we may remove the shock. The response does not extinguish immediately. It may in fact remain at a high rate for an extremely long period. In a common-sense analysis, the organism makes the avoidance response and thus does not come in contact with the aversive stimulus. When it is removed from the program, he does not have the opportunity to find out that it has, in fact, been deleted.

In the case of Scotty, the use of an avoidance schedule no doubt helped both to bring about and to maintain the high rate of clutching toys. Ultimately, he was released from the electronic program altogether and was maintained with only a stuffed animal. Since he also continued to show a high response rate of clutching the animal, he did not have an opportunity to learn that failing to clutch it would no longer result in shock. The theoretical explanations of the resistance of avoidance behavior to extinction have been many and varied and have included highly speculative notions. The fact that the phenomenon can be used to an advantage in the treatment of maladaptive behavior has been amply documented in Scotty's case.

The Executive Monkey

Dr. Brady's experiment with the executive monkey is of extreme importance to both psychology and medical science. It had been suspected for many years that situations which involved decisions and prompt actions such as those demanded of executives in business or the military brought about conditions which produced ulcers. Dr. Brady's research was the first clear-cut demonstration that this type of environmental condition could indeed produce ulcers. These findings, for obvious reasons, have not been experimentally reproduced in human beings although currently observations of blood contents have suggested that a similar situation probably obtains for humans.

One interesting finding of Dr. Brady's study was that the destructive effects of the avoidance behavior do not occur while the organism is in the responding situation, but rather become critical during the resting period following avoidance performance. The physiological concomitants which produce the ulcers occur as an aftermath to a period of avoidance responding. If we can generalize Dr. Brady's findings to humans, we might conclude that it is not the work or worry which causes ulcers in the executive. *It is the rest that he later allows himself* which brings them on. Perhaps the executive would do well to arrange his schedule so that he gradually diminishes his hectic activities before taking a vacation. In this way, physiological effects may be slowly dissipated before he takes his much-deserved rest.

The use of control procedures is one of the most important tools of science. In experimentation, we frequently speak of the experimental condition and the control condition. In a sense, we perform the experiment once under the control conditions and then make a slight modification and perform it again under what are now the experimental conditions. The only difference between the control and experimental procedure is the value of some independent variable which we have manipulated. If the experimental procedure yields a different result from the control procedure, then we say that result is due to the difference in that variable. You have seen many examples of this procedure throughout the text. When a scientist wishes to demonstrate that a presumed reinforcer is in fact controlling behavior, he continues treating the subject exactly as he had before; however, he discontinues the presentation of the reinforcer or, perhaps, presents it without regard to the occurrence of the response. The baseline procedure is a common control technique where the behavior of a single subject is observed for a period before some independent variable is manipulated. The baseline data are the control data; the data obtained after the variable has been manipulated are the experimental data.

Brady and his colleagues used one of the most elegant control procedures known to science in their study of shock avoidance on the production of duodenal ulcers. They used what has come to be known as the "yoked control." They placed the experimental monkey of each pair of monkeys on an avoidance schedule. Each bar press postponed the delivery of a brief electric shock for 20 seconds. Whenever the animal failed to press the bar within 20 seconds, a shock was delivered, and this was repeated thereafter every 5 seconds until the animal finally made a response. The control monkey received shocks at the same times as the experimental monkey. His bar press had no effect. Thus, the experimental and control monkey were treated exactly alike so far as physical restraint and delivery of electric shock were concerned. They were treated differently with regard to one potentially crucial variable; the effect of the bar-press response on the delivery of electric shock. As a result, the experimental animals developed ulcers whereas the control animals did not. This can be attributed to only one thing—that the experimental animals' behavior could affect the occurrence of the shock. The ulcers clearly were not due to physical stress or electric shock since the control monkeys did not get ulcers. The cause of the ulcers was behavioral in origin and was due to the interaction of the monkeys' behavior with the shock. It could be considered a result of psychological or behavioral stress rather than mere physical stress.

In a truly rigorously designed experiment, a control subject is treated the same as an experimental subject except for one condition. It is the effects of this condition which the experimenter wishes to assess. However, in certain behavioral experiments, this becomes somewhat difficult. One might think that an adequate control would be to have subjects seated in restraining chairs, but not on the avoidance schedule, and thus receiving no shocks. Such a control procedure obscures the effects of the physical stress of the shocks by themselves. This special sort of problem in the development of control procedure is limited to phenomena in which the output of the system studied affects the subsequent input to the system. In our example, the bar-press response is the output and the delivery of the electric shock is the input. Such systems make it difficult to develop an adequate control procedure. There are various approximations to the solution to this problem. For example, one might attempt to control the delivery of electric shock as a factor by noting the avoidance monkeys receive on the average one electric shock each hour. The experimenter could, in order to ensure that both animals receive shock, arbitrarily shock the control animal once each hour. In this way the control animal would receive the same number of shocks as the experimental animal. The problem with this is that the electric shock would occur at the fixed regular intervals for the control monkey whereas it would occur at variable intervals with the experimental monkey.

Of course, the experimenter could attempt to vary the actual time when the shock occurred. However, this sometimes becomes difficult. It is particularly difficult during the first few sessions of conditioning when the frequency and distribution of the electric shocks vary considerably throughout the session. Although it might not be possible for the experimenter to simulate the distribution and frequency of shocks the experimental monkey obtains, it is certainly much simpler to let the experimental monkey control the frequency of shocks not only for himself, but also for the control monkey. This then is the yoked control procedure. The output of the experimental subject controls the input not only for himself, but also for the control subject.

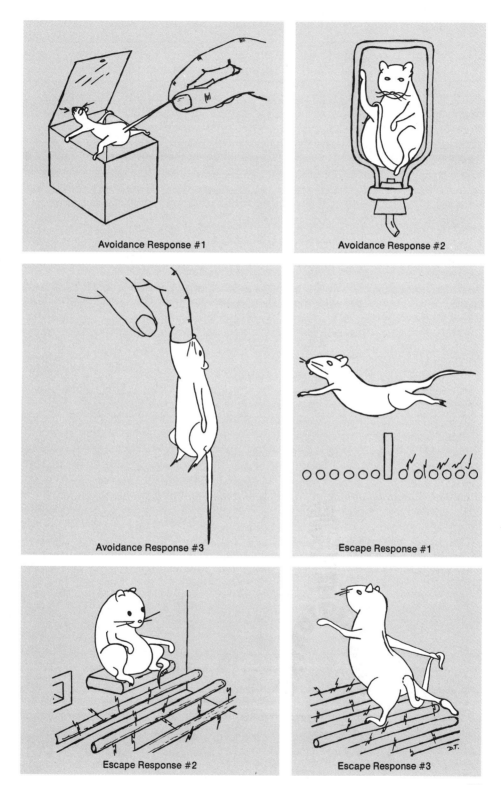

Avoidance Response #1

Avoidance Response #2

Avoidance Response #3

Escape Response #1

Escape Response #2

Escape Response #3

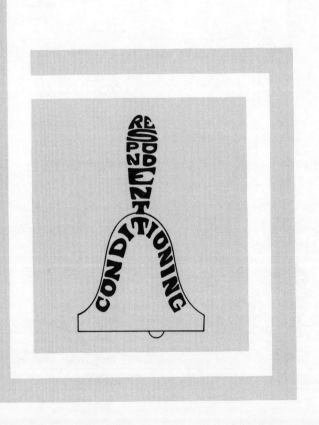

21

Commonly the psychologist, counselor, or psychiatrist engaged in psychotherapy seeks to make his patient aware of his behavior and what conditions produce it. Once these relationships have been understood, in many instances the patient is able to adjust his behavior so that more desirable consequences occur. In other cases, however, an individual's complete knowledge and apparent understanding of the origin, causes, and outcomes of his actions do not alter his behavior sequence to even a small degree. The following interview exemplifies one general class of this type of behavior problem.

A Case of Chicken Phobia

Therapist: If I understand correctly, you seem to have some kind of problem concerning birds. Could you tell me a little bit about it?

Client: Do you want the present part of it, or do you want me to tell you how it started?

Therapist: Both, but to begin with, I'd like to know what it is.

Client: Okay—the problem is a fear of birds in general, particularly pigeons and chickens! Especially if they're dead and in any sort of proximity to me.

Therapist: Any kind of birds?

Client: Any kind of birds—primarily large ones, chickens in particular, and so on going on down the scale.

Therapist: When you say a fear, what do you mean by that?

Client: An aversion to—I can't get close to them without having some sort of reaction.

Therapist: Suppose I were at this moment to approach you with a dead chicken; what would you do?

Client: Move to the other side of the room.

Therapist: Slowly?

Client: No, quickly.

Therapist: Would it be a deliberate thing? How would you feel while you were doing this?

Client: Very deliberate. I'd feel scared.

Therapist: What about yourself would tell you you were scared?

Client: Tenseness, I suppose. I get all tensed up. Like when I see a dead bird, I kind of clutch my hands and my stomach goes oooh.

Therapist: Do you notice your heart beating faster?

Client: Yeah, that's all I notice. It's been a long time since I've encountered a dead bird.

Therapist: You are a college graduate, isn't that true?

Client: Right.

Therapist: Have you had biology?

Client: A limited amount.

Therapist: Do you really believe that these chickens are going to hurt you in any way?

Client: No. Well, I can't say that, because if I didn't I would stay there with them.

Therapist: What do you think the chicken would do to you?

Client: A dead chicken can do nothing to me and no chicken or bird has ever attacked me or done anything in any particular way so I have no history of being attacked by birds or anything like that.

Therapist: Isn't your fear kind of ridiculous?

Client: Yeah.

Therapist: You really know that actually no harm can come to you, but still you're afraid.

Client: Yeah.

Therapist: Do you think it would help if someone would tell you that these animals can't hurt you?

Client: No, that's been done before.

Therapist: Has this ever caused you any problem, any kind of discomfort or inconvenience or actual harm?

Client: No harm. Inconvenience in that I can't work with pigeons in the experimental setting. And I suppose inconvenience when I was a child, like nightmares and things like that. There was more inconvenience to my parents than to me.

Conditioning a Phobia

The previous interview was made with a college student who suffered from what clinicians refer to as a phobia. A phobia is typically described as an irrational fear which seems to be fairly long-lasting and acute. The irrational aspect of the phobia is emphasized because the situation which the individual reacts to is not one which, under normal conditions, could do him any real harm. Phobias are frequently brought to the clinical psychologist. The reactions to the fears provoking situations are real and can be observed directly. Usually they involve avoidance responses of one type or another. The patient will attempt to remove himself from the situation as quickly as possible. Sometimes the escape or avoidance responses are extreme and in and of themselves may cause harm to the patient or to those about him. Even if an overt and dramatic escape or avoidance response does not occur, there are changes in the patient's behavior which are usually thought of as emotional responses. These may involve grimacing, becoming rigid, or turning pale. Furthermore, these emotional responses can be defined physiologically: often irregularities in heart rate, blood pressure, and the activity of the glandular system occur at the introduction of the phobic object.

Phobias have been documented early in the history of man and have been studied by many philosophers even before the formulation of a scientific psychology. With the development of a psychology of learning, it was believed that phobias occur because they are learned. Two pioneers in the field of behavioral psychology took it upon themselves to actually condition a phobic reaction in an infant.[1]

The subject for the study was a child who was only 11 months old at the time of the experiment. His name was Albert and he was the son of one of the nurses on the staff of the hospital where the two experimenters, John B. Watson and Rosalie Rayner, were conducting their experiments. Albert appeared to be an extremely healthy and robust infant in all respects, and for this reason he was subjected to the experiment. The two psychologists thought for a long time about undertaking this study for, after all, phobias may cause the patient real difficulty and discomfort, and in some instances make him careless or a poor judge, thus making possible real harm from other agents. Unlike many infants his age, Albert did not spend a great deal of time crying; he seemed an extremely happy baby.

1. This section based on Watson, J. B., and Rayner, R. Conditioned emotional reaction. *Journal of Experimental Psychology*, 1920, *3*, 1–4.

The experimenters found that he did become disturbed if two specific things were done. One response he made quite reliably was a startle response to loud noises. If, for instance, a resonant piece of metal was struck soundly with a hammer, the resulting clamor appeared to frighten Albert. If this was done two or three times in succession, Albert would begin to cry and exhibit many behaviors which looked a lot to the experimenters like fear responses. The second event was the sudden loss of support. If Albert was suddenly allowed to fall for just a few inches, he also exhibited the same type of startle reaction.

Prior to the experimental procedure, however, Albert did not seem to be offended or inordinately excited by any aspects of his environment. On various occasions animals and objects were presented to him without any of these responses occurring. These items included a white rat, a rabbit, a dog, a monkey, other toys, and a burning newspaper. Albert typically responded to these by reaching for them or otherwise exhibiting approach responses. Watson and Rayner decided to establish a phobic response to a white rat. The general design was to present the white rat to Albert and at the same time to strike the piece of metal behind him a blow with the hammer. This stimulus had previously brought about crying and other emotional responses. The precise procedure employed as presented by Watson and Rayner is presented below.

11 Months 3 Days

1. White rat suddenly taken from the basket and presented to Albert. He began to reach for rat with left hand. Just as his hand touched the animal, the bar was struck immediately behind his head. The infant jumped violently and fell forward, burying his face in the mattress. He did not cry, however.

2. Just as the right hand touched the rat, the bar was again struck. Again the infant jumped violently, fell forward, and began to whimper.

In order not to disturb the child too seriously no further tests were given for one week.

11 Months 10 Days

1. Rat presented suddenly without sound. There was steady fixation but no tendency at first to reach for it. The rat was then placed nearer, whereupon the infant began tentative reaching movements with the right hand. When the rat nosed the infant's left hand, the hand was immediately withdrawn. He started to reach for the head of the animal with the forefinger of the left hand, but withdrew it suddenly before contact. It is thus seen that the two joint stimulations given the previous week were not without effect. He was tested with his blocks immediately afterwards to see if they shared in the process of conditioning. He began immediately to pick them up, dropping them, pounding them, etc. In the remainder of the tests the blocks were given frequently to quiet him and to test his general emotional state. They were always removed from sight when the process of conditioning was under way.

2. Joint stimulation with rat and sound. Started to touch rat, then fell over immediately to right side. No crying.

3. Joint stimulation. Fell to right side and rested upon hands, with head turned away from rat. No crying.

4. Joint stimulation. Same reaction.

5. Rat suddenly presented alone. Puckered face, whimpered and withdrew body sharply to the left.

6. Joint stimulation. Fell over immediately to right side and began to whimper.

7. Joint stimulation. Started violently and cried, but did not fall over.

8. Rat alone. *The instant the rat was shown, the baby began to cry. Almost instantly he turned sharply to the left, fell over on left side, raised himself on all fours and began to crawl away so rapidly that he was caught with difficulty before reaching the edge of the table.*

It can be seen that after several pairings the rat alone brought about avoidance behavior and crying. Whereas before the rat had been at worst neutral, now it had apparently become a fear-provoking object.

Five days after this response had been established, Watson and Rayner conducted a further series of tests with Albert. Initially, the rat was presented to him and he responded without hesitation by beginning to cry and turning away, almost managing to crawl off the table. Later, colored blocks were offered to him, which he readily accepted, smiling and making gurgling sounds. Next the rat was reintroduced and again Albert scurried away from it on all fours as quickly as he could. It was obvious that the rat was still an object to be avoided as far as Albert was concerned and playing with the blocks showed that this response was not common to all offered objects.

In order to see if this avoidance generalized to other animate objects, a rabbit was presented. Albert leaned as far away from the animal as possible, whimpered, then burst into tears. When the rabbit was actually placed in contact with him, he buried his face in the mattress and crawled away, crying as he went. Next, a dog was presented. The dog did not produce as pronounced a reaction as the rabbit did. Albert did however appear to shrink from the animal and appeared to relax only when it was removed from his sight. In another test, a sealskin coat was presented. Albert immediately began to whimper and withdraw from the fur coat when it was brought near him. When the coat was placed on either side of him, he quickly turned away and moved from the direction of the object.

Albert was responding by crying and turning away and moving away from all objects which in any sense resembled the white rat. Also, it seemed as though the more similar the objects were in structure to the furry white rat, the more pronounced and violent were Albert's responses. His responses to the rabbit were extreme but responses to cotton wool were much less pronounced. This phenomenon is called stimulus generalization. We have discussed it in an earlier chapter and have found that generalization will predict that the organism will respond similarly to stimuli which are themselves similar.

The two psychologists believed at this point that they had established a phobia which would, in all probability, last for Albert's lifetime if further procedures were not enacted. These procedures involved gradually changing Albert's experiences with furry objects until they were always enjoyable and pleasant. In this way, they felt they could eliminate the phobia they had experimentally established. Unfortunately, they never had the opportunity to complete this phase of the experiment for Albert's mother removed him from the hospital after the last series of experimental procedures were enacted.

In some ways, the phobic behavior established by Watson and Rayner appears to be similar to escape and avoidance conditioning, which we have discussed in some detail earlier. Other components of the phobic behavior are different. First of all, the phobic behavior involves a variety of fear responses; consequently, it is commonly classified as emotional behavior. Unlike other behavior we have studied, emotional behavior does not appear to result immediately in any specific advantage or outcome to the organism. Emotional behavior seems to persist without any definite or identifiable reinforcement to the individual. It neither seems to yield positive reinforcement nor does it in any obvious way allow the organism to escape or avoid an unpleasant situation. While there are some variations in the specific responses therapists are referring to when they speak of emotional behavior, most agree that it involves physiological changes. These changes may include such events as alterations in blood pressure, increased activity of the sweat glands, and variations in heart rate or rhythms. All of these changes are behaviors which can be observed with the use of the proper physiological recording instruments. The often-mentioned lie detector is a device for measuring and recording certain physiological responses when a subject is confronted with various aspects of a supposed crime or misdeed. Some criminologists reason that the individual may attempt to obscure his deeds by distorting the truth. However, they feel that the individual cannot control his emotional responses, namely those physiological responses recorded by the lie detector.

This brings us to another important point about the phobia and emotional response. It appears that the individual cannot voluntarily control the occurrence of these physiological responses. As seen in the interview with the phobic patient, the fact that these birds could not harm the patient in any way did not seem to mitigate her fear reactions. Other responses such as lifting an arm or scratching the head, which deal primarily with gross muscle movement, seem to be modifiable if one simply asks the subject to execute particular movements. If the therapy patient is asked to move his arm or get up from a chair, he will in all likelihood find no difficulty in doing so. With any behavior involving an emotional component of a phobic response, telling or asking the individual to quit being emotional or afraid seems to have no effect on the behavior. When a criminal finds himself confronted by pertinent and incriminating evidence while connected to the lie detector, he can generally control his verbal behavior. However, measurements of his emotional behavior on the gauges and needles of the physiological recording instruments reveal that he cannot typically control these behaviors voluntarily.

The realization that emotional behavior appears to be different from other behaviors which involve gross muscle movements has led many writers to speculate that a different type of learning is involved in the conditioning of emotional responses. The type of conditioning which can possibly account for the acquisition of emotional responses is called respondent conditioning. Historically, the study of respondent conditioning preceded the investigation of the type of conditioning which we have studied up to this point, that involving positive and negative reinforcement. Let us now examine the procedure which many feel accounts for the conditioning of fear and other types of emotional responses.

Conditional Responses

Dr. Ivan Pavlov was already a physiologist of considerable international reputation when he first established the procedure which is now commonly called respondent conditioning. Pavlov worked for years in his native Russia conducting physiological experiments into the nature of the glands and the endocrine system. In his experimental work, he primarily studied the physiology of dogs, as they are of good size and have physiological systems somewhat comparable to those of humans. Since Pavlov was interested mainly in the secretion of glands, tubes were surgically inserted into certain of the dogs' glands in order to measure secretions directly. While under investigation, the dogs were usually placed in a type of restraining harness. Since the animals were fitted with fixed tubes, it was necessary to keep them restrained for long periods of time. Consequently, the dogs were fed while in restraint. Usually when food was presented to these animals, they would begin to salivate and drool extensively. This event is in no way unusual and can probably be observed in your own Fido at feeding time. However, after some experience with this general technique, Pavlov and his assistants noticed a curious thing when a certain assistant entered the experimental room. It was standard procedure in Pavlov's lab for one man always to feed the dogs. On several occasions, he entered the room when it was not feeding time. On these occasions he was not carrying food. The extraordinary event observed by Pavlov and his assistants was that the sight of the assistant produced the same effect as presentation of food. Upon observing him enter the room, the dogs would begin to salivate and drool as though food were being presented. It appeared as though the animals were responding to the assistant as if he himself were the lunch he generally brought.

From his studies, Pavlov knew that the salivation response was a reflexive type of response which occurs regularly in all animals when they are hungry and confronted with food. In terms of what he knew about physiology, there was no explanation for why the dogs salivated only when the assistant who typically fed them appeared, but not when other assistants entered the room. There was no reason for Pavlov to suspect that a particular assistant was any more delectable than the rest of his staff.

These initial observations led Pavlov to conduct a long series of experiments in which he systematically investigated the salivation response. His basic experiment entailed the following procedure. The dog was placed in restraint as before.

Meat powder was presented to the dog; as with other types of food, meat powder immediately produced salivation. Upon presentation of the powder, the experimenter now rang a bell. The ring was consistently paired with the presentation of the meat powder over a long series of trials. On all trials the presentation of the meat powder accompanied by the bell resulted in immediate salivation. Following the initial proceeding, a series of trials was conducted in which the meat powder was omitted and the bell presented alone. As you might suspect, the ringing of the bell produced salivation just as had the appearance of the assistant. Pavlov called the salivation response a conditioned response when the bell *alone* produced it. Pavlov reasoned that the occurrence of the salivation response when only the bell was presented was a result of a previous occasion in which meat powder and the bell were presented simultaneously. The salivation response to the bell was then conditional upon previous circumstances.

Pavlov developed a complete terminology to describe his conditioning procedures. He called the food or meat powder which always produced salivation the unconditioned stimulus (UCS). Meat powder unconditionally produced salivation whenever it was introduced. This salivation response was called the unconditioned response (UCR). The ringing of the bell was called the conditioned stimulus (CS). This stimulus would only produce salivation on the condition that it had been previously paired with the presentation of meat powder. Finally, salivation produced by the bell alone was called the conditioned response (CR). This response to the bell occurred only if previous pairings of the bell and meat powder had taken place. Figure 21-1 graphically presents Pavlov's terminology.

Conditioning Procedure

unconditioned stimulus—UCS
(Meat Powder)

conditioned stimulus—CS
(Bell)

unconditioned response—UCR
(Salivation)

Post-conditioning

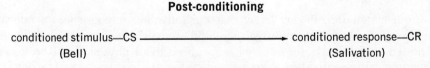

conditioned stimulus—CS
(Bell)

conditioned response—CR
(Salivation)

Figure 21-1   A schematic representation of Pavlov's conditioning terminology

At this point, it may be difficult for the student to see how the conditioning of salivation has anything to do with emotional responses. We have already established that emotional responses like salivation involve changes in physiological systems. It is generally thought that the individual cannot control either salivation or emotional responses in the same way as he controls his gross muscle behaviors.

In order to make a further comparison between the conditioning of emotional responses and salivation, let us reconsider the conditioning process that was involved in the establishment of a phobic reaction in Albert by Watson and Rayner. With Albert, the striking of the iron bar behind him produced a fright response. This type of response to loud noises is common in all infants and perhaps is a reflexive, unlearned behavior. Thus, since the sound created by striking a piece of metal with a handle unconditionally produced an unlearned fear response, in Pavlov's terminology it would be the unconditioned stimulus (UCS). The fear responses that resulted when the metal was struck could similarly be defined as the unconditioned response (UCR) since they were a natural reaction to the noise. In Albert's case, remember that Rayner presented the white rat at the same time as the noise; the white rat functioned as the conditional stimulus as it was repeatedly paired with the unconditioned stimulus, the loud noise. After several pairings, the white rat alone produced fear behavior. Thus, the fear response in Pavlov's terms was now a conditioned response (CR). Figure 21-2 shows the schematic presentation of the conditioning of a phobia in the same way as Pavlov explained the conditioning of salivation responses.

Conditioning Procedure

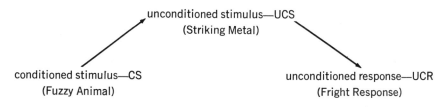

Post-conditioning

Figure 21-2   A schematic representation of the conditioning of a phobia

It is commonly believed that much emotional behavior is acquired through respondent or Pavlovian conditioning. The consistent pairing of naturally unpleasant objects or fear-producing stimuli with other objects or stimuli may bring about fear reactions to these objects, which did not originally produce fear responses. Young children who develop early illness and require a doctor's attention have been known to cry or exhibit other emotional behavior when the doctor approaches them. For these children, the doctor is associated with such things as needles and other unpleasant events; consequently, his presence produces fear responses. It is not surprising that these fear responses often generalize to other individuals, particularly to all persons wearing white coats, or in some instances to men in general.

In the case of phobias we can undoubtedly establish fear responses through accidental happenings. If an individual were struck by a lightning bolt during one of his first experiences with lighting a cigarette, he could early develop a phobic-type reaction to all aspects of cigarettes and cigarette smoking. Often, when the phobic patient makes his appearance at the physician's office, he does not know or remember what events resulted in the initial conditioning of his phobia. Some therapists spend session after session trying to uncover the initiating circumstances. Even if a patient does develop an insight and remembers specific events in his history which might have contributed to his phobic behavior, this knowledge in no way insures that he can overcome his fears. In fact, as we have mentioned previously, awareness of the conditions which initiated the phobia and full understanding that the phobic objects cannot do actual harm does not seem to mitigate the fear reaction when the phobic comes in contact with the fear-producing situation or object.

The respondent-conditioning procedures demonstrated by Watson and Rayner and by Pavlov differs in some respects from other types of conditioning procedures we have previously discussed. Formerly, we always spoke of the consequences of behavior. Behavior which yielded a reinforcer increased in rate. Responses which produced unpleasant events were punished and thus reduced in rate. In all instances, the primary concern was with the consequence the behaviors produced. In respondent conditioning as Pavlov and others after him have described it, reinforcement does not play a role. The only requirement is that the unconditioned stimulus and the conditioned stimulus be presented together over several trials. After such pairings, the conditioned stimulus produces the conditioned response. The conditioned response is similar in many respects to the unconditioned response which is produced by the unconditioned stimulus.

We have already said that Pavlov's type of conditioning is called respondent conditioning. Now we will reintroduce a term for the type of conditioning that we have discussed previously throughout this book. Since this type of response produces some kind of consequence, it can be said that the response operates on the environment to produce these consequences. The rat in an experimental chamber pushes the lever and thus operates the mechanisms which produce a food pellet. Similarly, a bear may emit climbing responses which operate to bring him close to apples in a tree. Conditioning which obviously involves responses which operate in the environment to produce direct consequences is commonly referred to as operant conditioning. Unlike respondent conditioning, which seems primarily to involve changes in glands, smooth muscles, or other physiological systems which are outside of voluntary control, operant conditioning involves responses which have to do with the gross muscle systems, which the organism regulates himself.

In our discussion of phobias, it was stated that they may be established through respondent conditioning. However, we have said nothing of the way phobias can be eliminated except that direct persuasion and argument seem to be of no value. Let us see how conditioning techniques employing fading procedures were used to eliminate a phobia in a young boy.

Elimination of a Car Phobia

Ever since he was eight years old John had been afraid of cars.[2] Two years earlier he had been in a car accident. This fear was without a doubt real and caused him and his parents distress and inconvenience. For instance, there was the time John's father had planned the excursion to the zoo.

"You'll like the zoo," John's father told him. "We can see elephants and monkeys, too. We'll have a great time, so let's have no nonsense. Okay?"

"Okay," John said.

All the while John was getting dressed to go to the zoo, he was strangely quiet. John's mother asked him if he felt well. John said that he did, but later, just as they were all ready to go to the garage and get into the car, he disappeared into the bathroom. The rest of the family waited in the car for him. Ten, fifteen minutes passed.

"This is ridiculous," John's father said. Five minutes later he got out of the car to go see John. "I'll settle his hash," he said.

When his father entered the house, John was standing outside the door to the bathroom. As his father approached, the boy lowered his head and looked sheepish.

"I've had enough," his father said and took his hand roughly. He half pulled John toward the car. When they were within about 30 feet, John ceased moving his feet and legs. His father dragged the child into the car and closed the door before he stopped to look closely at him.

"Now, John, I . . ." He stopped short. John had turned white. Beads of perspiration ran down his cheeks and his eyes looked funny and glazed. Just then he let out a wail of anguish which might easily have been heard for a block. His small body shook and trembled all over.

His father took the child back to the house and then returned to the car where the rest of the family waited.

"Well, we'll go to the zoo another time," his father said. They all got out of the car and walked slowly back to the house.

When Dr. Lazarus met John, it took him only a few minutes to diagnose his problem as a car phobia. This type of phobia occasionally occurred among children. Dr. Lazarus knew that John's fear of cars had been learned, and could therefore be unlearned.

In the initial session, Dr. Lazarus talked to John and got to know him. He found that John was fond of chocolate. During the next session, Dr. Lazarus began to treat John's phobia. While talking with him, Dr. Lazarus would steer the conversation onto the subject of trains, airplanes, buses, and other vehicles. Now, discussing motor vehicles seems a long way from actually riding in one, but even the confrontations with this stimulus initially produced mild fear reactions in John. However, Dr. Lazarus was sensitive to John's reactions and

2. This section based on Lazarus, A. A. The elimination of children's phobias by deconditioning. In H. J. Eysenck (Ed.), *Behavior Therapy and the Neurosis*. London: Pergamon, 1960, 114–122.

monitored them closely. Whenever John displayed fear reactions, he did not comfort the child or try to talk him out of his fear. However, as soon as John volunteered a positive comment about the subject, he would offer him a piece of his favorite chocolate. By the third session, John was talking freely at great length about all types of moving vehicles. He displayed no signs of being afraid. Dr. Lazarus felt that John was ready for the next phase of his treatment.

"Let's play a game today," Dr. Lazarus said. Slowly he pulled an object out of his pocket. It was a toy car. Immediately John stepped back a few steps and looked at Dr. Lazarus as if questioning his friendship. Before he said anything else, Dr. Lazarus popped a small piece of chocolate in John's mouth. Then he produced another car and proceeded to play a game in which he sent the two toy cars crashing into one another head on. John turned white and perspiration formed on his forehead. However, Dr. Lazarus didn't seem to notice John or his fearful state; he remained engrossed in his "play," time and time again acting out versions of accidents between the toy cars. Soon John began to recover some of his color and moved slightly toward Dr. Lazarus. At this point, Dr. Lazarus immediately lost momentary interest in his absorbing game, popped a piece of chocolate into John's mouth, and talked to the child. Then he turned back to his game. As John moved closer to Dr. Lazarus and the "accident prone" cars, he received more and more of his favorite chocolate and Dr. Lazarus' attention. After each "accident" in which John evidenced no fear, he received a chocolate. Soon John was touching the toy car without any apparent fear. Later Dr. Lazarus and John spent hours playing the "accident game" with the toy cars. The game was interspersed with "chocolate breaks" and John enjoyed the game considerably.

When the weather became acceptable, Dr. Lazarus and John played games outside. He arranged for a car to be parked nearby. They spent hours sitting in it discussing the accident in which John had been involved. As long as John entered into this conversation freely and showed no fear, he received pieces of chocolate and lots of attention from his new friend. After awhile, the two began to take very short imaginary rides. One day Dr. Lazarus searched through his pockets pretending to look for a piece of chocolate. "We're all out of candy, John. Sorry," he said. "Let's go get some more." While telling this to John he turned on the ignition and started the car, watching John closely as he did. There were no signs of fear. The store was only a block away, but he was in no hurry to get there. He backed the car out of the drive and out into the street. Once they reached the store and bought a good supply of chocolate, they got back into the car and began to drive around town. They laughed and acted like tourists. John chewed his chocolate and watched the sights; he was discovering the pleasures of travel.

When they returned to John's house his father was waiting in the drive. John jumped out of the car and ran to his Dad, and immediately began to talk about his wonderful recent excursion. John left Dr. Lazarus and his father alone and went inside to relate his adventures to his mother.

"I guess we're due to go on an outing," John's father said.

"Sounds like a good idea. I hear the zoo is good to visit this time of year," Dr. Lazarus smiled.

An analysis of Dr. Lazarus' interactions with John reveals the use of chocolate candy and attention as positive reinforcement. Successive approximations to the terminal behavior of riding in an automobile were reinforced systematically, and thus our old friend shaping played an integral role in John's recovery. Throughout, Dr. Lazarus was careful not to reinforce responses which were in any manner inconsistent with the terminal behavior. Verbalizations which revolved around John's fears where automobiles were concerned received no chocolate reinforcement and no attention.

Summary

We stressed that in clinical practice, some behavior patterns can be found which are apparently not under the subject's voluntary control, although the individual may thoroughly verbalize the relationship between his behavior and the conditions or situations which bring about this behavior. One clinical example of this type of behavior was mentioned: a narrative from the treatment of an irrational fear which is technically called a phobia. The distinctive features of this type of behavior are that the behavior does not appear to be under the voluntary control of the patient and involves extensive physiological responses such as deviations in heart rate, changes in skin resistance, and irregularities in blood pressure.

1. Watson and Rayner demonstrated how a phobic reaction could be established in the laboratory. A small child developed a severe phobic-type response to a rat. Prior to experimentation, the child was often seen to approach this animal without hesitation. After the experiment, the subject evidenced avoidance of the rat and exhibited much behavior which could be classified as emotional. These responses further generalized to other things and objects which bore resemblance to the rat; thus stimulus generalization was observed.

2. Avoidance or escape responses usually characterize a phobia. Another component of the phobic behavior involves what has been called emotional behavior. Emotional behavior appears to differ from other behavior previously considered in that it embraces changes and irregularities in the physiology of the glands, smooth muscle systems, and the autonomic nervous system in general. Emotional behavior also differs since it persists without producing a consequence which is reinforcing to the individual. Observation of emotional behavior does not yield the identification of definite reinforcers which are maintaining the behavior.

3. The differences between emotional behavior as seen in a phobia and other behavior which produces reinforcement and is maintained by reinforcement have led some writers to speculate that a different type of learning is needed to account for emotional responses. This type of learning is called *respondent conditioning;* the procedures for it were originally established by the Russian psychologist Ivan Pavlov. Pairing of the UCS and CS was a sufficient condition to bring about the establishment of the conditioned response.

4. A case of car phobia in a young boy was presented. Although it was suspected that the phobia had been established by an accidental case of respondent conditioning, its removal involved reinforcement techniques. Positive reinforcement and the use of fading and shaping technique were used; the child was

maintained on a positive reinforcement schedule with edibles and social reinforcement and was helped to overcome his avoidance of and emotional responses to automobiles.

QUESTIONS

1. What is the clinical name given an irrational fear?
2. While there is normally no real threat from the object or situation which brings about a phobia, the behavior exhibited by the patient could cause him real harm. (a) True; (b) False.
3. Watson and Rayner believed phobias, for the most part, came about through: (a) inheritance; (b) accidental conditioning; (c) imitation; (d) instincts.
4. What was the name of the child on whom Watson and Rayner conducted their experiment?
5. The child Watson and Rayner worked with showed fear responses to only two types of events. What were they?
6. Prior to the experimental procedure, Albert was also introduced to a series of things which included a rabbit, a rat, a dog, and others. What was Albert's response to these things?
7. The experimental procedure involved pairing: (a) the rat with the rabbit; (b) loss of support with the rat; (c) the loud noise with the rat; (d) the loss of support with the loud noise.
8. What response did Albert exhibit to the rat after the pairing procedure?
9. Five days after the basic experimental procedure, another series of tests was performed. At this time Albert was presented with several objects. Briefly describe his response to each of the following: (a) a toy block; (b) the rat; (c) the rabbit; (d) a fur coat.
10. Albert seemed to respond more violently and profoundly to some of the above objects than he did to others. Can you state a general pattern of his responding and how it related to the whole array of objects?
11. The fact that Albert responded similarly to objects which most resembled the rat illustrates a case of s_____ g_____.
12. One distinct component of phobic behavior is escape or avoidance behavior. The second component in which fear responses are included is called _____ behavior.
13. Emotional behavior appears to differ from other behavior in two important ways. One way is that it involves physiology—extensive activity of physiological processes such as heart rate, respiration, and sweat gland activity. What is the other way that emotional behavior seems to differ?
14. Emotional behavior always produces reinforcement. (a) True; (b) False.
15. The lie detector records the following responses: (a) leg movements; (b) physiological changes; (c) effectiveness of reinforcers; (d) extinction.
16. Which of the following responses seems to be more controllable by the individual? (a) Leg movements; (b) Movement of the toes and fingers; (c) Heart rate and heart beat; (d) Movement of the eyebrows.
17. The observation that emotional behavior appears to be different than other behaviors has led to the speculation that it is established by a different learning procedure. This procedure is called r_____ conditioning.
18. Pavlov is best known to psychology for his establishment of the procedures for _____ conditioning.

19. What experimental animals did Pavlov use?

20. Pavlov concluded that his experiment had made his dogs man-eaters since they would salivate when they saw one of the assistants. (a) True; (b) False.

21. Pavlov found that the presentation of food would bring about salivation in his dogs. In his conditioning experiment, the meat powder was called: (a) the unconditioned stimulus; (b) the unconditioned response; (c) the conditioned stimulus; (d) the conditioned response.

22. Salivation occurring when meat powder was presented was called the: (a) unconditioned stimulus; (b) conditioned stimulus; (c) unconditioned response; (d) conditioned response.

23. What event was paired with the presentation of meat powder and what terminology did Pavlov give this event?

24. After pairing the meat powder and the bell for a series of trials, the ringing of the bell alone would produce salivation. In this case, salivation was called the _____.

25. In the conditioning of a phobia in Albert by Watson and Rayner, four events were important. They were the white rat, the making of a loud noise with a hammer, fright responses produced by the sound of the hammer, and fright responses produced by the presentation of the rat. Categorize these as to unconditioned stimulus, conditioned stimulus, unconditioned response, and conditioned response.

26. The phobic response conditioned by Watson and Rayner and the salivation response conditioned by Pavlov are similar in two important ways. One is that they both involve physiological responses. What is the second?

27. In this chapter, two types of conditioning were mentioned. One was respondent conditioning and the other operant conditioning. Categorize the following into one of these types of conditioning: (a) phobias; (b) salivation responses; (c) avoidance response; (d) bar press for M&Ms.

NOTES

Conditioning a Phobia

We mentioned in the discussion of the Watson and Rayner experiment that their subject, the infant Albert, was taken from the experiment shortly after the phobia was conditioned. The experimenters had fully intended to attempt procedures to eliminate the phobia after they had once conditioned it. They had indeed felt obligated to do so. Albert's removal led them to speculate that in all likelihood he would retain the phobia throughout his life. A further suggestion made was that when Albert reached manhood, he might well have forgotten the circumstances under which his phobia first arose and might seek psychoanalytic help complaining of a dreadful fear of seal skins, fur coats, and all other furry objects. Watson and Rayner speculated how a well-meaning therapist who was uninformed as to the actual origin of the phobia might suggest that Albert's problem was linked to some early love for his mother.

It is indeed true that the clinical treatment of phobias has varied greatly in the past decade. Standard forms of therapy appeal to rational behavior or derive from a theory that has been unsuccessful. Phobias have been very successfully eliminated through the approaches involving behavior modification techniques, such as in the case reported in this chapter.

Another behavioral modification approach, similar to the technique used with John, is called systematic desensitization. This technique is unlike the treatment of the car phobia, for in systematic desensitization, the patient never leaves the therapist's office and no measures are instituted in order to bring him into direct contact with the environment outside the office. Instead of actually experiencing stimulus situations which approximate those which bring about the phobic reaction, the patient merely imagines such situations while relaxing in the therapist's office. The therapist employing systematic densensitization does not typically use chocolate candy as a reinforcer. Instead, he prefers semi-hypnotic relaxation induced through instructions. For most individuals, deep relaxation of this sort is extremely pleasant. Once the subject achieves deep relaxation, the therapist asks him to imagine various environmental situations or stimuli which normally produce a mild phobic reaction. If the patient can imagine these situations and yet remain deeply relaxed, the therapist moves on and asks the patient to imagine another environmental situation which more closely approaches the one to which the patient claims to have phobic responses. Eventually the therapist will instruct the patient to imagine the situation which seems to bring about the greatest fear responses. If he can imagine this situation and still remain deeply relaxed, he is effectively free of his phobia. After this procedure is completed, the patient should be capable of leaving the therapist's office and placing himself in the real situation without experiencing a phobic reaction. As unlikely as it seems, the patient usually finds he can do exactly this. Case reports of systematic desensitization indicate that it can be used to successfully treat many phobic behaviors. This technique along with other behavioral techniques has made phobic responses a relatively simple problem for the therapist to deal with. Thus, it becomes difficult to believe that the patient needs to spend as long as three to five years in psychoanalysis in order to be rid of a phobia which behavioral techniques can erase in two or three brief sessions.

Establishing Conditional Responses

The hypothesis that there are two basic types of conditioning, respondent and operant, is a distinction which has historical precedents in psychology. The basic distinctions between the two types of learning are typically made both on a procedural and behavioral level. It is traditional to state that responses involving smooth muscles and the autonomic nervous system can be conditioned respondently, but cannot be conditioned operantly. Responses of more gross muscle structures such as those of the limbs are obviously amenable to operant-conditioning techniques. Usually they can also be conditioned using respondent-conditioning procedures. Another distinction is that responses which are conditionable only by respondent procedures are not under voluntary control whereas responses conditioned by operant means can be regulated by the individual. While these guidelines are usually stated as established principles and distinguishing features, it has become apparent over the years that there are exceptions to these restrictions; in fact, they may not even be too meaningful.

There is a difference between the two procedures. With operant conditioning, a response must occur before it is conditioned. Generally the experimenters are not concerned with what situations caused the initial response. In the operant-conditioning procedure, a consequence is presented following the response once it does occur. The operant conditioner must wait for the response to occur before he can condition it. In respondent conditioning, the unconditioned stimulus immediately produces the unconditioned response. In Pavlov's study, once the meat powder was introduced, salivation immediately occurred. Thus, the experimenter can bring about the unconditioned response whenever he wishes. He has then only to pair the conditioned stimulus with the unconditioned stimulus. After he does this, the conditioned stimulus alone will produce a conditioned response which is similar in many respects to the unconditioned response.

22

During the last decade we have seen a rapidly increasing number of successful applications of the principles of behavior to the treatment of behavior problems. To date, modification of abnormal behavior is the most significant practical accomplishment of behavior technology. This has been reflected in the extensive coverage given to this area in the present text. Many other significant areas of application are yet to be developed. One very promising area which may see progress during the next decade is the application of the principles of behavior to education.[1] The need for improved educational practices is becoming more apparent. There is nation-wide concern about the level of achievement of students, the shortage of trained staff, the increasing number of students, and the rising costs of education. Helping to solve these problems may be the most exciting and fruitful task yet undertaken by the behavioral scientist and technologist.

By now, the relevance of the principles of behavior to education should be evident to the thoughtful reader. First, we must define the goals of education in terms of observable behavior changes. We should then attempt to reinforce those behaviors we want learned and extinguish those we find undesirable. We will shape complex response topographies of both a motor and verbal nature. We will condition complex discriminations and concepts using fading techniques. We will use schedules of reinforcement to maintain the highest and most consistent rates of educational behavior. In short, we will use the powerful set of behavioral tools that have been illustrated in the preceding chapters. The next section shows how the principles of behavior are being applied to teach an introductory psychology course to over one thousand students.

---

1. This section based on Malott, R. W., and Svinicki, J. G. Contingency management in an introductory psychology course for 1000 students. Paper presented at A.P.A., San Francisco, 1968.

A Modern College Course

This section describes an experimental college course designed to develop and demonstrate solutions to four major problems in higher education. These problems are (1) student underachievement, (2) large student/faculty ratios, (3) the high cost of education, and (4) the common complaint that a liberal education is difficult to achieve and irrelevant to the world of affairs.

Student Achievement

In a representative institution of higher education, 10 percent of the students are customarily on academic probation; many are eventually dismissed from school. This highlights the widespread problem of student underachievement which plagues higher education. In spite of this situation, it may be that all students meeting the normal entrance requirements of a college are capable of doing "A" level work at that college. Furthermore, it may be possible to design an educational system in which most students will attain this level.

Daily Reading Assignments and Quizzes

While some students work hard and earn the grade of "A" others work very little and earn much poorer grades. Nonetheless, grades may be effective reinforcers for nearly all college students. The problem is that the schedule of reinforcement is too intermittent to maintain the behavior of many students with deficient histories. Students who appear unmotivated may work industriously if the proper schedule of reinforcement is used. Without the proper history of training, laboratory animals required to make a large number of responses for each reinforcement may respond very poorly. However, if the reinforcements are programmed more frequently, they may respond well.

In the introductory psychology course at Western Michigan University, we eliminated the usual infrequent hour exams on large reading assignments. In their place are brief daily quizzes over one-hour daily reading assignments. This schedule seems to maintain more reading behavior than do the usual hour exams. In addition, the students avoid the tendency to wait until the day before the hour exam to try to cram a large amount of material. Cramming on only an hour's reading assignment is essentially not cramming. When first exposed to daily quizzes, students may object; however they soon come to prefer daily quizzes to hour exams (see Figure 22-1).

Clear Specification of the Responses to be Learned

In order to facilitate high student achievement, an attempt is made to specify as clearly as possible what will constitute mastery of the reading assignments. In

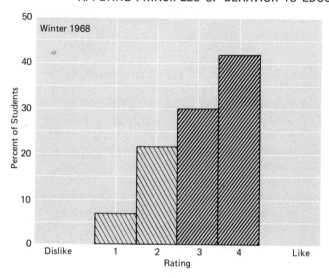

Figure 22-1 How do you feel about the daily quizzes?

the case of the programmed text material, there is little ambiguity; however, with the unprogrammed material, there is considerable room for judgment. For these latter materials we provide a set of reading objectives with each assignment. They indicate what the student should master.

Similarly, it may be that one of the reasons students have difficulty writing good laboratory reports is that it is not clear what is required. In order to eliminate some of this ambiguity, a detailed style manual and a sample laboratory report are provided.

Opportunities for Make-up Work

The regular daily quiz consists of six brief questions in which the proper terms are to be filled in. If the student misses one or more of these questions, he has the opportunity to attend one of several make-up quizzes on that reading assignment. The first make-up quiz is given the evening of the regular quiz and follows a 40-minute remedial lecture on the day's reading assignment. If the student does not answer all six questions correctly or does not attend the make-up quiz that evening, several other opportunities for make-up quizzes are given during the remainder of the week and weekend. No special remedial work is provided for these remaining make-up quizzes.

In order to provide the students with ample opportunity to acquire laboratory report writing skills, they are allowed to rewrite their reports as many times as needed until an "A" level report has been prepared.

To facilitate the completion of laboratory experiments, opportunities for extra laboratory sessions are provided on Friday and Saturday.

100 Percent Mastery Required

If the student does not pass with 100 percent accuracy one of the quizzes associated with each reading assignment, he must either drop the course or receive an "F" for the entire course depending upon the point in the term. This is known as the "Doomsday Contingency." The assignments are sufficiently clear and reasonable and the opportunities to take the quizzes sufficiently frequent that it is unnecessary for any conscientious student to face the Doomsday Contingency, and few do (see Figure 22-2).

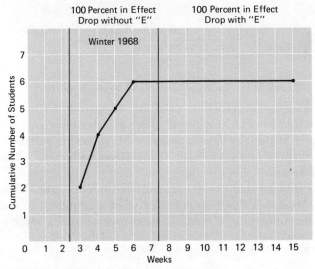

Figure 22-2 Students dropping Ψ 150 for failure to meet 100 percent

Even though an extremely aversive consequence is potentially available, it is so easy to avoid this consequence that the overall situation need not be particularly aversive, as the data seem to show (see Figure 22-3).

When these data were obtained, most of the make-up quizzes were given on Fridays and Saturdays, the main reason for objection. Since that time we have interspersed the quizzes throughout the week.

The laboratory was divided into four experiments to be completed in a total of 28 50-minute class periods. Because of the large number of students in each laboratory section, the manual apparatus, unattenuated test chamber, and various other factors, it was not clear whether it would be reasonable to expect the students to actually complete these experiments in the amount of time provided. They were informed that they were to perform the four experiments and write four laboratory reports for the semester; however, they were not explicitly informed of the consequences of failure to do this. The laboratory met twice a week for the entire term. During the first term this procedure was used, very few stu-

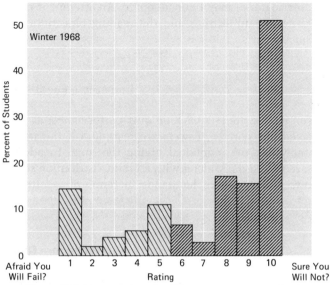

Figure 22-3 In regard to the 100 percent mastery criterion

dents completed all four experiments. The average number of experiments completed was between one and two. We prorated the students' grades on the experiments they had not completed on the basis of the grade for the laboratory reports they had turned in. We felt that this was entirely unsatisfactory and decided to adopt a more courageous procedure.

Several changes were put into effect simultaneously. Possibly the most important was the requirement that in order for the student to receive any credit for a laboratory experiment, he must complete the experiment and turn in an "A" level write-up. Before the experiment can be considered complete, the animal's behavior has to be demonstrated to the teaching apprentice. In addition, Friday and Saturday are available for make-up laboratory work each week. The laboratory was also changed from two days a week for 15 weeks to four days a week for 7½ weeks for either the first or second half of the term. The result of all this has been that, out of more than one thousand students, fewer than 12 failed to complete all four experiments and none failed to complete at least three experiments. Of those that failed to complete all four experiments, several were students for whom one or more rats died during the term.

Error Analysis

As anyone who has used test questions knows, an alarmingly high percentage of the questions are ambiguous or otherwise poor. An error analysis is made of the quiz questions and on the basis of this, all the questions are corrected and improved. Where there is a high level of error although the question appears satisfactory, the reading material may be inadequate. An attempt is made to compensate for this in the make-up lectures and the reading objectives by emphasizing the especially difficult parts.

Immediate Feedback

Students are given immediate feedback on quiz performance; as soon as the quiz papers are collected, the correct answers are read, and if the students have any questions, they may ask the individual giving the quiz. In addition all of the students' scores are posted daily along with a grade distribution so that each week the student knows exactly where he stands in terms of a letter grade for the course.

Procedure Quiz

No matter how clear the objectives and instructions are, the student must read them before they can be effective. We have observed that students tend to come to the laboratory unprepared. In order to reduce this, the students are given quizzes over the laboratory procedure sheets before experiment. In addition, a video tape is shown demonstrating proper techniques for each experiment.

Students are also given quizzes over the laboratory style manual and the general course procedures. In addition they are quizzed over the special material they are to analyze in the discussion sections; this reduces the likelihood that a student's discussion will be hampered by his not having recalled the material.

Absence Policy

During the first year that we taught this course, the correlation between unexcused absences and grades showed a tendency for students who had less than four unexcused absences to have final grades of "A" or "B" and for students who had more than four unexcused absences to have "C's" or lower. Though there are many possible interpretations of this correlation, the more absences the student has, the fewer the number of points he can earn; therefore the lower the grade he is likely to earn. A student might gradually slip from one grade to the next through repeated absences. No single absence is very important, but the cumulative deficit can be considerable. In order to prevent this we allow a maximum of four unexcused absences. The student receives no credit for the day if an unexcused absence occurs; and if he has more than four unexcused absences, he receives an "F" for the entire course. This has virtually eliminated excessive unexcused absences. Only absences which can be documented as legitimate are actually excused.

What has been the level of achievement attained as a result of these various procedures? The students work about 12 hours per week for 3 hours of credit;

80 percent to 90 percent earn a final grade of "A" and less than 2 percent receive an "F." This is the case even though high academic requirements are imposed.

Student/Faculty Ratio

A widely recognized problem in higher education is the rapidly increasing number of students for each faculty member (student/faculty ratio). A common method for dealing with this is the use of large lecture sections as the primary in-class teaching technique, combined with the redefinition of educational goals in terms amenable to multiple-choice, machine-scored, objective examinations. An alternative solution is needed. Laboratory experiences and small group discussions are valuable teaching techniques; but we should not neglect oral and written expression, creative behavior, and assessment of the student's mastery of the coursework throughout essay examinations.

One possible solution is based on the students' own evaluation of their performance in small discussion groups and laboratories, laboratory report writing, and essay examinations. In some instances, the grading is done by peers; in other instances, by more advanced students. Quality control is maintained by a sampling system involving other advanced students, teaching assistants, and faculty.

Peer Grading

One of the purposes of a course such as this is to develop written and oral fluency concerning the course subject matter. It is important that the students have an opportunity to emit verbal responses and for those responses to be reinforced. However, even in relatively small classes there is little opportunity for any but the most loquacious of students. In a 50-minute discussion class of 25 students, each student has an average of two minutes recitation time. Of course, even the most nondirective instructors utilize a large amount of this time and the rest is taken up by a small number of highly verbal students. Most students hardly recite at all.

Four-man student-led discussion groups were developed to deal with this problem. Students fill in detailed grading sheets each day evaluating the other three students in their groups. There are obviously many difficulties with this. One problem is that of collusion; all of the students may agree to give each other good grades. We have attempted to reduce this by rotating the students through the various discussion groups each day. Each discussion group sits at a separate table which contains a microphone. A student teaching apprentice listens to the various tables during the discussion. Although he only listens to one table at a time, the students never know which table it is. If the students' evaluation of the speakers varies considerably from that of the apprentice, they receive a zero for the day's seminar.

Another major problem with peer grading is whether or not the students are able to grade each other accurately even if they are being conscientious. We hope that the discussion text is programmed well enough so that the four students can come to a consensus about the correctness of the discussion which will be reasonably close to a correct response as defined by the instructor.

Teaching Apprentices

Each term, 52 of the best students in the introductory course are given the opportunity to act as teaching apprentices during the subsequent term. This requires 16 hours of work each week for which the student receives four hours of credit. Every effort is made to ensure that the experience justifies the academic credit received. Each teaching apprentice is responsible for a discussion/laboratory section of 28 students which meets four times per week. In addition, he helps monitor the weekly lecture sections. The teaching apprentice conducts the laboratory sessions and helps students who are having difficulty with their experiments. He also edits and grades all of the laboratory reports. He monitors the discussions, administers and grades the daily reading quizzes, does the bookkeeping for each section, and supervises the make-up laboratories and make-up quizzes.

After one term as a teaching apprentice, 13 teaching apprentices serve as advanced teaching apprentices the next term. The advanced teaching apprentice monitors the performance of the teaching apprentices in the discussion/laboratory sections. He has a rating form which he uses to grade the teaching apprentices. These grades are posted daily. The advanced teaching apprentice grades on the basis of classroom performance, reliability of performing clerical work, accuracy of seminar monitoring, quiz grading, and laboratory report grading. In addition, the advanced teaching apprentice helps with more advanced administrative aspects of the course.

Assistants

Four paid assistants each work 20 hours a week on the course. Two are graduate and two are undergraduate assistants. One assistant is primarily responsible for supervising the laboratory sections, another the seminar sections, and a third the reading quizzes and lecture sections. A fourth acts as a general administrative assistant. They are also responsible for evaluating the performance of the advanced teaching apprentices. Enough typing and other clerical activities are involved to require the services of a full-time secretary.

Faculty

Three faculty members are involved part-time with this course. One is primarily responsible for the seminars, one for the laboratories, and one for the lecture and reading assignments and overall management of the course. In addition, several faculty members serve as guest lecturers once a term. When the course was being established, a large amount of time was required of the faculty; however now their combined efforts probably equal the work of less than one half-time faculty member. At this point the course can essentially run without the involvement of the faculty, except for lectures. Faculty are now primarily concerned with maintaining and improving the standards of the course and developing new and better ways of administering the course and teaching the material.

We have been emphasizing mainly the solutions to problems of large student/faculty ratios in terms of the types of educational activities which are normally available only to students in small classes. Another dimension to this problem should also be considered. It is usually felt that as the student/faculty ratio increases, the faculty are less aware of the needs, interests, and problems of the individual student. We have made systematic attempts to deal with this problem by obtaining elaborate student evaluations of each reading assignment, laboratory experiment, discussion meeting, and lecture, as well as of the overall course. On the basis of the students' opinions of the interest, value, clarity, etc. of the many units of the course, these units have been drastically modified and in many instances eliminated. The faculty and assistants also conduct face-to-face interviews with a small sample of individual students. These techniques combined with the results of error analyses of the individual quiz questions give the students more than the customary degree of control over the course. We are able to be much more responsive to the wants and needs of the students in this large course than is usually the case with smaller courses using more traditional techniques.

Results

To what extent then, have these techniques been successful in dealing with large student/faculty ratios? A wide variety of complex activities are made available to the students. They have four hours of small group discussions or laboratory, one hour of lecture, and five daily reading assignments each week. In addition they write four laboratory reports per term and have a wide variety of remedial opportunities for the reading quizzes, laboratories and laboratory reports. These educational experiences are provided for an average of one thousand students per term by a paid staff which is the equivalent of one half-time faculty member, one full-time graduate assistant, one full-time undergraduate assistant, and one full-time secretary.

Cost of Education

A third problem faced by today's colleges and universities is the rising cost of education. Many fine institutions are in financial crisis. Yet the demand for their services is increasing. The crisis is largely a result of the high cost of personnel, equipment, and the physical plant. This trend may be reversed through careful planning and efficient use of these valuable commodities.

Two aspects of this solution to the cost of education have just been discussed. One is the evaluation of student performance by the students themselves and the other is the provision of an adequate supporting staff of assistants and secretaries for the faculty. Along the same line, the students in the course are also obliged to perform two or three hours of work during the term to help with the management of the course. These activities include animal care, laboratory maintenance, and clerical work. This allows the faculty member to spend his time on activities requiring his advanced training and to delegate other activities to his staff, the teaching apprentices, and the students themselves.

Another problem involved is the scheduling of class so that the classrooms operate at capacity throughout the day. By having laboratory and discussion sections meeting from 8:00 A.M. to 9:00 P.M., an average of four thousand student class hours per week are scheduled in two classrooms, totaling twelve hundred square feet of floor space. Extra laboratories as well as many of the make-up quizzes are scheduled in the same space on Friday and Saturday. Other make-up quizzes and lectures are scheduled elsewhere.

Relevant Liberal Education

Students often complain that a liberal or general education lacks sufficient relevance to world affairs to maintain their interest. Faculty members frequently confess that the goals of a liberal education are rarely achieved by education programs actually in existence. Furthermore, it is commonly stated that the attainment of a liberal education is incompatible with the attainment of a relevant or practical education. We believe that these two types of education may be achieved simultaneously and may in fact reinforce one another.

One of the problems of a curriculum aiming toward a liberal education is that no adequate framework has been developed to integrate the various traditional academic disciplines. A curriculum in behavioral science and technology, however, can illustrate the approaches of the various academic divisions and at the same time provide a framework for bringing them together.

By being sensitive to the interests of the students, we have developed an introductory course of obvious relevance and importance. Programmed texts are our primary means of teaching the principles of behavior; however, nearly half of the reading assignments and nearly all of the lectures are devoted to emphasizing the relevance, utility, and importance of the principles of behavior. Little effort is made in this introductory course to teach the value of an abstract science; instead, we emphasize the role of behavior principles in the analysis and control of significant human behavior. This has been greatly facilitated by the experimental material now available in behavior modification. No attempt is made in this first course to give an overview of all the various fields or approaches in psychology. Nonetheless, the general approaches and problems to be found in the natural sciences, social sciences, and humanities are illustrated in this course.

Discussion

Several features of this course may warrant additional comment.

Daily Reading Assignments and Quizzes

The rate at which quizzes on the reading assignments are given is determined by the instructor. In this sense they are "instructor-paced." This prevents the student from waiting until the end of the term when there will be insufficient time to attempt to master the semester's reading—an all too frequent phenomenon when the reading is entirely "student-paced." On the other hand, a student determines the rate at which he covers a specific assignment. In this sense, the course is "student-paced." In other words one student may need to spend only 15 minutes on the assignment whereas another student may need to spend two hours; the students may adjust their own personal daily work schedules accordingly. In this way individual differences in the rate of mastering the material may be accommodated within the instructor-paced assignment and quiz system.

Peer Grading

The notion of peer grading is important. If we are to shape complex behavioral repertoires in students, it is probably necessary that the students emit responses from these repertoires and that these responses be differentially reinforced. In most cases it is necessary to have humans evaluate the quality of the responses. In mass education the tendency has been to use professors as evaluators. This presents a severe constraint on the amount of behavior of a given student that a professor may evaluate. As an alternative, machine evaluation of relatively simple behavior, such as answering multiple-choice questions, may be used. If a system can be devised whereby peer evaluation is used effectively, then it may be possible to shape complex behaviors in a mass educational setting. This is what we are attempting.

Doomsday Contingency

It was hoped that there would not be any undesirable side effects resulting from our use of aversive control—the Doomsday Contingency. An analogous situation might be where an individual takes a pleasant stroll on the sidewalk adjoining a busy highway. There is a Doomsday Contingency ever present in that situation which is even more aversive than ours. If the individual indiscriminately steps onto the highway, there is a high probability that he will be run over by the oncoming traffic. The fact that this Doomsday Contingency is always there does not greatly decrease the pleasantness or reinforcing quality of the stroll along the sidewalk, since Doomsday is so easily avoided. This also seems to be the case in our course.

Daily Quizzes

Although students obtain a high level of mastery of the material on a daily basis— "immediate recall"—they do not do nearly as well on hour exams given at the end of the term—"long-term recall." We have been struggling with this problem constantly. We wish to obtain a high level of mastery of all of the material covered during the entire semester, even at the end of the term. Yet we wish to avoid the aversive side effect usually associated with final exams. We hope to be able to do this by giving occasional review quizzes which have the Doomsday Contingency in effect. Reviewing for these quizzes should be greatly facilitated through the use of the list of reading objectives.

Summary

Solutions to the problems of student achievement have been proposed in terms of daily reading assignments and quizzes, clear specifications of the responses to be learned, opportunities for make-up work, requirement of 100 percent mastery, error analysis, immediate feedback on quiz performance, procedure quizzes, and a strict absence policy. The problem of high student/faculty ratio has been dealt with in terms of peer grading, student teaching apprentices, and student assistants. These factors, and efficient classroom scheduling, are also involved in dealing with the high cost of education. The common complaint that a liberal education is difficult to achieve and irrelevant to the world of affairs may be more readily handled in a course in behavior science.

We have been discussing serious problems and the solutions we have attempted seem practicable. They have been demonstrated in a very large course but still only in one course. The establishment of an experimental college designed to further these notions seems to be a reasonable next step. Such a college will be of great value in its own right and will serve as a model which may shape the future of American education.

QUESTIONS

1. What were the four major problems in higher education discussed?
2. In a representative institution for higher education, what percentage of the students are customarily on academic probation: (a) 1; (b) 10; (c) 50; (d) 75.
3. What grade level of work do the authors feel should be attained by students meeting all entrance requirements for the college?
4. How is it that grades may be effective reinforcers for nearly all college students, when so many appear to be unmotivated by grades?
5. What was changed so that grades were made more effective reinforcers in the introductory psychology course at Western Michigan University?

6. What is the purpose of the reading objectives?
7. What opportunities were provided for make-up work?
8. What level of mastery was required of the reading assignments?
9. What was the consequence if 100 percent mastery was not obtained?
10. How was the credit given for laboratory experiments arranged so as to increase the number of laboratory experiments which the students completed?
11. What was done with the error analysis?
12. How was immediate feedback given for performance on quizzes?
13. What was the purpose of the procedure quiz?
14. What was the absence policy?
15. What was the rationale behind the absence policy?
16. What percentage of students earn "A"s in this course? (a) 10–20 percent; (b) 30–40 percent; (c) 50–60 percent; (d) 80–90 percent.
17. What is the common method for dealing with the problems generated by the increasing student/faculty ratio?
18. Briefly describe peer grading.
19. What is done to reduce the likelihood that students give each other good grades regardless of their actual performance?
20. What is done in an effort to ensure that the students are in fact able to grade each other?
21. What are the activities of an advanced teaching apprentice?
22. What efforts have been made to deal with the needs, interests, and problems of an individual student in large classes?
23. In what sense are the students paced?
24. What was the analogy between the Doomsday Contingency in the classroom and on the highway?
25. What is the problem of immediate recall versus long-term recall, and what is the proposed solution to the problem?

NOTES

We have seen how the principles of behavior are currently being applied to education. What about the future?

A Program of Accelerated Education

The graduate of an accelerated education program is 11 years old and has a Ph.D. degree. In this educational utopia, the student is typical. The only difference between the student of the future and the usual student of today is that one has attended a school with an accelerated education program while the other has attended today's school. A graduate of an accelerated education program differs from the typical student in three ways: he spends more time in school, he starts school at an earlier age, and he attends a school which uses advanced educational technology. Before we consider whether it is possible to produce 11-year-old Ph.Ds, let us consider whether it is desirable to do so.

The Disadvantages of Accelerated Education. It is usually argued that even if the 11-year-old could have all of the formal education of a Ph.D., he would lack the social, emotional, and intellectual maturity of a typical 26-year-old Ph.D. This argument assumes that psychological maturity is acquired simply through the process of aging. However, there is no evidence indicating that age by itself is an important determiner of psychological maturity. Rather, it appears that psychological maturity is primarily a result of experience, not of age. Experience seems to be the determining factor in the behavior of adults as compared to children. Similarly, proper emotional self-control and sound decision-making are not the result of age, but rather of experience.

Even though it may be conceded that psychological maturity is the product of experience and not age, it is frequently argued that it takes 26 years to have all of the experiences that result in the psychological maturity of a 26-year-old. This is questionable. For example, most of the time we are having experiences which contribute very little, if anything, to our maturity. It should be possible to condense most of these experiences (that normally occur throughout a 26-year period) into an 11-year period. This could be done by using a combination of methods based on real and vicarious experiences since much, if not most, of our psychological maturity is shaped by vicarious experience. Individual behavior appropriate to a family crisis is not necessarily learned through direct experience with similar crises; instead it may be learned vicariously through such media as television and movies. Whether or not we jump in the river to save a drowning child may be greatly determined by the comic books we have read. Much of our sexual behavior, when we reach sexual maturity, has already been determined by vicarious experiences occurring before sexual maturity. At an intermediate stage between vicarious and direct experience, the techniques of role-playing found in psychodrama might be used; the student could act in small classroom plays simulating real-life situations. Also, it might be possible on occasion to manipulate some real-life situations, such as fraternity rush or speech-making before a large audience, to give the student additional experience. Surely the combination of these techniques would result in a very mature 11-year-old.

It may be granted that a "crash" educational and maturational program could work, yet would it produce undesirable side effects? Would it require so much of the student's time that he would have little left for leisure? Would it have adverse effects on his mental health and adjustment? It is true that this intensive program would considerably lessen leisure time, and much of the remaining time for leisure would be highly organized to produce psychological maturity. The only answer thus far is that there is no evidence to indicate that a fairly rigorous work program *per se* will damage one's mental health. It is also reasonable to believe that organized leisure could be just as relaxing as disorganized leisure. For example, a well-prepared television show with a goal of enhancing psychological maturity could be just as entertaining as those which we currently view.

This program might not result in mental illness; but is its high degree of organization robbing man of one of life's greatest gifts, spontaneity? To some extent, people who raise this question may be confusing spontaneity with variety. There would most certainly be a much greater variety of experiences in the life of the student in this program than in the life of today's student. With regard to actual spontaneity, it is probably more myth than fact in the life of contemporary students. The life of today's student is in fact rather humdrum; lacking in variety, it contains relatively few surprises. If we find, however, that the student of an accelerated educational system is not getting enough surprises, we can arrange a few supplementary surprises for him, i.e., "planned spontaneity."

When we take away so much of the child's playtime, are we not taking from him much of the pleasure in his young life? The child with a B.A. degree in mathematics would probably get more pleasure from developing mathematical proofs and working on his M.A. thesis than from playing cowboys and Indians. Simply because an activity has long-range value does not mean that it cannot, at the time, be enjoyable.

It may be argued that although this extensive organization will not do any harm, it is simply immoral to exert so much control over the life of an individual. To this argument, one can only answer that most social advances have initially been criticized by some as being immoral.

Even if we can get our student through the Ph.D. program by the age of 11 and can prepare him adequately for society, will society be adequately prepared for him? The answer to this question depends on the nature of the society. If it is a society of 11-year-old Ph.D.s, then it will have no difficulty in accepting a new 11-year-old member. Much of our current society, however, would be very reluctant to accept an 11-year-old Ph.D.; therefore the transition period would undoubtedly be difficult. Just as the American black and American woman are having difficulties attaining and accepting their status as first-class citizens, so will these accelerated students have difficulties. In spite of the initial prejudices against the accelerated student there are many occupations which he could adopt until he had attained sufficient chronological age to be accepted by society, or until society had obtained sufficient mental age to accept him. Let us consider one example. Though most of this discussion is in terms of a Ph.D. program, it should be understood that 11-year-old M.D.s, L.L.B.s, etc., would also be produced. To state the problem bluntly, how would you like for your daughter to have her appendix removed by an 11-year-old M.D.? The answer, of course, is that you would not. Until he becomes acceptable, our young M.D. could serve as a nurse, a veterinarian, a laboratory technician, or an M.D. in underdeveloped areas where the population may be less squeamish.

Even when society has come to accept this student, will there be enough jobs requiring the education of a Ph.D., or will most Ph.D.s be educationally underemployed? This is difficult to answer. In our present society, we seem to have two relevant trends. On the one hand, automation is resulting in a general increase in the amount of education required for jobs; on the other hand, there appears to be a large segment of our population that is educationally underemployed. It is probably the case that most people are not making much use of their advanced education. This does not mean that there are not many important and as yet unaccomplished tasks which require advanced education. As long as there is ignorance, poverty, ill health, and unhappiness, there are tasks to be accomplished; as long as there are scientific questions to be answered and art objects to be created, there are tasks to be accomplished. Our current educational underemployment means that people are not being properly trained to use their education to accomplish these tasks, and even when they accomplish such tasks, they are not properly rewarded.

The question which is most frequently raised is "Who will decide what particular curriculum an individual student is taught?" This decision would probably be made by the same people who currently make such decisions, that is the student's parents, the teachers, and the student himself. While it is true that this means a student will make these decisions at a chronologically younger age, still he will be as educationally advanced as students are today.

Will the accelerated program result in all the students' being alike? In some respects it will increase their similarity. For example, under the accelerated program most students will be well educated. Few will be ignorant, so in that respect students would all be more alike than they are today. However, in terms of what the students learn, they would be much more different. By and large, there is very little diversity in today's curriculum. Most students take courses in essentially the same curriculum. However, in the accelerated program it would be possible to have a much greater variety of combinations of courses. For example, the student might study in three areas such as psychology, physics, and literature. Currently, few literary people have a good grasp of contemporary scientific psychology, let alone physics. In other words, most literary people have essentially the same background and are all very similar to each other. One can imagine that if a portion of the people in literature were well trained in scientific psychology and physics, their literature might be much different from that produced by current authors. This is just an example of the sort of diversity which could be but is not obtained under the present system.

It is often suggested that if everyone has a Ph.D., there will be little value in having a Ph.D. That is like saying that if everyone has a grade school education, then there is little value in having a grade school education. This is not true. The things you learn in school may be of value regardless of whether or not they put you ahead of your fellow man. It is worthwhile being able to read and write even though nearly everyone else can also. Similarly, it has been suggested that if everyone had a Ph.D., there would be no financial advantages to having one. This would not seem to be true. If everyone had a Ph.D., then everyone could be more productive, and the overall standard of living would be raised.

The Advantages of Accelerated Education. Several advantages of this program have been indicated or at least implied in the preceding discussion. A planned program to develop psychological maturity should produce individuals with more desirable traits than do our current haphazard practices. Early exposure to a rigorous work program should create good work habits which would carry over into adult life. The experiences of the accelerated student should be much more varied and interesting than those of today's student. The program should supply a greater amount of the highly educated manpower required to solve the problems which society faces. This would be done in two ways; it would produce a greater absolute number of Ph.D.s; and, by giving the Ph.D. at the age of 11, it would also give each Ph.D. an additional 15 years of professional life.

The economic advantages of this program are considerable. Since the child would attend school eight hours per day starting at the age of three years, the mother would be freed of her custodial duties sooner, and would be able to earn an income earlier. In spite of the increased amount of schooling per student, the absolute number of years of schooling per student would not be increased, and the absolute amount of facilities per student would not be increased. Finally, the accelerated student would earn a much greater total income in his lifetime. (It should be noted that due to our increased scientific and technological development, our standard of living has improved and continues to improve. With this increase in the number of Ph.D.s, the rate of improvement should be much greater.)

This program should provide a means of breaking the vicious cycle of the slum child whose present potential is geared toward becoming a slum parent and toward breeding more slum children. Once he has a Ph.D. and the values that usually accompany that degree, he will probably not return to the slums.

Presumably an educated person can appreciate a wider variety of things and find a more suitable job which is of interest to him. To the extent that this is true, then these are additional advantages that would accrue to the future students.

And finally, if our space program can be justified simply because it is a challenge so can our accelerated education program. The imminent possibility of a society of accelerated students so staggers the imagination that the challenge to develop the program must be accepted.

The Accelerated Education Program. SCHOOL CALENDAR. Although most of the features of this school are still in the developmental stage, the intensive school year could be put into effect tomorrow if we decided to do so. It normally takes about 21 years of schooling to prduce a Ph.D. (12 years for the high school diploma, 4 years for the B.A., 1 year for the M.A., and 4 years for the Ph.D.). A trimester program could greatly reduce the number of years required. The typical semester program consists of two 16-week semesters or 32 weeks of school per calendar year. The trimester program consists of three 16-week trimesters or 48 weeks per year. This would reduce the amount of time to produce a Ph.D. from 21 to 14 calendar years. If in addition, the students were to attend school on Saturdays, the 14 years could be reduced to 12.2 years. In other words, by changing only our school calendar it would be possible for students to get a Ph.D. in only a slightly longer time than it now takes them to get a high school diploma.

ENTRANCE AGE. Recent work by such people as Staats, Moore, and Ulrich indicates that, with special techniques, children can very profitably begin their formal schooling by the age of three years. Dramatic results have been obtained by Moore who has a six-year-old child writing, typing, and reading fourth to seventh grade material. One of his main devices is called a "talking typewriter." Initially the child is placed alone in a small room with an electric jam-proof typewriter. Whenever the child presses a key, a letter or symbol is typed in jumbo script and spoken by a soft voice through a loudspeaker. After the child has had experience with this arrangement, a letter is presented on a screen above the typewriter; the only key which will be effective is the key which produces the letter. When the child has learned to press the proper keys in response to projected letters, the situation is again changed. An entire word is projected on the screen with an arrow pointing to the first letter; the only key which will be effective this time is the one corresponding to the letter indicated by the arrow. When that key is pressed, the letter is typed and spoken as usual; in addition, the arrow moves on to the next letter. This process continues until the word is completed, at which time the word is spoken through the loudspeaker. The child, who is free to leave the laboratory whenever he wishes, usually spends less than ½ hour per day there, but within a few months he is writing, typing and reading.

Unfortunately, only a handful of people are doing research of this sort. But it seems reasonable to predict that if the amount of research in this area were significantly increased, within a few years it would be practical to start all students on their school work by the age of three. If this were combined with the previously mentioned calendar reform, students would receive their Ph.D. at the age of 15.2 years, the age when students today are entering the tenth grade.

EDUCATIONAL TECHNOLOGY. The final set of improvements will be the most difficult to achieve, although they will also be the most significant. They involve a complete re-evaluation of our educational practices, and the development of a scientifically based technology of education. Since education is one of the most conservative institutions in our society, reform will not be easy.

Modern psychology is gradually coming to recognize that behavior and not the mind is its subject matter; educational technology must come to a similar conclusion. When this conclusion is taken seriously, it becomes apparent that we must express the goals of education in terms of specific behaviors and general behavior patterns such as reading behavior, creative behavior, etc. The goals are not to increase the student's "knowledge" or improve his "mind." It is not sufficient to say that we are providing a "liberal education"; rather, we should say how we want our graduates to behave. Once we have expressed our general goals of education in terms of behavior, we must similarly express the goals of each course in the curriculum. We should eliminate those courses which produce behavior inconsistent with or irrelevant to our general behavioral goals. The small number of courses which profess goals compatible with our behavioral goals would then be evaluated in terms of whether they in fact accomplish these goals. In other words, will a person who graduated after taking a particular course behave any differently than one who has not had that course? On those rare occasions when there is a significant difference in behavior, is that difference in the desired direction? If the answer is "no" to either question, the course should be eliminated. Unfortunately, it is probable that very few courses live up to this criterion. If the dead wood were eliminated, our curriculum would probably be very small and obviously inadequate. Therefore it would be necessary to replace the eliminated courses with ones meeting our requirements. The old courses that would remain would probably be improved to such an extent that they would scarcely be recognized.

It is also possible, however, that many courses could be salvaged if a slightly different approach were taken. It may be that many general course areas suffer from insufficient exposure. The trend in education seems to be toward superficiality as indicated by the large number of survey courses offered. Consider, for example, the modern language requirement. In most liberal arts colleges, the student is required to take two years of a language. This represents a great deal of work and expense for each student; yet the percent of students who ever use the language is very small. A major reason for this is the low level of language proficiency attained, and the insufficient motivation to use the language. These deficiencies are in turn largely attributable to an insufficient exposure to the language and to situations where the language is functional.

If the above arguments are correct, the remedy is to increase and improve the exposure to the foreign language. The latest this should be started is when the student is three years old, though it would be wise to start at an earlier age.

It is easy to say that the student should spend more time studying language; but in order to do this he must spend less time studying other subjects. It is at this point that we should reconsider the liberal or general education objectives and procedures. Instead of the present objective of a liberal education, which is to broaden the individual's knowledge in many areas, we should strive toward having an individual who can and does behave proficiently in a few divergent areas. By insisting that the number of areas of proficiency be numerous, we get proficiency in almost no areas. Consequently we affect the behavior of our graduate very little; his education is nearly a total waste. It would be much better if he mastered a *few* divergent areas *well*.

Consider what might be an example of an improved curriculum. During grade school, the student would not only acquire the usual English language and arithmetical skills but would also have the opportunity to learn a foreign language and typewriting. In addition he would take a single sport and a single art and work extensively with them. These activities would be selected with the intention that they be continued for the rest of the individual's life. The curriculum for a given student might be the same from junior high school through graduate school to the point where the student begins work on his dissertation. During these years of advanced education, the individual would continue with his sport, art, and foreign language, but would also add three other disciplines for extensive study. These three disciplines might be equally emphasized so that if, for example, they were mathematics, history, and psychology, the only difference between a major in each of those fields would be the Ph.D. dissertation. Upon graduation, it is hoped that he would continue to make at least a vocational use of all of the disciplines he had studied.

The same approach might be used to improve the offerings of individual departments for students majoring in them. Instead of insisting that the student take one course in each of the many specialities within a discipline, he might be required to take several courses in each of a few such specialties. Similarly, most courses would probably profit greatly if they attempted to cover only a small portion of the material they now cover.

A revised curriculum would be just one of the results of an improved educational technology. After the accomplishment of the very difficult task of specifying the objectives of a course in behavioral terms, it should be possible to develop greatly improved techniques to accomplish these tasks. The current teaching machine and programmed instruction movement is a primitive beginning in the use of a behaviorally oriented technology of education; yet it represents a significant theoretical step in the right direction. Unfortunately, its practical results have not been very impressive thus far. It must be hoped that the current premature widespread use of unproven, low quality teaching-machine programs will not result in a permanent disillusionment with the entire movement. The approach has such great theoretical possibilities that its poor empirical results should move us only to work on the details, not abandon the general principles.

Generally speaking, a teaching program consists of a set of frames. Each frame presents a single concept, tests the student's understanding of the concept, and presents the correct answer to the test. Usually the frames vary in length from one sentence to one or two paragraphs. The preceding frames prepare the student so that he can properly answer the next frame; irrelevant frames are eliminated. If the student does not understand the concept, he will probably not respond correctly on the test at the end of the frame. He will then see the correct answer and realize his error. Sometimes it will be necessary to have the student study a few supplementary frames when he makes an error.

Programs are usually written so that the student makes very few errors. The requirement of a low error rate brings about one source of embarrassment to the programmed instruction movement. It is assumed that getting the correct answer to a frame serves as the reinforcement for reading the frame. The necessity of a low error rate, however, usually results in the answer to the frame being so obvious that it is a very small reinforcement for the student to know that he has responded correctly. Consequently, one of the most common criticisms of programmed instruction is that it is boring. Solving this problem will be a major accomplishment.

Two other concepts from the programmed instruction movement also have considerable significance. One is the notion of "terminal behavior." Terminal behavior is behavior which is acquired by the student studying the program. If one could specify the terminal behavior for a course, there would be no need to assign course grades; the student would simply study the material until he had acquired the terminal behavior, then he would pass the course. It would never be possible to "just barely pass" the course; for either the student learned or he did not. For courses in which the performance depends on what the student learned in the previous courses, such an approach is obviously important. This brings us to the other concept, that of "entering behavior."

The entering behavior for a program is the behavior which the student must be able to emit in order to study the program. For example, a program of calculus might require certain skills in algebra, trigonometry, and analytical geometry. It also assumes certain other skills which may be obscured because of their obviousness. It assumes a wide variety of reading skills, problem-solving skills, reasoning skills, and probably many other subtle behaviors such as paying attention and following instructions. Although there are various opinions, modern behavior theory indicates that most of the differences between individuals in such areas as scholastic performance are attributable to differences in individual past experiences. If this is true, then it should be insisted that, before proceeding to a new step in his education, the student must first demonstrate that he has the requisite entering behavior. This requirement might eliminate much of the individual differences in academic accomplishment. Since every student would be an "A" student, and because of the elimination of the snowballing effect of underachievement due to poor initial accomplishment, every student should proceed at about the same pace.

Dr. Skinner, who started the programmed instruction movement, has suggested that it could reduce the time required to learn a given amount of material by one-half. Let us make the more conservative assumption that programmed instruction plus the other products of an improved educational technology could reduce the time by only one-third. What implications does this have for our future student? Due to changes in the school calendar, the 21 years of schooling normally required to attain the Ph.D. could be reduced to 12.2 years. If the improved educational technology could reduce this time by one-third, it would be approximately 8.1 years. If the student begins school at the age of three, he would receive his doctorate at the age of 11.1 years.

Incredible as the results of this program seem, it is practicable. If the effort devoted to our space program were devoted to an accelerated education program, within only a few years we should be able to produce 11.1-year-old Ph.D.s as a matter of course.

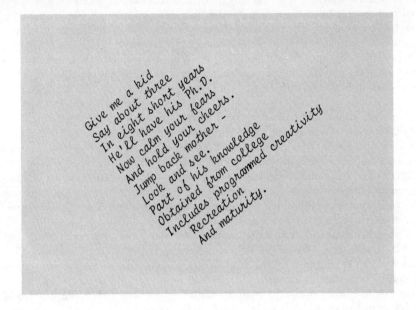

Give me a kid
Say about three
In eight short years
He'll have his Ph. D.
Now calm your fears
And hold your cheers.
Jump back mother —
Look and see.
Part of his knowledge
Obtained from college
Includes programmed creativity
Recreation
And maturity.

CONCLUSIONS

23

The story about the emperor and his new clothing is well known. Everyone swore they saw the clothing and commented on its beauty, but it took a child to point up the simple truth. "What manner of clothes are these?" the child must have reasoned. "They cannot be seen, nor can they be felt. Certainly they are of no value against the wind and the rain."

One point was made clear in the first chapter of this book. We were going to talk about behavior and we have done just that. We have spent precious little time on "feelings," "thoughts," "will," "purpose," "intention," and the "mind." Instead we have talked about behavior; that which can be seen, counted, and measured. In restricting our subject matter to observable behavior, we did not intend to imply that one could not fruitfully, interestingly, and intellectually talk about notions such as mind and feelings. Certainly eloquent and interesting words can be spent on the topic, but of course this is true of most any topic, including emperors and their attire.

But our intent was not to woo the reader with discussions of interesting and mysterious topics; we chose to speak of the less dramatic and more common-sense notion of behavior, which can be observed and recorded. We did so because the history of the science of psychology has taught us that this approach is the most practical for developing an accurate science. As the child reasoned, one may speak at length about nonexistent clothes, but they would not serve against the weather. We chose behavior because the relationships between what people do, or behavior, and other aspects of the environment have proven to be related in an orderly way. This approach has worked well in the past. Since other more exciting mental variables cannot be observed, little can be said about them. Perhaps when they can be observed, their relationships with the environment may prove intriguing. In the meantime, psychologists have relied on presently observable behavior as their basic datum. In keeping with a strict scientific tradition, we have endeavored to keep behavior the subject matter of this book, and have tried our best to demonstrate some of the relations between the basic datum of behavior and the world about us.

Also, in the initial chapter of this book, a single principle of behavior was distilled from a number of cases presented in those first pages. This single principle stated as economically as possible is: *behavior is controlled by its consequences.* If a response produces events which are reinforcing, the response will increase or maintain. If events which are commonly described as unpleasant or aversive follow the response, it will decrease in rate. In subsequent chapters this single principle has been developed in two directions. The first direction was complication. The reader was introduced to such procedures as extinction, discrimination, response differentiation, shaping, fading, schedules of reinforcement and other arrangements of contingencies which involved several of these simpler procedures.

The second direction related to diverse populations of individuals with a variety of behavioral problems. Behavioral consequences were employed to eliminate these problems and to make the existence of these individuals more enjoyable and more acceptable to society in general. Behavior was modified in a predicted and desirable direction by the scientific arrangement and application of consequences.

Although the authors have endeavored to show many instances in which behavior was controlled by its consequences, the student may find himself questioning the generality of this principle. After all, only a small portion of human behavior has been discussed in this book. Can this simple principle possibly account for all human behavior, or must new principles ultimately be introduced? Is it not presumptuous to assume that something so complex as human behavior can be explained and controlled by a simple principle which a grade school child could understand without difficulty?

The answer revolves around two points of science. While the concept of behavioral consequences is a simple one, the application of the principle to human behavior may be technically difficult. The analysis of the behavior of any given individual at a particular point in time and space may involve only amalgams of individual instances of this simple principle, but it presents a compound and intricately interrelated configuration. In order to determine what factors give rise to specific behavior patterns, we must consider the previous experiences of the individual, beginning as early as possible. We must also consider the numerous aspects of his environment which are currently affecting his behavior. Although final analysis may ultimately involve nothing more complex than positive and negative reinforcement acting on behavior in the many ways we have discussed in this book, untangling the various arrangements which have occurred over the years may preclude any immediate meaningful resolution.

Even in instances discussed in this volume where specific consequences were applied to modify existing behavior patterns, it was found that specialized equipment and detailed programming conditions were often necessary. Psychology is not, in this respect, unlike other sciences. The important concepts in science tend to be very simple but may involve the compounding of these simple principles into highly complex arrangements.

Thus it can be suggested that the reader should not discard beforehand a simple principle just because it must be used to explain a complex situation. It is difficult for the explorer who becomes buried in an avalanche to conceive that the tons of snow on top of him are merely a compounded version of tiny snow-flakes.

A second answer to this question evokes an analysis of the basic strategy of science. Most science which we know and which has so greatly benefited our culture is an empirical science. This type of science proceeds by the observation of phenomena and seeks to draw unifying principles from these observations. By employing in systematic ways principles which have been so derived, the scientists can predict outcomes. Early observers of behavior found that the consequences which behavior produced seemed to be a factor in the ultimate course of that behavior. We have seen throughout these pages how this principle has been extended to many problem areas and populations. In an empirical science, the principle becomes more highly validated each time it is extended to a new problem area or population.

However, it may also be that when more complex behavior is considered, the simple principle will not be adequate. We have seen one instance, in the chapter on respondent conditioning, where the general procedure of behavioral consequences may not totally explain the phenomena. For some behaviors, psychologists generally feel that the principle of behavioral consequences is not enough. They favor an explanation more closely aligned with Pavlov's method. Psychologists disagree as to whether or not respondent conditioning is qualitatively different from operant conditioning. Scientists may show in the future that this is indeed the case. As more and more human behavior comes under scientific scrutiny, it may become clear that there are many other important behavioral principles. It may be found that the principle of behavioral consequences is only one principle which alone is incomplete to explain all behavior.

Whether the principle of behavioral consequences is enough to account for all or most human behavior will only be found when more research is undertaken. The ultimate validity of the principle of behavioral consequences is an empirical question. It must be decided by students of psychology. The principle of behavioral consequences should not, however, be discarded before it has been tested to its limit. The horse must be ridden into the ground before it can be put out to pasture. If the studies reported within this volume and many others which were not reported here are any indication, then the principle of behavioral consequences is still a front runner. As its general application grows with each new successful use, it becomes yet stronger.

A twofold challenge is placed before today's psychologist. He is first challenged by the nagging insatiability of scientific curiosity. Scientists have been trained to pursue a line of inquiry to its absolute limit. They are possessed by the activity of finding out what makes the world and the people in it run. Even if there were no practical considerations, we would probably find psychologists who persevere at long and meticulous experiments for no reason other than amassing knowledge.

The second important challenge put to the psychologist concerns the practical aspect of human behavior. If one has ever questioned the need for behavioral science, he need only look at the problems which confront him and his fellow men at each new dawning. Problems of the emotionally disturbed remain salient, not only in terms of those currently in our institutions, but also in terms of what measures should be taken to prevent the costly and exasperating stage of behavior maladjustment which ends in institutionalization. The problems of education loom ahead. We are faced with students who must be educated and with a system which demands that education take place with more certainty and efficiency than it has in the past if we are to keep pace with our limited funds and an ever-expanding population. Interpersonal problems of the family and of race relations have been relatively untreated in any significant way by psychologists, as have behavior problems of the aged, handicapped, and the culturally deprived.

The student may say to himself, surely these massive problems cannot be tackled with an arsenal which contains only the simple principle of behavioral consequences and a few dozen techniques. Again, this is an empirical question. Certainly if the principle is to fail, these problems will offer an adequate challenge. There is always the possibility, however, that it may prove to be an effective tool, in even these highly complex areas. It is up to future students to mount this horse and ride it headlong into the massive and often foreboding problems which confront us. If the horse fails, we must then look for another. The quest is not, however, for steeds to ride, but rather for ambitious, serious-minded, and energetic young people with the fortitude to follow with all alacrity where their mount may lead.

QUESTIONS

1. In the story of the emperor, what did most people say about his new clothes?
2. Who was it that questioned the actual existence of the emperor's clothes?
3. What was the basis of the questioner's reasoning?
4. Did the child see any practical value in these clothes?
5. We spent a lot of time in this book talking about "feelings," "thoughts," "will," and the "mind." (a) True; (b) False.
6. What has the history of the science of psychology taught us that would lead us to choose behavior as the subject material rather than some of these interesting, mysterious topics such as the "mind," "feelings" and so on?
7. What have we discovered about the way in which behavior and other aspects of the environment are related?
8. Why have we been unable to eventually test whether or not mental variables such as "feelings" and "mind" are related to other aspects of the environment?
9. What is the single principle of behavior stated in the first chapter and stressed in the rest of the book?
10. What are the two types of consequences which affect behavior and what effect does each produce on behavior?
11. In what two directions was this principle developed following its introduction?
12. What question might a student have about the application of this principle to the explanation of human behavior?

13. In answering this question of generality, we must consider two points of science. In regard to the first point: (a) What considerations must be made before the question can be answered? (b) How is psychology in this respect like other sciences?

14. A reader should discard a simple principle because it must be used to explain a complex situation. (a) True; (b) False.

15. In regard to the second answer to this question of generality: (a) What is one name of the type of science which includes most of the science that we know and which has benefited us most? (b) How does this type of science proceed? (c) What can scientists do as a result of systematically using the principles that have been derived in this manner? (d) How can we validate such principles in an empirical science?

16. Each time the principle is successfully applied in a new situation, the principle increases in generality. (a) True; (b) False.

17. Which type of behavior may not be explained by this one principle?

18. What is the only way in which we can determine whether or not the principle of behavioral consequences accounts for all or most human behavior?

19. What is the twofold challenge confronting the psychologist in our society?

NOTES

We pointed out in this chapter that empirical science is the type of science which has produced the most benefits for our culture. Empirical science is also the younger type of

> Two bearded dudes,
> Both pretty hip,
> Say that Truth
> Is a functional relationship

science. It was preceded by years of intellectual endeavor which employed a different type of scientific logic, called deductive reasoning. A science based on deductive reasoning begins with basic assumptions and then seeks to derive specific facts from these broad assumptions. The procedure is that which one might encounter in formal logic courses. "Given that all men are mortal and given the further assumption that Socrates was a man, it can be concluded with certainty that Socrates was also mortal."

Early scientific endeavor was often carried on by individuals associated with the church. Since early religious orders were given the task of transmitting the culture to their members, much time was spent in thought and naturally these individuals began to turn their reflections to the nature of man and the universe. By and large, these early efforts which used strict deductive reasoning were of little or no practical value. This type of logic suffers from the problem that the conclusions drawn can never extend beyond the basic assumptions. Furthermore, if these basic assumptions are wrong, all of the conclusions which are drawn from them are also in error and will not obtain in a real world. This synthetic method rarely yielded conclusions which coincided with events in the physical world and therefore was of little value to people who were interested in predicting and controlling their environment.

Some years later, a new form of deductive science was developed, called hypothetical-deductive science. As with other deductive approaches, the hypothetical-deductive system begins with basic assumptions. From these assumptions are drawn logical conclusions or extensions. These extensions occur as predictions. One may observe behavior and draw a basic assumption about the nervous system. For instance, from observing an organism behave and from watching him as we apply various tactile stimuli, we might assume that he has a nervous system which is made up of tiny wires in much the same way a television set is. Beginning from this basic assumption, we may do various experiments to validate it. All of this experimentation is done without actual direct observation of the nervous system; it does not involve cutting open an organism and observing the nervous system through direct means. The basic problem with the hypothetical-deductive system is that there are many alternate assumptions which could possibly account for the observations and experimental outcomes. In the final analysis, since direct observation never comes into the picture, the scientist may end up with any number of alternate assumptions, all of which are basic and all of which explain the observations.

The strict inductive approach such as that presented throughout this book involves observation of events, formulation of a hypothesis regarding a specific principle which interrelates these events, and then observation to determine whether this hypothesis holds up in different cases. An interesting aspect of a strict inductive approach is that one cannot make a definite statement regarding all possible situations until all possible situations have been observed. If one observes only a limited number of cases, however, he can make a statement of probability and extend this to untested and unobserved situations. By observing behavior, psychologists arrived at the hypothesis that behavior is controlled by its consequences. This hypothesis was tested and found to hold true. Further, its generality was extended by testing it in other situations with other types of organisms and under a variety of conditions. If in a significant number of such instances, the basic hypothesis holds, one may conclude that it probably also holds for other behavior. As the principle is tried over and over again and continues to produce the same results, we gain faith in it and the probability that it is indeed true for all behavior. We become more comfortable with the general validity of the hypothesis.

The choice of behavior as a datum of an empirical science of psychology is not altogether arbitrary. It is a decision made from observing the progress of older sciences which used observable events as their basic data, from a long-term look at the history of science itself, and from the early inability of a science of psychology to evolve from other types of data.

Science is at best an endeavor to derive orderly relationships between two sets of variables. The science of physics is concerned with establishing relationships between physical operations on objects in space and time and the changes in motion, inertia, etc., which occur as a result of these physical operations. The strategy is to develop laws which will help us to predict the outcomes of the behavior of objects in the future. Practical applications of physics are obvious and should come to mind each time we cross a bridge, admire a huge skyscraper, or even observe a bar of soap, whose manufacturers brag will always float in the bathtub. If psychology is to pattern itself after the older and successful sciences, it must also seek to establish relationships. Early psychologists began by trying to find relationships between people's feelings, thoughts, and perceptions as revealed to the experimenter through verbal behavior. These data of feeling tones, perceptions, etc. were reported by the subject to the experimenter, who then sought to relate these introspective data to the world. Great time and effort was spent in trying to critically analyze the difference between a thought, a feeling, and a perception. This approach failed because the basic datum was the verbal behavior of the individual, which was taken as a direct representation of such things as feelings and emotions. Feelings and emotions were never observed directly; rather, verbal reports of these were the real data which went into equations and formulations. The failure of this type of psychology should not be taken to mean that verbal behavior itself cannot be studied scientifically. In earlier chapters of this book we have pointed out how indeed verbal behavior may be controlled and modified. The attempt, however, to view verbal behavior as synonymous with feelings and thoughts which cannot be observed has not proved valuable. Few if any meaningful relationships have come from these years of endeavor.

The reliance on overt behavior as the basic datum in psychology has come about because, first of all, this approach works. Psychology has progressed inasmuch as it has begun to be cognizant of behaviors which can be observed and measured. In the relatively short time that this approach has been used, many meaningful relationships have ensued. Often, however, this approach is criticized because it does not deal with notions such as mind, feelings, emotions, and most of the subject matter that the individual untrained in psychology will speak of when the study of psychology is mentioned. But can a science of psychology function without even considering these areas? Probably it can. Let us consider the following hypothetical situation. Assume we have developed a science of psychology which will allow us to predict an individual's behavior merely by manipulating his environment. Let us further assume that he is placed in a room and isolated from the experimenter who watches him through a television screen from a distant observation booth. The subject looks around and sees himself confined in the experimental chamber. He feels surrounded by all the stimuli and equipment but yet experiences a conscious feeling of choosing, feeling, and thinking. The experimenter in the meanwhile has little notion at all of the subject's feelings or thoughts. He is merely observing overt behavior. He pushes a button which introduces a stimulus. He predicts that when the stimulus is presented, the subject will respond by pushing a particular lever. The stimulus is presented to the subject, the subject sees the stimulus, experiences the act of choosing, and, with deliberation, depresses the lever. Inside the experimental booth, the experimenter records the response. It is precisely what he had predicted. He has been affecting overt behavior without ever considering thoughts or feelings. The experimenter then introduces new stimuli and makes predictions as to the subject's behavior which are fulfilled. Within the two booths, different levels of analysis are occurring. The subject is analyzing his own environment in terms of what he feels, thinks, and believes about it. The experimenter does not have knowledge of thoughts, feelings, or internal emotions. He merely controls the environment and accurately predicts the behavior. Inasmuch as the experimenter is able to control and predict the subject's behavior without reliance on the subject's wishes, feelings or experiences, he is demonstrating a successful science of behavioral psychology. The behavior he might wish to manipulate could involve any number of overt responses, which we might variously classify as emotion, affection, anger, rage, creativity, intellectual scholarship, passivity, aggression or laziness. Any behavior which can be observed in another individual can theoretically be brought under the control of the environment. The hope of an empirical behavioristic science of psychology is to empirically demonstrate this. It does not deny feelings, thoughts, and choosing; it merely does not admit these factors as basic data in his science. They cannot be observed and measured.

Morality

People in the business world have been concerned with the concepts of "obvious self-interest" and "enlightened self-interest." The notion is that business and industry should do what is in their own self-interest. Initially it appeared that their obvious self-interests would dictate that they should not be particularly concerned with the social welfare of their employees or of the community at large. On the other hand, enlightened self-interest requires a long-range view. For example, they need to be concerned about the purchasing power of the community in general if they are to sell their product.

A brief exposure to the basic principles of behavior may leave the student with the impression that there are no alternative types of morality. At first the student only thinks of primary reinforcement. Since he is an organism and behaves according to the principles of reinforcement, he should do only those things which produce unconditioned positive reinforcement and eliminate unconditioned negative reinforcement. He should eat his meals and come in out of the rain.

However, even a superficial analysis of our behavior indicates that there is more to it than that. Certainly we are also controlled by conditioned reinforcers; in fact it may be that more of our behavior is controlled by conditioned than by unconditioned reinforcers. We not only feed ourselves and come in out of the rain, but we make certain that others are fed and get in out of the rain as well. The notion of enlightened self-interest would indicate that we do this not because it is in any sense moral or right, but because in the long run, if we make sure that other people are taken care of, they will be likely to take care of us when our turn comes to be helped. In other words, behaving properly to other people is reinforced by conditioned reinforcers which are ultimately associated with unconditioned reinforcement.

In many cases this is true. However, the notion of enlightened self-interest implies that, in situations where the conditioned reinforcers for behaving properly will never be backed up with unconditioned reinforcers, we should not be expected to go out of our way to behave well toward others. In other words, when we learn to discriminate between those situations where conditioned reinforcement is followed by unconditioned reinforcement and those where it is never followed by unconditioned reinforcement, we should fail to respond when the sole reinforcement for responding is consistently the conditioned reinforcement. If it is very clear to you that you will not see a particular person again, then it might be thought that no reason exists for you to behave properly toward him. The mere fact that he might speak harshly to you should not matter since the negative reinforcing properties of such stimulation are merely of a conditioned nature and will never be backed up with any unconditioned negative reinforcers. Nonetheless, we behave in a reasonably civil and unselfish manner to complete strangers whom we will never see again. Our behavior is under the control of conditioned reinforcers in situations where we can discriminate that unconditioned reinforcers will never be forthcoming.

This analysis is consistent with laboratory studies by Zimmerman[1] which demonstrate similar findings with pigeons. Pecking a left response key was reinforced on a variable-interval schedule with a four-second presentation of a food magazine containing grain. Pecking a right key was reinforced by a one-half second presentation of the magazine. The presentation of the food magazine itself served as a conditioned rein-

1. Zimmerman, J. Technique for sustaining behavior with conditioned reinforcement. *Science*, 1963, *142*, 682–684.

forcer. When it was up for four seconds, following a left key-peck response, there was sufficient time for the animal to get its head to the food magazine and consume some of the grain, which acted as an unconditioned reinforcer. However the one-half second food magazine presentation following right key-peck responses was so short that the animal could not possibly reach the magazine in time to get any grain. The right key-peck response was nonetheless maintained by this mere conditioned reinforcer. The right key-peck response, maintained solely by the conditioned reinforcer, did not occur as high a rate as did the left key-peck response, maintained by both conditioned and unconditioned reinforcers. Nonetheless, the right key-peck response still occurred at a respectable rate.

Furthermore, it is not a question of whether the animal could discriminate between the right key and the left key. This is an easy discrimination for the animal as was demonstrated in this experiment by the relatively low response rate on the right key. To put it very crudely, the animal was not confused; the mere presentation of the food magazine by itself was reinforcing. In the same manner the young man who finds the presentation of the fold-out from *Playboy* reinforcing is not confused. It is quite clear that the young man is dealing with a mere picture, a conditioned reinforcer.

If one is willing to accept the notion that much of art, recreation, and sports is based on conditioned reinforcement, it should be obvious that, in these situations as well, it is sometimes clear that no unconditioned reinforcers will be forthcoming. This should not be taken to mean that if unconditioned reinforcers are never forthcoming, the conditioned reinforcers will maintain their reinforcing properties. That is not true. In the case of the pigeon study, if we withhold the food entirely for the left key-peck response, the mere brief presentation of the food magazine will lose its conditioned reinforcing power and the bird will stop pecking the right key.

A conditioned reinforcer must occasionally be paired with an unconditioned reinforcer, but it will maintain its effectiveness at some lesser degree in situations which are discriminately different from those where the unconditioned reinforcer will be forthcoming. This is important because it gets close to a fundamental issue of morality. As reinforcement theorists, we need not always justify our behavior in terms of forthcoming primary reinforcement. It is positively reinforcing to be good and negatively reinforcing to be bad even though we discriminate that in any particular instance we may never receive unconditioned positive or negative reinforcement for the particular act. Another way of putting it is that you should not feel yourself a traitor to the notion of reinforcement by simply being a good guy.

It is most fortunate that we do not have to be concerned with potentially backing up each conditioned reinforcer with an unconditioned reinforcer. There are many situations where it is desirable for people to behave properly, yet where there will obviously be no unconditioned consequences. It would be difficult to engineer a society so that unconditioned consequences were always potentially available. It is indeed fortunate for man and society that this is unnecessary. Man can be moral even when there is no potential unconditioned reinforcement involved.

INDEX

Accelerated education, 429–436
  advantages, 432
  disadvantages, 429–432
  program, 432–436
Accidental conditioning, 62–65, 75–76
Acquired unconditioned reinforcers, 310–315
  addictive, 311–313, 318–319
  imprinted, 314–315, 319
Addictive reinforcers, 311–313, 318–319
Adjunctive reinforcers, 309–310, 318, 327
Aggression, 309–310
Alcoholism, 103–107, 329–333, 341–342, 345–
    346
Allen, K., 11n, 136n
Anal gratification, 323–324
Animal behavior and human behavior, 8–9
Animal language system, 257–261
Animals, experiments with, as assembly line
    inspectors, 173–178
  as guided missiles, 159–163
  superstitious behavior, 63–64, 75
  See also specific animals; specific experiments
Anna State Hospital, 8, 249, 309
Anti-social behavior, 26–28, 35, 266, 270–272
Aphonia, 89–91
Arithmetic, teaching of, to animals, 251–255
Art appreciation, conditioning of, 192
Assembly line tedium, 171, 173–178, 190–191
Attenuation of reinforcing consequences, 218
Autistic children, 86–89, 97–98, 233–235,
    237–239
Avoidance behavior, 377, 381–389
  and extinction, 394
  in phobias, 411
  types of, 392–393
Ayllon, T., 45–46, 48, 247n, 249–251, 279–
    280, 287, 293n, 294–295
Azrin, N. H., 8, 247n, 249–251, 279–280, 309

Bachrach, A. J., 3n
Backward chaining, 298–299, 301–303
Backward conditioning, 76

Baer, D. M., 5n, 223n, 225–228, 231–232
Bangs, J. L., 90n
Baroff, G. S., 354n
Baseline, 330, 395
  behavioral, 143
Basic stimulus generalization experiment, 184,
    186–187
Battle fatigue, 96
Beard stroking, 324
Bed wetting, 266
Behavior, 12, 19
  See also specific problems
Behavior modification, see Conditioning
Behavior principles, 288–291, 316–317, 319,
    440
Behavioral psychology, 439–442, 445
Berryman, R., 297n
Birds, fear of, 399–401
"Bootleg" reinforcement, 48
Brady, J. V., 386n, 387, 394–395
Brain stimulation, electric, 307, 326
Brainwashing, 212–218, 220–221
Breast feeding, 323
Breland, K., 147–148, 153, 160, 163, 167, 169
Bright, G., 337n
Brodsky, G., 266n, 267–268, 271, 274
Buell, J., 11n
Burnbrauer, J., 41n
Butterfield, W. H., 155–158, 178

Cars, fear of, 409–412
Castration, fear of, 323
Chickens, fear of, 399–401
Chimpanzees, teaching of, arithmetic, 251–255
  value of "money," 277–278
Churchill, D. W., 237n
Clinical psychology, 45–46
College education, incentives for, 287
  relevance of, 426
  See also Education; Lectures, college
"Coming when called," 23–24, 34
Computer behavior, 291

Concept formation, 174–187, 190–192
    See also Stimulus class
Conceptual behavior, 174, 187
Conditioned punishers, 393
Conditioned reinforcement, 35, 278–285, 287–291
    defined, 278, 285
    generalized conditioned reinforcement, 280, 285
    and remedial education, 281–285
    and token economy, 278–281
Conditioning, accidental, 62–65, 75–76
    backward, 76
    checks, 55–57
        See also Control procedures
    defined, 21, 33
    operant, 32–33, 57, 408, 414
    respondent, 32–33, 57, 405–408, 411, 414
    See also specific problems (Hyperactivity, Temper tantrums, etc.); specific subjects (Infants, Retardates, etc.); specific techniques (Discrimination, Extinction, Fading, Generalization, Gradual change, Imitative behavior, Punishment, Reinforcement, Response differentiation, Schedules of reinforcement, Shaping, etc.)
Conrad, D. G., 386n
Continuous reinforcement (CRF), 102, 107–109, 112, 135–136
Control procedures, 56–57, 144, 365–366, 394–396
Conversation, art of, 68–69
Coral Gables VA Hospital, 103–107, 329–333, 342, 345–346
Coulter, S. K., 237n
Counting behavior in chimpanzees, 251–255
Cowart, J., 7n
Cowles, J. T., 277
Crying behavior, 10–11, 15, 17, 37–41, 53–54
    See also Temper tantrums
Cumming, W., 172–175, 177–178
Cumulative recorder, 34

Daily Worker, N. Y., 215
Debacha, P. C., 315n
Deductive reasoning, 443–444
Delinquents, juvenile, 155–159, 208–211, 218
Deprivation, use of, in reinforcing, 34, 280, 306, 313, 317, 326
Desensitization, systematic, 413–414
Determinism and free will, 367
Devine, J. V., 315n
Diagnosis of childhood disturbances, 97–98
Differential reinforcement, in psychotherapy, 70–72, 76–77
    in response differentiation, 65–70, 72
    in successive approximation, 91
Differential reinforcement of other behavior (DRO), 137–139, 141, 143–144, 230–231
Digital gratification, 323–324
Diogenes, 179

Discriminated extinction, 151–152, 163
Discrimination, errorless, 197, 202, 204–205
Discrimination training, 147, 163
    See also Stimulus discrimination
Discriminative stimulus (S^D), 148–149, 163–164, 288–289, 322–323
    See also Stimulus discrimination
Disruptive behavior, as a reinforcer, 315–316
Divers for coins, 101–102
Dogs and salivation response, 405–408
Doomsday Contingency, 420, 427–428
Dropouts, high school, 316
Drug addiction, 311–313, 346

Eating problems, manners, 249–250
    refusing to eat, 3–5, 293–294
Education, 417–428
    accelerated, 429–436
    cost of, 425–426
    reform, 433–436
    relevance of, 426
    remedial, 282–285
    teacher shortages, 423–425
    See also Grades, school; Learning; Students
Electric brain stimulation, 307, 326
Electric shock, use of, in conditioning, 8–11, 307, 309, 330–333, 335–337, 340–342, 345–348, 380–383, 387–388
Electro-convulsive shock therapy (ECS), 346–347
Elliott, R., 360n
Emotional behavior, characterized, 404, 406–407, 411
Enuresis, 266
Error analysis of quiz questions, 421–422
Errorless discrimination, 197, 202, 204–205
Erwin, W. J., 3n
Escape procedure, 376–377, 380–383, 389–394, 411
Excitement seeking, 346
Experimental psychology, 45–46
Explanatory fiction, 327
Extinction, and forgetting, 48–50
    as a procedure, defined, 40, 135
        use of, 38–44, 45–48, 309–310, 354
        for check purposes, 54–56
    as a result, 108, 136, 141, 151–152, 163, 348, 393–394

Fading, 196–202, 204–205, 207–208, 211, 218
    defined, 196, 202
    and shaping, 207–208, 211
    summary, 202
Falk, J., 308
Fear, 407
    See also Phobia
Ferster, C., 130–133, 143, 251–254
Findley, J., 108n, 248
Firecrest School, 225
Fishing, incentive for, 132
Fixed-interval schedule of reinforcement (FI), 132–135, 140–141

Fixed-ratio schedule of reinforcement (FR), 106–114, 129
  characteristics of, 113, 120–121
  defined, 106, 120–121
  extinction in, 108
  post-reinforcement pause in, 107, 113, 119, 121
  variable-ratio, comparison with, 118–119, 121
  as work incentive, 114
Food, fear of, 293
Forgetting, 48–50
Fort Custer State Home, 153
Freidinger, A., 90n
Freud, S., 323–324, 364, 391
Fuller, P. R., 20, 32, 34, 54

Gambling, 115–118
Generalization, 175–176
  gradient, 184–185, 187
  of imitation, 224–225, 227, 231–232, 239
  of reinforcement therapy, 263–272
  See also Stimulus generalization
Generalized condition reinforcers, 279–280, 285
General Mills, Inc., 160–161
Genital gratification, 323–324
Giles, D. K., 282n
Glasses, wearing of, conditioning a child to, 86–88, 97
Goldiamond, I., 80n, 371
Golding, W., 248
Grades, school, 282, 284, 287–288
  peer grading, 423–424, 427
  as reinforcers, 418, 422–423, 424
Gradient of reinforcement, 76
Gradual change techniques, 207–218, 220–221
  chart, 208
  summary, 218
Grant, D. A., 143n
Graphs, use of, to show behavior change, 24–25, 30
Guided missiles, use of animals as, 159–163

Hake, D. F., 309n
Hall, V. R., 282n
Hammer, C., 251–254
Happiness as a conditioned response, 229–230
Harris, F. R., 11n, 26n, 136n
Hart, B., 11n
Hart, C., 153n
Hartford, R. A., 384n
Haughton, E., 48, 293n, 294–295
Hawkins, T. C., 326
Head banging, 7–8, 355–357
Hearing, testing of, 199–202
Hefferline, R. F., 384–385, 392
Herrnstein, R. J., 76, 179
Hingtgen, J. N., 237
Hockett, C. F., 257–258, 261
Holland, J. G., 191n
Homme, L. E., 315n, 371
Hospitalization, defects of, 96–97, 109

Hostile behavior, 266, 269–270
Hutchinson, R. R., 309n, 310n
Hyperactivity, 28–29
Hypothetical construct, 327

Idiots, see Retardates
Illusion, perceptual, see Mueller-Lyer illusion
Imitative behavior, 223–240, 243–244
  defined, 239
  excess of, 233–239
  generalization of, 224–225, 227, 231–232, 239
  lack of, 223–232
  measurement of, 237–238
  summary, 239–240
  verbal instructions, 247–251, 255
Imprinted reinforcers, 314–315, 319
Inactivity, treatment of, 26–28, 35
Inconsistent parent, characterized, 75
Indoctrination, see Brainwashing
Inductive reasoning, 444
Infants, conditioning of, 22, 401–404
Initial behavior, 81, 84, 92
"Institutionalization," 96–97, 109
Instructions, verbal, 247–251, 255
Intelligence, as an intervening variable, 327
Intensity considerations in successive approximation, 89, 91–93
Intensive conditioning program, 237–239, 270–271
Intermittent reinforcement, 135–136, 176–177
  See also Schedules of reinforcement
Intuitive behavior concepts, 179, 187
Isaacs, W., 80n
Isolation, prolonged, effects of, 248

"John Henry," 290
Johnson, V. E., 290
Johnston, M. K., 26n

Keenan, B., 384n
Kelly, C., 26n
Kleptomania, 358
Knowles, P. A., 329n, 333n
Kolb, D. A., 209n
Korean War, brainwashing of prisoners, 212–218, 220–221
Kushner, M., 9n, 104

Language, requirements for, 257–261
  teaching of, to animals, 251, 255, 257–261
Law of Least Effort, 289
Lawler, M., 41n
Lazarus, A. A., 409–411
Learning, defined, 21
  errorless, 197, 202, 204–205
  incentives, 282–285, 287–288, 367–368
  See also Education; Students, study behavior of
Lectures, college, 322–323
Limited hold, 132, 140
Livingston, P., 103n
Location response, 65–68

Lord of the Flies, 248
Loveland, D. H., 179
Lying, 364

Machines and man, 289–291
Malott, R. W., 181*n*, 417*n*
Man, nature of, 288–289
Mantle, M., 61
Mason, J. W., 386*n*
Masters, W. H., 290
Masturbation, 290, 323–324
Matching of stimuli, 251–255
Mathie, J., 351–353, 354, 364
Maturity, psychological, 430
Mees, H., 86*n*
Mentally ill patients, conditioning of, 45–47, 57, 249–251
    See also Psychotics; Schizophrenics
Meyerson, L., 199
Michael, J., 45–46, 199
Mohr, J. P., 3*n*
Money, as a conditioned reinforcer, 278
Mongoloid child, self-injurious behavior in, 377–383
Monkeys, experimentally produced ulcers in, 386–388
Morality, 446–447
Motivation, 322
    See also Reinforcer effectiveness, factors influencing
Motor responses, generalization of verbal responses to, 231
Mueller-Lyer illusion, 181–187

Nalorphine, 313
National Aeronautic and Space Administration (NASA), 248
Negative reinforcement, 373, 392–396
    avoidance, 384–389
    defined, 373, 388
    escape, 376–377
    escape and avoidance combined, 380–383
    unconscious response, 385
Nondirective psychotherapy, 69–72
Nose picking, 323–324
Nursery school, controlling behavior in, 315

Olds, J., 307*n*
Operant conditioning, 32–33, 57
    defined, 408, 414
Oral gratification, 323–324

Paralysis, hysterical, 374–377, 391–392
Patterson, G. R., 28–29, 266–271, 274
Pavlov, I., 33, 213, 220, 405–408, 411, 414, 441
    See also Respondent conditioning
Peeping Tom, 351–353
Peer grading in colleges, 423–424, 427
"Pelican," pigeon guided missile, 161, 177–178
Penis envy, 323

Pep talk, as a discriminative stimulus, 322
Perceptual illusion, 181–184
Perthu, M., 153*n*
Pestering behavior, 26, 46–47, 149–153, 167–168
Peterson, R. F., 225*n*, 231
Phenylketonuria, 97
Phobias, 293, 323, 401–404, 408–411
Pica reinforcer, 310, 318
Pierrel, R., 298*n*
Plato, 179
Play behavior, 26–28, 35, 266, 269–270, 272
Playboy magazine, 289, 291, 447
Pliskoff, S. S., 326
Pokrzywinski, J., 181*n*, 185
Polydipsia, 308, 310
Porter, R. W., 386*n*, 387–388
Post-reinforcement pause, 107, 113, 119, 121
Potential positive reinforcers, 33
Premack Principle, 316–317, 319
Primary reinforcers, 278, 285, 288–289, 312
    See also Conditioned reinforcement
Prisoners, incentives for, 127–129
Prisoners of war, brainwashing of, 212–218, 220–221
Problem child, 266–272
    See also specific problems
Proctor, D., 48
Psychologist, as a parent, 53–54
Psychotherapy, 69–72, 399–401, 413–414
    getting unwilling subjects into, 208–211, 218
Psychotics, 7, 79–80, 233, 279–281
    See also Mentally ill patients; Schizophrenics
Psychotic talk, 47–48, 57
Punishment, in conditioning
    by contingent stimulation, 7–11, 16–17, 329–342, 345–348
    conditioned punishers, 393
    defined, 332, 341, 346
    with escape and avoidance procedures, 380–383, 387–388
    result of, 347–348
    and torture, difference between, 332, 341
    by contingent withdrawal of reinforcer, 353–362, 364–367
    defined, 353–354, 362

Quizzes, in education, 418–419, 421–422, 427–428

Rabbits, sexual behavior of, 305
Ranier School, 41
Rats, behavior training of, 296–300
Rayner, R., 401–404, 407–408, 411, 413
Reading, teaching of, to juvenile delinquents, 155–159
    to retardates, 195–198
Reinforcement, 14–15, 20, 26, 29, 33, 92, 98, 109
    accidental, 63–65
    conditioned, 278–285, 287–291

differential, 65–72, 76–77, 91
generalization of, 263–272
timing of, 22, 33, 61–62, 75–76
unauthorized, 48
See also Deprivation; Schedules of reinforcement; Stimulus discrimination
Reinforcer, removal of, *see* Punishment
Reinforcer effectiveness, factors influencing, 305–319, 322–327
acquired unconditioned reinforcers, 310–315, 318–319
adjunctive reinforcers, 309–310, 318, 327
concept of, 325–327
deprivation, 306, 313, 317, 326
increases, 307–308, 326
Premack Principle, 316–317, 319
satiation, 306–307, 317
theoretical status of, 326
Reinforcers, acquired unconditioned, 310–315, 318–319
addictive, 311–313, 318–319
adjunctive, 309–310, 318, 327
Reinforcers, conditioned and unconditioned, 35
effective, 54
potential, 33
presumed, 54
Reinforcing consequences, 208
attenuation of, 218
Relativism, 373
Relevance, in college courses, 426
Remedial education, 282–285
Respondent conditioning, 32–33, 57, 405–408, 411, 414
Response chains, 231
Response class, 30, 67–69, 72
Response differentiation, 65–69, 72, 91–93
Response topographies, 88–89, 91–93
Retardates, conditioning of, 20–21, 32, 118–119, 225–228, 230–232
diagnosis of, 97–98, 199
self-injurious behavior in, 354–357, 365–366
teaching of, 5–6, 153–155, 168–169, 195–198, 202, 204, 300
vomiting behavior in, 41–43, 54, 337–342
Reward, 8–9, 11, 14–15, 19, 29
See also Reinforcement
Rickert, E. J., 315n
Risley, T., 6n, 23, 86n, 110n, 233n, 234
Rogers, C., 70–72, 76
Rosenkranz, A., 103n, 329n, 333n
Rubin, H. B., 305n
Rumination, 337–342

Salesman, door-to-door, reinforcement of, 120
Salinger, J .D., 19
Saskatchewan Hospital, 46
Satiation, 306–307, 317
Schedules of reinforcement, 102–121, 129–141, 143–144, 208, 326, 418
continuous, 102, 107–109, 112
defined, 102, 120
fixed-interval, 132–135, 140–141

fixed-ratio, 106–114, 120–121, 129
time-dependent, 129–141
variable-interval, 130–132, 134, 140–141
variable-ratio, 114–121, 129
Schedules of Reinforcement, 130, 143
Schizophrenics, 293–296
Schuster, R., 311–313
Schwitzgebel, R., 209–211
Scratching, excessive, 136–139
Secondary reinforcers, 278, 285, 288–289
See also Conditioned reinforcement
Self-control techniques, 367–371
Self-help, teaching of, to retardates, 300
Self-injurious behavior, 7–8, 16–17, 354–357, 365–366, 377–383
Separation from mother problem, 266–269
Sexual behavior, 305–307
Sexual machines, 290
Sexual reinforcers, 307
Shaping, 86, 92, 207–208, 211, 217–218
See also Successive approximation
Shell shock, 374–377, 391–392
Sherman, J. A., 223n, 225n
Sherman, J. G., 298n
Shock treatments (ECS), 346–347
Sibley, S., 110n
Sidman, M., 392, 394
Siqueland, E. R., 22n
Skinner, B. F., 49–50, 63–65, 72, 75, 130–131, 133, 143, 148, 159–164, 173, 177–178, 191, 436
Skinner box, 248, 393
Sky-diving, 346
Smoking, cessation of, 323, 333–337, 342, 347, 360–361, 366–367
Sneezing, prolonged, 9–10, 17
Social reinforcers, 283–284
Speech problems, aphonia, 89–91
in the deaf, 199
excessive imitation, 233–237
lack of imitation, 223–232
overtalking, 110–113
psychotic talk, 47–48, 57
refusal to speak, 80–85
and stimulus control, 247–255
Spontaneity, planned, 430
Sports, incentives for, 35, 68, 120, 283
Staats, A. W., 155–158, 178, 433
Starvation, psychological, 3–5
Stealing behavior, 357–360
Steinhorst, R., 315n
Stimulus discrimination, 147–164, 167–169, 288–289, 322–323
discriminated extinction, 151–152, 163
discrimination training, 147, 163
successive discrimination, 168–169
use of, in conditioning pestering behavior, 149–153, 167–168
in teaching delinquents, 155–159
in teaching the retarded, 153–155, 168–169
in training animals, 147–149, 159–163, 167

Stimulus class, 174, 187
Stimulus control, 148, 163, 247–255
Stimulus dimensions, 198
Stimulus generalization, 174–187, 190–192
  defined, 174, 186
  summarized, 186–187
Stimulus matching, 243–244
Stimulus response chains, 295–303, 312–313
  backward chaining, 298–299, 301–303
  defined, 295, 301
  used with rats, 296–300
  used with schizophrenics, 293–296
Stock market trading, 132
Straining the ratio, 108
Students, in peer grading, 423–424
  study behavior of, 28–29
  as teacher aides, 424
  underachievers, 418–423, 428
  work incentives for, 287–288
Success, as a positive reinforcer, 102, 120
Successive approximation, 16, 83–91, 231
  explained, 80–81, 83–84, 86, 89, 92–93
  initial response, 81, 84, 92
  prerequisite behavior, 84–85
  and response differentiation, 91–93
  response intensity, 89, 91–93
  response typographies, 88–89, 91–93
  terminal response, 80–81, 83, 86, 88, 92
  See also Shaping
Successive discrimination, 168–169
Superstitious behavior, 63–65, 72, 75–76, 139–140, 386
Svinicki, J. G., 417n
Systematic desensitization, 413–414

Tabasco, use of, in conditioning, 339–340
Talking behavior, see Speech problems
Tate, B. G., 354n
Teacher shortage problems, 423–425
Television viewing, use of, in conditioning, 23–25, 34
Temper tantrums, 38–41, 266–270
Terminal response, 81, 83, 86, 88, 92, 207
Therapy, and experimentation, 273–274
  See also Psychotherapy
Thomas, J., 79n
Thompson, T., 311–313
Thornton, T., 333n
"Three on a match," 64, 76
Thumbsucking, 5, 16, 323
Thumb twitching, as an unconscious response, 384
Tighe, T. J., 360n
Time-dependent schedules of reinforcement, 129–141
  fixed-interval, 132–135, 140–141
  and superstition, 139–140
  variable-interval, 130–132, 140–141
Timing, factor in reinforcement, 22, 33, 61–62, 75–76
Toilet-training, 323
Token economy, with chimpanzees, 277–278
  in a mental hospital, 279–281

Topography, in successive approximation, 88–89, 91–93
Tough, J., 118n, 377–380
Trading stamp plan, 282
Truax, C. B., 70–71, 76–77
Twain, M., 35

Ulcers, experimentally produced, 386–388
  and relaxation, 394–395
Unauthorized reinforcement, 48
Unconditioned positive reinforcers, 35
Unconscious response, 385
Underachievement, student, 418–423, 428

Variable-interval schedule of reinforcement (VI), 130–132, 134, 140–141
Variable-ratio schedule of reinforcement (VR), 114–121, 129
  defined, 114, 121
  fixed-ratio, compared with, 118–119, 121
  as a gambling incentive, 115–118
  as a work incentive, 120
Verbal behavior, see Speech problems
Verbal reports, validity of, 364
Verbal responses, generalization of, to motor responses, 231
Verhave, T., 177–178, 192
Villarreal, J. E., 310n
Vomiting behavior, 41–44, 54, 57, 337–342
Voyeuristic behavior, 351–353

Walter Reed Army Institute of Research, 386
War neurosis, 96
Water reinforcement, 306, 308–309
Watson, J. B., 401–404, 407–408, 411, 413
Welt, K., 153n, 195n
Wetzel, R. J., 358n
Whaley, D. L., 7n, 23n, 103n, 110n, 149–152, 153n, 195n, 329n, 333n, 377n
Whining behavior, 10–11, 17
Williams, C. D., 38, 40
Williams, T., 41n
Will power, 367, 369–371
Wolf, M., 11, 26n, 41n, 42–43, 54, 56–57, 86n, 233n, 234, 282–283, 287
Work incentives, 114, 120, 128–129, 134–135
  on assembly line, 171, 190–191
  in a mental hospital, 144, 279–281
  for students, 134–135, 287–288, 367–368
World War I, battle fatigue, 96
  shell shock, 374–377
  "three on a match," 64, 76
World War II, battle fatigue, 96
  defense experiments, 159–163
  prisoners of war, 212

"XY" recorder, 34

Yealland, L. R., 374–377, 391
Yoked control, 395

Zimmerman, E. H., 40–41
Zimmerman, J., 40n, 446